D0897670

UA
23
R76

Rosi, Eugene J   comp.
    American defense and détente; readings in national security
policy. Edited by Eugene J. Rosi.   New York, Dodd, Mead,
1973.

    x, 532 p.   25 cm.

    Includes bibliographical references.

    1. United States—Military policy—Addresses, essays, lectures.   I. Title.

UA23.R76   355.03'3073   72-12034
ISBN 0-396-06622-4   MARC

Library of Congress   73

DAVID FELLMAN
Vilas Professor of Political Science
University of Wisconsin–Madison
ADVISORY EDITOR TO DODD, MEAD & COMPANY

American Defense and Détente

Readings in National Security Policy

American Defense and Détente

Readings in National Security Policy

edited by

EUGENE J. ROSI

DICKINSON COLLEGE

DODD, MEAD & COMPANY

New York   1973   Toronto

to Pamela, Christina, Ian, and Rocco

Preface

At the time when many people believe the cold war is over and some blame the United States for causing it, a book of readings on American national security policy may be dismissed as irrelevant or as a rationalization for American militarism. Irrespective of who caused the cold war or whether or not it is over, however, we cannot anticipate an early demise for national security affairs. Indeed, the ambiguities and subtleties of an era of détente require sophisticated analysis and discriminating judgment in order to overcome the frozen stereotypes of the early cold war period without jeopardizing fundamental values.

A belief that the American political system can be made to work better is one of the editor's biases; a second is that an important contribution to the functioning of the system comes from an interested and informed public which includes interested and informed college students. This book is intended, therefore, to provide some of the materials from various academic disciplines which will help students think rigorously about national security policy in an era of détente and improve the quality of their contribution to the opinion-policy process.

I am happy for an opportunity to acknowledge here some long-standing intellectual debts, especially to my teachers at Columbia University: above all to William T. R. Fox, Director of Columbia's Institute of War and Peace Studies, whose teaching and writing have enriched my understanding of international politics and national security affairs; to David B. Truman, now President of Mount Holyoke College, and to Herbert H. Hyman, presently Professor of Sociology at Wesleyan University, for their insights into the political process and public opinion. For their reading and commenting on the manuscript I am grateful to Professor Fox and to Robert Gilpin, Professor of Politics at Princeton University, a friend who has been a source of stimulation and encouragement for many years. Financial support in preparing the manuscript came from the Dickinson College Faculty Research Fund.

EUGENE J. ROSI

Contents

Introduction

One hundred and sixty-five years separate the Farewell Addresses of Presidents George Washington and Dwight Eisenhower, both of whom served the country in war and peace and left office with counsel to the nation on matters of "national security." During the first century after Washington delivered his advice, the nation followed the principles he enunciated:

permanent, inveterate antipathies against particular nations and passionate attachment for others, should be excluded; . . . Our detached and distant situation invites and enables us to pursue a different course. Why forego the advantages of so peculiar a situation? Why quit our own to stand upon foreign ground? Why, by interweaving our destiny with that of any part of Europe, entangle our peace and prosperity in the toils of European ambition, rivalship, interest, humor or caprice? It is our true policy to steer clear of permanent alliances with any portion of the foreign world; . . . Taking care always to keep ourselves by suitable establishments, on a respectable defensive posture, we may safely trust to temporary alliances for extraordinary emergencies.

America's preoccupation with the western hemisphere ended in the twentieth century, after what has been called the "passing of the European age." Following a withdrawal from European politics between the two world wars, American policy after World War II deviated almost entirely from Washington's counsels of noninvolvement, which were subordinated, as C. B. Marshall points out, to Washington's other principle of maintaining a "respectable defensive posture."[1]*

The primacy of the principle of national defense was reaffirmed in 1961 by President Eisenhower as he addressed himself to the technological revolution, the impact of which his predecessor could not have foreseen. Although he recognized the military establishment as a "vital element in keeping the peace," Eisenhower called attention to the uniqueness in the American experience of the existence in peacetime of a military establishment and a large arms industry. Despite the "imperative need" for such a development, the President issued his

* Footnotes, where used, appear at the ends of chapters and selections.

1

now famous warning that "in the councils of government we must guard against the acquisition of unwarranted influence, whether sought or unsought, by the military-industrial complex." The President saw the technological revolution as being largely responsible for the development of such a complex, with its influence on research, the universities, and the free scholar. He expressed his respect for scientific research and discovery but cautioned against both the possible domination of the nation's scholars by the federal government and the "equal and opposite danger that public policy could itself become the captive of a scientific-technological elite."

While the primacy of national defense provided a continuity between the two Farewell Addresses, vast changes had occurred domestically and internationally during the elapsed span of more than a century and a half. In 1796 the United States was a new nation of 4 million people on the east coast of a continent which was on the periphery of the Europe-dominated international system. In 1961 it was one of two superpowers, populated by 180 million people, bordered by two oceans, supporting a defense establishment of 2.5 million men, and possessing hundreds of military bases around the globe as well as alliances with 42 nations. National security was a goal of public policy, as William T. R. Fox has written, and no longer a premise of policy as it was during most of the nineteenth century.[2] During the one hundred years after Washington spoke his farewell, geography had more or less guaranteed the new nation considerable freedom of action and national security could be assumed. Recall, for example, Secretary of State Olney's assertion during the Venezuela boundary dispute in 1895 that "Today the United States is practically sovereign on this continent, and its fiat law . . . because . . . in addition to all other grounds, its infinite resources combined with its isolated position render it master of the situation and practically invulnerable as against any or all other powers." In the twentieth century, however, security became an objective. America was now a major actor in the world arena and, after World War II, with technology mastering geography in the form of long-range bombers and ICBM's, security could no longer be assumed. Moreover, the pursuit of national security in the nuclear age was fraught with dangers, both internal and external, some of which were alluded to by President Eisenhower.

In the years following Eisenhower's address, American involvement in the Vietnam war grew to enormous proportions—at its high point represented by more than half a million troops and $30 billion a year—becoming the prime example of what critics called US "globalism." For many of these same critics the war was linked to the military-industrial complex. The war's drain on American material resources and human life—more than 45,000 killed by 1972—exacerbated the problems in American society. A gradual withdrawal of American troops from Vietnam began in 1969, due in part to the domestic unrest. As the United States entered the early 1970's there were increasing signs that some of the American people were tired of the role of "world leadership" that was thrust upon (or seized by, depending on one's interpretation) the United States after World War II.

Since the end of that war, what George Washington referred to as a "respectable defense posture" has often been called "national security policy," with the National Security Act of 1947 placing an official stamp of approval on the use of the term. What is meant by "national security"?[3] As defined here, it means *the security a nation has when its core values are protected against external threats.* A nation's "core values" may include, for example, certain political, social, or economic institutions; liberty; welfare; the preservation of human life; or a whole "way of life." Basic to the concept of national security policy is the necessity for sacrificing some values in order to preserve others. Setting out two extremes may serve to illustrate: by fighting a war a nation may choose to sacrifice much human life in order to preserve a way of life; or it may do the reverse—by surrendering without bloodshed in the face of threat, it may choose to sacrifice a way of life in order to prevent the loss of human life. Whether the decision to be made involves an immediate issue of war or peace, as in the previous example, or simply peacetime defense planning, the essential questions to be asked in making the decision are which values are being threatened, by whom, and in what way? How much is to be sacrificed of which values in order to preserve how much of which other values? What means are to be used?

Questions such as these require answers even if no specific threat exists because security policy is conditioned by the very nature of the international environment: each nation is uncertain of the intentions of the other nations in the international system; each is ultimately dependent upon its own resources for the protection of its values. The way in which a particular nation answers the questions posed will depend upon the interaction of various participants in the political process—participants who may frequently disagree in their perceptions of a possible threat and in their judgments of values to be sacrificed and instruments to be applied. The policies which result from the domestic decision-making process will have an impact on both the international and domestic spheres in an interacting fashion. For example, one of the domestic consequences of America's worldwide security commitments has been the expansion of defense industries (the reverse is argued in some of the readings that follow, which suggest that defense industries have been instrumental in maintaining and extending America's worldwide commitments). In another example, the war in support of the Vietnam commitment has had a profound impact on American society; the domestic consequences of the war have in turn affected subsequent decisions, as the American climate of opinion put pressure on Presidents Johnson and Nixon to modify policy.

In the abstract, then, national security is concerned with the protection of a society's core values from external threat, the assumptions being that the system of nation states will continue to exist for some time and that external threat is a possible consequence of this condition. Although the concept of national security, as outlined here, assumes that military force will remain as an instrument for the protection of the nation, the concept is not narrowly restricted in scope to military affairs; rather it involves the interaction of domestic and international environments in various ways: political, military, economic, and social-psychological. Finally, the concept as given here does not prescribe for each state the particular values to be preserved or sacrificed, the policies for securing particular ends, or the political process by means of which the policies are formulated. To move from this abstract level to a world politics involving the sacrifice of men and resources, one would need to supply at a minimum the values, capabilities, political processes and policies of states X and Y as they reacted to threats from states A and B in the world environment of the year 19____.

It is appropriate at this point to describe briefly and in general the process for making national security decisions in the United States. (Further discussion on aspects of the process, including differing interpretations of how it works, appears in several of the editorial commentaries and selections that follow.) Policy-making in national security affairs is dominated by the executive sector of the government. Initiatives are chiefly in the hands of the President with the assistance of his close advisers, including the Special Assistant for National Security Affairs, the Secretary of Defense, the Secretary of State, and the Chairman of the Joint Chiefs of Staff. Among the advisers to the President in the 1960's, prominent roles were played by Defense Secretary Robert MacNamara and by Special Assistants such as McGeorge Bundy, W. W. Rostow, and Henry Kissinger. The Congress was clearly subordinate, with the influential Armed Services and Appropriations Committees taking the lead in support of substantial defense expenditures. Since the late 1960's, however, the Congress—especially the Senate—has been attempting to assume a stronger position in the defense-policy process, as evidenced by the Senate passage of the National Commitments Resolution in 1969 and the Cooper-Church Amendment in 1970, both of which seek to limit executive action overseas without Congressional approval. (Some of the subsequent Congressional actions in the early 1970's are mentioned in the introduction to Part III.)

Nongovernmental participants in the policy process include the mass media, interest groups such as labor and industry, and individual elites such as scientists and defense intellectuals, who frequently work for study centers like the Rand Corporation and the Hudson Institute.[4] The nongovernmental and governmental elites interact privately and engage in public debate before an audience made up of the attentive public, that small proportion of the general public which is informed and active. The general public is usually poorly informed and uninterested, tending to follow the cues of the president.[5]

The international context within which the domestic policy-making process occurs has been transformed in the twentieth century. The European age of the balance of power has been replaced by the Soviet-American bipolar balance of terror. Empires have been superseded by a Third World of nations, whose unfulfilled expectations have produced rising frustrations. A participation revolution has occurred, as the public's role has increased in the political systems of both developed and less developed nations; for, as Samuel Huntington has suggested, political modernization involves "the extension of political consciousness to new social groups and the mobilization of these groups into politics." [6] The impact of technology can be traced through all of these transformations, particularly in the form of nuclear weapons, mass communications techniques, the green revolution in agriculture, and the population explosion due to medical developments.

The interaction of two of these factors in the policy-making process will be singled out for comment: the exponential growth of technology and the rise of public participation in political systems. One consequence of the rise of public opinion and parliamentary democracy has been to enlarge the number of participants in the policy process. Technology, however, has provided a countervailing force—especially since World War II—a force which enhances the role of the executive branch of government in the formulation, implementation, and explanation of policy. It is difficult for public officials such as Congressmen, let alone for the general public, to understand the nature of modern weapons technology and the implications for policy. This is one of the reasons for Congressional acquiescence to the executive branch in the making of defense policy during much of the post-World War II period. Once policy has been formulated, modern communications technology permits greater executive control of policy implementation; witness President Johnson's virtual daily direction of tactical bombing in Vietnam. Furthermore, mass media techniques, particularly television, present the executive branch with powerful instruments for mobilizing public support of its policies. One need not accept C. Wright Mills's thesis (that the power elite manipulates mass opinion) to appreciate that the power of the executive, combined with the technological abstruseness inherent in such national security issues as nuclear strategy, can produce a feeling of impotence in the public.

Assuming that the interested and informed layman—and in the face of modern technology, the term "layman" probably includes most public officials—is not (and cannot become) a technological expert, what is his role in the policy process? "Technology," simply defined, is *the use of scientific knowledge for human purposes*. It is chiefly these purposes or human values that today constrain man as he faces his environment. Given the potential of modern technology, write Harold and Margaret Sprout, man is no longer restricted by physical factors like geography as in the past—but by purposes, social costs, priorities. [7] Thus, because of the advance of technology, the importance of value considerations is magnified: as Bernard Brodie has suggested, [8] it was easier to limit warfare in the eighteenth century because technology would not permit the destruction of continental proportions that is possible in the nuclear age. Today, judgments must be made about how much is to be allocated to the budget for Health, Education and Welfare compared to that for Defense; and in a democracy such value judgments are mainly comprised of the "expertise" of those who are laymen as far as technology is concerned, the political leaders and the publics they represent.

It may be argued that a state has certain basic "national interests"—with the

President and his national security advisers being the best judges of these—and that values not supportive of these national interests which are introduced into the policy process by various publics are detrimental to the most efficient promotion of national security. Yet as Arnold Wolfers wrote: "In losing sight of the individuals who comprise a state, exponents of the states-as-actors theory may come up with a relatively accurate analysis of national behavior in a period when value patterns remain static, but they are more likely to be mistaken in a period of upheaval in which elites and values are subjected to rapid and radical change." [9]

In such a period of change, not only might the analyst err in his prediction of national behavior but a President and his advisers who followed the states-as-actors-theory would be likely to misjudge the degree of opposition to particular security policies they seek to implement. Within a dynamic international system, American society, and in particular its youth, is obviously undergoing important changes which will affect its national security policy. [10]

The issue that Wolfers has pointed out in this passage is reflected throughout the preceding pages. It is the problem of finding the appropriate level of analysis. Which *is* the key variable in understanding national security policy: the individual, the state, or the international system? All three are important and must be taken into account, as Part I will suggest. So far, the present discussion has briefly covered several aspects of the national security policy process, including the constraints of the international system, the strength of the national executive, and the role of the public. The last aspect to be considered will be the significance of individual perception in the process.

The actions of a state in the international system can be reduced ultimately to the decisions of individual policy-makers. These decisions are based on how the policy-makers perceive an issue and the possible effects of their decisions on the values they consider most important. Policy-makers act on the basis of what have variously been termed as their "definitions of the situation," "theories of international relations," or "perceptions of reality." [11] What is important in making a decision, write Harold and Margaret Sprout, is not the "real" or "objective" environment, but how the decision-maker perceives the environment. In distinguishing between psychological and objective environments, the Sprouts point out that the consequences of a decision will be affected by the "real" environment, whether or not it has been correctly perceived by the decision-maker. Using their example, the Japanese fleet steaming toward the Hawaiian Islands in December 1941 was not in the psychological environment of the American decision-makers before the Pearl Harbor attack, although it was of course in the objective environment. The decisions of the American leaders, based on their perceptions of the environment, did not include preparations for such an attack; however, the consequences of their decisions, beginning with the destruction of the fleet at Pearl Harbor, were affected by what was in the objective environment.

The perceptions of the participants in the policy process are therefore of utmost importance. The student of national security affairs needs to keep in mind that conclusions are not based on facts which "speak for themselves" (a not infrequent assertion in public discussion). Whether intelligence gathering, strategy, or public attitudes are involved, facts are interpreted in some fashion through a theoretical perspective or perception of the situation. Furthermore, writes James Schlesinger in discussing the use of quantification, the higher the decision in the national security process, the more the decision becomes a matter of faith not susceptible to quantification.[12] Perceptions and theoretical perspectives are crucial in answering such questions as which American values are to be promoted and which are to be sacrificed? What are the intentions of the USSR, China? If there is a threat, should it be met by an ABM or a MIRV (multiple independently targeted reentry vehicle)? Will an ABM or a MIRV provoke a more dangerous response? Is the American national interest in Vietnam less vital in the 1970's than it was in the early or mid-1960's? Why? Will the American people support American intervention in the Middle East? Under what conditions would the American people support the use of nuclear weapons?

As the preceding questions suggest, misperception of the intentions, capabilities, or behavior of a state or of the nature of the international system can have dangerous consequences. For example, the origins of the cold war and the action-reaction arms spiral involving the two superpowers have been described as at least partly due to misperceptions on both sides.[13] "The frantic reflex action of intervention" by the United States in the developing countries has been viewed as being mainly the result of American misperceptions about the international system: that it is bipolar, unstable, and tightly coupled (i.e., that a disturbance in one part will affect the entire system).[14]

Safeguards against the pitfalls of misperception are offered in a study by Robert Jervis,[15] who encourages the use of devil's advocates among policymakers to ensure that differing interpretations or images of information are available. Responsible public debate would also seem to lend itself to this type of safeguard by the presentation of (1) alternative interpretations of the significance of events, (2) the possible consequences of alternative actions, and (3) the value implications of both.

This introduction has suggested some of the major themes to be developed in the selections included in this volume. Additional commentary will introduce the material in each of the four parts of the book and each of the selections. Each part introduction will discuss topics dealt with in that part, referring to various other perspectives, and the headnotes will place the selections in context. The task of specifically analyzing each selection and extracting its chief contributions has been left to the student. Following is a brief overview of how the readings are organized.

At the heart of national security policy is the use of power for the purpose of protecting a society's core values from external threats. The selections in Part I offer conflicting interpretations of important variables in this process: considering the nature of power, values, and the national interest; and whether or not American national security policy is the consequence of a pluralistic interaction of individuals, groups, and institutions or the result of manipulation by a power elite.

The sources of possible external threats to American values are the actors and forces in the international system. Part II, in dealing with the contemporary international environment, presents various perspectives on the international system—including a consideration of the balance of terror, technological acceleration, and the challenges of Russia, China, and the Third World nations.

How America responds to perceived challenges or threats in the international environment depends on the domestic environment. The articles in Part III analyze the domestic organization, process, and participants for making security decisions, and include discussion of weapons research and development, and the politics of defense decisions.

The selections in Part IV are intended to illustrate the interaction of the domestic and international environments, involving the implementation of American policy in the world arena and in turn the impact of the international system and American policies on American society. The first four articles in this part are concerned with alliances, military and economic assistance, arms control and disarmament, and limited war. The concluding set of articles deals with the interrelationship of national security policy, society, and the international system by considering the military-industrial complex and the choice between an imperial or exemplary America.

Although many of the readings that follow reflect the biases and premises of the editor, some of which have been made explicit, a number of the selections do not. Within an analytical framework which necessarily represents the editor's perspectives, the intention has been to provide sufficient differences in interpretation—for example, on power elite and pluralism, national interest, deterrence, war profiteering, the military-industrial complex—in order to furnish the kind of devil's advocacy that prevents frozen perspectives. Hopefully, enough of the complexity in the process will have been conveyed so that the reader will not feel inclined to classify the participants literally as the advocates either of the angels of darkness or the angels of light.

NOTES

1. C. B. Marshall, *The Limits of Foreign Policy* (New York: Henry Holt, 1954), p. 85.
2. William T. R. Fox, *The American Study of International Relations* (Columbia, S.C.: University of South Carolina Press, 1968), p. 59.
3. For useful discussions of "national security" both as a concept and as a field of study, see Morton Berkowitz and P. G. Bock, *American National Security* (New York: Free Press, 1965) and "National Security," *The International Encyclopedia of the Social Sciences* (1968). A classic article on the subject, Arnold Wolfers' "National Security as an Ambiguous Symbol," is reprinted in Part I of the present volume (selection 3); other aspects of the subject are discussed in the editorial commentary introducing Part I.
4. For a favorable assessment of the role of the Rand Corporation in the policy process, see Bruce L. R. Smith, *The Rand Corporation* (Cambridge: Harvard University Press, 1966). A critical viewpoint is expressed by Philip Green, "Science, Government, and the Case of RAND: A Singular Pluralism," *World Politics* (July 1968), pp. 592–605. A discussion of various national security centers appears in Gene Lyons and Louis Morton, *Schools for Strategy* (New York: Praeger, 1965).

5. This description of the opinion-policy process follows the pioneering analysis of Gabriel Almond, *The American People and Foreign Policy* (New York: Harcourt, Brace and World, 1950).

6. Samuel Huntington, *Political Order in Changing Societies* (New Haven: Yale University Press, 1968), p. 266.

7. Harold and Margaret Sprout, *Foundations of International Politics* (Princeton, N.J.: Van Nostrand, 1962). This is not to suggest that material factors are irrelevant. For example, with reference to nuclear weapons and strategy: geographic location, distance, and size are importantly related to missile accuracy, warhead yield, and dispersal; although producing a simple atomic bomb is not now a difficult problem, the industrial capacity of the United States and the USSR is required to produce a complex mix of weapons systems.

8. Bernard Brodie, *Strategy in the Missile Age* (Princeton, N.J.: Princeton University Press, 1959), p. 311.

9. Arnold Wolfers, "The Actors in International Politics," in W. T. R. Fox, *Theoretical Aspects of International Relations* (Notre Dame, Ind.: University of Notre Dame Press, 1959), p. 87.

10. For surveys of the attitudes of American youth, see Daniel Seligman, "A Special Kind of Rebellion," *Fortune* (January 1969), pp. 67ff., and Jeremy Main, "Dissidence Among College Students Is Still Growing and It Is Spreading Beyond the Campus," *Fortune* (June 1969), pp. 73–74.

11. See Richard Snyder, H. W. Bruck, and Burton Sapin, *Foreign Policy Decision Making* (New York: The Free Press, 1963); William T. R. Fox, "Theories as Forces in Modern World Politics," in *The American Study of International Relations* (Columbia, S.C.: University of South Carolina Press, 1967); Harold and Margaret Sprout, "Environmental Factors in the Study of International Politics," in James Rosenau, *International Politics and Foreign Policy* (New York: The Free Press, 1961), pp. 106–119.

12. James Schlesinger, "Quantitative Analysis and National Security," *World Politics* (January 1963), pp. 295–315.

13. This interpretation of the cold war origins is Marshall Shulman's in *Beyond the Cold War* (New Haven: Yale University Press, 1966); the interpretation of the arms race is Robert MacNamara's in *The Essence of Security* (New York: Harper and Row, 1968). This is not to imply that misunderstanding is all that separated the USSR and the United States, for as Shulman has written: "all that we know about Soviet behavior in [the early post-World War II period] suggests that had there been no risk in further expansion, and no effective resistance, in all probability Soviet probing would have been far less conservative than it was." *Ibid.,* p. 10.

14. Max Singer and Aaron Wildavsky, "A Third World Averaging Strategy," in Paul Seabury and Aaron Wildavsky, eds., *U.S. Foreign Policy: Perspectives and Proposals for the 1970s* (New York: McGraw-Hill, 1969), pp. 14–16.

15. Robert Jervis, "Hypotheses on Misperception," *World Politics* (April 1968), pp. 454–479.

PART I

Power, Values, and the Pursuit of National Interest

The protection of a nation's core values from external threats requires the mobilization of national power and its projection into the international system. "Mobilization" implies that power is "capacity" or "potential"; one implication of "projection" is that power involves the threat of "severe deprivations" for noncompliance with intended policies.[1] In the making of American national security policy, who does the mobilizing of what kinds of power to achieve what national interests abroad? Our discussion begins with a consideration of power and then turns to national interest and national security.

Power is relational, not simply an absolute and objective quantity that is or is not possessed. A power relationship exists, write Peter Bachrach and Morton Baratz, "when (a) there is a conflict over values or course of action between A and B; (b) B complies with A's wishes; and (c) he does so because he is fearful that A will deprive him of a value or values which he, B, regards more highly than those which would have been achieved by noncompliance."[2]

Here are three illustrations of the relational aspects of power. The first power relationship exists between the would-be wielder of power and the object. As the work of Thomas Schelling[3] has emphasized, the communication process is significant in understanding power: if the object of a threat does not perceive that he is being threatened, the wielder of power is in effect powerless, unable to achieve his desired ends by threatening deprivation, and compelled either to withdraw or use force. For example, a person can not be threatened with a pistol to "do such and such or else" if the person does not know what a pistol is, does not hear the threat, or misinterprets the message. Furthermore, in the wielder-object relationship, values as well as perceptions are important. The expectations of the wielder of power, State A, may not be fulfilled due to a misunderstanding of the values of the object nation. This may partly explain why the United States was unable to compel North Vietnam to the negotiating table on its own terms by threatening escalation (and escalating). Or the achievement of State A's external goals may be offset by a feedback effect on State A internally of its use of power or force externally. For example,

America's use of power and coercion in Vietnam has set in motion vast social and political forces in our own society.

The foregoing examples suggest a second power relationship: that which exists between decision-makers and the populace of their own country. Ultimately, the use of power rests on the support of the nation, whose willingness to sacrifice will be greater for some goals than others. In the process of using power, however, the values sacrificed (e.g., education, health) within the society for external goals may turn out to be more important than those gained in the pursuit of a foreign policy. "The security of the Nation is not at the ramparts alone. Security also lies in the value of our free institutions," wrote Judge M. I. Gurfein in denying governmental "prior censorship" in the *New York Times* "Pentagon Papers" case.[4]

A third power relationship links the states directly involved in the exercise of power with the international system. Each state must calculate its actions in light of the relativity of power in the international system, where a change in the power of State A relative to State B will necessarily have implications for the relationships of A and B with allies, adversaries, and neutrals.

Power was made the central concept of political science and international relations by the post-World War II "Realist" school, which maintained that "all politics is a struggle for power."[5] As many critics have indicated, such a definition reduces the analytical utility of the concept, since in it the term "power" is used so broadly that it explains everything and nothing. Rather than being an end in itself, power is usually a means to other ends, such as the shaping of a society according to a particular set of values and purposes, or the promotion of national interests. A broad definition of "the pursuit of American national interests" might be *the maintenance at least cost of American values or the American way of life.* Several questions arise from this general definition: What are the values to be maintained? What will be the cost to which other values? Who will decide such questions concerning the ends and means of national security policy?

We will deal with these questions by considering four ways of approaching the concept of national interest (see figure), two at opposite ends of a horizontal "yes" axis ("There are national interests") and two at opposite ends of a vertical "no" axis ("There are no national interests"). At the top of the no-national-interest axis appears the supranational interests approach—including concern for humanity, world government, and a classless world society— all of which are in opposition to national egotism. Expectations for the early demise of the nation state fall into this category, as well as some of the views of leaders like Woodrow Wilson, whom the Realists criticized for sacrificing national interest to universalist wishful thinking. For example, Hans Morgenthau maintained in *In Defense of the National Interest* that "Wilson's thought not only disregards the national interest, but is explicity opposed to it on moral grounds."[6]

At the bottom of the vertical "no" axis appears the subnational interests approach category. Here would fall those explanations which maintain that

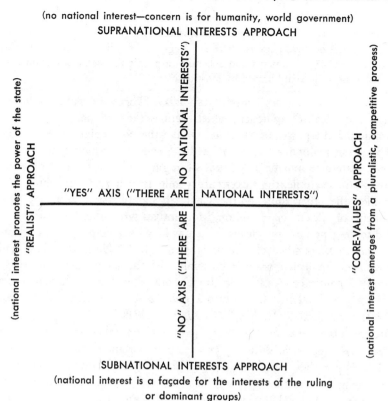

(no national interest—concern is for humanity, world government)
SUPRANATIONAL INTERESTS APPROACH

"YES" AXIS ("THERE ARE NATIONAL INTERESTS")

NO NATIONAL INTERESTS")

"NO" AXIS ("THERE ARE

(national interest promotes the power of the state)
"REALIST" APPROACH

"CORE-VALUES" APPROACH
(national interest emerges from a pluralistic, competitive process)

SUBNATIONAL INTERESTS APPROACH
(national interest is a façade for the interests of the ruling
or dominant groups)

**FOUR WAYS OF APPROACHING THE CONCEPT
OF NATIONAL INTEREST**

national interest is a facade for the interests of the ruling or dominant groups. C. Wright Mills argued in *The Power Elite,*[7] for example, that an overlapping elite composed of the corporate rich, the military, and the politicians dominated American society. This self-perpetuating, upper-class group with coinciding interests, according to Mills, determined policy—especially the "big decisions" like the Korean war and dropping the Atomic bomb on Japan. At the middle levels of power, which includes the Congress and interest groups, stalemate exists; at the broad base of the pyramid, the masses are manipulated by the elites. The following caveats, offered by one of Mills's supporters, G. William Domhoff, dilute the power-elite thesis, however:

The control is not complete; other groups sometimes have their innings, particularly when these groups are well organized and angry. Nor is the power elite always united in its policies; there are long standing disagreements between its moderate and conservative wings on some issues, as manifested, for example in the arguments between the Committee for Economic Development and the National Association of Manufacturers. Nor does the power elite automatically act in its best interests; to read case studies of specific decisions is to be aware that lack of information, misunderstandings, and personality clashes may lead to mistakes on issues that must be decided in a hurry. For all of these reasons, there is a degree of conflict and complexity in this country of 38,000 governments and 200 million people that lends a certain credence to the portrait of diversity drawn by most observers.[8]

On one side of the horizontal "yes" axis ("There are national interests") appears the "Realist" approach, which defines the national interest in terms of promoting the power of the state. Unlike the power-elite thesis, the Realist interpretation maintains that all states have enduring national interests which rational statesmen pursue regardless of regime, ideology, class, or economic interests—for example, the three-century-long British preoccupation with who controlled the other shore of the Channel. Paraphrasing with approval the sentiments of Alexander Hamilton, Morgenthau wrote that the statesman "can afford to be generous and idealistic . . . as long as generosity and idealism are not likely to affect adversely the national interest." [9] He must choose national interest over legalistic-moralistic principles. At the same time, however, "it is not only a political necessity but also a moral duty for a nation to follow in its dealings with other nations but one guiding star, one standard for thought, one rule for action: *THE NATIONAL INTEREST*." [10]

On the other end of the "yes" axis appears what may be called the "core-values" approach, differing in several important respects from the three previous approaches. Emphasizing that nations pursue multiple values rather than chiefly power, those who follow the core-values approach argue that conceptions of national interest emerge from a pluralistic, competitive process within American society as various groups with differing perceptions of national interests seek to persuade other elites, the attentive public, and the general public of the correctness of their particular interpretation. General agreement on fundamental and enduring national interests, according to this approach, exists only in times of clearly perceived crisis. A nation may feel secure when it perceives it has the power to protect its core values against external attack; it may feel insecure when the opposite is the case. Decisions to protect these values do not simply follow the Golden Rule; nor are they amoral reactions to the "necessities of power politics"—rather, both moral judgment and compromise are unavoidable. As Arnold Wolfers wrote:

Despite the difficulties of doing justice to the statesman and avoiding the pitfalls of politically dangerous as well as morally untenable condemnations, men who have non-perfectionist and non-nationalistic moral convictions dare not evade the task of moral judgment whether of their own political acts or of the acts of others. Where there is so much room for moral choice as there is in international politics and where the destiny of entire nations depends on these choices, attempts to evade, silence or ignore moral judgment merely play into the hands of those who relish the uncriticized use or abuse of their power. The Nazi leaders were helped by the climate of moral cynicism which prevailed in Germany. It made it easy for them to justify even the most brutal acts on the grounds of necessity of state or to glorify their freedom from any "decadent" moral inhibitions.[11]

Since the end of World War II, public debate over conceptions of national interest and national security has waxed and waned. Beginning in the late 1940's and lasting over a decade, the Realists and the Idealists argued over national interest, international organization, power, and moral principle. (The Idealists' position was presented in T. I. Cook and Malcolm Moos's *Power Through Purpose;* selections 1, 2, and 3 in this part were also important contributions to the debate.) The issue was initially joined over whether or not American policy-makers during World War II neglected political considerations for purely military victory in a moralistic crusade to free the world of balance of power politics. Both the Realist and Idealist positions were disputed in the 1960's by the cold war Revisionists, who maintained that the United States had been far from utopian, naive, and neglectful of American interests; to the contrary they argued that in the 1940's the United States had thrown its nuclear weight around and was itself the chief cause of the cold war.[12] A theoretical framework for some of these interpretations was available in Mills's *The Power Elite,* published in 1956, which foreshadowed many of the contemporary criticisms of the military-industrial complex in its allusions to America's "permanent war economy" and "military capitalism," as well as to the "military definition of world reality" and "crackpot realism" that Mills believed were the controlling perspectives for postwar American foreign policy. World War II marked the beginning of a new era for the United States, according to Mills, because the war permitted the power elite to assume its dominant position, thereby ending the political era of the 1930's. The fundamental shift from the domestic welfare concerns of the 1930's to the external security concerns of the postwar period was also noted by Arnold Wolfers who, unlike Mills, cited the importance of the external threat to American values that emerged after the war.

Three decades have passed since the United States entered World War II, and we appear now to be moving into another era, one in which internal welfare values will again receive greater emphasis. To the extent that national debates are ever "won" or "lost" and have an impact on decision-making, it may perhaps be concluded that in the postwar era, realism has prevailed over idealism—at least in a modified form. Discussions of American foreign policy are couched predominantly in terms of national interest, balance of power, spheres of influence, and arms control, rather than in terms of general and complete disarmament, world government, or considering the UN as the cornerstone of US foreign policy. Many academics and intellectuals seem to prefer being considered hard-nosed rather than woolly-headed.

The Vietnam war may further serve to support the generalization that realism has prevailed over idealism. It is true that, on the one hand, it can be said that American policy-makers never learned the lessons of realism—that the Vietnam war is an example of "illusions of omnipotence," "globalist pretentions," "a moral crusade for democracy against the communist monolith," the "rampant military mind"—all adding up to the fundamental neglect of the national interest. But on the other hand, one can argue that the war shows that the lessons of realism may have been learned quite well. Judging from the secret memoranda that were published in the Pentagon Papers, a number of analyses and recommendations concerning that war—many by civilian intellectuals and not the military—seemed to be inspired less by visions of a moralistic crusade against atheistic communism ·than by an essentially Realist conceptual framework, which based policy calculations on the "necessities" of superpower national interest and responsibilities for maintaining order and a world power balance. The following examples are suggestive:

U.S. aims—70%—to avoid a humiliating U.S. defeat (to our reputation as a guarantor). 20%—to keep SVN (and the adjacent) territory from Chinese hands. 10%— to permit the people of SVN to enjoy a better, freer way of life. . . . It is essential —however badly SEA may go over the next 1–3 years—that U.S. emerge as a "good doctor." We must have kept promises, been tough, taken risks, gotten bloodied, and hurt the enemy very badly. We must avoid harmful appearances which will affect judgments by, and provide pretexts to, other nations regarding how the U.S. will behave in future cases of particular interest to those nations—regarding U.S. policy, power, resolve and competence to deal with their problems . . . (memorandum dated March 24, 1965, by John T. McNaughton, then Assistant Secretary of Defense for International Security Affairs).

. . . our assets, as I see them are sufficient to see this thing through if we enter the exercise with adequate determination to succeed. I know well the anxieties and complications on our side of the line. But there may be a tendency to underestimate both the anxieties and complications on the other side and also to underestimate that limited but real margin of influence on the outcome which flows from the simple fact that at this stage of history we are the greatest power in the world—if we behave like it. (Letter dated November 16, 1964, by Walt W. Rostow, then Chairman of the State Department's Policy Planning Council.) [13]

Vietnam policy-makers in both the Johnson and Nixon Administrations might well see some of their own dilemmas reflected in the following passages from Morgenthau's In Defense of the National Interest:

The kind of thinking required for the successful conduct of foreign policy must at times be diametrically opposed to the kind of considerations by which the masses and their representatives are likely to be moved. The peculiar qualities of the statesman's mind are not always likely to find a favorable response in the popular mind. The statesman must think in terms of the national interest, conceived as power among other powers. The popular mind, unaware of the fine distinctions of the statesman's thinking, reasons more often than not in simple moralistic and legalistic terms of absolute good and absolute evil. The statesman must take the long view, proceeding slowly and by detours, paying with small losses for great advantages; he must be able to temporize, to compromise, to bide his time. The popular mind wants quick results; it will sacrifice tomorrow's real benefit for today's apparent advantage. . . . A tragic choice often confronts those responsible for the conduct of foreign affairs. They must either sacrifice what they consider good policy upon the altar of public opinion, or by devious means gain popular support for policies whose true nature they conceal from the public. . . . The framers of American foreign policy must possess a deep understanding of both our national interest and our national strength. They must be imbued with the moral determination to defend to the last what they know the national interest requires, and they must be prepared to face political defeat at home rather than gamble away the interests and perhaps the very existence of the nation for a fleeting triumph in the next elections.[14]

The Realists sought to restore national interest and power to their proper places in international politics following their depreciation and the failures of utopianism after the two world wars. However, an unintended contribution of Realist effort may have been to push the pendulum in the United States further than desired in the direction of a "security" or "power politics" perspective, one which has been oriented generally (and particularly in Vietnam policy) toward military instrumentalities more than political accommodation. A corrective to the swing of the pendulum may lie in some of the views of the Realists' *bête noire*, Woodrow Wilson. The termination of the "large-scale limited war" in Vietnam may be facilitated, writes William T. R. Fox, by a "peace of reconciliation" such as that implied in Wilson's *Fourteen Points*, which suggested, again according to Fox, that Wilson believed "magnanimity and moderation before the fighting had completely ended made for both an earlier and a better ending of War." [15]

NOTES

1. Various characteristics of power are discussed in the selection by Holsti (selection 4). On "potential," see Harold and Margaret Sprout, *Foundations of International Politics* (Princeton, N.J.: Van Nostrand, 1962). Power as "deprivation" is the usage of Harold Lasswell and Abraham Kaplan, *Power and Society* (New Haven: Yale University Press, 1950).

2. Peter Bachrach and Morton Baratz, "Decisions and Nondecisions: An Analytical Framework," *American Political Science Review* (September 1963), p. 635.

3. Thomas Schelling, *The Strategy of Conflict* (Cambridge: Harvard University Press, 1960).

4. *New York Times,* June 20, 1971.

5. A selection by the leader of this school, Hans Morgenthau, appears in this part (selection 1). Viewing the essence of politics as the "dependable coordination of human efforts and expectations for the attainment of the goals of the society," Karl Deutsch has criticized the narrow usage of power—"the ability to afford not to learn"—and offers a conception of power as the "currency" of politics. See Deutsch, *The Nerves of Government* (New York: Free Press, 1963) and *The Analysis of International Relations* (Englewood Cliffs, N.J.: Prentice-Hall, 1968).

6. Hans Morgenthau, *In Defense of the National Interest* (New York: Knopf, 1951).

7. C. Wright Mills, *The Power Elite* (New York: Oxford, 1956).

8. G. William Domhoff and Hoyt B. Ballard, *C. Wright Mills and The Power Elite* (Boston: Beacon Press, 1968), p. 277.

9. Hans Morgenthau, "National Interest and Moral Principle in Foreign Policy," *The American Scholar* (Spring 1949), p. 212.

10. *In Defense of the National Interest* (above, n. 6), p. 242.

11. Arnold Wolfers, "Statesmanship and Moral Choice," *World Politics* (January 1949), p. 194.

12. E.g., D. F. Fleming, *The Cold War and Its Origins* (New York: Doubleday, 1961); W. A. Williams, *The Tragedy of American Diplomacy* (New York: Dell, 1962); Gar Alperovitz, *Atomic Diplomacy: Hiroshima and Potsdam* (New York: Vintage, 1965).

13. *New York Times,* June 15, 1971, p. 20.

14. *In Defense of the National Interest* (above, n. 6), pp. 223, 224, 230.

15. William T. R. Fox, "The Causes of Peace and Conditions of War," *Annals of the American Academy of Political and Social Science* (November 1970), p. 13.

1.

Hans J. Morgenthau: *Another "Great Debate":* *The National Interest of the United States*

The active participation of the United States in world politics after World War II was quickly followed by disillusionment over the broken hopes for peace and world organization. The Realists attributed the lack of American preparation for postwar realities—chiefly the emergence of Soviet power—to the strain of legalistic-moralistic idealism in US policy, which had expected to replace nation states striving to maximize their strength in a world of power politics with the "coordinate state" based on the equal dignity and mutual interdependence of nations.

At the center of the Realist-Idealist debate, which began in the mid 1940's and continued to the early 1960's, was Professor Hans J. Morgenthau, for whom the neglect of American national interest in favor of supranational sentimentalism and wishful thinking was due to a half-century of "ever more complete intoxication with moral abstractions." Professor Morgenthau's numerous books and articles set forth the principles of political realism—including the national interest defined in terms of power—for colleagues, practitioners and thousands of college students. *Politics Among Nations,* first published in 1948 at the height of the Cold War, is in its fourth edition. Among Morgenthau's other works are *In Defense of the National Interest, Dilemmas of Politics,* and *A New Foreign Policy for the United States.* He is Professor of Political Science and Modern History at the University of Chicago and Leonard Davis Distinguished Professor of Political Science at the City University of New York.

The controversy which has arisen on the occasion of Ambassador Kennan's and my recent publications differs from the great historical debates on American foreign policy in two significant respects. It raises an issue more fundamental to the understanding of American foreign policy and of all politics than those with which the previous "great debates" were concerned, and it deals with the issue largely in terms which are not conducive to understanding.

The great debates of the past, such as the one over intervention vs. neutrality in 1793, expansion vs. the status quo before the Mexican and after the Spanish-American War, international cooperation vs. isolation in the 'twenties, intervention vs. abstention in the late 'thirties—all evolved around clear-cut issues

Hans J. Morgenthau, "Another Great Debate: The National Interest of the United States," *American Political Science Review* (December 1952), pp. 961–88. Footnotes omitted. Reprinted by permission of the American Political Science Association and the author.

of foreign policy. In 1793 you were in favor of going to war on the side of France or of remaining neutral. In the 1840's you approved of the annexation of Texas or you did not. At the turn of the century you supported overseas expansion or you were against it. In the 'twenties you advocated joining the League of Nations or staying out of it. In the late 'thirties you wanted to oppose the Axis Powers by all means short of war or you wanted to abstain from intervening. What separates the "utopian" from the "realist" position cannot be so sharply expressed in terms of alternative foreign policies. The very same policies can be and are being supported by both schools of thought. What sets them apart is not necessarily a matter of practical judgment, but of philosophies and standards of thought.

The issue which the present debate raises concerns the nature of all politics and, more particularly, of the American tradition in foreign policy. The history of modern political thought is the story of a contest between two schools which differ fundamentally in their conception of the nature of man, society, and politics. One believes that a rational and moral political order, derived from universally valid abstract principles, can be achieved here and now. It assumes the essential goodness and infinite malleability of human nature and attributes the failure of the social order to measure up to the rational standards to lack of knowledge and understanding, obsolescent social institutions, or the depravity of certain isolated individuals or groups. It trusts in education, reform, and the sporadic use of force to remedy these deficiencies.

The other school believes that the world, imperfect as it is from the rational point of view, is the result of forces which are inherent in human nature. To improve the world one must work with those forces, not against them. This being inherently a world of opposing interests and of conflict among them, moral principles can never be fully realized, but at best approximated through the ever temporary balancing of interests and the ever precarious settlement of conflicts. This school, then, sees in a system of checks and balances a universal principle for all pluralist societies. It appeals to historic precedent rather than to abstract principles, and aims at achievement of the lesser evil rather than of the absolute good.

This conflict between two basic conceptions of man and politics is at the bottom of the present controversy. It is the same conflict which found its classic expression in the polemic of Burke against the philosophy of the French Revolution. Given the sad state of political thought in our time, it would be vain to expect the spokesmen of political realism to speak with the voice of Burke and the defenders of political utopianism to measure up to the standards of Condorcet and Rousseau. Yet one has a right to expect that scholars discuss the issue without resort to invective and with proper regard for established facts.

I

In order to refute a theory which pretends to be scientific, it is first necessary to understand what a scientific theory is. A scientific theory is an attempt to bring order and meaning to a mass of phenomena which without it would remain disconnected and unintelligible. Anyone who disputes the scientific character of such a theory either must produce a theory superior in these scientific functions to the one attacked or must, at the very least, demonstrate that the facts as they actually are do not lend themselves to the interpretation which the theory has put upon them. When a historian tells us that the balance of power is not a universal principle of politics, domestic and international, that it was practiced in Europe only for a limited period and never by the United States, that it ruined the states that practiced it, it is incumbent upon him to tell us how we can dispose by means of theory of the historic data by which, for instance, David Hume demonstrated the universality of the balance of power and Paul Scott Mowrer and Alfred Vagts its practice by the United States; what Kautilya was writing about in the fourth century B.C. when he summarized the theoretical and practical tradition of Indian statecraft in terms of the balance of power; what the Greek city states, the Roman republic, and the medieval emperors and popes were doing if they did not apply the principles of the balance of power; and how the nations which either neglected these principles or applied them wrongly suffered political and military defeat and even extinction, while the nation which applied these principles most consistently and consciously, that is, Great Britain, enjoyed unrivalled power for an unparalleled length of time.

The historian who wishes to replace the balance of power as the guiding principle of American foreign policy with the "humanitarian and pacific traditions" of the "coördinate state" must first of all explain how it has come about that the thirteen original states expanded into the full breadth and a good deal of the length of a continent, until today the strategic frontiers of the United States run parallel to the coastline of Asia and along the River Elbe. If such are the results of policies based upon "humanitarian and pacific traditions," never in the history of the world has virtue been more bountifully rewarded! Yet our historian must explain not only the great sweep of American expansion, but also the specific foreign policies which in their historic succession make up that sweep. Is it easier to explain the successive shifts of American support from Great Britain to France and back again from the beginning of King George's War in 1744 to the War of 1812 in terms of the "coördinate state" than in terms of the balance of power? The same question might be asked about the postponement of the recognition of the independence of the Spanish colonies until 1822, when the Floridas had been acquired from Spain and Spain had thereby been deprived of the ability to challenge the United States from within the hemisphere. The same question might be asked about the Monroe Doctrine itself, about Lincoln's policies toward Great Britain and France, and about our successive policies with regard to Mexico and the Caribbean. One could go on and pick out at random any foreign policy pursued by the United States from the beginning to 1919 and one would hardly find a policy, with the exception perhaps of the War of 1812, which could not be made intelligible by reference to the national interest defined in terms of power—political, military, and economic—rather than by reference to the principle of the "coördinate state." This inevitable outcome of such an inquiry is well summarized in these words:

Ease and prosperity have made us wish the whole world to be as happy and well to do as ourselves; and we have supposed that institutions and principles like our own were the simple prescription for making them so. And yet, when issues of our own interest arose, we have not been unselfish. We have shown ourselves kin to all the world, when it came to pushing an advantage. Our action against Spain in the Floridas, and against Mexico on the coasts of the Pacific; our attitude toward first the Spaniards, and then the French, with regard to the control of the Mississippi; the unpitying force with which we thrust the Indians to the wall wherever they stood in our way, have suited our professions of peacefulness and justice and liberality no better than the aggressions of other nations that were strong and not to be gainsaid. Even Mr. Jefferson, philanthropist and champion of peaceable and modest government though he was, exemplified this double temper of the people he ruled. "Peace is our passion," he had declared; but the passion abated when he saw the mouth of the Mississippi about to pass into the hands of France. Though he had loved France and hated England, he did not hesitate then what language to hold. "There is on the globe," he wrote to Mr. Livingston at Paris, "one single spot the possessor of which is our natural and habitual enemy. The day that France takes possession of New Orleans seals the union of two nations, who, in conjunction, can maintain exclusive possession of the sea. From that moment we must marry ourselves to the British fleet and nation." Our interests must march forward, altruists though we are; other nations must see to it that they stand off, and do not seek to stay us.

This realist appraisal of the American tradition in foreign policy was published in 1901 in the *Atlantic Monthly*. Its author was a professor of jurisprudence and political economy at Princeton by the name of Woodrow Wilson.

Nothing more needs to be said to demonstrate that facts do not support a revision of American diplomatic history which tries to substitute "humanitarian and pacifist traditions" and the "coördinate state" for power politics and the balance of power as the guiding principle of American foreign policy. What, then, does support it? Three things: the way American statesmen have spoken about American foreign policy; the legal fiction of the "coördinate state"; finally, and foremost, an emotional urge to justify American foreign policy in humanitarian, pacifist terms.

It is elementary that the character of a foreign policy can be ascertained only through the examination of the political acts performed and of the foreseeable consequences of these acts. Thus we can find out what statesmen have actually done, and from the foreseeable consequences of their acts we can surmise what their objectives might have been. Yet examination of the facts is not enough. To give meaning to the factual raw material of history, we must approach historical reality with a kind of rational outline, a map which suggests to us the possible meanings of history. In other words, we put ourselves in the position of a statesman who must meet a certain problem of foreign policy under certain circumstances and ask ourselves, what are the rational alternatives from which a statesman may choose who must meet this problem under these circumstances, presuming always that he acts in a rational manner, and which of these rational alternatives was this particular statesman, acting under these circumstances, likely to choose? It is the testing of this rational hypothesis against the actual facts and their consequences which gives meaning to the facts of history and makes the scientific writing of political history possible. . . .

In truth, it is not the disinterested consideration of facts which has given birth to the theory of the "coördinate state." That theory is rather the response to an emotional urge, and since this emotion is not peculiar to a particular author but typical of a popular reaction to the new role which the United States must play in world affairs, it deserves a brief analysis.

One of the great experiences of our time which have impressed themselves upon the American mind is the emergence of the United States as a nation among other nations, exposed to the same opportunities, temptations, risks, and liabilities to which other nations have been traditionally exposed. This experience becomes the more shocking if it is compared with the expectation with which we fought the Second World War. We expected from that war a reaffirmation of the secure, detached, and independent position in world affairs which we had inherited from the Founding Fathers and which we had been successful in preserving at least to the First World War. By avoiding what we thought had been Wilson's mistakes, we expected to emerge from that war if not more independent, certainly more secure than we were when we entered it. In fact, probably not even in the early days of the Republic were we more exposed to danger from abroad than we are today, and never had we less freedom of action in taking care of our interests than we have today.

It is naturally shocking to recognize that a happy chapter in the history of the nation and in one's own way of life has come to an end. There are those who reconcile themselves to the inevitable, albeit with sorrow rather than with glee, and try to apply the lessons of the past to the tasks at hand. There are others who try to escape from a disappointing and threatening reality into the realm of fantasy. Three such escapist fantasies have arisen in our midst in response to the challenge of American world leadership and power: the fantasy of needless American participation in war, the fantasy of American treason, and the fantasy of American innocence.

The first of these fantasies presumes that the present predicament is a result not of necessity but of folly, the folly of American statesmen who needlessly intervened in two world wars. The second of these fantasies attributes the present predicament to treason in high places whereby the fruits of victory were handed to the enemy. The third of these fantasies denies that the predicament is real and prefers to think of it as an intellectual fraud perpetrated upon the American people. To support this fictional denial of the actualities of the present, it draws upon a fictional account of the past. The United States does not need to bear at present the intellectual, moral, and political burdens which go with involvement in power politics and the maintenance of the balance of power; for it has never borne them in the past, never having been thus involved. The golden age of past political innocence sheds its glow upon a but seemingly less innocent present and promises a future in which all the world will follow the example of America, forswear power politics and the balance of power, and accept the principle of the "coördinate state." Our rearmament program, as exemplified in the Atlantic Security Pact, we are told, has nothing to do with the balance of power but aims at the "organization of as much of the world as we can upon the basis of the coördinate state. . . . It may prove impossible under present conditions to build such a system without having to fight a war with Russia, but then at least we will be fighting, as we did before, for the thing we consider worth defending with our lives and treasure." Thus a fictional account of the American past, begun as an act of uncalled-for patriotic piety, issues in an ideology for a third world war. Escape we must from the unfamiliar, unpleasant, and dangerous present, first into the political innocence of the past and from there into the immediate future of a third world war, beyond which the revived and universalized innocence of the more distant future will surely lie.

We have said that to present the American tradition in foreign policy as having been free from concern with power politics and the balance of power is not warranted by the facts of American history. Yet it might still be argued, and it is actually being argued, that, regardless of the evidence of history, the American people will not be reconciled to power politics and the balance of power and will support only policies based upon abstract moral principles. While in the past the United States might have pursued balance of power policies and while it might be a good thing if it did so again, the American people will not stand for it. Here the emotional appeal to patriotic piety is joined by calculations of political expediency. Yet the case for misrepresenting American history has nothing to gain from either.

There is a strong tendency in all historiography to glorify the national past, and in popular presentations that tendency takes on the aspects of the jingoist whitewash. Even so penetrating a mind as John Stuart Mill's could deliver himself of an essay in which he proved, no doubt to the satisfaction of many of his English readers but certainly of few others, that Great Britain had never interfered in the affairs of European nations and had interfered in those of the Indian states only for their own good. Yet it is the measure of a nation's maturity to be able to recognize its past for what it actually is. Why should we not admit that American foreign policy has been generally hardheaded and practical and at times ruthless? Why should we deny Jefferson's cunning, say, in the Puget Sound affair, the cruelty with which the Indians were treated, and the faithlessness with which the treaties with the Indians were cast aside? We know that this is the way all nations are when their interests are at stake— so cruel, so faithless, so cunning. We know that the United States has refrained from seeking dominions beyond the seas not because it is more virtuous than other nations, but because it had the better part of a continent to colonize.

As has been pointed out elsewhere at greater length, the man in the street, unsophisticated as he is and uninformed as he may be, has a surer grasp of the essentials of foreign policy and a more mature judgment of its basic issues than many of the intellectuals and politicians who pretend to speak for him and cater to what they imagine his prejudices to be. During the recent war the ideologues of the Atlantic Charter, the Four Freedoms, and the United Nations were constantly complaining that the American soldier did not know what he was fighting for. Indeed, if he was fighting for some utopian ideal, divorced from the concrete experiences and interests of the country, then the complaint was well grounded. However, if he was fighting for the territorial integrity of the nation and for its survival as a free country where he could live, think, and act as he pleased, then he had never any doubt about what he was fighting for. Ideological rationalizations and justifications are indeed the indispensable concomitants of all political action. Yet there is something unhealthy in a craving for ideological intoxication and in the inability to act and to see merit in action except under the stimulant of grandiose ideas and far-fetched schemes. Have our intellectuals become, like Hamlet, too much beset by doubt to act and, unlike Hamlet, compelled to still their doubts by renouncing their sense of what is real? The man in the street has no such doubts. It is true that ideologues and demagogues can sway him by appealing to his emotions. But it is also true, as American history shows in abundance and as the popular success of Ambassador Kennan's book demonstrates, that responsible statesmen can guide him by awakening his latent understanding of the national interest.

II

Yet what is the national interest? How can we define it and give it the content which will make it a guide for action? This is one of the relevant questions to which the current debate has given rise.

It has been frequently argued against the realist conception of foreign policy that its key concept, the national interest, does not provide an acceptable standard for political action. This argument is in the main based upon two grounds: the elusiveness of the concept and its susceptibility to interpretations, such as limitless imperialism and narrow nationalism, which are not in keeping with the American tradition in foreign policy. The argument has substance as far as it goes, but it does not invalidate the usefulness of the concept.

The concept of the national interest is similar in two respects to the "great generalities" of the Constitution, such as the general welfare and due process. It contains a residual meaning which is inherent in the concept itself, but beyond these minimum requirements its content can run the whole gamut of meanings which are logically compatible with it. That content is determined by the political traditions and the total cultural content within which a nation formulates its foreign policy. The concept of the national interest, then, contains two elements, one that is logically required and in that sense necessary, and one that is variable and determined by circumstances.

Any foreign policy which operates under the standard of the national interest must obviously have some reference to the physical, political, and cultural entity which we call a nation. In a world where a number of sovereign nations compete with and oppose each other for power, the foreign policies of all nations must necessarily refer to their survival as their minimum requirements. Thus all nations do what they cannot help but do: protect their physical, political, and cultural identity against encroachments by other nations.

It has been suggested that this reasoning erects the national state into the last word in politics and the national interest into an absolute standard for political action. This, however, is not quite the case. The idea of interest is indeed of the essence of politics and, as such, unaffected by the circumstances of time and place. Thucydides' statement, born of the experiences of ancient Greece, that "identity of interest is the surest of bonds whether between states or individuals" was taken up in the nineteenth century by Lord Salisbury's remark that "the only bond of union that endures" among nations is "the absence of all clashing interests." The perennial issue between the realist and utopian schools of thought over the nature of politics, to which we have referred before, might well be formulated in terms of concrete interests vs. abstract principles. Yet while the concern of politics with interest is perennial, the connection between interest and the national state is a product of history.

The national state itself is obviously a product of history and as such destined to yield in time to different modes of political organization. As long as the world is politically organized into nations, the national interest is indeed the last word in world politics. When the national state will have been replaced by another mode of organization, foreign policy must then protect the interest in survival of that new organization. For the benefit of those who insist upon discarding the national state and constructing supranational organizations by constitutional fiat, it must be pointed out that these new organizational forms will either come into being through conquest or else through consent based upon the mutual recognition of the national interests of the nations concerned; for no nation will forego its freedom of action if it has no reason to expect proportionate benefits in compensation for that loss. This is true of treaties concerning commerce or fisheries as it is true of the great compacts, such as the European Coal and Steel Community, through which nations try to create supranational forms of organization. Thus, by an apparent paradox, what is historically relative in the idea of the national interest can be overcome only through the promotion in concert of the national interest of a number of nations.

The survival of a political unit, such as a nation, in its identity is the irreducible minimum, the necessary element of its interests vis-à-vis other units. Taken in isolation, the determination of its content in a concrete situation is relatively simple; for it encompasses the integrity of the nation's territory, of its political institutions, and of its culture. Thus bipartisanship in foreign policy, especially in times of war, has been most easily achieved in the promotion of these minimum requirements of the national interest. The situation is different with respect to the variable elements of the national interest. All the cross currents of personalities, public opinion, sectional interests, partisan politics, and political and moral folkways are brought to bear upon their determination. In consequence, the contribution which science can make to this field, as to all fields of policy formation, is limited. It can identify the different agencies of the government which contribute to the determination of the variable elements of the national interest and assess their relative weight. It can separate the long-range objectives of foreign policy from the short-term ones which are the means for the achievement of the former and can tentatively establish their rational relations. Finally, it can analyze the variable elements of the national interest in terms of their legitimacy and their compatibility with other national values and with the national interest of other nations. We shall address ourselves briefly to the typical problems with which this analysis must deal.

The legitimacy of the national interest must be determined in the face of possible usurpation by subnational, other-national, and supranational interests. On the subnational level we find group interests, represented particularly by ethnic and economic groups, who tend to identify themselves with the national interest. Charles A. Beard has emphasized, however one-sidedly, the extent to which the economic interests of certain groups have been presented as those of the United States. Group interests exert, of course, constant pressure upon the conduct of our foreign policy, claiming their identity with the national interest. It is, however, doubtful that, with the exception of a few spectacular cases, they have been successful in determining the course of American foreign policy. It is much more likely, given the nature of American domestic politics, that American foreign policy, insofar as it is the object of pressures by sectional interests, will normally be a compromise between divergent sectional interests. The concept of the national interest, as it emerges from this contest as the actual guide for foreign policy, may well fall short of what would be rationally required by the overall interests of the United States. Yet the concept of the national interest which emerges from this contest of conflicting sectional interests is also more than any particular sectional interest or their sum total. It is, as it were, the lowest common denominator where sectional interests and the national interest meet in an uneasy compromise which may leave much to be desired in view of all the interests concerned.

The national interest can be usurped by other-national interests in two typical ways. The case of treason by individuals, either out of conviction or for pay, needs only to be mentioned here; for insofar as treason is committed on behalf of a foreign government rather than a supranational principle, it is significant for psychology, sociology, and criminology, but not for the theory of politics. The other case, however, is important not only for the theory of politics but also for its practice, especially in the United States.

National minorities in European countries, ethnic groups in the United States, ideological minorities anywhere may identify themselves, either spontaneously or under the direction of the agents of a foreign government, with the interests of that foreign government and may promote these interests under the guise of the national interest of the country whose citizens they happen to be. The activities of the German-American Bund in the United States in the 'thirties and of Communists everywhere are cases in point. Yet the issue of the national interest vs. other-national interests masquerading as the national interest has arisen constantly in the United States in a less clear-cut fashion.

A country which had been settled by consecutive waves of "foreigners" was bound to find it particularly difficult to identify its own national interest against alleged, seeming, or actual other-national interests represented by certain groups among its own citizens. Since virtually all citizens of the United States are, as it were, "more or less" foreign-born, those who were "less" so have frequently not resisted the temptation to use this distinction as a polemic weapon against latecomers who happen to differ from them in their conception of the national interest of the United States. Frequently, this rationalization has been dispensed with and a conception of foreign policy with which a writer happened to disagree has been attributed outright to foreign sympathy or influence or worse. British influence and interests have served as standard arguments in debates on American foreign policy. Madison, in his polemic against Hamilton on the occasion of Washington's Neutrality Proclamation of 1793, identified the Federalist position with that of "the foreigners and degenerate citizens among us, who hate our republican government, and the French revolution," and the accusation met with a favorable response in a majority of Congress and of public opinion. However, these traditional attempts to discredit dissenting opinion as being influenced by foreign interests should not obscure the real issue, which is the peculiar vulnerability of the national interest of the United States to usurpation by the interests of other nations.

The usurpation of the national interest by supranational interests can derive in our time from two sources: religious bodies and international organizations. The competition between church and state for determination of certain interests and policies, domestic and international, has been an intermittent issue throughout the history of the national state. Here, too, the legitimate defense of the national interest against usurpation has frequently, especially in the United States, degenerated into the demagogic stigmatization of dissenting views as being inspired by Rome and, hence, being incompatible with the national interest. Yet here, too, the misuse of the issue for demagogic purposes must be considered apart from the legitimacy of the issue itself.

The more acute problem arises at the present time from the importance which the public and government officials, at least in their public utterances, attribute to the values represented and the policies pursued by international organizations either as alternatives or supplements to the values and policies for which the national government stands. It is frequently asserted that the foreign policy of the United States pursues no objectives apart from those of the United Nations, that, in other words, the foreign policy of the United States is actually identical with the policy of the United Nations. This assertion cannot refer to anything real in actual politics to support it. For the constitutional structure of international organizations, such as the United Nations, and their procedural practices make it impossible for them to pursue interests apart from those of the member-states which dominate their policy-forming bodies. The identity between the interests of the United Nations and the United States can only refer to the successful policies of the United States within the United Nations through which the support of the United Nations is being secured for the policies of the United States. The assertion, then, is mere polemic, different from the one discussed previously in that the identification of a certain policy with a supranational interest does not seek to reflect discredit upon the former, but to bestow upon it a dignity which the national interest pure and simple is supposed to lack.

The real issue in view of the problem that concerns us here is not whether the so-called interests of the United Nations, which do not exist apart from the interests of its most influential members, have superseded the national interest of the United States, but for what kind of interests the United States has secured United Nations support. While these interests cannot be United Nations interests, they do not need to be national interests either. Here we are in the presence of that modern phenomenon which has been variously described as "utopianism," "sentimentalism," "moralism," the "legalistic-moralistic approach." The common denominator of all these tendencies in modern political thought is the substitution for the national interest of a supranational standard of action which is generally identified with an international organization, such as the United Nations. The national interest is here not being usurped by sub- or supranational interests which, however inferior in worth to the national interest, are nevertheless real and worthy of consideration within their proper sphere. What challenges the national interest here is a mere figment of the imagination, a product of wishful thinking, which is postulated as a valid norm for international conduct, without being valid either there or anywhere else. At this point we touch the core of the present controversy between utopianism and realism in international affairs; we shall return to it later in this paper.

The national interest as such must be defended against usurpation by non-national interests. Yet once that task is accomplished, a rational order must be established among the values which make up the national interest and among the resources to be committed to them. While the interests which a nation may pursue in its relation with other nations are of infinite variety and magnitude, the resources which are available for the pursuit of such interests are necessarily limited in quantity and kind. No nation has the resources to promote all desirable objectives with equal vigor; all nations must therefore allocate their scarce resources as rationally as possible. The indispensable precondition of such rational allocation is a clear understanding of the distinction between the necessary and variable elements of the national interest. Given the contentious manner in which in democracies the variable elements of the national interest are generally determined, the advocates of an extensive conception of the national interest will inevitably present certain variable elements of the national interest as though their attainment were necessary for the nation's survival. In other words, the necessary elements of the national interest have a tendency to swallow up the variable elements so that in the end all kinds of objectives, actual or potential, are justified in terms of national survival. Such arguments have been advanced, for instance, in support of the rearmament of Western Germany and of the defense of Formosa. They must be subjected to rational scrutiny which will determine, however tentatively, their approximate place in the scale of national values.

The same problem presents itself in its extreme form when a nation pursues, or is asked to pursue, objectives which are not only unnecessary for its survival but tend to jeopardize it. Second-rate nations which dream of playing the role of great powers, such as Italy and Poland in the interwar period, illustrate this point. So do great powers which dream of remaking the world in their own image and embark upon world-wide crusades, thus straining their resources to exhaustion. Here scientific analysis has the urgent task of pruning down national objectives to the measure of available resources in order to make their pursuit compatible with national survival.

Finally, the national interest of a nation which is conscious not only of its own interests but also of that of other nations must be defined in terms compatible with the latter. In a multinational world this is a requirement of political morality; in an age of total war it is also one of the conditions for survival.

In connection with this problem two mutually exclusive arguments have been advanced. On the one hand, it has been argued against the theory of international politics here presented that the concept of the national interest revives the eighteenth-century concept of enlightened self-interest, presuming that the uniformly enlightened pursuit of their self-interest by all individuals, as by all nations, will of itself be conducive to a peaceful and harmonious society. On the other hand, the point has been made that the pursuit of their national interest by all nations makes war the permanent arbiter of conflicts among them. Neither argument is well taken.

The concept of the national interest presupposes neither a naturally harmonious, peaceful world nor the inevitability of war as a consequence of the pursuit by all nations of their national interest. Quite to the contrary, it assumes continuous conflict and threat of war, to be minimized through the continuous adjustment of conflicting interests by diplomatic action. No such assumption would be warranted if all nations at all times conceived of their national interest only in terms of their survival and, in turn, defined their interest in survival in restrictive and rational terms. As it is, their conception of the national interest is subject to all the hazards of misinterpretation, usurpation, and misjudgment to which reference has been made above. To minimize these hazards is the first task of a foreign policy which seeks the defense of the national interest by peaceful means. Its second task is the defense of the national interest, restrictively and rationally defined, against the national interests of other nations which may or may not be thus defined. If they are not, it becomes the task of armed diplomacy to convince the nations concerned that their legitimate interests have nothing to fear from a restrictive and rational foreign policy and that their illegitimate interests have nothing to gain in the face of armed might rationally employed.

III

We have said before that the utopian and realist positions in international affairs do not necessarily differ in the policies they advocate, but that they part company over their general philosophies of politics and their way of thinking about matters political. It does not follow that the present debate is only of academic interest and without practical significance. Both camps, it is true, may support the same policy for different reasons. Yet if the reasons are unsound, the soundness of the policies supported by them is a mere coincidence, and these very same reasons may be, and inevitably are, invoked on other occasions in support of unsound policies. The nefarious consequences of false philosophies and wrong ways of thinking may for the time being be concealed by the apparent success of policies derived from them. You may go to war, justified by your nation's interests, for a moral purpose and in disregard of considerations of power; and military victory seems to satisfy both your moral aspirations and your nation's interests. Yet the manner in which you waged the war, achieved victory, and settled the peace cannot help reflecting your philosophy of politics and your way of thinking about political problems. If these are in error, you may win victory on the field of battle and still assist in the defeat of both your moral principles and the national interest of your country.

Any number of examples could illustrate the real yet subtle practical consequences which follow from the different positions taken. We have chosen two: collective security in Korea and the liberation of the nations that are captives of Communism. A case for both policies can be made from both the utopian and realist positions, but with significant differences in the emphasis and substance of the policies pursued.

Collective security as an abstract principle of utopian politics requires that all nations come to the aid of a victim of aggression by resisting the aggressor with all means necessary to frustrate his aims. Once the case of aggression is established, the duty to act is unequivocal. Its extent may be affected by concern for the nation's survival; obviously no nation will commit outright suicide in the service of collective security. But beyond that elemental limitation no consideration of interest or power, either with regard to the aggressor or his victim or the nation acting in the latter's defense, can qualify the obligation to act under the principle of collective security. Thus high officials of our government have declared that we intervened in Korea not for any narrow interest of ours but in support of the moral principle of collective security.

Collective security as a concrete principle of realist policy is the age-old maxim, "Hang together or hang separately," in modern dress. It recognizes the need for nation A under certain circumstances to defend nation B against attack by nation C. That need is determined, first, by the interest which A has in the territorial integrity of B and by the relation of that interest to all the other interests of A as well as to the resources available for the support of all those interests. Furthermore, A must take into account the power which is at the disposal of aggressor C for fighting A and B as over against the power available to A and B for fighting C. The same calculation must be carried on concerning the power of the likely allies of C as over against those of A and B. Before going to war for the defense of South Korea in the name of collective security, an American adherent of political realism would have demanded an answer to the following four questions: First, what is our interest in the preservation of the independence of South Korea; second, what is our power to defend that independence against North Korea; third, what is our power to defend that independence against China and the Soviet Union; and fourth, what are the chances for preventing China and the Soviet Union from entering the Korean War?

In view of the principle of collective security, interpreted in utopian terms, our intervention in Korea was a foregone conclusion. The interpretation of this principle in realist terms might or might not, depending upon the concrete circumstances of interest and power, have led us to the same conclusion. In the execution of the policy of collective security the utopian had to be indifferent to the possibility of Chinese and Russian intervention, except for his resolution to apply the principle of collective security to anybody who would intervene on the side of the aggressor. The realist could not help weighing the possibility of the intervention of a great power on the side of the aggressor in terms of the interests engaged and the power available on the other side.

The Truman administration could not bring itself to taking resolutely the utopian or the realist position. It resolved to intervene in good measure on utopian grounds and in spite of military advice to the contrary; it allowed the military commander to advance to the Yalu River in disregard of the risk of the intervention of a great power against which collective security could be carried out only by means of a general war, and then refused to pursue the war with full effectiveness on the realist grounds of the risk of a third world war. Thus Mr. Truman in 1952 is caught in the same dilemma from which Mr. Baldwin could extricate himself in 1936 on the occasion of the League of Nations sanctions against Italy's attack upon Ethiopia only at an enormous loss to British prestige. Collective security as a defense of the status quo short of a general war can be effective only against second-rate powers. Applied against a major power, it is a contradiction in terms, for it means necessarily a major war. Of this self-defeating contradiction Mr. Baldwin was as unaware in the 'thirties as Mr. Truman seems to be in 1952. Mr. Churchill put Mr. Baldwin's dilemma in these cogent terms: "First, the Prime Minister had declared that sanctions meant war; secondly, he was resolved that there must be no war; and thirdly, he decided upon sanctions. It was evidently impossible to comply with these three conditions." Similarly Mr. Truman had declared that the effective prosecution of the Korean War meant the possibility of a third world war; he resolved that there must be no third world war; and he decided upon intervention in the Korean War. Here, too, it is impossible to comply with these three conditions.

Similar contradictions are inherent in the proposals which would substitute for the current policy of containment one of the liberation of the nations presently the captives of Russian Communism. This objective can be compatible with the utopian or realist position, but the policies designed to secure it will be fundamentally different according to whether they are based upon one or the other position. . . .

From the utopian point of view there can be no difference between the liberation of Esthonia or Czechoslovakia, of Poland or China; the captivity of any nation, large or small, close or far away, is a moral outrage which cannot be tolerated. The realist, too, seeks the liberation of all captive nations because he realizes that the presence of the Russian armies in the heart of Europe and their cooperation with the Chinese armies constitute the two main sources of the imbalance of power which threatens our security. Yet before he formulates a program of liberation, he will seek answers to a number of questions such as these: While the United States has a general interest in the liberation of all captive nations, what is the hierarchy of interests it has in the liberation, say, of China, Esthonia, and Hungary? And while the Soviet Union has a general interest in keeping all captive nations in that state, what is the hierarchy of its interests in keeping, say, Poland, Eastern Germany, and Bulgaria captive? If we assume, as we must on the historic evidence of two centuries, that Russia would never give up control over Poland without being compelled by force of arms, would the objective of the liberation of Poland justify the ruin of western civilization, that of Poland included, which would be the certain result of a third world war? What resources does the United States have at its disposal for the liberation of all captive nations or some of them? What resources does the Soviet Union have at its disposal to keep in captivity all captive nations or some of them? Are we more likely to avoid national bankruptcy by embarking upon a policy of indiscriminate liberation with the concomitant certainty of war or by continuing the present policy of containment? . . .

IV

The foregoing discussion ought to shed additional light, if this is still needed, upon the moral merits of the utopian and realist positions. This question, more than any other, seems to have agitated the critics of realism in international affairs. Disregarding the voluminous evidence, some of them have picked a few words out of their context to prove that realism in international affairs is unprincipled and contemptuous of morality. To mention but one example, one eminent critic summarizes my position, which he supposes to deny the possibility of judging the conduct of states by moral criteria, in these words: "And one spokesman finds 'a profound and neglected truth,' to use his words, in the dictum of Hobbes that 'there is neither morality nor law outside the state.' " These are indeed my words, but not all of them. What I actually said was this:

There is a profound and neglected truth hidden in Hobbes's extreme dictum that the state creates morality as well as law and that there is neither morality nor law outside the state. Universal moral principles, such as justice or equality, are capable of guiding political action only to the extent that they have been given concrete content and have been related to political situations by society.

It must be obvious from this passage and from all my other writings on the subject that my position is the exact opposite from what this critic makes it out to be. I have always maintained that the actions of states are subject to universal moral principles and I have been careful to differentiate my position in this respect from that of Hobbes. Five points basic to my position may need to be emphasized again.

The first point is what one might call the requirement of cosmic humility with regard to the moral evaluation of the actions of states. To know that states are subject to the moral law is one thing; to pretend to know what is morally required of states in a particular situation is quite another. The human mind tends naturally to identify the particular interests of states, as of individuals, with the moral purposes of the universe. The statesman in the defense of the nation's interests may, and at times even must, yield to that tendency; the scholar must resist it at every turn. For the light-hearted assumption that what one's own nation aims at and does is morally good and that those who oppose that nation's policies are evil is morally indefensible and intellectually untenable and leads in practice to that distortion of judgment, born of the blindness of crusading frenzy, which has been the curse of nations from the beginning of time.

The second point which obviously needs to be made again concerns the effectiveness of the restraints which morality imposes upon the action of states.

A discussion of international morality must guard against the two extremes either of overrating the influence of ethics upon international politics or else of denying that statesmen and diplomats are moved by anything else but considerations of material power.

On the one hand, there is the dual error of confounding the moral rules which people actually observe with those they pretend to observe as well as with those which writers declare they ought to observe. . . .

On the other hand, there is the misconception, usually associated with the general depreciation and moral condemnation of power politics, discussed above, that international politics is so thoroughly evil that it is no use looking for ethical limitations of the aspirations for power on the international scene. Yet, if we ask ourselves what statesmen and diplomats are capable of doing to further the power objectives of their respective nations and what they actually do, we realize that they do less than they probably could and less than they actually did in other periods of history. They refuse to consider certain ends and to use certain means, either altogether or under certain conditions, not because in the light of expediency they appear impractical or unwise, but because certain moral rules interpose an absolute barrier. Moral rules do not permit certain policies to be considered at all from the point of view of expediency. Such ethical inhibitions operate in our time on different levels with different effectiveness. Their restraining function is most obvious and most effective in affirming the sacredness of human life in times of peace.

In connection with this passage we have given a number of historic examples showing the influence of moral principles upon the conduct of foreign policy. An example taken from contemporary history will illustrate the same point. There can be little doubt that the Soviet Union could have achieved the objectives of its foreign policy at the end of the Second World War without antagonizing the nations of the West into that encircling coalition which has been the nightmare of Bolshevist foreign policy since 1917. It could have mitigated cunning for its own sake and the use of force with persuasion, conciliation, and a trust derived from the awareness of a partial community of interests and would thereby have minimized the dangers to itself and the rest of the world which are inherent in the objectives of its policies. Yet the Soviet Union was precluded from relying upon these traditional methods of diplomacy by its general conception of human nature, politics, and morality. In the general philosophy of Bolshevism there is no room for honest dissent, the recognition of the intrinsic worth of divergent interests, and genuine conciliation between such interests. On all levels of social interaction opposition must be destroyed by cunning and violence, since it has no right to exist, rather than be met half way in view of its intrinsic legitimacy. This being the general conception of the political morality of Bolshevism, the foreign policy of the Soviet Union is limited to a much more narrow choice of means than the foreign policies of other nations.

The United States, for instance, has been able, in its relations with the nations of Latin America, to replace military intervention and dollar diplomacy with the policy of the Good Neighbor. That drastic change was made possible by the general conception of political morality which has been prevalent in the United States from its very inception. The United States is a pluralist society which presupposes the continuing existence and legitimacy of divergent interests. These interests are locked in a continuing struggle for supremacy to be decided by force only as a last resort, but normally through a multitude of institutional agencies which are so devised as to allow one or the other interest a temporary advantage but none a permanent supremacy at the price of the destruction of the others. This morality of pluralism allows the United States, once it is secure in that minimum of vital interests to which we have referred above, to transfer those principles of political morality to the international scene and to deal with divergent interests there with the same methods of genuine compromise and conciliation which are a permanent element of its domestic political life.

The third point concerns the relations between universal moral principles and political action. I have always maintained that these universal moral principles cannot be applied to the actions of states in their abstract universal formulation, but that they must be, as it were, filtered through the concrete circumstances of time and place. The individual may say for himself: *"Fiat justitia, pereat mundus";* the state has no right to say so in the name of those who are in its care. Both individual and state must judge political action by universal moral principles, such as that of liberty. Yet while the individual has a moral right to sacrifice himself in defense of such a moral principle, the state has no moral right to let its moral disapprobation of the infringement of liberty get in the way of successful political action, itself inspired by the moral principle of national survival. There can be no political morality without prudence, that is, without consideration of the political consequences of seemingly moral action. Classical and medieval philosophy knew this and so did Lincoln when he said: "I do the very best I know how, the very best I can, and I mean to keep doing so until the end. If the end brings me out all right, what is said against me won't amount to anything. If the end brings me out wrong, ten angels swearing I was right would make no difference." The issue between utopianism and realism, as it bears on this point, has been put most succinctly by Edmund Burke, and what he has to say in the following passage about revolution, that is, civil war, may well be applied *mutatis mutandis* to all war.

Nothing universal can be rationally affirmed on any moral or any political subject. Pure metaphysical abstraction does not belong to these matters. The lines of morality are not like the ideal lines of mathematics. They are broad and deep as well as long. They admit of exceptions; they demand modifications. These exceptions and modifications are not made by the process of logic, but by the rules of prudence. Prudence is not only the first in rank of the virtues political and moral, but she is the director, the regulator, the standard of them all. Metaphysics cannot live without definition; but Prudence is cautious how she defines. Our courts cannot be more fearful in suffering fictitious cases to be brought before them for eliciting their determination on a point of law than prudent moralists are in putting extreme and hazardous cases of conscience upon emergencies not existing. Without attempting, therefore, to define, what never can be defined, the case of a revolution in government, this, I think, may be safely affirmed—that a sore and pressing evil is to be removed, and that a good, great in its amount and unequivocal in its nature, must be probable almost to a certainty, before the inestimable price of our own morals and the well-being of a number of our fellow-citizens is paid for a revolution. If ever we ought to be economists even to parsimony, it is in the voluntary production of evil. Every revolution contains in it something of evil.

Fourth, the realist recognizes that a moral decision, especially in the political sphere, does not imply a simple choice between a moral principle and a standard of action which is morally irrelevant or even outright immoral. A moral decision implies always a choice among different moral principles, one of which is given precedence over others. To say that a political action has no moral purpose is absurd; for political action can be defined as an attempt to realize moral values through the medium of politics, that is, power. The relevant moral question concerns the choice among different moral values, and it is at this point that the realist and the utopian part company again. If an American statesman must choose between the promotion of universal liberty, which is a moral good, at the risk of American security and, hence, of liberty in the United States, and the promotion of American security and of liberty in the United States, which is another moral good, to the detriment of the promotion of universal liberty, which choice ought he to make? The utopian will not face the issue squarely and will deceive himself into believing that he can achieve both goods at the same time. The realist will choose the national interest on both moral and pragmatic grounds; for if he does not take care of the national interest nobody else will, and if he puts American security and liberty in jeopardy the cause of liberty everywhere will be impaired.

Finally, the political realist distinguishes between his moral sympathies and the political interests which he must defend. He will distinguish with Lincoln between his "*official* duty" which is to protect the national interest and his "*personal* wish" which is to see universal moral values realized throughout the world. . . .

The contest between utopianism and realism is not tantamount to a contest between principle and expediency, morality and immorality, although some spokesmen for the former would like to have it that way. The contest is rather between one type of political morality and another type of political morality, one taking as its standard universal moral principles abstractly formulated, the other weighing these principles against the moral requirements of concrete political action, their relative merits to be decided by a prudent evaluation of the political consequences to which they are likely to lead.

These points are re-emphasized by the foregoing discussion. Which attitude with regard to collective security and to the liberation of the captive nations, the utopian or the realist, is more likely to safeguard the survival of the United States in its territorial, political, and cultural identity and at the same time to contribute the most to the security and liberty of other nations? This is the ultimate test—political and moral—by which utopianism and realism must be judged.

2.

William T. R. Fox: *The Reconciliation of the Desirable and the Possible*

The preceding selection by Hans J. Morgenthau modulated the more extreme tones of some of his previous writings on political realism. Three years earlier, for example, in debating national interest and moral principle in the *American Scholar* with William T. R. Fox, he had seen no compromise possible between the latter two concepts and asserted that the statesman must choose between

William T. R. Fox, "The Reconciliation of the Desirable and the Possible," *The American Scholar,* Vol. 18, No. 2 (Spring 1949), pp. 212–16. Copyright © by the United Chapters of Phi Beta Kappa. Reprinted by permission of *The American Scholar* and the author.

national interest and moral principle. This view was rebutted by Professor Fox, who contended that there was no escape from compromise—the essence of politics was precisely the reconciling of "the desirable and the possible," which of necessity involved a moral choice.

In the forefront of writing on international relations theory and national security policy for two decades, Professor Fox is the author of *The Superpowers;* coauthor with his wife, Annette Baker Fox, of *NATO and the Range of American Choice;* and editor of the *Theoretical Aspects of International Relations.* He has written numerous articles on civil-military relations, diplomacy, arms control, theory and the teaching of international relations, some of which are collected in *The American Study of International Relations.* Professor Fox is James T. Shotwell Professor of International Relations at Columbia University and Director of its Institute of War and Peace Studies, a research center which has contributed a number of excellent analyses relevant to national security policy.

C an one successfully assert the irrelevance of "moral principle" to the conduct of foreign relations? This is what Professor Morgenthau says he is doing when he declares that "national interest" provides the sole valid criterion in making decisions in the field of foreign affairs.

A doctrine of this character will shock those many men of good will who believe the world is suffering from an excess of devotion to national interest rather than from the opposite. The doctrine will seem even more frightening to them because of the tone of pessimism which pervades the whole analysis. The casual reference to "those potentially unlimited power drives which are latent in all men" suggest that Power, Evil, and Original Sin are three names for the same thing, that the Kingdom of God is not to be brought down on this earth whatever we do, that peace on earth and good will to men is something to be sung about in Christmas carols and not to be translated into actuality.

The "men of little faith" have been the traditional objects of public scorn when things go amiss with the world. Professor Morgenthau instead turns his neo-Calvinist verbal artillery on the men of too great faith. It is perhaps time that they be put on the moral defensive. Serious students of politics will share with Professor Morgenthau a profound skepticism regarding any man whose faith in the virtue of his particular design for universal peace is so great that he would have us if necessary fight a third world war to make the Russians accept his plan.

There is a further difficulty. "Politics," says Max Weber, "is a slow boring of hard boards." Advocates of utopian programs almost invariably short-circuit the political process. Their faith in the virtue of a particular plan is buttressed by their faith in the possibility of its being put into effect. Whether a given utopian plan would be put into effect by threatening war or by making a series of dramatic concessions, its supporters generally propose to avoid the necessity for painful negotiation and for the hard intellectual analysis that accompanies such negotiation. But neither the avenging God of the Old Testament, who would have us deal harshly with His enemies, nor the merciful God of the New, who would turn the other cheek however great the provocation, can furnish the model for the responsible politician who abjures both holy war and fatuous gesture.

The demagogues of the Right and of the Left can afford to offer simple solutions. Their freedom to criticize is unlimited by any substantial prospect that they will come to power. There is little chance that they will be forced to demonstrate how much passion and how little dispassionate analysis entered into their program-making. Advocacy of one-way atomic war is not yet socially acceptable, but some of the more extreme Russophobes who call for firmness without patience only imperfectly conceal their anxiety to have the United States begin dropping atomic bombs. At the other extreme, are the protagonists of patience without firmness, of unlimited concession, of choking Stalin with kindness. Such a course of action may conceivably evoke a complete change in the hearts of the men of the Kremlin. But if it did not, and all available historical evidence suggests that it would not, the United States would then be under the necessity of opposing a Russia which it had materially strengthened.

The patient exploration of every avenue for peace and the day-by-day assessment of the country's security position are twin tasks which the responsible leader cannot escape. Neither can be performed simply by imposing on a refractory world some moral principle of universal applicability. But how shall he decide when to be firm and when to be conciliatory?

According to Professor Morgenthau, war is never necessary solely to uphold a moral principle; but one must always be prepared to make war when a fundamental national interest is involved. National interest turns out to be another name for national security, and this in its turn is revealed to mean the maintenance of the state's territorial integrity *and* its basic institutions. Now which institutions are basic? Can this question be answered except in the language of moral principle?

Here, it seems to me, is a basic flaw in Professor Morgenthau's choice of language. The flaw appears to me to be more in his choice of words than in his underlying analysis. He protests too vehemently his amorality. His uncompromising support of national interest as *the* guiding principle does not wholly conceal the moral foundations of his position.

"Respect for the existence and the individuality of its members is," he declares, "of the essence of the Western state system." This is the principle of live and let live. It is the democratic principle which recognizes the equal integrity and right of autonomous and full development of *other* personalities or groups. It is a principle which determines when one is to be unyielding and when compliant. It is a moral principle.

One is not bound absolutely to respect the existence and the individuality of every other member of the state system, but only so long as the actions of the other do not threaten the existence and the individuality of one's "self." (The "self" of which we are here talking, in a world politics context, is the nation-state.) Stated in concrete present-day terms, Red totalitarianism is all right in Russia, provided its existence there does not threaten the American national interest. It must, of course, be in the national interest to frustrate the policies of another state if that state's national interest were defined in terms which menaced that of one's own state. Therefore, only compatible national interests ought to be recognized.

Is the national interest of any given state capable of objective determination except in terms of some explicitly declared set of value preferences? The camel's nose of moral principle is already under the tent when one admits that it is territorial integrity *plus* basic institutions which must "in the national interest" be protected. By the time the responsible leader has taken the next step and decided which foreign policies of other powers are compatible with this national interest he will be consulting his conscience as well as his intellect.

We are sometimes told that a responsible statesman would recognize that there really is no such thing as national interest. Charles Beard denounced the whole idea of national interest as a pious fraud to cloak the internal struggle between the trade-hungry merchants and the land-hungry planters for control of United States foreign affairs. He could see only sub-national interests. But he rejected the idea of supranational interest even more emphatically than he did the idea of national interest. It was only, he maintained, because the American people became infected with a sense of world mission, that they have in the twentieth century blundered into other peoples' wars. Thus, even he, in a negative sort of way recognized an American national interest—in avoiding taking sides in "other peoples' wars."

To Woodrow Wilson, on the other hand, is attributed the belief that formulation of policy in terms of national self-interest is wrong per se. Wilson undoubtedly believed that what was good for the world was good for the United States, and he believed that democracy, national self-determination and a world commonwealth of nations would together usher in the reign of universal peace. But he was quite as ready to outbuild Britain in a naval arms race to crush "British navalism" as he had been to lead the United States to victory over Prussian militarism. Wilson clearly understood the need for protecting what he believed to be American interests in a stubborn and imperfect world.

That Wilson, in the Fourteen Points and at Versailles, may have been mesmerized by his own skill in phrase-making—some think he had been earlier when he coined the phrase "too proud to fight"—is more than possible. The moral effect of solemn invocations of principle uttered by Cordell Hull was negated by his recurring explicit warning that the United States would assume no risk of war or of political or military involvement in defense of these principles. In our own decade the too sweeping phraseology of the Atlantic Charter and the Truman Doctrine have aroused unfulfillable expectations in many parts of the world. All these point to the undesirability of careless, irresponsible and unconditional invocation of moral principle.

The chief task of the policy-maker lies in the reconciliation of the desirable and the possible. Moral principle is *not* irrelevant, but it can provide by itself no sure guide to policy. It is in weighing the risks and the gains—the value losses and the value increments to the self in whose name one is acting, i.e., the nation-state—that judgments about the possible emerge. It is in formulating this judgment that one arrives at a conception of the national interest.

What is judged to be absolutely impossible is the pursuit of a policy which endangers the very existence of the nation-state itself. Such a policy will be rejected however imperative may appear the moral precept which gave rise to the policy. Thus if one arranges political objectives in hierarchical order, survival will take precedence over all the others. But it is not the survival of the individual, but of his state, for which the ultimate sacrifice of life is in our century ordinarily made. Stated in other language, the nation-state is the "survival self," but the self in whose name moral principle is invoked may be either broader or narrower in scope.

The applicability of moral principle in a situation threatening survival may be illustrated by an admittedly far-fetched example. The Truman Doctrine seems to promise American aid to freedom-loving peoples *everywhere* in the world against the forces which would impose on them tyranny, and especially Moscow-dominated tyranny. Let us suppose that it is freedom-loving but totally inaccessible Afghanistan which calls for help against an expansionist Soviet Union in accordance with that country's interpretation of the Truman Doctrine.

Is the Afghan claim for help any less valid because Afghanistan is so inconveniently located from the point of view of American capacity to help? It is not, and yet hardly anyone expects the United States to take great risk to support a prospective victim of aggression, especially if that victim is believed to be beyond the reach of its aid in any case. No distinction can be made between such a power and a near neighbor of the United States *solely* by reference to some moral principle of universal and unconditional applicability.

The difference between the Morgenthau position and my own is partly but not wholly verbal. He contends that policy must be based *either* on national interest *or* on moral principle. My own view is that moral principle necessarily enters into any valid formulation of national interest, which must itself reconcile the desirable and the possible. Against the view that there can be no compromise, I assert that there can be no escape from compromise. This is what makes politics a vocation only for the mature, for the responsible, for the man who does not despair when he discovers incommensurate values placed in such a juxtaposition that one or another has to be sacrificed.

It is this to which Alexander Hamilton had reference when he pointed to the "disproportion" between the risk to which strict fulfillment of the French Alliance would have exposed the United States and the advantages either to the United States or to France which would have flowed from American intervention in that European war. Then as now, treaty observance depended upon continuing mutuality of interest.

These things must be said if only because stability and responsibility in American foreign policy require that the American people not appear to themselves as more generous than they really are. Leadership in the United Nations, Truman Doctrine and Marshall Plan are none of them exclusively the result of a developing sense of world citizenship in the United States or a manifestation of American belief in the brotherhood of man.

It was fear of the consequences for American security if Greece were overrun or if European recovery were longer delayed that has stimulated the military aid to Greece and the economic aid to Western Europe. The E.R.P. appears unselfish in a context in which material values alone are considered; but it is more correctly assessed as based on *mutual* interest, including the American national interest, once the non-material values of freedom and survival are also brought into the analysis.

If Americans persuade themselves that present aid to Western Europe, Greece and China is due primarily to American generosity, they may feel free to suspend that aid whenever they feel piqued about the behavior of one of the beneficiaries. A British decision to nationalize the steel industry or a Chinese decision to abandon the capital city to the Communists may disappoint the American people. If, however, they understand the self-interest which motivated the original aid, they will find that the threat to American security has increased, and that pique is a luxury which not even the American people can afford in a crisis. Nor will the American people, resentful because they were oversold in 1945 as to the benefits which would flow from United Nations membership, abandon that organization of substantial though not unlimited utility.

That the American national interest seems to be in so little conflict with the interests of the other powers on the outer side of the Iron Curtain is fortunate indeed. It shows that the national interest of the United States is in our time formulated in terms which can be supported by any other power whose diplomatic watchword is "live and let live."

3.

Arnold Wolfers: "National Security" as an Ambiguous Symbol

The Realists maintained that American foreign policy must follow, in Hans J. Morgenthau's words, "but one guiding star—The National Interest"—the implication being that the security of the nation provided a clear and objective standard for deciding the ends and means of foreign policy. In one of the classic writings on national security, Professor Arnold Wolfers explores the ambiguities of this concept. Differentiating between subjective and objective security, he

Arnold Wolfers, "National Security as an Ambiguous Symbol," *Political Science Quarterly*, Vol. 67, No. 4 (December 1952), pp. 481–502. Reprinted by permission of the *Political Science Quarterly* and the author.

argues that nations pursue a variety of values, not just survival or protection from external attack. Thus, foreign policy choices must be seen as resting on moral judgments as to what values will be sacrificed to maintain a particular level of security.

The late Arnold Wolfers was Director of the Washington Center of Foreign Policy Research. His books include *Britain and France Between Two Wars* and *Alliance Policy in the Cold War*. Some of his finest essays, such as "Statesmanship and Moral Choice," are collected in *Discord and Collaboration*.

Statesmen, publicists and scholars who wish to be considered realists, as many do today, are inclined to insist that the foreign policy they advocate is dictated by the national interest, more specifically by the national security interest. It is not surprising that this should be so. Today any reference to the pursuit of security is likely to ring a sympathetic chord.

However, when political formulas such as "national interest" or "national security" gain popularity they need to be scrutinized with particular care. They may not mean the same thing to different people. They may not have any precise meaning at all. Thus, while appearing to offer guidance and a basis for broad consensus they may be permitting everyone to label whatever policy he favors with an attractive and possibly deceptive name.

In a very vague and general way "national interest" does suggest a direction of policy which can be distinguished from several others which may present themselves as alternatives. It indicates that the policy is designed to promote demands which are ascribed to the nation rather than to individuals, sub-national groups or mankind as a whole. It emphasizes that the policy subordinates other interests to those of the nation. But beyond this, it has very little meaning.

When Charles Beard's study of *The Idea of National Interest* was published in the early years of the New Deal and under the impact of the Great Depression, the lines were drawn differently than they are today. The question at that time was whether American foreign policy, then largely economic in scope and motivation, was aimed not at promoting the welfare interests of the nation as a whole but instead at satisfying the material interests of powerful sub-national interest or pressure groups. While it was found hard to define what was in the interest of national welfare or to discover standards by which to measure it, there could be no doubt as to what people had in mind: they desired to see national policy makers rise above the narrow and special economic interests of parts of the nation to focus their attention on the more inclusive interests of the whole.

Today, the alternative to a policy of the national interest to which people refer is of a different character. They fear policy makers may be unduly concerned with the "interests of all of mankind." They see them sacrificing the less inclusive national community to the wider but in their opinion chimeric world community. The issue, then, is not one of transcending narrow group selfishness, as it was at the time of Beard's discussion, but rather one of according more exclusive devotion to the narrower cause of the national self.

There is another difference between the current and the earlier debate. While it would be wrong to say that the economic interest has ceased to attract attention, it is overshadowed today by the national security interest. Even in the recent debates on the St. Lawrence Seaway, clearly in the first instance an economic enterprise, the defenders of the project, when seeking to impress their listeners with the "national interest" involved, spoke mainly of the value of the Seaway for military defense in wartime while some opponents stressed its vulnerability to attack.

The change from a welfare to a security interpretation of the symbol "national interest" is understandable. Today we are living under the impact of cold war and threats of external aggression rather than of depression and social reform. As a result, the formula of the national interest has come to be practically synonymous with the formula of national security. Unless explicitly denied, spokesmen for a policy which would take the national interest as its guide can be assumed to mean that priority shall be given to measures of security, a term to be analyzed.[1] The question is raised, therefore, whether this seemingly more precise formula of national security offers statesmen a meaningful guide for action. Can they be expected to know what it means? Can policies be distinguished and judged on the ground that they do or do not serve this interest?

The term national security, like national interest, is well enough established in the political discourse of international relations to designate an objective of policy distinguishable from others. We know roughly what people have in mind if they complain that their government is neglecting national security or demanding excessive sacrifices for the sake of enhancing it. Usually those who raise the cry for a policy oriented exclusively toward this interest are afraid their country underestimates the external dangers facing it or is being diverted into idealistic channels unmindful of these dangers. Moreover, the symbol suggests protection through power and therefore figures more frequently in the speech of those who believe in reliance on national power than of those who place their confidence in model behavior, international coöperation, or the United Nations to carry their country safely through the tempests of international conflict. For these reasons it would be an exaggeration to claim that the symbol of national security is nothing but a stimulus to semantic confusion, though closer analysis will show that if used without specifications it leaves room for more confusion than sound political counsel or scientific usage can afford.

The demand for a policy of national security is primarily normative in character. It is supposed to indicate what the policy of a nation should be in order to be either expedient—a rational means toward an accepted end—or moral, the best or least evil course of action. The value judgments implicit in these normative exhortations will be discussed.

Before doing so, attention should be drawn to an assertion of fact which is implicit if not explicit in most appeals for a policy guided by national security. Such appeals usually assume that nations in fact have made security their goal except when idealism or utopianism of their leaders has led them to stray from the traditional path. If such conformity of behavior actually existed, it would be proper to infer that a country deviating from the established pattern of conduct would risk being penalized. This would greatly strengthen the normative arguments. The trouble with the contention of fact, however, is that the term "security" covers a range of goals so wide that highly divergent policies can be interpreted as policies of security.

Security points to some degree of protection of values previously acquired. In Walter Lippmann's words, a nation is secure to the extent to which it is not in danger of having to sacrifice core values, if it wishes to avoid war, and is able, if challenged, to maintain them by victory in such a war.[2] What this definition implies is that security rises and falls with the ability of a nation to deter an attack, or to defeat it. This is in accord with common usage of the term.

Security is a value, then, of which a nation can have more or less and which it can aspire to have in greater or lesser measure.[3] It has much in common, in this respect, with power or wealth, two other values of great importance in international affairs. But while wealth measures the amount of a nation's material possessions, and power its ability to control the actions of others, security, in an objective sense, measures the absence of threats to acquired values, in a subjective sense, the absence of fear that such values will be attacked. In both respects a nation's security can run a wide gamut from almost complete insecurity or sense of insecurity at one pole, to almost complete security or absence of fear at the other.[4]

The possible discrepancy between the objective and subjective connotation of the term is significant in international relations despite the fact that the chance of future attack never can be measured "objectively"; it must always remain a matter of subjective evaluation and speculation. However, when the French after World War I insisted that they were entitled to additional guarantees of security because of the exceptionally dangerous situation which France was said to be facing, other Powers in the League expressed the view that rather than to submit to what might be French hysterical apprehension the relative security of France should be objectively evaluated. It is a well-known fact that nations, and groups within nations, differ widely in their reaction to one and the same external situation. Some tend to exaggerate the danger while others underestimate it. With hindsight it is sometimes possible to tell exactly how far they deviated from a rational reaction to the actual or objective state of danger existing at the time. Even if for no other reasons, this difference in the reaction to similar threats suffices to make it probable that nations will differ in their efforts to obtain more security. Some may find the danger to which they are exposed entirely normal and in line with their modest security expectations while others consider it unbearable to live with these same dangers. Although this is not the place to set up hypotheses on the factors which account for one or the other attitude, investigation might confirm the hunch that those nations tend to be most sensitive to threats which have either experienced attacks in the recent past or, having passed through a prolonged period of an exceptionally high degree of security, suddenly find themselves thrust into a situation of danger.[5] Probably national efforts to achieve greater security would also prove, in part at least, to be a function of the power and opportunity which nations possess of reducing danger by their own efforts.[6]

Another and even stronger reason why nations must be expected not to act uniformly is that they are not all or constantly faced with the same degree of danger. For purposes of a working hypothesis, theorists may find it useful at times to postulate conditions wherein all states are enemies—provided they are not allied against others—and wherein all, therefore, are equally in danger of attack.[7] But, while it may be true in the living world, too, that no sovereign nation can be absolutely safe from future attack, nobody can reasonably contend that Canada, for example, is threatened today to the same extent as countries like Iran or Yugoslavia, or that the British had as much reason to be concerned about the French air force in the twenties as about Hitler's *Luftwaffe* in the thirties.

This point, however, should not be overstressed. There can be no quarrel with the generalization that most nations, most of the time—the great Powers particularly—have shown, and had reason to show, an active concern about some lack of security and have been prepared to make sacrifices for its enhancement. Danger and the awareness of it have been, and continue to be, sufficiently widespread to guarantee some uniformity in this respect. But a generalization which leaves room both for the frantic kind of struggle for more security which characterized French policy at times and for the neglect of security apparent in American foreign policy after the close of both World Wars throws little light on the behavior of nations. The demand for conformity would have meaning only if it could be said—as it could under the conditions postulated in the working hypothesis of pure power politics—that nations normally subordinate all other values to the maximization of their security, which, however, is obviously not the case.

There have been many instances of struggles for more security taking the form of an unrestrained race for armaments, alliances, strategic boundaries and the like; but one need only recall the many heated parliamentary debates on arms appropriations to realize how uncertain has been the extent to which people will consent to sacrifice for additional increments of security. Even when there has been no question that armaments would mean more security, the cost in taxes, the reduction in social benefits or the sheer discomfort involved has militated effectively against further effort. It may be worth noting in this connection that there seems to be no case in history in which a country started a preventive war on the grounds of security—unless Hitler's wanton attack on his neighbors be allowed to qualify as such—although there must have been circumstances where additional security could have been obtained by war and although so many wars have been launched for the enhancement of other values. Of course, where security serves only as a cloak for other more enticing demands, nations or ambitious leaders may consider no price for it too high. This is one of the reasons why very high security aspirations tend to make a nation suspect of hiding more aggressive aims.

Instead of expecting a uniform drive for enhanced or maximum security, a different hypothesis may offer a more promising lead. Efforts for security are bound to be experienced as a burden; security after all is nothing but the absence of the evil of insecurity, a negative value so to speak. As a consequence, nations will be inclined to minimize these efforts, keeping them at the lowest level which will provide them with what they consider adequate protection. This level will often be lower than what statesmen, military leaders or other particularly security-minded participants in the decision-making process believe it should be. In any case, together with the extent of the external threats, numerous domestic factors such as national character, tradition, preferences and prejudices will influence the level of security which a nation chooses to make its target.

It might be objected that in the long run nations are not so free to choose the amount of effort they will put into security. Are they not under a kind of compulsion to spare no effort provided they wish to survive? This objection again would make sense only if the hypothesis of pure power politics were a realistic image of actual world affairs. In fact, however, a glance at history will suffice to show that survival has only exceptionally been at stake, particularly for the major Powers. If nations were not concerned with the protection of values other than their survival as independent states, most of them, most of the time, would not have had to be seriously worried about their security, despite what manipulators of public opinion engaged in mustering greater security efforts may have said to the contrary. What "compulsion" there is, then, is a function not merely of the will of others, real or imagined, to destroy the nation's independence but of national desires and ambitions to retain a wealth of other values such as rank, respect, material possessions and special privileges. It would seem to be a fair guess that the efforts for security by a particular nation will tend to vary, other things being equal, with the range of values for which protection is being sought.

In respect to this range there may seem to exist a considerable degree of uniformity. All over the world today peoples are making sacrifices to protect and preserve what to them appear as the minimum national core values, national independence and territorial integrity. But there is deviation in two directions. Some nations seek protection for more marginal values as well. There was a time when United States policy could afford to be concerned mainly with the protection of the foreign investments or markets of its nationals, its "core values" being out of danger, or when Britain was extending its national self to include large and only vaguely circumscribed "regions of special interest." It is a well-known and portentous phenomenon that bases, security zones and the like may be demanded and acquired for the purpose of protecting values acquired earlier; and they then become new national values requiring protection themselves. Pushed to its logical conclusion, such spatial extension of the range of values does not stop short of world domination.

A deviation in the opposite direction of a compression of the range of core values is hardly exceptional in our days either. There is little indication that

Britain is bolstering the security of Hong Kong although colonies were once considered part of the national territory. The Czechs lifted no finger to protect their independence against the Soviet Union and many West Europeans are arguing today that rearmament has become too destructive of values they cherish to be justified even when national independence is obviously at stake.

The lack of uniformity does not end here. A policy is not characterized by its goal, in this case security, alone. In order to become imitable, the means by which the goal is pursued must be taken into account as well. Thus, if two nations were both endeavoring to maximize their security but one were placing all its reliance on armaments and alliances, the other on meticulous neutrality, a policy maker seeking to emulate their behavior would be at a loss where to turn. Those who call for a policy guided by national security are not likely to be unaware of this fact, but they take for granted that they will be understood to mean a security policy based on power, and on military power at that. Were it not so, they would be hard put to prove that their government was not already doing its best for security, though it was seeking to enhance it by such means as international coöperation or by the negotiation of compromise agreements—means which in one instance may be totally ineffective or utopian but which in others may have considerable protective value.

It is understandable why it should so readily be assumed that a quest for security must necessarily translate itself into a quest for coercive power. In view of the fact that security is being sought against external violence—coupled perhaps with internal subversive violence—it seems plausible at first sight that the response should consist in an accumulation of the same kind of force for the purpose of resisting an attack or of deterring a would-be attacker. The most casual reading of history and of contemporary experience, moreover, suffices to confirm the view that such resort to "power of resistance" has been the rule with nations grappling with serious threats to their security, however much the specific form of this power and its extent may differ. Why otherwise would so many nations which have no acquisitive designs maintain costly armaments? Why did Denmark with her state of complete disarmament remain an exception even among the small Powers?

But again, the generalization that nations seeking security usually place great reliance on coercive power does not carry one far. The issue is not whether there is regularly some such reliance but whether there are no significant differences between nations concerning their over-all choice of the means upon which they place their trust. The controversies concerning the best road to future security that are so typical of coalition partners at the close of victorious wars throw light on this question. France in 1919 and all the Allies in 1945 believed that protection against another German attack could be gained only by means of continued military superiority based on German military impotence. President Wilson in 1919 and many observers in 1945 were equally convinced, however, that more hope for security lay in a conciliatory and fair treatment of the defeated enemy, which would rob him of future incentives to renew his attack. While this is not the place to decide which side was right, one cannot help drawing the conclusion that, in the matter of means, the roads which are open may lead in diametrically opposed directions.[8] The choice in every instance will depend on a multitude of variables, including ideological and moral convictions, expectations concerning the psychological and political developments in the camp of the opponent, and inclinations of individual policy makers.[9]

After all that has been said little is left of the sweeping generalization that in actual practice nations, guided by their national security interest, tend to pursue a uniform and therefore imitable policy of security. Instead, there are numerous reasons why they should differ widely in this respect, with some standing close to the pole of complete indifference to security or complete reliance on non-military means, others close to the pole of insistence on absolute security or of complete reliance on coercive power. It should be added that there exists still another category of nations which cannot be placed within the continuum connecting these poles because they regard security of any degree as an insufficient goal; instead they seek to acquire new values even at the price of greater insecurity. In this category must be placed not only the "mad Caesars," who are out for conquest and glory at any price, but also idealistic statesmen who would plunge their country into war for the sake of spreading the benefits of their ideology, for example, of liberating enslaved peoples.

The actual behavior of nations, past and present, does not affect the normative proposition, to which we shall now turn our attention. According to this proposition nations are called upon to give priority to national security and thus to consent to any sacrifice of value which will provide an additional increment of security. It may be expedient, moral or both for nations to do so even if they should have failed to heed such advice in the past and for the most part are not living up to it today.

The first question, then, is whether some definable security policy can be said to be generally expedient. Because the choice of goals is not a matter of expediency, it would seem to make no sense to ask whether it is expedient for nations to be concerned with the goal of security itself; only the means used to this end, so it would seem, can be judged as to their fitness—their instrumental rationality—to promote security. Yet, this is not so. Security, like other aims, may be an intermediate rather than an ultimate goal, in which case it can be judged as a means to these more ultimate ends.

Traditionally, the protection and preservation of national core values have been considered ends in themselves, at least by those who followed in the footsteps of Machiavelli or, for other reasons of political philosophy, placed the prince, state or nation at the pinnacle of their hierarchy of values. Those who do so today will be shocked at the mere suggestion that national security should have to be justified in terms of higher values which it is expected to serve. But there is a large and perhaps growing current of opinion—as a matter of fact influential in this country for a long time—which adheres to this idea. We condemn Nazis and Communists for defending their own totalitarian countries instead of helping to free their people from tyranny; we enlist support for armaments, here and in Allied countries, not so much on the grounds that they will protect national security but that by enhancing such security they will serve to protect ultimate human values like individual liberty. Again, opposition in Europe and Asia to military security measures is based in part on the contention that it would help little to make national core values secure, if in the process the liberties and the social welfare of the people had to be sacrificed; the prevention of Russian conquest, some insist, is useless, if in the course of a war of defense a large part of the people were to be exterminated and most cities destroyed.[10]

While excellent arguments can be made to support the thesis that the preservation of the national independence of this country is worth almost any price as long as no alternative community is available which could assure the same degree of order, justice, peace or individual liberty, it becomes necessary to provide such arguments whenever national security as a value in itself is being questioned. The answer cannot be taken for granted.

But turning away now from the expediency of security as an intermediate goal we must ask whether, aside from any moral considerations which will be discussed later, a specific level of security and specific means of attaining it can claim to be generally expedient.

When one sets out to define in terms of expediency the level of security to which a nation should aspire, one might be tempted to assume that the sky is the limit. Is not insecurity of any kind an evil from which any rational policy maker would want to rescue his country? Yet, there are obvious reasons why this is not so.

In the first place, every increment of security must be paid by additional sacrifices of other values usually of a kind more exacting than the mere expenditure of precious time on the part of policy makers. At a certain point, then, by something like the economic law of diminishing returns, the gain in security no longer compensates for the added costs of attaining it. As in the case of economic value comparisons and preferences, there is frequently disagreement among different layers of policy makers as to where the line should be drawn. This is true particularly because absolute security is out of the question unless a country is capable of world domination, in which case, however, the insecurities and fears would be "internalized" and probably magnified. Because nations must "live dangerously," then, to some extent, whatever they consent to do about it, a modicum of additional but only relative security may easily become unattractive to those who have to bear the chief burden. Nothing renders the task of statesmen in a democracy more difficult than the reluctance of the people to follow them very far along the road to high and costly security levels.

In the second place, national security policies when based on the accumulation of power have a way of defeating themselves if the target level is set too high. This is due to the fact that "power of resistance" cannot be unmistakably distinguished from "power of aggression." What a country does to bolster its own security through power can be interpreted by others, therefore, as a threat to their security. If this occurs, the vicious circle of what John Herz has described as the "security dilemma" sets in: the efforts of one side provoke countermeasures by the other which in turn tend to wipe out the gains of the first. Theoretically there seems to be no escape from this frustrating consequence; in practice, however, there are ways to convince those who might feel threatened that the accumulation of power is not intended and will never be used for attack.[11] The chief way is that of keeping the target level within moderate bounds and of avoiding placing oneself in a position where it has to be raised suddenly and drastically. The desire to escape from this vicious circle presupposes a security policy of much self-restraint and moderation, especially in the choice of the target level.[12] It can never be expedient to pursue a security policy which by the fact of provocation or incentive to others fails to increase the nation's relative power position and capability of resistance.

The question of what means are expedient for the purpose of enhancing security raises even more thorny problems. Policy makers must decide how to distribute their reliance on whatever means are available to them and, particularly, how far to push the accumulation of coercive power. No attempt can be made here to decide what the choice should be in order to be expedient. Obviously, there can be no general answer which would meet the requirements of every case. The answer depends on the circumstances. A weak country may have no better means at its disposal than to prove to stronger neighbors that its strict neutrality can be trusted. Potentially strong countries may have a chance to deter an aggressor by creating "positions of strength." In some instances they may have no other way of saving themselves; while in others even they may find it more expedient to supplement such a policy, if not to replace it, by a policy intended to negotiate their opponent out of his aggressive designs.

The reason why "power of resistance" is not the general panacea which some believe it to be lies in the nature of security itself. If security, in the objective sense of the term at least, rises and falls with the presence or absence of aggressive intentions on the part of others, the attitude and behavior of those from whom the threat emanates are of prime importance. Such attitude and behavior need not be beyond the realm of influence by the country seeking to bolster its security. Whenever they do not lie beyond this realm the most effective and least costly security policy consists in inducing the opponent to give up his aggressive intentions.

While there is no easy way to determine when means can and should be used which are directed not at resistance but at the prevention of the desire of others to attack, it will clarify the issue to sketch the type of hypotheses which would link specific security policies, as expedient, to some of the most typical political constellations.

One can think of nations lined up between the two poles of maximum and minimum "attack propensity," with those unalterably committed to attack, provided it promises success, at one pole and those whom no amount of opportunity for successful attack could induce to undertake it at the other. While security in respect to the first group can come exclusively as a result of "positions of strength" sufficient to deter or defeat attack, nothing could do more to undermine security in respect to the second group than to start accumulating power of a kind which would provoke fear and countermoves.

Unfortunately it can never be known with certainty, in practice, what position within the continuum one's opponent actually occupies. Statesmen cannot be blamed, moreover, if caution and suspicion lead them to assume a closer proximity to the first pole than hindsight proves to have been justified. We believe we have ample proof that the Soviet Union today is at or very close to the first pole, while Canadian policy makers probably place the United States in its intentions toward Canada at the second pole.

It is fair to assume that, wherever the issue of security becomes a matter of serious concern, statesmen will usually be dealing with potential opponents who occupy a position somewhere between but much closer to the first of the two poles. This means, then, that an attack must be feared as a possibility, even though the intention to launch it cannot be considered to have crystallized to the point where nothing could change it. If this be true, a security policy in order to be expedient cannot avoid accumulating power of resistance and yet cannot let it go at that. Efforts have to be made simultaneously toward the goal of removing the incentives to attack. This is only another way of saying that security policy must seek to bring opponents to occupy a position as close to the second pole as conditions and capabilities permit.

Such a twofold policy presents the greatest dilemmas because efforts to change the intentions of an opponent may run counter to the efforts to build up strength against him. The dangers of any policy of concessions, symbolized by "Munich," cannot be underestimated. The paradox of this situation must be faced, however, if security policy is to be expedient. It implies that national security policy, except when directed against a country unalterably committed to attack, is the more rational the more it succeeds in taking the interests, including the security interests, of the other side into consideration. Only in doing so can it hope to minimize the willingness of the other to resort to violence. Rather than to insist, then, that under all conditions security be sought by reliance on nothing but defensive power and be pushed in a spirit of national selfishness toward the highest targets, it should be stressed that in most instances efforts to satisfy legitimate demands of others are likely to promise better results in terms of security.[18] That is probably what George Kennan had in mind when he advised policy makers to use self-restraint in the pursuit of the national interest. While in the face of a would-be world conqueror who is beyond the pale of external influence it is dangerous to be diverted from the accumulation of sheer defensive power, any mistake about his true state of mind or any neglect of opportunities to influence his designs, where it has a chance of being successful, violates the rules of expediency. It should always be kept in mind that the ideal security policy is one which would lead to a distribution of values so satisfactory to all nations that the intention to attack and with it the problem of security would be minimized. While this is a utopian goal, policy makers and particularly peacemakers would do well to remember that there are occasions when greater approximation to such a goal can be effected.

We can now focus our attention on the moral issue, if such there be.[14] Those who advocate a policy devoted to national security are not always aware of the fact—if they do not explicitly deny it—that they are passing moral judgment when they advise a nation to pursue the goal of national security or when they insist that such means as the accumulation of coercive power—or its use—should be employed for this purpose.[15]

Nations like individuals or other groups may value things not because they consider them good or less evil than their alternative; they may value them because they satisfy their pride, heighten their sense of self-esteem or reduce their fears. However, no policy, or human act in general, can escape becoming a subject for moral judgment—whether by the conscience of the actor himself or by others—which calls for the sacrifice of other values, as any security policy is bound to do. Here it becomes a matter of comparing and weighing values in order to decide which of them are deemed sufficiently good to justify the evil of sacrificing others. If someone insists that his country should do more to build up its strength, he is implying, knowingly or not, that more security is sufficiently desirable to warrant such evils as the cut in much-needed social welfare benefits or as the extension of the period of military service.[16]

Many vivid examples of the moral dilemma are being supplied by current controversies concerning American security policy. Is a "deal with fascist Spain" morally justified, provided it added an increment to our security, though principles valued highly by some were being sacrificed? Should we engage in subversive activities and risk the lives of our agents if additional security can be attained thereby? Should we perhaps go so far as to start a preventive war, when ready, with the enormous evils it would carry with it, if we should become convinced that no adequate security can be obtained except by the defeat of the Soviet Union? In this last case, would not the exponents of amoralism have some moral qualms, at least to the point of rationalizing a decision favoring such a war by claiming that it would serve to satisfy not primarily an egotistical national demand for security but an altruistic desire to liberate enslaved peoples? It is easier to argue for the amorality of politics if one does not have to bear the responsibility of choice and decision!

Far be it from a political scientist to claim any particular competence in deciding what efforts for national security are or are not morally justified. What he can contribute here is to point to the ambiguities of any general normative demand that security be bought at whatever price it may cost. He may also be able to make it more difficult for advisers or executors of policy to hide from themselves or others the moral value judgments and preferences which underlie whatever security policy they choose to recommend or conduct.

The moral issue will be resolved in one of several ways depending on the ethical code upon which the decision is based. From one extreme point of view it is argued that every sacrifice, especially if imposed on other nations, is justified provided it contributes in any way to national security. Clearly this implies a position that places national security at the apex of the value pyramid and assumes it to constitute an absolute good to which all other values must be subordinated. Few will be found to take this position because if they subscribed to a nationalistic ethics of this extreme type they would probably go beyond security—the mere preservation of values—and insist that the nation is justified in conquering whatever it can use as *Lebensraum* or otherwise. At the opposite extreme are the absolute pacifists who consider the use of coercive power an absolute evil and condemn any security policy, therefore, which places reliance on such power.

For anyone who does not share these extreme views the moral issue raised by the quest for national security is anything but clear-cut and simple. He should have no doubts about the right of a nation to protect and preserve values to which it has a legitimate title or even about its moral duty to pursue a policy meant to serve such preservation. But he cannot consider security the supreme law as Machiavelli would have the statesman regard the *ragione di stato*. Somewhere a line is drawn, which in every instance he must seek to discover, that divides the realm of neglect, the "too-little," from the realm of excess, the "too-much." Even Hans Morgenthau who extols the moral duty of self-preservation seems to take it for granted that naked force shall be used for security in reaction only to violent attack, not for preventive war.

Decision makers are faced with the moral problem, then, of choosing first the values which deserve protection, with national independence ranking high not merely for its own sake but for the guarantee it may offer to values like liberty, justice and peace. He must further decide which level of security to make his target. This will frequently be his most difficult moral task though terms such as adequacy or fair share indicate the kind of standards that may guide him. Finally, he must choose the means and thus by scrupulous computation of values compare the sacrifices, which his choice of means implies, with the security they promise to provide.

It follows that policies of national security, far from being all good or all evil, may be morally praiseworthy or condemnable depending on their specific character and the particular circumstances of the case. They may be praised for their self-restraint and the consideration which this implies for values other than security; they may instead be condemned for being inadequate to protect national values. Again, they may be praised in one instance for the consideration given to the interests of others, particularly of weaker nations, or condemned in another because of the recklessness with which national values are risked on the altar of some chimera. The target level falls under moral judgment for being too ambitious, egotistical and provocative or for being inadequate; the means employed for being unnecessarily costly in other values or for being ineffective. This wide range of variety which arises out of the multitude of variables affecting the value computation would make it impossible, and in fact meaningless, to pass moral judgment, positive or negative, on "national security policy in general."

It is this lack of moral homogeneity which in matters of security policy justifies attacks on so-called moralism, though not on moral evaluation. The "moralistic approach" is taken to mean a wholesale condemnation either of any concern with national security—as being an expression of national egotism—or of a security policy relying on coercive and therefore evil power. The exponent of such "moralism" is assumed to believe that security for all peoples can be had today by the exclusive use of such "good" and altruistic means as model behavior and persuasion, a spirit of conciliation, international organization or world government. If there are any utopians who cling to this notion, and have influence on policy, it makes sense to continue to disabuse them of what can surely be proved to be dangerous illusions.

It is worth emphasizing, however, that the opposite line of argument, which without regard for the special circumstances would praise everything done for national security or more particularly everything done for the enhancement of national power of resistance, is no less guilty of applying simple and abstract moral principles and of failing to judge each case realistically on its merits.

In conclusion, it can be said, then, that normative admonitions to conduct a foreign policy guided by the national security interest are no less ambiguous and misleading than the statement of fact concerning past behavior which was discussed earlier. In order to be meaningful such admonitions would have to specify the degree of security which a nation shall aspire to attain and the means by which it is to be attained in a given situation. It may be good advice in one instance to appeal for greater effort and more armaments; it may be no less expedient and morally advisable in another instance to call for moderation and for greater reliance on means other than coercive power. Because the pendulum of public opinion swings so easily from extreme complacency to extreme apprehension, from utopian reliance on "good will" to disillusioned faith in naked force only, it is particularly important to be wary of any simple panacea, even of one that parades in the realist garb of a policy guided solely by the national security interest.

NOTES

1. Hans Morgenthau's *In Defense of the National Interest* (New York, 1951) is the most explicit and impassioned recent plea for an American foreign policy which shall follow "but one guiding star—the National Interest." While Morgenthau is not equally explicit in regard to the meaning he attaches to the symbol "national interest," it becomes clear in the few pages devoted to an exposition of this "perennial" interest that the author is thinking in terms of the national security interest, and specifically of security based on power. The United States, he says, is interested in three things: a unique position as a predominant Power without rival in the Western Hemisphere and the maintenance of the balance of power in Europe as well as in Asia, demands which make sense only in the context of a quest for security through power.

2. Walter Lippmann, *U.S. Foreign Policy* (Boston, 1943), p. 51.

3. This explains why some nations which would seem to fall into the category of *status quo* Powers *par excellence* may nevertheless be dissatisfied and act very much like "imperialist" Powers, as Morgenthau calls nations with acquisitive goals. They are dissatisfied with the degree of security which they enjoy under the *status quo* and are out to enhance it.

France's occupation of the Ruhr in 1923 illustrates this type of behavior. Because the demand for more security may induce a *status quo* Power even to resort to the use of violence as a means of attaining more security, there is reason to beware of the easy and often self-righteous assumption that nations which desire to preserve the *status quo* are necessarily "peace-loving."

4. Security and power would be synonymous terms if security could be attained only through the accumulation of power, which will be shown not to be the case. The fear of attack—security in the subjective sense—is also not proportionate to the relative power position of a nation. Why, otherwise, would some weak and exposed nations consider themselves more secure today than does the United States?

Harold D. Lasswell and Abraham Kaplan, *Power and Society* (New Haven, 1950), defining security as "high value expectancy" stress the subjective and speculative character of security by using the term "expectancy"; the use of the term "high," while indicating no definite level, would seem to imply that the security-seeker aims at a position in which the events he expects—here the continued unmolested enjoyment of his possessions—have considerably more than an even chance of materializing.

5. The United States offers a good illustration and may be typical in this respect. For a long time this country was beyond the reach of any enemy attack that could be considered probable. During that period, then, it could afford to dismiss any serious preoccupation with security. Events proved that it was no worse off for having done so. However, after this happy condition had ceased to exist, government and people alike showed a lag in their awareness of the change. When Nicholas J. Spykman raised his voice in the years before World War II to advocate a broader security outlook than was indicated by the symbol "Western Hemisphere Defense" and a greater appreciation of the rôle of defensive military power, he was dealing with this lag and with the dangers implied in it. If Hans Morgenthau and others raise their warning voices today, seemingly treading in Spykman's footsteps, they are addressing a nation which after a new relapse into wishful thinking in 1945 has been radically disillusioned and may now be swinging toward excessive security apprehensions.

6. Terms such as "degree" or "level" of security are not intended to indicate merely quantitative differences. Nations may also differ in respect to the breadth of their security perspective as when American leaders at Yalta were so preoccupied with security against the then enemy countries of the United States that they failed or refused to consider future American security vis-à-vis the Soviet Union. The differences may apply, instead, to the time range for which security is sought as when the British at Versailles were ready to offer France short-run security guarantees while the French with more foresight insisted that the "German danger" would not become acute for some ten years.

7. For a discussion of this working hypothesis—as part of the "pure power" hypothesis —see my article on "The Pole of Power and the Pole of Indifference" in *World Politics,* vol. IV, No. 1, October 1951.

8. Myres S. McDougal ("Law and Peace" in the *American Journal of International Law,* vol. 46, No. 1, January 1952, pp. 102 *et seq.*) rightly criticizes Hans Morgenthau (and George Kennan for what Kennan himself wrongly believes to be his own point of view in the matter; see fn. 15 *infra*) for his failure to appreciate the rôle which non-power methods, such as legal procedures and moral appeals, may at times successfully play in the pursuit of security. But it is surprising how little aware McDougal appears to be of the disappointing modesty of the contributions which these "other means" have actually made to the enhancement of security and the quite insignificant contributions they have made to the promotion of changes of the *status quo*. This latter failure signifies that they have been unable to remove the main causes of the attacks which security-minded peoples rightly fear.

9. On the problem of security policy (*Sicherheitspolitik*) with special reference to "collective security" see the comprehensive and illuminating study of Heinrich Rogge, "Kollektivsicherheit Buendnispolitik Voelkerbund," *Theorie der nationalen und internationalen Sicherheit* (Berlin, 1937), which deserves attention despite the fact that it was written and published in Nazi Germany and bears a distinctly "revisionist" slant.

10. Raymond Dennett goes further in making the generalization that, "if economic pressures become great enough, almost any government, when put to the final test, will moderate or abandon a political association" (such as the alliance system of the United

States with its usefulness to national security) "if only an alteration of policy seems to offer the possibility of maintaining or achieving living standards adequate enough to permit the regime to survive." "Danger Spots in the Pattern of American Security," in *World Politics,* vol. IV, No. 4, July 1952, p. 449.

11. Not everyone agrees that this can be done. Jeremy Bentham wrote that "measures of mere self defense are naturally taken for projects of aggression" with the result that "each makes haste to begin for fear of being forestalled." *Principles of International Law,* Essay IV.

12. The Quakers, in a book on *The United States and the Soviet Union: Some Quaker Proposals for Peace* (New Haven, 1949), p. 14, state that "it is highly questionable whether security can be achieved in the modern world through an attempt to establish an overwhelming preponderance of military power." This can be read to mean that a less ambitious military target than overwhelming preponderance might be a means of achieving security.

13. As A. D. Lindsay puts it, "The search for perfect security . . . defeats its own ends. Playing for safety is the most dangerous way to live." Introduction to Thomas Hobbes, *Leviathan,* p. xxii.

14. On the moral problem in international relations see my article on "Statesmanship and Moral Choice" in *World Politics,* vol. I, No. 2, January 1949, pp. 176 *et seq.,* especially p. 185. In one of his most recent statements on the subject, Reinhold Niebuhr, *The Irony of American History* (New York, 1945), points specifically to the moral problem involved in security policy—"no imperiled nation," he writes, "is morally able to dispense with weapons which might insure its survival" (p. 39).

15. It is not without irony that of the two authors who have recently come out for a policy of the national interest, the one, George F. Kennan, who calls for a policy of national self-restraint and humility, usually identified with morality, should deny "that state behavior is a fit subject for moral judgment" (*American Diplomacy, 1900–1950,* Chicago, 1952, p. 100), while the other, Hans Morgenthau (*op. cit.*), calling for a policy of unadulterated national egotism, claims to speak in the name of morality.

16. It would be unrealistic to assume that policy makers divide their attention strictly between ends and means and only after having chosen a specific target level as being morally justified decide whether the means by which it can be attained are morally acceptable. Moral judgment is more likely to be passed on the totality of a course of action which embraces both the desired end and the means which lead to it.

4.

K. J. Holsti: *The Concept of Power in the Study of International Relations*

According to the Realists, all politics is a struggle for power: the national interest must be defined in terms of the need to maximize power, which is offered as the central organizing concept for international politics. Upon closer examination, however, "power," like "national security," turns out to be a very ambiguous term. In an article which attempts to clarify the concept of power, Professor K. J. Holsti suggests that power—the process in international politics of one state influencing another in its own interests—can be viewed as well as a relationship, as a means to other ends, as a quantity, and as a capability.

K. J. Holsti, "The Concept of Power in the Study of International Relations," *Background,* Vol. 7, No. 4 (February 1964), pp. 179–93. Some footnotes omitted and bibliographical references omitted. Reprinted by permission of the publisher, Sage Publications, and the author.

Associate Professor of Politics at the University of British Columbia, K. J. Holsti is editor of *International Studies Quarterly* and author of *International Politics*.

Students of international politics have for years argued that the concept of power can be used as a fruitful approach in studying processes in international systems. Unfortunately, there has been little systematic examination of the concept so that, like the balance of power, its meaning has remained ambiguous. Some have claimed that the concept can be used to analyze every major phenomenon in international politics. Others have defined power roughly as a means to an end. Some use the term to denote a country's military forces, but when used in this way they are really discussing only a country's military capability and not the amount of influence the country wields in the system.

Hans Morgenthau is the foremost advocate of the concept of power as the theoretical core of international politics. In his view, all politics is a struggle for power. He derives this dictum from the assumption that the desire to dominate is "a constitutive element of all human associations." Thus, regardless of the goals and objectives of government, the immediate aim of all state action is to obtain and to increase power. Since by definition all states seek to maximize their power, international politics can be conceived of and analyzed as a struggle between independent units seeking to dominate others.

Professor Morgenthau unfortunately fails to submit the concept of power to further examination so that some ambiguity remains. He implies, for example, that power is also a major goal of policy or even a determining motive of any political action. Elsewhere, however, he suggests that power is a relationship and a means to an end. Because of this ambiguity, we do not know what the concept explains or fails to explain in international politics. Does the term "struggle for power" shed light on the many processes that go on within an international system? The word "struggle" certainly does not tell us much about the relations between Norway and Sweden or between Canada and the United States. Does the term "power," defined as the immediate goal of all governments, explain the major external objectives of Nicaragua or Chad or Switzerland?

In contrast to the "struggle for power" concept is the "anti-power theory" of international relations. The proponents of this theory (including Woodrow Wilson) claim that there is a distinction between "power politics" and some other kind of politics. Not pessimists regarding human nature, they assume that man is essentially tolerant and pacific and that the human community is united through many bonds. Statesmen, they claim, have a choice between practicing "power politics" and conducting foreign relations by some other means. Wilson and others made the further assumption that there is a correlation between a nation's social and political institutions and the way it conducts its foreign relations. To them, autocracies which did not consult "the people" usually engaged in deception, duplicity, and saber-rattling. Democracies, on the other hand, displayed tolerance, morality, and justice, and sought only peace and stability. In the new order which they envisaged for the post World War I period, negotiations would replace threats of war, and world-wide consensus on the desirability of peace would sustain democratic statesmen. In other words, power politics was synonymous with autocracy. But how democratic governments were supposed to achieve their objectives is left unexplained.[1] This view is also of limited use because it is mostly prescriptive: it enunciates how international processes *should* be carried on, but it fails to help us understand what actually occurs.

A third view of power is found in past and contemporary texts on international relations. Authors present the student with a brief and formal definition of power, often equating power with the physical assets a nation possesses. Most texts, in fact, concentrate on the analysis of these assets (often called the "elements of national power") without discussing the actual relations between governments and the techniques by which these assets are brought to bear on the pursuit of national objectives.

Should we not, however, define power in a way which best clarifies what we observe and what we wish to know? A definition should suggest areas of inquiry and reality, though no definition is likely to account for the totality of the subject. Thus, one definition of the concept may be useful for describing and analyzing social relations within a political party or within a family, but it may not be useful for studying international relations. Let us first describe an *act* which we conceive to be central to the process of international politics; that is, the act or acts that A commits toward B so that B pursues a course of behavior in accordance with A's wishes. The act can be illustrated as follows:

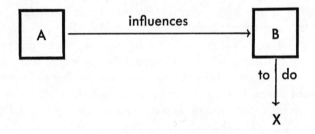

A seeks to influence B because it has established certain goals which cannot be achieved (it is perceived) unless B (and perhaps many other actors as well) does X. If this is an important act in international political processes, we can see that it contains several elements:

1. Influence (an aspect of power) is essentially a *means* to an end. Some governments or statesmen may seek influence for its own sake, but for most it is instrumental, just like money. They use it primarily for other goals, which may include prestige, territory, souls, raw materials, security, or alliances.

2. The act also implies a base of capabilities which the actor uses or mobilizes to use in his efforts to influence the behavior of B. A capability is any physical or mental object or quality available as an instrument of inducement. The

concept of capability may be illustrated in the following example. Suppose an unarmed man walks into a bank and asks the clerk to give him all her money. The clerk observes clearly that the man has no weapons and refuses to comply with his order. The man has sought to influence the behavior of the clerk, but has failed. The next time, however, he walks in armed with a pistol and threatens to shoot if the clerk does not give him the money. This time, the clerk complies. In this instance the man has mobilized certain resources or capabilities (the gun) and has succeeded in influencing the clerk to do as he wished. The gun, just like a nation's military forces, *is not synonymous with the act of influencing,* but it is the instrument that was used to induce the clerk to change her behavior to comply with the robber's objectives.

3. The act of influencing B obviously involves a *relationship* between A and B, though as we will see later, the relationship may not even involve communication. If the relationship covers any period of time, we can also say that it is a *process*.

4. If A can get B to do something, but B cannot get A to do a similar thing, then we can say that A has more power than B *vis-à-vis* that action. Power, therefore, is also a *quantity*. But as a quantity it is only meaningful when compared to the power of others. Power is therefore relative.

To summarize, then, power may be viewed from several aspects: it is a means, it is based on capabilities, it is a relationship, and a process, and it can also be a quantity.

But for purposes of analyzing international politics, we can break down the concept of power into three separate elements: power is (1) the act (process, relationship) of influencing other factors; (2) it includes the capabilities used to make the wielding of influence successful; and (3) the responses to the act. The three elements must be kept distinct. However, since this definition may seem too abstract, we can define the concept also in the more operational terms of policy makers. In formulating policy and the strategy to achieve certain goals, they would explicitly or implicitly ask the four following questions:

1. Given our goals, what do we wish B to do or not to do? (X)
2. How shall we get B to do or not to do X? (implies a relationship and process)
3. What capabilities are at our disposal so that we can induce B to do or not to do X?
4. What is B's probable response to our attempts to influence its behavior?

Before discussing the problem of capabilities and responses we have to fill out our model of the influence act to account for the many patterns of behavior that may be involved in an international relationship. First, as J. David Singer points out, the exercise of influence implies more than merely A's ability to *change* the behavior of B. Influence may also be seen where A attempts to get B to *continue* a course of action or policy which is useful to, or in the interests of, A. The exercise of influence does not always cease, therefore, after

B does X. It is often a continuing process of reinforcing B's behavior. Nevertheless, power is "situational" to the extent that it is exercised within a framework of goals.[2]

Second, it is almost impossible to find a situation where B does not also have some influence over A. Our model has suggested that influence is exercised only in one direction, by A over B. In reality, however, influence is multilateral. State A, for example, would seldom seek a particular goal unless it had been influenced in a particular direction by the actions of other states in the system. At a minimum, there is the problem of feedback in any relationship: if B complies with A's wishes and does X, that behavior may subsequently prompt A to change its behavior, perhaps in the interest of B. Suppose, for example, that state A, after making threats, persuades B to lower its tariffs on the goods of state A. This would seem to be influence travelling only in one direction. But where state B does lower its tariffs, that action may prompt state A to reward state B in some manner. The phenomenon of feedback may be illustrated as follows:

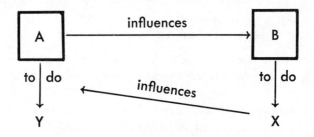

Third, the number of times a state becomes involved in acts of influence depends upon the general level of involvement of that particular actor in the system. The first requisite for attempting to wield influence is a perception that somehow state B (or any other) is related to the achievement of state A's goals and that there is, or will be, some kind of relationship of interdependence. If the relationship covers only inconsequential matters, few acts of influence may be necessary; but the greater the involvement of an actor in the system, the greater the necessity to wield influence over other actors. For example, except for limited trade relations, there is little perception of interdependence between Iceland and Uganda, hence little need for the government of Iceland to attempt to influence the domestic or external policies of the African country.

Fourth, there is the type of relationship which includes what Herbert Simon has called "anticipated reaction." This is the situation, frequently found in international relations, where A might wish B to do X, but does not try to influence B for fear that B will do Y instead, which is an unfavorable response from A's point of view. In a hypothetical situation, the government of India might wish to obtain arms from the United States to build up its own defenses, but it does not request such arms because it fears that the United States would insist on certain conditions for the sale of arms which might compromise India's neutrality. This "anticipated reaction" may also be multilateral, where

A wishes B to do X, but will not try to get B to do it because it fears that C, a third actor, will do Y, which is unfavorable to A's interests. India wants to purchase American arms, but does not seek to influence the United States to sell them for fear that Pakistan (C) will then build up its own armaments and thus start an arms race. In this situation, Pakistan (C) has influence over the actions of the Indian government even though it has not deliberately sought to influence India on this particular matter or even communicated its position in any way. The Indian government has simply perceived that there is a relatively high probability that if it seeks to influence the United States, Pakistan will react in a manner that is contrary to India's interests.

Fifth, power and influence may be measured quite objectively by scholars and statesmen, but what is important in international relations is the *perceptions* of influence and capabilities that are held by policy-makers. The reason that governments invest millions of dollars for the gathering of intelligence is to develop or have available a relatively accurate picture of other states' capabilities and intentions. Where there is a great discrepancy between perceptions and reality, the results to a country's foreign policy may be disastrous. To take our example of the bank robber again, suppose that the man held a harmless toy pistol and threatened the clerk. The clerk perceived the gun to be real and hence complied with his demand. In this case the robber's influence was far greater than the "objective" character of his capabilities, and the distorted perception by the clerk led her to act in a manner that was unfavorable to her and her employers.

Finally, as our original model suggests, A may try to influence B *not to do* X. Sometimes this is called "negative" power, where A acts in a manner to *prevent* a certain action it deems undesirable to its interests. This is a very typical relationship and process in international politics. By signing the Munich treaty, for example, the British and French governments hoped to prevent Germany from invading Czechoslovakia: the Soviet government by using a variety of instruments of foreign policy, has sought to prevent West Germany from obtaining nuclear weapons; by organizing the Marshall Plan and NATO, the United States sought to prevent the growth of communism in western Europe and/or a Soviet military invasion of this area.

Capabilities

The second element of the concept of power consists of those capabilities that are mobilized in support of the act of influencing. It is difficult to understand how much influence an actor is likely to wield unless we also have some knowledge of the capabilities that are involved.[3] Nevertheless, it should be acknowledged that social scientists do not understand all the reasons why some actors—whether people, groups, governments, or states—wield influence successfully, while others do not.

It is clear that in political relationships not everyone possesses equal influence. We frequently use the terms "great powers" and "small powers" as a shorthand way of suggesting that some actors make commitments abroad and have the capacity to meet them that others lack. The distinction between the "great powers" and the "small powers" is usually based on some rough estimation of tangible and intangible factors which we have called capabilities. In domestic politics it is possible to construct a lengthy list of those capabilities and attributes which seemingly permit some to wield influence over large numbers of people and over important public decisions. Dahl lists such tangibles as money, wealth, information, time, political allies, official position, and control over jobs, and such intangibles as personality and leadership qualities. But not everyone who possesses these capabilities can command the obedience or influence the behavior of other people. What is crucial in relating capabilities to influence, according to Dahl, is that the person *mobilize these capabilities for his political purposes,* and that he possess skill in mobilizing them. A person who uses his wealth, time, information, friends, and personality for political purposes will likely be able to influence others on public issues. A person, on the other hand, who possesses the same capabilities but uses them to invent a new mousetrap is not likely to be important in politics.

The same propositions also hold true in international politics. Capabilities may also be tangible or intangible. We can predict that a country in possession of a high Gross National Product, a high level of industrial development, sophisticated weapons systems, and a large population will have more influence and prestige in the system than a state with a primitive economy, small population, and old fashioned armaments. And yet, the intangibles are also important. In addition to the physical resources of a state, such factors as leadership and national morale have to be assessed. We could not, for example, arrive at an estimation of India's influence in world politics unless we regarded the prestige and stature of its leadership abroad.

Moreover, the amount of influence a state wields over others can be related, as in domestic politics, to the capabilities that are *mobilized* in support of foreign policy objectives. Or, to put this proposition in another way, we can argue that a capability does not itself determine the uses to which it will be put. Nuclear power can be used to provide electricity or to coerce and perhaps to destroy other nations. The use of capabilities depends less on their quality and quantity than on the external objectives that a government formulates for itself.

However, the *variety* of foreign policy instruments available to a nation for influencing others is partly a function of the quantity and quality of capabilities. What a government will seek to do, and how it attempts to do it will depend at least partially on the resources it finds available. A country such as Thailand which possesses relatively few and underdeveloped resources cannot, even if it desired, construct nuclear weapons with which to intimidate others, or establish a world-wide propaganda network, or dispense several billion dollars annually of foreign aid to try to influence other countries. And in other international systems, such as in the ancient Hindu interstate system, the level of technology limited the number of capabilities that could be used for external purposes. Kautilya suggested in the *Arthasastra* that only seven elements made up the capability of the state: the excellence (quality) of the king and the ministers, and the quality and quantity of the territory, fortresses, treasury, army, and allies. In general, advanced industrial societies are able to mobilize a wide variety of capabilities in support of their external objectives. We can conclude, therefore, that how states *use* their capabilities depends on their external objectives, but the choice of objectives and the instruments to achieve those objectives are limited or influenced by the quality and quantity of available capabilities.

The Measurement of Capabilities

For many years students of international politics have made meticulous comparisons of the mobilized and potential capabilities of various nations. Comparative data relating to the production of iron ore, coal, hydroelectricity, economic growth rates, educational levels, population growth rates, military resources, transportation systems, and sources of raw materials are presented as indicators of a nation's power. Unfortunately, few have acknowledged that in making these comparisons they are not measuring a state's power or influence, but only its base. Our previous discussion would suggest that such measurements and assessments are not particularly useful unless they are related to the foreign policy objectives of the various states. Capability is always the capability to do something; its assessment, therefore, is most meaningful when carried on within a framework of certain goals and foreign policy objectives.

The deduction of actual influence from the quantity and quality of potential and mobilized capabilities may, in some cases, give an approximation of reality, but historically there have been too many discrepancies between the basis of power and the amount of influence to warrant adopting this practice as a useful approach to international relations. One could have assumed, for example, on the basis of a comparative study of technological and educational level, and general standard of living in the 1920's and 1930's that the United States would have been one of the most influential actors in the international system. A careful comparison of certain resources, called by Simonds and Emeny the "great essentials," revealed the United States to be in an enviable position. In the period 1925 to 1930, it was the only major country in the world that produced from its own resources adequate supplies of food, power, iron, machinery, chemicals, coal, iron ore, and petroleum. If actual influence had been deduced from the quantities of "great essentials" possessed by the major actors the following ranking of states would have resulted: (1) United States, (2) Germany, (3) Great Britain, (4) France, (5) Russia, (6) Italy, (7) Japan. However, the diplomatic history of the world from 1925 to 1930 would suggest that there was little correlation between the capabilities of these countries and their actual influence. If we measure influence by the impact these actors made on the system and by the responses they could invoke when they sought to change the behavior of other states, we would find for this period quite a different ranking, such as the following: (1) France, (2) Great Britain, (3) Italy, (4) Germany, (5) Russia, (6) Japan, (7) United States.

Other historical discrepancies can also be cited. How, for example, can we explain the ability of the French after their defeat in the Napoleonic wars to become, within a short period of time, one of the most influential members in the Concert of Europe? More recently, how could such figures as Dr. Castro, Colonel Nasser and Marshal Tito successfully defy the pressure of the great powers? The answer to these questions lies not solely in the physical capabilities of states, but partly in the personalities and diplomacy of political leaders, the reactions of the major powers, and other special circumstances. Hence, the ability of A to change the behavior of B is enhanced if it possesses physical capabilities which it can use in the influence act; but B is by no means defenseless because it fails to own a large army, raw materials, and money for foreign aid. Persuasiveness is often related to such intangibles as personality, perceptions, friendships, traditions, and customs, all of which are almost impossible to measure accurately.

The discrepancy between physical capabilities and actual influence can also be related to credibility. A nuclear capability, for example, is often thought to increase radically the diplomatic influence of those who develop it. Yet, the important aspect of a nuclear capability is not its possession, but the willingness to use it if necessary. Other actors must know that the capability is not of mere symbolic significance. Thus, a leader like Dr. Castro possesses a particular psychological advantage over the United States (hence, influence) because he knows that in almost all circumstances the American government would not use strategic nuclear weapons against his country. He has, therefore, effectively broken through the significance of the American nuclear capability as far as Cuban-American relations are concerned.

Finally, discrepancies between actors' physical capabilities and their actual influence can be traced to the habit of analyzing capabilities only in terms of a single state. The wielding of influence in modern international politics is, however, seldom a bilateral process. In a system where all states perceive some involvement and relationship with all other actors, governments seek to use the capabilities and diplomatic influence of other actors by forming diplomatic or military coalitions. Indeed, modern diplomacy is largely concerned with eliciting support of friends and neutrals, presumably because widespread diplomatic support for an actor's policies increases the legitimacy of those objections, thereby increasing the influence of the actor. "Small" states in particular can increase their influence if they can gain commitments of support from other members of the system.[4] If there is no direct relationship between physical capabilities and actual influence, how do we proceed to measure influence? Assessment of physical capabilities may be adequate for rough estimations of influence or war potential and in some circumstances it may suffice to rely on reputations of power. But for precise knowledge, we have to refer to the actual processes of international politics and not to charts or indices of raw materials. We can best measure influence, according to Dahl, by studying the *responses* of those who are in the influence relationship. If A can get B to do X, but C cannot get B to do the same thing, then in reference to that particular action, A has more influence. Or, if B does X despite the protestations of A, then we can assume that A, in this circumstance, did not enjoy much influence over B. It is meaningless to argue that the Soviet Union is more powerful than the United States unless we cite how, for what purposes, and in relation to whom, the Soviet Union and the United States are exerting influence. We may conclude, then, that capabilities themselves do not always lead to the successful wielding of influence and that other variables have to be considered as well. In general, influence varies with (1) the type of goals an actor pursues, (2) the quality and quantity of capabilities (including allies and intangibles) at its disposal, (3) the skill in mobilizing these capabilities in support of the goals, and (4) the credibility of threats and rewards.

How Influence Is Exercised

Social scientists have noted several fundamental techniques that individuals and groups use to influence each other. In a political system which contains no one legitimate center of authority (such as a government, or a father in a family) that can command the members of the group or society, bargaining has to be used among the sovereign entities. A. F. K. Organski, Charles Schleicher, and Quincy Wright suggest four typical bargaining techniques in international politics: persuasion, offering rewards, threatening punishments, and the use of force. These categories are very useful for analyzing the wielding of influence in the system, but they can be expanded and refined to account for slightly different forms of behavior. Recalling that A seeks one of three courses of conduct from B (e.g., B to do X in the future, B not to do X in the future, and B to continue doing X) it may use six different tactics.

1. *Persuasion*. Persuasion may include threats, rewards and actual punishments, but we will mean here those situations in which an actor simply initiates or discusses a proposal or situation with another and elicits a favorable response without explicitly holding out the possibility of rewards or punishments. We cannot assume that the exercise of influence is always *against* the wishes of others and that there are only two possible outcomes of the act, one favoring A, the other favoring B. For example, state A asks B to support it at a coming international conference on the control of narcotics. State B might not originally have any particular interest in the conference or its outcome, but decides, on the basis of A's initiative, that something positive might be gained not only by supporting A's proposals, but also by attending the conference. In this case there might also be the expectation of gaining some type of reward in the future, but not necessarily from A.

2. *The offer of rewards*. This is the situation where A promises to do something favorable to B if B complies with the wishes of A. Rewards may be of almost any type in international relations. To gain the diplomatic support of B at the narcotics conference, A may offer to increase foreign aid payments, to lower tariffs on goods imported from B, to support B at a later conference on communications facilities, or it may promise to remove a previous punish-

ment. The latter tactic is used often by Soviet negotiators. After having created an unfavorable situation, they promise to remove it in return for some concessions by their opponents.

3. *The granting of rewards.* In some instances, the credibility of an actor is not very high and state B, before complying with A's wishes, may insist that A actually give the reward in advance. Frequently in armistice negotiations neither side will unilaterally take steps to demilitarize an area or to demobilize troops until the other shows evidence of complying with the agreements. One of the cliches of cold war diplomacy holds that deeds, not words, are required for the granting of rewards and concessions.

4. *The threat of punishment.* Threats of punishment may be further subdivided into two types:

   (a) positive threats, where, for example, state A threatens to increase tariffs, to cut off diplomatic relations, to institute a boycott or embargo against trade with B, or to use force.

   (b) threats of deprivation, where A threatens to withdraw foreign aid or in other ways to withhold rewards or other advantages that it already grants to B.

5. *The infliction of non-violent punishment.* In this situation, threats are carried out in the hope of altering B's behavior which, in most cases, could not be altered by other means. The problem with this tactic is that it usually results in reciprocal measures by the other side, thus inflicting damage on both, though not necessarily bringing about a desired state of affairs. If, for example, A threatens to increase its military capabilities if B does X and then proceeds to implement the threat, it is not often that B will comply with A's wishes because it, too, can increase its military capabilities easily enough. In this type of a situation, then, both sides indulge in the application of punishments which may escalate into more serious form unless the conflict is resolved.

6. *Force.* In previous eras when governments did not possess the variety of foreign policy instruments that are available today, they had to rely frequently in the bargaining process upon the use of force. Force and violence were not only the most efficient tactics, but in many cases they were the only means possible for influencing. Today, the situation is different. As technological levels rise, other means of inducement become available and can serve as substitutes for force.[5]

Patterns of Influence in the International System

Most governments at one time or another use all of these techniques for influencing others, but probably over ninety percent of all relations between states are based on simple persuasion and deal with relatively unimportant technical matters. Since such interactions seldom make the headlines, however, we often assume that most relations between states involve the making or carrying out of threats. But whether a government is communicating with another over an unimportant technical matter or over a subject of great consequence, it is likely to use a particular type of tactic in its attempts to influence, depending on the general climate of relations between those two governments. Allies, for example, seldom threaten each other with force or even make blatant threats of punishment. Similarly, governments which disagree over a wide range of policy objectives are more likely to resort to threats and to the imposition of punishments. We can suggest, therefore, that just as there are observable patterns of relations between states in terms of their foreign policy strategies (alliances, isolation, neutrality, etc.), there are also general patterns of relations between actors with reference to the methods used to influence each other. The methods of exerting influence between Great Britain and the United States are *typically* those of persuasion and rewards, while the methods of exerting influence between the Soviet Union and the United States in the early post World War II era were typically those of threatening and inflicting punishments of various types. Since such typical patterns exist, we can then construct rough typologies of international relationships as identified by the typical techniques used in the act of influence.

1. *Relations of consensus.* Relations of consensus would be typical between actors that had few disagreements over foreign policy objectives, and/or had a very low level of interaction and involvement in each other's affairs. An example of the former would be Anglo-American relations, and of the latter, the relations between Thailand and Bolivia. In the relations of consensus, moreover, influence is exercised primarily by the technique of persuasion and through the subtle offering of rewards. Finally, since violence as a form of punishment is almost inconceivable between two countries, the military capabilities of neither actor are organized, mobilized, and "targeted" toward the other.

2. *Relations of overt manipulation.* Here, there may be some disagreement or conflict over foreign policy objectives, or state A might undertake some domestic policy which was disapproved by state B, such as a form of racial discrimination. Since there is some conflict, there will also be at least a modest degree of involvement between the two actors, or a perception that A and B are in some kind of a relationship of interdependence. The techniques used to influence will include, if normal persuasion fails, (a) offers of rewards, (b) the granting of rewards, (c) threats to withhold rewards (e.g., not to give foreign aid in the future), or (d) threats of non-violent punishment, including, for example, the raising of tariffs against B's products. Militarily, in relations of overt manipulation, there is still no mobilization or targeting of military capabilities toward state B. Examples of overt manipulation would include the relations between China and the Soviet Union, 1960–1963, and the relations between France and the United States during this same period.

3. *Relations of coercion.* In relations of coercion, there are fundamental disagreements over foreign policy objectives. Almost all actions that A takes externally are perceived by B to be a threat to its own interests. Involvement is, therefore, high. A seeks to influence B's behavior typically by (a) threatening punishments, (b) by inflicting non-violent punishments and under extreme provocation, (c) by the selective and limited use of force as, for example, in a peace-time blockade. Military capabilities, finally, are likely to be targeted towards each other. Examples would include the Soviet Union and the western coalition for most of the period since 1947, Cuba and the United States between 1960 and 1963, Nazi Germany and Czechoslovakia between 1937 and 1939, and Egypt and Israel since 1948.

4. *Relations of force.* Here, there is almost total disagreement on foreign policy objectives and the areas of consensus are limited to a few necessities such as communications. The degree of involvement is obviously extremely high. The typical form of exercising influence is through the infliction of violent punishment, though in some instances rewards (e.g., peace offers) might be offered. National capabilities are mobilized primarily with a view to conducting the policy of punishment. However, the quantity of military capabilities that is used will vary with the geographic and force-level boundaries which the disputants place on the conflict.

Though most relations between states could be placed in one of the previous categories, it should also be apparent that under changing circumstances, governments are required to resort to techniques of influence toward others that they would normally avoid. However, the cold war represents a curious phenomenon in the history of international politics because in the relations between east and west *all* of the techniques of influence are being used simultaneously. There are several areas of policy where consensus exists between the Soviet Union and the leaders of the west and where agreements—either in treaties or through "understandings"—can be reached without making threats or imposing punishments.[6] There are also areas of great controversy where the antagonists commit military capabilities and seek to influence each other's behavior most of the time by making threats and carrying out various forms of punishment.

To summarize this analysis of power, we can suggest that power is an integral part of all political relationships, but in international politics we are interested primarily in one process: how does one state influence the behavior of another in its own interests. The act of influencing becomes, therefore, a central focus for the study of international politics and it is from this act that we can best deduce a definition of power. If we observe the act of influencing, we can see that it is a process, a relationship, a means to an end, and even a quantity. Moreover, we can make an analytical distinction between the act of influencing, the basis, or capabilities, upon which the act relies, and the response to the act. Capabilities are an important determinant of how successful the wielding of influence will be, but they are by no means the only determinant. The nature of a country's foreign policy objectives and the skill with which an actor mobilizes its capabilities for foreign policy purposes are equally important.

The act of influencing may be carried out by a variety of means, the most important of which are the offer and granting of rewards, the threat and imposition of punishments, and the application of force. The choice of means used to induce will depend, in turn, upon the general nature of relations between two governments and on the degree of involvement among actors in the system.

This formulation of the power concept will not, of course, be useful for all aspects of the study of international relations. The categories are mental constructs imposed upon reality for the purpose of clarifying certain aspects of reality. They cannot be expected to cover all international relationships, however. They fail to account for such questions as the determination of national goals or governmental decision-making processes. They will not alert the investigator or student to certain processes in bilateral or multilateral systems that contain complex patterns of economic, technical, and military relations. Questions dealing with trade relations, export credits, or investment incentives —all areas of interest in the study—are often decided on the basis of technical criteria by specialists who cannot mobilize national capabilities for bargaining purposes. Power, no matter how defined, seems particularly inappropriate as a tool for analyzing relations in a highly integrated international community, such as exists in Scandinavia or North America. The concept of leadership might be more appropriate for these relations. In addition, the state A-state B relationship does not seem to account for the activities of various international functional groups (technical, scientific, and economic) which act in concert across traditional national jurisdictions. In short, the concept of power cannot serve, as many have argued, as the core of a theory of international relations. But it can indicate areas of inquiry for further research in international processes and, if formulated carefully, it may become for the first time an important teaching device as well.

NOTES

1. There is room for disagreement on this characterization of the Wilsonian theory of power. Wilson was obviously aware of the role of power as military force and as public opinion. His concept of collective security, where all peaceful nations would band together to enforce the peace, implies that democracies no less than autocracies, should use force when necessary.

2. State A might also wish state B to do w, y, and z, which may be incompatible with the achievement of X.

3. We might assess influence for historical situations solely on the basis of whether A got B to do X, without having knowledge of either A's or B's capabilities.

4. This is one reason why international conflicts seldom remain confined to the original disputants. Recognizing the dangers of increasing the number of parties to a dispute, the United Nations has sought to "isolate" conflicts as much as possible.

5. Presumably, therefore, disarmament and arms control would become more feasible because other instruments of policy can be used in the influence act. In previous eras, to disarm would have led to the collapse of the most important—if not only—capability that could be mobilized for foreign policy purposes.

6. Areas of agreement between the Soviet Union and the west which have resulted either in treaties or "understandings" would include the cessation of nuclear tests, the demilitarization of the Antarctic and, possibly, outer space, the renouncing of nuclear war as an instrument of policy, and efforts to prevent the spread of nuclear weapons.

5.

C. Wright Mills: *The Power Elite*

Power is organized at home and projected abroad in pursuit of national interests. But whose interest is the national interest? From the Realist perspective, the fundamental national interest exists irrespective of political system or political party, and its legitimacy, writes Professor Morgenthau, "must be determined in the face of possible usurpation by subnational, other-national, and supranational interests." According to the power-elite thesis, however, the national interest is in reality the interest of a dominant, interlocking, self-perpetuating, and irresponsible elite composed of the corporate rich, the military, and the politicians. The classic statement of this position is C. Wright Mills's *The Power Elite,* from which the following selection is taken.

At the time of his death C. Wright Mills was Professor of Sociology at Columbia University. He was the author of many works including *White Collar, The Causes of World War Three,* and *The Sociological Imagination.* A number of reviews of *The Power Elite* and Mills's rejoinder have been compiled by G. William Domhoff and Hoyt B. Ballard in *C. Wright Mills and The Power Elite.*

We study history, it has been said, to rid ourselves of it, and the history of the power elite is a clear case for which this maxim is correct. Like the tempo of American life in general, the long-term trends of the power structure have been greatly speeded up since World War II, and certain newer trends within and between the dominant institutions have also set the shape of the power elite and given historically specific meaning to its fifth epoch:

I. In so far as the structural clue to the power elite today lies in the political order, that clue is the decline of politics as genuine and public debate of alternative decisions—with nationally responsible and policy-coherent parties and with autonomous organizations connecting the lower and middle levels of power with the top levels of decision. America is now in considerable part more a formal political democracy than a democratic social structure, and even the formal political mechanics are weak.

The long-time tendency of business and government to become more intricately and deeply involved with each other has, in the fifth epoch, reached a new point of explicitness. The two cannot now be seen clearly as two distinct worlds. It is in terms of the executive agencies of the state that the rapproche-

From C. Wright Mills, *The Power Elite,* pp. 274–97. Some footnotes omitted. Copyright © 1956 by the Oxford University Press, Inc. Reprinted by permission of the publisher.

ment has proceeded most decisively. The growth of the executive branch of the government, with its agencies that patrol the complex economy, does not mean merely the "enlargement of government" as some sort of autonomous bureaucracy: it has meant the ascendancy of the corporation's man as a political eminence.

During the New Deal the corporate chieftains joined the political directorate; as of World War II they have come to dominate it. Long interlocked with government, now they have moved into quite full direction of the economy of the war effort and of the postwar era. This shift of the corporation executives into the political directorate has accelerated the long-term relegation of the professional politicians in the Congress to the middle levels of power.

II. In so far as the structural clue to the power elite today lies in the enlarged and military state, that clue becomes evident in the military ascendancy. The warlords have gained decisive political relevance, and the military structure of America is now in considerable part a political structure. The seemingly permanent military threat places a premium on the military and upon their control of men, materiel, money, and power; virtually all political and economic actions are now judged in terms of military definitions of reality: the higher warlords have ascended to a firm position within the power elite of the fifth epoch.

In part at least this has resulted from one simple historical fact, pivotal for the years since 1939: the focus of elite attention has been shifted from domestic problems, centered in the 'thirties around slump, to international problems, centered in the 'forties and 'fifties around war. Since the governing apparatus of the United States has by long historic usage been adapted to and shaped by domestic clash and balance, it has not, from any angle, had suitable agencies and traditions for the handling of international problems. Such formal democratic mechanics as had arisen in the century and a half of national development prior to 1941, had not been extended to the American handling of international affairs. It is, in considerable part, in this vacuum that the power elite has grown.

III. In so far as the structural clue to the power elite today lies in the economic order, that clue is the fact that the economy is at once a permanent-war economy and a private-corporation economy. American capitalism is now in considerable part a military capitalism, and the most important relation of the big corporation to the state rests on the coincidence of interests between military and corporate needs, as defined by warlords and corporate rich. Within the elite as a whole, this coincidence of interest between the high military and the corporate chieftains strengthens both of them and further subordinates the role of the merely political men. Not politicians, but corporate executives, sit with the military and plan the organization of war effort.

The shape and meaning of the power elite today can be understood only when these three sets of structural trends are seen at their point of coincidence: the military capitalism of private corporations exists in a weakened and formal democratic system containing a military order already quite political in outlook and demeanor. Accordingly, at the top of this structure, the power elite has been shaped by the coincidence of interest between those who control the major means of production and those who control the newly enlarged means of violence; from the decline of the professional politician and the rise to explicit political command of the corporate chieftains and the professional warlords; from the absence of any genuine civil service of skill and integrity, independent of vested interests.

The power elite is composed of political, economic, and military men, but this instituted elite is frequently in some tension: it comes together only on certain coinciding points and only on certain occasions of "crisis." In the long peace of the nineteenth century, the military were not in the high councils of state, not of the political directorate, and neither were the economic men—they made raids upon the state but they did not join its directorate. During the 'thirties, the political man was ascendant. Now the military and the corporate men are in top positions.

Of the three types of circle that compose the power elite today, it is the military that has benefited the most in its enhanced power, although the corporate circles have also become more explicitly intrenched in the more public decision-making circles. It is the professional politician that has lost the most, so much that in examining the events and decisions, one is tempted to speak of a political vacuum in which the corporate rich and the high warlord, in their coinciding interests, rule.

It should not be said that the three "take turns" in carrying the initiative, for the mechanics of the power elite are not often as deliberate as that would imply. At times, of course, it is—as when political men, thinking they can borrow the prestige of generals, find that they must pay for it, or, as when during big slumps, economic men feel the need of a politician at once safe and possessing vote appeal. Today all three are involved in virtually all widely ramifying decisions. Which of the three types seems to lead depends upon "the tasks of the period" as they, the elite, define them. Just now, these tasks center upon "defense" and international affairs. Accordingly, as we have seen, the military are ascendant in two senses: as personnel and as justifying ideology. That is why, just now, we can most easily specify the unity and the shape of the power elite in terms of the military ascendancy.

But we must always be historically specific and open to complexities. The simple Marxian view makes the big economic man the *real* holder of power; the simple liberal view makes the big political man the chief of the power system; and there are some who would view the warlords as virtual dictators. Each of these is an oversimplified view. It is to avoid them that we use the term "power elite" rather than, for example, "ruling class." [1]

In so far as the power elite has come to wide public attention, it has done so in terms of the "military clique." The power elite does, in fact, take its current shape from the decisive entrance into it of the military. Their presence and their ideology are its major legitimations, whenever the power elite feels the need to provide any. But what is called the "Washington military clique" is not composed merely of military men, and it does not prevail merely in Washington. Its members exist all over the country, and it is a coalition of generals in the roles of corporation executives, of politicians masquerading as admirals, of corporation executives acting like politicians, of civil servants who become majors, of vice-admirals who are also the assistants to a cabinet officer, who is himself, by the way, really a member of the managerial elite.

Neither the idea of a "ruling class" nor of a simple monolithic rise of "bureaucratic politicians" nor of a "military clique" is adequate. The power elite today involves the often uneasy coincidence of economic, military, and political power.

Even if our understanding were limited to these structural trends, we should have grounds for believing the power elite a useful, indeed indispensable, concept for the interpretation of what is going on at the topside of modern American society. But we are not, of course, so limited: our conception of the power elite does not need to rest only upon the correspondence of the institutional hierarchies involved, or upon the many points at which their shifting interests coincide. The power elite, as we conceive it, also rests upon the similarity of its personnel, and their personal and official relations with one another, upon their social and psychological affinities. In order to grasp the personal and social basis of the power elite's unity, we have first to remind ourselves of the facts of origin, career, and style of life of each of the types of circle whose members compose the power elite.

The power elite is *not* an aristocracy, which is to say that it is not a political ruling group based upon a nobility of hereditary origin. It has no compact basis in a small circle of great families whose members can and do consistently occupy the top positions in the several higher circles which overlap as the power elite. But such nobility is only one possible basis of common origin. That it does not exist for the American elite does not mean that members of this elite derive socially from the full range of strata composing American society. They derive in substantial proportions from the upper classes, both new and old, of local society and the metropolitan 400. The bulk of the very rich, the corporate executives, the political outsiders, the high military, derive from, at most, the upper third of the income and occupational pyramids. Their fathers were at least of the professional and business strata, and very frequently higher than that. They are native-born Americans of native parents, primarily from urban areas, and, with the exceptions of the politicians among them, overwhelmingly from the East. They are mainly Protestants, especially Episcopalian or Presbyterian. In general, the higher the position, the greater the proportion of men within it who have derived from and who maintain connections with the upper classes. The generally similar origins of the members of the power elite are underlined and carried further by the fact of their increasingly common educational routine. Overwhelmingly college graduates, substantial proportions have attended Ivy League colleges, although the education of the higher military, of course, differs from that of other members of the power elite.

But what do these apparently simple facts about the social composition of the higher circles really mean? In particular, what do they mean for any attempt to understand the degree of unity, and the direction of policy and interest that may prevail among these several circles? Perhaps it is best to put this question in a deceptively simple way: in terms of origin and career, who or what do these men at the top represent?

Of course, if they are elected politicians, they are supposed to represent those who elected them; and, if they are appointed, they are supposed to represent, indirectly, those who elected their appointers. But this is recognized as something of an abstraction, as a rhetorical formula by which all men of power in almost all systems of government nowadays justify their power of decision. At times it may be true, both in the sense of their motives and in the sense of who benefits from their decisions. Yet it would not be wise in any power system merely to assume it.

The fact that members of the power elite come from near the top of the nation's class and status levels does not mean that they are necessarily "representative" of the top levels only. And if they were, as social types, representative of a cross-section of the population, that would not mean that a balanced democracy of interest and power would automatically be the going political fact.

We cannot infer the direction of policy merely from the social origins and careers of the policy-makers. The social and economic backgrounds of the men of power do not tell us all that we need to know in order to understand the distribution of social power. For: (1) Men from high places may be ideological representatives of the poor and humble. (2) Men of humble origin, brightly self-made, may energetically serve the most vested and inherited interests. Moreover (3), not all men who effectively represent the interests of a stratum need in any way belong to it or personally benefit by policies that further its interests. Among the politicians, in short, there are sympathetic *agents* of given groups, conscious and unconscious, paid and unpaid. Finally (4), among the top decision-makers we find men who have been chosen for their positions because of their "expert knowledge." These are some of the obvious reasons why the social origins and careers of the power elite do not enable us to infer the class interests and policy directions of a modern system of power.

Do the high social origin and careers of the top men mean nothing, then, about the distribution of power? By no means. They simply remind us that we must be careful of any simple and direct inference from origin and career to political character and policy, not that we must ignore them in our attempt at political understanding. They simply mean that we must analyze the political psychology and the actual decisions of the political directorate as well as its social composition. And they mean, above all, that we should control, as we have done here, any inference we make from the origin and careers of the political actors by close understanding of the institutional landscape in which they act out their drama. Otherwise we should be guilty of a rather simple-minded biographical theory of society and history.

Just as we cannot rest the notion of the power elite solely upon the institutional mechanics that lead to its formation, so we cannot rest the notion solely upon the facts of the origin and career of its personnel. We need both, and we have both—as well as other bases, among them that of the status intermingling.

But it is not only the similarities of social origin, religious affiliation, nativity, and education that are important to the psychological and social affinities of the members of the power elite. Even if their recruitment and formal training were more heterogeneous than they are, these men would still be of quite homogeneous social type. For the most important set of facts about a circle of men is the criteria of admission, of praise, of honor, of promotion that prevails among them; if these are similar within a circle, then they will tend as personalities to become similar. The circles that compose the power elite do tend to have such codes and criteria in common. The co-optation of the social types to which these common values lead is often more important than any statistics of common origin and career that we might have at hand.

There is a kind of reciprocal attraction among the fraternity of the successful —not between each and every member of the circles of the high and mighty, but between enough of them to insure a certain unity. On the slight side, it is a sort of tacit, mutual admiration; in the strongest tie-ins, it proceeds by intermarriage. And there are all grades and types of connection between these extremes. Some overlaps certainly occur by means of cliques and clubs, churches and schools.

If social origin and formal education in common tend to make the members of the power elite more readily understood and trusted by one another, their continued association further cements what they feel they have in common. Members of the several higher circles know one another as personal friends and even as neighbors; they mingle with one another on the golf course, in the gentleman's clubs, at resorts, on transcontinental airplanes, and on ocean liners. They meet at the estates of mutual friends, face each other in front of the TV camera, or serve on the same philanthropic committee; and many are sure to cross one another's path in the columns of newspapers, if not in the exact cafes from which many of these columns originate. As we have seen, of "The New 400" of cafe society, one chronicler has named forty-one members of the very rich, ninety-three political leaders, and seventy-nine chief executives of corporations.

"I did not know, I could not have dreamed," Whittaker Chambers has written, "of the immense scope and power of Hiss' political alliances and his social connections, which cut across all party lines and ran from the Supreme Court to the Religious Society of Friends, from governors of states and instructors in college faculties to the staff members of liberal magazines. In the decade since I had last seen him, he had used his career, and, in particular, his identification with the cause of peace through his part in organizing the United Nations, to put down roots that made him one with the matted forest floor of American upper class, enlightened middle class, liberal and official life. His roots could not be disturbed without disturbing all the roots on all sides of him."

The sphere of status has reflected the epochs of the power elite. In the third epoch, for example, who could compete with big money? And in the fourth, with big politicians, or even the bright young men of the New Deal? And in the fifth, who can compete with the generals and the admirals and the corporate officials now so sympathetically portrayed on the stage, in the novel, and on the screen? Can one imagine *Executive Suite* as a successful motion picture in 1935? Or *The Caine Mutiny?*

The multiplicity of high-prestige organizations to which the elite usually belong is revealed by even casual examination of the obituaries of the big businessman, the high-prestige lawyer, the top general and admiral, the key senator: usually, high-prestige church, business associations, plus high-prestige clubs, and often plus military rank. In the course of their lifetimes, the university president, the New York Stock Exchange chairman, the head of the bank, the old West Pointer—mingle in the status sphere, within which they easily renew old friendships and draw upon them in an effort to understand through the experience of trusted others those contexts of power and decision in which they have not personally moved.

In these diverse contexts, prestige accumulates in each of the higher circles, and the members of each borrow status from one another. Their self-images are fed by these accumulations and these borrowings, and accordingly, however segmental a given man's role may seem, he comes to feel himself a "diffuse" or "generalized" man of the higher circles, a "broad-gauge" man. Perhaps such inside experience is one feature of what is meant by "judgment."

The key organizations, perhaps, are the major corporations themselves, for on the boards of directors we find a heavy overlapping among the members of these several elites. On the lighter side, again in the summer and winter resorts, we find that, in an intricate series of overlapping circles; in the course of time, each meets each or knows somebody who knows somebody who knows that one.

The higher members of the military, economic, and political orders are able readily to take over one another's point of view, always in a sympathetic way, and often in a knowledgeable way as well. They define one another as among those who count, and who, accordingly, must be taken into account. Each of them as a member of the power elite comes to incorporate into his own integrity, his own honor, his own conscience, the viewpoint, the expectations, the values of the others. If there are no common ideals and standards among them that are based upon an explicitly aristocratic culture, that does not mean that they do not feel responsibility to one another.

All the structural coincidence of their interests as well as the intricate, psychological facts of their origins and their education, their careers and their associations make possible the psychological affinities that prevail among them, affinities that make it possible for them to say of one another: He is, of course, one of us. And all this points to the basic, psychological meaning of class consciousness. Nowhere in America is there as great a "class consciousness" as among the elite; nowhere is it organized as effectively as among the power elite. For by class consciousness, as a psychological fact, one means that the individual member of a "class" accepts only those accepted by his circle as among those who are significant to his own image of self.

Within the higher circles of the power elite, factions do exist; there are conflicts of policy; individual ambitions do clash. There are still enough divisions of importance within the Republican party, and even between Republicans and Democrats, to make for different methods of operation. But more powerful than these divisions are the internal discipline and the community of interests that bind the power elite together, even across the boundaries of nations at war.

Yet we must give due weight to the other side of the case which may not question the facts but only our interpretation of them. There is a set of objections that will inevitably be made to our whole conception of the power elite, but which has essentially to do with only the psychology of its members. It might well be put by liberals or by conservatives in some such way as this:

"To talk of a power elite—isn't this to characterize men by their origins and associations? Isn't such characterization both unfair and untrue? Don't men modify themselves, especially Americans such as these, as they rise in stature to meet the demands of their jobs? Don't they arrive at a view and a line of policy that represents, so far as they in their human weaknesses can know, the interests of the nation as a whole? Aren't they merely honorable men who are doing their duty?"

What are we to reply to these objections?

I. We are sure that they are honorable men. But what is honor? Honor can only mean living up to a code that one believes to be honorable. There is no one code upon which we are all agreed. That is why, if we are civilized men, we do not kill off all of those with whom we disagree. The question is not: are these honorable men? The question is: what are their codes of honor? The answer to that question is that they are the codes of their circles, of those to whose opinions they defer. How could it be otherwise? That is one meaning of the important truism that all men are human and that all men are social creatures. As for sincerity, it can only be disproved, never proved.

II. To the question of their adaptability—which means their capacity to transcend the codes of conduct which, in their life's work and experience, they have acquired—we must answer: simply no, they cannot, at least not in the handful of years most of them have left. To expect that is to assume that they are indeed strange and expedient: such flexibility would in fact involve a violation of what we may rightly call their character and their integrity. By the way, may it not be precisely because of the lack of such character and integrity that earlier types of American politicians have not represented as great a threat as do these men of character?

It would be an insult to the effective training of the military, and to their indoctrination as well, to suppose that military officials shed their military character and outlook upon changing from uniform to mufti. This background is more important perhaps in the military case than in that of the corporate executives, for the training of the career is deeper and more total.

"Lack of imagination," Gerald W. Johnson has noted, "is not to be confused with lack of principle. On the contrary, an unimaginative man is often a man of the highest principles. The trouble is that his principles conform to Cornford's famous definition: 'A principle is a rule of inaction giving valid general reasons for not doing in a specific instance what to unprincipled instinct would seem to be right.'"

Would it not be ridiculous, for example, to believe seriously that, in psychological fact, Charles Erwin Wilson represented anyone or any interest other than those of the corporate world? This is not because he is dishonest; on the contrary, it is because he is probably a man of solid integrity—as sound as a dollar. He is what he is and he cannot very well be anything else. He is a member of the professional corporation elite, just as are his colleagues, in the government and out of it; he represents the wealth of the higher corporate world; he represents its power; and he believes sincerely in his oft-quoted remark that "what is good for the United States is good for the General Motors Corporation and vice versa."

The revealing point about the pitiful hearings on the confirmation of such men for political posts is not the cynicism toward the law and toward the lawmakers on the middle levels of power which they display, nor their reluctance to dispose of their personal stock. The interesting point is how impossible it is for such men to divest themselves of their engagement with the corporate world in general and with their own corporations in particular. Not only their money, but their friends, their interests, their training—their lives in short—are deeply involved in this world. The disposal of stock is, of course, merely a purifying ritual. The point is not so much financial or personal interests in a given corporation, but identification with the corporate world. To ask a man suddenly to divest himself of these interests and sensibilities is almost like asking a man to become a woman.

III. To the question of their patriotism, of their desire to serve the nation as a whole, we must answer first that, like codes of honor, feelings of patriotism and views of what is to the whole nation's good, are not ultimate facts but matters upon which there exists a great variety of opinion. Furthermore, patriotic opinions too are rooted in and are sustained by what a man has become by virtue of how and with whom he has lived. This is no simple mechanical determination of individual character by social conditions; it is an intricate process, well established in the major tradition of modern social study. One can only wonder why more social scientists do not use it systematically in speculating about politics.

IV. The elite cannot be truly thought of as men who are merely doing their duty. They are the ones who determine their duty, as well as the duties of those beneath them. They are not merely following orders: they give the orders. They are not merely "bureaucrats": they command bureaucracies. They may try to disguise these facts from others and from themselves by appeals to traditions of which they imagine themselves the instruments, but there are many traditions, and they must choose which ones they will serve. They face decisions for which there simply are no traditions.

Now, to what do these several answers add up? To the fact that we cannot reason about public events and historical trends merely from knowledge about the motives and character of the men or the small groups who sit in the seats of the high and mighty. This fact, in turn, does not mean that we should be intimidated by accusations that in taking up our problem in the way we have, we are impugning the honor, the integrity, or the ability of those who are in high office. For it is not, in the first instance, a question of individual character; and if, in further instances, we find that it is, we should not hesitate to say so plainly. In the meantime, we must judge men of power by the standards of power, by what they do as decision-makers, and not by who they are or what they may do in private life. Our interest is not in that: we are interested in their policies and in the *consequences* of their conduct of office. We must remember that these men of the power elite now occupy the strategic places in the structure of American society; that they command the dominant institutions of a dominant nation; that, as a set of men, they are in a position to make decisions with terrible consequences for the underlying populations of the world.

Despite their social similarity and psychological affinities, the members of the power elite do not constitute a club having a permanent membership with fixed and formal boundaries. It is of the nature of the power elite that within it there is a good deal of shifting about, and that it thus does not consist of one small set of the same men in the same positions in the same hierarchies. Because men know each other personally does not mean that among them there is a unity of policy; and because they do not know each other personally does not mean that among them there is a disunity. The conception of the power elite does not rest, as I have repeatedly said, primarily upon personal friendship.

As the requirements of the top places in each of the major hierarchies become similar, the types of men occupying these roles at the top—by selection and by training in the jobs—become similar. This is no mere deduction from structure to personnel. That it is a fact is revealed by the heavy traffic that has been going on between the three structures, often in very intricate patterns. The chief executives, the warlords, and selected politicians came into contact with one another in an intimate, working way during World War II; after that war ended, they continued their associations, out of common beliefs, social congeniality, and coinciding interests. Noticeable proportions of top men from the military, the economic, and the political worlds have during the last fifteen years occupied positions in one or both of the other worlds: between these higher circles there is an interchangeability of position, based formally upon the supposed transferability of "executive ability," based in substance upon the co-optation by cliques of insiders. As members of a power elite, many of those busy in this traffic have come to look upon "the government" as an umbrella under whose authority they do their work.

As the business between the big three increases in volume and importance, so does the traffic in personnel. The very criteria for selecting men who will rise come to embody this fact. The corporate commissar, dealing with the state and its military, is wiser to choose a young man who has experienced the state and its military than one who has not. The political director, often dependent for his own political success upon corporate decisions and corporations, is also wiser to choose a man with corporate experience. Thus, by virtue of the very criterion of success, the interchange of personnel and the unity of the power elite is increased.

Given the formal similarity of the three hierarchies in which the several members of the elite spend their working lives, given the ramifications of the decisions made in each upon the others, given the coincidence of interest that prevails among them at many points, and given the administrative vacuum of the American civilian state along with its enlargement of tasks—given these trends of structure, and adding to them the psychological affinities we have noted—we should indeed be surprised were we to find that men said to be skilled in administrative contacts and full of organizing ability would fail to do more than get in touch with one another. They have, of course, done much more than that: increasingly, they assume positions in one another's domains.

The unity revealed by the interchangeability of top roles rests upon the parallel development of the top jobs in each of the big three domains. The interchange occurs most frequently at the points of their coinciding interest, as between regulatory agency and the regulated industry; contracting agency and contractor. And, as we shall see, it leads to co-ordinations that are more explicit, and even formal.

The inner core of the power elite consists, first, of those who interchange commanding roles at the top of one dominant institutional order with those in another: the admiral who is also a banker and a lawyer and who heads up an important federal commission; the corporation executive whose company was one of the two or three leading war materiel producers who is now the Secretary of Defense; the wartime general who dons civilian clothes to sit on the political directorate and then becomes a member of the board of directors of a leading economic corporation.

Although the executive who becomes a general, the general who becomes a statesman, the statesman who becomes a banker, see much more than ordinary men in their ordinary environments, still the perspectives of even such men often remain tied to their dominant locales. In their very career, however, they interchange roles within the big three and thus readily transcend the particularity of interest in any one of these institutional milieux. By their very careers and activities, they lace the three types of milieux together. They are, accordingly, the core members of the power elite.

These men are not necessarily familiar with every major arena of power. We refer to one man who moves in and between perhaps two circles—say the industrial and the military—and to another man who moves in the military and the political, and to a third who moves in the political as well as among opinion-makers. These in-between types most closely display our image of the power elite's structure and operation, even of behind-the-scenes operations. To the extent that there is any "invisible elite," these advisory and liaison types are its core. Even if—as I believe to be very likely—many of them are, at least in the first part of their careers, "agents" of the various elites rather than themselves elite, it is they who are most active in organizing the several top milieux into a structure of power and maintaining it.

The inner core of the power elite also includes men of the higher legal and financial type from the great law factories and investment firms, who are almost professional go-betweens of economic, political and military affairs, and who thus act to unify the power elite. The corporation lawyer and the investment banker perform the functions of the "go-between" effectively and powerfully. By the nature of their work, they transcend the narrower milieu of any one industry, and accordingly are in a position to speak and act for the corporate world or at least sizable sectors of it. The corporation lawyer is a key link between the economic and military and political areas; the investment banker is a key organizer and unifier of the corporate world and a person well versed in spending the huge amounts of money the American military establishment now ponders. When you get a lawyer who handles the legal work of investment bankers you get a key member of the power elite.

During the Democratic era, one link between private corporate organizations and governmental institutions was the investment house of Dillon, Read. From it came such men as James Forrestal and Charles F. Detmar, Jr.; Ferdinand Eberstadt had once been a partner in it before he branched out into his own investment house from which came other men to political and military circles. Republican administrations seem to favor the investment firm of Kuhn, Loeb and the advertising firm of Batten, Barton, Durstine and Osborn.

Regardless of administrations, there is always the law firm of Sullivan and Cromwell. Mid-West investment banker Cyrus Eaton has said that "Arthur H. Dean, a senior partner of Sullivan & Cromwell of No. 48 Wall Street, was one of those who assisted in the drafting of the Securities Act of 1933, the first of the series of bills passed to regulate the capital markets. He and his firm, which is reputed to be the largest in the United States, have maintained close relations with the SEC since its creation, and theirs is the dominating influence on the Commission."

There is also the third largest bank in the United States: the Chase National Bank of New York (now Chase-Manhattan). Regardless of political administration, executives of this bank and those of the International Bank of Reconstruction and Development have changed positions: John J. McCloy, who became Chairman of the Chase National in 1953, is a former president of the World Bank; and his successor to the presidency of the World Bank was a former senior vice-president of the Chase National Bank. And in 1953, the president of the Chase National Bank, Winthrop W. Aldrich, had left to become Ambassador to Great Britain.

The outermost fringes of the power elite—which change more than its core—consist of "those who count" even though they may not be "in" on given decisions of consequence nor in their career move between the hierarchies. Each member of the power elite need not be a man who personally decides every decision that is to be ascribed to the power elite. Each member, in the decisions that he does make, takes the others seriously into account. They not only make decisions in the several major areas of war and peace; they are the men who, in decisions in which they take no direct part, are taken into decisive account by those who are directly in charge.

On the fringes and below them, somewhat to the side of the lower echelons, the power elite fades off into the middle levels of power, into the rank and file of the Congress, the pressure groups that are not vested in the power elite itself, as well as a multiplicity of regional and state and local interests. If all the men on the middle levels are not among those who count, they sometimes must be taken into account, handled, cajoled, broken or raised to higher circles.

When the power elite find that in order to get things done they must reach below their own realms—as is the case when it is necessary to get bills passed through Congress—they themselves must exert some pressure. But among the power elite, the name for such high-level lobbying is "liaison work." There are "liaison" military men with Congress, with certain wayward sections of industry, with practically every important element not directly concerned with the power elite. The two men on the White House staff who are *named* "liaison" men are both experienced in military matters; one of them is a former investment banker and lawyer as well as a general.

Not the trade associations but the higher cliques of lawyers and investment bankers are the active political heads of the corporate rich and the members of the power elite. "While it is generally assumed that the national associations carry tremendous weight in formulating public opinion and directing the course of national policy, there is some evidence to indicate that interaction between associations on a formal level is not a very tight-knit affair. The general tendency within associations seems to be to stimulate activities around the specific interests of the organization, and more effort is made to educate its members rather than to spend much time in trying to influence other associations on the issue at hand . . . As media for stating and re-stating the over-all value structure of the nation they (the trade associations) are important . . . But when issues are firmly drawn, individuals related to the larger corporate interests are called upon to exert pressure in the proper places at the strategic time. The national associations may act as media for co-ordinating such pressures, but a great volume of intercommunication between members at the apex of power of the larger corporate interests seems to be the decisive factor in final policy determination."

Conventional "lobbying," carried on by trade associations, still exists, although it usually concerns the middle levels of power—usually being targeted at Congress and, of course, its own rank and file members. The important function of the National Association of Manufacturers, for example, is less directly to influence policy than to reveal to small businessmen that their interests are the same as those of larger businesses. But there is also "high-level lobbying." All over the country the corporate leaders are drawn into the circle of the high military and political through personal friendship, trade and professional associations and their various subcommittees, prestige clubs, open political affiliation, and customer relationships. "There is . . . an awareness among these power leaders," one first-hand investigator of such executive cliques has asserted, "of many of the current major policy issues before the nation such as keeping taxes down, turning all productive operations over to private enterprises, increasing foreign trade, keeping governmental welfare and other domestic activities to a minimum, and strengthening and maintaining the hold of the current party in power nationally."

There are, in fact, cliques of corporate executives who are more important as informal opinion leaders in the top echelons of corporate, military, and political power than as actual participants in military and political organizations. Inside military circles and inside political circles and "on the sidelines" in the economic area, these circles and cliques of corporation executives are in on most all major decisions regardless of topic. And what is important about all this high-level lobbying is that it is done within the confines of that elite.

The conception of the power elite and of its unity rests upon the corresponding developments and the coincidence of interests among economic, political, and military organizations. It also rests upon the similarity of origin and outlook, and the social and personal intermingling of the top circles from each of these dominant hierarchies. This conjunction of institutional and psychological forces, in turn, is revealed by the heavy personnel traffic within and between the big three institutional orders, as well as by the rise of go-betweens as in the high-level lobbying. The conception of the power elite, accordingly, does *not* rest upon the assumption that American history since the origins of World War II must be understood as a secret plot, or as a great and co-ordinated conspiracy of the members of this elite. The conception rests upon quite impersonal grounds.

There is, however, little doubt that the American power elite—which contains, we are told, some of "the greatest organizers in the world"—has also planned and has plotted. The rise of the elite, as we have already made clear, was not and could not have been caused by a plot; and the tenability of the conception does not rest upon the existence of any secret or any publicly known organization. But, once the conjunction of structural trend and of the personal will to utilize it gave rise to the power elite, then plans and programs did occur to its members and indeed it is not possible to interpret many events and official policies of the fifth epoch without reference to the power elite. "There is a great difference," Richard Hofstadter has remarked, "between locating conspiracies *in* history and saying that history *is,* in effect, a conspiracy . . ."

The structural trends of institutions become defined as opportunities by those who occupy their command posts. Once such opportunities are recognized, men may avail themselves of them. Certain types of men from each of the dominant institutional areas, more far-sighted than others, have actively promoted the liaison before it took its truly modern shape. They have often done so for reasons not shared by their partners, although not objected to by them either; and often the outcome of their liaison has had consequences which none of them foresaw, much less shaped, and which only later in the course of development came under explicit control. Only after it was well under way did most of its members find themselves part of it and become gladdened, although sometimes also worried, by this fact. But once the co-ordination is a going concern, new men come readily into it and assume its existence without question.

So far as explicit organization—conspiratorial or not—is concerned, the power elite, by its very nature, is more likely to use existing organizations, working within and between them, than to set up explicit organizations whose membership is strictly limited to its own members. But if there is no machinery in existence to ensure, for example, that military and political factors will be balanced in decisions made, they will invent such machinery and use it, as with the National Security Council. Moreover, in a formally democratic polity, the aims and the powers of the various elements of this elite are further supported by an aspect of the permanent war economy: the assumption that the security of the nation supposedly rests upon great secrecy of plan and intent. Many higher events that would reveal the working of the power elite can be withheld from public knowledge under the guise of secrecy. With the wide secrecy covering their operations and decisions, the power elite can mask their intentions, operations, and further consolidation. Any secrecy that is imposed upon those in positions to observe high decision-makers clearly works for and not against the operations of the power elite.

There is accordingly reason to suspect—but by the nature of the case, no proof—that the power elite is not altogether "surfaced." There is nothing hidden about it, although its activities are not publicized. As an elite, it is not organized, although its members often know one another, seem quite naturally to work together, and share many organizations in common. There is nothing conspiratorial about it, although its decisions are often publicly unknown and its mode of operation manipulative rather than explicit.

It is not that the elite "believe in" a compact elite behind the scenes and a mass down below. It is not put in that language. It is just that the people are of necessity confused and must, like trusting children, place all the new world of foreign policy and strategy and executive action in the hands of experts. It is just that everyone knows somebody has got to run the show, and that somebody usually does. Others do not really care anyway, and besides, they do not know how. So the gap between the two types gets wider.

When crises are defined as total, and as seemingly permanent, the consequences of decision become total, and the decisions in each major area of life come to be integrated and total. Up to a point, these consequences for other institutional orders can be assessed; beyond such points, chances have to be taken. It is then that the felt scarcity of trained and imaginative judgment leads to plaintive feelings among executives about the shortage of qualified successors in political, military, and economic life. This feeling, in turn, leads to an increasing concern with the training of successors who could take over as older men of power retire. In each area, there slowly arises a new generation which has grown up in an age of co-ordinated decisions.

In each of the elite circles, we have noticed this concern to recruit and to train successors as "broad-gauge" men, that is, as men capable of making decisions that involve institutional areas other than their own. The chief executives have set up formal recruitment and training programs to man the corporate world as virtually a state within a state. Recruitment and training for the military elite has long been rigidly professionalized, but has now come to include educational routines of a sort which the remnants of older generals and admirals consider quite nonsensical.

Only the political order, with its absence of a genuine civil service, has lagged behind, creating an administrative vacuum into which military bureaucrats and corporate outsiders have been drawn. But even in this domain, since World War II, there have been repeated attempts, by elite men of such vision as the late James Forrestal's, to inaugurate a career service that would include periods in the corporate world as well as in the governmental.

What is lacking is a truly common elite program of recruitment and training; for the prep school, Ivy League College, and law school sequence of the metropolitan 400 is not up to the demands now made upon members of the power elite. Britishers, such as Field Marshal Viscount Montgomery, well aware of this lack, recently urged the adoption of a system "under which a minority of high-caliber young students could be separated from the mediocre and given the best education possible to supply the country with leadership." His proposal is echoed, in various forms, by many who accept his criticism of "the American theory of public education on the ground that it is ill-suited to produce the 'elite' group of leaders . . . this country needs to fulfill its obligations of world leadership."

In part these demands reflect the unstated need to transcend recruitment on the sole basis of economic success, especially since it is suspect as often involving the higher immorality; in part it reflects the stated need to have men who, as Viscount Montgomery says, know "the meaning of discipline." But above all these demands reflect the at least vague consciousness on the part of the power elite themselves that the age of co-ordinated decisions, entailing a newly enormous range of consequences, requires a power elite that is of a new caliber. In so far as the sweep of matters which go into the making of decisions is vast and interrelated, the information needed for judgments complex and requiring particularized knowledge, the men in charge will not only call upon one another; they will try to train their successors for the work at hand. These new men will grow up as men of power within the co-ordination of economic and political and military decision.

The idea of the power elite rests upon and enables us to make sense of (1) the decisive institutional trends that characterize the structure of our epoch, in particular, the military ascendancy in a privately incorporated economy, and more broadly, the several coincidences of objective interests between economic, military, and political institutions; (2) the social similarities and the psychological affinities of the men who occupy the command posts of these structures, in particular the increased interchangeability of the top positions in each of them and the increased traffic between these orders in the careers of men of power; (3) the ramifications, to the point of virtual totality, of the kind of decisions that are made at the top, and the rise to power of a set of men who, by training and bent, are professional organizers of considerable force and who are unrestrained by democratic party training.

Negatively, the formation of the power elite rests upon (1) the relegation of the professional party politician to the middle levels of power, (2) the semi-organized stalemate of the interests of sovereign localities into which the legislative function has fallen, (3) the virtually complete absence of a civil service that constitutes a politically neutral, but politically relevant, depository of brainpower and executive skill, and (4) the increased official secrecy behind which great decisions are made without benefit of public or even Congressional debate.

As a result, the political directorate, the corporate rich, and the ascendant military have come together as the power elite, and the expanded and centralized hierarchies which they head have encroached upon the old balances and have now relegated them to the middle levels of power. Now the balancing society is a conception that pertains accurately to the middle levels, and on that level the balance has become more often an affair of intrenched provincial and nationally irresponsible forces and demands than a center of power and national decision.

But how about the bottom? As all these trends have become visible at the top and on the middle, what has been happening to the great American public? If the top is unprecedentedly powerful and increasingly unified and willful; if the middle zones are increasingly a semi-organized stalemate—in what shape is the bottom, in what condition is the public at large? The rise of the power elite, we shall now see, rests upon, and in some ways is part of, the transformation of the publics of America into a mass society.

NOTES

1. "Ruling class" is a badly loaded phrase. "Class" is an economic term; "rule" a political one. The phrase, "ruling class," thus contains the theory that an economic class rules politically. That short-cut theory may or may not at times be true, but we do not want to carry that one rather simple theory about in the terms that we use to define our problems; we wish to state the theories explicitly, using terms of more precise and unilateral meaning. Specifically, the phrase "ruling class," in its common political connotations, does not allow enough autonomy to the political order and its agents, and it says nothing about the military as such. It should be clear to the reader by now that we do not accept as adequate the simple view that high economic men unilaterally make all decisions of national consequence. We hold that such a simple view of "economic determinism" must be elaborated by "political determinism" and "military determinism"; that the higher agents of each of these three domains now often have a noticeable degree of autonomy; and that only in the often intricate ways of coalition do they make up and carry through the most important decisions. Those are the major reasons we prefer "power elite" to "ruling class" as a characterizing phrase for the higher circles when we consider them in terms of power.

6.

Arnold M. Rose: The Power Structure: Political Process in American Society

In contrast to the economic-elite dominance hypothesis of C. Wright Mills and his followers, Arnold Rose offered in his book *The Power Structure: Political Process in American Society* a multi-influence hypothesis, which maintained that both political power in American society and society itself were pluralistic. Drawing on his own research and political experience as well as on the work of sociologists and political scientists, Professor Rose concluded that the power structure in the United States is "highly complex and diversified (rather than unitary and monolithic), that the political system is more or less democratic (with the glaring exception of the Negro's position until the 1960's), that in political processes the political elite is ascendant over and not subordinate to the economic elite, and that the political elite influences or controls the economic elite at least as much as the economic elite controls the political elite." Although he agreed with Mills that the role of the military elite has become increasingly important, Rose argued that the military were becoming more "civilianized" and were more exposed to the constraints of politics and public opinion than ever before.

The late Arnold Rose was Professor of Sociology at the University of Minnesota and the author of many works in sociology, including *Theory and Method in the Social Sciences.*

[In his book, *The Power Elite*] Mills's general thesis is that there is a national power elite which forms a self-conscious integrated unity, and "Insofar as national events are decided, the power elite are those who decide them" (p. 18).

The people of the higher circles may also be conceived as members of a top social stratum, as a set of groups whose members know one another, see one another socially and at business, and so, in making decisions, take one another into account. The elite, according to this conception, feel themselves to be, and are felt by others to be, the inner circle of "the upper social classes." They form a more or less compact social and psychological entity; they have become self-conscious members of a social class. People are either accepted into this class or they are not, and there is a qualitative split, rather than merely a numerical scale, separating them from those who are not elite. They are more or less aware of themselves as a social class and they behave toward one another differently from the way they do toward members of other classes. They accept one another, understand one another, marry one another, tend to work and to think if not together at least alike. [Page 11.]

The unity of the power elite, however, does not rest solely on psychological similarity and social intermingling, nor entirely on the structural coincidences of commanding positions and interests. At times it is the unity of a more explicit co-ordination. To say that these three higher circles are increasingly co-ordinated, that this is *one* basis of their unity, and that at times—as during the wars—such co-ordination is quite decisive, is not to say that the co-ordination is total or continuous, or even that it is very sure-footed. Much less is it to say that willful co-ordination is the sole or the major basis of their unity, or that the power elite has emerged as the realization of a plan. But it is to say that as the institutional mechanics of our time have opened up avenues to men pursuing their several interests, many of them have come to see that these several interests could be realized more easily if they worked together, in informal as well as in more formal ways, and accordingly they have done so. [Pages 19–20.]

Mills gives the impression of not being consistent in his thesis, however, especially regarding the role of politicians, for he considers them as subordinates to the economic elite (now integrated with the military elite): "What is usually taken to be the central content of politics, the pressures and the campaigns and the congressional maneuvering, has, in considerable part, now been relegated to the middle levels of power" (p. 28). Elsewhere he speaks of the top politicians as the "lieutenants" of the economic elite. His chapter on the political elite (chapter 10) is the shortest in the book, and almost half of it deals with the civil service rather than the superordinate elected or appointed government officials. Even when he deals with the political elite, he considers it to consist only of those in the Executive branch; there are only a few casual references to the Legislative and Judicial branches. Thus, despite Mills's initial reference to three elites, the book portrays the population of the United States as a *single* power pyramid: The economic-military elite are on top, their appointed henchmen plus the politicians form a secondary level of power, and at the large base are the powerless undifferentiated masses (pp. 28–29). This national pattern prevails also in each of the several communities of the United States, at least in the major ones, except that the military may be absent from the local community power structure:

Local society is a structure of power as well as a hierarchy of status; at its top there is a set of cliques or "crowds" whose members judge and decide the important community issues, as well as many larger issues of state and nation in which "the community" is involved. Usually, although by no means always, these cliques are composed of old upper-class people; they include the larger businessmen and those who control the banks who usually also have connections with the major real-estate holders. Informally organized, these cliques are often centered in the several economic functions: there is an industrial, a retailing, a banking clique. The cliques overlap, and there are usually some men who, moving from one to another, co-ordinate viewpoints and decisions. There are also the lawyers and administrators of the solid *rentier* families, who, by the power of proxy and by the many contacts between old and new wealth they embody, tie together and focus in decision the power of money, of credit, or organization.

Immediately below such cliques are the hustlers, largely of new upper-class status, who carry out the decisions and programs of the top—sometimes anticipating them and always trying to do so. Here are the "operations" men—the vice-presidents of the banks, successful small businessmen, the ranking public officials, contractors, and executives of local industries. This number two level shades off into the third string men—the heads of civic agencies, organization officials, the pettier civic leaders, newspaper men and, finally, into the fourth order of the power hierarchy—the rank and file of the professional and business strata, the ministers, the leading teachers, social workers, personnel directors. [Pages 36–7.]

Actually, Mills is not quite as inconsistent about the existence of *three* power elites as he at first appears to be, for later in his book he explains that, in his view, the economic-military elite have taken over the top "command" positions in the political elite. Thus his view is that a political elite might be said to exist, but it is manned and controlled by certain members of the economic-military elites. Nevertheless his initial statement that there are three power elites is quite misleading; it does not reflect his true views, and it allows his thesis to appear more acceptable than it should in view of the facts about the distribution of power.

Mills does not assume that the unity and integration of the power elite rests on elite consciousness or on deliberate co-ordination among all its members. He thus departs from European aristocratic theories of the elite and from conspiracy theories circulated in both Europe and the United States. Nevertheless, Mills's conception of the power elite is that it is more or less integrated and unitary, but he considers this integration and unity to be based on three other factors: "psychological similarity," "social intermingling," and "coinciding interests." The main *empirical* evidence he brings to these points is on "social intermingling"; he offers no data on "psychological similarity" and little on "coinciding interests," but infers that these result from extensive social interaction from childhood on. While our own inclination is to believe that the United States is too large and too heterogeneous to permit the economic leadership to be as integrated, in any of the three respects, as Mills says it is, we shall not present any direct data on these matters. We shall, however, consider how the *political* elite is subject to diverse pressures, to external limitations not subject to control by the economic elite, and to tendencies which on many occasions resist the interests of the economic elite.

But even at this early stage of our analysis we must express our amazement at the rationalistic nature of Mills's interpretation that an economic elite can control American society. In the first place, there are large-scale historical forces—often of an economic character—which constrain, limit, push, and direct any society in ways beyond the control of any segment in it. If Mills was a student of Marx and Veblen, among others, he apparently did not learn his lesson well. The substructure of any society—its geography, technology, economic organization, and basic institutions of family and religion—are only to a very limited extent manipulable by any one group, no matter how powerful or rational it is in the pursuit of its material interests. Related to this, but somewhat more manipulable, are the demands and requirements of that large-scale organization, the government. Perhaps Mills took these as given, and did not feel the need even to mention them.

In the second place, there are cultural values—both on the high plane of ideals and the low plane of everyday norms—which are also subject to only limited manipulation. The "American creed" of liberty, equality, fair play, justice, etc., and the more universal religious and humanistic ideals are not mere words which can be completely twisted and distorted to serve the interests of any group, even though man's ability to rationalize them away while pursuing his individual or sub-group interests is considerable. The everyday norms of mutual expectations in interpersonal relations set further limits on rational behavior, and these norms also are internalized by power elites no less than by the masses. Rational manipulation can take place within their framework, but not in spite of it, and if Mills wished to point out the facts of manipulation and the "higher immorality" in American society, he would be required to start from the general cultural framework of values and norms. Thirdly, there are the constraints on power, embodied in the Constitution and other forms of law, that are supported by public opinion in principle if not always in detail. Powerful leaders can sometimes get around basic law or change it, but not with ease or speed. In the fourth place, there are limits on rational pursuit of individual and group interests imposed by counter-elites (such as civil-rights groups, youth groups, and trade unions), kinship and friendship loyalties, public opinion, and voluntary associations. Mills explicitly denies the importance of these factors in American society, but we shall later adduce evidence that they are not without significance. Even if Mills were correct on this last point, we should have to consider his analysis sociologically inadequate through his neglect of the first three considerations. If the economic elite uses its power to make decisions for its own advantage in many instances, it lacks alternatives in other instances, and does not always behave rationally where there are alternatives.

It is because of the great social imperatives—that is, the physical, institutional, and cultural forces—that there is a certain similarity of action among the contending groups within a society (and sometimes even across national lines). Mills interprets this as the imposition on the political elites and other "secondary" leaders of the dominant will of the top economic elite, whereas usually it is nothing more than the lack of alternatives. That is, when leaders of the major political parties, or the leaders of the Western nations, or even the leaders of the United States and the Soviet Union came to an agreement, it is usually a case of reason bowing to the inevitable, rather than of lieutenants bowing to a hidden economic elite. Of course, there are the extremists—said to be at both ends—who refuse to believe this, and who, if they accede to political power, use that power to fly in the face of the inevitable. They either get smashed or reverse course without any directions from the economic elite. In world affairs we see this in the actions of Communist China; in the United States we see it in the local communities where right-wing extremists have been elected to public office.

Mills accepts the Marxist assumption of "false consciousness" in the masses— arising out of ignorance, apathy, and deliberate distortion (often with the aid of the mass media). He is supported here by much sociological research on anomie in an urbanized and mass culture, voting and non-voting patterns, alienation from work, the effects of the mass media, individualistic forms of social pathology, and the findings of vast body of research since Durkheim's study of suicide (1897). But, as we shall also attempt to show later, Mills's use of the facts of false consciousness in the mass suffers from two defects. First, Mills assumes that it is avoided by the economic elite, whereas the facts show that this is true only in degree. The economic power elite also has contracted some of the "illness" of the mass society. It sometimes deliberately and con- sciously works against its own interests, although perhaps less frequently than do the lower classes. Even its incidence of mental illness, addiction, and irra- tional crime is only somewhat lower than that found in the lower classes. Second, there are certain "reactions to the mass society" developing in all strata of American society which can be expected to operate against false conscious- ness to some extent. For example, mass education has some effect in immunizing people against ignorance and the distortions of the mass media; some voluntary associations bring their members into realistic participation in politics. Mills gives the impression that the inert masses in the United States are the great majority, whereas studies of participation in voluntary associations suggest that they are not over 40 percent of the population, and are probably slowly de- creasing in proportion. Such conditions and trends will be discussed more fully in subsequent chapters.

Mills's rebuttal to arguments about mass participation in voluntary associa- tions and social movements rests on his opinion that such things are not impor- tant. This is not only a personal value judgment; it also leads to circular reasoning: the only important things in American life are those things the economic elite successfully seeks; since the economic elite has shown little interest in the civil-rights movement, either for or against it, then *ipso facto,* the civil-rights movement is not important, even though it involves the social energies and life chances of a sizable minority of the population.

Whereas Hunter says nothing regarding the means by which the economic elite control the government, Mills lists three such means (pp. 165–70 of *The Power Elite*).

He states, first, that the Constitution, particularly since the adoption of the Fourteenth Amendment, gives free rein to the corporate rich to run the economy. I would not basically quarrel with this statement standing alone, for the American economy is overwhelmingly one of free private enterprise and semi-monopoly capitalism, rather than of state capitalism or guild socialism. However, when Mills carries this over to the political realm, he cites only evidence that supports his view: "In virtually every case of [governmental] regulation that we examine the regulating agency has tended to become a corporate outpost" (p. 166). He ignores the numerous and powerful governmental restraints and limitations on corporations—through the power to tax, to license, to set rates in interstate commerce, to control conditions of marketing (of securities as well as of products), to control the accuracy of labeling and advertising, to set the conditions of collective bargaining and the labor contract, and dozens of lesser governmental powers. It is of course true that in some of these areas (particularly rate-setting and licensing), the economic elite has found means of influencing the government administrators, but even here the fact that they must work through the government administrators (appointed by the President with the consent of the Senate) is a limitation on their power. It is simply incorrect to consider that the relation of government to the economy is the same in 1960 as it was in 1860 except insofar as the government today is even more controlled by the interests of the economic elite than it was then—which is Mills's position. The difficulty lies with Mills's contrast-conception, which is one of state capitalism, or guild socialism, or populism; for implicit in his remarks about the lack of government interference with the economy is his belief that the only real alternative to complete private enterprise is complete state or "worker" ownership, control, and operation of the economy.

The second means by which Mills considers that the economic elite controls the government is that of the large political campaign contribution. I agree that this is a major means of influence, though not of control, and I deal with it in Chapter 13. However, Mills pays very little attention to this factor, which could provide the main factual basis for his thesis. I do not know why Mills considers it so unimportant, but I suspect it is probably because he has little understanding of how politics works.

The third means of elite control over government, which Mills considers the most important of all, he states in the following words: "As the corporate world has become more intricately involved in the political order, these executives have become intimately associated with the politicians, and especially with the key 'politicians' who form the political directorate of the United States government" (p. 167). More specifically:

During World War II they served on innumerable advisory committees in the prosecution of the war. They were also brought into the military apparatus more permanently by the awarding to many businessmen of commissions in the reserve officer corps. All this has been going on for a long time and is rather well known, but in the Eisenhower administration the corporate executives publicly assumed the key posts of the executive branch of the government. Where before the more silent power and the ample contract was there, now there was also the loud voice. [Pages 167–8.]

During the last three decades, since the First World War in fact, the distinction between the political and the economic man has been diminishing; although the corporation managers have, in the past, distrusted one of their own who stays too long in the political arena. They like to come and go, for then they are not responsible. Yet more and more of the corporate executives have entered government directly; and the result has been a virtually new political economy at the apex of which we find those who represent the corporate rich. [Page 169.]

I understand these and other statements by Mills to mean that the economic elite has taken over control of the Executive branch of the government. But just exactly how they have done that, he does not say. To point to many specific businessman appointments in the Eisenhower Administration does show a major (not exclusive) reliance of a Republican Administration on businessmen. It does not explain the means of control, and it does not prove that the businessman appointees are running the government for the benefit of business. I suspect that businessmen who go to work for the government develop a quite different point of view toward government from that of businessmen who never have government experience. The latter, I would hypothesize, remain largely alienated from, and hostile to, government even when it is in Republican hands. Mills himself acknowledges this when he states that the business elite become suspicious of their colleagues who remain in government service "too long." Part of the businessmen's antagonism to even Republican administrations, I suspect, is toward the permanent top civil servants, but mainly it is due to a lack of understanding of political processes. The Kennedy Administration made some major business appointments too; it made even more appointments of college professors. Despite the facetious observations, this does not mean that Harvard University (or the academic profession in general) has assumed political control of the nation. The activities of the Executive branch suggest that President Kennedy was mainly in control of his businessman and professor appointees. In Chapter 11 the process by which Kennedy achieved the nomination for the presidency is traced. It was a political process, involving very little special dependence on the economic elite.

Mills does not give much consideration to the Congress, and does not claim that any significant number of businessmen have entered the Congress. Rather he holds, without evidence, that Congress is subordinate to the Executive branch and consists of persons who take orders from the economic elite. I do not doubt that a small number of congressmen have been "bought" by the economic elite, and that a larger number have viewpoints identical to those of the economic elite and contrary to the wishes of the majority of their constituencies. But I believe political processes are such that most congressmen are most of the time responsive to the wishes of the majority of their constituents. And I believe, contrary to Mills, that congressional action is important to the outcome of key national issues. I do not claim to "prove" that these statements are correct, nor do I claim that congressmen or other elected officials are mere passive registers of the wishes of their constituencies. I seek in later chapters to illustrate the complexity of political processes, and to show how largely independent they are of controls from the economic elite. I seek to show this for the selection of the political elite in certain states (Chapter 10) and for the passage of a specific piece of federal legislation (Chapter 12). Insofar as the facts presented about the political process in these studies are representative, they do not confirm Mills's portrayal of economic elite control, although they are not inconsistent with a statement that the economic elite has political influence considerably beyond its proportion in the population. . . .

PART II

The Contemporary World Environment and National Security

National security policy rests on a number of assumptions, one set of which involves the nature of the world environment. Thus, the premises on which policy is constructed are implicit in the answers to questions like these: What are the causes of war in the international system? Is nuclear terror in balance? Are there alternatives to balancing terror? Are the Soviet and Chinese challenges to the United States military or political, both, or neither? Is technology accelerating beyond man's control when peaceful nuclear reactors can produce 10,000 bombs' worth of plutonium by the end of the 1970's? [1] Is the population bomb more to be feared than the atomic bomb?

One premise of the present volume is that nation states—the chief actors in the international system—exist in a condition of uncertainty as to each other's intentions and must therefore be prepared to defend themselves against possible threats to their basic values. External threats may include the violent policies of an adversary or the nonviolent policies of an ally—for example, the impact on the American economy of British entry in the European Economic Community in 1973. Due primarily to mutual uncertainty, suspicion, and fear (and not because of man's innate evil or lust for power), nation states are caught in what John Herz has called the "security dilemma." [2] They feel compelled to seek power in order to achieve security (the protection of their cherished values). Gains by some stimulate striving by others, with the pursuit of "absolute" or "perfect" security being self-defeating. This situation, existing since the origins of the western state system, is a continuing one which may be ameliorated, however, by mutual accommodation based on mutual recognition of security interests.

With the security dilemma at its center, the contemporary world environment is a kaleidoscope of complex patterns. Cutting across the traditional nation-state divisions are the activities of multinational corporations or of subnational actors like insurgent groups; pressure inside and outside nations emanates from forces such as nationalism, race, communism, and modernization. Exponentially growing technology, for example, has had an enormous impact on the international system, its participants, and the methods of conducting relations between them. Compare the most lethal form of "interaction," the capacity of a single weapon in 1944 (a B-29 bomber) and 1972 (an ICBM): range has increased four to ten times (2000 miles for the bomber; 8000 miles for the ICBM; around the globe for the fractional orbital bombardment system); speed has increased 50 times (300 miles per hour compared to 15,000); the explosive power of a single weapon has multiplied more than eight million times (from 3 tons of TNT in 1944 to 25 million tons for the present Soviet SS 9 missile). Nation states have been raised to great or superpower status or reduced to third- or fourth-rate level, depending on the growth of their technology, as the number of computers a nation produces seems to provide a better indication of future world status than the traditional index of coal or steel production. Changes in the international law of the sea have been stimulated by new methods of exploiting the resources on or below the ocean bottom.

Various analytical distinctions are possible in attempting to understand these complexities. For example, three levels of the international system have been offered by Stanley Hoffmann: the bipolar, polycentric, and multipolar. The first, seen in the Soviet-American relationship and on whose balance nuclear peace is most dependent, is the foundation for the system; the second suggests the growing political flexibility of middle and small powers, due largely to superpower fears of using force which may escalate to nuclear conflict; the third can be seen in the destabilizing trend toward an increase in the number of nuclear powers.[3] Geographic metaphors have also been used as frames of reference, with the East-West (cold war) division being supplemented by the North-South (rich-poor) dichotomy. Throughout the system, touching each point of the compass, modernization is occurring: national integration, a primary goal of modernization, is a vital issue not only in Pakistan or Nigeria but also in Italy (with its problem of the south), Belgium (the Flemings and the Walloons), Canada (the French "nation"), the United States (the blacks), and the Soviet Union (with its non-Russian nationalities now comprising more than half the Soviet population).

A precondition for the continuance of the international system is the bipolar Soviet-American relationship. It is necessary, therefore, to consider what is involved in the "balance of terror," the mutual nuclear deterrence of the United States and the USSR. However, before turning to the particular question of Soviet-American balance, let us discuss various components of deterrence—psychological, political, technological—on a more abstract level. Simply put, deterrence means that State A seeks to prevent State B from doing Z by threatening B with unacceptable costs if it does Z. One requirement for deterrence is that decision-makers act rationally—the leaders of State B must calculate the costs and benefits of the action that State A is seeking to deter and rationally conclude not to act. A second psychological factor is the will or credibility of the deterrer—the leaders of State B must believe that the leaders of State A will indeed do what they threaten to do (recall the discussion of power in the introduction to Part I). Third, in view of the devastating consequences of a successful surprise nuclear attack, is the importance of the offensive (since an effective defense against saturation attack is not in sight). Fourth is the important distinction between an offensive first strike and a retaliatory second strike, with the most meaningful consideration under this factor being the forces a state has remaining after it has absorbed an attack. Deterrence, in other words, is based on communicating to the adversary that even after a first strike has been received, a sufficient amount of second-strike retaliatory forces will remain to cause unacceptable damage.

A number of factors could contribute to an instability of the balance that now exists between the United States and the USSR, such as accidental launching of a missile; miscalculation of intentions and capabilities; irrationality; nuclear proliferation; escalation of a small conflict; or a technological breakthrough such as a perfected defense system, which would permit one side to threaten the other with impunity. These destabilizing factors can be offset, however, by mutual invulnerability of retaliatory forces and by arms control measures. With mutual invulnerability, for example, neither side need be panicked into causing a thermonuclear holocaust because of an accidental launching. Invulnerability can be achieved by dispersal, "hardening," mobility, and mixing (planes, missiles, and submarines) of strategic forces. Past arms control measures have included the Soviet-American hot line; the Test Ban Treaty of 1963; the Non-Proliferation Treaty of 1969; and the 1972 Moscow summit agreement limiting the United States and the Soviet Union to two ABM systems each and freezing land-based and submarine-launched ballistic missiles (ICBM, SLBM) at the numbers in existence or under construction.

The impact of technology has been pervasive in the development of missile generations since the late 1950's: reaction time has been reduced from hours with the liquid-fueled missiles to 30 seconds with the solid-fueled missiles; "hardened" sites can withstand 1000 pounds per square inch overpressure, or a near direct hit; the reduced weight-to-yield ratio permits smaller but powerful warheads; accuracy has been sharpened from within miles of a target to within .2 of a mile (a twofold increase in accuracy is reportedly equivalent to about an eightfold increase in explosive yield); single warhead missiles are being replaced by MIRV's, multiple independently targeted reentry vehicles with 3 to 14 warheads. Increased accuracy and the MIRV have diminished the invulnerability of the fixed land-based missile relative to the mobile and concealed submarine-launched missile system.

Indeed, until the late 1950's, the importance of invulnerable retaliatory forces was not fully appreciated. To place this assertion and the foregoing discussion in context, let us briefly review some phases in the evolution of American strategic doctrine. For about the first decade of the nuclear age, the atomic bomb was generally considered a "city-buster." American strategy was essentially "first strike/counter city"—that is, the United States, having a monopoly of nuclear weapons, threatened the use of nuclear weapons against the cities of an aggressor nation. The testing of a Soviet atomic bomb in 1949 and a deliverable thermonuclear weapon in 1953, accompanied by the growth of its strategic air force, undermined the first strike/counter city strategy, since it would leave Soviet nuclear forces intact for a retaliatory attack on American cities. To the extent that the "massive retaliation" statement by Secretary Dulles in 1954 (the United States would "retaliate, instantly, by means and at places of our own choosing") implied an American first strike/counter city strategy, mutual suicide would be the result. The predominant belief that the two superpowers were in a stable mutual stalemate with strategic forces aimed at each other's cities was upset in the late 1950's. The work of Albert Wohlstetter of the RAND Corporation was instrumental in shifting the emphasis away from the belief in a stable stalemate toward one which called for a protected second-strike force, as it came to be understood that not a stable but a delicate balance of terror existed—since a surprise attack by the USSR on the strategic forces of the United States (i.e., a first strike/counter force attack) would leave the United States helpless.

A drastic shift in strategic doctrine occurred in the early 1960's, usually identified with a speech by Secretary of Defense McNamara at Ann Arbor in 1962. The "controlled response, city-sparing" doctrine enunciated in this speech was in effect a second strike/counterforce strategy whose aim was to prevent nuclear holocaust after deterrence has broken down. By retaliating in a controlled manner against military targets in the USSR, while avoiding Russian cities, the United States would seek to negotiate a truce before an all-out, city-destroying attack was launched by either side. Among the numerous criticisms of the strategy at the time were that it would not work when targets were "hardened" and that the Soviet Union would reject the strategy since it was numerically inferior in ICBM's (the Soviets argued that the important thing was not to limit damage in a nuclear war but instead to do all that was possible to avert a nuclear war). From 1965 on, the city-sparing strategy dropped out of the posture statements of the Secretary of Defense, to be replaced by "assured destruction," which has essentially remained as the basic American nuclear doctrine. Assured destruction, a second strike/counter city strategy, means that after absorbing an attack by the Soviet Union, the United States could still retaliate to destroy about one-third of the Soviet population and two-thirds of its industrial capacity. The Soviet Union, declared Secretary McNamara in 1968, had the capability to inflict roughly the same amount of damage on the United States if the latter attacked first. By the late 1960's, therefore, mutual invulnerability of retaliatory forces precluded a disarming first strike by either side, resulting in a balance of terror more stable than in the 1950's.[4]

But the late 1960's also brought technological innovations—MIRV, the ABM, and a rapid Soviet build-up—which diluted the confidence of some in the future stability of the balance. The Nixon Administration seemed to raise questions about assured destruction and called its own doctrine "strategic sufficiency." Although few basic differences are apparent between strategic sufficiency and assured destruction, passages in the President's foreign policy statements in 1970 and 1971 were reminiscent of McNamara's city-sparing strategy.[5]

Should a President, in the event of a nuclear attack, be left with the single option of ordering the mass destruction of enemy civilians, in the face of the certainty that it would be followed by the mass slaughter of Americans? (1970, p. 122)

I must not be—and my successors must not be—limited to the indiscriminate mass destruction of enemy civilians as the sole possible response to challenges. This is especially so when that response involves the likelihood of triggering nuclear attacks on our own population.

It would be inconsistent with the political meaning of sufficiency to base our force planning solely on some finite—and theoretical—capacity to inflict casualties presumed to be unacceptable to the other side.

But sufficiency also means numbers, characteristics, and deployments of our forces which the Soviet Union cannot reasonably interpret as being intended to threaten a disarming attack. (1971, pp. 170–71)

A second strike/counter force strategy can be inferred from the foregoing quotations. Although no elaboration appeared in the President's document, reminiscent of the McNamara city-sparing doctrine was this scenario, which was evidently elicited from State and Defense Department spokesmen: if in a crisis a Soviet attack destroyed most of American bombers and land-based missiles, the President might not want to launch an attack on the Soviet population; instead he might order an attack on Soviet bomber bases, nuclear weapons depots, hydroelectric plants, and attempt to negotiate a cease-fire.[6]

Now that the Soviet Union has reached parity with the United States in nuclear weapons, is it possible that both sides would be willing to move away from the "assured destruction" balance of terror to a "no cities" doctrine, in combination with a limited ABM, in case the unthinkable should materialize?[7]

The Soviet drive to parity in strategic forces has been one of the significant developments of the past decade. The following table illustrates the growth of land-based (ICBM) and submarine-launched (SLBM) ballistic missiles for both countries, with the United States remaining at the level reached in 1967:

		1960	1962	1965	1969	1972	1977
USA	ICBM	18	294	854	1054	1054	1054 (1000)
	SLBM	32	144	496	656	656	656 (710)
USSR	ICBM	35	75	270	1050	1530	1618 (1408)
	SLBM	—	some	120	160	560	740 (950)

The figures in the 1977 column represent the limits (on missiles in existence or under construction) agreed upon at the 1972 Nixon-Brezhnev summit meeting.[8] Although the USSR has the greater number of ICBM's and SLBM's, the United States has superiority in weapons technology, strategic bombers (530 to 140), and deliverable warheads (5700 to 2500). If the two superpowers can reach further agreement before 1977, these figures could represent a longer-term ceiling or might even be reduced.

Some observers view facts presented in the above table not as a reflection of the growth of parity but of American inferiority. By emphasizing comparative megatonnage (USSR—10,330; US—1,730), the American Security Council maintained in 1970 that the Soviet Union had quadrupled its total megatonnage in five years, while the United States had reduced its megatonnage by more than 40 percent.[9] In a criticism of the Moscow 1972 summit agreement, the duration of the 2:1 American advantage in warheads was questioned by columnist Stewart Alsop because of the possible "MIRVing" of Russia's "enormous new missile" (50 megatons of explosive power).[10] The foregoing discussion and the table have suggested three ways of measuring comparative strength: the number of vehicles or launchers, megatonnage, and the number of warheads. Although the summit agreement placed a limit on the number of launchers, the modernization of launchers and warheads as well as multiplication of warheads can continue. A Soviet attempt to match the American warhead total, and a possible US reaction, could bring in the late 1970's the confrontation of perhaps 8,000 warheads on each side.

Thus, a crucial question for the future is whether the USSR will be satisfied with the present configuration of parity or will continue the growth of its missile forces. Testifying before Congress, Soviet specialist Thomas Wolfe offered his interpretation of the background to Soviet military policy and possible future trends. Wolfe suggested that the basically continental dimensions of Stalin's foreign policy were enlarged to global interests by Khrushchev, and that the Brezhnev-Kosygin leadership has striven to provide the previously unavailable capabilities for the pursuit of these expanded objectives. The assumptions behind the military policy of the present Soviet leaders, according to Wolfe, are:

1. that nuclear war must be avoided; 2. that deterrence based on Soviet strategic nuclear power, both offensive and defensive, offers the best guarantee against a general nuclear war; 3. that the Soviet Union must maintain a traditionally strong continental military position, both to back up its interest in the crucial political arena of Europe and to cope with the problems created by the rise of a rival seat of Communist power in Peking; and 4. that the Soviet Union must also develop more mobile and versatile conventional forces—including Soviet naval and maritime capacities—in order to support its interests in the Third World and to sustain its role as a global competitor of the U.S.[11]

In response to the specific question of future strategic trends, Dr. Wolfe offered two interpretations. A more optimistic one held that the USSR would rest at parity due to domestic consumer concerns, other internal pressures for resources, belief that parity would be favorable to the pursuit of political objectives, and belief that superiority might not last long enough to make the gains significantly greater. A more skeptical interpretation maintained that the Soviet Union would strive for superiority due to doctrinal pressures, the assessment that the USSR was still making respectable economic gains, belief that the United States was troubled with internal difficulties and would be unable to compete, and belief that the Soviet leaders would be more confident in achieving political objectives if they had recognized superiority.[12] Viewing the 1972 summit agreement through these two perspectives one could observe: (1) that the optimistic interpretation has been confirmed by the Soviet agreement to limit ABM's and missile launchers; or (2) that if the USSR "MIRVs" its already more potent and more numerous missiles it could overcome the primary US missile advantage, in the number of warheads.

Is the balance of terror that we have been describing rooted in the cold war, the ideological tension dividing East and West? Perhaps so in part, yet it can be argued that the centuries-old security dilemma is at the heart of the Soviet-American competition, with ideological hostility serving to exacerbate the inherent tension. Indeed a book written in 1946,[13] at the beginning of the atomic age, sketched without cold war ideological polemics some of what were to become the chief characteristics of Soviet-American relations in the following decades: bipolarity, nuclear deterrence (then called "determent"), and arms control but not disarmament. A reader in the 1970's may wonder if the past quarter-century would have been very different without the communist-free world dichotomy.

Assuming that the cold war has contributed in some way to the shape of the contemporary world environment and the Soviet-American rivalry, do the origins of that war lie in the behavior of the United States or the Soviet Union or both? The Revisionists blame the United States for cutting off Lend Lease, encircling the Soviet Union, and brandishing the bomb.[14] Some Kremlinologists suggest other reasons for the cold war: Herbert Dinerstein has stressed the internal causes for Soviet foreign policy; Adam Ulam asks why the Soviet Union demobilized in 1948 if it felt so threatened by US aggression.[15]

A number of factors seem to have interacted in causing the postwar Soviet-American rivalry. Start with the uncertainty, suspicion, and fear associated with the security dilemma; add the misperceptions on both sides of intentions and capabilities, misperceptions conditioned by ideological and theoretical frameworks; then add technology—and the result is a kind of action-reaction-overreaction pattern. One example of this pattern occurred in the late 1950's, when many Americans were concerned with Soviet economic growth (later information indicated it was slowing down) and space achievements; at that time "worst-case" estimates of the capabilities of the USSR (encouraged by Khrushchev's claims of manufacturing 250 missiles annually) produced the "missile gap" and the crash program to develop American missiles. The result in the early 1960's was a vast American missile superiority over Russia instead of the reverse. One Soviet reaction to American strategic superiority was its attempt to affect the balance by placing missiles in Cuba in 1962. The failure of this policy not only spurred the development of USSR strategic missiles but also its naval capabilities. Consider another possible action-reaction cycle: George Rathjens speculates that the Soviet Tallinn air defense system may have been constructed in the expectation that the American B-70 bomber would be deployed (it was not); in turn the Tallinn system was initially and incorrectly believed by some in the US intelligence community to be an ABM system and may have contributed to development of new American missiles and penetration aids.[16]

A decade of Soviet military progress has provided depth and flexibility in strategic and tactical land, sea, and air forces. These increased capabilities may encourage Soviet intervention around the globe to the ultimate disadvantage of the USSR, much as critics of American policy have attributed "globalism" in part to the flexible response capabilities provided by the Kennedy-McNamara Administration. The Soviet Union is overextended, writes Herbert Dinerstein, and not yet fully appreciative of the distinctions between the present age of clientism and the past era of colonialism.[17] Despite increasing Soviet activity around the world, however, the judgment of the Institute for Strategic Studies is that the USSR acted with moderation in the Middle East in 1970 and that the bonds which linked Moscow and Washington, "whose composition consisted in part of fear and suspicion and which existed within the framework of fundamental adversity . . . still implied more of a common interest in strategic restraint than a separate interest in strategic adventure.[18] Continued confidence in the latter assessment seemed warranted by the results of the 1972 Nixon-Brezhnev summit conference, which took place in Moscow despite American bombing of North Vietnam and mining of its major ports. From the intensive negotiations emerged agreements on such issues as arms control; space cooperation; science and technology; environmental protection; and on twelve "basic principles of relations" between the United States and the USSR, including the "major importance" attached to "preventing the development of situations capable of causing a dangerous exacerbation of their relations."[19]

Does strategic "restraint" or "adventure" best characterize the policies of the world's most populous nation, China? Not too long ago the People's Republic of China (then commonly referred to as Red China) was frequently represented as an expansionist power whose leaders might even welcome a nuclear war from which 300 million Chinese would emerge victorious. Although Khrushchev was criticized by China for "adventurism" in putting missiles in Cuba, he was also attacked by them for "capitulationism" in removing them under pressure from the American "paper tiger." (Khrushchev reportedly replied that the "paper tiger has nuclear teeth.") The Chinese were condemned as aggressors in Korea, Tibet, and India; as supporters of North Vietnamese aggression in South Vietnam; and as fomenters of revolution in Africa and Indonesia. The change in Chinese policy from "adventure" to "restraint" seems due partly to an actual shift toward a pragmatic policy and partly to a reappraisal by western observers that emphasizes, for example, the caution and prudence in much of past Chinese policy (separating rhetoric from action), the legitimate Chinese concerns with possible threats to their interests, and those misperceptions on both sides during the Korean War which lead to Chinese intervention. Pragmatism should be a stabilizing ingredient in the foreign policy of leaders whose perceptions of the United States may derive from reading Admiral Mahan's geopolitical theories and whose visions of Maoist thought as the center of communist world theory may have replaced traditional geographic and cultural perceptions of China's central position in the global environment.

A few early signs of American flexibility toward China appeared during the "containment but not isolation" period of the 1960's, but increased progress in opening trade relations and cultural exchange came during the Nixon Administration, climaxed by the President's visit to Peking in early 1972. The 1971 foreign policy statement of President Nixon, who was a hard-line anticommunist during the Korean War years, noted that the "doctrines of violence and revolution" of the People's Republic of China (not so named in the 1970 statement) were "proclaimed more often than followed as principles of foreign relations." [20] The Chinese pragmatism reflected in the "ping-pong diplomacy" of 1971 was continued by the admission into China of visiting American scholars and journalists. In a series of articles in the *New York Times,* Seymour Topping reported his impression that internally "the basic needs of the people are being met and the foundation being laid for a modern industrial country . . . agricultural production is increasing while the birth rate is dropping. . . ." [21]

The country that centuries ago invented gunpowder and the rocket has tested atomic and thermonuclear weapons, launched a satellite, and is expected to have 10 to 25 operational ICBM's by the mid-1970's which could reach the United States or European Russia. (The prediction in 1967 was 50 to 150 operational ICBM's by the mid-1970's; the delay in the timetable has been attributed to the Cultural Revolution.) Stressing a "no first use" doctrine, the Chinese have refused to sign the Test Ban Treaty or the Non-Proliferation Agreement, both of which it considers attempts to freeze the nuclear superiority of the superpowers. Presumably its goals in the construction of a nuclear capacity are to increase its influence vis-à-vis the Soviet Union and the United States, and both regionally and globally as a leader of the Third World. [22] Indeed, the Chinese appear to be deemphasizing their own superpower potential and accenting their leadership, not only of the Third World, but of middle and small powers which are concerned about superpower hegemony. Declaring in June 1971 that China would assume a superpower role "neither now nor ever in the future," Premier Chou En-Lai said: "We will always stand together with oppressed countries and peoples in firmly opposing the power politics of superpowers." [23] China's entrance into the United Nations in the fall of 1971 offered a world forum for pursuing these ends: attacking Soviet and Indian policy during the India-Pakistan war, China classified India as a potential "subsuperpower" in partnership with the USSR in committing aggression against Asians, and advised "all the countries in the world which are subjected to injury and threat by superpowers or subsuperpowers" not to relax their vigilance. [24]

The possibility that China may lead Third World opposition to superpower (and subsuperpower) hegemony is a useful reminder that the emphasis in this discussion on the superpower balance of terror, although necessary, is not nearly sufficient for understanding the contemporary international environment. Let us return briefly to some of the other forces at work in the system. Futurists foresee in the year 2000 perhaps 1 billion Indians and 1.5 billion Chinese in a world of 7.5 billion people. The gap between the rich, largely white (except for Japan) North and the poor, largely nonwhite South may increase, as the leading nations move into the "politics of abundance" of post-industrial society and the Third World poor remain at pre-industrial levels.[25] The world's resources will continue to be consumed in disproportionate quantities by the North—today about 40 percent of world resource consumption is America's, whose population is 6 percent of the world total. Urbanization will continue worldwide: although migrants to cities in the developing nations have not proved to be the source of violence that was anticipated, later generations of these migrants are more likely to fulfill the predictions.[26] As the poor of the new nations are frustrated in their striving for economic betterment, national identity, equality, and independence, will the incidence and scale of war multiply? Although the major wars of the twentieth century were not due to poverty, the awakening poor of today may indeed be a greater potential source of internal and international war than the predominantly inert poor of the past.

This brief attempt to penetrate what C. B. Marshall called the "impenetrable blank of the future" may perhaps be best concluded with three illustrations which clearly indicate the changing perceptions and realities of the twentieth-century environment. At the turn of the century English geopolitician Halford Mackinder described the world as a "closed system" with technology reducing the continents to islands; in 1965 then Chinese Defense Minister Lin Piao portrayed the basic conflict in the world system as that of the cities versus the countryside; today, continents and islands, cities and countryside are all part of what some ecologists have called Spaceship Earth, with attendant implications regarding resource exhaustion and pollution that transcend traditional security concerns.

NOTES

1. Albert Wohlstetter, "Strength, Interest, and New Technologies," in *The Implications of Military Technology in the 1970's,* Adelphi Papers No. 46 (London: Institute for Strategic Studies, 1968), p. 1. India, which has not signed the Non-Proliferation Treaty, will conduct underground nuclear tests for peaceful purposes when it has developed the necessary technology, according to a statement by its Defense Minister (*International Herald-Tribune,* May 3, 1972).

2. John Herz, *International Politics in the Atomic Age* (New York: Columbia University Press, 1959).

3. Stanley Hoffman, *Gulliver's Troubles* (New York: McGraw-Hill, 1968), pp. 22ff.

4. For discussions of deterrence, see Bernard Brodie, *Strategy in the Missile Age* (Princeton, N.J.: Princeton University Press, 1959); Henry A. Kissinger, *The Necessity for Choice* (New York: Harper, 1960); Thomas Schelling, *Arms and Influence* (New Haven: Yale University Press, 1966); Herman Kahn, *On Escalation* (Baltimore: Pelican, 1968).

5. Richard M. Nixon, *U.S. Foreign Policy for the 1970's: A Report to the Congress,* February 18, 1970; February 25, 1971.

6. *New York Times,* February 26, 1971.

7. An opponent of what he calls the present MAD posture (Mutual Assured Destruction), Donald Brennan has suggested greater emphasis on making defense more effective, along with an agreed reduction of offensive forces (*New York Times,* May 24, 25, 1971). The 1972 Presidential report to Congress continued the emphasis on both retaliatory strength and a capability for flexible application, with the "assured destruction" doctrine being described as inadequate for the latter purpose (*U.S. Foreign Policy for the 1970's: A Report to Congress,* February 9, 1972, pp. 157–58).

8. A protocol to the Moscow Agreement provided that additional SLBM's could become operational as replacements for equal numbers of older ICBM's or SLBM's on older submarines, up to a total of 950 SLBM's and 62 modern ballistic missile submarines for the USSR, and 710 SLBM's and 44 submarines for the U.S.

9. *New York Times*, October 27, 1970. Most of the data in the table is drawn from *The Military Balance 1972–73* (London, International Institute for Strategic Studies, 1972), p. 67, an annual publication which is indispensable for the student of security policy; see pp. 83–86 for a concise analysis of the impact of the SALT agreements on the strategic balance.

10. *Newsweek* (Atlantic Edition), June 5, 1972, p. 8.

11. Thomas Wolfe, "Diplomatic and Strategic Impact of Multiple Warhead Missiles," *Hearings*, Subcommittee on National Security Policy, Committee on Foreign Affairs, House of Representatives, 91st Congress, 1st Session, July 22, 1969, p. 139. Also see his *Soviet Power and Europe 1945–70* (Baltimore: Johns Hopkins Press, 1970).

12. Ibid., Subcommittee on National Security Policy *Hearings*, pp. 139–44.

13. Bernard Brodie, F. S. Dunn, P. E. Corbett, W. T. R. Fox, and Arnold Wolfers, *The Absolute Weapon* (New York: Harcourt, Brace, 1946).

14. See, for example, Gar Alperovitz, *Atomic Diplomacy: Hiroshima and Potsdam* (New York: Vintage, 1965).

15. Herbert S. Dinerstein, "The Soviet Outlook," in *America and the World*, Robert E. Osgood *et al.*, eds. (Baltimore: Johns Hopkins Press, 1970); Adam Ulam, *Expansion and Coexistence* (New York: Praeger, 1968).

16. George Rathjens, *The Future of the Strategic Arms Race* (New York: Carnegie Endowment, 1969).

17. Dinerstein, *op. cit.*

18. *Strategic Survey 1970* (London: Institute for Strategic Studies, 1971), p. 11.

19. *International Herald Tribune*, May 30, 1972.

20. *U.S. Foreign Policy for the 1970's*, February 25, 1971, p. 106.

21. *New York Times*, June 27, 1971.

22. Morton Halperin, "Chinese Attitudes toward the Use and Control of Nuclear Weapons," in *China in Crisis*, Tang Tsou, ed., Vol. 2 (Chicago: University of Chicago Press, 1968).

23. *New York Times*, June 9, 1971. Also see editorials quoted in *Strategic Survey 1970* (see above, n. 18), p. 32.

24. *New York Times*, December 17, 1971.

25. Herman Kahn and Anthony Weiner, "The Next Thirty Years," in "Toward the Year 2000," *Daedalus* (Summer 1967), pp. 705–32; on the "politics of abundance," see A. F. K. Organski, *The Stages of Political Development* (New York: Knopf, 1965).

26. Samuel Huntington, *Political Order in Changing Societies* (New Haven: Yale University Press, 1968), p. 278ff.; Joan Nelson, "The Urban Poor: Disruption or Political Integration in Third World Cities?" *World Politics* (April 1970), pp. 393–414.

THE INTERNATIONAL SYSTEM

7.

Kenneth Waltz: *Man, the State, and War*

The "pictures in the heads" of decision-makers—their preconceptions or theoretical frameworks—influence how they select and evaluate information. Three "images" of international relations are offered in the following selection by Kenneth Waltz, who suggests that the major causes of war are to be found in

From Kenneth Waltz, *Man, the State, and War*, Columbia University Press, 1959, pp. 12–15, 224–38. Reprinted by permission of the publisher.

man, in the structure of the separate states, and in the state system itself. Although the first and second images help clarify the forces that affect security policy, the search for a solution to the problem of war can not ignore the third image: that of the interaction of states in the international system, in which the peace strategy of each state depends upon the strategies of the other states in the system.

Professor of Politics at the University of California, Berkeley, Dr. Waltz is author of *Foreign Policy and Democratic Politics,* and coeditor of *Use of Force* and *Conflict in World Politics.*

. . . Where are the major causes of war to be found? The answers are bewildering in their variety and in their contradictory qualities. To make this variety manageable, the answers can be ordered under the following three headings: within man, within the structure of the separate states, within the state system. The basis of this ordering, as well as its relevance in the world of affairs, is suggested in the preceding pages. These three estimates of cause will subsequently be referred to as images of international relations, numbered in the order given, with each image defined according to where one locates the nexus of important causes.

Previous comments indicate that the views comprised by any one image may in some senses be as contradictory as are the different images *inter se.* The argument that war is inevitable because men are irrevocably bad, and the argument that wars can be ended because men can be changed, are contradictory; but since in each of them individuals are taken to be the locus of cause, both are included in the first image. Similarly, acceptance of a third-image analysis may lead to the false optimism of the world federalists or to the often falsely defined pessimism of a *Realpolitik* position. Since in all respects but one there may be variety of opinion within images and since prescription is related to goal as well as to analysis, there is no one prescription for each image. There are, however, in relation to each image-goal pairing, logical and illogical prescriptions.

One can say that a prescription is wrong if he can show that following it does not bring about the predicted result. But can one ever show that a prescription was actually followed? One often hears statements like this: "The League of Nations didn't fail; it was never tried." And such statements are irrefutable. But even if empirical disproof were possible, the problem of proving a prescription valid would remain to be solved. A patient who in one period of illness tries ten different medications may wonder just which pill produced the cure. The apportioning of credit is often more difficult than the assigning of blame. If a historical study were to show that in country A increases in national prosperity always followed increases in tariffs, to some observers this might seem to prove that high tariffs are a cause of prosperity; to others, that both of these factors are dependent on a third; and to still others, nothing at all. The empirical approach, though necessary, is not sufficient. The correlation of events means nothing, or at least should not be taken to mean anything, apart from the analysis that accompanies it.

If there is no empirical solution to the problem of prescription verification, what solution is there? Prescription is logically impossible apart from analysis. Every prescription for greater peace in the world is then related to one of our three images of international relations, or to some combination of them. An understanding of the analytical terms of each of the images will open up two additional possibilities for accepting or rejecting prescriptions. (1) A prescription based on a faulty analysis would be unlikely to produce the desired consequences. The assumption that to improve men in a prescribed way will serve to promote peace rests on the further assumption that in some form the first image of international relations is valid. The latter assumption should be examined before the former is made. (2) A prescription would be unacceptable if it were not logically related to its analysis. One who suffers from infected tonsils profits little from a skillfully performed appendectomy. If violence among states is caused by the evilness of man, to aim at the internal reform of states will not do much good. And if violence among states is the product of international anarchy, to aim at the conversion of individuals can accomplish little. One man's prognosis confounds the other man's prescription. If the validity of the images themselves can be ascertained, the critical relating of prescription to image becomes a check on the validity of prescriptions. There is, however, an additional complicating factor. Some combination of our three images, rather than any one of them, may be required for an accurate understanding of international relations. We may not be in a situation where one can consider just the patient's tonsils or his appendix. Both may be infected but removing either may kill the patient. In other words, understanding the likely consequences of any one cause may depend on understanding its relation to other causes. The possible interrelation of causes makes the problem of estimating the merit of various prescriptions more difficult still.

What are the criteria of merit? Suppose we consider again the person who argues that "bad" states produce war, that "good" states would live peacefully together, that therefore we must bring states into accord with a prescribed pattern. To estimate the merit of such a series of propositions requires asking the following questions: (1) Can the final proposition be implemented, and if so, how? (2) Is there a logical relation between prescription and image? In other words, does the prescription attack the assigned causes? (3) Is the image adequate, or has the analyst simply seized upon the most spectacular cause or the one he thinks most susceptible to manipulation and ignored other causes of equal or greater importance? (4) How will attempts to fill the prescription affect other goals? This last question is necessary since peace is not the only goal of even the most peacefully inclined men or states. One may, for example, believe that world government and perpetual peace are synonymous, but one may also be convinced that a world state would be a world tyranny and therefore prefer a system of nation-states with a perpetual danger of war to a world state with a promise of perpetual peace. . . .

Throughout the first half of the present century, Norman Angell has argued with persistence, eloquence, and clarity the proposition that war does not pay.

Increasingly, under the influence of "the balance of terror," one finds men speaking as though the argument Angell first popularized fifty years ago has been made true by recent advances in the technology of warfare. But, in the sense Angell intended, it has always been true. Angell was a rationalist and individualist in the ninteenth-century mold, much less concerned with the relative gains and losses of this or that nation than with the unchallengeable fact that war at best takes men away from the work that produces the necessities and comforts of life, at worst destroys what they have already produced. War may achieve a redistribution of resources, but labor, not war, creates wealth. Perhaps not from the perspective of a nation or a tribe but from the perspective of mankind, war has never "paid."

Yet war recurs. The beast in man may glory in the carnage; the reason in man rebels. War and the threat of war stimulate speculation upon the conditions of peace. Seemingly critical thought may, however, embody uncritical reactions to the immediately impressive aspects of the situation faced. Peace programs, whether they would rely for their efficacy upon irenic diplomacy, armed crusade, moral exhortation, or psychic-cultural readjustment, are based at least implicitly on the ideas of the causes of war we entertain. As was argued in the introductory chapter, our estimates of the causes of war are determined by our presuppositions as much as by the events of the world about us. A systematic study of the assumed causes of war then becomes a direct way of estimating the conditions of peace. Our primary concern has not been with building models from which policies promoting peace can be derived but with examining the presuppositions upon which such models are based. This puts the problem in academic terms. Its relevance is much broader, for the policies of statesmen as well as the interests and procedures of scholars are the product of a conjunction of temper, experience, reason, and event. The practice of politics is greatly influenced by the images the politicians entertain.

When Ranke argued that the external relations of states determine their internal conditions, his argument had considerable cogency. So great was the importance of diplomacy in nineteenth-century Europe and so many were the statesmen trained in its ways that even internal governance at times corresponded in method to the techniques by which affairs among states were conducted. One need mention only Metternich and Bismarck. Diplomacy then, as it often has, took on many of the qualities of a game of chess. Perhaps the last illustration of this on the grand scale is provided by Bismarck's manipulations in the Balkan crises of 1885–87. But already by the dawn of the nineteenth century, factors internal to states were becoming more important in international relations. And with their greater importance, one finds a growing tendency to explain relations among states in terms of their internal condition. Most notably among English liberals, the practice of Metternich as well as the dictum of Ranke was reversed. Attempts were made to apply the supposed methods and sanctions of internal governance—judicial settlement, public opinion—to affairs among states.

The vogue of an image varies with time and place, but no single image is ever adequate. Thus Bismarck's skepticism about a possible alliance with Russia was based in part on fear of her internal instability. One who would play a game of chess has to consider the weight of the different pieces as well as the possible moves, and in international politics the weights change with time. Thus John Stuart Mill, writing to an Italian correspondent in June of 1859, expressed England's sympathy for the cause of Italian national freedom but justified England's inaction by pointing out that Austria was the only ally on which England could count should she have to fight for her liberty against France and Russia united.[1] Mill's thoughts and Bismarck's policies can often be adequately described in terms of the second and third images, respectively, but especially when considering the possibilities of state policy the calculations of each comprehended elements from more than one image. This is generally the case. Yet the firmness with which a person is wedded to one image colors his interpretation of the others. Bismarck was inclined more than Mill to keep his eye on the map of Europe, the chessboard; Mill more than Bismarck to focus upon the qualities of peoples and their governments, the chessmen.

In contrast to Metternich and Bismarck, who were diplomatists in domestic as well as international affairs, statesmen of the twentieth century more frequently transfer the methods of the party politician to external politics. Woodrow Wilson, to cite an example used earlier, saw clearly one of the essential elements of a third-image analysis, that everyone's policy depends upon everyone else's. With many authoritarian states in the world, he realized that even the nonauthoritarian state must on occasion be prepared to use force in order to defend its interests. But, convinced that democratic states are peaceful because their governments reflect the aspirations of the people, he foresaw a day when the internal condition of all states would mean not the constant possibility of war but rather the assurance of perpetual peace. Wilson's emphasis upon the second image led him to particular interpretations of the first and third, rather than to a complete ignoring of them.

According to the third image, there is a constant possibility of war in a world in which there are two or more states each seeking to promote a set of interests and having no agency above them upon which they can rely for protection. But many liberals and socialist revisionists deny, or at least minimize, the possibility that wars would occur in a world of political or social democracies. An understanding of the third image makes it clear that the expectation would be justified only if the minimum interest of states in preserving themselves became the maximum interest of all of them—and each could rely fully upon the steadfast adherence to this definition by all of the others. Stating the condition makes apparent the utopian quality of liberal and socialist expectations. The criticism could be extended by questioning as well their interpretations of the first image. But the point as it applies here—that emphasizing one image frequently distorts, though it seldom excludes, the other two—is perhaps sufficiently clear. It may profit us more to shift our attention briefly to similar effects that may follow from concentration upon the third image.

While from the sociologist's perspective government is simply one of many social institutions, it is at the same time a precondition of society. The first perspective without the second is misleading, as was illustrated in one way in Chapter III, in another way in Chapter VI. The state of nature among men is a monstrous impossibility. Anarchy breeds war among them; government establishes the conditions for peace. The state of nature that continues to prevail among states often produces monstrous behavior but so far has not made life itself impossible. The ahistorical analyses of Spinoza, Rousseau, and Kant lay bare the logic of civil society and at the same time make clear why the logic does not carry men past the establishment of separate states to the founding of a world state. Yet in the international as in the domestic sphere, if anarchy is the cause, the obvious conclusion is that government is the cure; and this is true even though the disease in the former case is not fatal. The problem, however, becomes a practical one. The amount of force needed to hold a society together varies with the heterogeneity of the elements composing it. World federalists write as though the alternatives before us were unity or death. "World government is necessary and therefore possible," Robert Maynard Hutchins avers.[2] But demonstrating the need for an institution does not bring it into existence. And were world government attempted, we might find ourselves dying in the attempt to unite, or uniting and living a life worse than death.

The third image, like the first two, leads directly to a utopian prescription. In each image a cause is identified in terms of which all others are to be understood. The force of the logical relation between the third image and the world-government prescription is great enough to cause some to argue not only the merits of world government but also the ease with which it can be realized.[3] It is of course true that with world government there would no longer be international wars, though with an ineffective world government there would no doubt be civil wars. It is likewise true, reverting to the first two images, that without the imperfections of the separate states there would not be wars, just as it is true that a society of perfectly rational beings, or of perfect Christians, would never know violent conflict. These statements are, unfortunately, as trivial as they are true. They have the unchallengeable quality of airtight tautologies: perfectly good states or men will not do bad things; within an effective organization highly damaging deviant behavior is not permitted. The near perfection required by concentration upon a single cause accounts for a number of otherwise puzzling facts: the pessimism of St. Augustine, the failure of the behavioral scientists as prescribers for peace, the reliance of many liberals on the forces of history to produce a result not conceivably to be produced by the consciously directed efforts of men, the tendency of socialists to identify a corrupting element every time harmony in socialist action fails to appear. It also helps to explain the often rapid alternation of hope and despair among those who most fully adopt a single-cause approach to this or to almost any other problem. The belief that to make the world better requires changing the factors that operate within a precisely defined realm leads to despair whenever it becomes apparent that changes there, if possible at all, will come slowly and with insufficient force. One is constantly defeated by the double problem of demonstrating how the "necessary changes" can be produced and of substantiating the assertion that the changes described as necessary would be sufficient to accomplish the object in view.

The contrary assertion, that all causes may be interrelated, is an argument against assuming that there is a single cause that can be isolated by analysis and eliminated or controlled by wisely constructed policy. It is also an argument against working with one or several hypotheses without bearing in mind the interrelation of all causes. The prescriptions directly derived from a single image are incomplete because they are based upon partial analyses. The partial quality of each image sets up a tension that drives one toward inclusion of the others. With the first image the direction of change, representing Locke's perspective as against Plato's, is from men to societies and states. The second image catches up both elements. Men make states, *and* states make men; but this is still a limited view. One is led to a search for the more inclusive nexus of causes, for states are shaped by the international environment as are men by both the national and international environments. Most of those whom we have considered in preceding chapters have not written entirely in terms of one image. That we have thus far been dealing with the consequences arising from differing degrees of emphasis accounts for the complexity of preceding chapters but now makes somewhat easier the task of suggesting how the images can be interrelated without distorting any one of them.

The First and Second Images in Relation to the Third

It may be true that the Soviet Union poses the greatest threat of war at the present time. It is not true that were the Soviet Union to disappear the remaining states could easily live at peace. We have known wars for centuries; the Soviet Union has existed only for decades. But some states, and perhaps some forms of the state, are more peacefully inclined than others. Would not the multiplication of peacefully inclined states at least warrant the hope that the period between major wars might be extended? By emphasizing the relevance of the framework of action, the third image makes clear the misleading quality of such partial analyses and of the hopes that are often based upon them. The act that by individual moral standards would be applauded may, when performed by a state, be an invitation to the war we seek to avoid. The third image, taken not as a theory of world government but as a theory of the conditioning effects of the state system itself, alerts us to the fact that so far as increasing the chances of peace is concerned there is no such thing as an act good in itself. The pacification of the Hukbalahaps was a clear and direct contribution to the peace and order of the Philippine state. In international politics a partial "solution," such as one major country becoming pacifistic, might be a real contribution to world peace; but it might as easily hasten the coming of another major war.

The third image, as reflected in the writings of Rousseau, is based on an analysis of the consequences arising from the framework of state action. Rousseau's explanation of the origin of war among states is, in broad outline, the final one so long as we operate within a nation-state system. It is a final explanation because it does not hinge on accidental causes—irrationalities in men, defects in states—but upon his theory of the framework within which *any* accident can bring about a war. That state A wants certain things that it can get only by war does not explain war. Such a desire may or may not lead to war. My wanting a million dollars does not cause me to rob a bank, but if it were easier to rob banks, such desires would lead to much more bank robbing. This does not alter the fact that some people will and some will not attempt to rob banks no matter what the law enforcement situation is. We still have to look to motivation and circumstance in order to explain individual acts. Nevertheless one can predict that, other things being equal, a weakening of law enforcement agencies will lead to an increase in crime. From this point of view it is social structure—institutionalized restraints and institutionalized methods of altering and adjusting interests—that counts. And it counts in a way different from the ways usually associated with the word "cause." What causes a man to rob a bank are such things as the desire for money, a disrespect for social proprieties, a certain boldness. But if obstacles to the operation of these causes are built sufficiently high, nine out of ten would-be bank robbers will live their lives peacefully plying their legitimate trades. If the framework is to be called cause at all, it had best be specified that it is a permissive or underlying cause of war.

Applied to international politics this becomes, in words previously used to summarize Rousseau, the proposition that wars occur because there is nothing to prevent them. Rousseau's analysis explains the recurrence of war without explaining any given war. He tells us that war may at any moment occur, and he tells us why this is so. But the structure of the state system does not directly cause state A to attack state B. Whether or not that attack occurs will depend on a number of special circumstances—location, size, power, interest, type of government, past history and tradition—each of which will influence the actions of both states. If they fight against each other it will be for reasons especially defined for the occasion by each of them. These special reasons become the immediate, or efficient, causes of war. These immediate causes of war are contained in the first and second images. States are motivated to attack each other and to defend themselves by the reason and/or passion of the comparatively few who make policies for states and of the many more who influence the few. Some states, by virtue of their internal conditions, are both more proficient in war and more inclined to put their proficiency to the test. Variations in the factors included in the first and second images are important, indeed crucial, in the making and breaking of periods of peace—the immediate causes of every war must be either the acts of individuals or the acts of states.

If every war is preceded by acts that we can identify (or at least try to identify) as cause, then why can we not eliminate wars by modifying individual or state behavior? This is the line of thinking followed by those who say: To end war, improve men; or: To end war, improve states. But in such prescriptions the role of the international environment is easily distorted. How can some of the acting units improve while others continue to follow their old and often predatory ways? The simplistic assumption of many liberals, that history moves relentlessly toward the millennium, is refuted if the international environment makes it difficult almost to the point of impossibility for states to behave in ways that are progressively more moral. Two points are omitted from the prescriptions we considered under the first and second images: (1) If an effect is produced by two or more causes, the effect is not permanently eliminated by removing one of them. If wars occur because men are less than perfectly rational and because states are less than perfectly formed, to improve only states may do little to decrease the number and intensity of wars. The error here is in identifying one cause where two or more may operate. (2) An endeavor launched against one cause to the neglect of others may make the situation worse instead of better. Thus, as the Western democracies became more inclined to peace, Hitler became more belligerent. The increased propensity to peace of some participants in international politics may increase, rather than decrease, the likelihood of war. This illustrates the role of the permissive cause, the international environment. If there were but two loci of cause involved, men and states, we could be sure that the appearance of more peacefully inclined states would, at worst, not damage the cause of world peace. Whether or not a remedy proposed is truly a remedy or actually worse than none at all depends, however, on the content and timing of the acts of all states. This is made clear in the third image.

War may result because state A has something that state B wants. The efficient cause of the war is the desire of state B; the permissive cause is the fact that there is nothing to prevent state B from undertaking the risks of war. In a different circumstance, the interrelation of efficient and permissive causes becomes still closer. State A may fear that if it does not cut state B down a peg now, it may be unable to do so ten years from now. State A becomes the aggressor in the present because it fears what state B may be able to do in the future. The efficient cause of such a war is derived from the cause that we have labeled permissive. In the first case, conflicts arise from disputes born of specific issues. In an age of hydrogen bombs, no single issue may be worth the risk of full-scale war. Settlement, even on bad grounds, is preferable to self-destruction. The use of reason would seem to require the adoption of a doctrine of "non-recourse to force." One whose reason leads him down this path is following the trail blazed by Cobden when in 1849 he pointed out "that it is almost impossible, on looking back for the last hundred years, to tell precisely what any war was about," and thus implied that Englishmen should never have become involved in them.[4] He is falling into the trap that ensnared A. A. Milne when he explained the First World War as a war in which ten million men died because Austria-Hungary sought, unsuccessfully, to avenge the death of one archduke.[5] He is succumbing to the illusion of Sir Edward Grey who, in the memoirs he wrote some thirty years ago, hoped that the horrors of the First World War would make it possible for nations "to find at least one common ground on which they should come together in confident understanding: an agreement that, in the disputes between them, war must be ruled out as a means of settlement that entails ruin." [6]

It is true that the immediate causes of many wars are trivial. If we focus upon them, the failure to agree to settlement without force appears to be the ultimate folly. But it is not often true that the immediate causes provide sufficient explanation for the wars that have occurred. And if it is not simply particular disputes that produce wars, rational settlement of them cannot eliminate war. For, as Winston Churchill has written, "small matters are only the symptoms of the dangerous disease, and are only important for that reason. Behind them lie the interests, the passions and the destiny of mighty races of men; and long antagonisms express themselves in trifles." [7] Nevertheless Churchill may be justified in hoping that the fear induced by a "balance of terror" will produce a temporary truce. Advancing technology makes war more horrible and presumably increases the desire for peace; the very rapidity of the advance makes for uncertainty in everyone's military planning and destroys the possibility of an accurate estimate of the likely opposing forces. Fear and permanent peace are more difficult to equate. Each major advance in the technology of war has found its prophet ready to proclaim that war is no longer possible: Alfred Nobel and dynamite, for example, or Benjamin Franklin and the lighter-than-air balloon. There may well have been a prophet to proclaim the end of tribal warfare when the spear was invented and another to make a similar prediction when poison was first added to its tip. Unfortunately, these prophets have all been false. The development of atomic and hydrogen weapons may nurture the peace wish of some, the war sentiment of others. In the United States and elsewhere after the Second World War, a muted theme of foreign-policy debate was the necessity of preventive war—drop the bomb quickly before the likely opponent in a future war has time to make one of his own. Even with two or more states equipped with similar weapon systems, a momentary shift in the balance of terror, giving a decisive military advantage temporarily to one state, may tempt it to seize the moment in order to escape from fear. And the temptation would be proportionate to the fear itself. Finally, mutual fear of big weapons may produce, instead of peace, a spate of smaller wars.

The fear of modern weapons, of the danger of destroying the civilizations of the world, is not sufficient to establish the conditions of peace identified in our discussions of the three images of international relations. One can equate fear with world peace only if the peace wish exists in all states and is uniformly expressed in their policies. But peace is the primary goal of few men or states. If it were the primary goal of even a single state, that state could have peace at any time—simply by surrendering. But, as John Foster Dulles so often warns, "Peace can be a cover whereby evil men perpetrate diabolical wrongs." [8] The issue in a given dispute may not be: Who shall gain from it? It may instead be: Who shall dominate the world? In such circumstances, the best course of even reasonable men is difficult to define; their ability always to contrive solutions without force, impossible to assume. If solutions in terms of none of the three images is presently—if ever—possible, then reason can work only within the framework that is suggested by viewing the first and second images in the perspective of the third, a perspective well and simply set forth in the *Federalist Papers,* especially in those written by Hamilton and Jay.

What would happen, Jay asks, if the thirteen states, instead of combining as one state, should form themselves into several confederations? He answers:

Instead of their being "joined in affection" and free from all apprehension of different "interests," envy and jealousy would soon extinguish confidence and affection, and the partial interests of each confederation, instead of the general interests of all America, would be the only objects of their policy and pursuits. Hence, like most *bordering* nations, they would always be either involved in disputes and war, or live in the constant apprehension of them.[9]

International anarchy, Jay is here saying, is the explanation for international war. But not international anarchy alone. Hamilton adds that to presume a lack of hostile motives among states is to forget that men are "ambitious, vindictive, and rapacious." A monarchical state may go to war because the vanity of its king leads him to seek glory in military victory; a republic may go to war because of the folly of its assembly or because of its commercial interests. That the king may be vain, the assembly foolish, or the commercial interests irreconcilable: none of these is inevitable. However, so many and so varied are the causes of war among states that "to look for a continuation of harmony between a number of independent, unconnected sovereigns in the same neighborhood, would be to disregard the uniform course of human events, and to set at defiance the accumulated experience of the ages."[10]

Jay and Hamilton found in the history of the Western state system confirmation for the conclusion that among separate sovereign states there is constant possibility of war. The third image, as constructed in Chapter VI, gives a theoretical basis for the same conclusion. It reveals why, in the absence of tremendous changes in the factors included in the first and second images, war will be perpetually associated with the existence of separate sovereign states. The obvious conclusion of a third-image analysis is that world government is the remedy for world war. The remedy, though it may be unassailable in logic, is unattainable in practice. The third image may provide a utopian approach to world politics. It may also provide a realistic approach, and one that avoids the tendency of some realists to attribute the necessary amorality, or even immorality, of world politics to the inherently bad character of man. If everyone's strategy depends upon everyone else's, then the Hitlers determine in part the action, or better, reaction, of those whose ends are worthy and whose means are fastidious. No matter how good their intentions, policy makers must bear in mind the implications of the third image, which can be stated in summary form as follows: Each state pursues its own interests, however defined, in ways it judges best. Force is a means of achieving the external ends of states because there exists no consistent, reliable process of reconciling the conflicts of interest that inevitably arise among similar units in a condition of anarchy. A foreign policy based on this image of international relations is neither moral nor immoral, but embodies merely a reasoned response to the world about us. The third image describes the framework of world politics, but without the first and second images there can be no knowledge of the forces that determine policy; the first and second images describe the forces in world politics, but without the third image it is impossible to assess their importance or predict their results.

NOTES

1. J. S. Mill, *Letters,* ed. Elliot, I, 222.
2. Hutchins, "The Constitutional Foundations for World Order," in *Foundations for World Order,* p. 105.
3. Cf. Popper, *The Open Society and Its Enemies,* pp. 158–59, 574–79; Esslinger, *Politics and Science, passim.*
4. Cobden, *Speeches,* ed. Bright and Rogers, II, 165.
5. Milne, *Peace with Honour,* p. 11.
6. Grey, *Twenty-five Years,* II, 285.
7. Churchill, *The World Crisis, 1911–1914,* I, 52.
8. "Excerpts from Dulles Address on Peace" (Washington, April 11, 1955), in New York *Times,* April 12, 1955, p. 6.
9. *The Federalist,* pp. 23–24 (No. 5).
10. *Ibid.,* pp. 27–28 (No. 6); cf. p. 18 (No. 4, Jay), and pp. 34–40 (No. 7, Hamilton).

NUCLEAR DETERRENCE: THE BALANCE OF TERROR

8.

Klaus Knorr: The Great Nuclear Powers

A dominant characteristic of the contemporary international system is the nuclear balance of terror—mutual deterrence resting on the exploitation by the super-powers of the fear of atomic holocaust. In explaining the balance of terror, Klaus Knorr points out that in the nuclear age it is the risk of nuclear war which is manipulated, rather than war itself; the utility of military force has been reduced due to the potential scale of destruction, the superiority of the offensive, uncertainties about capabilities, and the range and speed of nuclear weapons. Political, psychological, and technological factors are joined as uncertainty about future developments provides "perhaps the best available basis for a lasting balance of terror."

Professor of International Affairs at Princeton University and former director of Princeton's Center of International Studies, Klaus Knorr is the author of many national security policy studies, including *War Potential of Nations* and *Military Power and Potential.*

The preceding chapter discussed some "costs," and hence restraints, on the use of national military power as if nuclear arms did not exist. But these restraints, though now of greater magnitude and impact than they were even three decades ago, are precipitants of social, economic, and political forces that have been operating over a considerable past, and that would have generated these effects even if nuclear weaponry had not been invented. They are connected with the development of modern science and technology, and the progressive industrialization and economic development of human societies. Nuclear armaments, and the particular restraints on the employment of military power that their characteristics stimulated, are also, of course, a product and result of modern science and technology. But they are a precipitant more recent in origin.

As suggested in Chapter I, if we are interested in changes in the utility of military power, we are concerned with the utility of international war, the utility of military threats, and the utility derived from the mere possession of military forces. These distinctions serve a purpose since, although the different kinds of utilities are obviously related, any changes in the utility of military power need not produce equal changes in the other utilities. Unhappily for the purpose of clear exposition, all these utilities are a function of many variable factors, and concentration on any one runs the danger of seemingly ignoring or belittling the others. Thus, any one of the utilities is a function (1) of how the military capabilities of possible opponents compare quantitatively and qualitatively in military effectiveness; (2) of the stakes involved in a clash of interests; (3) of the skill of statesmen and military leaders; (4) of the propensity of governments and generals to accept risks and to behave rationally; (5) of the character and strength of domestic political support; and (6) of moral, political, and legal restraints. But they are also a function of what concerns us at this point—namely, the properties of military technology. Focusing now on this factor, we may argue as follows: If, as a general phenomenon in the international system, the utility of international war rose or declined, one would logically expect the utility of military threats and of military capabilities to change in the same direction, and this especially if one disregards, as this essay does, the domestic uses of military forces. After all, a threat would be useless if the flat disutility of proceeding to war were known to all parties concerned; and the mere possession of armed forces is useful as long as they are usable—that is, if they enable a government to utter a threat or counter-threat, or to precipitate or join in war. It is on this usability of military forces, and the anticipation that they may be used, that their value rests. However, even if—as a result of changes in military technology—the several utilities change in the same direction, these changes tend not to be proportionate. Thus, if the utility of resorting to war declines as a result of technological factors, the utility of threats will tend to decline less, since the threatening party need not be compelled to make good its threat and since the recipient of a threat may not be sure whether the threatening government is purely bluffing or apt to behave irrationally. The utility derived from the mere possession of armed forces should also decline less, since the potential threat or counterthreat implicit in the possession of armed forces produces this value without the disadvantage attached to an explicit threat—namely, that an unheeded threat may compel the threatening power to choose between executing the threatening action or having its threat revealed as a bluff.

The New Military Technology

We have said, and must reiterate, that observable shifts in the utility of national military power—and changes in the usability of military forces—make it clear that these effects are highly sensitive to variable conditions. The form of military force is one of these conditions. As we all know, the emergence of nuclear weapons—by which we mean nuclear explosives, associated delivery vehicles, and supporting infrastructure—has had a truly revolutionary impact on the nature of armed conflict and, indeed, on the nature of military security. It has sharply impinged on the usability of military capabilities, primarily as the result of five properties and consequences.

First is the enormous increase in the scale of destruction. One should not forget, to be sure, that scientific and technological advance, and the ability of industrial nations to pour huge amounts of capital into the military sector, had been rapidly increasing the destructiveness of weapons for some time. The devastation visited on Germany in World War II was unprecedented in terms of previous experience; and, had nuclear arms not been introduced, weapons of greater destructive power would no doubt have been developed in any case. However, the destructive capacity of nuclear weaponry represents a revolutionary progression; it involves a "quantum jump" of stupendous and awesome proportions. The two nuclear superpowers possess the means to snuff out human life on a gigantic, if not exhaustive, scale.

Second, there is at present the enormous technological superiority of offensive over defensive forces. Although the offensive has enjoyed technological superiority over the defensive at various times in the past, such superiority was not coupled with the immense destructive power now available. Over the hundred or so years preceding 1945, defensive weaponry was technologically somewhat superior to offensive arms, so that offensive victory was usually the fruit of great superiority in numbers, tactical surprise, vastly better generalship or morale, or was achieved at the expense of disproportionately large casualties.

The decisive domination of the offense that prevails at the present time has made the nation-state, and especially its population and accumulated wealth, strikingly more vulnerable than was the case before. According to the brilliant analysis of John Herz, the very *raison d'être* of the nation-state resided in its ability to lend military protection and security to the population it encompassed by surrounding itself with a "hard shell" of armies and fortifications that were effective in obstructing foreign penetration into the "soft interior," and thus afforded a basic "impermeability."[1] As Herz notes, this impermeability began, in fact, to diminish as—with increasing economic development and international economic specialization—the nation-state became, at least for a time, less self-sufficient and thus vulnerable to economic blockade in time of war. The new trend toward "total war" observable during World War I, which led to civilians being regarded as legitimate objects of warfare by means of economic blockade, exploited this vulnerability; and with the development of efficient aircraft, "the roof blew off the territorial state," [2] as World War II amply demonstrated. This development has now culminated in the huge destructiveness of nuclear explosives, against which, so far at least, there is no effective defense affording protection to territories and populations. The "hard shell" of the nation-state has been shattered and, as Herz suggests, the age of "territoriality" has passed. The classic nation-state has perhaps lost its principal *raison d'être*.[3] Today it looks as if unlimited might is associated with absolute impotence.[4] If and to the extent that this is true, military superiority has ceased to be meaningful, and it will remain so as long as offensive forces retain the towering dominance they have achieved as a result of the number and relative invulnerability of nuclear weapons, the speed with which attack can be launched and consummated, and the unlimited choice of targets available to the attacker.

The third characteristic concerns the greatly enhanced uncertainties about the capabilities of military forces and about international relationships of military power—coupled as these uncertainties are with the certitude of immense destructiveness. Nations lack experience with the strategic and tactical use of sophisticated nuclear weapons, and governments disposing of nuclear armament are today far less knowledgeable than they were before the nuclear age about the military effectiveness of their own armed forces and especially about those of their prospective opponents. Not surprisingly, the experts are setting more store by gaming exercises. War gaming has acquired greater conceptual refinement and uses the new powerful tool of the electronic computer. Yet the results of simulation are necessarily sensitive to the design of programs. The good design presupposes an input of knowledge that is hard to come by, harder to validate, and incapable of commanding full confidence.

The decrease in military knowledge stems chiefly from the fact that highly qualitative technical features of increasingly sophisticated nuclear weapons, delivery mechanisms and facilities for command and control have become crucially important to their functioning; that the pursuit of the technological arms race leads to the continuous "improvement" and change of these features; and that their design is readily surrounded by a wall of secrecy. In consequence, international differences in military capabilities are much harder to estimate, and the outcome of any future contest of arms has become more chancy than used to be the case.

To be sure, military power has never been easy to measure, and international differences in military strength were therefore always difficult to calculate and easy to misapprehend. In addition to constituents that could be counted readily—battleships, regiments, and guns—there were always the imponderables of qualitative differences in generalship and troop morale, and the possible intervention of accidental conditions, such as weather and disease.

Nor were generals free from ignorance and often grossly mistaken ideas about the implications of new weaponry. Before 1914, for instance, Marshall Foch based his famous and fatal strategy of *l'offensive à l'outrance* on the flat assumption, subsequently proven wrong, that all improvements in firearms added to the strength of the offensive.[5]

But the problem of calculating and comparing military power has now become still more difficult. Who, for example, can trust his imagination to foresee the pace of battle fought with tactical nuclear weapons on both sides? Moreover, the problem has become more important as the consequences of a mistaken estimate have grown more fatal. Error was more tolerable when war was —for technological as well as political reasons—less destructive of civilian populations and more limited in its consequences; decisions to go to war were more readily made. Today, the consequences of error have become dire. The uncertainties make any but the grossest known imbalances in military strength a dubious basis for military planning and high decisions of states. Technical military uncertainties are thus compounded by uncertainty about what hostile governments—facing doubts and the colossal risks of a false step—will choose to do in an emergency. Finally, should belligerents blunder into all-out nuclear war, they might be unable to end the war fast enough to prevent mutual mass destruction. These various uncertainties, in fact, contribute appreciably to deterring any decision to precipitate war.

Fourth, there is the dramatically increased, and indeed global, reach of nuclear weaponry. Nuclear warheads capable of delivery by long-range aircraft, intercontinental rockets, and roaming ships can be launched against targets anywhere on the globe, and exploded on target with great dispatch. Until these appalling weapons appeared on the scene, the military power of a nation inevitably declined as it moved away from its home base. The cost of transmitting power over space, this "loss-of-strength gradient,"[6] is still effective for conventional—that is, non-nuclear and non-strategic—forces; and, to that extent, geography and distance remain important. If nuclear weapons are not available or usable, it still makes a big difference to military operations that Korea is a peninsula and Taiwan an island—and both therefore subject to the influence of sea power, with its relatively low transportation costs—that South Vietnam has a very long coastline, and that Manchuria, the main area of China's industrial war potential, is far from South Vietnam. But as far as long-range nuclear weapons are concerned, the cost of transmitting military power has fallen dramatically. In this respect, too, the world has "shrunk." Against a nuclear great power there is no safety anywhere.

Finally, there is the fabulous speed with which nuclear weapons can reach their targets. This also represents an important difference between the present and the pre-nuclear past. Although the phenomenon of the *Blitzkrieg* has been observable through the ages, armies and navies were cumbersome and slow; belligerents relied on the mobilization of additional military strength while hostilities were in progress; and war was therefore ordinarily slow in gathering momentum. This ponderousness gave governments time to consider and reconsider, especially when war had been precipitated by mistake, and enabled them to negotiate its end before destruction reached too large a scale. This potential margin of security may have gone, or at least become much less reliable, with the advent of nuclear armament.

All five changes tend to restrict, singly and together, the usability and hence the political utility of national military power in various ways. Their overall impact is indeed easy to perceive. However, in order to improve our understanding of these developments, and their consequences, we must once again note how they vary with circumstance.

The Confrontation of the Superpowers

As between the two major nuclear powers, the strategic nuclear weapons of each are capable of visiting quick and enormous destruction on the civilian populations of the other. Adequate defenses do not at present exist, if by "adequate" we mean defenses capable of reducing casualties to a magnitude approaching the levels sustained by Germany, Japan, and the Soviet Union during the Second World War. The United States is at present following a policy aimed at damage limitation, in the event of strategic war, as well as one aimed at deterring attack. However, according to Mr. McNamara, the Secretary of Defense, this country would suffer civilian casualties numbered in the tens of millions if the Soviet Union were to launch a large-scale and efficient attack and did not go out of its way to minimize the destruction of cities. "Damage limitation" apparently cannot prevent catastrophic damage. The present position of the USSR is estimated to be no better, and almost certainly is appreciably worse. Nor can civilian populations at this time receive adequate protection by the execution of a pre-emptive strike against the opponent's attack forces. The "survivability" which missile launchers have acquired by means of hardening, dispersion, mobility, concealment, and sheer numbers discourages pre-emption. In the pre-nuclear age, a state was unable to inflict such an enormous degree of damage before it had defeated the opponent's armed forces and, after victory, it had normally no cause to inflict such damage, since the vanquished power gave in. The war was over. As long as the outcome of battle was sufficiently indeterminate, as it frequently was, and military defeat uncertain, the risk of war was often accepted; that is, the value at stake in international conflict seemed to justify acceptance of the estimated consequences of hostilities. The prospects of large-scale nuclear war are utterly different now that the offense has an overwhelming advantage over defensive forces.

As long as these conditions—the conditions of the mutual balance of terror—prevail, it is hard to think of conflict objectives valuable enough to justify the deliberate initiation of large-scale nuclear war. The disproportion between the military means and any conceivable foreign-policy objective is so vast that such an act would be irrational. It is true, of course, that deterrence depends, strictly speaking, not only on the devastation an attacking nation must expect to absorb but also on the gains expected from nuclear war. As long as both antagonists must expect to suffer enormous damage, however, no conceivable gains could offset or exceed the losses, and self-deterrence results unless irrationality intervenes. Under this condition, it is widely deduced, the threat of precipitating such a war for the purpose of enforcing foreign-policy demands on a major nuclear power is bound to lack credibility. It is not surprising that Herman Kahn speaks of a widespread feeling of "nuclear incredulity." [7]

In terms of the national effort expended on them, strategic nuclear forces are certainly very important military capabilities maintained in the United States and the Soviet Union. Military forces of this importance have in the past served as a useful instrument in the pursuit of a wide range of foreign-policy objectives. However, strategic nuclear forces do not command this broad and diffuse usefulness. This does not mean, of course, that they lack utility from the viewpoint of one nuclear power confronting another. But their usefulness is narrow and specific, for it rests primarily on the ability to deter nuclear attack. Now that nuclear arms exist, this deterrent value may afford the leaders of the major nuclear powers utility as great as, or greater than, the utility that military power has ever offered to political leaders. What we are compelled to deduce, however, is that strategic nuclear forces do not have the *scope* of usefulness that non-nuclear powers possessed in the past.

Moreover, the existence of strategic nuclear weapons casts a shadow on the value of hypothetical limited conflicts in which strategic weapons are not employed. Any limited conflict—for instance, a conventional war—between nuclear powers carries the risk of escalating to the strategic level at which, as long as the mutual balance of terror prevails, the pay-offs are hugely negative for both contestants. The risk of *deliberate* escalation may be small, if not infinitesimal, under these conditions; the risk of *inadvertent* escalation may be greater. To the extent that this risk inhibits lesser military conflict between nuclear powers, the existence of strategic nuclear weapons also reduces the scope of useful purposes to which limited-war capabilities, especially non-nuclear forces, may be put. The risk of the inadvertent outbreak of strategic nuclear war, while the balance of terror prevails, is hard to estimate; and when the consequences involved are so fatal, even a small risk is a serious matter. In the pre-nuclear past, certainly, war has often come about by mistake. World War I was in 1914 unpremeditated by all major governments involved; and in 1939, Hitler did not expect his aggressive moves to entail the large-scale prolonged war which World War II became. Such precedents would be ominous indeed were it not for the fact that the governments of the two superpowers are keenly aware of this danger and utterly determined to escape it. This is part of the self-deterrence which is implicit in mutual deterrence. As a result, these governments treat each other with great circumspection when entangled in a serious crisis.

The two governments acted with such caution in the several crises in and over Berlin. In each case the Soviet government, which initiated these crises, increased the pressure step by cautious step, taking discriminating care that no new move was apt to provoke a violent response. By using the government of the German Democratic Republic for implementing many of the moves—a classical example of acting by proxy—the Soviet Union left itself avenues for retreat that it could tread without intolerable loss of face; and in each instance the Soviet Union eventually withdrew from its extreme demand and accepted a compromise. Again, both governments exhibited exemplary prudence when they confronted one another in the course of the Cuban missiles crisis in 1962. Though we know nothing about the deliberations that took place in the Kremlin, the record of Khrushchev's acts and his communications to President Kennedy give evidence of the care he took to prevent a further intensification of the crisis. On the American side, several firsthand accounts of the labors in the White House have been made public. They disclose the most painstaking dedication to prudence and restraint, even though the government was staunchly determined to have the Soviet missiles removed from Cuban soil.[8] It can also be taken for granted that both powers have taken utmost care to prevent the sort of failure in command and control that figures so luridly in fictional accounts of how a future nuclear war might break out.

And yet the inadvertent precipitation of nuclear war remains a substantial risk. One crisis, or even several crises, well managed do not insure that every crisis will subside or be terminated without a fatal misstep. Governments *are* capable of blunder; and, after all, Khrushchev evidently acted on a serious miscalculation of likely United States reactions when he authorized Soviet missiles to be emplaced in Cuba. Risks are hard to calculate. As we shall develop below, communication may well fail at the critical moment; an actor may be tempted to sail too close to the wind in pressing his opponent; the assumption of perfect rationality is not calculated to dissipate worry; and too often in the human situation events dominate intentions.

Thus, against whatever utility nuclear powers derive from their ability to deter strategic war and, to a lesser extent, limited war between one another must be set the *disutility* that general war, which it is in the strongest interest of each to avoid, may nevertheless occur by mistake or accident. The proponents of disarmament are aware of this. They are convinced that this situation puts a premium on greater human wisdom, rationality, and restraint, on safer containment of imprudence, passion, and stupidity, than past governments have been able to muster over any length of time. To the disarmer, national armaments evidently represent a net disutility.

However, the conclusion so far reached calls for refinement. Several qualifications come to mind. First, nuclear weapons are not, of course, all alike in purpose, explosive yield, and other relevant properties. At least by objective standards, they differ in the threatened scale of destruction, and should also differ in their escalatory potential. Might they not also differ in usability, and hence in utility? For instance, how do essentially defensive systems such as atomic demolition munitions and anti-submarine and anti-aircraft weapons, with nuclear warheads, differ in the threatened scale of destruction from similar non-nuclear weapons? If a bridge is destroyed by a nuclear demolition charge, and a submarine sunk or an aircraft shot down by means of a nuclear explosive, no more destruction has taken place than if non-nuclear ammunition had been used, except for the effects of a small amount of radioactive fall-out, and that can be minimized by proper design of the explosive and a judicious choice of yield.

And, are certain "clean" tactical nuclear weapons of very small yield not simply accomplishing a given destructive mission more economically, in terms of delivery effort, than a larger mass of conventional explosives? Are nuclear weapons detonated over one's own territory as escalatory as such weapons exploded on the territory of an adversary? Will even one strategic nuclear weapon, fired in order to symbolize resolve in an intense crisis—perhaps while a local military conflict is in process—and with due care to minimize or avoid damage, necessarily touch off a large-scale exchange involving disaster on both sides?

These questions cannot be answered now, at least with anything approaching confidence. What matters here is not so much that weapons and modes of employing them differ appreciably by objective standards, as how the governments of the great nuclear powers structure their perceptions and responses; and this would seem to depend upon whether or not opponents agree—either at the time of crisis or beforehand, and either tacitly or formally—that these distinctions are relevant and should guide their conflict behavior. Whether this agreement will occur or not, we do not know at this time. However, if it did come about, such agreement would tend to make nuclear weapons of some types, or in particular forms of employment, more widely usable—that is to say, extend their utility beyond the narrow range likely to obtain without such agreement.

Second, in the United States, and to some extent also in the Soviet Union, there has been a keen speculative interest in the notion of "firebreaks"—restraints on the conduct of military conflict designed to prevent, or at least impede, escalation from lower to higher levels of violence. They are marked by distinctions, easily recognized, for limiting force.[9] One function attributed to "firebreaks" is that of controlling inadvertent escalation, by giving two nuclear powers suddenly caught in the unplanned eruption of a minor conflict time to ascertain the opponent's intentions, to come to their senses, and to terminate the conflict before it moves up the escalation ladder. Another function sometimes attributed to "firebreaks" is that of permitting the conduct of low-level, and presumably localized, conflict without an unacceptable risk of escalation to a level of warfare which it is in the interest of both adversaries to avoid.[10] Thus, some experts believe that there is a great difference in escalatory potential between the use of conventional armaments and tactical nuclear weapons, and that escalation of limited conflict could be more easily controlled if the use of any nuclear arms were forgone. Others have argued that, if both nuclear powers have an overwhelming interest in shunning mutual mass destruction, even the employment of non-strategic nuclear weapons, or the non-strategic use of nuclear weapons, should be safe.

This second function of "firebreaks" would serve the purpose of extending the utility of conventional or non-strategic nuclear armaments in conflicts between nuclear powers, though they would do so by depriving strategic weapons of their ability to deter all kinds of conflicts between such powers. War at a restricted level of violence would become more feasible than it would be if escalation were impossible or very hard to control.

If limited local war is to provide a terminal stage of military conflict between the superpowers, both must necessarily find an outcome more appealing than exposure to more violent levels of conflict. Regarding the threshold marked by the introduction of tactical nuclear arms in a local war, it has indeed been argued forcefully that this firebreak is broad and reliable as long as the governments of both powers are inspired by a stark fear of all-out strategic war, and are afraid that escalation is much more probable once any kind of nuclear arms, especially tactical nuclear weapons, are introduced. The more they fear that escalation may be automatic after the nuclear threshold has been crossed, the more they should be aware of the fact that crossing that threshold means entrusting one's destiny to a possibly reckless opponent. Under these circumstances, it is said, the fear of violating the most critical threshold will induce the superpowers to proceed with utmost restraint, and make them most reluctant to escalate a local engagement conducted with non-nuclear arms.[11] In the United States, under the administration of President Kennedy, this set of arguments led to a considerable build-up of conventional forces, based on the so-called doctrine of flexible response. According to this strategic doctrine, the United States must have military capabilities enabling it to proportion any military response to its particular provocation and not to remain excessively dependent on a threat of nuclear retaliation, for this deterrent threat might confront the country with the awful dilemma, in the event that a crisis involves important values, of whether to escalate to the holocaust of mutual annihilation or to give in to the adversary's pressure and ruthlessness. Such an "impossible choice" would almost surely produce a "paralysis of decision."[12]

Several arguments can be raised against this line of reasoning. It may well be true that military escalation can be controlled as long as the application of force remains highly localized and adheres to an exceedingly low level of violence. This happened during the Cuban missiles crisis, which was satisfactorily resolved, although under the shadow of strategic nuclear capabilities. In this instance, progressive escalation was not at all automatic; there proved to be "down escalators" as well as "up escalators."[13] On such a relatively low level of conflict, the communication of resolve or despair may restrain an opponent from proceeding to a more serious provocation, and thus in effect prevent war. Yet it is hard to see that escalation would be as easy to control if troops of the two superpowers were engaged in considerable and prolonged combat with one another, if casualties had occurred, and if—as would be likely—the original stakes of conflict had become inflated by the very fact that a military engagement was taking place. Several factors might push one or the other government to make the conflagration leap across the firebreak. A belligerent enjoying superiority on the conventional level might be tempted to press his advantage and raise the price of settlement in various ways. Contrariwise, a belligerent doing poorly in limited conflict might be tempted to improve his position by escalating to a degree. In fact, even if the governments involved were prepared to keep cool heads in a situation fraught with enormous dangers, the public in either nation—unless it were fully aware of the risks being run—might become aroused to righteous indignation and urge its government to abandon restraint.

And escalation to the employment of tactical nuclear weapons might occur because of a failure of command and control in a tense situation, or because one antagonist or both, thinking escalation imminent or unavoidable sooner or later, decided to pre-empt; and unlike present conditions on the strategic level, the advantage of striking first in a tactical situation might be considerable and attractive.

Another question may be posed. If escalation can be controlled because the interest of both antagonists to avoid large-scale strategic war is overwhelming, why should not all rungs on the escalation ladder, short of this extreme level of violence, keep conflict limited? Why should the restriction of hostilities to non-nuclear weapons be the crucial threshold? Why would a hard-pressed power not bring tactical nuclear arms into play, although perhaps with a defensive mode of employment? No matter which lower level of conflict were reached, one might speculate, the great-power belligerents would do their utmost to prevent the final step up the escalation ladder. Perhaps even limited strategic war might then be possible without escalation to the cataclysmic level.[14]

But this line of speculation also suggests that the lower-level thresholds are not very high. It can therefore be argued that the emphasis on limited war on a low level, and especially on the "conventional option," has the grave disadvantage of encouraging the aggressive initiation of such conflicts. As has been argued, this is not in the interest of nuclear great powers, for any proposed preference for limiting war to a conventional contest tends to degrade the deterrent value of their nuclear stockpiles.[15] The United States, for example, might find it far harder, with such a policy, to cope with massive Chinese aggression in Asia.[16] As we pointed out above, this is indeed a fair criticism. To increase the feasibility of limited war is to deprive, under the balance of mutual terror, strategic capabilities of their power to deter all but the mildest applications of military force against a nuclear great power. And there is a further implication to be pondered. Whichever school of thought is more realistic, it can scarcely be denied that any military conflict between nuclear powers has *some* probability of escalating—abruptly or gradually—to the large-scale strategic level, if only as a result of inadvertence. We do not wish to exaggerate this possibility, for knowledgeable leaders everywhere might well hesitate to the point of paralysis before doing anything likely to touch off a catastrophic train of events. But it cannot be taken for granted that they will succeed in averting disaster. However small, the possibility cannot be ignored. If this is conceded, then it is possible that a policy of firebreaks that encourages the initiation of limited military conflicts, or discourages them less than would be the case otherwise, may actually increase the probability of the nuclear holocaust more than a policy that keeps the danger of escalation high and thus gives the powers the strongest incentive to shun all military conflict, at least as long as the balance of terror obtains.

Since nuclear powers have hitherto avoided direct military clashes, and we lack pertinent experience, the speculations discussed above are wholly hypothetical. So much turns on the subjective perceptions of the key actors, and these are practically impossible to predict. We have no way of knowing whether, in the event of a direct military confrontation between nuclear powers, the maintenance of firebreaks would be feasible and, if so, where they would be located on the spectrum of increasing violence. It seems plausible to assume that the chances for viable firebreaks would be increased if nuclear powers firmly embedded this concept in their military doctrine and war plans, if they adjusted their military capabilities accordingly, and if—in one way or another —they let each other know that they had done so. There is no conclusive evidence that this has happened.

Soviet strategic thinking, as expressed in public, has until recently derided any idea of keeping a war between the nuclear superpowers restricted. This expression of Soviet doctrine may have been intended to serve the deterrent posture of the Soviet Union—that is, have constituted a part of its declaratory policy—and may not therefore have reflected actual Soviet thinking on the subject. It is also true that Soviet writings have expressed more recently some grudging interest in the possibility of limited local—and even entirely conventional—war in Europe and, more so, outside Europe. Yet the dominant Soviet emphasis is still on the risk that small conflicts will rapidly expand into general war; and that, once tactical nuclear weapons are brought into action, it is infeasible to distinguish between tactical and strategic targets.[17]

One is led to suspect, in conclusion, that escalation from limited conflict between nuclear powers should not be assumed to be automatic. The interests in halting it are, at present at least, very solid indeed. On the other hand, the uncertainty about whether escalation can be avoided looms very large. And this uncertainty itself is therefore apt to deter these powers from lightly initiating even the most limited application of military force against each other. This means that, given the reigning balance of terror, a structure of strategic capabilities that, in Herman Kahn's nomenclature,[18] should afford only "Type I Deterrence" affords also a considerable degree of "Type II Deterrence"—the ability to deter escalation to nuclear war from lesser and local clashes.

Another qualification that we must now introduce turns on our assumptions regarding an existing mutual balance of terror and the consequences of this balance. These assumptions must now be questioned. To begin with, the foregoing analysis treated the two nuclear powers as if they were interchangeable— that is, as if both were equally determined to avoid large-scale nuclear war. This may, in fact, be the case, at least at this juncture. Even if it is, however, it does not follow that they are of necessity equally eager to avoid or minimize the risk of such a war. Usually, the value at stake in a conflict, and other factors such as the personalities of the decision-makers, also bear on behavior under the restraint of risk. It may be assumed, of course, that such differences are likely to be of negligible or no consequence when the risk involves the disaster of nuclear war. Yet this might not be true, especially if there is an expectation that some sort of firebreak will operate in a limited conflict and greatly minimize the risk. To be sure, in such conflict each opponent would face not only the other's limited-war forces, but also *some* risk of uncontrolled escalation. But this suggests that the risk is capable of different estimation. Moreover, these conflicts would be contests of will in which opponents may attempt to manipulate the risk to their advantage. They may have a strong incentive to do so if their stake is of high value, and particularly if it seems to them more valuable than what is at stake for the other antagonist. A balance of motivation, or of resolution, thus becomes part of the effective balance of bargaining strength. There is, furthermore, also a very important skill element in the reciprocal manipulation of risk. The skill of rightly estimating the opponent's nerve and control in the course of a tense crisis may permit bargaining exploitation of what one expert has called "the narrow margin of freedom of action that eludes nuclear deterrence." [19] Perhaps not too much should be made of these possibilities, but they should not be ruled out.

What if we drop the assumption of a stable mutual balance of terror, based, as it must be, on the assured and known second-strike capability of each nuclear power to cause disastrous damage to the other's cities and population? If only one of two nuclear powers possessed this capability, it would enjoy significant military superiority over the other, and could exploit its position in order to press the other to make concessions about foreign-policy issues. Subject to restraints to be noted later, the superior power could then derive a great deal of utility from its strategic and limited-war capabilities—not perhaps from brazenly initiating or threatening war but from its lesser fear of war in the course of a diplomatic crisis; and should limited hostilities break out, it would clearly enjoy "escalation dominance." Even if the known balance of nuclear forces were such as to produce serious doubts about whether a truly mutual balance of terror prevailed, or whether one power was strategically superior to the other, the beneficiary of the doubt would be in a position to press harder than its opponent for a satisfactory settlement of disputes.

Instabilities in the Balance of Terror

The widespread conviction that the balance of terror now believed to exist between the Soviet Union and the United States will endure for a long time to come, and thus constitute a fixed datum, has been endorsed in recent years with amazing certitude. Not only has the short history of nuclear competition between the two powers been marked by remarkable ups and downs in their relative capabilities, with the United States enjoying a significant degree of superiority much of the time; this history has also revealed serious limitations to estimating and comparing the true military relationship between the two strategic capabilities without a considerable time lag. The widespread belief, in the late 1950's and in 1960, in the existence of a "missile gap" greatly favoring the USSR—a belief that was subsequently proven erroneous—is a case in point. How, then, can one be sure that the balance of terror, assuming it to hold at present, will endure in the future?

Current belief in a balance of terror is based on the assumption that each of the powers possesses an unquestionable offensive capacity to obliterate the other, even if one launches a first strike against the other's means of nuclear re-prisal, and that technology is unable to come up with active defenses against nuclear missiles efficient enough to rob the offense of its present decisive superiority. To be sure, anti-ballistic-missile (ABM) defenses have been developed, but it has been generally assumed, at least until very recently, that if one opponent deployed such defenses, the other could always saturate them if he produced—at an expense falling far short of the expense of ABM's—more missiles and a variety of penetration aids such as decoys on which ABM forces would waste the short precious time available for action against incoming missiles.

It is entirely possible, and perhaps probable, that neither the Soviet Union nor the United States will develop and deploy large-scale and near-perfect defenses. Perhaps the development of an improved ABM technology will fail to touch off a new phase in the arms race between the nuclear superpowers—a race between the means of penetration and the means of interception, between the forces for assuring the destruction of the opponent and those designed to limit the damage he can inflict. And even if both sides deploy substantial defensive capabilities, the outcome may well be that neither side will develop confidence in its ability to fend off the other's attack. But even under these assumptions, the balance of terror might be seriously affected and look more fragile than it does at the present time. Of course, the balance would gain in stability if ABM's were deployed only for protecting the retaliatory forces, thus rendering them less vulnerable than they might be otherwise, and adding assurance to each antagonist's ability to devastate the other. Yet if they were installed to afford substantial protection to populations, then they would—even were they far from perfect—introduce new uncertainties, and thus tend to destabilize the condition of nuclear terror; and this particularly if only one side proceeded to large-scale deployment.

Modern science and technology, however, are too dynamic to make one sure that ABM's will not be developed with an efficiency capable of seriously undermining, if not ending completely, the present superiority of the offense.[20] What if technology comes up with a "splendid defense"? Of course, if for a time only one side developed and installed effective defenses, it would gain a decisive strategic superiority, completely upsetting the balance of terror. Yet this is very unlikely to happen, since both sides are devoting considerable resources to relevant research and development, and since the large-scale deployment of ABM systems would probably be a gradual process, and one that could hardly be concealed from a watchful opponent. Still, a degree of temporary advantage might result. This advantage would probably not be great enough to preclude the other power's ability to deter a direct attack on itself; but it might make it attractive to the advantaged power to engineer serious crises, possibly including limited military conflict, and exact a high price for their settlement. In brief, the power with ABM success might be far less deterred than the other from initiating courses of action now considered too risky. By diminishing the opponent's confidence in his offensive power, superior defensive capabilities would encourage an aggressive posture.

Should both powers develop and deploy very good though not splendid ABM systems, mutual nuclear deterrence would certainly become more complicated than it is at present. The vulnerability of both populations, and hence their role as hostages to the good behavior of their governments, would be more or less diminished, and so would the power to deter. Even if neither side had an incentive to attack the other directly, the risks that lesser provocations might escalate to the intolerable round of destruction would be seriously impaired. Stability at the strategic level—an appreciably different stability from the present one—would be accompanied by greater instability at lower levels of international violence. In fact, the political utility of military power might be extended considerably beyond its present narrow scope.

As already acknowledged, none of this may happen. Large-scale ABM systems may not be installed, or parallel advances in offensive capabilities may checkmate the new defenses. It cannot be taken for granted, however, that it will not happen. Viewed in retrospect, the balance of terror may never have been "delicate," especially when intangibles are taken into account. But it is "too complex and too changeable" to warrant belief in its permanence.[21] This is so for several reasons. It may be upset by the development of new technology, perhaps because one power possesses better research and development resources than the other, or administers them to better effect, or is lucky in invention, or owns more skill in innovation[22]—that is, in the military exploitation of evolving technological choices. With technological invention and innovation being rather unpredictable, as they notably were during the past twenty-five years, important differences between the two powers might—for this and other reasons—develop in force structures and magnitudes, in military doctrine and in facilities for command and control; and such differences might make the balance of terror less "mutual." Differences in the information which each side possesses about the other's capabilities and plans might, from time to time, generate significant asymmetries in their ability to deter. Finally, there are various political and psychological factors that condition deterrent power, all subject over time to change that may prove destabilizing in the overall balance rather than compensatory. Leaders will change and may differ in skill, in their ability to keep cool under the stresses of crisis, in their disposition to run risks and to gamble, and in the political pressures to which they are subjected, especially in crises, by rivals for leadership, by larger publics, and by allies. The values at stake in conflict are highly variable. In other words, there is no such thing—as is too often assumed—as an absolute ability to deter, fixed in power and constant at all times regardless of changeable circumstances. Rather, the power to deter is the power to deter a particular adversary in a particular situation. These particulars are apt to change over time; and deterrence cannot be insensitive to all these changes.

Uncertainties even about the present balance of terror, dissatisfaction with the present restricted utility of military power, and uncertainties about whether the strategic balance will remain stable give the governments of both superpowers an incentive to continue the quantitative, and especially the qualitative, arms race, and thus to set in motion forces capable of upsetting the present conditions of stability. Given various uncertainties, a margin of military superiority looks desirable. The incentive to escape from their present position of being locked in a stalemate of strategic threat and counterthreat—provided there are means of escape that are technologically, economically, politically, and perhaps morally feasible—is reinforced by the desire to reduce damage in the event of inadvertent war and to counter any threat from new nuclear powers that are incapable of mounting an attack with which even ABM's of presently available properties cannot cope. Nor is the problem only one of efficient ABM's. More advanced and "exotic" weapons systems may issue from the laboratories.

It is true that the arms race is expensive and its outcome uncertain. Each side must fear that it might confer a degree of temporary advantage on the other. For each the future might be worse than the present; larger defense efforts might lead to lesser security. In terms of long-run security, therefore, both governments might recognize an interest in preserving present conditions and hence in calling off or slackening the race. The trouble is that this shared interest can be satisfied only if the suspension of the arms race is jointly organized, formally or informally. Unfortunately, the suspension of the qualitative arms race, of the pursuit of military research and development, is practically impossible to verify. Given the profusion of laboratories in each country, the evasion of an agreement, whether formal or tacit, is relatively easy; and if only for protection against the other's possible evasion, the inducement to evade is considerable. Under these circumstances, it requires a good deal of optimism to believe that the great powers will do anything else but pursue courses of action likely to undermine the degree of stability now extant. They might refrain from deploying new systems by mutual understanding; they are less likely to refrain from pressing their development; and if they believe a developed system spells a more than marginal improvement in their military capabilities, the temptation to deploy would be strong, and perhaps irresistible.

To conclude, the leaders of the two superpowers cannot know now what the opponent's force structure will be five or ten years hence. Existing known types of arms may be vastly improved, and entirely novel weapons may show up in the armories. A host of relevant political conditions may change. It is fair to ask: What does "mutuality" of deterrence mean as one tries to look into the future? Perhaps the best available basis for a lasting balance of terror will be that—although many factors in the present strategic equation change—their implication will be highly uncertain, singly and especially in combination. Utter lack of confidence in what would happen if *the* "button," or any one of a series of buttons, were pushed might for some time to come preserve the present degree of stability between the nuclear great powers.

The Restricted Usability of Military Forces

Unquestionably, the conditions, and especially the costs, of using force as an instrument of foreign policy have undergone a major permutation in the nuclear age. As between the two nuclear great powers locked in a balance of terror, military power is actively usable for a far smaller range of political purposes than was the case between great powers before the nuclear era. The very behavior of the two powers toward one another can be regarded as evidence to this effect. Even though tension between them has been high, and conflicts often sharp, they have treated each other with great circumspection in the military area; and this caution is generally credited to their eagerness to avoid general war. Indeed, this caution makes them shun any direct military confrontation. They prefer war by proxy to war between themselves. They prefer vague threats to specific threats of war. They do not seem eager to have diplomatic disputes escalate into intense crises. Hitherto their fear of monstrous destruction seems to have made them unwilling to use force or the threat of force bluntly as a sanction in diplomatic bargaining; and the movement toward a *détente* in Soviet-American relations that set in after the Cuban missiles crisis can be interpreted as manifesting a mutual desire to avoid dangerous crises.

This behavior, of course, expresses a profound appreciation of military force. Deterrence of provocative behavior rests on such appreciation. But, as we have seen, there is more to it than that. Within this tightly restrained situation, these powers tend to use their military strength on behalf of foreign-policy objectives in a subtle and highly controlled manner. The risk of escalation may be very dangerous to both; yet, if foreign-policy stakes are sufficiently high, they do not refrain from manipulating this risk to their advantage. In each past crisis, both faced the risk that a direct military confrontation might occur, and if it did, the further risk that a limited conflict would escalate. This presence of deadly risk makes each crisis a dangerous test of wills—a test in which the threat of military force is likely to be used only in a most discreet fashion, as, for example, in the course of several crises over Berlin and the crisis over the Cuban missiles. As has been observed by others, in pursuing their foreign policies and in arriving at crisis settlements, the great nuclear powers do not use nuclear war, but exploit the fear of it.[23] They exploit the risk of war rather than relative military power; they negotiate less from strength than from relative susceptibility to fear and worry.[24]

In order to understand this introduction of military power by the great powers in crisis management, we must look at the components of crisis behavior. A crisis between great powers is an unstable sequence of interactions, of tacit or explicit bargaining moves, at an intense level of confrontation that increases the probability of international violence. Nevertheless, one must not exaggerate the function of military power in crisis situations, important as it is. The personality of leaders, the freedom of action they have in terms of national politics and commitment to alliances, and the skill of governments are also important determinants of the outcome of crises, of whether they end in peaceful adjustment, or unresolved deadlock, or cause the eruption of military hostilities. The personality of leaders is important in affecting their ability to stand up under pressures, including the pressures resulting from anxiety and the speed with which events take place. Leaders also differ in rationality, the degree to which they are subject to emotion in making decisions, in their propensity to gamble and act with daring in managing a severe crisis, and so on. The freedom of action that leaders enjoy affects the range of feasible options open to them. The skill of leaders is important in how they cope with domestic pressure and the entreaties of allies; and it is crucial in managing the intergovernmental bargaining process with the adversary. This management may involve attempts to alter the opponent's perception of the situation by giving him information about one's arms, capabilities, and resolve. It involves the holding out of rewards since no crises, and especially no crisis proceeding under the shadow of nuclear capabilities, is lacking in common interests, and hence, in the language of game theory, is not merely a "zero-sum game"; it has a cooperative as well as a competitive aspect.[25] The derivation of influence from the promise of reward may take such forms as the offer of acceptable concessions to the opponent's demands and the offer of a line of retreat from excessive demands that enables him to save face before his domestic and the international public. And skill is obviously crucial in the manipulation of threats, tacit or explicit, of impending military action. The trading of threats and counter-threats goes to the heart of the test of wills; and it is the manipulation of military threats between great nuclear powers that has become so dangerous because of the looming disaster of all-out nuclear war, and the risk that lesser military confrontations may escalate to this level. As long as a balance of terror prevails between the opponents, and the temptation of a pre-emptive strike by surprise is accordingly small, there is less pressure to make fateful decisions without deliberation; and there is also hope that abrupt moves up the escalation ladder can be avoided even if a rather limited application of force takes place. Nevertheless, the trading of military threats is much more risky when the opponents are nuclear powers than usually was the case before the nuclear age. The willingness to assume the risk and, by increasing it for the opponent, also to increase it for oneself depends on the factors already mentioned (e.g., the personalities of the leaders, their freedom of action) and, in addition, on the relation of military strength, as perceived by each opponent, and on the stakes for each involved in the crisis. Thus, the risks are, or appear to be, unequal because one antagonist has, or believes he has, a significant degree of military superiority; and the issue at stake may be of much greater value to one actor than to the other. One may minimize risk by assuming bargaining positions that leave acceptable options of retreat, that balance ends and means at the least dangerous level of crisis interaction; one may raise risks by assuming positions from which one cannot extricate oneself without large disadvantages in terms of loss of face, political influence, self-respect, etc.—that is, by deliberately making commitments from which it is extremely hard to be relieved. The mutual manipulation of military threats is apt to lead to change in the actor's perceptions as the crisis proceeds, and produces a kind of quick learning process through which risks and resolve are reevaluated. Mao points out that "war is a contest of strength," but that "the original state of strength changes in the course of war."[26] So it is with severe crises. They are a contest of wills, but the initial relation of their strengths is apt to change, and perhaps fluctuate, in the course of the crisis. When war can be a massive disaster to both contestants, there is the temptation to paralyze the opponent by threatening this disaster; but the trading of such monstrous threats may end in one's own paralysis.[27] Threat manipulation is so dangerous a game because so much can go wrong in the trading of risks. Under the pressure of time and anxiety, errors may be made, decision-making may become stereotyped rather than flexible and adaptive, more emotional and less rational, and information may be hard to communicate and to receive. In part, the opponent's intentions are seldom known and easily misunderstood. Even if he tries to communicate his real intentions, his message may be suspect, and his intentions are subject to change, and indeed rapid change, in a fast-moving crisis.

Under these circumstances, it is not hard to see why the governments of the two superpowers tread with care, and rarely make explicit threats of violence when in the throes of a crisis; and why—were they ever involved in a direct but low-level military clash—they might understand that "underretaliation" is preferable to "overretaliation." [28] The fear of escalation tends to be inhibiting. In the course of the Cuban missiles crisis, certainly, the specific threat of force was very low-level, although "threats of higher levels of violence were implicit at every stage in the developing crisis," [29] and were no doubt effective. Where the stakes are high, as in Europe—and, as in the Caribbean, anywhere close to the territories of the two great powers—a direct military confrontation between the two antagonists appears at this time so dangerous that it is virtually inconceivable, except by inadvertence. Even over South Vietnam, in 1965, when the United States greatly increased its commitment, including the commitment of its prestige, the Soviet Union as well as China behaved with extreme caution. As a British commentator put it, the conflict in Vietnam "appeared to have reduced the international scene to a state of frozen immobility." [30] Even a small risk of precipitating nuclear war obviously serves to inhibit the use of military power; its most valuable payoff is the payoff of the threat rather than its execution, and of the implicit rather than of the explicit threat. Nevertheless, military power has been used in a fashion—over Berlin, over Cuba, and over South Vietnam. Even under conditions of nuclear parity, and the competitive manipulation of a deadly risk, strategic nuclear power is of instrumental value, and thus of some political utility.

There is indeed a weighty factor running counter to the posture of caution assumed by the Soviet Union and the United States. This factor is inherent in the role of protector which the two great powers have taken on. Not only do both have numerous allies, but there are also other states whose policy toward one great power is partially governed by the expectation its government has of receiving support in a pinch from the other great power. The so-called "domino theory," at times espoused in the United States, expresses an awareness of this circumstance. According to this doctrine, Thailand will fall under Communist control if South Vietnam does, Burma will if Thailand does, and so on. In its crude form, the domino theory may serve to distort reality more than to illuminate it, for the behavior of the "domino" states is not simply a product of the condition singled out by this view. Yet the value of Soviet and United States protection tends to fluctuate delicately with a vast range of behavior taken as indicative of their ability and willingness to intervene on behalf of a nation pressed by the other great power or one of its allies. Changes in military capabilities, deployment, and expenditures, and in the content and tone of official and unofficial announcements, are watched and interpreted from this point of view by the interested parties. The pattern of behavior in international crises is indubitably regarded as the most telling indicator of "protective worth." Thus, the value of the United States as a protector tends to go down if this country is deemed to act with timidity in a crisis over Berlin or Laos, and it tends to go up if it acts with forthright vigor in South Vietnam or the Caribbean. It is not rare, when the United States acts with especial military aplomb and pugnacity, as it did in Lebanon in 1958, for a foreign critic to berate the United States on political or moral grounds while simultaneously deriving assurance from the display of the American willingness to act boldly. The United States and the Soviet Union are thus sometimes placed in the difficult position of having to decide whether or not the penalties of non-involvement in a crisis exceed the advantages.

But in direct confrontations, it is in subtle, indirect, and severely restrained ways that military power is exerted between the nuclear states. The importance of this fact cannot be overstressed. But, though this amounts to an important qualification of our first conclusion, that conclusion is by no means dissipated. When risks are suicidal, or close to suicidal, war and the threat of war are shunned and compromise more readily accepted.

Past behavior exhibits the painstaking care the two superpowers take in avoiding a direct military confrontation even of a highly localized and limited sort. When one of them intervenes abroad militarily, the other will rigorously castigate such action but refrain from military counterinvention. Thus, the United States stood by when the Soviet Union crushed the Hungarian uprising; and the Soviet Union remained on the sidelines when the United States directly intervened in the South Vietnamese civil war. It is interesting to note the very gradual way, carefully circumscribed in each stage, in which the United States stepped up its military intervention in 1965, including the limited bombardment of North Vietnam. The highly controlled escalation in which the United States engaged was probably dictated by several prudential considerations. One may speculate that a regard for world public opinion, including American public opinion, was a consideration, and that another was the aim not to put the Soviet Union at any one time under too much pressure to resort to a form of intervention that would be risky for both superpowers. Nevertheless, the Kremlin probably felt and yet resisted considerable pressure, made especially acute by Peking's accusations, to come effectively to the aid of Communist North Vietnam. Both powers were pulling their military punches. Using military power more boldly would have meant exposure to mortal danger.

NOTES

1. John H. Herz, *International Politics in the Atomic Age*, New York: Columbia University Press, 1959, pp. 40f.

2. *Ibid.*, p. 104.

3. *Ibid.*, pp. 5, 42.

4. *Ibid.*, p. 169.

5. This point and the example have been called to my attention by Professor Norman Gibbs of Oxford University.

6. Kenneth E. Boulding, *Conflict and Defense: A General Theory*, New York: Harper, 1962, pp. 230ff. See also Modelski, "Agraria and Industria," *op. cit.*, p. 133.

7. Herman Kahn, *On Escalation: Metaphors and Scenarios*, New York: Praeger, 1965, p. 89.

8. Cf. Theodore C. Sorensen, "Kennedy vs. Khrushchev: The Showdown in Cuba," *Look*, September 7, 1965, pp. 43–54.

9. Thomas C. Schelling, *The Strategy of Conflict*, Cambridge: Harvard University Press, 1960, pp. 257ff.

10. For detailed presentation and analysis of such "firebreaks," see Kahn, *On Escalation*.

11. Cf. Otto Heilbrunn, *Conventional War in the Nuclear Age*, New York: Praeger, 1965, pp. 17ff.

12. *Ibid.*, chap. 1.

13. See the analysis of Albert and Roberta Wohlstetter, *Controlling the Risks in Cuba*, Adelphi Papers (London), No. 17 (April 1965), pp. 18f.

14. Cf. Klaus Knorr and Thornton Read (eds.), *Limited Strategic War*, New York: Praeger, 1962, esp. chaps. 1, 2, 3, 8.

15. Cf. Bernard Brodie, "What Price Conventional Capabilities in Europe?" *The Reporter*, May 23, 1963, pp. 25–29.

16. Bernard Brodie, "The McNamara Phenomenon," *World Politics*, XVII (July 1965), p. 682.

17. Thomas W. Wolfe, *Trends in Soviet Thinking on Theater Warfare, Conventional Preparations, and Limited War*, RAND Corp., Memorandum RM-4505-PR, pp. 41ff.

18. Kahn, *On Thermonuclear War*, pp. 126–44.

19. Général André Beaufré, *Introduction à la stratégie*, Paris: Armand Colin, 1963, p. 98.

20. For an argument showing that technological change may not, and is perhaps unlikely to, upset the currently stable balance of deterrence, see Arnold M. Kuzmack, "Technological Change and Stable Deterrence," *Journal of Conflict Resolution*, IX (September 1965), pp. 309–17.

21. Wohlstetter, *Controlling the Risks in Cuba*, p. 24.

22. On the difference between military invention and innovation, and their conditions, see Klaus Knorr and Oskar Morgenstern, *Science and Defense*, Center of International Studies, Princeton University, Policy Memorandum No. 32, 1965.

23. Robert Dickson Carr, "A New Cold War?" *Survival*, VII (March–April 1965), pp. 79ff.

24. Coral Bell, *Negotiation from Strength*, New York: Knopf, 1963, chap. 7.

25. Cf. Schelling, *The Strategy of Conflict*, esp. chap. 4.

26. Mao Tse-tung, *On the Protracted War*, Peking: Foreign Languages Press, 1954, p. 87.

27. Wohlstetter, *Controlling the Risks in Cuba*, p. 20.

28. Cf. Deutsch, *The Nerves of Government*, p. 194.

29. Wohlstetter, *Controlling the Risks in Cuba*, p. 22.

30. *Manchester Guardian Weekly*, July 15, 1965, p. 1.

9.

George W. Rathjens and Albert Wohlstetter:
The ABM—Two Analyses

Do new developments in weapons systems, such as the anti-ballistic missile (ABM) and the multiple independently targeted reentry vehicle (MIRV), portend the possible upsetting of the balance of terror? The following exchange— over the feasibility of the ABM—took place between two specialists in strategic studies in Congressional hearings and in the pages of the *New York Times*. It not only illustrates many of the complexities in deterrence theory and modes of analysis, but also the differing sets of assumptions about Soviet intentions and capabilities, and their implications for American policy and international stability. (A report by the Operations Research Society of America which criticized expert testimony on both sides of the ABM controversy singled out several ABM proponents and opponents, including Dr. Rathjens, for misleading argumentation. *New York Times,* October 1, 1971.)

George Rathjens is a Professor of Political Science at Massachusetts Institute of Technology and the author of *The Future of the Strategic Arms Race*. Albert Wohlstetter, Professor of Political Science at the University of Chicago, has long been involved in national security analysis, beginning with his work at the RAND Corporation; his many strategic studies include the classic article, "The Delicate Balance of Terror."

Statement of Dr. George W. Rathjens to the Senate Committee on Armed Services, April 23, 1969 [1]

(Excerpt)

I welcome the opportunity, and am honored, to appear before you to comment on the question of our deployment of an anti-ballistic missile defense system. . . .

In considering defense of our strategic retaliatory forces two questions must be asked:

1. Are they likely to be so vulnerable to preemptive attack in the near future that a decision must be made now to remedy that vulnerability?

2. If so, is the deployment of the proposed Safeguard ABM defense for Minuteman the preferred way of dealing with the problem?

The Administration's decision implies an affirmative answer to both questions. In my judgment the answer is almost certainly negative.

Our strategic forces now have the capability to deliver over four thousand

From *Planning-Programming-Budgeting—Defense Analysis: Two Examples,* Subcommittee on National Security and International Operations of the Committee on Government Operations, U.S. Senate, September 10, 1969, pp. 1–12, 17–21.

nuclear warheads against an adversary. Less than one tenth of that force could, according to former Secretary of Defense McNamara, destroy over 75% of the industry and 30% of the population of the Soviet Union, the latter figure being almost certainly a low estimate since it is based on immediate and easily calculable fatalities with those that are delayed and difficult to quantify being neglected. During the time when Safeguard is being deployed the number of warheads our strategic force can deliver will be increased to ten thousand or so assuming implementation of present plans to replace large fractions of our Minuteman and Polaris force with new missiles carrying several warheads each.

While these new warheads will each be of lower yield than those they replace, they will nevertheless be very much more powerful than those that destroyed Hiroshima and Nagasaki. The net effect of these changes is that our capability for inflicting damage on an adversary will go up sharply during the next few years. Even without adding to this the fact that we also have several thousand nuclear warheads in Europe, some of which could be delivered by tactical forces against the USSR, a preemptive strike against us in the mid-70's would seem like madness on the part of the Soviet leadership unless they could have extremely high confidence of being able to destroy at least 95%, and more likely 98%, of our retaliatory force.

This implies an ability to destroy nearly simultaneously our ICBM and our Polaris forces, a requirement that could be met only if the Soviet Union were to develop very large numbers of highly accurate missiles and an extremely effective anti-submarine warfare capability. In this connection it is to be noted that we are probably ahead of the USSR in all of the relevant technologies: the development of MIRV's, the attainment of very high accuracies with our missiles, and in ASW developments. Yet even if the Soviet SS-9 missile force were to grow as rapidly as the Defense Department's most worrisome projections, even if the Soviet Union were to develop and employ MIRV's with those missiles and even if they achieved accuracies as good as we apparently expect with our MIRV forces (according to figures released in late 1967 by former Deputy Secretary of Defense Nitze), a quarter of our Minuteman force could be expected to survive a Soviet preemptive SS-9 attack. That quarter would alone be more than enough to inflict unacceptable damage on the USSR. The possibility of the Soviet Union attaining an ASW capability that would imperil our Polaris force is even more remote. Despite our superiority in ASW there is no reason to believe that even we will have really effective ASW capabilities during the next few years. (If there were any real basis for hope we would presumably be expanding our forces when in fact the Nixon Administration budget involves a cut of $105 million for attack submarines.)

In addition to means of destroying our ICBM's and SLBM's, the Soviet Union would also have to have a highly effective air defense including capability to cope with improved air-to-surface missiles if it were to rationally consider a preemptive attack against us. This follows because of the impossibility of coordinating a preemptive strike against all our retaliatory forces, and because of the possibility that some of our aircraft may be airborne at the time of attack. If an adversary were to time an attack so that our ICBM's and bomber bases would be struck at the same time, early warning of the attack against our ICBM's would permit us to launch at least 40 percent of the bomber fleet. If an attempt were made to strike the bomber bases by surprise using FOB's or SLBM's, then we would have at least 20 minutes after destruction of the bombers during which to launch our ICBM's. Thus, a coordinated attack that would knock out ICBM's, SLBM's, and bombers would appear to be impossible.

From the Soviet point of view an effective first strike is an even more difficult undertaking than the above implies. While we have designed our ICBM force so that it can "ride out" an attack against it, Soviet decision makers could never be sure that the force would not be launched before their weapons actually detonated.

Thus, the determination that action is now needed to cope with a potential mid-70 threat to our retaliatory capability seems decidedly premature. I know of no basis for believing that the concatenation of events required to place our retaliatory forces in peril by the mid-70's is even a remote possibility.

But, however tenuous the basis for the argument, the Administration has clearly decided that our retaliatory capability may be threatened in the mid-70's, and that action is now required to insure that it will not be. If indeed such an essential element of American strength as our retaliatory posture may be in jeopardy, I would suggest that defense of Minuteman using Safeguard is hardly a high confidence solution.

There is, as I am sure you are aware, substantial doubt in the scientific community about whether such a complex system as Safeguard can be counted on to function reliably, particularly considering that it will never be possible to test it in an environment that even remotely simulates that in which it will have to operate. Experience with far less complex systems reinforces those doubts. Recollection of our experience with our ICBM programs should certainly give us pause.

Despite the fact that the requirements for reliable performance in the case of a defense of ICBM's may not be as high as for defense of cities, it seems to me that the Administration is asking great forbearance on the part of the American public when it attempts to persuade them that our retaliatory capability is in jeopardy, and then offers as a solution to the problem a system in which they can have no more confidence than in Safeguard.

However, even if Safeguard could be counted on with high confidence to perform exactly in conformance with specifications, there would still be reason to doubt that it would be a good solution to the question of possible Minuteman vulnerability. . . .

APPENDIX: DEFENDING MINUTEMAN MISSILES WITH THE SAFEGUARD SYSTEM

I

The Administration has stated that the total cost of Phase I of its Safeguard plan will be 2.1 billion dollars. Two ICBM sites at Great Falls, Montana, and Grand Forks, North Dakota, will be defended.

It is unlikely that either will have more than 75 Sprint missiles considering that the Administration has announced that the number of Sprints would not be increased significantly over the earlier plan, and that all twelve Safeguard sites are now to have Sprint defenses.

If one assumes accuracy for Soviet SS-9 missiles comparable to that expected for U.S. MIRV programs, an optimum Soviet attack would employ MIRV warheads in the yield range near one megaton and each Soviet SS-9 missile could carry several of these. Several such warheads would have to be targeted on each Minuteman to have a reasonable chance of destroying it, but one such warhead could easily destroy the missile site radar.

The defense would have to assume that the radar would be targeted in any attack, and it would have to be defended. If the defense assumes its interceptors will work perfectly it might allocate only one to each Soviet reentry vehicle that might destroy the radar. More reasonably the defense might allocate at least two Sprints to attempt intercept of each incoming reentry vehicle. To exhaust the defenses in these circumstances the Russians would have to allocate at most 200 reentry vehicles to attack the two MSR's. If they did so they would be able to destroy some 40 fewer Minuteman than if there had been no defense.

Thus, the defense will have saved that number of Minuteman for a cost of $2.1 billion, or at a cost of 50 million per Minuteman saved.

There are many reasons why this estimate is likely to be much too low.

(1) If some of the Sprints are deployed too far away from the MSR to defend it, or if there are fewer than 75 Sprints per base, the costs per Minuteman saved could go up sharply—perhaps severalfold.

(2) If the offense could count on at least two Sprints being allocated to attack each reentry vehicle targeted against the radar, and it probably could, it would have to allocate only half as many reentry vehicles to radar attack to exhaust the defenses, the effect being to double the cost per Minuteman saved.

(3) If the adversary warheads did not have a kill probability of one against the Minuteman (or the radar), the number of Minuteman saved will be decreased assuming, as is likely, that at least some warheads that would have gone wide of their marks would nevertheless have been intercepted.

(4) If, after review, the Administration should decide to terminate the program after completing only the Montana and North Dakota bases, then all of the development and production tooling costs would have to be written off against just the two sites.

(5) While we might hope that the Administration's $2.1 billion cost estimate is correct, costs of similar programs have generally escalated upon implemen-

tation. (Note also that the $2.1 billion figure does not include AEC costs for Safeguard.)

Considering these reasons, the 50 million dollar figure above should be multiplied—perhaps by a factor of three to ten. Obviously then, an estimate of 50 to 100 million dollars per Minuteman saved is very conservative.

Two arguments can be made against the foregoing line of reasoning:

(1) It can be said that the discussion neglects the effects of Spartan missiles in degrading an adversary attack. On technical grounds this seems like a reasonable approximation. While the offense would of course have to allocate some effort to insuring penetration of Spartan defenses, it would hardly be enough to change significantly the above estimates. In any case, the Administration can scarcely argue otherwise since, in claiming as it has that the Soviet Union need not react to a nationwide Spartan defense by improving its offensive forces, it has implicitly acknowledged Spartan's inutility as a defense against a sophisticated attack.

(2) It can be argued that the discussion fails to consider the bonus effect implicit in the fact that the sites at Grand Forks and Malstrom would offer protection of population against Chinese attack. It is probably reasonable to neglect this considering that the relatively small cities in this area, particularly in the area protected by the Malstrom site, would be unlikely to be hit by the Chinese. This would be particularly so if only the Phase I program were implemented in view of the fact that they could as easily attack other far more populous targets which would not be defended at all.

II

For the Soviet Union to have a capability to destroy 90% of the Minuteman force in a preemptive attack using a MIRVed SS-9 force, about 850 missiles would be required (assuming accuracies similar to those we expect and reliabilities of about 75%). For the capability to be achieved by January 1975 requires production at the rate of about one missile every three days. Assuming 4 or 5 MIRV's per missile, from about 20 to 50 missiles would be needed to exhaust 150 Sprint interceptors, the number depending on the reliability of the offensive missile and the number of Sprints to be used against each attacking reentry vehicle. With a production rate of one ICBM every three days, from two to five months' production would suffice to neutralize the Safeguard Phase I deployments. If the offense chose to use somewhat smaller yield reentry vehicles for radar attack than would be optimal for ICBM attack the production time would be further reduced.

Statement of Dr. Albert Wohlstetter to the Senate Committee on Armed Services, April 23, 1969 [2]

(Excerpt)

I appreciate the honor of testifying before this Committee on the role of an anti-ballistic missile system in the 1970's. . . .

Understanding of the complex problems of designing a protected and responsible nuclear strategic force has grown slowly among scientists as well as laymen, civilians as well as soldiers, Democrats as well as Republicans. But it has grown, and I think decisively. The United States has designed and deployed a second strike force capable of riding out an attack; and there have been large improvements in protecting responsible command.

This was accomplished not by merely expanding nuclear bombardment forces, but in essence by shifting to forces with protection against the changing threat. The stereotype repeated throughout the 1960's that our security has declined while our strategic force grew at an accelerating rate is grossly wrong on both counts.

In the past some key programs increased the protected second strike capacity of the force, while cutting at the same time billions of dollars from the spending projected, and our security is much greater in the 1960's, since we have protected and made more responsive our strategic force.

In the 1970's, unless we continue to make appropriate decisions to meet technological change, once again the viability of a large part of our second strike force will be put in question. Several related innovations, but in particular the development of a rocket booster carrying many reentry vehicles each aimed precisely at a different target (MIRV's), raise once again the possibility of attack ratios favoring the attacker. One reentry vehicle may kill a booster carrying several. One booster can carry the means of destroying many boosters.

Raising a question about the future second strike capacity of any part of our strategic force implies nothing about the present intentions of an adversary to strike first or even to be able in the future effectively to strike first. The recent debate on whether the SS-9 is a "first strike weapon" or whether the Russians intend it to be seems beside the point. If by maintaining our second strike capability we can make the risks of striking very great, this can affect an adversary's intentions favorably to ourselves.

It can deter him even in a crisis, like the one over missiles in Cuba, when the alternative to striking may look bad, but not, if we are careful, as bad as striking. Moreover, we ought not to talk of "first strike weapons" and "second strike weapons" as if this could be settled simply by looking at the weapons on one side.

Whether or not a weapons system can preclude substantial retaliation will depend on many uncertain future performance characteristics of the forces on both sides. The test of whether one has a responsible second strike capability is whether one can, under nuclear attack, preserve vehicles, decision centers and the flow of communications among them, whether one can transmit the order to retaliate and penetrate adversary defenses to reach targets.

If we were unwilling even to entertain the hypothesis of a first strike, we would do nothing to protect any part of our strategic forces or its control centers by making them mobile or hard or by ABM. Some leading scientists who oppose currently deploying ABM say they will favor it for the defense of Minuteman when precise MIRV's and the related offense technologies are likely to be available to the Russians. That calendar date, and not present Soviet intent, is then a major substantive issue for these opponents. And their position recognizes that we want to maintain the second strike capacity—not of just one, but of all major vehicles types in our strategic force: Minuteman, bombers, and Poseidon.

In designing a second strike force, there are excellent reasons for making it a substantial mixture of vehicles of several quite different types: land as well as sea based, manned as well as unmanned, each with its own mode of protection. Such systems have differing limitations, are subject to varied and independent uncertainties, require distinct modes of attack and, if each type is protected, greatly complicate the attack. It is a serious matter, then, if a large part of this mixture is badly affected by changing adversary forces and technologies. The forces deployed and the state of the art available to the Russians will influence other parts of our strategic force than Minuteman silos. And ABM has a role to play, for example, in protecting the important fixed elements of a mobile force, including the politically responsible command centers. Preserving command, control and communications is always hard, and particularly so for mobile sea-based systems.

My remarks, however, center, so far as the second strike function of ABM is concerned, on the problem of protecting Minuteman. We have good cause to preserve the second strike capability of so large a proportion of our strategic force. Even if it were true that the United States needed only a few strategic vehicles surviving, buying and paying for the operation of a great many that had become vulnerable to attack would be a very poor way to obtain those few surviving. There are safer and cheaper ways of getting a force of a given size than to buy a much larger one, most of which is susceptible to annihilation.

How does the planned timing of our ABM deployment compare to the date when it is reasonably likely that Russian offense technology could badly worsen the effectiveness of our projected Minuteman III? The first point to note is that the proposed Safeguard deployment has very extended leadtimes. It can stretch out further if continuing review of intelligence suggests it may, but the shortest schedule calls for completing this program early in 1976. If, as ABM opponents stress in other connections, there is likely to be a substantial shakedown period, we are talking of 1977 or later. If, as has been suggested, we delay decision for another year or more and then proceed to design and develop an entirely new ABM, we are talking of the 1980's.

Second, predicting exact calendar dates at which technologies will be available to adversaries and what their strategic significance will be is very hard, and we are not very good at it. Moreover, we have erred not only on the side of overestimating Russian capabilities, but often by underestimating them. At earlier dates we were surprised by the rapid Soviet achievement of the A-bomb, the H-bomb, advanced jet engines, long-range turbo-prop bombers, airborne intercept radars, and large-scale fissile-material production. And scientists have been surprised; not only military men.[3]

Third, the public discussion has not stressed how sensitively the accuracy of attack affects the viability of the hardened force attacked. Accuracy affects the number of weapons required to destroy a hard target very much more than the bomb yield or the overpressure resistance of the target. Roughly speaking, for such targets, improving accuracy by a factor of slightly more than two is the same as increasing bomb yield tenfold and serves essentially to offset a tenfold increase in overpressure resistance.

I have tried with some effort to reconstruct various numerical proofs recently presented or distributed to the Congress that purport to show our Minuteman will be quite safe without any extra protection; these proofs depend heavily on optimistic estimates of limitations in Russian delivery accuracies, reliabilities, and associated offense capabilities and sometimes on very poor offense tactics. Suppose, however, that by 1976 when Safeguard is deployed, or by 1977 when it may be shaken down, the Russians have:

(1) Accuracies like those of the systems we are deploying now.

(2) Overall reliabilities currently attributable to them.

(3) Methods familiar to us for using extensive and timely information as to which missiles have failed so that others can replace them, the technique known as shoot-look-shoot.

(4) Continued production of SS-9 boosters at past rates.

(5) Modest numbers of MIRV's per booster (e.g., the three five-megaton reentry vehicles stated by Secretary Laird for the SS-9).

Then the percentage of the Minuteman force that would be destroyed, if undefended, comes to about 95 percent.

These results are based on quite moderate assumptions about Russian capabilities. Better accuracies, for example, may be expected in the late 1970's, and higher degrees of MIRVing. Reliabilities of any given offense missile system improve with use. Do those who favor a hardpoint defense but would postpone a start really consider these Russian capabilities I have outlined "extremely implausible"? Or at all implausible?

There is a striking inconsistency in the way ABM opponents treat the Chinese and the Russians. In contemplating the possibility of a Russian offense against our Minuteman, they assume Russians who cannot by 1976 or 1977— 20 years after Sputnik—do what we know how to do now. When considering the ability of the Chinese to penetrate an ABM defense, they attribute to them penetration systems that cost us many billions of dollars, a dozen years of trials and many failures to develop—and they assume this frequently for first-generation Chinese missiles.

These are rather backward Russians and very advanced Chinese. Moreover, since in the Russian case we are considering a potential threat to our second-strike capability and we want this to be highly reliable, we want particularly to avoid underestimating the threat. But we should undertake a modest defense of population if it works in the expected case, even if on extremely pessimistic assumptions it might not. Here again it seems to me the ABM critics get things exactly backwards. . . .

The major components of the Safeguard system have received elaborate study and testing. Ideas for brand new ABM systems to defend hard points that I am familiar with are not serious competitors in this time period. We should start deploying the system now on the schedule suggested and we should expect, as in the case of every other offense and defense system, that we shall learn a great deal from operational experience, make some changes and retrofits. This seems to me a sound way to supplement the protection of the Minuteman in a period when we can expect it to be endangered. . . .

Supplementary Statement by Dr. Albert Wohlstetter, May 23, 1969

Supplement on Purported Proofs That the Minuteman Will Be Safe Without Further Protection

In preparing my testimony for the Senate Armed Services Committee on the role of ABM in the 1970's, I undertook to review and test my past views on the subject and once again to form my own independent judgment. I therefore did not rely on calculations of either the government or its critics. I took the relevant classified and public data and performed my own analysis.

The kind of analysis involved in obtaining a protected and responsible strategic force has been my principal concern for eighteen years starting with the study that gave rise to the first-strike/second-strike distinction and to a good many other concepts and modes of protecting and controlling strategic forces cited by both sides in the present debate. The ABM has other functions that I support, but my testimony in the space available focussed on its role in defending Minuteman. As I stressed there, these are complex and intrinsically uncertain matters. Where scientists differ on them, laymen may be tempted simply to throw up their hands and choose to rely on the authority of those scientists they favor. I feel, however, that the substantive differences among the scientists, if carefully explained, are quite accessible to the members of this Committee and that such careful explanation can help them form their own judgment as to which conclusions are sound.

ON THE SAFETY OF MINUTEMAN

In my statement to the Senate Armed Services Committee on April 23, I said, "I have tried to reconstruct various numerical proofs recently presented or distributed to the Congress that purport to show our Minuteman will be safe without any extra protection; these proofs depend heavily on optimistic estimates of limitations in Russian delivery accuracies, reliabilities, associated offense capabilities, and sometimes on poor offense tactics." In response to questions from members of the Committee, I illustrated several troubles with these attempted proofs of the safety of Minuteman, but there was no time to explain their defects adequately. I would like to try to do that now, and to comment specifically on the calculations of Dr. Rathjens, Dr. Lapp, and of the Federation of American Scientists. Some of the comments, particularly those of Dr. Lapp, bear also on some unevidenced statements on this subject by Prof.

Chayes and Dr. Panofsky, and more recently, by Dr. Wiesner and Dr. Steven Weinberg.

Though my own calculations were based on classified as well as public data, my summary of results, like that of Dr. Rathjens, was unclassified and so are the comments I am about to make. This will prevent explicit specification of some of the numbers assumed by Dr. Rathjens and by myself and inevitably it forces some roundaboutness of expression. I am able to state, for example, that Dr. Rathjens and I assume the same accuracy for the Russian SS-9 in the mid- and late 1970's. I can say that the SS-9 is now expected (and, before the Nixon administration, was expected) to achieve that accuracy years in advance of this late time period. And I can say, as Dr. Rathjens did, that the accuracy we have assumed for the Russians, in this late time period, is essentially the same as that estimated for our own MIRV carrying missiles, namely Poseidon and Minuteman III.[4] But I cannot say what that accuracy is.

I am, therefore, submitting a classified statement in which the essential numerical assumptions are explicit and related to intelligence estimates. However, even without the classified statement, some essential defects of the calculations of Dr. Rathjens, Dr. Lapp, and the Federation of American Scientists can be made clear.

Dr. Rathjens' calculations. Dr. Rathjens has stated, "Even if the Soviet SS-9 missile force were to grow as rapidly as the Defense Department's most worrisome projections, even if the Soviet Union were to develop and employ MIRVs with those missiles and even if they achieved accuracies as good as we apparently expect with our MIRV forces (according to figures released in late 1967 by former Deputy Secretary of Defense Nitze), a quarter of our Minuteman force could be expected to survive a Soviet preemptive SS-9 attack. That quarter alone would be more than enough to inflict unacceptable damage on the USSR."[5]

My own parallel calculations for the mid- and late 1970s, using what I described as moderate assumptions, show about 5% surviving. What explains the difference? Since Dr. Rathjens and I compared notes on April 22, I am able to fix quite precisely where we agreed and where we differed.

Our assumptions agreed in the accuracy assumed for the SS-9, in the overall reliability rate, in the number of SS-9 boosters (500) and in the use of several independently aimed reentry vehicles in each booster. Our assumptions differed on three key points: in the degree of blast resistance assumed for our Minuteman silos, in the yield of the Russian reentry vehicles, and in the use or non-use by the Russians of substantial information about what missiles are unready at launch or fail in early stages.

On the first point, I have explained that Dr. Rathjens assumed that Minuteman silos were two-thirds more blast resistant than I did, and two-thirds more blast resistant than they are officially estimated to be. He derived his assumption by reading several points off an unclassified chart showing the probability of a Minuteman silo being destroyed as a function of accuracy for various bomb yields. Then by using standard rules for weapons effects he inferred the over-

pressure resistance of Minuteman silos. However, the curves on the unclassified chart cannot be correctly read to imply the overpressure resistance Dr.
Rathjens infers. His reading of the curves was in error.

Second, I assumed three 5-megaton reentry vehicles for each SS-9, as in Secretary Laird's public statements. Dr. Rathjens assumed four 1-megaton reentry
vehicles. More than four reentry vehicles can be fitted on the SS-9, if the payload is only one megaton. However, the three 5-megaton reentry vehicles, given
the accuracy we both assume, and given the actual blast resistance of the Minuteman, do enough for the attacker. Using his lower Russian bomb yield and
his overestimated Minuteman blast resistance, Dr. Rathjens derived a probability of about 60 percent that one arriving Russian reentry vehicle would
destroy one Minuteman silo. If he had used the officially estimated 5-megaton
reentry vehicle and the actual blast resistance of the Minuteman silo, the probability would have been nearly 99%. If he had used three 5-megaton reentry
vehicles per booster for the SS-9 and the correct estimate for blast resistance, he
would have found only 16%, instead of 25% of the Minuteman force surviving.
Alternatively, if he had used the classified estimates of the number of 1-mega-
ton reentry vehicles that can be fitted on an SS-9 booster, his calculations would
have shown about 7.3 percent surviving. The combined significance of these
first two points of difference between Dr. Rathjens and myself is then considerable.

The third point of difference between our calculations is that Dr. Rathjens
assumes that the Russians would have to salvo all of their missiles with no information as to which had been unready or failed in time to be discovered, or
at any rate with no use of such information. However, it is familiar that better
methods are available and are of considerable utility for an offense that wants to
assure a very high percentage of destruction of the force attacked. Most missiles
that are counted as "unreliable" (excluded from the figure of overall reliability)
are either not ready for launch or fail at launch, and this information can be
made available immediately. A substantial additional fraction that fail do so at
burnout, and information as to whether burnout velocity is within expected
tolerances can also be made quickly available. For radio-guided missiles this is
almost automatic, but inertial systems can also radio this information back, as
the telemetering in missile flight test program shows. Later flight information
is also feasible. While some fraction of the failures will remain unknown, a
large proportion can be known. Therefore, instead of salvoing all extra missiles
blindly, to make up for all unreadiness and all failures without knowing where
they occur, one can reprogram some extra missiles to replace the large proportion of known failures. Using a current planning factor for the proportion of
the unreliable missiles that cannot be replaced on the basis of timely information, the calculations using three 5-megaton reentry vehicles show considerably
greater destruction. Instead of 16 percent surviving, the approximate 5 percent
survival that I mentioned in my statement results. Such techniques of using
substantial timely information as to which missiles cannot be relied on are less

important for cases where smaller yields and larger numbers of reentry vehicles per booster are used. For the 1-megaton multiple reentry vehicle case I have referred to, the expected number of Minuteman surviving reduces from approximately 7.3 percent without using such techniques to 5 percent using them.

A table follows summarizing differences between Dr. Rathjens and my calculations:

CALCULATIONS ON THE VULNERABILITY OF THE MINUTEMAN FORCE IN THE LATE 1970's IF NO EXTRA PROTECTION

Difference Between Assumptions Used by Dr. Rathjens and Myself

	Assumption	*Difference*
Number of SS-9's	Same (500)	
Overall reliability	Same	
Accuracy	Same	
Minuteman blast resistance	Dr. Rathjens'	⅔ higher than official estimate
	Mine	Official estimate
SS-9 payload	Dr. Rathjens'	4 reentry vehicles at 1 MT (less than SS-9 capability)
	Mine	3 at 5 MT (SS-9 capability)
Use of partial information on missile malfunctions	Dr. Rathjens'	Not used
	Mine	Used

Effect of Assumptions on Minuteman Survivability

	Percent of Minuteman Surviving
Dr. Rathjens' result	25
Adjust for correct Minuteman blast resistance and three 5 MT MIRV per SS-9	16
Alternative adjust for correct Minuteman blast resistance and number of 1 MT MIRV warheads the SS-9 is capable of carrying . . .	7.3
Using correct Minuteman blast resistance, either three 5 MT MIRV per SS-9, or the correct number of 1 MT warheads per SS-9, and information as to missile malfunctions	5

Exchange of Letters Between Dr. George W. Rathjens and Dr. Albert Wohlstetter, The New York Times, June 15, 1969

DR. RATHJENS' LETTER

To the Editor:

You recently carried a story[6] about Albert Wohlstetter's criticisms of an estimate I made that 25 percent of our Minuteman force could be expected to survive a pre-emptive attack by a Soviet SS-9 missile force in the mid-1970's. Mr. Wohlstetter is reported to claim that the "correct" number is 5 percent.

I have dealt with Mr. Wohlstetter's criticisms in a classified letter, but also feel I should comment on them publicly.

First, there is the question of whether I used the right "hardness" for Minuteman silos in my calculation. I used a chart released by Deputy Secretary of Defense Packard and data made available by former Deputy Secretary of Defense Nitze on Nov. 8, 1967.

One cannot determine unambiguously either the hardness of a Minuteman silo or the accuracy we expect with MIRV's from this data. However, by using both releases one can derive a probability for a Minuteman silo being destroyed without knowing the exact hardness. This I did. Any error in estimation of hardness is irrelevant because it is offset by a compensating difference in estimation of accuracy.

PLAUSIBLE THREAT

Second, it is alleged that I made an error in assuming four one-megaton [MT] warheads per SS-9 missile rather than three five-MT warheads as Mr. Wohlstetter assumed. My statement for Senator Albert Gore's subcommittee was prepared before anyone had suggested that the Soviet Union could employ the latter option with the SS-9. I saw no reason to change it, since I continue to regard a payload of less than three five-MT warheads as a plausible threat and because the difference is small compared with the following more important points.

The major difference between Mr. Wohlstetter's analysis and mine is with respect to the extent to which the Russians could retarget some of their missiles to take account of failures of others.

Mr. Wohlstetter has assumed perfect information would be available to them about missile launch failures, failures during powered flight, and failures in separation and guidance of the individual warheads, and that they would be able to use that information with the high confidence required to make a preemptive attack a rational choice. I have assumed they would not be able to obtain and use information about such failures in a timely fashion. This accounts for most of the difference in our estimates of Minuteman survival.

There are five far more important points to be made.

There is no hard evidence that the Russians are determined to build a capability to effectively attack our ICBM's.

If they wish to do so, they can build such a capability by the mid-1970's.

If they do so, implementation of the Safeguard plan could be offset by a very small additional Russian effort. Even an expanded Safeguard system would be less satisfactory than other alternatives for strengthening our retaliatory capabilities.

Even if the Russians built the capability to destroy our Minuteman force, pre-emptive attack by them would be madness unless they could discount completely the possibility that we might launch some Minutemen before the arrival of their ICBM's, and unless they could be highly confident of also destroying the other components of our retaliatory strength essentially simultaneously, a possibility that is all but incredible.

The most effective means of insuring the continued viability of the Minuteman force is early agreement to stop MIRV testing and to preclude a large build-up in Soviet ICBM strength. Negotiations to achieve these ends clearly merit higher priority than the deployment of Safeguard.

GEORGE W. RATHJENS,
Cambridge, Mass., June 5, 1969.

DR. WOHLSTETTER'S LETTER

To the Editor:

Responsible scientists like Drs. Bethe and Ruina, who feel we can delay starting ABM to protect Minuteman, testify that "any one . . . system, bombers, Polaris, Minuteman, has its own vulnerability;" that we need all three; that a threat to Minuteman concerns us gravely. One key issue then is whether that threat will develop by 1976 or 1977 when at the earliest Safeguard will be shaken down—or whether it is safe to wait years for a better ABM.

A disparate variety of calculations by Drs. Rathjens, Weinberg, Wiesner, and Lapp purport to show that it is safe to wait, that an attack by 500 Russian SS-9 missiles would leave untouched anywhere from one-fourth to three-quarters of our Minutemen.

They claim to square with official intelligence. Such confident inferences by scientists carry great authority and ought to be made with the utmost professional care. But despite their widely publicized claims, it is they (not those who would start ABM) who are careless of pre- as well as post-Nixon intelligence, and quite casual in their calculation.

They attribute to an SS-9 in the late 1970's poorer combinations of bomb yield, number of MIRV's, and accuracy than intelligence expects in the early 1970's; and compound these errors by presuming poor Russian tactics or higher blast resistance than designed.

BASIS FOR CALCULATION

In a note to me on his calculations, Dr. Rathjens assumed our silo could resist overpressures two-thirds higher than its design performance; and derived a probability some three-fourths too high that it could survive a 1-MT burst. He bases his probability calculations on doubtfully relevant 1967 testimony about U.S. attacks on adversary silos of unspecified hardness with a range of destruction probabilities. Dr. Rathjens applies the low end of this range to late 1970 SS-9's attacking our silos—which hardly fits a proof that "the most worrisome projections" leave us nothing to worry about. The other end of the range yields roughly the appropriate lower survival probability.

Dr. Rathjens assumes only four one-MT MIRV's in the late 1970's SS-9. But (a) more than four one-MT MIRV's were attributed by pre-Nixon intelligence to the SS-9 in the early 1970s; and (b) an alternative of three 5-MT MIRV's is now public. 500 SS-9's equipped with either of these MIRV options could destroy about 95 percent of Minuteman if the Russians use well-established techniques for reprogramming missiles to replace known failures. Using no reprogramming at all, the 1-MT MIRV force would destroy 92 or 93 percent of Minuteman. The ability of the five-MT force to destroy 95 percent of Minuteman presumes only half the failures after launch are replaced—a figure well within the state of the art.

Even limiting the use of information to missile malfunctions before or during launch, the five-MT MIRV force would leave only 8 or 9 percent surviving. These numbers are intrinsically uncertain—sensitive especially to changing accuracy.

400 SS-9's with one-MT MIRV's and accuracies better by only 250 feet would destroy more Minutemen than 500 with the accuracy expected in the early 1970's.

Dr. Rathjens' belief that variants of Safeguard help retaliation less than available alternatives is based on estimates of costs of these alternatives which I find as casual as his calculations on the threat to Minuteman.

Finally, unlike him, I don't believe a stable, monitorable agreement to limit strategic offense and defense would freeze ABM at zero. ABM can counter improvements in offense accuracy unlikely to be monitored; and can protect population against smaller powers that violate or do not sign the agreement. I doubt the Russians would accept a total ban on ABM.

ALBERT WOHLSTETTER,
University of Chicago,
Los Angeles, June 11, 1969.

Letter by Dr. George W. Rathjens to The New York Times, *June 22, 1969*

To the Editor:

In your issue of June 15 you published a letter from me regarding Safeguard and a rebuttal by Albert Wohlstetter imputing to me assumptions and statements I did not make.

Mr. Wohlstetter implies that my calculations were meant to apply to the late 1970's. They were not, as perusal of my letter and Congressional statements will show. All references by me are to the mid-1970's or in one case specifically to 1975. I have never denied that by the late 1970's the Soviet Union could, if it wished, have a capability to destroy nearly all of our Minuteman force in a preemptive attack.

He states that, in using information released by former Deputy Secretary Nitze regarding MIRV effectiveness against hardened missile sites, I used the low end of Mr. Nitze's estimates. I did not. Had I done so I would have calculated 30 percent survival for our Minuteman force. I used the median of the two values given by Mr. Nitze.

Mr. Wohlstetter charges me with having used "casual" cost estimates in my analysis. No cost estimates appeared in my letter. The only relevant figure in testimony by me was a marginal cost for Minuteman procurement of $4 million per missile, a figure consistent with testimony provided by various Defense officials over the last years.

He implies that I believe a "stable, monitorable agreement to limit strategic offense and defense would freeze ABM at zero." I have neither said nor implied any such thing. I have said that I believe nationwide ABM deployment by either side would be a serious impediment to reaching an arms limitation agreement.

The quality of the debate regarding Safeguard would be improved if Mr. Wohlstetter would try to make his case by arguing its merits and by rebutting his opponents' analyses, not by misrepresenting their views. In doing the latter, he imposes on The Times, its readers, and the nation.

GEORGE W. RATHJENS,
Cambridge, Mass., June 16, 1969.

Letter by Dr. Albert Wohlstetter to The New York Times, *June 29, 1969*
To the Editor:

Space permits only brief reply to George W. Rathjen's defense of his calculations that 25 percent of Minuteman would survive an attack by 500 SS-9's.

One key point: his results, no matter how derived, simply do not jibe with the designed blast resistance of Minuteman silos and pre-Nixon intelligence estimates of SS-9 performance by 1972.

He says he used the median rather than the lower of Deputy Defense Secretary Nitze's two hypothetical kill probabilities. But he wrote me earlier that he assumed a .6 probability for a one-megaton [MT] weapon against a Minuteman silo. The lower of Mr. Nitze's two probabilities, not their median, scales to .61 at one-MT using the familiar cube root approximation; and even higher —to .69—using more exact methods.

Mr. Rathjens erred in stating his assumptions; or in his inference from this doubtfully relevant 1967 hypothetical; or both. The gist of the matter is that with expected MIRV performance 500 SS-9's could destroy some 95 percent of Minuteman.

Safeguard will not be deployed until 1976, or shaken down until 1977. It is plainly directed at a threat in the late nineteen-seventies. For Mr. Rathjens to suggest that his calculations don't apply after 1975 is to suggest they don't apply at all.

One alternative to Safeguard is to expand Minuteman. Mr. Rathjens cites a $4-million cost for a Minuteman. The relevant marginal systems costs are twice that or more.

The Defense Department was much criticized for omitting the incremental cost of ABM warheads—which made a difference of a few percent. For Minuteman, Mr. Rathjens appears to leave out silos, initial personnel training, training equipment, spares, land purchase and much else. On the other hand, the ABM costs he cites include land purchased, construction, all hardware investment, and initial training, and are a phase of a program serving several functions besides the defense of Minuteman.

These are only some of the flaws. To say that Mr. Rathjens's costs are casual, as I do, is to be courteous.

I should think the quality of the debate on this complex issue might improve if less time were spent in propagating quick analyses and more in improving their quality, if we used the authority of science less and its methods more.

ALBERT WOHLSTETTER,
University of Chicago,
Chicago, June 25, 1969.

NOTES

1. From hearings, "Authorization for Military Procurement, Research and Development, Fiscal Year 1970, and Reserve Strength," Senate Committee on Armed Services, 91st Congress, 1st session, part 2.

2. From hearings, "Authorization for Military Procurement, Research and Development, Fiscal Year 1970, and Reserve Strength," Senate Committee on Armed Services, 91st Congress, 1st session, part 2.

3. We have not been very good at predicting our own or our adversary's technologies. These matters are intrinsically uncertain. Eminent scientists at the end of the 1940's predicted that fusion weapons would be infeasible, and if feasible undeliverable, and if delivered of no strategic significance, since they thought (erroneously) they could be used only against cities. (Some of those who then thought the threat of fusion bombs against cities neither moral nor important strategically now take it to be both.) In February 1953 an important scientific study group expected the Soviets would have no ICBM's before the late 1960's—a prediction plainly in error by the end of the year. Writing in October 1964 some scientists opposing ABM were quite sure that no technological surprises could substantially change the operational effectiveness of intercontinental delivery systems, and thus entirely missed the major strategic potential of precisely aimed MIRV's, a concept that was at that very time emerging in the classified literature. These were able and informed men. But exact prediction on these matters defies confident assertion.

4. Poseidon and Minuteman III have been test flown and are in the process of deployment. (The first of these should be operational in about a year and a half.)

5. Testimony of April 23 before the Senate Armed Services Committee. See also his testimony of March 28, Part 1, p. 359 of *Strategic and Foreign Policy Implications of ABM Systems.* Hearing before a subcommittee of the Senate Committee on Foreign Relations.

6. Story in *The New York Times,* May 26, 1969, based on May 23 Supplementary Statement by Dr. Wohlstetter to the Senate Armed Services Committee.

10.
Philip Green: Deadly Logic: The Theory of Nuclear Deterrence

Many of the assumptions, analyses, and conclusions of the deterrence theorists are rejected by Philip Green. In his view, "pseudo-scientists" of strategic analysis overemphasize rationality and pretend objectivity, when in fact they are politically and ethically committed to a cold war perspective. In the book from which

From Philip Green, *Deadly Logic: The Theory of Nuclear Deterrence,* pp. 255–65, 266–68, 271–76. Some footnotes omitted. Published originally by the Mershon Center for Education in National Security. Copyright © 1966 by the Ohio State University Press. Reprinted by permission of Schocken Books, Inc.

the following selection was taken, Professor Green writes that deterrence theory "(1) presumes that no conduct is absolutely prohibited . . . (2) treats all violence and destruction as qualitatively indistinguishable . . . (3) makes moral distinctions between weapons and targets difficult to justify . . . (4) assumes that a deep psychological and physical commitment to the possibility of wreaking destructive violence on foreign populations is morally neutral . . . (5) tends to subordinate all political considerations to military ones . . . (6) is culture bound; it shares the most important American cold war biases . . . and (7) has an antipopular political bias."

A political scientist at Smith College, Philip Green is the author of several articles criticizing aspects of national security policy, and is co-author of *Power and Community: Dissenting Essays in Political Science*.

1. *The Non-Political Character of Deterrence Theory*

Several cardinal points emerge from this study of the methodology of theoretical deterrence studies. First, the questions that deterrence theorists seem habitually to ask—whether "rationality" can control the arms race, and whether "scientific" analysis seems to favor certain kinds of wartime strategies rather than others—are of the most limited value. It is important to understand just what that value is and to see in what way it has been oversold.

If one accepts all the assumptions that go into a deterrence study or into the verbal presentation of deterrence logic, and *if* one feels that the analysis has been truly rigorous, *then* one will be prone to accepting the conclusions generated by the analysis. This is to say that like-minded people will reach the same conclusions if they reason logically. No doubt; but the statement is trivial, for why should we all be like-minded? Let us consider a number of propositions concerning international policies, suggested by my earlier discussion, on which we may *not* be like-minded.

A. The Communist powers will seize and exploit every military advantage we allow them, even outside the peripheries of their own borders—or they will not.
   1. The German problem can be "solved" only by military deterrence strategies—or it can be "solved" by political accommodation.
B. The arms race can be stabilized through arms control—or, within the presently anarchic international system, it cannot.
C. Continued prosecution of the cold war is in our interest—or it is not.
   1. The West German demand for nuclear proliferation of one sort or another presents a problem soluble by strategic means—or it does not.
   2. The continual fighting of limited wars, such as that in Vietnam, probably will not lead to all-out-war—or it probably will.
D. The Soviets are not serious about disarmament—or they are.
   1. The world would be a worse place after the conclusion of a "bad" disarmament agreement—say one based on Soviet proposals—than it would be given the prospect of a continued arms race—or it would not. (Another way of putting some of the implications of these first four points is to say that, in Aaron Wildavsky's terms, the *greatest* danger of the

present confrontation may be seen as, on the one hand, appeasement of an implacable enemy à la 1938, or as, on the other hand, the prospect of getting into an uncontrollable, spiralling arms race with an opponent who could be dealt with successfully on a non-militarized basis.)

E. The domestic political, social, and moral effects of a continual emphasis on anti-Communist ideology can be controlled—or they cannot.

F. It may be worthwhile going through the uncertain catastrophe of nuclear war at some level to attain our policy ends—or it may not.

G. The use of nuclear weapons is morally supportable in some instances—or it is not.

H. It is not reasonable for the United States unequivocally to adopt a no-first-use policy—or it is.

I hope it is obvious that these are among the crucial propositions one can make about world conflict in the nuclear era (doubtless there are several others I have left out). The point is that deterrence theorists have simply not discussed these propositions. They have, on the one hand, wasted their time and ours by asking what we have seen to be essentially meaningless questions about the prospects for something called rational behavior. Even worse, they have, on the other hand, settled matters regarding the specific propositions presented here by making either explicit or implicit assumptions about them. Thus, the argument that the balance of terror was delicate directly depended on an assumption about Communist aggressiveness. But this is to say that Wohlstetter did not really show the balance of terror to be delicate; he merely assumed it. Again, Kahn's civil-defense-not-incredible-first-strike strategy depends directly on assumptions about Communist aggressiveness; the lack of a political solution in Europe; the neutral long-run political effects of the cold war; the potential utility of nuclear war; the morality of using nuclear weapons; and the reasonableness of a first-use policy. He does not show it to be a feasible strategy, as he claims to, but merely tells us what we have to believe to think it is. Similarly, Schelling's theory of brinksmanship depends on assumptions about the uses of limited war and the prospective feasibility of nuclear war; in the long run, his views on arms control and the prospective stability of limited war depend on additional assumptions about most of the propositions listed above. In fact, the whole notion of the workability and preferability of a deterrence strategy depends on the making of assumptions about *all* the above propositions.

Furthermore, there is something special about the assumptions deterrence theorists make. In the first place, they are uniformly tendentious, and the tendency is always and simply to support the moderate or liberal American view of the cold war—that is, to make an unquestioning application of the appeasement model to the present international conflict (see note 102, Chapter V). If Communism is not innately militarily aggressive; if the arms race is technologically uncontrollable; if the N-country problem or the German problem or the Vietnam problem or the China problem or the cold war ethos in general may lead to military breakdown or domestic dissolution; if a disarmament agreement would by changing expectations about international behavior make disarmament workable; if nothing is worth the potential catastrophe of nuclear war; if moral qualms about the use of nuclear weapons cannot be overcome; if, generally, the international system as it now stands is unsatisfactory both practically and morally—then the sophisticated deterrence strategy that has come to prominence in the past few years is not really defensible when compared with disarmament and minimum deterrence strategies.

In the second place, by constantly assuming away, as we have seen, the most important questions in the field of inquiry being investigated, deterrence theorists engage in what I have elsewhere called the vice of the depoliticalization of the political: the attempt to fit essentially political questions into the straitjacket of so-called scientific analysis.

The root error in all theorizing of this type, which is finally unpersuasive because it claims to demonstrate so much more than it possibly can, lies in the attempt somehow to separate the "analytical" components of a policy problem from the political and moral ones. It is necessary to insist that this cannot be done: policy proposals rest on assertions about politics, and such assertions consist primarily of complex and indissoluble political *judgments*. A judgment is an expression of belief based on one's entire training and experience, and is thus inevitably both "moral" and "analytical," "technical" and "political," "subjective" and "objective." Whether "in principle" political judgments can eventually be broken down into analytic categories is an interesting but irrelevant question, in that the basic issues of "the arms debate" relate not to abstract matters of principle but to immediate practical needs. All we can do at present is to recognize that there are various kinds of inseparable evaluative elements in all political judgments, and not attempt to hide this frustrating fact under the camouflage of theoretical social science. With regard to statements such as Kahn's,

Despite a widespread belief to the contrary, objective studies indicate that even though the amount of human tragedy would be greatly increased in the postwar world, the increase would not preclude normal and happy lives for the majority of survivors and their descendents.

or even Wohlstetter's calmer, ". . . at critical junctures in the 1960's we may not have the power to deter rational attack," the notion that we can distinguish between the factual and the evaluative parts of a political judgment is useless.

Thus we are led back to the statement that sophisticated deterrence theory is of only the most limited value. If one thinks that over-all questions of policy are beyond debate, then there is certainly a sense in which strategic analysis can be both "scientific" and useful. The virtue of the RAND study of overseas bases was precisely that by the nature of its commission it assumed the need for some kind of strategic Air Force role; within the bounds set by that assumption alternatives could be fairly rigorously compared. The same considerations apply generally to the kind of weapons system comparisons that Hitch and McKean have explained in their *Economics of Defense in the Nuclear Age*. And more broadly, once one accepts the need for some policy of nuclear deterrence, it certainly becomes helpful to have as policy consultants persons who can think logically about such a policy, and who understand the basically intuitive insight into the process of mutual deterrence.

But when one is dealing with the choice of fundamental policies itself, about which debate is still widespread among the interested public, deterrence theorizing becomes simply delusive. There is still much value in the rebuttal that Brodie, Kaufmann, and a few others delivered to the early Dulles version of massive retaliation—but the latter is not today the most intellectually respectable alternative to mutual deterrence. And nothing of any obvious usefulness has been added to the original insights of deterrence theory. The elaborations that have been suggested since then are all based on unassessed assumptions and are therefore of no value unless one happens for one's own reasons to agree with them. The refined methods of justifying these strategies, we have observed, merely take one possible outcome of a certain kind of international conflict, trick it out in a "scenario" or a set of matrices or a complicated systematic-looking argument, manipulate it if possible with numbers to make the exercise look "scientific," and then treat the result as though it represented not a vague possibility but a near certainty. The general notion of rationality, similarly though less definitively, accomplishes the same result of substituting abstract propositions about theoretically possible human behavior for concrete propositions, such as the ones I have outlined above, about the probable behavior of relevant persons. And the result is essentially irresponsible strategic thinking.

The problems of deterrence are treated as problems of calculation, in which any overbalancing of probable cost by probable gain leads inevitably to action, and any overbalancing of probable gain by probable cost to inaction. It is this oversimplified view of policy-making that leads Wohlstetter to extol the "scientific method" of policy analysis, leads Glenn Snyder to conceive of a "national interest" which rises above "politics," and leads deterrence theorists generally to neglect all considerations of public opinion and its effects in presenting their proposals. Thus are naturally produced such ideas as that the balance of terror is or was "delicate" and needs or needed strengthening on our side; that the astonishing ideas of "limited strategic war" or "controlled central war," conceived in a void of abstract speculation, are necessary and reasonable types of war to plan for; that complicated arms control arrangements are more likely to be the genesis of enduring agreement than uncomplicated, dramatic disarmament arrangements; and that a counterforce first strike backed up by a massive civil-defense program is less likely to lead to the end of civilization as we know it than is even the most unreasonable of disarmament schemes. No other reason but sheer assertion is offered for giving credence to any of these ideas, in the works of professional "expertise" that have been analyzed in this thesis. Virtually everywhere one looks for serious discussion, one finds airy speculations about what rational men might or might not do.[1]

Some of these ideas seem irrelevant to reality. Others are all too relevant, for they have helped stretch out the arms race farther and faster than might have been the case if the real world of, say, Soviet behavior had been investigated, instead of the abstract world of decision-makers who all seem to think exactly like

Wohlstetter and Kahn. In the near future we may be once again encountering, with Communist China, the same kinds of problem that we have had to face in constructing a strategy for dealing with the Soviet Union; and given the apparent inevitability of further nuclear proliferation before the arms race is brought under control (if it ever is) we shall be doing this in an even more complex and tense situation than has existed so far. The ideological rigidity with which we approach the needs of policy-making will be, it can safely be predicted, even greater than it has been in the past, because of the special relationship that the American national psyche appears to be in with Communist China. Under these circumstances, the need for control will be even more vital than it has been, and the penalties for making "self-negating prophecies" may be even greater. The abstracted, Hobbesian rationalism with which we have hitherto viewed, and added fuel to, the arms race will have only a negative contribution to make in meeting these difficulties.

It hardly needs adding, finally, that what we are talking about has nothing to do with "science." To use inappropriate techniques that permit analysis to consist wholly of the manipulation of one's own prejudices; to rest one's theorizing on an assumption that already contains in it the conclusions that one wishes to reach—this is exactly the opposite of what genuine scientists in any field actually do.[2]

As for Wohlstetter's claim that the people who do this kind of work are more qualified to offer policy advice than the people who sign letters from Pugwash conferences, it should be juxtaposed with his comment that "today it is hardly necessary to argue for deterrence." Among deterrence theorists the case for deterrence apparently has the epistemological status of the case for electromagnetism. No doubt such true believers can find a commonly perceived framework within which to exchange their rigorous and convincing studies of each other's assumptions. For others, however, such a mode of thought hardly seems so systematic or analytic as to call for, let alone compel acceptance of, its conclusions.

2. The Political Significance of Deterrence Theory

Why, we might ask, does such an overwhelming proportion of the academic theorists of deterrence leap from a world of inappropriate or unverified theorizing into a world of national policy-making with such confidence? The most likely answer raises some disturbing questions about the future of social science in democratic society.

No doubt a large part of the explanation of this phenomenon is to be found in the desire of some persons to be influential, even at the cost of misusing their claims to professional authority. But this tells only a part—and a relatively unimportant part—of the story. What is more important and disturbing is the impression one gets that some of these writers genuinely imagine themselves to be unable to make meaningful statements unless these be cast in the form of "scientific" propositions, which have either been in some sense tested, or are soon to be so. . . .

. . . [The] methodological stance of the scientist may easily become a façade behind which another *persona* of the scientist—the would-be policy-maker who hides within his psyche—manipulates his esoteric knowledge to convince the public of the scientific reputability of statements which as science are really spurious. I do not mean to suggest, either, that such a misuse of science must always—or even often—be conscious or wilful. It may simply be that in the act, repeated again and again, of assuring one's self that one is a scientist, one may gradually forget that skill through the exercise of which one learns to detect one's own departures from the standard of scientific detachment. In any event, is the public record of those who consciously cast their work in a "scientific" mold any better than the record of those whose type of mind favors speculation and poetic metaphor on the one hand, or "mere" scholarly and systematic immersion in subject matter, without "scientific" rigor, on the other? If there is any evidence for an affirmative answer to that question, it is certainly a well-kept secret.

Of course, as Wohlstetter and Brodie have argued, one hardly wants to replace the analysts' efforts at scientific reasoning with the military man's supposed reliance on authority, unimpressive intuition, common sense, and assumptions that are even more arbitrary and unstated than, say Kahn's. But that is not really what most serious critics propose; and thus it is not true that, as several practitioners of systems analysis have suggested, the limitations of the scientific method for studying policy problems are shared by all the serious alternative methods. For the gist of the case against the methods described in this book is that, applied to politics, they demonstrate political obtuseness and moral obscurantism. And what is proposed is that, for this reason above all, such methods be replaced with that traditional scholarly or even intelligent lay analysis that does not slight fundamentals but rather begins with them: that we rely not on easily impeachable "common sense" but on the *uncommon sense* of the thoughtful student of politics.

Certainly there have been scholars and other writers willing to discuss the crucial issues in international politics. In recent years alone, the names of Louis J. Halle, Hedley Bull, Hans Morgenthau, John Strachey, George Kennan, Walter Lippmann, David Lilienthal, D. F. Fleming, John Herz, and others come immediately to mind. Many of these have made substantive proposals which are ultimately not too unlike those offered by deterrence theorists. They have done so without benefit of conflict systems designs, formal behavioral models, matrices and calculi, and theories of rationality, and without the pretention to being more scientific or rigorous than their colleagues. Their analyses have consisted of a willingness to state what they believe about the world, the evidence which leads them to believe it, and what conclusions seem to follow from such beliefs. No doubt the more systematically such an argument is put, the better an argument it is—rigorous thought is always preferable to sloppiness. But rigor is not a substitute for thought, and rigorous deterrence analysis has been empty of real thought about the major problems of national policy. . . .

. . . The constant false references to a workable theory (or theories) of strategy can only have a deleterious effect on public debate. By this I mean much more than that deterrence theorists themselves are, as I have claimed, discussing the wrong propositions. In addition, they threaten to affect public discussion generally in other unfortunate ways, which can be indicated by reference to some selected examples. What is central to all of these examples is the suggestion that, instead of being at worst an alternative mode to the one I have suggested, of dealing seriously with the issues of national security, deterrence theory is beginning to *replace* it.

Thus a well-known student of international law and organization remarks that "the science of game theory has shown that an understanding of international relations may be acquired by comparing the rules of governmental conduct to those of a game." Again, Kenneth Thompson, who has written widely on the subject of power politics and diplomacy, now forsakes his own tradition of scholarly investigation of political phenomena to accept unquestioningly the claims of Herman Kahn on the virtues of civil defense, with Kahn being metamorphosed into "experts in the government and the RAND Corporation. . . ." As a *reductio ad absurdum* of the uses of deterrence theory, a newspaper reporter writes a book (lauded on the dust jacket by Kahn) consisting mostly of semiofficial statements in justification of a "no-cities" nuclear strategy, in which the proposed strategy is justified entirely by reference to scenarios and war games that have been played on computers in the Pentagon; the book contains hardly a reference to the real political world that exists outside the minds of those who decide what assumptions shall be fed into the computers.

Finally, and in a way most significantly, an economist, Michael D. Intriligator, has seized on the formal discussion of deterrence theory to present a paper on the supposed economic analysis of deterrence, which is not only useless but is highly misleading as well. The paper treats of all the abstract economic models I have referred to in this thesis, and some that I have not, in the most technical possible manner (so technical indeed as to be incomprehensible to the non-economist); but there is not one word in it that even vaguely relates to the problems of deterrence: that is, problems of international relations in the nuclear era. Intriligator's paper thus not only distorts the nature of the economist's contribution to matters of policy but—and this is its broader significance—like most formal deterrence theory it has the political effect of suggesting that "deterrence" refers to an area of study rather than to a specific political proposal. In fact, Intriligator seems merely to be one would-be exemplar of Bernard Brodie's remark that "RAND and other comparable institutions have played a role very much like certain great universities and research centers in the past, where some dedicated scholars and their students have opened up whole new fields of knowledge."

If the pseudo-science of strategic analysis comes to be viewed generally in the light Brodie casts on it, the results can only be unfortunate. Those who discuss international politics in a more traditional—one might say a more historically conscious—fashion, whether in support of, or in opposition to, current American nuclear policy, have hardly lost their voices. But certainly such persons do not have as much of the public ear as they used to have. Rather we find a public reaction suggested by the laudatory quotations about the new deterrence theorists, which I have noted earlier in Chapter II. And since, as we have seen, the overt content of deterrence theorizing is always an analysis of the *military* significance of a proposition, the growth of deterrence theory further puts immense pressure on whatever opponents remain to cast their own arguments also in as militarized a framework as possible: to prove that they too can be guardians of the national security. Thus the very content of debate, as well as its method, is changed by one of the parties to the debate.

Nor is distortion of genuine public debate the only possible consequence of the new intellectual imperialism. Considering the nature of the deterrence theorist's use of the supposed materials of social science, one can only understand those materials as having been selectively adapted to bolster an already internalized political stance. To dignify such a posture by calling it "expert," and to give those who adopt it special access to the public ear and to policy-makers for that reason, are actions that must have significant consequences.

One probable consequence lies in what appears to have become a permanent fact of modern life, in the United States at least. In a given area of knowledge "experts" command both more prestige and higher salaries, on the whole, than do "amateurs." The temptation for those who are intelligent and interested in a given field is thus to become experts in it. If becoming "expert" requires not only the possession of a technical education but also the adoption of a particular political and ethical stance, then there is trouble ahead for democratic politics. In the course of a gloss on ex-President Eisenhower's famous remarks about the threat posed by "the military-industrial complex," John Bennett has described this problem trenchantly:

Increasingly the close connection between the scientific community and, even more broadly, the academic community with defense policy adds to the complex of power which Eisenhower mentions. . . . The link between the RAND Corporation with the air force on the one hand and with the universities on the other dramatizes what I have in mind. Herman Kahn's book, *On Thermonuclear War,* is a great intellectual achievement and deserves much attention but it was designed by agencies within the defense department [sic] to change the attitudes of the American people about nuclear war and it was published by the press of a great university. The contribution of the academic community to government, including the defense department, is in itself not subject to criticism. And we may welcome, first of all, the sophistication and intellectual ferment that it has brought government. But in the long run there is a great danger that those who are most competent to criticize the policies of government will be inhibited by their responsibility in relation to those policies. There is danger that we shall confront one vast "establishment" which includes business, the military, the civilian government, the scientific community, foundations and the universities, and that informed public debate about the great moral issues concerned with national defense will be inhibited.

One can also describe the problem differently by looking at it the other way around. An elite can be defined, as Bennett defines it, by specifying those who are included in it. An elite may also be defined by specifying those who are *excluded* from it, and, further, by specifying the grounds on which they are excluded. When an "elite" consists merely of those who happen to hold political power at the present moment, and the struggle to replace them is an open one, then by the most usual definition of political democracy we may say that they are subject to replacement by its natural processes. However, when the elite is also defined by its possession of some particular expertise, then it will be relatively "open" or "closed" depending on the extent to which capability for attaining that expertise is evenly distributed throughout the different political and social groups in the society. The very worst case, I should think, is one in which so-called technical expertise is in actuality defined by one's explicit or tacit adherence to the substantive political position of those already in power. And that case is precisely the one that seems to obtain with regard to "expertise" in the field of national security policy. The intellectual imperialism of deterrence theory is not just an academic fact, but a political act. *If* game theory, systems analysis, and the naïve deterrence theory assumption of rationality are in fact the relevant techniques and assumptions for learning to think about such problems; *and* if thinking about those problems in this way is invariably associated with programmatic support of a deterrence policy, *then* a committed advocate of, say, general and complete disarmament who wishes to attain the status of a consulting "expert" is confronted with an arbitrary political obstacle.

Of course, deterrence theory may not have quite the importance attributed to it here. It may be that the actual public policy function of deterrence theory is not to influence policy-makers, but rather to provide them with rationalizations for decisions already made by more conventional methods. Or it may be that the course of American policy is already too rigidly set for the sources of that policy to be of practical concern.

With regard to the first possibility, however, the argument that one's work is not really influential hardly relieves one of the intellectual obligation to do it properly; and one should not provide rationalizations unless one believes in their validity. As to the more profound question concerning American political reality, if deterrence theory really has "won" whatever debate its proponents were engaging in, it still at least stands as an object lesson about how such debates ought *not* to be conducted in the future.

For the more solidified the reputation of "experts" becomes, the more, to that extent, will opposing viewpoints be blocked from getting a hearing. The possibility of influencing governmental decision-making, through available techniques of petition and pressure, is what chiefly defines the ability of different social groups to participate effectively in the democratic political process. The false attribution of expertness to an intellectual elite, which has in effect passed a test of political acceptability, narrows rather than enlarges the channels of influence. Pseudo-science such as that of deterrence theorists thus constitutes a disservice not only to the scholarly community, but ultimately to the democratic political process as well.

NOTES

1. The abstracted rationalism of deterrence theory finds its apotheosis in Morton Kaplan's remark that "If, in the real world, it is not possible for political or emotional reasons to adopt the strategy indicated in this article [the strategy of 'limited nuclear reprisals'] the calculus employed can be used to discover whether a reasonably effective alternative exists and, if so what it is." Why a calculus that has already given one worthless answer should be employed to find alternatives to that answer, Kaplan does not make clear.

2. It is sometimes claimed on behalf of biased work that anyway science can never be "objective." Extended discussion of such a viewpoint is profitless since regardless of whether the premise is true, the implied conclusion does not follow. Even if we can't be objective, still scientists and philosophers of diverse schools have little difficulty agreeing on what constitutes the *ideal* of objectivity. Therefore we can at the very least always judge how closely a given piece of scientific work approximates the condition of being bias-free. A genuine scientist will feel no hesitancy to claim that under certain conditions hydrogen and oxygen combine to make water, for the statement that they do so is true whether we like it to be or not. But the statement that the assumption of rationality makes a given strategy preferable to another is true only if we *like* it to be true—and a genuine scientist will therefore never claim that such a statement is factually descriptive. Although it may in a given instance be impossible to avoid subjectivity, we can at least avoid the pretense that it is objectivity.

11.

Hedley Bull: *Strategic Studies and Its Critics*

A few of the criticisms leveled against deterrence theorists—such as oversimplification and distortion of political reality—are accepted by Hedley Bull in the selection that follows. Unlike other critics, however, he believes that the civilian students of strategy have had a beneficial effect on strategic policy. (It should be noted that the selections by Bull, Green, Rathjens, Wohlstetter, and Knorr illustrate how assumptions—for example, those concerning the role of military force in the international system—can lead deterrence theorists and their critics to conflicting policy prescriptions for national security.)

Author of *Control of the Arms Race* and numerous other works in international relations and national security, Hedley Bull is Professor of International Relations at Australian National University, Canberra, and formerly (1964–67) director of the Arms Control and Disarmament Research Unit of the British Foreign Office.

The civilian strategic analysts who now constitute a distinct profession in the Western world have from the first been subject to criticism that has called in question the validity of their methods, their utility to society, and even their integrity of purpose.[1] Some of it is directed at particular strategists

Hedley Bull, "Strategic Studies and Its Critics," *World Politics*, Vol. 20, No. 4 (July 1968), pp. 593–605. Copyright © 1968 by Princeton University Press. Reprinted by permission of the publisher.

or at particular techniques they employ, but much of it purports to expose deficiencies that are characteristic of the genre. Some of this is of so scurrilous a nature as not to deserve a reply, but some raises issues of real importance. What are in fact the distinguishing features of the new style of strategic analysis? What has given rise to the criticisms that have been made of it? And what substance do the criticisms have?

Strategy in its most general sense is the art or science of shaping means so as to promote ends in any field of conflict. In the special sense in which I am using it here, the sense in which "strategy" is interchangeable with "military strategy," it is the art or science of exploiting military force so as to attain given objects of policy. If we contrast the strategic thinking of contemporary military analysts with the classical tradition of strategic thought from Clausewitz to Douhet, certain of its peculiarities are at once apparent.

First, strategic thinking at the present time is no longer exclusively concerned with the efficient conduct of war. From the time of Napoleon to that of Hitler, strategy was conceived of as an aspect of war. Contrasting it with tactics, which was the art of winning battles, Clausewitz defined strategy as "the art of employment of battles as a means to gain the object in war." [2] How to gain the object in war remains a central preoccupation of contemporary strategic thinking, but it is no longer the only one or necessarily the most important. Attention has shifted away from war as an instrument of policy toward the threat of war, and studies of actual violence have given place to analyses of "deterrence," "crisis management," "the manipulation of risk"—or, as we call it when it is practiced by our opponents rather than ourselves, "blackmail." Moreover, gaining the object in war, even when it remains the concern of strategists, is no longer always seen in Clausewitz' sense of attaining victory by imposing our will on the adversary. In discussions of the conduct of strategic nuclear war the object of victory over the opponent has in fact taken second place to that of our own survival. It has sometimes been argued that the chief mission of United States strategic nuclear forces in the event of general war is that of the limitation of damage suffered by the United States and its allies—an object that is not relative to the amount of damage suffered by the enemy, but absolute.

Second, strategic thinking is no longer the preserve of the military. The great strategic writers of the past, like Liddell Hart, Fuller, and Mao Tse-tung in our own time, were soldiers (or sailors or airmen) or ex-soldiers. They were often quite bad soldiers; and they had quailties of mind that soldiers, good and bad, do not often have. But underlying all their theorizing was the assumption that strategy was in some sense a practical business, that experience of the management of forces and weapons in war, even if it was not a sufficient condition of strategic understanding, was at least a necessary one.

The military profession today is very far from having vacated the field of strategy; in wide areas of strategic policy the chiefs of staff responsible to governments remain the preponderant influence. But in the United States and to a lesser extent elsewhere in the Western world, the civilian experts have made great inroads. They have overwhelmed the military in the quality and quantity of their contributions to the literature of the subject; no one would now think of turning to the writings of retired officers rather than to the standard academic treatments of deterrence, limited war, or arms control for illumination of the problems of the nuclear age. They increasingly dominate the field of education and instruction in the subject—the academic and quasi-academic centers of strategic studies have displaced the staff colleges and war colleges, except in narrow fields of professional knowledge. And, most prominently in the United States, the civilian strategists have entered the citadels of power and have prevailed over military advisers on major issues of policy.

A third peculiarity of strategic thinking at the present time is its abstract and speculative character. There has not yet been a nuclear war, and the possibility that there will be one has not yet existed long enough for it to have become clear how the structure of international life will be affected. Anyone who has embarked upon a discussion of what the conditions are under which one country can deter another from doing something, of whether or not limitations are possible in nuclear war, of whether the nuclear stalemate makes conflict at lower levels more likely or less, or of whether one country can credibly threaten to use nuclear weapons on behalf of another must have experienced the sense of being at sea in an argument in which, it seems, almost any position can be plausibly defended and almost none is safe from attack.

Strategic thinking, of course, has always been speculative. It has always had to deal with the future, and it has always involved the making of plans, the fulfilment of which depends on decisions taken by the opponent as well as on those we take ourselves. And the conditions of war and crisis under which these decisions have to be made make them peculiarly difficult to anticipate and peculiarly unlikely to follow the lines of assumed standards of rationality. The advent of nuclear and missile technology, however, has rendered strategic thinking speculative to a degree that it had not previously attained. It is not the physical effects of nuclear explosives and missiles that are speculative; indeed, in this respect war has become more predictable and measurable than before. What cannot be confidently foreseen is how statesmen, governments, and societies will behave under the stress of the use of these weapons or the threat to use them. In a period of vast changes in warfare and its place in human affairs, the relevance of history and experience, and the competence of those whose expertise is founded in them, have rightly been called in question.

A fourth characteristic of strategic thinking at the present time is its sophistication and high technical quality. Many students of strategy today take the view that until our own time military affairs escaped sustained scientific study and received only the haphazard attention of second-rate minds. Accordingly they see themselves as presiding over the birth of a new science, eliminating antiquated methods and replacing them with up-to-date ones. Some take the view that there is a close analogy between strategic studies and economics, and they hold out the hope that the former subject, when it emerges from its birth pangs, will enable us to rationalize our choices and increase our control of our environment to the same extent that the latter has done.

This view does less than justice to the classical tradition of strategic thinking, while it also fails to recognize the very slight extent to which the new scientific rigor in strategic studies has so far circumscribed the domain of speculation. Nevertheless, it is clear that the intellectual resources now being devoted to strategic studies are without precedent and that this has resulted in a literature of higher technical quality and a discussion of a higher standard of sophistication than have existed before. One incidental consequence of this is the emergence of strategic studies as an appropriate subject for inclusion in university curricula. Although I do not myself believe that it is desirable to separate strategic studies from the wider study of international relations, it can be argued that it compares very favorably with some other branches of political science both in its moral and social relevance and as an intellectual discipline.

A number of factors account for the barrage of criticism that the civilian strategists have had to face. For those who feel guilt about modern war or have fear of it—and in some degree this includes all persons who are sensitive and aware—the strategists have undoubtedly provided a scapegoat. The political influence that the civilian strategists have come to command, especially though not exclusively in the United States, has caused resentment—on the one hand among the older generation of soldiers and civil servants whose influence they have displaced, and on the other hand among their fellow intellectuals who have remained outsiders. Their willingness to treat strategy as a specialist's subject, even as an esoteric one, has irritated those who are unable to understand or to emulate them. Their insistence on the complexity of the problems of strategy and arms control has been unwelcome to purveyors of simple solutions of one kind or another. Most basically, perhaps, the position of the professional strategist is and will remain controversial because the legitimacy of the question he sets himself—What shall the state do with its military force?—is itself controversial. While there continues to be disagreement in modern society as to whether or not the state should ever use military force or possess it at all, there will not be general agreement about the worth and utility of students of strategy, in the way in which there is now (although there has not always been) about that of students of medicine, architecture, or economics.

To show that the motives that underlie criticism of the strategist are sometimes discreditable is not, of course, to say that it is only from these sources that criticism arises, still less to provide a rebuttal of the criticisms themselves. Many of the criticisms are worth sympathetic consideration. In my view they do not constitute, either singly or collectively, a valid indictment of the work of the civilian strategists. But we should be grateful that they have been made, for they do draw attention to some false paths along which strategists might stray and sometimes have strayed. Here I shall consider five of the charges.

The first and most common complaint is that the strategists leave morality out of account. Strategists are often said to be technicians and calculators who are indifferent as to the moral standing of the causes for which war is undertaken or of the means by which it is carried on.

There is a sense in which strategic thinking does and should leave morality out of account. Strategy is about the relationship between means and ends, and an exercise in "pure" strategy will exclude consideration of the moral nature of the means and the ends, just as it will exclude anything else that is extraneous. If what is being said is that strategic judgments should be colored by moral considerations or that strategic inquiry should be restricted by moral taboos, this is something that the strategist is bound to reject. If what the critics of Herman Kahn have in mind is that he should not have thought about the unthinkable or that he should have thought about it with his heart instead of his head, then they are obstructing him in his essential task.

What can be said, however, is that while strategy is one thing and morals are another, the decisions that governments take in the field of military policy should not be based on considerations of strategy alone. If the charge against the strategists is that their advice to governments is drawn up in purely strategic terms, as if strategic imperatives were categorical imperatives, or that they themselves have no other dimension in their thinking than the calculation of means and ends, then this is a serious and legitimate complaint.

But so far as one can judge, such a charge is not true of any of the strategists. It is easy to see that their works, dealing as they do with strategy and not with other subjects, might give the impression that decisions should be determined by the logic of this subject alone, but there is no reason to believe that this impression is correct. Strategists as a class, it seems to me, are neither any less nor any more sensitive to moral considerations than are other intelligent and educated persons in the West.

Why, then, is the charge so frequently made? Can all the critics be wrong? Surely as between Herman Kahn and his critic James Newman, as between Irving Horowitz and those he calls "the new civilian militarists," or as between Anatol Rapoport and the various unnamed strategists who are his targets there is some sort of moral disagreement. I believe that there is, but that what is at issue is not whether or not moral questions should be asked before decisions are taken but what the answers to the moral questions are.

In almost any disagreement as to whether or not to resort to war or to threaten it, or as to how a war should be conducted or what risks in it should be run, there are moral arguments to be advanced on both sides. What the critics take to be the strategists' insensitivity to moral considerations is in most cases the strategists' greater sense of the moral stature of American and Western political objectives for which war and the risk of war must be undertaken. The notion that virtue in international conduct lies simply in avoiding risk of war and never in assuming it, always in self-abnegation and never in self-assertion, only in obeying the rules a world community might legislate if it existed and never in pursuing the different moral guides that are appropriate in a situation in which it does not—such a notion is of course untenable. But it forms part of the perspective of many of the critics. What chiefly characterizes the so-called idealist school to which they belong is not (as is often said) that it exaggerates the force of moral considerations, still less that it alone is endowed with moral vision, but that it fails to appreciate the full range of the moral argument, that it embraces what Treitschke called "the monkish type of virtue" without being able to see that there is any other.

There is, I think, a related moral disagreement between the strategists and their critics, which concerns the role of the strategist as an adviser to governments. It is said that there is something unbecoming to an intellectual—or at all events to a university man, with his allegiance to the universal republic of science—in bestowing the fruits of his strategic advice upon any particular government. Since governments use this advice to further their conflicts with one another, the strategic adviser is in a different position from the scholar or scientist who gives advice about the economy or health or education, since in these fields the interests of one nation may be advanced without injuring those of others. The scholar may legitimately proffer advice, if he has any, about the conditions of peace, so the argument goes, but he is disloyal to his calling if he provides advice about war.[3]

Some of this criticism may be met readily enough. One may point out that the strategic interests of nations are not wholly exclusive of one another and that contemporary strategists have been inclined to draw attention to the common interests that nations have in avoiding nuclear war and in limiting it if it occurs. One may say that one of their contributions has been the systematic study of arms control, which may be defined as cooperation among antagonistic states in advancing their perceived common interests in military policy. Arms-control policy is, I should say, subsumed under strategy as a special case. It may also be pointed out that it is facile to regard war and peace as alternative objects of policy, as if peace did not need to be enforced or war were not an outgrowth of diplomacy.

Yet it remains true that the strategic adviser does assist the government he serves to advance its objectives at the expense of those of other governments. But whether or not there is anything in the position of such an adviser unbecoming to a scholar or a scientist will depend on what we take the moral nature of that government and its objectives to be. Few of the critics would, I think, argue that the scientists who assisted the British and American governments during the Second World War, and whose position the contemporary strategists have inherited, were acting in an improper way. Not everyone will agree that the position is the same now; but at least it is not possible to maintain that there is any general incompatibility between assisting a state to augment its relative military position and remaining faithful to scholarly or scientific values.

The second criticism that I wish to discuss is that strategists take for granted the existence of military force and confine themselves to considering how to exploit it, thereby excluding a whole range of policies such as disarmament or nonviolent resistance that are intended to abolish military force or to provide substitutes for it.

It is true that strategists take the fact of military force as their starting point. The question is whether any other starting point is possible at all, whether the doctrine of disarmament that is implicit in this complaint is not inherently untenable. The capacity for organized violence between states is inherent in the nature of man and his environment. The most that can be expected from a total disarmament agreement is that it might make armaments and armed forces fewer and more primitive.

If what is meant by "total disarmament" is a state of affairs in which war is physically impossible, in which states cannot wage war even when they want to (this is what Litvinov meant when he first put forward the proposal in 1927), then we must say that such a state of affairs cannot be. If, on the other hand, what is meant is a situation in which military force has been reduced to very low qualitative and quantitative levels, then this is something that can in principle occur and may well seem worth trying to bring about. But the view that security against war is best provided by a low level of armaments rather than a high one is a particular strategic theory; the arguments for it and against it belong to the same mode of discourse as that we apply in evaluating any other proposition about the relationship between military force and possible ends of policy.

Either, then, the second criticism is a nonsense or it represents an attempt to contribute to strategic reasoning, not a statement about it from outside. In fact, it would seem to me, proposals for radical disarmament and for nonviolent resistance have received a fair hearing within the Western community of strategists. No doubt strategists are inclined to think too readily in terms of military solutions to the problems of foreign policy and to lose sight of the other instruments that are available. But this is the occupational disease of any specialist, and the remedy for it lies in entering into debate with the strategist and correcting his perspective.

The third criticism is that strategists are inclined to make unreal assumptions about international politics and that in comparing alternative strategies and computing their costs and benefits they make assumptions that simplify and distort political reality, that do not allow for change, and that in the course of the subsequent analysis become lost to sight.

This is a complaint that has a great deal of force. The technical rigor and precision of much strategic analysis has been achieved at the cost of losing touch with political variety and change. If the political terms in the strategists' equations were more complex and were changed more frequently, the beauty of much of the ratiocination would be destroyed.

Some of the now-classic analyses of America's problem in choosing her weapons and military posture were founded upon the assumption that there was only one significant relationship in nuclear international politics, that between the United States and the Soviet Union, and that this consisted only of hostility. Not only, as it were, was the game two-person and zero-sum, but the two persons were assumed to be identical twins, Country A and Country B. Even when these analyses were first made they were a simplification of reality, but with their survival into the age of the Soviet-American détente and of the disintegration of the Atlantic Alliance and the Communist bloc, they became dangerously unreal. The greatest absurdities of this sort in recent times formed part of the debate that took place in the United States during the Kennedy administration about the control of nuclear weapons in NATO. The various solutions were set out in programmatic form—a United States nuclear monopoly, national nuclear forces, a NATO nuclear force, a European nuclear force—and their advantages and disadvantages were spelled out on the basis that NATO was a single person and that the sole requirement of that person was to deter attack by the Soviet Union. Not all those who contributed to the debate, of course, formulated the problem in this way, but many a weighty treatise appeared that did so. General de Gaulle has now demonstrated what was perhaps all along clear, that Paris and London are not Washington and that nuclear forces have diplomatic functions as well as military ones; but it is extraordinary for how long, under its own momentum, this strange logic persisted.

All that one can say in defense of the strategists against this charge is that follies of this sort are not inherent in what they do, that technical precision must often be sacrificed so as to allow for political variety and change, and that enough of the strategists are aware of this to ensure that the corrections can come from inside the strategic community.

The fourth criticism is that the civilian strategists are pseudoscientific in their methods, that specialist techniques they employ—such as game theory, systems analysis, simulation, and the writing of scenarios—are bogus when used to arrive at strategic decisions and serve to give an air of expertise to positions arbitrarily and subjectively arrived at. This is the theme of the book *Deadly Logic,* by Philip Green, and it is also part of the meaning of the wrong-headed but subtle and powerful book *Strategy and Conscience,* by Anatol Rapoport.

The crux of the matter is the attack on game theory, which more clearly than any of the other techniques mentioned does represent an impressive expertise. Rapoport presents some strong arguments against the application of game theory to strategic decision-making. Exercises in game theory, he says, deal in numerical probabilities, but these cannot be assigned to unique events. Such exercises assume the unlimited ability of each party to think and compute with no limit of time—which actual decision-makers cannot do. The exercises assume that the goals of each party are single, simple, and unchanging, whereas historical individuals and groups have objectives that are plural, complex, and subject to constant revision. And so on.

This attack on the use of game theory is bewildering. As Donald Brennan has pointed out in a review of Rapoport, the great majority of civilian strategists do not use game theory and indeed would be at a loss to give any account of it.[4] There are, certainly, a number of strategists, like Thomas Schelling, who have mastered this technique, but in their work exercises in game theory serve only to illustrate points that are independently arrived at; they have not employed game theory in order to determine solutions to strategic problems. As far as I know, the only person who has claimed that game theory presents a method of solving strategic problems is Oskar Morgenstern of Princeton University. Morgenstern collaborated with John von Neumann in producing *Theory of Games and Economic Behavior* and has also written a book on strategy, *The Question of National Defense*.[5] But even in Morgenstern's book, which contains much rhetoric about the value of game theory, it is not possible to find an instance in which he makes use of it. I do not despair of finding an example of what Green and Rapoport are talking about, but I must say I have not so far come across one. It may be that although game theory is not an essential or even a significantly used technique of the civilian strategists, some of the logic of game theory is implicit in the way some strategists do their thinking, and a critique of the former is a way of providing a critique of the latter.[6] The basic point of Philip Green's book, that the technique and rigor that the civilian strategists have brought to the subject do not provide a means of circumventing political choices and that they can be and sometimes are employed as a political weapon in support of one arbitrarily chosen policy or another, is undoubtedly correct. This, however, is an argument for recognizing the limits of rigor and precision and for being on guard against their misuse, not for abandoning rigor and precision in favor of something else.

Both in the domestic defense debates in Western countries today and in international rivalries over arms control or the sharing of military burdens within alliances, the strategist is constantly finding that his works are pressed into the service of political objectives that are pursued on different grounds. The army, the navy, the air force, each has its strategic ideology; the United States, France, and Great Britain, in contending with one another as to how nuclear weapons shall be controlled in NATO, as to where and in what way a war in Europe would be fought, as to what contributions shall be made to the shield forces in central Europe—each develops a strategic doctrine that points to the end it has in view, and each is anxious to exploit the authority of studies independently undertaken and scientifically followed through.

The strategist himself, however, cannot be held responsible for the use that others make of his ideas. Moreover, the fact that strategic expertise has come to have a political function as an ideology is inevitable and, I believe, by no means wholly regrettable. Scientific expertise has become the idiom of debate, within governments and between them, not only in the strategic field but in many others. If it is pressed into service by one party, the other parties must acquire it themselves or go under. The British Foreign Office now finds it necessary to employ its own economic experts to do battle with the Treasury and the Department of Economic Affairs, its own scientific experts to deal with the Ministry of Technology and the Atomic Energy Authority, and its own strategic experts to contend with the Ministry of Defence. The governments of Western Europe in the last decade have found themselves constantly at a most serious political disadvantage in relation to the United States in defense matters because they have not had a body of strategic expertise of their own with which to frustrate American attempts to overawe them. That they will acquire such expertise there can be no doubt.

These developments are not wholly to be regretted because they do raise the standard and tone of strategic debate at the highest levels of decision; the necessity under which governments, and departments of governments, labor of developing strategic ideologies does show that somewhere in the process of decision, independent and expert studies are being carried out and that these cannot be ignored.

Is it the case that the civilian strategists in America have been consistent endorsers of the main lines of United States foreign policy and that they have hidden this policy outlook beneath a pretense of objectivity? The work of the most prominent of these persons originated in criticism and questioning of the established policies of the Eisenhower Administration. No doubt it still has proceeded on the basis of assumptions held in common with official thinking, which looked at from the outside appear as orthodox. In the writings of some of the strategists, more particularly those Rapoport calls the "neo-traditionalists," the assumptions (e.g., about the existence of a "threat," the need for military strength, the morality of providing it, and so on) are spelled out and defended. In the writings of others they are not, and in these cases it is important that critics should identify the assumptions and question them. But the shaping of United States military policy is not an exercise in philosophy or theology; at some point firm assumptions have to be made, and on the basis of them the costs and benefits of alternatives worked out. It is inevitable that in this process the assumptions will be taken as read and also that books and papers will be written in which the authors address themselves to others who make the same assumptions, rather than to the public at large.

The fifth criticism, although it also comes from Anatol Rapoport, is in some ways at loggerheads with the fourth. It is that the sin of the strategist, far from being his covert commitment to political purposes, is his objectivity. This is really the distinctive contribution of Rapoport's book. The strategist is detached and aloof, but he has no right to be. The effect of his cold appraisal of the world as he sees it is to perpetuate the nightmare around him or to create it where it does not exist. Given the dangers of the world as it is now, the appropriate attitude is not to describe it but to go to work on it. The strategists, who have the ear of the powerful, might accomplish great things if they abandoned the strategic mode of reasoning for the conscientious; but instead they are collaborators in the system and are speeding up its movement toward catastrophe.

If there is a kernel of truth in what Rapoport says it is that the strategist, like all students of social affairs, is related to what he studies not only as subject to object but also as cause to effect. It is always important to recognize in foreign policy, as in the conduct of Western policy toward Russia and China now, that the intentions and goals of a country, whether they are peaceful or aggressive, are not fixed and given, but are always in part the product of our own action toward them.

But this basis of truth does not sustain the strange construction that Rapoport erects upon it. There are certain things that Russia will do whatever policies the United States follows toward her, certain conflicts in the world that simply have to be taken as given. Arthur Burns has pointed out in a review that one of Rapoport's errors is to make the common American assumption of a fundamentally two-person situation.[7] From the perspective of a small country on the sidelines of the international arena, the Soviet-American conflict simply appears as a datum, something that has arisen quite independently of anything that small country did or might have done. It is, to say the least, greatly to exaggerate the influence of the strategists to hold them responsible for the rise of Russian power and for the overflowing beyond Russian borders of the revolution of 1917.

But even if Rapoport is right and America, if not her strategists, has it in her power to mold the behavior of Russia or China, this does not necessarily support the conclusions that Rapoport would like to draw from this. If United States policy in recent years has contributed to the changes that have made the Soviet Union a more satisfied power and a more conservative influence in world affairs, this may have as much to do with America's strength and firmness as will her overtures of conciliation or readiness to make concessions.

The doctrines that the civilian strategic analysts in the West have evolved in the last decade are scarcely the last word on strategy in the nuclear age, but should be seen as first, faltering steps in defining a problem that will be with us for as far into the future as we can see. The three notions that have been most central in these doctrines—"deterrence," "limited war," and "arms control"—have all been elaborated chiefly in the context of the Soviet-American confrontation, and their implications for the more polycentric diplomatic field that now exists have not been thought out. They have all been put forward in relation to classical international conflict between states that are internally stable and armed with the most advanced weapons, and they have not been adapted to the different but now more prominent circumstances of civil conflicts within unstable states with primitive military equipment. Moreover, even in the narrow field in which, quite rightly, the civilian strategists have concentrated their efforts, their most fundamental assumptions are open to challenge, as the debate about ballistic missile defense is now showing.

Yet the work of the civilian strategists has at least charted some reasoned course where otherwise there might well have been only drift. It has provided some solid intellectual fare that subsequent generations, even though they reject it, are at least likely to recognize as a serious attempt to come to grips with the problem. When one asks oneself what the history of strategic policy in the West might have been in the last ten years had this influence not been brought to bear, or when one contemplates the moral and intellectual poverty of the debate about nuclear affairs (or of that part of it we are able to see) in the Soviet Union where in fact no such influence exists, it is difficult to escape the conclusion that even though the civilian strategists have sometimes committed the errors I have been exploring, they have served us well.

NOTES

1. See, e.g., James R. Newman, review of Herman Kahn's *On Thermonuclear War*, *Scientific American*, CCIV (March 1961), 197–98; P. M. S. Blackett, *Studies of War, Nuclear and Conventional* (New York, 1962), chap. 10; Sir Solly Zuckerman, *Scientists and War: The Impact of Science on Military and Civil Affairs* (New York, 1967), chap. 5; Irving L. Horowitz, *The War Game: Studies of the New Civilian Militarists* (New York, 1963); Anatol Rapoport, *Strategy and Conscience* (New York, 1964); Philip Green, *Deadly Logic: The Theory of Nuclear Deterrence* (Columbus, 1966).

2. *On War*, Book III, chap. 1.

3. See, e.g., Max Teichmann, "Strategic Studies or Peace Research?" *Arena* (Melbourne), No. 12 (Autumn 1967), 9–16.

4. *Bulletin of the Atomic Scientists*, XXI (December 1965), 25–30.

5. *Theory of Games and Economic Behavior* (Princeton, 1944); *The Question of National Defense* (Princeton, 1959), esp. 61, 164, 269.

6. In his reply to Brennan's review, Rapoport says, "My complaint against the strategists was not that they use or misuse game theory (although one of my earlier articles was so entitled). On the contrary, my complaint was that they have not learned some important lessons of game theory" (*Bulletin of the Atomic Scientists*, XXI [December 1965], 31–36). This is a slippery reformulation that does not answer Brennan's charge, viz., that Rapoport implies that strategists use game theory, whereas they do not.

7. Arthur Lee Burns, "Must Strategy and Conscience Be Disjoined?" *World Politics*, XVII (July 1965), 687–702.

THE USSR AND CHINA: WHAT KIND OF CHALLENGES?

12.

Marshall D. Shulman: *The Future of the Soviet-American Competition*

The cold war hostility of the first postwar decade has evolved into the present limited adversary relationship between the United States and the USSR. Marshall Shulman examines the conditions in the international system which are affecting the superpowers, as well as the trends within these countries. Looking to the late 1970's he suggests that the Soviet-American competition can be viewed positively as a learning process, one which may eventually produce a new cooperation between the two giants on problems of mutual concern.

Marshall D. Shulman, "The Future of the Soviet-American Competition," *Soviet-American Relations and World Order: The Two and the Many*, Adelphi Paper No. 66 (March 1970), pp. 1–10. Reprinted by permission of the Institute for Strategic Studies, London, and the author.

Marshall Shulman is Professor of Government and Director of the Russian Institute at Columbia University. A leading authority on the Soviet Union, he has published *Stalin's Foreign Policy Reappraised* and *Beyond the Cold War,* among other works.

Politics delights in surprises, and predictions about anything so complex as the adversary relationship between the Soviet Union and the United States are probably best written in ink that is guaranteed to fade almost immediately.

Nevertheless, the exercise of trying to anticipate what form the Soviet-American competition may take in the 1970's can be useful. It obliges us to order our thoughts about the changes in international politics that will affect this relationship. It compels us to come to some tentative conclusions about the nature of the two political and economic systems and how they are evolving. And if we believe it is important to moderate the conflict and to move it in the direction of cooperation—as all reasonable men must believe—a clear-eyed view of how it now seems to be moving is a good place to begin.

Since there are differences of opinion about the essential nature of the conflict, it might be well to make explicit at the outset the approach followed in this paper, that since World War II, the Soviet-American relationship has been mainly a nation-state rivalry for military power and for political influence, complicated by differences in political culture and ideology. This rivalry has also been complicated by the fact that these two countries became world powers at a time when former power relationships were dissolving, and new lines of influence were being drawn upon a starkly bipolar map of the world. Coincidentally, the arrival of nuclear weapons led each country to see its vital security as threatened by the power of the other.

To approach the problem in this way does not mean that we treat the two nations as simple entities. There are forces and pressures within each complex political system that we may not be able to delineate with precision, but we are aware that the declaration of strategic or foreign policy as though it were the product of a unified and rational process may often represent an after-the-fact rationalization of the interplay of these forces and pressures. We therefore approach Soviet-American relations as the interaction between two complex systems, and we are necessarily concerned with their inner dynamics, both in the near-term shifts in the tides of politics, and in longer-term evolutionary changes.

Some will argue that ideology is a greater determinant in the behaviour of the two systems than it appears to be in the following analysis, which treats it as a secondary and transitional factor. This is of course a matter of belief, difficult to prove or disprove. Those who share this objection would as a consequence find it difficult to accept the main conclusion of this paper, that the exercise of political will on each side could reverse present trends which otherwise appear to lead towards a more intense military competition and exacerbated political tensions.

II

We begin with some conditions of change in international politics which seem likely to affect the background against which the Soviet-American competition will operate in the 1970's.

1. The first and most important condition is *the accelerating pace of technological innovation*. This has two aspects:

(*a*) The rapid introduction of *qualitative and quantitative changes in strategic weapons systems*. After a period of relative stability and an approach to approximate parity, the strategic weapons balance is being affected by the introduction of new systems of greater complexity and higher performance. If this trend is not deflected by conscious effort on the part of the two countries, the effects will be to increase costs, uncertainties and consequently tensions. It is also likely to increase the influence of soldiers and military interest groups on the decision-making process within both countries.

(*b*) The rapid introduction of *new industrial technology*. The advanced industrial countries, including not only the United States and the Soviet Union but also Japan and Western Europe, are experiencing a new phase of industrialization, involving the accelerated introduction of technological innovation. If this trend continues, it will change the relative economic power relationships among the industrial countries, to the advantage in particular of West Germany and Japan. It will also widen the gap between the industrialized and the developing countries. Equally important, it is already beginning to have profound social and political consequences within the industrial countries.

2. *Changes in the structure of the world power system*. Given the continuing force of nationalism in the present period, and the limited capacity of strategic power to influence political developments, the trend in international politics appears to be towards a diffusion of power and a diminishing bipolarity in regard to all forms of power other than the capacity to wage general nuclear war. What appears to be emerging is a multiple balance of power system, based upon the rising potential of Japan, China, West Germany—or Western Europe, if the momentum towards West European integration is resumed.

3. *The continuing rise of the North-South problem as a source of international tension*. The continued growth of the industrial countries and the incapacity of the developing countries to cope with the food-population balance and the problems of nation-building, as well as innumerable potential sources of conflict throughout the developing areas (religious, tribal, borders, etc.), will generate tensions which will cut across the Soviet-American competition, exacerbating it in some cases but producing common or parallel interests in others.

4. The *intensification of social and political changes within the industrialized countries*. For reasons which may be partly a consequence of advancing industrialization but are partly still obscure, domestic forces are becoming a larger source of political dynamism in the present period and are likely to have increasing effects upon international politics in many ways that are difficult to fore-

cast. This is reflected in the rejection of traditional values by a young generation in search of new political formulations, in the shifting coalitions of political power in many countries (especially in Western Europe), in the groping adaptations of political institutions to the changing requirements of modern technology. One consequence is an increasing domestic preoccupation within the industrialized countries, and the relatively greater role of domestic factors in the determination of foreign policies. In both the Soviet Union and the United States, social tensions are increased by the paradoxical rise in pressures for change and, at the same time, strong conservative resistance to change.

III

This leads us to a brief consideration of some trends within the United States and the Soviet Union and in their respective foreign policies that may be expected to affect their relationship during the coming decade.

The situation in the United States is characterized by a polarization in political life. The rise of serious domestic tensions, reflected in student activism, militancy in the Negro civil rights movement, protests concerning poverty, urban and environmental problems, and a generalized mood of irascibility and anger, has begotten a backlash movement of ascending strength, expressed in a pendular swing towards conservatism. (As we shall see in a moment, the backlash reaction to pressures for change appears to be common to the current Soviet experience as well.)

Economic trends in the United States also reflect contrasting developments. There has been an extraordinary growth in advanced technology and a widening involvement in economic operations abroad through the remarkable expansion of multinational corporations—themselves a new structural factor in international politics. But at the same time, the United States has been experimenting with monetary controls in an effort to check a persistent inflationary trend during a period of decline in the rate of growth of the gross national product, seeking to avert a recession and an increase in unemployment to serious levels. In the event of a recession, the tide of domestic politics could be reversed.

In foreign policy, it would be difficult to overestimate the scarring domestic effect of the Vietnam war. The Vietnam issue has stimulated both general disaffection and specific pressures against foreign commitments and against the military establishment. These have weakened support for foreign policy, foreign aid programmes and military expenditures in favour of domestic programmes, although they have not resulted in any substantial shift of resources towards the domestic front. The debate over the anti-ballistic missile system, in addition to expressing cumulative resistance to military influences, served an educational function in creating a wider understanding of the implications of the new phase of the strategic weapons race. The prospect for parity with the Soviet Union is beginning to gain *some* public acceptance, and talks with the Soviet Union on strategic weapons have been well received as a general proposition, but it should be said that progress towards specific arms limitation will require further development of national opinion about the nature of security under present conditions. The population as a whole has not yet been weaned from the "little blue blanket" of security through superiority. Traditionally, the professional military interests, together with that part of the business community directly involved as military suppliers and the small circle in the Congress with special interests in military affairs, have had a relatively free hand in determining military procurement policies, but a countervailing force has been developing in American political life which cuts across the political spectrum. This coalition draws strength not only from liberal anti-military sentiments, reacting to Vietnam and concern about domestic priorities, but also from conservative opposition to the expansion of the federal budget and the level of taxation. (It is indicative of the attitude of a large part of the business community that the stock-market, in the midst of a general decline, has bounded upward with every rumour of progress towards peace in Vietnam.) Despite the conservative tide in politics, therefore, the balance between these contending pressures appears to be fairly even, but it would be a mistake to underestimate the latent political strength of conservative preference for military muscle. This balance is sensitive to international developments, such as Czechoslovakia. If events raise the level of apprehension about Soviet capabilities or intentions, conservative support for higher military capabilities would undoubtedly weigh more heavily in the balance. In the absence of hard evidence, however, manipulation of the "Soviet threat" is more sceptically received than it was in the past.

Unlike the situation of two decades ago, there appears to be no tendency to displace domestic tensions upon foreign objects. The "cold war" has little emotional appeal, but it may also be observed that the movements of radical protest do not find their inspiration in the Soviet Union. Except for the Vietnam issue, foreign policy is not in the forefront of American politics. Although the mood of retrenchment is strong, it has limits: it does not, for example, call into question the basic principle of the commitment to the defence of Western Europe. Moreover, the effort of the Administration to define a post-Vietnam policy for Asia as a whole which will continue to maintain an American influence in that area while avoiding involvement in internal disputes has met with general support. There is also general support for the steps advanced by the Administration for the gradual improvement of relations with China, but despite Soviet suspicions on this score there is no widespread or responsible inclination to try to exploit the Sino-Soviet conflict.

In sum, given the domestic preoccupations, the conservative tide in politics, and the balance of pressures around military issues, the United States is capable of moving cautiously over time towards a reduction of tensions with the Soviet Union and away from a commitment to overwhelming superiority, if no shocks intervene to change these balances. Although past events have left a residual scepticism about purely atmospheric swings between eras of good-will and sharp hostility, perhaps the most important point to note is the interdependent effect of the balance of forces within each country upon the other.

If it is hazardous to generalize so broadly and so impressionistically about the United States, how much more so is it in the case of the Soviet Union. Unfortunately, many of our impressions concerning Soviet trends are necessarily speculative, where more direct knowledge might help to dispel some of the dark suspicions which multiply our troubles. But until more direct knowledge is possible, we have no choice but to make the best judgments we can, with as much detachment as possible, on trends in the Soviet situation that may have a bearing on her relations with the United States in the coming decade.

Beginning with the domestic economic side, we can observe that while the Soviet economy has overcome the decline in its growth rate which set in during the early 1960's, it is not showing the buoyant growth of the 1950's and faces some institutional problems likely to be of mounting concern. Soviet statistics claim an overall growth rate of a little over 7 percent. Most Western analysts believe the figure is between 5 and 6 percent at the most, which would still be impressive by international standards.

The general improvement in material conditions for Soviet citizens appears to be continuing its upward course, for recent Soviet investment policies have favoured the consumer and the military sectors at the expense of production growth. Nevertheless, although Soviet consumers have more money to spend, they have experienced difficulty in finding goods and services on which to spend it, and they have particularly felt the effects of shortcomings in such agricultural items as meat, fresh fruit and vegetables.

In addition to the agricultural sector, Soviet analysts have been frank to acknowledge some persistent difficulties in labour productivity, capital investment and construction.

Of more fundamental concern to Soviet planners, however, have been the problems of technological innovation and management administration. Despite the fact that the Ministry of Instrumentation, Automation and Guidance Systems has been registering the highest growth rate of the entire industrial sector, and that scientific research and development has been greatly enlarged and re-organized (with emphasis, however, upon military and space activities), Soviet authorities have expressed a continuing preoccupation with the vital problem of improving the process by which new technology emerges from research and development and is applied to industry, along with accompanying improvements in modern management. On this score, the Soviet Union has not kept pace with the technological revolution which has been manifest in Western Europe, Japan and the United States, except in the military and space fields and in certain limited sectors of metallurgy and machinery.

This sector of the economy, of evident importance to the future industrial power of the Soviet Union, raises problems fundamental to the political system. To an outside observer, the most significant aspect of Soviet political life today is the interplay between two tendencies: one, to adapt the system and its policies to the requirements of modern technology and management; the other, to preserve as a matter of the highest priority the leading role of the Communist Party bureaucracy. The latter tendency represents a form of conservative backlash. It relies upon exhortation and coercion to maintain its position. It has been intensifying campaigns for ideological conformity, narrowed the latitudes within which intellectuals and nationality groups may express themselves, and narrowed politics and policy-making to the small circle at the top of the Party hierarchy. The Soviet Union is not lacking in talented scientists, technicians and economic administrators, but their efforts to modernize the system would require a more flexible political administration at the top in order to be effective.

There is evidence of many impulses towards modernizing the archaic impedances to economic progress. Within recent years, sociological studies have begun to deal more realistically with the attitudes and desires of the work force. Theorists have been cautiously re-working the standard ideological formulations to bring them closer to a realistic appreciation of the scientific and technological revolution in the world, and the nature of contemporary capitalism. Scientific research has sought to overcome its isolation from the experience of other countries in such matters as automation, the applications of advanced technology, including computer techniques and administrative theory and practice. In time these efforts towards modernization may be successful, but this does not appear likely until the political leadership is prepared to accept greater resiliency in its mode of governance, which is to say that it shall have to come to terms with the crucial question of what is to be the role of the Communist Party under conditions of advanced industrialization.

If the system is to adapt itself successfully, political leadership of great vitality and of pragmatic flexibility will be required. Given the age of the present leadership (the oldest of any major country) and its accumulation of problems, some change of personnel may be expected in the near future, but the next half-generation on the scene does not appear to be less orthodox. What this would suggest is that the evolutionary development to be anticipated is less likely to be smooth and gradual than an uneven dialectical alternation between advance towards modernization and regression towards orthodoxy, particularly because of the absence of constitutional procedures governing succession.

The character of the political leadership has an obvious bearing upon Soviet choices in the field of foreign policy. In Eastern Europe, the orthodox interpretation of the "doctrine of the Socialist community" has required tight Party, military and police control. The dilemma this presents is that while coercion could at one time impose crude industrialization, it cannot now after twenty-five years modernize the economies of the area, raise productivity and win the allegiance of the people. This dilemma helps to explain why the Soviet leadership is so prone to interpret "bridge-building" as "perfidious subversion," when faced with East European pressures for new technology and investment funds from Western Europe. Under these circumstances, bureaucratic orthodoxy would not seem likely to provide lasting and viable answers to the problem of instability in Eastern Europe.

The mark of Party orthodoxy is also evident in Soviet relations with the foreign Communist Parties. It was seen in the compulsive urge to elicit some kind of symbolic show of unity against the Chinese, however hedged, and in the contradictory efforts to organize a broad-front anti-imperialist rally while at the same time holding the Communist Parties to a narrow ideological path.

The crisis in Soviet relations with China has reinforced the tendency towards orthodoxy in several ways: by providing a justification for a tighter mobilization of the society; and—so long as China poses a militant challenge to Soviet leadership of the international Communist movement—by stimulating a tone of militancy and fidelity to revolutionary goals on the part of the Soviet leadership, while inhibiting overt and substantial improvement of relations with the West.

The high level of tension on her border with China affects Soviet foreign policy in several contradictory directions. It imposes a requirement for a partial quietus in the West, in order not to have to face active fronts in several directions at once and to inhibit the United States from taking advantage of the Sino-Soviet conflict. It is a matter of genuine and lively apprehension to the Soviet Union that the United States might try to exploit Soviet problems in Eastern Europe or with China; the President's visit to Bucharest and the small steps towards the normalization of relations with China have been interpreted in this light. But the tension with China also raises the prospect for a considerable expansion of Soviet influence in Asia, which is seen as a necessity in order to assure Soviet security in the East. This prospect was suggested in the tentatively advanced notion of a collective security system in Asia, intended both to contain China and to replace the anticipated reduction in the American presence in Asia. The Soviet Union has not yet made it clear whether she intends to work towards a regional collective security arrangement in Asia, or whether she will proceed through a network of bilateral agreements. Increased Soviet maritime activity in the Indian Ocean and intensified diplomatic, economic and cultural bilateral contacts with nations on the southern periphery of China are steps that have already been set in motion; even more marked is a systematic drive for increased influence in Japan, whose growing industrial strength is seen as a major factor in any new power configuration in Asia. The effect of this strategy will be to pit Soviet support for existing governments in Asia against Chinese support for revolutionary movements, and the effectiveness of this strategy may depend upon the level of resources the Soviet Union is able and willing to invest in this effort, and also upon the extent to which the United States does in fact reduce her presence in this area. So long as Soviet political strategy continues to move in this direction, its efforts will be competitive but in a parallel direction with American interests in stabilizing existing governments in this area, with the exception of Vietnam, which is regarded as a symbol of Soviet support for "national liberation movements."

Relations with the United States, perhaps more than any other aspect of Soviet foreign policy, reflect the interplay of opposing tendencies. From the point of view of those who see the strengthening and modernization of the Soviet economy as the primary requirement for Soviet power in the future, the present need is to reduce the drain on resources from military expenditures and to increase trade and scientific contacts with the West. This pragmatic judgment is expressed in statements of interest in strategic arms talks with the United States and in a policy of reduced tension.

On the other hand, from the point of view of the orthodox wing of the Party bureaucracy, any slackening of opposition to the United States presents serious operational difficulties. Times of reduced tension and increased contacts with the West invariably complicate matters for the Party orthodoxy by encouraging non-conformist thought among intellectuals, artists, scientists, economists and the youth, not only at home but also in Eastern Europe. This apprehension is reflected in drum-fire campaigns by the Party in liaison with the police against "bourgeois ideology" and "subversive ideas from the West." It is also reflected in campaigns in liaison with some sections of the military leadership to trumpet the threat of "aggressive American imperialism" preparing for another world war, to express resistance to arms limitations and support for further military appropriations. (It is only fair to observe that this tactic has its analogue in the United States.) There is no doubt that the intensification of the American involvement in Vietnam after 1964, and the military build-up associated with that war, contributed greatly to the Soviet perception of the United States as militant and imperialistic, and served to strengthen the military pressures in the Soviet Union.

What all this suggests is that any effort to project the future state of Soviet-American relations must take account of the uncertainty as to which tendency is likely to prevail in the Soviet Union, for each is accompanied by different perceptions of the United States and of Soviet interests. So long as Party orthodoxy remains the dominant consideration, the Soviet Union is likely to accept higher economic and political strains rather than to exercise restraints against her military interests groups; to push naval and conventional forces in the anticipation of contests for influence in remote areas; to accept relatively higher risks in the Mediterranean and the Middle East in the hope of getting a dominant influence in the Arab world. Also, she would be more likely to heighten the political rivalry by pressing an "anti-imperialist" campaign to contest American influence in various parts of the world, and by asserting her revolutionary zeal in responding defensively to polemical charges from the Chinese.

If however this policy direction proves unsuccessful and the view comes to prevail that Soviet interests will be best advanced over the long run by the enhanced power of a strengthened and modernized economy, we can more hopefully anticipate restraint in the arms race and in the political rivalry and perhaps some measures of limited co-operation. It is worth emphasizing here the point suggested earlier that the workings of Soviet internal politics are influenced in some degree by developments within the United States. Trends towards moderation in Soviet policy could be inhibited either by bellicosity and an unrestrained military spiral in the United States, or by a collapse of American strength and will.

IV

Putting these external and internal trends together, what can be anticipated for the Soviet-American relationship in the 1970's?

The first and most important question is: what are the prospects for the strategic military rivalry between the two super-powers? There seems little doubt that the security of the Soviet Union and of the United States would be no less, and probably would be considerably improved, if the level of effort now being devoted by the two countries to strategic weapons were half of what it now is. And yet the probabilities appear to be that the upward spiral of the strategic arms race will continue, at least in the near future. Although the two countries have entered into talks for the purpose of limiting the strategic weapons competition—a welcome and long overdue beginning—there are reasons for anticipating that these talks may not begin to show substantial effects for several years, at best. Among the factors which lead to this projection are the following:

1. The sheer complexity of the subject—infinitely greater than the partial test ban, for example. Although the margins of safety in the present deterrent balance would be ample to sustain a simple freeze, at least as a temporary first step, the legacy of mistrust on both sides is likely to mire down even the simplest freeze proposal in intricate discussions of the equivalency of weapons systems with widely different performance characteristics.

2. The powerful upward tug of technological innovations. If research and development continue at high levels (and they may be increased as a result of arms limitation talks) it is likely that further innovations will make their appearance, each generating new pressures for deployment, which could only be aborted by very strong resistance from civilian authorities. Moreover, some of the qualitative improvements now emerging may have the effect of increasing counter-force capabilities—a further source of anxieties regarding adversary doctrines and intentions, and therefore a source of instability.

3. Despite strong anti-military pressures, public opinion in the United States does not yet appear to be prepared to accept the parity in strategic relations which the Soviet Union would require as a basis for negotiations. The residual level of mistrust of the Soviet Union, the consequent commitment to security through superiority, and the strength of military and associated pressure groups are limiting factors in the American approach to negotiations. As we have seen, the balance between military and anti-military pressures is however sensitive to international developments. Moreover, the notion of parity requires a psychological adjustment which has not yet taken place. Until habits of thinking are accustomed to the reality that superiority confers no actual advantage over a deterrent balance and entails risks and costs, anxieties will persist that parity—however it is measured—might weaken the credibility of the American commitment to Western Europe, or would make Soviet political behaviour more adventurous or American less resolute.

4. For its part, the present Soviet leadership does not appear prepared to surmount its ideologically rooted mistrust of American intentions, nor to exercise forceful restraint against pressures from its various military interests by asserting a clear priority for economic considerations.

5. Dynamic energy for the continued upward spiral of the strategic arms race is generated by the large areas of uncertainty in the perception by each side

of the intentions, strategic doctrines and hidden potential capabilities of the other.

6. Time lags in the reaction cycle have generally required several years for strategic conceptions to penetrate the bureaucracies and become reflected in actions visible to the other side. In the interval, conservative planning against worst possible contingencies, plus the long lead-times required for planning, exert an upward force on military preparations.

7. In the present period, apprehensions about Chinese policies and potential power have been a limiting factor in any substantial arms limitations by the United States and the Soviet Union. There is nothing immutable about present Chinese policies, however, and this factor may be subject to change.

The foregoing considerations do not necessarily mean that the strategic arms competition is bound to go through the roof. Also present in the situation are a number of factors which can be expected in time to work in favour of moderating the arms race:

1. Both countries are experiencing budgetary pressures against the high and increasing costs of new strategic weapons systems. The United States, despite her economic and technological advantages, would be limited by serious domestic tensions from exploiting that advantage in a high-level arms race. In the Soviet Union, the drain of personnel, research facilities and specialized resources to military research and procurement directly limits progress in industrial technology. The atmosphere generated by the onset of arms limitation talks, if entered into with evident seriousness and substantiality, may be expected to strengthen the political effectiveness of budget reduction pressures in both countries.

2. Both countries have come to accept as a matter-of-course satellite reconnaissance, which increases the possibility for verification with less political intrusiveness and contributes to stability by reducing areas of uncertainty. If this were not the case, the arms race would be more virulent than it is.

3. Improvement in missile accuracy and yield may in the foreseeable future lead the two powers to reduce their reliance upon fixed-site land-based missiles in favour of submarine-based retaliatory forces, which could contribute to a stable balance of deterrents at moderate levels.

4. The preparations by each government for the talks is itself a useful educational exercise and this, plus the exchange of positions could help to widen understanding of the process of interaction which makes an anachronism of former concepts of security through weapons superiority. This is a process of learning, on both sides.

What this balance of considerations suggests is that perhaps the strategic arms race may continue to move upward for several years, after which the counter-pressures and the experience of living with the new military technology may help to establish a new equilibrium at a higher level than has prevailed over the past decade. Even in the absence of a formal agreement, conditions may then favour informal understandings or tacit and reciprocated measures of restraint. In the meantime, however, the political climate may be adversely affected by the uncertainties, costs and strains of the weapons race, as well as by a discouraged reaction on the part of those who had expected quick and dramatic results from the arms limitation talks. This prospect underlines the importance of educating public opinion to regard these talks as a process involving learning-time and the acceptance of new conceptions of security, rather than as an event likely to produce immediate results.

The adverse effects of the strategic spiral can be mitigated if some restraint is shown in interim deployment decisions, and in those local conflict situations where parallel interests exist (as for example, in Southern Asia), and if there is progress in some secondary aspects of the military competition, such as non-proliferation and the seabed. The essential condition required is the growth of the conviction on each side that the political leadership on the other side is serious about the need to find ways to damp down the mutually disadvantageous, and potentially dangerous, competition in strategic weapons.

A second major group of questions for the future concerns the level of political rivalry to be expected in the 1970's between the Soviet Union and the United States. Will the strategic limitation talks, even if not immediately productive, moderate political rivalry? If the political competition continues more or less unabated, what will be its intensity and where will it tend to be concentrated geographically?

A popular impression persists that the symbolic effect of the Big Two meeting to discuss strategic weapons inevitably signifies a spheres-of-influence agreement, and this prospect for a condominium of the super-powers has been faced with alarm by some Europeans and with nervousness by the Soviet Union.

There are a number of reasons why this is not likely to be the case. One is that the strategic arms limitation talks, if our preceding analysis is correct, are more likely to have their effects over a number of years rather than immediately. Another is that it is becoming more widely appreciated that the nuclear-missile weapons systems have limited political applications, and for all practical political purposes, a gross deterrent balance between the super-powers has the same political effect whether it operates at a high, medium or low level—providing only that it does not approach the point at which the probabilities of general nuclear war appear to be substantially increased. Therefore, although strategic weapons are of course not without symbolic political effect, they can vary through a fairly wide middle range more-or-less independently from the course of the political competition. There is of course some flow of influence in the opposite direction: a certain confidence is required for successful negotiations on strategic weapons and this confidence would be impaired by grievously provocative actions on the political front by either side. Short of this, however, it is not likely that the curves of military and political competition will move in close congruence. Both countries have been at pains to reassure their respective allies that the political interests of other countries will not be disposed on the backs of envelopes in two-power talks. Moreover, the disposition of the Soviet leadership is not to extend the scope or effect of the talks to a general *détente* in the political rivalry with the United States. If the Sino-Soviet conflict remains at more-or-less the same level as it has been in the recent past, it can be expected to inhibit any Soviet tendencies towards a general *détente* with the United States, but at the same time to keep tensions in this relationship within moderate limits.

In Europe, the near-term prospect is for a continued moderate-level political rivalry, in a situation of greater fluidity and manoeuvre than was the case during the decade just passed. The major elements involved are: instability in Eastern Europe, a loosening of West German policies, Soviet interest in trade and technology from the West, and a flux in the political life of the West European countries.

The problem faced by the Soviet leadership in Eastern Europe of reconciling tight Party control with local nationalist sentiment and the needs for economic reform is likely to be a continuing source of tension and suspicion. Soviet sensitivities to the political effects of Western influences in Eastern Europe will probably keep the expansion of economic, political and cultural contacts between this area and the West to moderate levels, although Soviet interest in Western trade and technology may produce loosening effects in Eastern Europe not easy to control.

In Western Europe, the reshuffling of centre-left coalitions will continue to encourage Soviet efforts to stimulate neutralist trends by an expansion of bilateral relations. In the case of West Germany—the source of the greatest concern to the Soviet Union in Europe particularly with the decline of the Gaullist influence in France—Soviet policy involves a two-pronged approach: one which experiments with the offer of improved relations in exchange for West German surplus capital and for moves in a neutralist direction (that is, a less close tie to Washington), and the other which thunders intimidatory charges of *revanchisme,* militarism and neo-fascism intended to isolate West Germany and restrain her growth of influence in Europe. It is in this context that the Soviet proposal for a European Security Conference has taken on particular significance in Soviet policy.

At the popular level in Western and Northern Europe, there has been some responsiveness to the European Security Conference idea, and it seems likely that such a conference may be held in the early 1970's. What form it will take, and whether it will achieve the effect intended for it by the Soviet Union (stabilization of the Soviet position in Eastern Europe, a framework for containing the expansion of West German influence, and perhaps secondarily the reduction of United States influence in Europe) is hard to predict. Western Europe will try to edge the conference idea from atmospherics to concrete settlements; the Eastern European countries will find in it a greater freedom of manoeuvre. It seems possible that such a conference, or series of conferences, by multiplying the number of contacts between East and West Europe, may move Europe towards a *de facto* softening of its dividing line.

It does not seem likely, however, that this movement towards practical accommodation will take the form of a spheres-of-influence agreement, much as the Soviet leadership would like to have a formal recognition of its primary interests in Eastern Europe. Even if the United States and Western Europe were disposed to try to stabilize the situation by such an agreement—which they are not likely to be—a Soviet hegemony in Eastern Europe is unlikely to be stable or productive, for reasons I have suggested earlier. What seems more probable is a general acceptance of a modified spheres-of-influence understanding: an unchallenged recognition of Soviet security interests in Eastern Europe (which already exists), without however sanctioning Soviet political hegemony over the area. An implicit codification of this distinction would permit an enlargement of political, economic and cultural contacts between East and West Europe, and would offer the practical advantages to the Soviet Union of stability and productivity. The conception that a Soviet zone of vital security interest could and would be respected without Soviet political control is doubtless too difficult to legislate; it might however come into being by a gradual process once the present alternative is seen as unproductive.

Outside Europe, the political rivalry between the United States and the Soviet Union may be expected to operate with cautious restraint for long-term gains, with the exception of the Middle East, where the prospect of gaining decisive influence in the Arab world encourages the Soviet leadership to play close to the marginal risk of loss of control over a possible conflict situation. The interest of the Soviet Navy in offsetting American naval supremacy in the Mediterranean can be expected to increase, as will its interest in opening up the Suez route to the Indian Ocean, but although this competition is aimed at valuable political prizes, it is being managed with tacit restraint on both sides.

As we have seen, the political and economic competition in Asia is becoming more intense, partly in response to the Sino-Soviet conflict and partly in anticipation of a contraction of United States influence in the area, but the essential characteristic of this competition is that both sides are seeking to increase their influence with established governments, and therefore some parallelism of interest, as in the Tashkent episode, may keep the rivalry within accepted norms of international behaviour, and may lead to forms of tacit co-operation. The main hazard in this area, as in Africa, is that unpredictable revolutionary developments could bring forward claimants to the title of "national liberation movements," whom the Soviet Union would feel compelled to support to demonstrate her fidelity to revolutionary goals, particularly while the Chinese, because of their appeal for radical protest groups, are able to exert a catalytic disruptive influence. Given the fact that both the Soviet Union and the United States have since 1965 greatly increased their capabilities for intervening in local conflict situations, the potentiality exists for explosive encounters despite the evident reluctance of either power to become involved. The United States is clearly in no mood to repeat her Vietnam experience elsewhere, and the Soviet Union has made plain her desire to increase her influence with established national governments in the developing world rather than to work for the revolutionary overthrow of these governments. The factor of chance, however, cannot be discounted, nor the risk that local conflicts in some remote and unanticipated area might develop independently of the will or the control of the super-powers.

V

Perhaps man's irrepressible optimism exposes him to the danger of wishful thinking, but the compensation for this danger is that it also encourages him to reject fatalism and to act. Over a somewhat longer time perspective—that is, towards the end of the decade of the 1970's—it seems reasonable to believe that the logic of the situation would work towards an amelioration of this conflict relationship.

We have seen that the trends in international politics are towards the rise of other political forces, whose effect is to relieve the stark bipolarity of this competition. Middle and smaller powers have found their voices, and are not content to accept the will of the super-powers. The Soviet-American competition less and less holds the centre of the stage, except as the level of tension might rise to the point where nuclear war is thought to be a possibility. Even here, the prospect that other nations may within the coming decade have some military nuclear capabilities, or acquire bacteriological or chemical weapons, serves to fragment the political map of the world, and to cause common concern to the Soviet Union and the United States. The inexorable rise of the North-South division of the world will put the Soviet Union and the United States, along with other industrialized countries, back-to-back against a breaking storm of poverty, hunger—too many people for too little food—and violent despair. These common interests may not dissolve the differences that now drive the Soviet-American competition, but they may in time come to make these differences seem less important.

Advancing technology is certain to exert long-term effects upon this relationship in a number of ways. The internal evolution of the two systems may move each country in its own way in the direction of pragmatism and flexibility, or it may in time bring both societies to resemble Kafkaesque bureaucratic nightmares. We shall each have to learn how to live with the computer and the technocrat. Just as each child experiences the problems of adolescence according to its distinctive nature and temperament, so each nation may face the imperatives of advanced technology according to its political culture and institutions. Nevertheless, all advanced industrial societies will face some problems in common: the pollution of the environment, the congestion of cities, the food-population imbalance in the developing world, the exploration of the universe. These present opportunities, if not the necessity, for practical co-operation.

Perhaps the future of the Soviet-American competition can be seen as a series of stages, each representing a learning process. If the two countries can learn to moderate the hazards of nuclear war as a first step, and to conduct their political competition with restraint as a second step, they may be prepared to advance to the third step of beginning to co-operate to make the earth's environment habitable for the human race.

To expect nations to behave rationally requires one to believe that there are enough reasonable men on both sides to keep the competition between their respective systems within the bounds of sanity, until a more rational international order becomes possible. I believe this to be true.

13.

Michel Oksenberg: The Strategies of Peking

What kind of challenge to the stability of the international system and the position of the United States can be anticipated from the People's Republic of China? A few years ago one author described China as the "greatest dissatisfied power in the world." Noting that until recently more Americans had been to the moon with government permission than to China, Michel Oksenberg examines in the following selection four interpretations of the new phase in Chinese foreign policy that emphasize, respectively, "no change," "fundamental change," "oscillation," and the dominance of a trend toward increasing moderation.

Michel Oksenberg, an Associate Professor of Political Science at Columbia University, is writing a book on the politics of water conservancy in China.

After a period of studied withdrawal from the world scene from 1966 to 1969, the People's Republic of China has returned to the international diplomatic and trading arenas with vigor and imagination. President Nixon's projected visit to Peking symbolizes the rapid turnabout. Three years ago U.S. bombs were falling within miles of the Chinese border and fears of a Sino-American war were rampant in the two countries. Indeed, in 1967–68, when China had only one ambassador abroad, its trade had dropped and its relations with its neighbors had reached all-time lows, many students of Chinese foreign policy (this author included) thought it entirely possible that Chinese leaders had become overwhelmed by domestic problems of an enduring nature. As a result, it was thought that China was turning inward and was unlikely to play an active role on the world scene in the early 1970's.

That view was wrong. Ambassadors have returned to their posts. China's trade has resumed its upward growth. Peking has embarked upon its largest aid program to date, the construction of the railroad from Tanzania to the Zambian copper fields. Limited tourism to China has resumed, with Japanese visitors particularly again flocking to the mainland. Following the armed clashes in April 1969 over the disputed islands in the Ussuri River in Manchuria, Sino-Soviet relations have improved somewhat; Peking and Moscow plan increases in their trade and are engaging in border talks.

A major development has been the surge of international recognition that it is the People's Republic of China and not the rival Republic of China on Tai-

Michel Oksenberg, "The Strategies of Peking," *Foreign Affairs,* October 1971, pp. 15–29. One footnote omitted. Copyright by the Council on Foreign Relations, Inc., New York. Reprinted by permission of *Foreign Affairs.*

wan which is the legitimate government of China. Beginning with Canada in October 1970 a variegated group of nations have established diplomatic relations with Peking: Equatorial Guinea, Italy, Ethiopia, Chile, Nigeria, Kuwait, Cameroon, San Marino and Austria. Announcement of the Nixon visit dramatically strengthens the trend. In the fall of 1970, for the first time, a majority in the General Assembly voted that the Peking government was entitled to the Chinese seat in the United Nations; the motion failed because earlier in the session a majority had voted that this was an "important" one, requiring a two-thirds vote for passage. Now that the United States has announced support for the seating of China, while attempting to preserve a seat for Taiwan, it seems certain that Peking will be voted a seat in the United Nations this year.

The most significant change is in Sino-American relations. Since 1960 the United States has made halting efforts to improve relations with China. Washington's relationship with Taipei and its involvement in the Vietnam war—particularly the rationale that it was being fought to stop alleged Chinese expansionism—made improvement difficult. But as the influence of Taipei in American domestic affairs ebbed and the Vietnam war began to "wind down," the Nixon administration was able to change its China policy. By early 1971, it had largely eliminated restrictions on American travel to China, relaxed the trade embargo on the sale of selected goods and allowed limited tourist purchases of Chinese products. Perhaps most significantly, the Seventh Fleet terminated its regular patrolling of the Formosa Strait. And the Nixon administration indicated that it believed the Peking government, not Taipei, was the effective, long-term ruler of the mainland. Peking responded to these gestures by purchasing machinery with American-made parts and by toning down the vehemence of its anti-American statements.

Then came the developments of late March and April, 1971. The United States removed all travel restrictions to the People's Republic, and soon thereafter Peking invited the U.S. table tennis team to tour the mainland. Two U.S. pressmen accompanied the group, and invitations to other journalists followed. With the exception of Edgar Snow's visits in 1960, 1964 and 1970, these were the first visits by American journalists to territory under the control of the Chinese Communist Party (CCP) since its Yenan days. To underline Peking's intent, Huang Hua was announced as the first ambassador to Canada. Huang has had extensive dealings with Americans before and is one of the most senior of the Chinese diplomatic corps. China apparently envisions its Canadian Embassy as more than that and is preparing for wider contacts with the American people and government. Also during this time, plans proceeded for Henry Kissinger's visit to Peking, which culminated in the invitation to President Nixon.

Clearly, a new phase in Chinese foreign policy has begun, including, as Chou En-lai has stated, a new page in Sino-American relations. How might the characteristics of this foreign policy be summarized? The Chinese operate on three levels of relations: state-to-state, party-to-party, and "people-to-people." Unlike its approach in the late 1950's or mid-1960's, Peking is not stressing party-to-party relations, nor is it currently seeking to establish a world organization of revolutionary movements. With a few exceptions—such as a March 1971 statement commemorating the Paris Commune—it has muted its direct Party polemics aimed at other communist states. Concomitantly, China has emphasized normal state relations in its dealings with all sorts of governments around the world. But this emphasis on state relations has not lessened the emphasis on peoples' diplomacy. Large numbers of "friendly personages" currently are visiting China. The Chinese continue to present Mao's thoughts as an answer to the intellectual questioning of people around the world, although less exuberantly than they did during the peak of the Cultural Revolution. In fact, a distinctive aspect of current Chinese foreign policy is the attempt to combine both state relations and peoples' diplomacy.

The Chinese are paying proportionately more attention to the developed capitalist world than probably has ever been the case in their 22 years of rule. They continue, of course, to give primacy to neighboring countries, and of the developing areas they take a particularly keen interest in the Middle East. As to their techniques of influence, the new phase appears to involve an increased use of trade and aid as a way of influencing world events. Possibly the best example of this is that China has ceased to purchase Australian wheat in order to put pressure on Canberra to change its China policy. (This move was coupled with the extension of an invitation to a group of opposing Labor Party parliamentarians to visit the mainland.) The extension of aid to Tanzania and Pakistan are other examples of the use of aid to enhance Chinese influence.

The current phase of China's foreign policy involves building a broad united front to alter its strategic position. The invitation to President Nixon signals the beginning of China's diplomatic efforts toward not only the United States but perhaps eventually the U.S.S.R. and Japan to reduce the military threats directed at it. The Chinese also hope to isolate and permanently rid China of one set of adversaries: the groups that have denied its legitimacy and perpetuated the existence of the Republic of China on Taiwan. These enemies are Chiang Kai-shek and his principal supporters in Japan and the United States. At the same time, now that this broad front of support has begun to be mobilized, the Chinese are using it to gain entry into the United Nations and to support their claim to a voice in the shaping of world affairs.

After 22 years of unyielding enmity, the improvements in Sino-American relations have produced a sense of relief and optimism about the future. After all, prior to the ping-pong visit, Americans were more familiar with the moon than the People's Republic; the moon has received wider TV coverage and more Americans had been there with government permission. The euphoria of the moment is to be welcomed. Yet, overoptimism would be tragic. For the history of Sino-American relations is the story of high hopes on both sides dashed by misunderstandings and conflicts of interest, leaving legacies of mutual recriminations. It is better to greet and advocate improvements in relations with a sense of the problems ahead, so that when and if they arise they will not end in another era of hostility.

II

How is one to interpret current Chinese foreign policy? Does it really represent a departure from the past? Or are the Chinese employing the same strategies in an altered context? Students of contemporary Chinese foreign policy, disagreeing among themselves, basically offer four explanations: (1) that it represents no change in Chinese policy but is a response to changed policies on the part of the U.S.S.R., United States and others; (2) that it involves a fundamental change in Chinese intentions and strategies in world affairs; (3) that it manifests the latest swing in a foreign policy characterized by oscillations between periods of fervor and periods of moderation; and (4) that after the aberrations of the Cultural Revolution, it is a return to an earlier trend toward increasing moderation and willingness to conduct diplomacy along Western lines. Let us examine each interpretation.

One wing of the "no change" school argues that Chinese policy now, as in the past, has largely been reactive. China has neither the economic resources nor the military might to underwrite an assertive foreign policy. Peking lives in a world which it has not shaped. Thus, Chinese foreign policy responds to the initiatives of others. And the Chinese tend to react in kind. They responded militarily to the advancing U.N. forces in Korea in the fall of 1950 and to the advancing Indian military positions on the Sino-Indian border in 1962. On the other hand, when approached in a conciliatory manner, as in the attempts to achieve a compromise settlement over Indochina problems in the Geneva conferences of 1954 and 1961–62, the Chinese played a constructive role in the pursuit of peace.

According to this line of reasoning, current Chinese foreign policy is a response to a number of friendly overtures. The Nixon administration has changed its China policy. The Soviet Union has adopted a less militant posture, following the war scares of the spring of 1969 and Kosygin's September 1969 visit to Peking. And the United Nations opens up prospects for China that had never existed before. Always eager to have state-to-state relations with nations that recognize it as the legitimate government of all of China, Peking is responding to opportunities it simply never had before. There has been no change in foreign policy; there has only been a change in the way others perceive and deal with Peking.

Others conclude "no change," but for totally different reasons. They view Chinese manœuvrings as mere tactics to camouflage China's aims. The wolf has temporarily donned sheep's clothing to enter the United Nations and wreak havoc once it gets in. They note that in spite of the changes in posture, Peking has yet to make any overt, major concessions, such as on the Taiwan issue or apparently on the Sino-Soviet border conflict.

Others, however, suggest that a fundamental change has occurred in China's approach to the world. They note shifts away from what they characterize as the hallmarks of Peking's policy during the late 1950's and most of the 1960's: the open encouragement of many revolutionary movements around the world;

the attempts to create a new world revolutionary movement under Peking's leadership; the energetic pursuit of the Sino-Soviet dispute; the severance of meaningful cultural exchanges with developed countries. To these analysts, current Chinese foreign policy, with its emphasis on state-to-state relations, its quest for membership in the United Nations and its willingness to host the leader of the "imperialist powers" represents considerable movement, although to be sure not a total abandonment of the old policies.

People who subscribe to this view differ among themselves concerning the reasons for the fundamental change. Some argue that the Chinese have learned from past policies which basically ended in failure. And indeed, a plausible case can be made that the policies pursued from the late 1950's through the late 1960's yielded few tangible rewards. By the end of this time, China was encircled by enemies who were strengthening their military positions on China's periphery. China had made little headway in gaining recognition in the developing world; indeed, on the eve of the Cultural Revolution, the Chinese suffered serious reversals in Indonesia, in Africa and in Afro-Asian organizations. In 1968–69 Peking came frighteningly close to nuclear war with Moscow. China faces a potentially threatening Japan. The Cultural Revolution left China more isolated in world affairs than ever before. Recognizing their deteriorating position, Chinese leaders have altered their approach to world affairs.

On the other hand, equally plausibly, it could be argued that the current phase is based on strength and optimism rather than on necessity and adversity. The Cultural Revolution may have made the leaders of China more willing to take part in world activities, confident that their people, now more ideologically prepared, could deal with foreigners without being corrupted and losing their revolutionary commitment. Moreover, as a result of the Cultural Revolution, the leaders of China may feel that they now have more to offer the world, in terms of their bold and often innovative experiments in public health, education, industrial management, bureaucratic controls, penology and so on. Hence they may feel that any participation in world affairs would be truly reciprocal in the flow of ideas. In sum, after putting their own revolutionary house in order, the leaders of China may be more prepared to risk state-to-state relations and participation in "bourgeois" organizations.

A third interpretation is that current policy represents neither continuity with the past phase nor a fundamental change, but a swing back to moderation after the ideological militance of the Cultural Revolution. Indeed, this view concentrates upon a distinctive characteristic of Chinese foreign policy; its marked fluctuations over the past 22 years between the periods of fervor and the periods of moderation. (China's domestic politics evidence similar oscillations between the periods of maximum mobilization and revolutionary advance and the periods of consolidation.) The current phase represents a return roughly to the kinds of policies pursued during the Bandung phase of Chinese foreign policy in the mid-1950's or the policies of the early 1960's. With the exception of 1955 and early 1956, these periods of external moderation have tended to correspond to periods of internal moderation in policies. Similarly, periods of internal revolutionary militancy tend to be reflected soon in greater fervor and rigidity abroad. According to this cyclical interpretation of China's foreign relations, coupled with the close relationship it sees between domestic and foreign policies, current Peking actions abroad flow from the more moderate domestic policies intended to consolidate the gains of the Cultural Revolution.

Finally, some people emphasize that the current policies fit into a long-term trend of China's involvement in world affairs. They see an historical process unfolding in China as in the Soviet Union before it. The revolutionary régime is in the process of gradually losing its commitment to violence and radical change, with its leadership increasingly technically proficient and aware of the complexities of the world. Moreover, with the passage of time, it increasingly acquires acceptance in the world at large. And the recent phase in Chinese foreign policy merely testifies to the strengths of those trends—the triumph of "reasonableness" and "pragmatism."

What is so striking about these varying interpretations is how they are rooted in more basic assumptions about American domestic and foreign affairs, the consequences of the Cultural Revolution, the relationship between domestic and foreign policies, and the long-term intentions and capabilities of the Chinese in world affairs. For example, people who are convinced of the essential rationality of American policies and who consider radical ideologies ill-suited to the modern world are inclined also to believe in a long-run moderating trend in Chinese foreign policy. Militant anti-communists have proclivities toward the "wolf in sheep's clothing" interpretation of present Chinese policies; and people who are deeply disturbed by American military activities in East Asia tend to interpret Chinese foreign policy as essentially reactive.

Actually, the search for a single interpretation is misdirected. The interpretations outlined above focus upon different aspects of Chinese policy. All are partially correct. Peking's approach to world affairs is the most recent of several swings toward moderation, but it is not exactly like earlier ones. In this sense, Chinese foreign policy has fundamentally changed, for the current policies contain elements that have not come together before. Not all can be interpreted in terms of new departures and oscillations, however. Certain long-run trends are also evident in terms of China's increasing capabilities and role in world affairs. Finally, there is no clear sign of a basic change in China's international goals and strategies.

III

The foreign policies of all countries appear to fluctuate between periods of zealousness and periods of moderation or quiescence. Certainly the United States has been more willing at some times than at others to become engaged militarily abroad and to use its economic resources to shape the course of world events. The Chinese fluctuations, however, appear to be more extreme than elsewhere.

Certainly one reason for the oscillations is Mao Tse-tung himself. He seeks to take advantage of possibilities for forward movement, but recognizes that when inevitable restraints are encountered, consolidation must begin. Mao advocates mass mobilization, struggle and militancy during the periods of advance, and emphasizes unity, to a certain extent harmony, and an effort to build institutions during the consolidation periods.

The reasons go deeper than Maoist theory. Although Western observers do not yet clearly understand the precise relationship, the fluctuations appear to be connected to Chinese economic conditions. A large portion of China's sales abroad are derived from agricultural production, so that a bad harvest leads to decreases in China's exporting capacity and changes in the composition and direction of trade. Further, government revenue and hence expenditures in this "balanced budget-minded" régime drop when the economy falters. As in capitalist countries, the Chinese economic performance over the past 22 years has been unsteady, cycling between periods of maximum productivity and recessions of varying degrees. Indeed, some scholars believe China's economic cycle is an inherent part of this régime, the result of its pursuit of both rapid social change and economic growth.

Yet another reason for the oscillating nature of Chinese foreign policy may be the existence of different opinion groups among the leadership, and fluctuations in their relative power. Indeed one detects the continued presence of three approaches which have existed since the late 1800's to the basic question: how to respond to the Western challenge? That is, how much "Chineseness" to preserve in order to retain the essence of China and to make a distinctive contribution to the world? And how much to accept from abroad in order to defend and transform China? (Of course, another deep difference is over what the "essence" of China is.) One response could be labelled "ideological militancy." This is the nativistic response, inflexible and unyielding, which seeks to preserve ideological purity even at the risk of temporary military defeat. It places utmost confidence in the long-run capabilities of the Chinese people to outlast any adversary as long as they remain armed ideologically. To be sure, the ideological militants of today differ from their forebears over the values to be guarded—Maoism rather than Confucianism. A second position is to accept Western technology and Western strategies, and even to accept a Western presence in China, but primarily for the purpose of controlling, manipulating and perhaps eventually defeating the West. It is an attempt to use the West against itself. Seemingly compromising and flexible, this approach none the less seeks to preserve a distinctive Chinese identity. A third approach advocates the pursuit of national greatness as a Westernized country. It urges participation in world affairs on Western terms, confident that eventually China would emerge as a wealthy and powerful country. This latter group has always been a distinct minority. Since 1949, the major line of contention has been over the two other positions.

Why has not one of these approaches remained dominant? This question probes the limits of our knowledge about the dynamics of this vast society. It may well be, however, that the advocates of the differing approaches to China's foreign policy problems, in an imprecise and subtle way, are embodiments or representatives of various social interests in China. That is, the available evidence suggests that the "ideological militants" find their greatest appeal among some of the young, perhaps a large portion of the peasantry, and perhaps more in the interior regions than on the coast. On the other hand, scientists, commercial personnel, and in general the urban dwellers along the coast may be more receptive to Western influence. (The fact that the present leaders of Shanghai are among the most vociferous supporters of "ideological militancy," to be sure, detracts from the force of the argument.) Thus fluctuations in policy lines in China may to a certain extent reflect changes in the political strength of the various constituencies which these spokesmen indirectly represent or whom they consider to be their "referent groups."

This situation probably is not unlike the American scene. The foreign policy of Republican presidents must reflect, to some extent, the mood of the major sources of Republican strength in the country, particularly in the Middle West, while the Democratic Party must be more responsive in its foreign policy to its constituencies, such as the intellectuals and labor. As a nation undergoing rapid change, Chinese society is riven by many cleavages between the young and the old, between the privileged and the deprived, between the urban and rural dwellers, between people in different bureaucracies and in different geographical areas, and so on. Now the leaders of any country must rest their rule upon the strong support of certain segments of society, but the leaders of China apparently have had difficulty forging a supportive coalition of different social groups that can endure. The coalitions that have been formed thus far are subject to sharp tensions. The oscillations in Chinese foreign policy, then, reflect to some extent the continually shifting social basis of the régime and the differing foreign policy predilections of the coalitions that have been put together. Admittedly, it is difficult to provide the hard evidence to sustain this interpretation, but it grows out of a long historical perspective of Chinese foreign policy, where it seems to hold.

Whether considered from an economic, political or sociological perspective, the forces that produce the fluctuations appear deeply embedded. For the foreseeable future, therefore, Chinese policy is likely to continue its gyrations between periods of fervor and moderation. In the past, Chinese and American policies have been out of phase. Chinese moderation in the mid-1950's confronted U.S. assertiveness, while American accommodations of the late 1960's encountered Chinese militance. For the first time, the two are in phase, which may help explain the rapidity of the progress. And the task for Washington in the future, in the current idiom, will be to swing with the Chinese.

IV

Chinese foreign policy also has exhibited certain underlying continuities over the past 22 years. In the broadest terms, the goals have remained the same. The leaders of China have searched for national security, for dignity and for the ability to make a contribution to world affairs. As the French and Russian Revolutions, the Chinese Revolution faced a largely hostile world; for understandable reasons the established countries feared what its consequences might be. Since the Chinese face military might deployed at their very doorstep, they have made the quest for security fundamental.

But even more fundamental has been the concern with their dignity. Interstate relations as we know them today grew out of the Western experience, and were brought to the rest of the world during the past 300 years by Western military men, adventurers, traders and missionaries. Except for the third opinion group mentioned above, most Chinese believe this to be inequitable. China seems quite willing to join the world, but not on dictated terms. That solution would entail a loss of dignity. In many areas of interstate relations, the Chinese are dissatisfied with current international practices—how borders have been delineated, what the limits of territorial waters are, how trade should be conducted, how shipping insurance should be set, and so on. In sum, a world in which China will feel it has a dignified role will be one in which China helps write some of the rules of interstate intercourse. China is the last great cultural area to hold out on this point. This is what makes the bringing together of China and the rest of the world so difficult, for the Chinese, more than any other nation, raise profound questions about the present structure of interstate relations.

Related to the search for dignity is China's desire to assist the impoverished peoples of the world, and to be the spokesman for the smaller countries. Certainly these efforts seek to expand its influence and control. But American aid programs can be seen in a similar light. In both instances, though, the aid programs also spring from the belief that they can truly benefit the recipients. However, the American and the Chinese views of what constitutes an improved life and how to achieve it usually come into direct conflict. None the less, this impulse of the Chinese to assist the downtrodden probably will remain strong, because of their pride in their domestic achievements and because of the belief that they are relevant to the plight of others.

There are also continuities in Chinese strategy. The Chinese do not divide the world into the strong and the weak. That is a static view of power. Rather, perhaps because of their long history, they consider power as something dynamic, ever-changing. Thus, they see a world divided into the "powerful-becoming-weaker" and the "weaker-becoming-stronger." The Chinese leaders believe themselves to be in the latter category and their task is to hasten the process. They adopt strategies which they perceive appropriate to this condition: (1) garbing actions in the cloak of virtue (to become the "aggrieved" party in a dispute, to make sure the stronger party appears as a bully); (2) hiding their weakness through secrecy and dissimulation; (3) employing stratagems to provoke conflict among their rivals; (4) playing upon the internal tensions and weaknesses of the enemy; (5) maximizing their leverage by becoming a balancer (to become an object of a bidding game between stronger and competing powers); (6) depriving stronger powers of threatening options through prolonged negotiations or temporary agreements that do not surrender their own flexibility; and (7) when possible, luring the stronger power into untenable positions and then vanquishing him. These are the strategies of protracted struggles.

Indeed, traditional Chinese strategic thinking is rich with analysis concerning the conditions favorable to the use of each of these stratagems, the range of problems and opportunities involved in employing them, and so on. But one lesson above all others emerges from this literature: to employ any of these strategies, a nation must retain its independence. Mao Tse-tung is in keeping with this tradition when he asserts, "We must keep the initiative in our own hands." A weak nation can not hasten its growth if it is enmeshed in a net of entangling alliances and mutual obligations that deprive it of flexibility in manipulating its environment.

V

Against this background, what are the principles upon which American policy must be based? A number of essential characteristics immediately come to mind: self-awareness, realism, flexibility, imagination and sensitivity.

Washington's approach toward Peking must be based on an awareness of self. While Vietnam has demonstrated the limits and dangers of U.S. capabilities, Washington none the less is still fond of saying: "We are still the greatest, richest and most powerful nation on earth." But this view of the world—that there is a clear hierarchy of nations—is simplistic and outmoded. To be sure, the United States is the greatest power, in that it believes it has interests in every area of the globe; no other nation makes this claim. On the nuclear level, admittedly there are but two giants—the United States and the U.S.S.R. But it is foolish to rank nations according to a single dimension. One must consider many dimensions—a nation's quality of life, the strength of its currency in international markets, its conventional military capability, the vitality of its intellectual activity, the extent of social equity and so on. America is not on top in all of these, and probably is surpassed by China in some of them. A balanced view of the world provides the basis for a more successful relationship with China, encouraging neither arrogance nor servility, but a recognition that each can benefit from the other's strengths.

Nor should American policy stem from a paternalistic desire to draw China out of its isolation. It is not clear that the leaders of China are more isolated from the world than their American counterparts. Rather, the leaders of the two countries have contact with different aspects of the world. While China's leaders are unacquainted with the offices of the multinational corporation, America's leaders have demonstrated that they are isolated from the lives of an aroused, impoverished peasantry. Moreover, the plain fact is that the Chinese have had wider contacts with Western nations than is often believed. We should pursue improvements in Sino-American relations, then, in order to end our isolation from an important current in the world.

Our search for self-awareness also requires that we understand the Chinese view of America. Remarkably little is known about what the Chinese leaders truly think about U.S. policies. But as contacts multiply, they must be encouraged to speak to this point. Their undue fears should be allayed; our past misunderstood actions must be explained; our current actions—such as at the Strategic Arms Limitation Talks (SALT)—must be interpreted. Washington must strive to establish the validity of U.S. policies in terms understandable to the Chinese.

A sense of realism must also pervade U.S. policies. Nothing could be more detrimental at this stage than believing that the 22-year legacy of mutual bitterness and distrust could disappear swiftly or that the Taiwan issue is all that separates Washington from friendship with Peking. In short, improving Sino-American relations involves the bringing of two different social systems and cultures together. No countries in the world—including those which recognize Peking's claim to Taiwan—have enjoyed easy relations with China. The Chinese are developing nuclear weapons. The need for a military balance of power in the region remains. While the long-run goal should be to develop a close relationship, Washington's minimal goal should be to remove the rancor from, and introduce mutual respect into, what probably will remain an adversary relationship. The outbursts and setbacks which undoubtedly will occur during periods of ideological militancy must be endured. We also must recognize China's legitimate security interests around its periphery. We must cease rewarding states for their hostility toward China. And the various intelligence-gathering operations aimed at China should be closely scrutinized in order to balance the hostility generated against the value of information acquired.

In addition, the American public and the Chinese must be made aware of the constraints within which the United States currently operates. Improvements in Sino-American relations should be sought in ways that would not unduly harm U.S.-Japanese relations, U.S.-Soviet relations (especially with regard to SALT), or Sino-Japanese relations. In particular, any U.S. military disengagement from the Western Pacific—especially from Taiwan—must be done in such a way as to maintain Japan's confidence in its own security. Sino-American hostility must not be replaced by a new era of Sino-Japanese enmity. Nor should the motivation for improving Sino-American relations be to manipulate Sino-Soviet tensions.

In a number of areas Chinese and American interests coincide. Both long for a reduction in the American military presence in East Asia; Washington should specify to China what Chinese actions might hasten the process of withdrawal to acceptable levels. Neither side desires a nuclear-armed Japan; perhaps Tokyo should be included in quiet trilateral talks to allay Chinese fears of revived Japanese militarism. While Chinese science is advanced in some areas, it lags in other nonstrategic fields; for our government to encourage the inclusion of Chinese scientists in international gatherings would have mutual benefit. Both parties could profit from Chinese purchase of American capital equipment, financed by U.S. extensions of credit. Each might be interested in opening permanent news and trade offices in the other's capital. Finally, as previously noted, the Chinese on two occasions have participated constructively in conferences on Indochina. Perhaps they may be interested in doing so again.

Setbacks should be expected and endured. The first American journalists who visited the mainland wrote glowing reports of the achievements of the past 22 years, and indeed those achievements have occurred. But the day will come when journalists begin to inquire into the fate of imprisoned intellectuals, and report a seamier side of Chinese life. If tourism increases and trade increases, some Americans are bound to transgress Chinese law. American journalists may be expelled and other Americans arrested. A more serious reversal will occur when the pendulum swings toward the ideological militants who even now give evidence of opposing the overtures toward Washington.

Above all, we must learn to be more sensitive to the Chinese than we have heretofore. Words are extremely important. The President's reference to the "People's Republic of China" is important, as is his reference to "Peking" rather than "Peiping." Crucial in this regard, obviously, is our handling of the Taiwan issue, where misunderstandings could arise not only out of substance but out of the choice of words—such as whether there is only "one China."

Historic opportunities are now present to involve China more fully in world affairs. We should welcome the challenge which previous generations have shunned, to build with a unified China the institutions which would draw China and the rest of the world closer together. This course must be pursued with no illusions that old problems will be solved. The new problems, however, will be more worthy of our attention than those faced in Asia in the past decade.

TECHNOLOGICAL ACCELERATION: CAN WE SURVIVE IT?

14.

Victor Basiuk: The Impact of Technology in the Next Decades

Many of the effects of technological acceleration on the international system and on the chief participants in the system—the nation states—are evident. An obvi-

Victor Basiuk, "The Impact of Technology in the Next Decades," *Orbis,* Vol. 14 (Spring 1970), pp. 17–42. Some footnotes omitted. Reprinted by permission of *Orbis.* This article is based in part on research sponsored by the U.S. Arms Control and Disarmament Agency under contract with the Institute of War and Peace Studies, Columbia University, and in part on research sponsored by the Institute for the Study of Science in Human Affairs, Columbia University. The judgments expressed are those of the author and do not necessarily reflect the views of the U.S. Arms Control and Disarmament Agency or any other agency of the U.S. government.

ous example is to be found in the revolution in military technology of the past two decades. After evaluating numerous technological developments, Victor Basiuk suggests that a stalemate in the military sector is likely in the future, with the result that nonmilitary technology will become more significant for national security due to its impact on the distribution of world and regional power.

Adviser to the Chief of Naval Operations, Dr. Basiuk was for a number of years on the staff of Columbia University's Institute of War and Peace studies. He is author of the forthcoming book, *Technology, the Future, and American Policy.*

Looking ahead a quarter of a century, one can discern technological developments certain to affect the economies of every advanced industrial society: (1) Development of large-scale generation of power to meet expanded needs, accompanied by important reductions in the cost of energy. (2) Growth of telecommunications by means of global satellites ringing the earth. (3) Exploitation of the untapped marine resources of the world. (4) Refinement of weather prediction and expanded capability for weather and climate modification.

Significant in themselves, they loom even more important because of the way they will interact with and shape some dominant scientific and technological trends: e.g., the change of scale on which science and technology have to be conducted today and the impetus to integration—economic and perhaps political. For the essential fact is that the cost of developing these new technological areas is so great that only giant industrial nations, or combinations of nations, will be able to afford to do so. The unfolding of the new technology of the next twenty-five years and its enormous political ramifications are the subjects this article will explore.

Decline in the Deterministic Effect of Resource Location

Historically, technology has always played a major role in creating new resources or helping to exploit the traditional ones, but in most instances it tended to be tied down to its physical resource base. Major industrial centers were built around coal-iron ore complexes, such as those in the Durham-Cleveland, Great Lakes-Pennsylvania, Ruhr, and Krivoi Rog-Donbas regions. The development of railroads was fairly closely tied to the availability of resources— either mineral or agricultural—on the land the railroads crossed. Electricity made water power a significant source of energy, but hydroelectric stations and the economic activity stimulated by them were narrowly confined to rivers and their vicinity.

What is noteworthy today is the decline in importance of the location of raw materials and sources of energy as a determining factor in economic development and the rise of new power centers. No single invention was responsible for this decline, but the most significant technologies initially responsible were chemistry and transportation. By combining and recombining elements and thus converting them into more useful products, chemistry undertook to make "resources" out of the most ubiquitous materials, such as air, water and sand. Substitution of raw materials became relatively easy and prevalent; e.g., if natural rubber was not locally available, synthetic rubber could be produced from coal, oil or foodstuffs.

Technological advance in transportation, resulting in the reduction of costs, greatly increased the mobility of raw materials. Perhaps the most striking example in this respect is the post-World War II development of the steel industry in Japan, which by 1964 had become the third largest in the world (after the United States and the Soviet Union). In 1965, Japan imported 88 percent of her iron ore and 64 percent of her coking coal at an average distance of 5,500 miles. The magnitude of Japan's achievement (aided, besides transportation, by other technological improvements) was driven home in April 1969 when the merger of the two largest Japanese steel companies generated serious concern on the part of both American and European steel manufacturers about their ability to compete with the Japanese. It has been estimated that if the two companies, Yawata Iron and Steel and Fuji Iron and Steel, merge and continue to grow at their present rate, they will overtake United States Steel by the middle 1970's, thus becoming the largest steel company in the world.

In brief, the availability of superior technology—and not the location of raw materials or sources of energy—has become the principal factor in the emergence of new industrial centers and the economic viability of nations and regions. The extent of this trend is illustrated by the nuclear agro-industrial centers which have been proposed for the 1970's. These centers, located on the coast of a water-deficient area, would combine desalinization of water for irrigation purposes with large-scale production of those chemicals, fertilizers and metals which require cheap and abundant electricity. Seawater and air would provide the raw material for such chemicals as hydrochloric and nitric acids and ammonia, while other raw materials (e.g., bauxite and phosphorus) would be imported. These centers would offer many millions of people new sources of food and employment.

The decline in the deterministic effect of resource location has a number of implications. The vistas for organized human will backed by advanced technology have broadened immensely. On the other hand, the historically built technological superstructure of advanced societies creates rigidity and a deterministic effect of its own. Thus, what will increasingly matter in producing differential benefits from science and technology among the advanced nations will be not so much the extent of the present advance, but rather farsightedness in planning, determination in the pursuit of selected goals, and willingness to reshape and restructure the existing social institutions and technological superstructure to meet the requirements of future technology.

The Integrative Effect of Technology

With the freeing of technology from a resource base has come a different trend: the integrative effect of technology on society and the integrative process within technology itself. Many loose statements have been made in this connection: e.g., progress in transportation and telecommunications has "shrunk" the world; the peoples of the world or a given region have become interdependent. In fact, the integrative influence of technology is a highly complex and multifaceted phenomenon that has not been fully understood and probably will not be for some time. It operates on different levels, and its impact on society frequently runs at cross currents.

One level is the integration of human activity and spatial units into one global geo-technical system. The advanced industrial societies are highly interrelated, technologically and politically. The three remaining areas which have not been fully—or at all—integrated into the global system are the underdeveloped regions, the scarcely inhabited regions (the Amazon, the Arctic), and the ocean floor. Technological developments in the next decade or so will contribute significantly toward the integration of these areas.

Thanks largely to satellites, costs of telecommunications are rapidly decreasing; by 1980 it may be possible to telephone anywhere in the world for one dollar during off-business hours. The drop in telecommunications costs will be a major factor in the process of integrating the less developed countries internally and with the world system. A satellite-based television network for less developed nations as large as India could be developed, built, and made operational in about four years. To construct a comparable terrestial network would take perhaps as long as two or three decades and the cost would be about twice as great. Provided the government of the receiving state cooperates, such a network would make possible direct transmission of programs from an advanced nation into community receivers of the less developed countries. If the presently available receivers are appropriately augmented (at a cost of at least $40 each), a global television network, involving direct transmission through satellites into home receivers, could be operational by the late 1970's. Without such augmentation, a highly advanced country could develop, at substantial cost, the capability for transmitting programs directly into home receivers of foreign nations by the early 1980's.

Preferences of the public in advanced countries for local programs, the time differential, and political considerations will probably hinder the establishment of a truly global television network in the next twenty-five years. It is likely that a greater interchangeability of programs among the advanced nations will take place in the near future; selected programs from abroad will be transmitted, with the aid of a satellite, through local television stations. Since the less developed countries have only limited resources for their own programs, they will rely to a greater extent on programs from abroad, beamed into community receivers or perhaps directly into home sets. New audio-visual techniques of instruction, combined with satellite-aided television, promise not only a much more rapid integration of the less developed societies with the rest of the world, but a social transformation whose effects are not entirely clear.

The nuclear agro-industrial complexes described above will contribute to the integration of arid and hitherto sparsely inhabited areas. Even now, conventional means of desalinization of water combined with controlled-environment greenhouses of air-inflated plastic are beginning to be used successfully to convert deserts into economically productive areas. The techniques for controlling rainfall will improve significantly by 1980, thus helping to increase geographic areas capable of sustaining agricultural productivity and possibly to expand the areas of human habitat in general. It appears that, by diverting the flow of ocean currents, large-scale changes in climate are economically feasible even at the present cost of energy. As the cost of energy declines, projects designed to implement such changes will become increasingly more attractive; eventually, they may lead to freeing huge areas of permafrost for agriculture and other economic activity and improve the means for converting present deserts into productive regions.

The use of the earth resource survey satellites, to be introduced in the early 1970's, is expected to facilitate the discovery of mineral resources, thus generating economic activity in geographic regions hitherto not considered to be economically attractive and perhaps not even habitable.

Exploitation of oil and gas from the sea bed has advanced rapidly in recent years; the present gross annual revenue of the U.S. offshore oil industry exceeds $9 billion. Human underwater missions of long duration at a depth of 600 to 1,000 feet are expected to take place in the near future. It has been predicted that commercial capability for extensive and prolonged engineering operations on continental slopes as deep as 3,000 feet will take place by 1980, while commercial deployment of vehicles and machines at 6,000 feet and beyond is expected sometime in 1980–1990.

Computers, capable of processing vast amounts of data, provide a major instrument of in-depth integration. They greatly facilitate large-scale organization, control of both men and materials, and regional and national planning. Computations on a scale that would have taken months and years before—or could not have been made at all—are either possible now or will soon become possible within seconds and at very low cost. Sometime in the period between 1976 and 1981, computing is likely to become a public utility, with many thousands of remote terminals for the use of individuals and organizations to obtain the information they need. A concomitant development will be the replacement of money and checks by the computer-controlled credit card. The present trend in computer technology is great increase in memories and the speed of retrieval. The main memories of some two million characters and the auxiliary memories of half a billion characters are considered to be large in the present generation of computers. In the next computer generation, to become available in the late 1970's, the main memories will contain hundreds of millions of characters, while the auxiliary memories will have many billions of characters. The retrieval of information will be increased to about twenty to forty million characters per second between the auxiliary and the main memory, as compared with the one to three million per second now.

Last but not least, integration proceeds within science and technology itself. The combination of computers, satellites, atmospheric sciences and oceanography opens up broad vistas for weather prediction and modification. Transplantation of body organs and their increasing substitution by synthetic items —which is revolutionizing medicine—represents the meeting of medicine, mechanics and chemistry. The combination of electronics and chemistry, electronics and physics, biological sciences and chemistry are further examples of the growing trend. It appears that the synergistic effect resulting from the meeting and integrating of two or more sciences and technologies produces the most rapid progress.

What are the implications of this integrative trend? Instrumentally speaking, the capability to understand and control the integrative trend of technology is highly important and will be increasingly crucial in the future. There is a growing need for conceptual instruments on how to integrate various technologies to achieve particular social goals. Systems analysis is but one such instrument, and it has not yet been adequately developed. The ability to control the forms and phases of the integrative trend—particularly on the "horizontal" level—is an increasingly important leverage of international power and influence. A better understanding and the fostering of integration between the various sciences and technologies will accelerate technological innovation and progress.

The integrative trend of technology creates an appreciable measure of global, regional and local interdependence, but it does not necessarily create unity. Indeed, in a number of its forms this trend can create or exacerbate conflict. A growing settlement and integration of Northern China and Eastern Siberia may increase rather than diminish conflict between the USSR and China, and the better integrated instruments of military force are likely to intensify a clash. There is no conflict for the sea bed in the deep ocean areas at this time, but such a conflict looms as a definite possibility in the future as the ocean floor begins to be integrated into global economic activity.

These examples are not intended to confirm the somewhat simplistic statement that "technology unites, while humans divide." Technology itself, as an independent variable, may divide. Computers, by integrating human and material resources of educational institutions, make it possible to create a mega-university, but these same computers, by facilitating impersonality, may split asunder the mega-university and even the entire society. In terms of political division or unification or political impact in general, it is not always clear what the general integrative trend signifies for the future. The rise of multinational corporations (of which the Intelsat is but one) and the technological integration of the ocean floor—which may involve companies of various nationalities working, and eventually multinational personnel living, side by side on the bottom of the sea—are truly major developments. They might modify, if not undermine, the present nation-state system in the next decades. But it will take some time before the exact nature of their political impact becomes clearly discernible.

Global Projection of Influence Through Technology

The integrative impetus of technology is accompanied by the increasingly versatile, global projection of national influence and power through technology. In the nineteenth century this phenomenon was manifested by Great Britain's global projection of power, first through the Royal Navy and later through telecommunications (cables and radio). In the post-World War II period, the United States eclipsed all other powers by a wide margin in the magnitude of its global projection and the multiplicity of its instruments. After the massive display of U.S. military power in both Europe and Asia during World War II, the United States made an effort to withdraw, but was compelled to stay. The forms of its military power grew in variety and size—from bombers to ICBM's and Polaris IRBM's trained on various targets in Eurasia. Global military operations have been improved—and are continuously improving—through nuclear propulsion in naval vessels, better communications systems, more effective logistics support, worldwide surveillance through satellites and other means, and long-range airlift.

On the nonmilitary level, the Voice of America provides another form of projection of global influence. Physically, the recent lunar landings were aimed at the moon, but politically they were aimed at Earth. Foreign aid is, in part, a means of extending America's influence through more advanced technology into the less developed world. The multinational corporation—primarily a subsidiary of the technologically and managerially superior American companies —is a projection mainly into industrialized nations.

The Kremlin imitated the American global strategic nuclear projection, and now the Soviets are expanding their global capability in subnuclear military technology. The Soviet Union is roughly equal to the United States in global extension of its influence through outer space technology (but not communications satellites), broadcasting and oceanology. In other respects, its efforts at projecting Soviet power are less significant than those of the United States.

In comparison with the United States and the Soviet Union, Western Europe has not scored conspicuously in the global projection of its power and influence. In the first place, Western Europe lacks the unified political will required for such an undertaking. The foreign aid programs of the largest West European states have grown recently from about a half to almost two-thirds of that of the United States, but they are not effectively coordinated. Europe participates in Intelsat, the Europeans have an outer space program of their own, and Great Britain and France have a nuclear striking capability; but, on the whole, the present capability of Western Europe to project its power and influence globally is small when compared with U.S. and Soviet capabilities. Perhaps the only exception is the large West European merchant marine. In 1967, the gross tonnage of the merchant fleets of the EEC countries and the United Kingdom amounted to 44,194,000 tons, compared with 19,179,000 tons under U.S. registry and 8,562,000 tons flying the Soviet flag. Under peacetime conditions, however, a nation's merchant marine is not one of the most important instruments of power and influence. By shipping goods (rather than people) and having low visibility, the merchant marine has relatively limited impact on human psychology and values and is basically at the disposal of the customer, of whatever nationality he might be. One European power with formerly global interests, Great Britain, is in the process of retrenchment rather than augmentation of her projection capabilities.

Technological instruments for projecting one's power and influence globally will be significantly improved in the next decade or two, and entirely new instruments will appear. We noted above that global voice communications will become cheap and readily useable within the next ten years. In the 1970's, some highly advanced nations will have the technological capability for beaming television programs directly into the receivers of the less developed world, and this capability will probably be used. It is conceivable that in the 1980's the superpowers will increasingly project themselves through television broadcasts directly into the receivers of the more advanced countries, such as those of Western Europe. Computers, global communications and high-speed transportation make it possible to control a scattered international enterprise from a central point; further progress in all of these areas will enhance the role of foreign investment in extending a nation's influence. The era of global mass travel is just beginning and will witness rapid growth with the introduction of "air buses" and, later, supersonic aircraft. Control of the means of telecommunications and of mass travel—through ownership of manufacturing facilities, the media themselves, or both—is an important lever of power. Quite apart from this leverage, proliferation of global mass travel and mass communications tends to favor those who are technologically more powerful, affluent and numerous: they have much more to project, and can afford to project more. The influence exerted may produce important modifications in the value systems of those who are the primary objects of the projection.

Major developments will likely occur in large-scale climate modification, perhaps as early as the late 1970's, and with a correspondingly greater certainty in subsequent years. If unilaterally developed, climate and weather modification provides a valuable instrument for projecting one's power externally. The cost of energy is likely to be dramatically reduced in the next ten to twenty-five years. According to present and admittedly conservative projections based on "surprise-free" developments in nuclear technology, the cost of power to U.S. industry will decline from about 8 mills/kw-hr. to 1.5 mills/kw-hr. (in 1968 dollars) by the year 2000. However, technological breakthroughs might reduce the cost of energy to this level—and possibly below—much sooner than estimated. The nations that capitalize on technologies where major breakthroughs are likely to occur—which would include such areas as controlled thermonuclear reaction (CTR), superconductivity, and magnetohydrodynamics (MHD) —and possess the capability of utilizing them on a sufficiently large scale, will be in a position to control world markets through superior and cheaper products. Marine resources development represents still another important area. It will permit the projection of national substance into hitherto unoccupied and unexploited parts of the globe, and its geopolitical impact will grow in the next decades.

We live in a period when attributes of power and influence become increasingly diffuse; differing from attributes in the pre-World War II decades, they do not necessarily accrue narrowly to individual nations. In an integrating world, where regional differences are perhaps more important now than national, it would be an oversimplification to equate each manifestation of ability for global projection by a nation with the actual attainment of power and influence. The effect of some external projections of national substance will be neutralized by other developments, and still other projections are likely to be counterproductive in terms of power and influence. This, in particular, may pertain to the potential impact of global projections on the values and motivations of those peoples who become their targets. However, we are still far from attaining a homogeneous world, and, on balance, the ability for global projection through technology will be an important attribute of power of nations, regions, and those international institutions capable of commanding the necessary resources for it.

The Growing Scale and Costs of Technology

To this list of basic consequences of the new technology one has to add its growing scale. Large economies of scale entail enormous costs and require enormous resources. Even in such "conventional" items as transformers for power networks, the minimum economic size of a plant needed to produce the huge transformers to take advantage of the economies of scale is pushing producers into cooperation or mergers. Most European companies are incapable of producing the huge transformers needed for the continuously increasing voltage in the networks. This development has forced even such giants as Siemens and Telefunken to join forces in the heavy electrical engineering field. In the United States, five producers supply the entire market, while in Europe there are as many as thirty.

The scale and cost of the present advanced technology—outer space, particle accelerators for advanced nuclear research, supersonic transport, and nuclear weapons development—are of gigantic proportions, and they are imposing a heavy burden even on a country of America's wealth and resources. Future technologies will become even more demanding in this respect. The benefits from the nuclear agro-industrial complexes are expected to be important, but the economic scale of operation requires an investment of between half a billion and a billion dollars for each complex. Economies of scale are important in advanced technology of power generation.

Recent progress in controlled thermonuclear reaction led to anticipation that operational prototype reactors would be ready in the United States perhaps as early as the late 1970's. While these reactors are expected to be relatively small (2,000 megawatts), commercial fusion reactors may have a capacity as large as 10,000 megawatts, and reactors of 20,000 megawatts are conceivable and would be even more economical. A reactor of this size would have a generating capacity more than twice as large as that of Poland in 1967. MHD power is particularly responsive to economies of scale. If the expected progress in the technology of MHD power materializes, the economies of scale might push the size of generating plants even higher than the above figures suggest; furthermore, huge MHD plants are likely to become operational before commercial CTR becomes a reality.

There are other technologies on the horizon which will require major initial outlays. Current projections anticipate the availability of nuclear-propelled surface-effect ships, perhaps as large as an aircraft carrier, in 1985–1990. These vessels, moving at a speed of 100 knots, would have both land and sea mobility. Since there will be no need to construct roads and dock facilities and since they will be highly automated, they are expected to be attractive commercially after the initial R & D costs are met. Various schemes for large-scale climate modifications will demand immense expenditures. The present exploitation of ocean resources is limited to relatively shallow depths. To move to greater depths and to widen the scope of exploitable resources, the necessary exploration and research and development will require billions of dollars.

In a somewhat different category—but nonetheless real—are the costs generated by undesirable by-products of technological progress. The present highly advanced nations have been developing and applying science and technology with little or no heed to how this activity might affect the environment in the future. The result has been badly polluted rivers, lakes and the air; ecological imbalances that annihilated, or threaten to annihilate, certain species, vegetation and other substances important to man's livelihood, health and the beauty of his environment; and direct hazards to human health and life through such phenomena as excessive chemicals in food and unsafe means of transportation. These characteristics of technological advance in the highly developed nations are no longer tolerable. It will require vast expenditures to compensate for many years of neglect and to effect the necessary planning and readjustment for the future.

The foregoing discussion suggests at least three points. First, rising costs are such that even the superpowers will not be able individually to take advantage of the full potential of future technology. This factor will increasingly generate pressure for international cooperation in technological development among the middle-rank powers, between the superpowers and the middle-rank powers— and perhaps between the superpowers themselves. Second, huge scales of effort will be needed to utilize advanced technology. This will put pressure on the middle-rank powers and smaller nations to cooperate in its utilization—a step that would involve restructuring institutions and the existing "technological superstructure"—or to forgo the advantages of the technology altogether. Third, some forms of future technology—such as large-scale climate modification— will require international cooperation not so much because of the costs involved but because more than one geographic region will be affected and the participation of those concerned will be essential. All three considerations have significant implications for functionalism either as an independent variable affecting the future world order or as an instrument of national policy for the attainment of specific objectives in international affairs.

The Rapidity of Technological Change

The continuously accelerating growth of technological innovation and change constitutes another major trend. Over half of the products manufactured by American industry today did not exist twenty years ago. Only ten years ago it used to take from five to seven years for a chemical product to advance from the laboratory to the production stage; the process has now been shortened to from one to three years. When the Communications Satellite Corporation was established, it was viewed as an investment in a technology several years away; its operational capability and earnings potential proved to be much faster and greater than originally anticipated. Only a year ago it was expected that commercial use of controlled thermonuclear reaction would be available sometime after the year 2000; now nuclear scientists are thinking in terms of an operational prototype reactor in the late 1970's, which would make CTR economical perhaps in the late 1980's or the early 1990's.

The total body of currently existing science and technology is so large and so versatile that a particular socially significant impact need not depend on progress in one area of technology. It may come from an advance or a breakthrough in one area or another, or it may come from all of them at about the same time, in which case the impact is likely to be truly revolutionary. This can be illustrated by the case of future progress in reducing the cost of energy. It can be achieved by technological advance in the application of superconductivity; indeed, major progress in that area is currently taking place. Cheap energy can be obtained through controlled thermonuclear reaction. Progress in the technology of MHD power would also result in lower costs of energy. But if significant advance is achieved in all of these, the cost of energy would be drastically reduced, since the three technologies are complementary and can be applied in a single power station. Quite apart from any major technological innovation that may take place in a particular field, synergistic effects involving innovations from various fields which reinforce each other provide a major dynamic force in modern technological change.

Technological Impact and Social Discontinuities

In the past twenty-five years, the incidence of the technological impact on society was in the military field: through nuclear weapons and missiles, it revolutionized military planning and warfare. It is only recently that advanced technology has begun to affect the daily lives of individuals and the work of institutions. The case may well be that the impact of technology on society will produce some important discontinuities in social and political trends in a not-so-distant future. There are signs that these discontinuities might be taking place in the United States now. They are reflected in the changing values of American youth.

Recent *Fortune* magazine surveys of college and non-college youth shed some light on this subject.[1] According to the surveys, three-fifths of American college students are "practical-minded"; for them, college is a natural road to career, status and financial success. About two-fifths of college students, however, reject these values, and since they appear to be growing into a majority of college students in the future, the surveys call them the "forerunner group." The forerunners are not concerned about money. They are more likely than the practical students to have privileged backgrounds; they take affluence for granted, are disdainful of "careerist" values and vague about their own career expectations. The forerunner group is most likely to major in humanities and seems to be interested in finding work that is intellectually challenging and related to its social concerns.

About half of the forerunners believe that the United States is a "sick society," and nearly a fifth of them have a sense of "solidarity and identification" with the New Left. They tend to be scornful of patriotism. However, only a relatively small percentage (between 3 and 4 percent) of college students in general were classified as "revolutionary," and less than 10 percent as "radical dissidents." The vast majority (76.4 percent) falls into the categories of "reformers" and "moderates," while a little over 10 percent are "conservatives." Non-college youth takes nearly as critical a view of society as college youth.

Not all aspects of this development can be attributed to technological impact, but its important role (direct and indirect) is unmistakable. The "affluent society," and the values and attitudes stemming from it, is largely a result of the high productivity made possible by modern technology—a new factor that opens up the option of completely eradicating poverty, something that was unthinkable before. The penetrating influence of technology makes the irrelevance of some old attitudes obvious: what matters now is the skill to operate computers, to conduct research in laboratories, not whether one is black or white, Protestant or Catholic. The rise of what Kenneth E. Boulding calls the "superculture"—"the culture of airports, throughways, skyscrapers, hybrid corn and artificial fertilizers, birth control and universities" [2]—worldwide in scope, with science as its common ideology, induces questions in the minds of young people about the relevance of nationalism in the present world system.

The rapid pace of technological change (practically all of the socially conscious life of the "now" generation has been within the last ten years, marked by the impact of such innovations as the transistor radio, worldwide jet transportation, the Pill, the landing on the moon, and other near-miracles) creates among the young a different perspective on how long it takes to get things done. When this perspective is applied to social problems like poverty, racial prejudice and wars, it not only widens the generation gap but makes a large percentage of young people action-prone. Today's affluence provides money, transportation, bullhorns and duplicating machines to translate the propensity to action into organizational and politically meaningful terms. Nearly instantaneous television coverage also fosters organizational efforts: it shows the radically inclined students all over the nation where the action is and makes rapid response possible. Perhaps more important, television compels emotional involvement in the coverage of violence (such as clashes of demonstrators on the streets or the torments of wounded soldiers in Viet Nam), but is much less effective with complex, abstract issues. It thus encourages "commitment" and discourages rational resolution of social problems.[3]

Other factors contributing to the new trend in value orientation, exemplified by the forerunner group, include the high complexity of modern technological society. A young man has to go through many years of schooling and then many years of work in routine or subordinate capacity before he reaches a stage where he can do something important or be influential. The impersonality of the existing institutions, their huge size and complexity producing rigidity and poor adaptability to change, induces a feeling of helplessness and alienation from the society as presently governed. Furthermore, as young people observe the rapidity of change they begin to wonder whether the skills they obtain through long years of schooling will be applicable to the society they will live in. As they try to look into the post-industrial society of coming years [4] —with its emphasis on superior knowledge, meritocracy, and highly complex, even more impersonal, computerized decision-making by increasingly larger organizations—many young people find the picture not particularly reassuring. Hence the shift to social and moral concerns, the humanitarian aspects of life, to "feeling" and "simple justice," as distinguished from the highly rational, complex, impersonal and, at times, quite arbitrary realities induced by technological advance.[5]

As one examines the impact of technology on the value system of the young generation, one can hardly escape the question: What sort of social discontinuities will result when institutions and daily lives of individuals are much more strongly affected by future technology? The late 1970's and the early 1980's, in particular, seem to be important in this respect. At that time, a number of technological impacts will converge and may produce major, perhaps radical, changes in society. Among the relevant factors can be mentioned the pervasive impact of computers; truly global mass communications and travel; development of ocean resources; the multiple problems of the post-industrial society then in full swing; and the imponderable effects of biomedicine. Moreover, it will be a time when nations will have to begin adjusting their technological superstructure and institutions for the even larger scale of the technologies of the later 1980's and the early 1990's: MHD power; thermonuclear plants; large-size, high-speed, surface-effect vehicles with both ocean and land mobility, and large-scale climate modification.

The nature and extent of the social discontinuities that might result will inevitably depend on a timely appreciation of the emerging problems and on effective policies to cope with them. It will also depend on the recognition of the extent to which the change being introduced by the technological impact is inevitable and legitimate, and on the adjustment of institutions and the creation of new ones to meet the requirements of this change. For a variety of reasons, all societies will not be equally successful in coping with the impact of technology. The price for failure, however, could be large: it may involve extensive social dislocation, widespread personal insecurity, severe social instability, and a serious weakening, if not collapse, of governmental authority and capability for defense.

While the exact consequences of the accelerating impact of future technologies are impossible to foresee, it is clear that the traditional view of technology as producing "long-range impact" no longer applies. Social, political and institutional changes induced by technology may be rapid, either as a result of a pent-up response to the already existing technology which has not yet come to the surface, or as a result of a swift advance in technology itself inducing concurrent socio-political change.

The Growing Importance of Nonmilitary Technology for National Security

Still another trend in the technological impact has been a changing relationship between military and nonmilitary technologies with regard to their effect on national security, especially that of the superpowers. Nonmilitary technology is gaining in importance as an area of direct relevance to national security, mainly because its role in changing the distribution of world and regional power is growing faster than the role of military technology.

Historically, national power has been changed through both military and nonmilitary technology. Through wars and conquest, qualitative or quantitative gains in weapons could change the distribution of power much more swiftly and more dramatically. Hence, it was the military sector on which the nations' concern for security was focused. In the long run, however, nonmilitary technology accounted for at least as much change in the distribution of world power as military technology. In more recent times, the rise of states has been principally determined by the technologies that made it possible for them to become great industrial centers.[6] Military power usually followed in the wake of industrial capability.

The acquisition of nuclear weapons by the United States at the end of World War II was a revolutionary development that gave the United States vast superiority in military power over the rest of the world in the immediate postwar years. Politically, however, nuclear weapons have proven to be a "power-unrewarding" area. Their great destructiveness and the unwillingness to use them came to mean that even an overwhelming nuclear superiority had but limited transferability into political power. The picture was further complicated by the progress of the Soviet Union in the development of nuclear technology, which accounted in large measure for the rise of Soviet power in the last two decades. However, after a certain point in weapons technology and the accumulation of "hardware" had been reached, the technological achievements of the two superpowers merely tended to neutralize each other, without any serious prospect for changing the distribution of world power.[7]

The acquisition of nuclear weapons by third states will not radically change the picture. If developed by responsible industrial powers (e.g., Japan) and accompanied by advanced means of delivery, they will have prestige value and will enhance the nation's military power to a point. But they will soon be absorbed and largely neutralized in the overall nuclear umbrella. If acquired by smaller states (e.g., Israel, Argentina), the weapons will temporarily change the regional distribution of power, but will eventually result in rudimentary regional nuclear umbrellas also characterized by mutual neutralization of power.

There are signs that, for political, technological and military reasons, the stalemate dominating nuclear affairs is beginning to spread into the conventional military sector as well. Concerned that a local conflict may escalate and trigger a nuclear war, the superpowers appear to be eager to restrict or smother it in an early stage, thus forestalling the stronger party from significantly changing the local balance of power through the force of arms (e.g., in the Middle East). The growing global projection of Soviet military power tends to deter potential American military action at various points of the globe; for example, the Soviet naval presence in the Mediterranean would make the U.S. government think twice before undertaking another Lebanon. The stalemate over Viet Nam suggests that substitution of technology for political solutions in limited conflict does not necessarily provide a solution. Viet Nam also indicates that modern conventional military technology, pitted against itself, has a tendency to manifest symptoms of a deadlock: American technology has been fighting not only the Vietnamese but also the products of Soviet and Chinese factories. Our aircraft, though superior, were practically stalemated by the effectiveness of the Soviet-built surface-to-air missile sites, assisted by anti-aircraft batteries.[8]

Future technology is likely to reinforce the growing stalemate. Nearly instantaneous satellite surveillance will help the United States and the Soviet Union to be well and swiftly informed about the location of each other's forces, particularly at sea. Improving air and sea mobility will afford both sides the possibility of blocking each other's moves. If, as predicted by some sources, lasers are developed into operational weapons,[9] resort to warfare on the subnuclear umbrella level will be further discouraged. However, unlike the case of the nuclear umbrella, the subnuclear umbrella military level can only be partially stalemated; for a number of reasons, changes in the distribution of power on this level are still likely to take place.[10]

While the military sector is thus kept in check, there is no sign of a stalemate —either now or in the future—in the ability of nonmilitary technology to effect a change in world power distribution. To mention but a few examples: Computers can provide a major impetus to the growth of a nation by facilitating economic planning and the investment and marketing strategy of corporations, thus providing differential advantage to the countries and regions leading in this field. Technological capability for the development of marine resources opens up new vistas in three-quarters of the globe that is virtually unexplored, unexploited and unsettled, with concomitant geopolitical implications. Nations that succeed in reducing the costs of energy sooner than others will be able to gain important advantages in the world markets, and strengthen their industrial capability and leverages of influence in the less developed world. The capability for controlling hurricanes, for covertly removing moisture from the atmosphere over a foreign nation, or for interfering with the layer of ozone surrounding the earth (and thus subjecting the ground underneath to severe burns by ultraviolet rays of the sun) [11]—for all of which the technologies could be developed by the late 1980's, if not sooner—would provide a more direct and dramatic means of changing the power distribution. The internal impact of technology on society and the resultant social discontinuities, which we have discussed previously, may also have implications of consequence for national power.

The speed of modern developments, which may prove many present estimates conservative, accentuates the importance of nonmilitary technology to national security. While the military sector may become increasingly stabilized in the next decades, nonmilitary technology might generate serious instability in foreign affairs which would be difficult, if not impossible, to control.

Implications for American Policy

Technology of the future will bring both great benefits and serious perils to society. The problem is to *control* it and its impact; the alternative is to be controlled by it. Control of technology requires a systematic effort by society to maximize its benefits and minimize its harmful effects in the context of social goals and purposes. As a corollary, it also requires analytical insights into the nature of the technological impact and the existence of appropriate institutions capable of generating and implementing the needed policies.

Since the dimensions of the technological impact range from local to global, in the last analysis its control can be effective only if it is undertaken on a worldwide scale. The political organization of the contemporary world does not permit effective control on such a scale at present. This suggests at least two criteria for American policy. (1) It is important that the United States be earnest and persistent in its efforts to subject technology and its impact to control in cooperation with other nations. (2) It is even more important that we as a society concentrate on improving our own capability in this regard. There can be little hope of being able to control technology globally if we are incapable of providing the requisite instruments of control within our own nation.

Improvements in the last twelve years notwithstanding, the United States is still inadequately equipped institutionally for this purpose. At the pinnacle of the U.S. government hierarchy, the principal responsibility for science and technology falls on the Science Adviser to the President and on his staff institutionalized in the Office of Science and Technology (OST). However, they can hardly be expected to cope with the staggering task of controlling technological impact. OST is a small body consisting of some twenty professional people who are mostly involved in immediate problems and issues. Its effectiveness has been strengthened by the President's Science Advisory Committee (PSAC) and it has also been assisted by the Federal Council for Science and Technology (FCST),[12] but OST has been unable to develop, or stimulate the development of, the needed conceptual instruments which would view the impact of science and technology as a continuum from its domestic origins to global implications and would attempt to control it accordingly. In actual operational capacity, OST's power with regard to major governmental agencies dealing with science and technology (such as the AEC, NASA and the Department of Defense) has been limited. OST has not been able to overcome a dispersion of responsibility for science and technology policy or to allocate resources in accordance with an overall plan, as distinguished from merely mitigating some excesses of the existing pluralism.

New institutions have been created in the past year to deal with the problem of controlling technology's impact. In May 1969 the President established a new interagency Environment Quality Council, with himself as chairman and the Secretaries of the principal departments concerned with the environment as members.[13] In January 1970 a three-member Council on Environmental Quality was set up at the White House. According to Washington observers, it is expected to fulfill a role with respect to the nation's environment similar to the one performed by the Council of Economic Advisers with respect to the national economy. At the same time, the President announced that the existing Environmental Quality Council was to be renamed the Cabinet Committee on the Environment and would be used as a forum for consideration of environmental issues by the President and Cabinet members. As of April 1970, the new Council on Environmental Quality was in the process of organizing its activities.

The National Goals Research Staff, established at the White House in July 1969, is somewhat less directly concerned with the problem of controlling the impact of technology, because it covers a broader spectrum of activity involving forecasting future developments and estimating the range of social choice. As a "think tank" for controlling technology, the NGRS is limited in two important respects: (1) considering the breadth of its mandate, its staff of ten professional people is small; (2) it is oriented toward U.S. internal problems, whereas technology needs to be analyzed in a global context.[14]

The proliferation of institutions at the highest level of government dealing with the impact of technology raises questions of the primacy of responsibility, of a sufficient comprehensiveness in approach, and of an effective coordination of activity among the institutions concerned. These questions can be fully answered only over a period of time.[15]

Aside from the need to strengthen our institutions, there is also a need to reexamine our policies with regard to science and technology. Some specific policy issues and problems can be briefly mentioned here.

In the past the United States had adequate resources to develop and take full advantage of practically the entire spectrum of potentially available technology. Because of the rapid proliferation of sciences and technologies and their initially high costs, the United States in the future will have the resources to develop and effectively utilize only a part of the spectrum. This will require a careful selection of priorities. In the postwar decades, priorities for the federally-supported development of science and technology were primarily determined by competition from the Soviet Union (nuclear-missile and outer space technologies) and by the interplay of various constituencies, inside and outside the U.S. government, competing for resources in support of their interest in a particular development (e.g., nuclear energy, marine sciences and technologies). A more rational and comprehensive approach to the determination of priorities in science and technology, which would consider the interests of the nation as a whole and anticipate the future, is needed.

A new look at nonmilitary technology, from the point of view of both control of its impact and priorities for support, might be in order. This is the technology which is not only growing in importance for national security, but is and will remain the principal instrument for increasing the nation's productivity and hence its ability to solve the multiple internal social and environmental problems contingent on the availability of resources. A number of key technological areas of major significance—such as MHD, CTR, superconductivity, weather modification and marine resources development—are currently either inadequately supported by the federal government or almost completely neglected. A comprehensive development of policies is needed with regard to such areas as the effect of technology on environment (including ecology), and the impact of computers, leisure (a result of the growing productivity) and biomedicine on society.

Last, there is a need for a clearer understanding of how technological developments can serve as a functional instrument of foreign policy and how to apply it wisely. In particular, the direct and indirect impact of technology as an independent variable on the future world order deserves close examination. The next step would be the formulation of a conscious policy, involving the use of technological instruments, to steer the development of the world order in a desirable direction.

NOTES

1. The two surveys commissioned by *Fortune* were conducted by Daniel Yankelovich, Inc., in October 1968 and March–April 1969. They interviewed 2,058 individuals and were reported in Daniel Seligman, "A Special Kind of Rebellion," *Fortune*, January 1969, p. 67ff., and Jeremy Main, "Dissidence Among College Students Is Still Growing, and It Is Spreading Beyond the Campus," *ibid.*, June 1969, pp. 73–74. This and the following paragraphs are based on the data supplied by these two articles.

2. Kenneth E. Boulding, "The Emerging Superculture," in Kurt Baier and Nicholas Rescher, editors, *Values and the Future* (New York: The Free Press, 1969), p. 347.

3. Seligman, *op. cit.*, p. 174.

4. For characteristics of the post-industrial society, see Daniel Bell, "Notes on Post-Industrial Society," *The Public Interest*, Winter 1967, pp. 24–35.

5. Cf. Seligman, *op. cit.*, pp. 174–175.

6. To illustrate: The initial industrial lead of Great Britain was undermined by the invention of the Bessemer process of steel production (1856) which, by allowing for mass production, made the United States the leading steel producer by the end of the nineteenth century. The Thomas-Gilchrist process (1879) enabled Germany to utilize the phosphoric iron ores of Alsace-Lorraine, thus making Germany the greatest European steel producer by

1893. Railroads were a major factor in the rise of the United States and Russia as great powers. Exploitation of hydroelectric power, chemical resources, telecommunications and cheap water transportation were important in Japan's rise to power before World War II.

7. For a good summary of what has come to be called "the nuclear umbrella," see The Washington Center of Foreign Policy Research, Johns Hopkins University, "Developments in Military Technology and Their Impact on United States Strategy and Foreign Policy," in U.S. Senate, Committee on Foreign Relations, *United States Foreign Policy* (Washington: GPO, 1961), pp. 718–730.

8. See Anthony Verrier, "Strategic Bombing—the Lessons of World War II and the American Experience in Vietnam," *The Royal United Service Institution Journal*, May 1967, pp. 157–158.

9. Lt. Col. Martin Blumenson, "The Incredible Laser," *Army*, April 1968, p. 35ff.; Herman Kahn and Anthony J. Wiener, *The Year 2000* (New York: Macmillan, 1967), p. 51.

10. The superpowers may not choose to stalemate each other (e.g., the USSR may let the United States defeat Red China in a localized conflict); or they may not succeed in restraining each other because of certain characteristics of the particular situation.

11. For potential developments in weather modification and how they relate to national power, see Gordon J. F. McDonald, "How to Wreck the Environment," in Nigel Calder, editor, *Unless Peace Comes* (New York: Viking, 1968), pp. 187–191.

12. PSAC has been helpful in examining issues referred to it by the Science Adviser to the President, but it has certain important limitations in developing a comprehensive science and technology policy: (1) It is a part-time advisory committee with no such broad responsibilities. (2) As a body consisting almost exclusively of scientists and engineers, it has not always provided impartial judgments; at times it has tended to take positions determined by the special background of this group, legitimate as these positions might be.

Unlike PSAC, the FCST consists of "insiders"—the heads of the independent agencies concerned with science and technology (NASA, AEC and NSF) and Assistant Secretaries for Science and Technology or their equivalent from the various departments. The FCST has suffered from the customary ailments of inter-agency committees, in particular the considerable degree of independence its members have. For a comprehensive discussion of key U.S. institutions for science and technology policy, see Eugene B. Skolnikoff, *Science, Technology, and American Foreign Policy* (Cambridge: The M.I.T. Press, 1967), pp. 226–248 and *passim,* and OECD, *Reviews of National Science Policy: The United States* (Paris, 1968), pp. 63–80 and *passim.*

13. For a more extensive discussion of the Environment Quality Council, see Luther J. Carter, "Environmental Quality: Nixon's New Council Raises Doubts," *Science,* July 4, 1969, pp. 44–46.

14. For details about the establishment of the National Goals Research Staff and its functions, see "The White House Looks to the Future," *The Futurist,* August 1969, pp. 99–101.

15. It should be noted that activity aimed at subjecting technology to greater control is not limited to the Federal Executive. In particular, on the suggestion of Representative E. Q. Daddario (Chairman of the Subcommittee on Science, Research and Development of the Committee on Science and Astronautics, House of Representatives), the National Academy of Sciences, the National Academy of Engineering and the Library of Congress undertook studies on how to secure a more effective assessment of technological impact for public policy. Among other things, the NAS Report on this subject recommended institutional innovations for "technology assessment." However, the "assessment mechanisms" proposed by the NAS are limited *ab initio* because they would apply to *publicly funded* technology only. See the Report of the National Academy of Sciences, *Technology: Processes of Assessment and Choice* (Washington: Committee on Science and Astronautics, U.S. House of Representatives, July 1969).

THE THIRD WORLD: RISING FRUSTRATIONS

15.
C. E. Black: Dynamics of Modernization

The contemporary international environment with respect to American national security policy is a revolutionary one not only because of superpower rivalry or nuclear weapons but also because of the vast transformations now occurring in Third World nations. All aspects of human activity, writes C. E. Black—including intellectual, political, economic, social, and psychological—are undergoing a revolutionary change which is on an order of magnitude comparable to the emergence of human civilization thousands of years ago. The potentials of this press toward modernization are great both for human betterment and for violence and destruction.

C. E. Black, an authority on Soviet Studies, is Professor of History at Princeton University and Director of the Center of International Studies.

Prologue: The Challenge of a Revolutionary Age

We are experiencing one of the great revolutionary transformations of mankind. Throughout the world in widely different societies man is seeking to apply the findings of a rapidly developing science and technology to the age-old problems of life. The resulting patterns of change offer unprecedented prospects for the betterment of the human condition, but at the same time threaten mankind with possibilities of destruction never before imagined. The search for an understanding of these forces of change is compelling, for failure may lead to catastrophe. The mastery of this revolutionary process has become the central issue of world politics—the ultimate stake for which peoples struggle in peace and risk annihilation in war. The initiative in guiding this transformation in a manner beneficial to human welfare belongs to those who understand most clearly the ways in which different societies around the world are affected, what must unavoidably be changed, and what must at all costs be preserved.

The change in human affairs now taking place is of a scope and intensity that mankind has experienced on only two previous occasions, and its significance cannot be appreciated except in the context of the entire course of world history. The first revolutionary transformation was the emergence of human beings, about a million years ago, after many thousands of years of evolution from primate life. . . .

The second great revolutionary transformation in human affairs was that from primitive to civilized societies, culminating seven thousand years ago in three locations, the valleys of the Tigris and Euphrates (Mesopotamia), the valley of the Nile, and the valley of the Indus. . . .

The process of change in the modern era is of the same order of magnitude as that from prehuman to human life and from primitive to civilized societies; it is the most dynamic of the great revolutionary transformations in the conduct of human affairs. What is distinctive about the modern era is the phenomenal growth of knowledge since the scientific revolution and the unprecedented effort at adaptation to this knowledge that has come to be demanded of the whole of mankind. Man perceives opportunities and dangers that for the first time in human existence are global in character, and the need to comprehend the opportunities and master the dangers is the greatest challenge that he has faced. . . .

"Modernization" as it is used here refers to the dynamic form that the age-old process of innovation has assumed as a result of the explosive proliferation of knowledge in recent centuries. It owes its special significance both to its dynamic character and to the universality of its impact on human affairs. It stems initially from an attitude, a belief that society can and should be transformed, that change is desirable. If a definition is necessary, "modernization" may be defined as the process by which historically evolved institutions are adapted to the rapidly changing functions that reflect the unprecedented increase in man's knowledge, permitting control over his environment, that accompanied the scientific revolution. This process of adaptation had its origins and initial influence in the societies of Western Europe, but in the nineteenth and twentieth centuries these changes have been extended to all other societies and have resulted in a worldwide transformation affecting all human relationships. Political scientists frequently limit the term "modernization" to the political and social changes accompanying industrialization, but a holistic definition is better suited to the complexity and interrelatedness of all aspects of the process. . . .

The Agony of Modernization

This rapid and rather impressionistic review of the main differences between tradition and modernity has purposely stressed the elements of expansion and amelioration, and may have conveyed the idea that mankind has benefited greatly from this process. This is certainly the case up to a point; indeed, it has often been asserted that an era of "progress" has arrived in which the benefits of man's new knowledge can be made available to all. A variety of utopias have been conceived of, in which it is anticipated that all manner of human ills will be overcome; even serious students of society with less utopian goals discuss the possibility of a world rid of war and poverty within a foreseeable future. Yet it is well known that modernization has been accompanied by the greatest calamities that mankind has known. Now that man has perfected weapons capable of destroying all human life, it is unavoidably clear that the problems modernity poses are as great as the opportunities it offers.

Of these problems, one of the most fundamental has been that the construction of a new way of life inevitably involves the destruction of the old. If one thinks of modernization as the integration or the reintegration of societies on the basis of new principles, one must also think of it as involving the disintegration of traditional societies. In a reasonably well-integrated society institutions work effectively, people are in general agreement as to ends and means, and violence and disorder are kept at a low level. When significant and rapid changes are introduced, however, no two elements of a society adapt themselves at the same rate, and the disorder may become so complete that widespread violence breaks out, large numbers of people emigrate, and normal government becomes impossible—all of which has happened frequently in modern times.

Modernization must be thought of, then, as a process that is simultaneously creative and destructive, providing new opportunities and prospects at a high price in human dislocation and suffering. The modern age, more than any other, has been an age of assassinations, of civil, religious, and international wars, of mass slaughter in many forms, and of concentration camps. Never before has human life been disposed of so lightly as the price for immediate goals. Nationalism, a modernizing force in societies struggling for unity and independence, easily becomes a force for conservatism and oppression once nationhood is achieved. Few political leaders have had the vision to place the human needs of their peoples above national aims. Too often the means for achieving modernization have become ends in themselves, and are fought for with a fanaticism and ruthlessness that risk the sacrifice of these ends.

Systems of knowledge based on age-old principles have been undermined, and numberless individuals in the modern world have found no other basis of orientation than immediate needs and goals. Eternal truths, generally embodied in religious dogmas and in conceptions of divinity, have been unthinkingly discarded because they were expressed in a manner that had come to be regarded as old-fashioned. Not infrequently these truths were later rediscovered and proclaimed as the latest revelation of modern science. The paradox of the dual nature of man—simultaneously rational and irrational—which was well understood in earlier times, had to be reasserted by modern psychology after several generations during which learned men had advocated the cult of reason. The desire to be modern has often led to the glorification of the transitory and to the frequent rejection of fundamental values as expressed in traditional institutional forms.

The process of political integration and centralization has been particularly destructive of men and institutions. National histories celebrate the success of rulers in defeating regional and local authorities, in bringing the church under control, and in winning prized pieces of territory from neighbors. Each of these acts may have contributed to the strength and integrity of the country, hence to its ultimate ability to forge a modern society, yet they involved not only a great deal of slaughter but also the destruction of institutions and organizations that had functioned successfully for generations. Frequently, after drowning in blood an entire network of local officials, the central authorities have had to find other people—usually less capable and experienced—to perform the same functions.

An inherent contradiction in the process of modernization is the tendency toward the concentration of authority at the level of politically organized societies and at the same time toward the integration of most aspects of human activity within a much larger framework, in some cases embracing all of mankind. When for the first time systems of knowledge of universal validity have been developed; when societies are increasingly dependent for their security on factors that extend far beyond their boundaries; when systems of production require raw materials, markets, and skills that no one society can provide; when social relationships and cultural institutions overlap national confines; and when the orientation of the individual is developing toward acquiring values that know no national frontiers—at this very time the effect of organizational controls within which all aspects of human activity must operate is being concentrated increasingly at the level of national states, of politically organized societies. This growing contradiction between independence and interdependence at the present stage of modernization lies at the heart of the contemporary international crisis.

One sometimes thinks of the modern age as being especially conducive to internationalism, but this has not thus far been the case. In traditional societies diverse peoples often have shared common religions, enjoyed fluid political allegiances and economic ties within large and loosely knit empires, and in a few cases employed languages recognized to some extent as universal. Today the inexorable requirements of modernization have been concentrated to such an extent at the national level that international organizations vital for national security can be formed only on the condition that they be forbidden to intervene in matters that are essentially within the domestic jurisdiction of member states. Intervention is permitted only if there is a threat to peace so grave that the great powers are willing to compromise their differences and take appropriate measures to prevent a major war.

Another source of unrest characteristic of the modern age has been the threat that the developing modern integrated society has posed to traditions and values evolved at a time when these were nurtured by a relatively small group of privileged leaders. The problem has led serious students to question whether education of a high quality can survive if everyone must be educated, whether ideas and standards will not erode if they must be presented in a form in which everyone can understand them—indeed, whether democracy is workable if everyone can make his influence felt. To some extent such fears no doubt are present among the former privileged leadership groups, which resent the necessity of sharing their privileges. Yet the problems of maintaining quality in an integrated or mass society cannot be said to have been solved. When a national budget must be approved by persons representing innumerable discordant interests, and when literature and art must be adapted to a mass audience at the risk of losing financial support—to cite only two examples—the problem is real.

Other social concomitants of modernization are equally grave. In many undeveloped countries, where the birth rate has remained high long after the death rate has declined, the growth in population may outstrip by a considerable margin any possible expansion in the output of food and manufactured goods. In these cases, even though agriculture and industry are stimulated by local efforts and foreign aid, production per capita may decline. The reluctance of the peoples of these countries to adopt methods of birth control is due to traditional values and behavior patterns that in their rate of change lag far behind medical care. In India, which has a serious population problem, not only are birth-control methods not employed but the many millions of Hindus refuse to eat the cattle that wander uncontrolled and often damage crops, or to kill the monkeys that devour enormous quantities of fruit and nuts. In such a case traditional scruples take precedence over human needs, and millions suffer.

The population problem is further compounded by the fact that in the early stages of economic growth, consumption on the part of the bulk of the population must be kept stable in order to provide the necessary investments. But how can this be done when the population is already growing faster than the production? In the more acute cases the answer has not yet been found. In the relatively developed countries, such as Britain in the mid-nineteenth century and Russia in the twentieth, the real income of wage earners appears to have declined absolutely for a generation or more before the benefits of the new industrial production became widely available. These countries started their growth at a much higher level than that of the newer states, however, and enjoyed more favorable conditions of development.

The effects of modernization on the stability and identity of personality have also been serious. The relatively stable personality characteristic of traditional societies is formed by an environment in which the elders are the unquestioned trustees of a cultural heritage that has changed only slowly through the centuries. Children are brought up within the immediate family in an atmosphere of emotional security, and enjoy face-to-face relations with the members of their community in relative isolation from peoples of a different heritage. This environment and set of relations make for a strong sense of identity and self-assurance, which for the overwhelming majority of members of traditional societies is never strained by confrontations with conflicting norms and values.

Although the fundamental psychological problems of individual adjustment may not change through the ages, and the incidence of aggressive and passive personalities and of neurotic and psychotic individuals may vary little, the environment in which these adjustments are made is greatly altered in the course of modernization. The traditional cultural heritage, rapidly undermined, gives way to a fundamental uncertainty as to norms and values. The environment in which children are raised and the norms that govern their upbringing are directly affected by a number of trends. Urbanization alters the family structure, and the local community dissolves as rural inhabitants desert the villages for cities and not infrequently for foreign countries. Changes in the relations between men and women attendant upon the mechanization of labor profoundly affect the centuries-old patterns of identity that have distinguished masculine and feminine roles.

The individual is less under the domination of his environment in modern than in traditional societies, and to this extent he is freer, but at the same time he is less certain of his purpose and in times of great unrest is prepared to surrender his freedom in the interest of purposeful leadership. This is what is meant by the loss of identity characteristic of individuals in societies undergoing rapid social change. The modern environment tends to atomize society, depriving its members of the sense of community and belonging without which individual fulfillment cannot be satisfactorily achieved. Many regard personal insecurity and anxiety as the hallmarks of the modern age, which can be traced directly to the profound social disintegration that has accompanied modernization.

This disintegration of traditional norms and values is apparent in the many forms of pathology that characterize modern societies. It is generally believed, although it is difficult to prove, that all categories of social disorganization—crime, delinquency, divorce, suicide, mental illness—have seen an increase in frequency as societies have become more modern. Underlying this trend is the circumstance that the close ties of individuals to others in the immediate environment are loosened as individuals by the millions migrate from rural to urban areas and the conformity to norms and effectiveness of sanctions characteristic of traditional societies are weakened. In a general sense this isolation of the individual is referred to as alienation.

At the heart of alienation is the impersonality of the societies in which the entire life of an individual—work, home, nourishment, health, communication, recreation—is managed by a variety of bureaucratic organizations that tend to treat individuals as numbers, bodies, or abstract entities. People may live in apartment houses where they do not know their neighbors, work in offices or factories where their colleagues change every few months, prepare food purchased from or delivered by unknown persons, eat among strangers in restaurants, enjoy entertainment either transmitted by electronic devices or seen in theaters or stadiums filled with persons one has never seen before, worship in churches where ceremony, clergymen, and congregation are unfamiliar, and grow up as children without close relations with parents and in environments where danger lurks in the street, and trees and animals are rarely seen. Indeed, individual social and spiritual needs receive more attention in modern armies than they do in the ever-growing metropolises in advanced societies. In terms of the relations of individuals to their environment this impersonal way of life in a modern metropolis—perhaps somewhat overdrawn for emphasis, but not untypical of the way many millions live—lies at the opposite extreme from life in the closely knit communities of traditional rural societies. No large numbers of individuals have been able thus far to adjust satisfactorily to the modern environment, and forms of social organization conducive to healthy personal adjustments have yet to be developed.

Related to these changes, in ways that are not entirely clear, is the increase in violence that has accompanied modernization. Painstaking but inevitably inconclusive worldwide estimates for the period 1820–1949 indicate that large wars have become more frequent and have taken a toll of 46.8 million lives. By comparison, 2.9 million lives have been lost in the same period from minor forms of group violence, and 9.7 million lives have been lost in murders involving one to three persons. One may gain some comfort from the fact that the increase in loss of life through violence has not exceeded the growth in world population. It nevertheless seems clear, although comparable statistics are not available for earlier periods of history, that the loss of life due to violence is significantly greater in proportion to population in modern than in traditional societies.

Some of this violence may be attributed no doubt to the willful malevolence of political leaders, but most of it can be explained by the radical character of the changes inherent in modernization. Involving the totality of human behavior patterns, these changes are correspondingly unsettling in terms of the identity and security of individuals and institutions. Traditional functions and institutions must be changed, but they do not surrender without a struggle. At the domestic level violence has taken the form of efforts to consolidate national authority, to suppress revolts, and to overthrow governments. The transition from traditional to modernizing political leaders has invariably involved violence and not infrequently civil wars of considerable intensity and duration. At the international level the dissolution of multinational empires, the liberation of subject peoples, the unification of territories to form new states, and the preservation of the national security of states both new and old have likewise been fraught with violence. Much of this violence has centered in the European and English-speaking societies that were the first to modernize, and it is possible that the inventiveness and vigor that enabled these peoples to develop modern knowledge and apply it to human affairs may be accompanied by an unusual bellicosity. It remains for the societies of Latin America, Asia, and Africa to demonstrate that they can achieve a comparable level of modernity with less violence.

The more modern societies are not freer than traditional societies from the problems inherent in personal and social relations; nor are they more civilized in any general or absolute sense. Modern societies, with a greater understanding of their physical and human environment, have a greater capacity for assuring the material welfare of mankind; yet at the same time, they face more complex personal and social problems and possess a greater capacity for violence and destruction. It is the task of the modern societies to make the best of their opportunities and to safeguard themselves as best they can against the destructive capabilities of their power.

PART III

The Domestic Environment and National Security

National security policies are not "necessities" imposed upon America by the world environment, even though some aspects of that environment are more fixed than others. External forces and events are assessed by decision-makers at different levels of the administrative structure and, under various constraints, choices are made. Although participants in the domestic sphere include the Congress, nongovernmental individuals and groups, the attentive and general publics, and the communications media, predominant in the process is the executive branch—with the President being advised chiefly by the Secretary of Defense, the Special Assistant for National Security Affairs, the Joint Chiefs of Staff, the National Security Council, the Secretary of State, and the Director of the Central Intelligence Agency. Generalizing about who among these "made the decisions" or wielded the most political "clout" is difficult. The organization charts do not reveal the informal lines of communication and influence. Policy documents and memoranda (including classified ones) do not disclose decisions made or influence exerted over the telephone.

"Although Presidents have rivals for power in foreign affairs," writes Aaron Wildavsky, "the rivals do not usually succeed. Presidents prevail not only because they may have superior resources but because their potential opponents are weak, divided, or believe that they should not control foreign policy." [1] Yet even in national security affairs presidential power is limited; "presidential *power* is the power to persuade," as Richard Neustadt observed. Anticipating the prospects of an Eisenhower presidency, President Truman said "He'll sit here and he'll say, 'Do this. Do that!' *And nothing will happen*. Poor Ike—it won't be a bit like the Army. He'll find it very frustrating." [2] Although the National Security Council and the Joint Chiefs of Staff are theoretically only the advisers of the President, writes Samuel P. Huntington, "Surely the President does not override united opinion among his top advisers much more often than he vetoes acts of Congress." [3] This view would tend to support the interpretations of those who concluded from a reading of the Pentagon Papers that President Johnson had deceived the American people during the 1964 election campaign concerning the decision to expand the Vietnam war and bomb North

Vietnam. But one may also argue that contingency papers are part of the policy-making process and until the President chooses, no decision has been made. Might not a reading of certain "Vietnam papers" from the Chairman of the Joint Chiefs of Staff and the Secretary of State in 1954 be as convincing that the decision had already been made to use American air power in Indochina, a step that the President subsequently refused to take?

At the top of the national security organizational pyramid is the National Security Council (NSC) which has been used according to the predilections of the President. It has functioned at various times, according to one author, for coordination, policy advice, policy planning, policy legitimation, crisis decision-making, budget influencing, education and communication, and creating a national security community.[4] The "institutionalization" of the National Security Council took place under Presidents Truman and Eisenhower, with Eisenhower in particular using it in the formalized manner suited to his preference for "completed staff work." The "desinstitutionalization" of the NSC occurred under Presidents Kennedy and Johnson, both of whom preferred a more personal, informal, ad hoc approach with presidential immersion in detail. Criticisms of the formal approach have included its routinization, excessive paper work, and insufficient action; of the informal approach, its inadequate concern for the long term, due to its detailed day-to-day crisis management.[5]

The Nixon Administration has "reinstitutionalized" the NSC system, combining several features of previous approaches and accelerating a major trend of the past decade, the centralization of decision power in the White House staff—in this administration under Henry Kissinger, Special Assistant to the President for National Security Affairs. The statements in 1970 by the latter and the President (see selection 16) indicate an awareness of previous shortcomings and a conscious effort to modify the system to suit the needs and preferences of the incumbent. The President's foreign policy reports to the Congress in 1971 and 1972 cite the importance of a conceptual framework for interpreting facts in terms of purposes and longer-range objectives and describe the establishment of several new interagency groups and committees for policy analysis. The basic committees are the Interdepartmental Groups (geographically and functionally organized), which report to the Senior Review Group, "the work horse of the system"; the Intelligence Committee; the Vietnam Special Studies Working Group; the Verification Panel, for arms control; and the Defense Program Review Committee, dealing with major issues of defense policy, posture, and budgetary support. Two groups whose task is the implementation of decisions are the Under Secretaries Committee and the Washington Special Actions Group.[6]

The chief adviser to the President in defense matters is formally the Secretary of Defense; and the role he plays depends on the man, the president, and the situation. President Eisenhower, with his military prestige, was more or less his own Secretary of Defense. Robert McNamara had an activist philosophy and the confidence of President Kennedy, who had lost faith in a sluggish State Department. McNamara exploited the potential of national security legislation to centralize decision-making and control and to institute systems analysis and cost-effectiveness techniques. One of the results (contrary to the "military ascendancy" thesis of C. Wright Mills) was to subordinate military influence as it had not been before—with the creation of the Office of Systems Analysis—and to continue the ascent of Pentagon civilians relative to the State Department by establishing a Pentagon "State Department," the Office of International Security Affairs (ISA).

With the arrival of the Nixon Administration and a Secretary of Defense more sympathetic to the military point of view—Melvin Laird—an increase in military influence occurred, marked for example by the downgrading of the Office of Systems Analysis and the ISA. The Joint Chiefs of Staff (JCS) began initiating more proposals rather than reacting to a bombardment of papers from the "whiz kids" in the Office of Systems Analysis.[7] This seemed a step toward correcting what Clark and Legere viewed as "one of the most serious shortcomings within the Defense Department during the past several years . . . the absence of an effective contribution by the professional military cadres to defense planning and programming."[8] Nearly a year and a half into the new administration, however (June 1970), Secretary Laird was reportedly reasserting some of the authority of the Pentagon civilians because he felt that they had been inadequately informed and involved during the Cambodia crisis, with direct contacts being maintained essentially between the White House and the JCS.[9]

The process of making decisions within the foregoing organizational structure is an intricate one. It is possible to sketch an analytical model for instructive purposes but nothing can capture the flow and the imponderables of the process. In the classical model of the rational decision-maker, for example, the decision-maker gathers information, calculates costs and benefits of various alternatives, ranks his preferences, and chooses the "least worst" alternative. But in the real world, information is seldom enough; time is short; the hierarchy of values is never explicit; and the consequences and their costs are never clear. Another analysis suggests that the decision-making process is one of "muddling through." For Charles Lindblom, politically feasible decisions consist of marginal, incremental changes in previous policy.[10] "Politically feasible" suggests that decisions are not made in a political vacuum but involve bargaining among the various participants as they compete for scarce resources. In decision-making, rationality is essential in the calculation of costs and benefits, in the balancing of objectives and capabilities, and in the evaluation of alternatives. But the decision-maker is affected also by his value preferences, his moral judgments, his perceptions of the environment; in other words, what may seem "rational" to an American may not seem rational to a Chinese.

Through mental lenses colored by his preconceptions, the decision-maker focuses on the evaluated information—intelligence—that links him with the external environment. The Washington intelligence community includes the Central Intelligence Agency (CIA; the chief collecting and coordinating body in the national security system), the Defense Intelligence Agency (DIA), the State Department, and the National Security Agency (the maker and breaker of codes). Differing institutional roles and perspectives, as well as personal judgments, may contribute to produce variations in the intelligence estimates sent to the decision-makers. Several years ago, for example, the CIA and the DIA were reportedly in disagreement over whether the weapons system being developed by the USSR at Tallinn was antiaircraft or anti-missile; in the spring of 1971, the CIA and the DIA were again reported as disagreeing over the functions of sites being excavated in the USSR—disagreeing as to whether they were for newer and more powerful missiles or for hardening the present missiles.[11] In both of these instances a "greater-than-expected-threat" perspective was more evident in the evaluation of the DIA.

Once it is received by the decision-maker, intelligence is used according to his judgment of the many variables involved in the situation. With hindsight (which of course is not available at the time of decision), it may be determined whether intelligence estimates were correct or incorrect: as they were incorrect, for example, on the "missile gap" or on Russia's placing of missiles in Cuba (as Klaus Knorr has suggested, this error may have been due in part to a failure of Soviet intelligence to estimate correctly the possible American response to such an action[12]); and correct, as indicated in the Pentagon Papers, in the estimate by the CIA of the prospects for success of bombing North Vietnam.

To improve decision-making in the Defense Department—not only for strategic planning but for the management of a huge establishment with assets estimated at $150 billion and with more than three million employees— new methods were introduced as part of the "McNamara revolution." Before McNamara, planning and decisions on weapons systems and the budget were largely separate, with costs not introduced systematically. The Programming-Planning-Budgeting System (PPBS) was instituted by McNamara to close the gap between the strategic and the budgetary processes. PPBS involved reorganizing all the activities of the Defense Department—men and equipment —into more than 1,000 program elements related to national security objectives; the defense budget was divided into nine new categories instead of into simply Army, Navy, Air Force, and Marines—they were Strategic and Retaliatory, Continental Defense, General Purpose, Airlift and Sealift, Reserve and National Guard, Research and Development, General Support, Retired Pay, and Military Assistance. According to the chief architect of the reform, Charles J. Hitch, the methods used in PPBS—systems analysis and cost-effectiveness techniques—seek to find that strategy (force or system) that offers the greatest amount of military effectiveness for a given expenditure; or, put another way, the objective is a given level of military effectiveness at least cost. Both cost and effectiveness are important, not simply cheapest unit cost. The armored knight of the middle ages, for example, was the most effective weapons system of the period, with high unit cost; the musket-and-powder system, permitting mass deployment, was a low-unit-cost system that replaced the bow and arrow, which had been high in cost due to the skill and training required; the most recent shift has been to a high-unit-cost system, nuclear weapons. For Hitch, systems analysis is not a panacea but a tool to assist the decision-maker in "defining military objectives, designing alternative systems to achieve these objectives, evaluating these alternatives in terms of their effectiveness and cost, questioning the objectives and other assumptions underlying the analysis, opening new alternatives and establishing new military objectives." [13]

One important feature of systems analysis is the use of quantification. Some of the early enthusiasts exaggerated the powers of the method and thus drew criticism from various quarters. The military were disturbed by what they considered the pretensions of inexperienced armchair generals.[14] Basically sympathetic critics who were practitioners themselves, such as James Schlesinger, argued that "Sophisticated costing may provide considerable assistance in revealing tradeoffs among various alternatives—but the ultimate decision, the choice of the strategic approach to the problem, remains a matter of faith that will always elude rigorous quantification. . . . The higher one goes in the decision making process the less quantitative and less systematic becomes the analysis." [15] Unsympathetic critics like Philip Green attacked the systems analysts for their false objectivity, asserting that a cold war bias was a basic assumption of the method.[16] Rejecting the views of the enthusiasts who claim panacea and the extreme critics who would discard analysis and rely on experience and intuition, a critic who has offered a more balanced assessment concludes that systems analysis is very useful to "sharpen . . . intuition and judgment." [17]

A primary area for the application of systems analysis and cost-effectiveness techniques is that of weapons procurement. The costs of procurement—$44 billion in 1968 alone—have raised cries of fraud and waste as more "cost overruns" on weapons production have been documented. The General Accounting Office reported in 1970 that the overrun on 38 weapons systems had been a total of $23.8 billion; the average cost for each F-111 fighter plane had grown from $3.2 million as originally estimated in the early 1960's to nearly $14 million per plane in 1970. Explanations for the huge cost expansion vary: some point to waste, mismanagement, inefficiency, high profits, and the practice of "buying in"—defined as follows in a Joint Economic Committee report: "a contractor may bid a lower price, higher performance, and earlier delivery than his rivals, knowing Pentagon officials will accept increased costs, less than promised performance, and late delivery." [18] Others stress rapid weapons obsolescence driven by the cold war competition and the high cost of sophisticated technology, materials, and personnel. A related explanation locates the basic problem in the nature of the weapons acquisition process, which has more inherent risk and uncertainty than ordinary production for the market. While demanding high performance products, changing strategic requirements make cost prediction difficult and the role of government essential.[19]

Though not in the public eye at the time, cost overruns in the 1950's—ranging from two to seven times the original estimates for 12 major weapons systems—were among the reasons for the attempt to assert greater civilian control over the procurement process during the McNamara revolution. One of Secretary McNamara's most controversial decisions involved his choice of General Dynamics over Boeing to produce the TFX (F-111) aircraft. Institutional roles, perspectives, and judgments were significant in this early example of civilians overruling the military, as Robert Art has shown in *The TFX Decision*.[20] As they compared the two "paper airplanes" (no prototypes had been built), the military saw the promise of extra performance in the Boeing proposal. Looking at the same facts but from a different perspective, the civilian secretaries saw cost and risk where the military saw promise. To them Boeing seemed to be "buying in"—the company with less experience in building fighter planes had submitted a lower estimate for what was technologically a far riskier design. McNamara's decision illustrated the application of the technique discussed previously: a technique "that (1) required him to consider alternative ways of satisfying a military requirement, (2) that required him to calculate the cost of each alternative, (3) that required him to weigh the military effectiveness of each alternative, and (4) that required him to compare all alternatives in terms of their cost and effectiveness." [21] The production of the F-111 was plagued with technical difficulties and spiraling costs, as the overrun indicates. Ultimately the Navy version of the plane was dropped and the numbers finally produced were considerably less than originally planned. (One wonders what the cost might have been if the technically riskier Boeing proposal had been selected instead.)

Among the criticisms of the McNamara methods in procurement were the lack of prototype development ("paper competition" was used instead) and, as Klaus Knorr and Oscar Morgenstern put it, lesser opportunity was afforded for healthy interservice and interinstitutional rivalry: "As long as resources are scarce, economy is a legitimate social objective. But the military must make their claims for resources; the economic evaluation—whether the country can 'afford' all that is demanded—clearly belongs to the higher civilian levels of decision-making." [22] Changes along some of these lines were instituted by the Nixon Administration, including increased military participation and the development of prototypes: under this administration a production contract would be signed only after a weapon was tested and evaluated ("fly before you buy").

That defense policy-making is essentially a political process has been implicit in this discussion of participants and organization. Let us set out two contrasting views regarding this thesis before elaborating briefly. The first view subordinates politics and maintains the distinctiveness of the military policy area:

To a much greater degree than in most other policy areas, military policy is a problem of factual analysis, informed prediction, and logical deduction, although value questions cannot be entirely excluded. Of course there is plenty of room for disagreement, and when the disagreeing parties possess both particular organizational interests and power, "politics" is bound to take place. But it is not clear why a compromise representing the relative power of the various interests will produce a policy closer to the logical imperatives of the national interest than an authoritative decision by "one man" or several men whose interests and outlook are truly national.[23]

In a second, contrary view, Bernard Cohen favors building a "theory of national security around a political model of military policy-making rather than a rational model—a model that builds the competition over values and preferences into the theory instead of treating given values as inputs which theory can handle."[24]

The view to be set forth in this discussion, similar to the views of Cohen and others,[25] maintains that in the formulation of national security policy, politics is not transcended in the name of the national interest or rationality. Governmental and nongovernmental groups and individuals compete to influence the allocation of scarce national resources according to their particular value preferences. Differing preferences and interpretations of the facts make conflict unavoidable despite the sincerity and honesty of the participants. Since rationality in decision-making can sharpen intuition but cannot guarantee a single, agreed-upon truth, persuasion and bargaining are therefore required to bring consensus out of conflicting institutional and personal perspectives.

This pluralistic process of conflict and consensus-building occurs in three overlapping arenas: (1) both within and between the military services and the civilian agencies; (2) within and between the executive and the legislative branches; and (3) in the public arena. One interesting study of the executive arena which illustrates the pressure-group model is Michael H. Armacost's *The Politics of Weapons Innovation.*[26] Investigating the controversy over building the Thor and Jupiter missiles in the 1950's, Armacost found broad military and civilian participation in the policy struggles, contrary to the rational model and the power-elite thesis: ". . . the fragmentation of power within the defense policy making system and the high stakes which important institutional interests invested in weapons decisions militated against leaving a monopoly of power over these 'cardinal choices' to a 'handful of men.'"[27] This conflict spilled over into the public arena as the Army and the Air Force leaked information to counteract the claims of the others. This interservice strife of the 1950's, observes Armacost, was displaced during the McNamara administration of the 1960's by a conflict between the civilians and the military. The establishment of civilian predominance in the early 1960's was facilitated by expanded budgets and reduced political risks and responsibilities for the military.[28] Healthy service rivalry was therefore not merely suppressed by the civilians, as some critics have argued, but ameliorated by expansion in strategic doctrine and military budgets. Beneath the surface, however, interservice politics has continued in a lower key, without contributing as extensively to the public policy debate as it did in the Thor-Jupiter controversy.[29]

The second arena of political conflict and consensus-building involves the executive branch and the Congress, whose rivalry is built into the system by the Constitution, which does not, observes Richard Neustadt, provide for a government of separated powers but one of "separated institutions sharing powers."[30] Institutional and personal perspectives have inevitably clashed over executive and Congressional interpretations of their respective powers as the domestic and world environments have been transformed in the twentieth century. Toward the end of the nineteenth century, Woodrow Wilson in his book entitled *Congressional Government* viewed Congress as "predominant over its so called coordinate branches. . . ." The presidency, Wilson said, was not a position of "recognized leadership in our politics . . . [it was] too silent and inactive"; ". . . [The] business of the President, occasionally great, is usually not much above routine."[31] In the early 1960's, in contrast, Senator J. W. Fulbright echoed the judgment of most scholars that the executive role in foreign and defense policy was preeminent, and that was as it should be.[32] Congress has generally acquiesced to its subordinate role in national security policy, deferring to the President and the military experts. Indeed, writes Bruce Russett, the Congress never in 25 years voted down a major weapons system proposal, sometimes voted more than was requested, and frequently protested the economies of the executive branch.[33] Congressional reasons for this financial support of the military included a concern for their constituencies, which a member of Congress cannot afford to ignore if he wishes to remain in office. In 1969 even liberal New York Republican Senators Javits and Goodell issued a joint statement announcing their intention to investigate the possibility that New York had suffered a disproportionate share of military base closings.[34] During the Johnson Administration, Russett observes, "defense spending became an agent of redistribution of income in favor of some of the poorer areas of the country, especially the South, and most particularly Texas."[35]

In the past three years, however, spurred by the profound effects of the Vietnam war, the Congress and particularly the Senate have been active in seeking a stronger role in the national security policy process. The manifestations of Congressional restiveness have included: (1) attacks on cost overruns; (2) passage by the Senate in 1969 of the National Commitments Resolution, which stated that "it is the sense of the Senate that a military commitment by the United States result only from affirmative action taken by the Legislative and Executive branches of the U.S. government by means of a treaty, statute, or concurrent resolution of both houses of Congress specifically providing for such a commitment"; (3) the six-week Senate debate in the Spring of 1970 over the Cambodian incursion, culminating in the passage of the Cooper-Church Amendment, which specified that Congressional approval would be necessary for funds to retain American troops in Cambodia;[36] (4) the passage by the Senate in June 1971 of an amendment to the Selective Service bill calling for the withdrawal of all US forces from Indochina within nine months if American prisoners of war are released; and (5) the Senate's rejection of the foreign aid authorization bill in October 1971;[37] and (6) passage by the Senate in spring 1972 (68–16) of a bill limiting Presidential use of American troops overseas without Congressional approval to 30 days.

The relative powers of the President and the Congress in national security affairs are not simply legalistic constitutional questions; an eighteenth-century constitution cannot be applied literally in a world fast approaching the twenty-first century. Just as the relationship of the executive and the legislative branches changed in the twentieth century in response to the dynamics of the domestic and world environments, political forces are now working to modify the sharing of powers by the executive and the Congress.

At some point the policy process we have been discussing becomes an opinion-policy process involving the public arena. As the three arenas interact, how does the public contribute? In a democracy does public opinion hamstring the leadership? Or is the process all a facade for irresponsible power-elite manipulation of the masses through control of the mass communications media?—as C. Wright Mills wrote, "with the increased means of mass persuasion that are available, the public of public opinion has become the object of intensive efforts to control, manage, manipulate, and increasingly intimidate." [38]

Contrary to Mills's interpretation of the opinion-policy process and the public arena, we offer a pluralistic interpretation: a "division of labor" framework derived from the model set forth by Gabriel Almond two decades ago.[39] According to this interpretation, public debate on national security policy is engaged in by governmental and nongovernmental elites chiefly before the "attentive public," the small portion of the people (3 to 10 percent) that are informed, interested, and regularly attuned to public policy discussion. The general public, usually passive and poorly informed, is aroused only in time of crisis. Through various techniques—speeches, press conferences, leaks, trial balloons, Congressional hearings—governmental actors attempt to gain support for or build a consensus behind their preferred policies. Nongovernmental actors such as general and special interest groups also participate in the process, seeking to mobilize other groups and publics and to influence governmental actors. Individuals with special expertise may be active in the process too: scientists, for example, have been especially prominent, at times with their advice on technical issues being intermingled with their policy preferences.[40]

The mass communications media perform a number of functions: they report remote events, selecting and emphasizing events according to "newsworthiness"; they transmit information and opinion on these events among the various participants, contributing to the structure of debate on controversial issues; and they may "create" events, such as the disclosure of the Pentagon Papers. As the foregoing comments suggest, the media—especially the quality media which serve the elites and the attentive public—are not simply transmitters of various points of view but participants who may support or criticize governmental policy. Even the television networks with their "history . . . of impartiality, even blandness," writes Bernard Hennessy, have been "liberalized" on public policy issues such as Vietnam, the military-industrial complex, and others. The concentration of power in the three networks can have a significant impact on public debate, Hennessy suggests, in view of the fact that "Not only do most Americans get most public affairs information from TV but they *trust* TV more than any other sources." Calling for forthright editorializing on television, Hennessy's "remedy for dishonest and covert partisanship, whether liberal or conservative, is honest and overt partisanship, both liberal and conservative." [41]

The operation of a twentieth-century democracy with 205 million people can not resemble an eighteenth-century town meeting. Decisions involving highly technical or strategic questions can not be made by laymen. Yet these decisions rest ultimately on value choices which in a democracy should be debated in the public arena. In the incremental process of making policy, governmental elites may choose with an eye to the possible reaction of publics; or fearing lack of support, they may seek to mobilize public opinion by emphasizing crisis. Occasionally the mobilization may border on manipulation. Given the uncertainties of the security dilemma in the present international system, the vital problem is to define and provide for the needs of national security while still preserving the requisites of democracy.

NOTES

1. Aaron Wildavsky, "The Two Presidencies," *TRANS-action* (December 1966), p. 7.
2. Richard E. Neustadt, *Presidential Power* (New York: Wiley, 1960), pp. 9, 10.
3. Samuel P. Huntington, "Strategic Planning and the Political Process," *Foreign Affairs* (January 1960), p. 299. (Reprinted as selection 25 in this part.)
4. Robert H. Johnson, "The National Security Council: The Relevance of its Past to Its Future," *Orbis* (1969), pp. 709–35.
5. Keith C. Clark and Laurence J. Legere, *The President and the Management of National Security* (New York: Praeger, 1969). (A portion of this book is reprinted in selection 17 in this part.)
6. *U.S. Foreign Policy for the 1970's: A Report to the Congress,* February 25, 1971; February 9, 1972. Excepting the Interdepartmental Groups and the Under Secretaries Committee, the above groups are chaired by Presidential Assistant Henry A. Kissinger. The core membership of these committees is basically the same and includes the Under Secretary of State, Deputy Secretary of Defense, Chairman of the JCS, and the Director of the CIA (*New York Times,* January 19, 1971).
7. *New York Times,* June 30, 1969.
8. Clark and Legere (above, n. 5), p. 210.
9. *New York Times,* June 13, 1970.
10. Charles Lindblom, "The Science of Muddling Through," *Public Administration Review,* Vol. 19 (1959), pp. 79–88. Also see James G. March and Herbert A. Simon, *Organizations* (New York: Wiley, 1958); Joseph Frankel, *The Making of Foreign Policy* (New York: Oxford University Press, 1963); Richard Snyder, H. W. Bruck, and Burton Sapin, *Foreign Policy Decision Making* (New York: Free Press, 1963); and Graham Allison, "Conceptual Models and the Cuban Missile Crisis," *American Political Science Review* (September 1969), pp. 689–715.
11. *New York Times,* May 26, 1971. For an informative analysis of the intelligence community, see Harry Howe Ransom, *The Intelligence Establishment* (Cambridge: Harvard University Press, 1970).
12. Klaus Knorr, "Failures in National Intelligence Estimates," *World Politics* (April 1964), pp. 455–467.
13. Charles J. Hitch, *Decisionmaking for Defense* (Berkeley: University of California Press, 1965), p. 52 and *passim.*
14. A high-ranking military officer tells this story: a man who feared flying because a bomb might be on the plane was assured by a systems analyst that the odds were one million to one against a bomb being aboard. When the man was still afraid, the systems analyst advised him to bring a bomb with him since the odds were 100 million to one against two bombs being aboard the plane.
15. James R. Schlesinger, "Quantitative Analysis and National Security," *World Politics* (January 1963), pp. 298, 302. (A selection by Dr. Schlesinger—selection 20—is reprinted in this part.)

16. Philip Green, *Deadly Logic* (Athens, Ohio: Ohio State University Press, 1966). (See selection 10, which is taken from *Deadly Logic*.)

17. Gene H. Fisher, "The Role of Cost-Utility Analysis in Program Budgeting," in *Program Budgeting,* David Novick, ed. (Cambridge: Harvard University Press, 1965), p. 77.

18. *The Economics of Military Procurement,* Report of the Subcommittee on Economy in Government, Joint Economic Committee, U.S. Congress, May 1969, p. 5.

19. M. J. Peck and F. M. Scherer, *The Weapons Acquisition Process* (Boston: Harvard University Press, 1962).

20. Robert J. Art, *The TFX Decision* (Boston: Little, Brown and Company, 1968).

21. *Ibid.,* p. 158.

22. Klaus Knorr and Oscar Morgenstern, *Science and Defense* (Princeton, N.J.: Center of International Studies, Princeton University, 1965), pp. 28, 29.

23. Glenn Snyder, "The Politics of National Defense: A Review of Samuel P. Huntington, The Common Defense," *Journal of Conflict Resolution* (December 1962), pp. 371–72.

24. Bernard Cohen, "Military Policy Analysis and the Art of the Possible: A Review," *Journal of Conflict Resolution* (June 1962), p. 159. This article is a review of Glenn Snyder's *Deterrence and Defense.*

25. Samuel P. Huntington, *The Common Defense* (New York: Columbia University Press, 1961); Gabriel Almond, *The American People and Foreign Policy* (New Haven: Yale University Press, 1950); Roger Hilsman, *The Politics of Policy Making in Defense and Foreign Affairs* (New York: Harper & Row, 1971); Warner R. Schilling, "The Politics of National Defense: Fiscal 1950," in *Strategy, Politics, and Defense Budgets,* Warner R. Schilling, Paul Y. Hammond, and Glenn Snyder (New York, Columbia University Press, 1962).

26. Michael H. Armacost, *The Politics of Weapons Innovation* (New York: Columbia University Press, 1961).

27. *Ibid.,* p. 253.

28. Armacost quotes Warner Schilling: "Who is going to object to systems analysis when the result is all systems go? Who is going to object to program budgeting when all programs are budgeted?" (p. 289). Paul Y. Hammond points to increased budgets and lessened responsibilities in "A Functional Analysis of Defense Department Decision-Making in the McNamara Administration," *American Political Science Review* (March 1968), pp. 57–69.

29. Secretary Laird's "disillusionment" with interservice logrolling was reported by the *New York Times* (August 1, 1970); logrolling was also referred to by the Blue Ribbon Defense Panel's *Report to the President and the Secretary of Defense on the Department of Defense* (July 1, 1970, p. 33).

30. Neustadt (above, n. 2), p. 33.

31. Quoted in Emmette E. Redford *et al., Politics and Government in the United States* (New York: Harcourt, Brace, and World, 1965), p. 316.

32. J. W. Fulbright, *Prospects for the West* (Cambridge: Harvard University Press, 1963).

33. Bruce Russett, *What Price Vigilance?* (New Haven: Yale University Press, 1970), p. 26.

34. *New York Times,* October 27, 1969.

35. Russett (above, n. 33), p. 68.

36. For the debate on Cambodia from the *Congressional Record,* see Eugene P. Dvorin, ed., *The Senate's War Powers* (Chicago: Markham, 1971).

37. Reduced sums for military and economic aid were subsequently authorized by the Senate; in signing a military procurement authorization bill, the President announced he would disregard the amendment calling for prompt withdrawal from Vietnam contingent on the release of prisoners of war (*N.Y. Times,* November 17, 1971).

38. C. Wright Mills, *The Power Elite* (New York: Oxford University Press, 1956), p. 310.

39. *The American People and Foreign Policy* (above, n. 25).

40. As Don K. Price has pointed out in *The Scientific Estate* (Cambridge: Belknap-Harvard University Press, 1967), pp. 275–76, it is important to understand that "practically all policies are based on a mixture of ideas that only scientists can understand with other ideas that most of them do not bother to—such as considerations of cost, administrative effectiveness, political feasibility, and competition with other policies. As a result policy questions cannot be solved like an equation or disposed of by a statute." For studies of scientists and policy-making, see Robert Gilpin, *American Scientists and Nuclear Weapons*

Policy (Princeton, N.J.: Princeton University Press, 1962) and Robert Gilpin and Christopher Wright, *Scientists and National Policymaking* (New York: Columbia University Press, 1964).

41. Bernard Hennessy, "Welcome, Spiro Agnew," *The New Republic,* December 13, 1969, p. 14. On the role of the press, see Bernard Cohen, *The Press and Foreign Policy* (Princeton, N.J.: Princeton University Press, 1963).

ORGANIZATION FOR DEFENSE

16.
The National Security Council: *Comment by Henry A. Kissinger*

At the apex of the national security organizational machinery is the National Security Council, the principal advisory body to the President. How the NSC is used depends upon the President; and problems have arisen both from the formalized use of the system during the Eisenhower years and from the ad hoc, informal approach of the Kennedy and Johnson Administrations. In revitalizing the formal organization, the Nixon Administration sought to avoid the difficulties of earlier years. The following selection presents a comment on the NSC system by Henry A. Kissinger, Special Assistant to the President for National Security Affairs, and a description from President Nixon's foreign policy report of February 1970. Both of these documents were published by the Subcommittee on National Security and International Operations of the Senate Committee on Government Operations, which for more than a decade through its hearings and reports has contributed substantially to the understanding of the policy process.

Professor Kissinger's numerous publications include *The Troubled Partnership, The Necessity for Choice,* and *Nuclear Weapons and Foreign Policy,* which was one of the earliest analyses of the implications of atomic weapons.

Letter to Senator Henry M. Jackson Concerning the National Security Council from Henry A. Kissinger, Assistant to the President for National Security Affairs

THE WHITE HOUSE,
Washington, March 3, 1970.

Hon. HENRY M. JACKSON,
U.S. Senate, Washington, D.C.

DEAR SENATOR JACKSON: In your letter of October 30, 1969, you asked me for "a memorandum or letter . . . describing the current approach to the NSC and its use in Presidential decision-making."

From *The National Security Council: Comment by Henry A. Kissinger,* Subcommittee on National Security and International Operations of the Committee on Government Operations, U.S. Senate, March 1970, pp. 1–7.

I have given your request the most careful consideration, and I am happy to comply. No student of policymaking could fail to appreciate the enormous contribution which you and your subcommittee have made to the body of learning on this subject. I hope I can be of assistance.

Enclosed is a copy of the section of the President's Report to the Congress on United States Foreign Policy which discusses the National Security Council system. The President intended this section of the Report to be a clear description of how the NSC system works and, more importantly, of what its purposes are. We prepared it with your request in mind. I believe it is a suitable document for your subcommittee to add to the body of literature on the subject of national security policymaking.

Perhaps I can add some background on our new NSC system which places it in historical perspective.

A staff report issued by your subcommittee nine years ago pointed out that "each successive President has great latitude in deciding how he will employ the Council to meet his particular needs. He can use the Council as little, or as much, as he wishes. He is solely responsible for determining what policy matters will be handled within the Council framework, and how they will be handled." [1] President Nixon's decisions as to the new role and structure of the NSC were influenced by his direct experience with the NSC machinery as it was used during the Eisenhower Administration, and also by the accumulated national experience of a variety of approaches to the utilization of the NSC machinery.

During the period of transition between election and inauguration, the President-elect devoted considerable attention to devising a system and procedure that would be efficient, effective, and suited to his own style of leadership. As a result, President Nixon announced at the outset of his Administration that the National Security Council and the NSC system would be the central machinery in the process of policymaking for national security. As the White House announced on February 7, 1969, "The President . . . indicated that the Council will henceforth be the principal forum for the consideration of policy issues on which he is required to make decisions."

It is not, of course, the NSC which makes decisions. The *President* makes decisions, in accordance with his Constitutional responsibility, and the NSC remains an advisory body as conceived by the 1947 National Security Act. Nor does the President necessarily make his decisions in the NSC meetings; rather, this is usually done after further private deliberation, subsequent to NSC consideration of the issues. The NSC is a forum for discussion, in which the interested departments and agencies of the U.S. Government are asked by the President to state issues, present alternatives, and discuss implications, in order that the President may elicit and receive the advice he requires.

The chapter from the President's Foreign Policy Report indicates the purposes which the new NSC system is meant to serve. We recognize, of course, that no institutional arrangement can guarantee that these objectives will all be realized. Nor can we claim that the structure and procedures we have devised are the only way to go about the business of policymaking. But the orderly and regularized procedures which the NSC system provides have advantages which President Nixon prefers to exploit.

The more ad hoc approach of the 1960's often ran the risk that relevant points of view were not heard, that systematic treatment of issues did not take place at the highest level, or that the bureaucracies were not fully informed as to what had been decided and why. Flexible procedures used in place of NSC meetings can enjoy the advantages which come with informality —speed, frankness, convenience, and so forth—but they may also suffer from the lack of fixed agenda, methodical preparation, and systematic promulgation or explanation of decisions. Of course, there is nothing to preclude a President from supplementing formal with informal machinery—as indeed has frequently been the case in this Administration.

President Nixon prefers to make use of the NSC and the NSC system, with occasional recourse to less structured groups. Almost all major issues are now treated within the framework of the NSC system. The Council meets regularly, usually once a week, and its agenda specifies for discussion a problem which has been through the process of review in the NSC system. In most cases, Presidential decisions follow in writing.

At the same time, we have tried to avoid some of the problems of the NSC system of the 1950's. One such problem was that the papers which came to the President from the NSC system, and the decision papers based upon them, were often not specific enough to provide effective guidance to the bureaucracy. Incoming papers often reflected compromises reached among agencies at a lower level. The machinery gave too much emphasis to interdepartmental consensus and too little to the presentation of distinct points of view and distinct policy alternatives.

As the chapter from the Foreign Policy Report makes clear, President Nixon wanted a system which provided him with analytical papers focusing on issues for decision and on clear policy alternatives. The system of supporting subcommittees which the President set up is intended to present distinct options, together with their pros and cons and implications and costs, rather than a single policy recommendation founded on bureaucratic consensus. We thus try to identify the real issues for Presidential decision instead of burying them in "agreed language." Formal agency positions are taken only at the level of the Council itself, and are argued out in front of the President. In focusing on the issues, we try to ask first the crucial policy question of where we want to go. We formulate the alternative answers to this question, and the President's decision then guides our inquiry into the operational issues.

Finally, we have sought to avoid some of the problems of the formality of the NSC system of the 1950's, by introducing some flexibility as to the channel through which a subject travels to presentation to the Council. The Foreign Policy Report identifies some of the special groups and channels in the new NSC system, and indicates that they serve the same purposes that the regular groups and channels serve: systematic review and analysis, bringing together all the departments and agencies concerned.

There are inevitable kinks in the system, and we will continue to be flexible in order to iron them out. Further experience will no doubt give us a better perspective on how well the system is working. Further modifications will no doubt be made.

As the chapter from the President's Report concludes, there is no textbook prescription for organizing the system and staff for national security policy-making. The only basic rule is that the structure be suited to the wishes and style of the President. As your subcommittee's staff report of 1960 pointed out, the National Security Council is "the President's instrument," and it "exists only to serve the President." [2]

Warmest regards,

HENRY A. KISSINGER.

Enclosure.

The National Security Council System [3]

If we were to establish a new foreign policy for the era to come, we had to begin with a basic restructuring of the process by which policy is made.

Our fresh purposes demanded new methods of planning and a more rigorous and systematic process of policymaking. We required a system which would summon and gather the best ideas, the best analyses and the best information available to the government and the nation.

Efficient procedure does not insure wisdom in the substance of policy. But given the complexity of contemporary choices, adequate procedures are an indispensable component of the act of judgment. I have long believed that the most pressing issues are not necessarily the most fundamental ones; we know that an effective American policy requires clarity of purpose for the future as well as a procedure for dealing with the present. We do not want to exhaust ourselves managing crises; our basic goal is to shape the future.

At the outset, therefore, I directed that the National Security Council be reestablished as the principal forum for Presidential consideration of foreign policy issues. The revitalized Council—composed by statute of the President, the Vice President, the Secretaries of State and Defense, and the Director of the Office of Emergency Preparedness—and its new system of supporting groups are designed to respond to the requirements of leadership in the 1970's:

—Our policy must be *creative:* foreign policy must mean more than reacting to emergencies; we must fashion a new and positive vision of a peaceful world, and design new policies to achieve it.

—Our policymaking must be *systematic:* our actions must be the products of thorough analysis, forward planning, and deliberate decision. We must master problems before they master us.

—We must know the *facts:* intelligent discussions in the National Security Council and wise decisions require the most reliable information available. Disputes in the government have been caused too often by an incomplete awareness or understanding of the facts.

—We must know the *alternatives:* we must know what our real options are and not simply what compromise has found bureaucratic acceptance. Every view and every alternative must have a fair hearing. Presidential leadership is not the same as ratifying bureaucratic consensus.

—We must be prepared if *crises* occur: we must anticipate crises where possible. If they cannot be prevented, we must plan for dealing with them. All the elements of emergency action, political as well as military, must be related to each other.

—Finally, we must have effective *implementation:* it does little good to plan intelligently and imaginatively if our decisions are not well carried out.

Creativity. Above all, a foreign policy for the 1970's demands imaginative thought. In a world of onrushing change, we can no longer rest content with familiar ideas or assume that the future will be a projection of the present. If we are to meet both the peril and the opportunity of change, we require a clear and positive vision of the world we seek—and of America's contribution to bringing it about.

As modern bureaucracy has grown, the understanding of change and the formulation of new purposes have become more difficult. Like men, governments find old ways hard to change and new paths difficult to discover.

The mandate I have given to the National Security Council system, and the overriding objective of every policy review undertaken, is to clarify our view of where we want to be in the next three to five years. Only then can we ask, and answer, the question of how to proceed.

In central areas of policy, we have arranged our procedure of policymaking so as to address the broader questions of long-term objectives first; we define our purposes, and then address the specific operational issues. In this manner, for example, the NSC first addressed the basic questions of the rationale and doctrine of our strategic posture, and then considered—in the light of new criteria of strategic sufficiency—our specific weapons programs and our specific policy for the negotiations on strategic arms limitation. We determined that our relationship with Japan for the 1970's and beyond had to be founded on our mutual and increasingly collaborative concern for peace and security in the Far East; we then addressed the issue of Okinawa's status in the light of this fundamental objective.

Systematic Planning. American foreign policy must not be merely the result of a series of piecemeal tactical decisions forced by the pressures of events. If our policy is to embody a coherent vision of the world and a rational conception of America's interests, our specific actions must be the products of rational and deliberate choice. We need a system which forces consideration of problems before they become emergencies, which enables us to make our basic determinations of purpose before being pressed by events, and to mesh policies.

The National Security Council itself met 37 times in 1969, and considered over a score of different major problems of national security. Each Council meeting was the culmination of an interagency process of systematic and comprehensive review.

This is how the process works: I assign an issue to an Interdepartmental Group—chaired by an Assistant Secretary of State—for intensive study, asking it to formulate the policy choices and to analyze the pros and cons of the different courses of action. This group's report is examined by an interagency Review Group of senior officials—chaired by the Assistant to the President for National Security Affairs—to insure that the issues, options, and views are presented fully and fairly. The paper is then presented to me and the full National Security Council.

Some topics requiring specialized knowledge are handled through different channels before reaching the National Security Council. But the purpose is the same—systematic review and analysis, bringing together all the agencies concerned:

—The major issues of defense policy are treated in systematic and integrated fashion by the NSC Defense Program Review Committee. This group reviews at the Under Secretary level the major defense policy and program issues which have strategic, political, diplomatic, and economic implications in relation to overall national priorities.

—Through other NSC interagency groups, the United States Government has undertaken its first substantial effort to review all its resource programs within certain countries on a systematic and integrated basis, instead of haphazardly and piecemeal.

Determination of the Facts. Intelligent discussions and decisions at the highest level demand the fullest possible information. Too often in the past, the process of policymaking has been impaired or distorted by incomplete information, and by disputes in the government which resulted from the lack of a common appreciation of the facts. It is an essential function of the NSC system, therefore, to bring together all the agencies of the government concerned with foreign affairs to elicit, assess, and present to me and the Council all the pertinent knowledge available.

Normally NSC Interdepartmental Groups are assigned this task. But other interagency groups perform this function for certain special topics. For example:

—The Verification Panel was formed to gather the essential facts relating to a number of important issues of strategic arms limitation, such as Soviet strategic capabilities, and our potential means of verifying compliance with various possible agreements. This Panel was designed not to induce agreement on policy views, but to establish as firmly as possible the *data* on which to base policy discussions. It helped to resolve many major policy differences which might otherwise have been intractable. As the section on Arms Control in this report explains in detail, the Panel played a central part in making our preparation for the Strategic Arms Limitation Talks with the Soviet Union the most thorough in which the U.S. Government has ever engaged.

—The Vietnam Special Studies Group (VSSG) gathers and presents to the highest levels of the United States Government the fullest and most up-to-date information on trends and conditions in the countryside in Vietnam. This group is of key assistance in our major and sustained effort to understand the factors which will determine the course of Vietnamization.

Full Range of Options. I do not believe that Presidential leadership consists merely in ratifying a consensus reached among departments and agencies. The President bears the Constitutional responsibility of making the judgments and decisions that form our policy.

The new NSC system is designed to make certain that clear policy choices reach the top, so that the various positions can be fully debated in the meeting of the Council. Differences of view are identified and defended, rather than muted or buried. I refuse to be confronted with a bureaucratic consensus that leaves me no options but acceptance or rejection, and that gives me no way of knowing what alternatives exist.

The NSC system also insures that all agencies and departments receive a fair hearing before I make my decisions. All Departments concerned with a problem participate on the groups that draft and review the policy papers. They know that their positions and arguments will reach the Council without dilution, along with the other alternatives. Council meetings are not rubber-stamp sessions. And as my decisions are reached they are circulated in writing, so that all departments concerned are fully informed of our policy, and so that implementation can be monitored.

Crisis Planning. Some events in the world over which we have little control may produce crises that we cannot prevent, even though our systemized study forewarns us of their possibility. But we can be the masters of events when crises occur, to the extent that we are able to prepare ourselves in advance.

For this purpose, we created within the NSC system a special senior panel known as the Washington Special Actions Group (WSAG). This group drafts contingency plans for possible crises, integrating the political and military requirements of crisis action. The action responsibilities of the departments of the Government are planned in detail, and specific responsibilities assigned in an agreed time sequence in advance. While no one can anticipate exactly the timing and course of a possible crisis, the WSAG's planning helps insure that we have asked the right questions in advance, and thought through the implications of various responses.

Policy Implementation. The variety and complexity of foreign policy issues in today's world places an enormous premium on the effective implementation of policy. Just as our policies are shaped and our programs formed through a constant process of interagency discussion and debate within the NSC framework, so the implementation of our major policies needs review and coordination on a continuing basis. This is done by an interdepartmental committee at the Under Secretary level chaired by the Under Secretary of State.

Conclusions. There is no textbook prescription for organizing the machinery of policymaking, and no procedural formula for making wise decisions. The policies of this Administration will be judged on their results, not on how methodically they were made.

The NSC system is meant to help us address the fundamental issues, clarify our basic purposes, examine all alternatives, and plan intelligent actions. It is meant to promote the thoroughness and deliberation which are essential for an effective American foreign policy. It gives us the means to bring to bear the best foresight and insight of which the nation is capable.

NOTES

1. "The National Security Council," A Staff Report of the Subcommittee, December 12, 1960, in *Organizing for National Security.* Inquiry of the Subcommittee on National Policy Machinery, Committee on Government Operations, U.S. Senate, Vol. 3, p. 31 (1961).

2. *Ibid.,* p. 38.

3. From the President's Report to the Congress on United States Foreign Policy, February 18, 1970.

17.
Keith C. Clark and Laurence J. Legere:
The President and the Management of National Security

Among the chief advisers to the President in the use of military force for the achievement of national objectives are the Secretary of Defense and the Joint Chiefs of Staff. The multiple roles of the Secretary, the JCS, and the Chairman of the JCS, as well as the basic outlines of the McNamara revolution in the Defense Department are discussed in the following selection. The study from which the selection is taken is a product of one of the government-sponsored "think tanks," the Institute for Defense Analyses.

Keith C. Clark was on leave from the CIA at the time of writing and Laurence J. Legere is a former military officer with the IDA.

The life and security of the nation may depend on the President's ability to assert effective control over the Department of Defense. The Defense Department budget amounts to about half of the national budget, and this alone forces close attention on the far-reaching decisions of the President and his secretary of defense about defense expenditures. This will be true if such expenditures continue at present levels or increase; it will be even more true if they are to be cut back.

From Keith C. Clark and Laurence J. Legere, *The President and the Management of National Security: A Report by the Institute for Defense Analysis,* pp. 173–84. Praeger Publishers, 1969. Reprinted by permission of the publishers.

In earlier times, military forces were organized into armies and navies, depending on whether they fought on land or sea. War was war and peace was peace, and it seemed a simple matter to decide whether a question was purely "military," or "political," or "economic," or whatever. Today there is no simple, widely accepted principle for organizing armed forces, and there are very few problems which are purely military or purely civilian. Nevertheless, those who man the Department of Defense and the armed forces do come from either civilian or military backgrounds, and their instinctive habits of mind often result in different ways of addressing problems. Well-defined professional and vocational backgrounds generate different approaches and perspectives. It is vital that such different approaches and perspectives be brought to bear on national-security affairs, but a President does have to decide on the basic mix between civilians and professional military men in the leadership of the Department of Defense.

"Civilian control" in the narrow sense is not really the issue. We automatically have civilian control by the very fact that the President is a civilian, and the secretary of defense is his personal appointee. The real issue is: What kinds of questions can best be decided by civilian executives? What kinds of questions can best be decided by professional military leaders? And what kinds of questions require combined judgments? The essential problem is: How can political authorities establish and maintain appropriate control without jeopardizing or inhibiting the expression of professional military judgment?

At the top of the civilian and military sides of the Department of Defense are the Office of the Secretary of Defense (OSD) and the Office of the Joint Chiefs of Staff (OJCS), respectively. There has been a steady growth in the authority and power of both, but the growth has not been even or in all respects parallel. Moreover, the civilian and the military officials have not always had a clear conception of the roles and contributions of their respective opposite numbers. Misunderstandings have sometimes produced confusion, and men of talent and good will on both sides of the line have often appeared to be in conflict, when actually they merely failed to appreciate the roles of the other side. Moreover, statutes and directives have often contributed to these misunderstandings because they were not precise in delineating roles and relationships.

The "McNamara Revolution"

What is now called the "McNamara Revolution" in the Department of Defense is in part the continuation of an evolutionary process started in the 1940's and accelerated in the 1950's. Centralization in national-security affairs began with the National Security Act of 1947, which created the position of secretary of defense but failed to provide him with staff or a department. The 1949 legislative amendments carried the process further by creating the Department of Defense. President Eisenhower's 1953 and 1958 Defense Department reorganizations shifted the balance of authority and responsibility in the military establishment away from the separate services, toward the secretary of defense and the collective Joint Chiefs of Staff. The 1958 reorganization was particularly significant because it put the secretary squarely in the military chain of command, just under the President, and directly over the unified and specified operating commands. Before that, the service departments had acted as "executive agents" for operational matters affecting particular unified and specified military commands—for example, army for Europe, navy for the Pacific, and air force for the Strategic Air Command. The 1958 legislation confined the service departments to administrative, training, and logistical functions.

The reorganizations of 1953 and especially of 1958 created the base for what was to follow, but for the most part it did not follow until after 1960. Probably the main reason why it did not was the extraordinary status of President Eisenhower in the eyes of almost all Americans. He was regarded by virtually everyone as the nation's foremost military hero and military expert, and the defense secretaries who served under him shared this widespread attitude. Those who say that Eisenhower was served by "weak" defense secretaries have not perceived the true nature of the situation. His defense secretaries were able executives, but they worked for a President who had relatively little need for a "strong" secretary in either the military-adviser or command role. President Eisenhower was almost unavoidably his own secretary of defense. Where he felt the need for a "strong" Cabinet member was in coping with the other aspects of foreign affairs; hence, Secretary of State John Foster Dulles emerged in this role.

Whether or not Secretary Robert S. McNamara's innovations amounted to a "revolution," it was he who fully exploited the implications of the 1958 legislation. He moved decisively from the moment he took office, and he was apparently convinced that new legislation was not required for him to carry out his duties with aggressive vigor. More importantly, he was imbued with the philosophy that industrial management required strong executive leadership, and he conceived of the job of being secretary of defense somewhat along the industry-manager model. He was determined to be an activist leader and not merely the judge of competing alternatives or a negotiator among competing interests.

Asserting this role from the outset, McNamara prepared a list of subjects for extensive review, including existing defense policies, strategies, and programs. The review tasks were assigned to appropriate offices in the Department of Defense, within the Joint Chiefs of Staff arena, to the separate services, and elsewhere. The results of the reviews generally displeased the secretary for at least two reasons. First, each document tended to reflect the institutional perspective of the office drafting it, and second, most seemed to rely on verbal, conventional wisdom instead of hard, fresh analysis.

McNamara quickly determined the need for two courses of action. First, he wanted to introduce new analytical techniques to replace the traditional, mainly verbal-philosophical methods of the past. Second, he wanted a strong staff capability within OSD, which, sharing his departmentwide perspective, could exercise those techniques. The first of these two concerns led to PPBS, which was initially centered in the Office of the Comptroller of the Department of Defense, at first Charles Hitch and later Robert Anthony. The second resulted in creation of the Office of Systems Analysis (SA), initially a part of the Defense Department Comptroller's Office but later established at assistant secretary level in 1965, with Alain Enthoven heading it throughout. Other key individuals and offices in OSD that worked closely with Secretary McNamara in the early years of the Kennedy Administration were Paul Nitze, assistant secretary of defense for international security affairs (ASD/ISA), and Harold Brown, director of defense research and engineering (DDR & E).

Reinforcing McNamara's disenchantment with the many organizations he inherited were particular reservations concerning the Joint Chiefs of Staff. In connection with the deteriorating situation in Laos during the spring of 1961, the President had invited McNamara and the five members of the JCS to the White House to discuss the matter. On that occasion, the President found himself exposed to five divergent but vigorously defended military points of view. This unsettling experience followed shortly after the Bay of Pigs episode, which had begun to engender some loss of confidence in the JCS on the part of the President and his defense secretary. After this meeting, McNamara sought and quickly obtained the President's permission to use the JCS chairman as principal spokesman for the chiefs as a whole. However, the incumbent chairman had been associated with the Bay of Pigs debacle, and, in addition, the President found it generally difficult to communicate easily with him. In late June, 1961, therefore, the President appointed retired General Maxwell Taylor (Army Chief of Staff, 1955–59) as his "Military Representative" in the White House, a post the general held until he was appointed chairman of the joint chiefs in October, 1962.

These, then, are the basic dimensions of the "McNamara Revolution," but in a way it should perhaps be called the "Kennedy Revolution." The relationship between the President and any Cabinet officer is both institutional and personal, and the rapport and mutual confidence emerging between the two men is always a major factor in determining the institutional relationship. Rapport and confidence developed very quickly between President Kennedy and McNamara, partly because their temperaments were similar in many respects. Both were impatient for quick but carefully researched solutions, and both were more than willing to experiment with new leadership and new organizational arrangements. Finally, when confronted with a deficient organizational component, both were inclined to bypass or overlook it, rather than overhaul it for the long pull. In dealing with the White House, McNamara took care to keep the President fully informed at the outset, including the registering of dissenting opinions in the JCS or elsewhere, but he proceeded on the assumption that it was basically his responsibility as secretary to settle Pentagon disagreements. This left the President the option of reversing any decision, but it relieved him of the need to dig repeatedly into complex Pentagon issues.

McNamara was a blessing to Kennedy because the new President needed the kind of detailed, systematic evidence that McNamara's procedures provided before he ran the risk of overruling the professional military. By contrast, President Eisenhower's status as the nation's leading military expert had allowed him to do so with relative impunity. Moreover, McNamara's systematic methods in the Pentagon enabled the President to be somewhat less formal and systematic at the White House level when considering national-security matters. During the first weeks and months of his administration, President Kennedy occasionally doublechecked some of McNamara's decisions with various officials of the separate armed services, but, as he developed more and more confidence in his defense secretary, the President was increasingly willing to let McNamara really run his department. McNamara, of course, continued to keep the President informed of major problems. The close relationship between the President and the secretary became, if anything, even closer in the Johnson Administration than in the Kennedy Administration, the most notable difference being a tendency on President Johnson's part to meet longer and more frequently with his secretary and other defense advisers than President Kennedy had (in part this resulted from President Johnson's preoccupation with the Vietnam War).

Roles of the Secretary of Defense

The trends discussed above, which enlarged the authority of the secretary of defense, highlighted a number of his roles or functions, which, for purposes of analysis, should be distinguished from each other. In short, the secretary of defense wears several hats, and those who work with and for him can become confused not only about which hat he may be wearing at any given time, but also by the particular requirements of any one of the hats. And these functional distinctions are only part of the story, because so much depends on the personalities of key individuals—especially the President and the secretary of defense—and the nature of the relationship that emerges between them. In any case, at least three critical roles can be identified for the secretary of defense.

First, the secretary is a personal adviser to the President. He is "the President's man," chosen to lead and direct the Department of Defense, a member of the Cabinet, and in recent years one of the closest members of the President's inner circle. Ideally, the secretary ought to be the most knowledgeable man in government concerning any subject pertaining to the role of military force in the attainment of national objectives. In practice, however, this is difficult to achieve because he is seldom a man of military background. He is therefore provided with elaborate staff assistance, including the Joint Chiefs of Staff themselves—the nation's top professional military men.

Any President will no doubt reach out for a variety of advice on most national-security issues, but if the secretary of defense has gained the President's confidence, the President will want to rely primarily on him for advice on the defense aspects of national-security matters.

The second role of the secretary of defense, that of military commander, is more formal and structured than the first, which is a highly personal and perhaps even intimate relationship. The second role derives from the Defense Reorganization Act of 1958, which designates the secretary as first in the chain of command under the President.

The secretary's third role is that of "manager" or chief executive officer of the Department of Defense. While it is misleading to push too far the analogy between a major governmental department and a large industrial corporation, there are some evident parallels—the receipt and disbursement of money, the maintenance of plant and equipment, procurement and distribution, and the support of personnel. The Department of Defense in all of these respects is larger by far than any other governmental department (as well as larger than any industrial corporation), and hence the secretary of defense as the "big boss" of this enterprise has enormous managerial responsibilities. If the President is likened to a chairman of the board, then the secretary of defense is clearly the chief executive officer and general manager of that part of the over-all governmental corporation which is the Department of Defense. One can take issue with any particular managerial decision by the secretary of defense—for example, the decision to purchase the TFX aircraft—on the grounds that the decision was poorly staffed, or that the wrong or inappropriate sources of advice were heeded, or on other grounds, but one can scarely argue that the secretary was not the final and appropriate locus of authority for this kind of decision.

Roles of the Joint Chiefs of Staff

The JCS, considered as a collective entity, also plays several roles, and in some respects these are parallel to those of the secretary of defense.[1] By law, it has a responsibility to serve corporately, as principal military adviser to the President, the secretary of defense, and the National Security Council (or presumably to such other comparable organization as the President may prefer to use). The particular relationship between the JCS on the one hand, and the President and the NSC on the other, is one of the sources of confusion and occasional dismay in the policy-making process because, on those occasions when the secretary and the chiefs may disagree, it can appear that the secretary of defense and the JCS are rival and competitive military advisers to the President.

Recent Presidents have seldom wanted to create the impression of having cut themselves off from direct consultation with the military chiefs, especially during shooting wars or other situations when the American people expect the President to listen to his professional military men. But while the members of the JCS are certainly distinguished military men, they come from different military backgrounds and often have diverging perspectives. It is therefore easier for the President to turn to a single man for his military advice (for example his secretary of defense) than to solicit the views of the chiefs—who may differ among each other or with the secretary. The President may face the dilemma that if he heeds only his secretary, he may undermine the morale and the usefulness of the chiefs and of the armed forces as a whole; whereas, if he heeds the chiefs too often, he may undermine the secretary's position. Equally important, to listen to one to the exclusion of the other can deprive the President of alternative sources of well-informed advice.

The second corporate role of the JCS is to serve as the military operational staff for the secretary of defense. If there is some ambiguity and lack of clarity as to the first JCS role, the role of the JCS in the chain of military command is clear. The secretary exercised his right under the 1958 reorganization legislation to specify the chain of command beneath him, and a Department of Defense directive accordingly provided that the chiefs as a corporate body would serve as a staff link in the chain between the secretary and the unified and specified commands. Inasmuch as a committee is seldom an efficient vehicle for transmitting military command, the JCS has occasionally, in time of crisis, designated a single chief to monitor a unified command in its name— but only in a specified field or for a specific purpose. It must be stressed that the particular chief who performs in this capacity does so as the agent of the JCS as a whole, which in turn is serving as the military staff of the secretary.

The third role of the JCS, closely related to its other advisory functions, is in planning and programing the military forces and matériel it believes will be required in the future, given the policy objectives of the nation. The performance of this task results in advice to the secretary in his role as general manager of the department, because all forces and matériel must be provided for in the department's annual budget, which every year is the adjusted current increment of the department's five-year plan. The Joint Strategic Objectives Plan (JSOP) of the JCS is probably the most prominent planning document produced in this area; projected at least five years into the future, it is revised annually by the joint chiefs and sent to the secretary. (The JSOP is discussed in some detail later in this chapter.)

In contrast to the first three roles of the JCS, which are corporate in nature, the fourth function is their respective individual roles as the nation's senior soldier, sailor, and airman, each responsible to the secretary of his particular service. In this sense, the JCS traces its origin back to the kind of loose confederation improvised at the outset of World War II to deal with the organization of the British military chiefs of staff after President Franklin D. Roosevelt had decided to fight the war in alliance with Great Britain. The National Security Act of 1947 gave the JCS a statutory existence, but it did little to resolve some of the fundamental anomalies inherent in the JCS system. One of these anomalies was that the armed forces continued to be organized along traditional lines into armies and navies, supplemented by air forces as a result of the invention of the airplane but without any recognition that the true impact of the airplane in effect called into question the traditional way of organizing armed forces. Moreover, there still remained problems inherent in the fact that the separate armed forces, as traditionally constituted, were rival tribes complete with separate tribal customs, philosophies, professional styles, and life styles—who really knew very little about each other.

Nevertheless, it still requires the better part of a man's career to train him to command a division of troops in the field, a fleet at sea, or a wing in the air. As long as this remains true, there will be men who are soldiers or sailors or airmen, with all their differences in custom, tradition, and outlook. The evolution of the Joint Chiefs of Staff in recent years, along with the growing support for "joint thinking" within the separate armed services, may well be the best way to proceed toward the best solution in practice, but these trends will require constant stimulation if the nation is to be served in the future by senior professional military officers whose experience will have fully qualified them to participate actively at the highest interdepartmental levels of the policy-making process.

Roles of the Chairman of the Joint Chiefs of Staff

The chairman of the Joint Chiefs of Staff (CJCS), like the President, the secretary of defense, and the chiefs themselves, also wears several hats. Unlike the others, however, little of his authority derives from statutes and directives. In terms of formal written charters, he is merely one among equals within the JCS, but in terms of precedent and practice, he has come to enjoy a substantial range of powers. The precedents include the ways in which several extremely able chairmen—especially Admiral Arthur W. Radford under President Eisenhower, General Maxwell D. Taylor under President Kennedy, and General Earle G. Wheeler under President Johnson—were able to make themselves highly useful and valuable to the Commanders in Chief whom they served. The practices include the ways in which these recent Presidents and several secretaries of defense have responded to the contributions of notable chairmen by informally "institutionalizing" the latters' important functions. The practices also include the way in which the other chiefs have in some respects gradually come to defer to the chairman and have even explicitly delegated some of their collective authority to him.

A certain degree of authority inheres in the very designation as chairman of any collective group. It often provides a man with a constituency and a power base from which to operate. This is less true of the CJCS than of other kinds of chairmen, because he is not elected or appointed by the collectivity which he represents. Moreover, he has no service or other "constituency" from which he can draw support but must borrow his help from the other chiefs. In short, he is appointed by the President, presumably in most cases with the concurrence of the secretary of defense, yet he would serve the President and the secretary rather poorly if he did not have or acquire the confidence and trust of the other chiefs. He is thus in the difficult position of holding office because of an appointment from above, but being effective in office only if he can acquire the support of the peers over whom he presides. It is a tribute to the personal abilities of a number of CJCS that this office has gradually increased to a very considerable position of power and prominence.

The first of the chairman's roles is that of the officer serving as senior military adviser to the President and to the secretary of defense, and in some cases, also to the secretary of state. This is a *de facto* role, almost wholly unsupported by *de jure* authority, and yet it is extremely important. Partly for the same reason that recent Presidents have turned for advice more and more to their secretaries of defense—the simple fact that it is easier to deal with a single individual than with a faceless institution such as the Department of Defense or the Office of the Joint Chiefs of Staff—the Presidents have also tended to turn to the CJCS as a primary military adviser in uniform.

The most noteworthy of the chairman's informally "institutionalized" roles have perhaps been his regular membership in President Johnson's Tuesday lunch group, the highest-level policy forum in the national-security field during the Johnson Administration, and his membership on the State Department-chaired Senior Interdepartmental Group (SIG). In recent years, the chairman has also accompanied the secretary of defense on important trips and has participated with the secretary in many—perhaps most—of the latter's informal and formal policy-making tasks.

The Chairman is not formally a member of the military staff of the secretary-commander, except insofar as he is a member of the joint chiefs. In practice, however, he has occasionally been deputized by the chiefs to serve as their agent for certain operational and advisory matters. To that extent, he has from time to time exercised a role of senior officer on the military staff that is the JCS.

As the chairman's position has evolved under recent incumbents, perhaps his most important role is to serve as an "ambassador" between the secretary of defense and the joint chiefs. As suggested above, the chairman's role is anomalous in that he is subject to the President and to the secretary, although much of his actual power derives from the respect and trust that he enjoys among his fellow chiefs. In earlier years some chiefs tended to view the chairman with the suspicion that he was "one of them, and not one of us," that he was primarily loyal to the President and the secretary, and that he therefore was not enthusiastic about defending views held by the chiefs. This suspicion has been largely overcome in recent years because the chairman has been able to act as a goodwill messenger and ambassador between the secretary and the JCS, helping both to establish effective rapport and cooperation between the central civilian and military leadership within the Pentagon. This has been a constructive and useful development, although it has depended in large part on the nature of the personalities involved. Like other developments, however, it may have become sufficiently institutionalized to survive changes in key personnel. . . .

NOTES

1. The Joint Chiefs of Staff (JCS) evolved early in World War II and was given statutory status in the National Security Act of 1947. Its members are the chairman, the chief of staff of the army, the chief of naval operations, and the chief of staff of the air force. The commandant of the marine corps sits as an equal on the JCS whenever a matter of direct concern to the corps is under consideration.

DECISION-MAKING

18.

Roberta Wohlstetter: *Cuba and Pearl Harbor:* Hindsight and Foresight

Intelligence—sometimes defined as evaluated information—links the decision-maker and the international environment. In comparing two cases—the Cuban missile crisis and the Pearl Harbor attack—the following selection describes how true "signals" were embedded in lots of "noise" and emphasizes that mountains of information do not themselves speak to the decision-maker but require a conceptual framework or set of assumptions for interpretation.

Roberta Wohlstetter is the author of *Pearl Harbor: Warning and Decision.*

To recall the atmosphere of September and October 1962 now seems almost as difficult as to recreate the weeks, more than two decades earlier, before the attack on Pearl Harbor. But if we are to understand the onset of the Cuban missile crisis, it is worth the effort. Indeed we may learn something about the problems of foreseeing and forestalling or, at any rate, diminishing the severity of such crises by examining side by side the preludes to both these major turning points in American history. In juxtaposing these temporally separate events, our interest is in understanding rather than in drama. We would like to know not only how we felt, but what we did and what we might have done, and in particular what we knew or what we could have known before each crisis.

Afterthoughts come naturally following the first wave of relief and jubilation at having weathered the missile crisis and forced the withdrawal of the missiles. But it is good to keep in mind the obvious contrast with Pearl Harbor. At the least, Pearl Harbor was a catastrophe, a great failure of warning and decision. At the very worst, the missile crisis was a narrow escape. Taken as a whole, however, its outcome must be counted as a success both for the intelligence community and the decision-makers. But a comparison of the failure at Pearl Harbor and the Cuban success reveals a good deal about the basic uncertainties affecting the success and failure of intelligence.

It is true for both Pearl Harbor and Cuba that we had lots of information about the approaching crisis. In discussing this information it will perhaps be useful to distinguish again between signals and noise. By the "signal" of an action is meant a sign, a clue, a piece of evidence that points to the action or to an adversary's intention to undertake it, and by "noise" is meant the back-

Roberta Wohlstetter, "Cuba and Pearl Harbor: Hindsight and Foresight," *Foreign Affairs* (July 1965), pp. 691–707. Copyright by the Council on Foreign Relations, Inc., New York. Reprinted by permission of *Foreign Affairs.*

ground of irrelevant or inconsistent signals, signs pointing in the wrong directions, that tend always to obscure the signs pointing the right way. Pearl Harbor, looked at closely and objectively, shows how hard it is to hear a signal against the prevailing noise, in particular when you are listening for the wrong signal, and even when you have a wealth of information. (Or perhaps especially then. There are clearly cases when riches can be embarrassing.)

After the event, of course, we know: like the detective-story reader who turns to the last page first, we find it easy to pick out the clues. And a close look at the historiography of Pearl Harbor suggests that in most accounts, memories of the noise and background confusion have faded quickly, leaving the actual signals of the crisis standing out in bold relief, stark and preternaturally clear.

After the crisis, memories fade and recriminations take their place. For a time the Cuban missile crisis figured as an outstanding triumph for the United States—in the swift discovery of "hard evidence," in the retention of American initiative, in the strict security maintained and in the taut control of power by the Executive Committee. Today, some of these aspects of the Cuban crisis have been thrown into doubt, and in particular, critics talk of a significant intelligence failure in anticipating the crisis. In both Pearl Harbor and Cuba the notion of a conspiracy of silence has been raised, the suggestion that we knew all along and failed to act, that Kennedy, like Roosevelt, had some special information which he withheld, or that information was so obvious that even a layman could have interpreted it correctly.

New York's Senator Keating, for example, was explicit and articulate in insisting that he believed long-range or medium-range missiles and Soviet combat troops were in Cuba as early as August. On August 31 he said in the Senate that he had reliable information on landings between August 3 and August 15 at the Cuban port of Mariel of 1200 troops wearing Soviet fatigue uniforms. He also reported that "other observers" had noted "Soviet motor convoys moving on Cuban roads in military formation," the presence of landing craft, and of suspicious cylindrical objects that had to be transported on two flatcars, and so on. He claimed that his statements had been verified by official sources within the U.S. Government. Between August 31 and October 12 he made ten Senate speeches warning of the Soviet military build-up.

After the crisis, Congressmen naturally wondered why we had not listened to Senator Keating, why it was possible to have had these warnings and many others and still be surprised on October 15. But failures to foresee and to forestall catastrophes are by no means abnormal. Military men and statesmen have no monopoly on being taken by surprise. The example of the Dallas police department springs to mind, and the murder of Oswald which gave rise, like Pearl Harbor, to rumors of conspiracy in high places and in local governments. Nor are American businessmen and financiers immune. Witness the $150 million De Angelis vegetable-oil scandal, where normally cautious bankers suddenly found they were holding empty storage tanks as security for their loans.

Conspiracy with the culprit, however, is hardly a universal line of explanation, as is suggested by a recent natural catastrophe—the earthquake in and near Alaska that sent a tidal wave to shatter the northern shore of California and caught some towns unprepared in spite of timely warnings. For the warnings sounded just like many others in the past that had not been followed by tidal waves. These are all American examples, but Singapore, "Barbarossa" (the German attack on Russia) and many others suggest that we are not dealing with a purely national susceptibility to surprise.

II

Defense departments and intelligence agencies, of course, continually estimate what an opponent can do, may do, intends to do. They try to gauge the technical limits within which he is operating, to determine his usual ways of behavior, under what conditions he will probe, push or withdraw. They try to measure what risks he will take, and how he might estimate the risks to us of countering him. Much of this work by American analysts is sound, thorough, intelligent, frequently ingenious and sometimes brilliant—but not infallible. Unhappily, any of these estimates may be partly, but critically, wrong. A wealth of information is never enough.

To get a rapid idea of the mass of data available for predicting the Cuban crisis and the Pearl Harbor attack, let us run through the main intelligence sources. In the case of Cuba, there was first of all magnificent photographic coverage as well as visual reconnaissance. The Navy ran air reconnaissance of all ships going in and out of Cuba, especially ships originating in Soviet or satellite ports during the summer of 1962, and intensified this sort of coverage during September. High-level photographic reconnaissance by U-2s over the island of Cuba was taking place at the rate of one flight every two weeks until the month of September, when it increased to once a week.[1] Low-level photographic reconnaissance began only after the President's speech of October 22—the first being on October 23. In addition to photography, we had voluminous accounts from Cuban refugees who were leaving the island in a steady stream. We had agents stationed on the island who were reporting, and we were listening to radio broadcasts from Cuba. The Cuban press, while carefully controlled, was making some announcements which are interesting in retrospect. A number of European correspondents stationed on the island were reporting to their newspapers, though the American press was not welcome.

Finally, but by no means least, we had Castro's pronouncements. His casual interviews with reporters, debates with students, interrogations of prisoners, and nearly interminable television speeches offer a rich fount of information. If you wait long enough, it seems, Castro will tell you everything. The only problem in a crisis is that you may not be able to wait that long. Castro is noted for his slyness, and he is perhaps better able than most Cubans to keep a secret. But sometimes he cannot resist hints that may reveal a trap before his victim falls into it. And often in real rather than calculated anger he will show his hand.

For predicting the Pearl Harbor attack, the United States Government had an equally impressive array of intelligence sources. Though aerial surveillance of the Japanese fleet was limited, the Navy had developed a system of pinpointing the location of ships and deducing their types by radio-traffic analysis. This was accomplished by analyzing the call signs of various ships, even though we could not read the content of the messages. Any change in call signs was in itself a cause for alarm, and it took usually several weeks of close listening to an enormous amount of traffic to re-identify the call signs. Call signs were changed on November 1, 1941, and again on December 1. We had not identified the new ones by December 7.

While we had not broken any military codes, we did have one superlative source that is perhaps comparable to the evidence provided by U-2 photography. That was the breaking of the top-priority Japanese diplomatic code, known as MAGIC, as well as some less complicated codes used by Japanese consular observers. We were listening in on diplomatic messages on all the major Tokyo circuits—to Rome, Berlin, London, Washington and so on. Colonel Friedman, an Army cryptographer, had devised a machine for rapidly decoding these messages, so that, in general, we knew what a message said before its intended Japanese recipients. Our ground observers, stationed in key ports along the coast of China and Southeast Asia, were reporting in by radio.

Ambassador Grew and his Embassy staff in Tokyo were experienced observers of local economic and political activities. Grew himself had a very sound estimate of Japanese character and diplomacy, but as Japanese censorship closed in during the last few weeks before the attack, Grew had to warn Washington that he was unable to report accurately on any military preparations then under way. American newspaper correspondents in Japan were also quite well informed and shrewd in their reporting. In addition to our own sources, we exchanged information with British intelligence. At that date, our own intelligence officers did not trust British intelligence fully. They expressed a certain amount of unease over British methods of picking up information, which they regarded as sophisticated but underhanded. As General Sherman Miles put it, U.S. intelligence preferred to be "above board." However, the British provided us with some good leads and lots of corroborative information. And there was, of course, the Japanese press, which proclaimed Japan's undying hostility to the American presence in Asia, and announced with increasing violence the Japanese intention to expand to the south.

In sum, for each of the two crises there was plenty of information suggesting its advent. Even though Cuba is a closed society, and even though Japan, in the last weeks, was under heavy censorship and tight security, the data provided by U.S. intelligence agencies were excellent. Once more, then, we come to the question, what went wrong? With all these data, why didn't we know that Japan would attack Pearl Harbor on December 7? Why, when it seems so clear in retrospect, didn't we anticipate that Khrushchev might put medium-range missiles into Cuba? Why didn't we seize the first indications that such installations were on the way? Weren't these early signs clear enough?

Unfortunately, they were not, and almost never are. Even with hindsight, we are not able to reconstruct the exact sequence of events that led to the Cuban missile crisis. Most of our sources are alive, and some of them are talking. But what can we say with certainty about Cuban and Soviet motives? Castro, for example, has spoken on many occasions about why missiles were put into Cuba. But he swings between the view that he requested them and the view that Khrushchev suggested the idea and that he, Castro, felt so indebted economically he had to accept. He has mentioned two motives—one, defense against an American invasion that he believed was imminent, and the other, the need to advance the international cause of socialism, which implied that the missiles were for offense as well as defense. Khrushchev's story is more consistent, but also more "official": he cites only the need to help Cuba prepare against an American invasion. But of course for active Cuban defense, long-range missiles are not necessary. Speculation on Soviet and Cuban motives still continues.

With hindsight, we can look back now and see that during the crisis there were naturally many confusions embedded in the mass of intelligence reports. A report of a "missile" might refer to a surface-to-air missile which is approximately 30 feet long, to the nose cone of a surface-to-surface missile which is about 14 feet long, to its body which is almost 60 feet long, or to a fuel storage tank. Or perhaps it might just represent the imagination of an excited Cuban refugee. Most of these objects were seen at night through closed shutters and in motion. Visual observation, except by a highly trained observer, was not likely to be accurate even as to the length of the object. And Senator Keating did not act altogether responsibly in perpetuating this confusion centering around the word "missile." He was right when he described the total build-up as alarming, but he was proceeding beyond the evidence in suggesting, as he did, that he had positive proof of the presence of medium-range missiles,[2] and of the capability for rapid transformation of surface-to-air missiles into medium-range surface-to-surface missiles.

Or take the presence of Soviet combat troops. President Kennedy's critics noted after the crisis that in his October 22 speech he made no mention of combat troops in Cuba, although the American public was later informed of their presence. Actually, Soviet troops, organized into four regimental units, totaled approximately 5,000 men. They were located at four different spots, two near Havana, one in Central Cuba and one in Eastern Cuba. They were equipped with modern Soviet ground-force fighting equipment, including battlefield rocket launchers similar to the American "Honest John." This equipment, along with the accompanying barracks and tent installations, was not identifiable, or at least was not identified, until we started photographing at low level. For this reason, President Kennedy made no demand about removal of troops on October 22, but kept to the colorless term, "Soviet technicians." While U-2 photography is almost as magical as the MAGIC code at the time of Pearl Harbor, like the code, it is limited; it cannot reveal all.

III

For the layman, the feeling persists that there must be some marvelous source that will provide a single signal, a clear tip-off that will alert the American forces and tell them exactly what to do. Unfortunately, there is no instance where such a tip-off arrived in time, except perhaps in the Philippines in 1941, when General MacArthur had a minimum of nine hours' warning between his knowledge of the Pearl Harbor attack and the initial Japanese assault on his own forces. The news of the attack on Pearl Harbor clearly did not tell him what alert posture to take, since his planes were found by the Japanese attackers in formation, wing-tip to wing-tip on their bases.

Instead we must wait for a number of signals to converge in the formation of a single hypothesis about the intentions and actions of an opponent. This is a necessary but slow process. In 1962, for example, General Carroll, head of the Defense Intelligence Agency, became suspicious of Soviet activities on the basis of several pieces of data from different sources. According to Secretary McNamara's testimony,

. . . [Carroll] had had thousands of reports like this. What gradually formed in his mind was a hypothesis based on the integration of three or four pieces of evidence, one of which was not a report at all, one of which was a recognition through photographic analysis that a SAM (surface-to-air missile) site appeared to be in a rather unusual place. . . . Gradually over a period of time—I do not know over what period of time—but sometime between the 18th of September and the 14th of October, there was formulated in his mind a hypothesis specifically that there was the possibility of a Soviet ballistic missile installation in a particular area, a hypothesis that had been formulated previously and had been tested previously and found to be in error with respect to other locations.

His only action here—I think quite properly his only action here—was to test that hypothesis, to submit it to the targeting group that targets the reconnaissance missions, and place that target on the track for the next reconnaissance mission, which was the October 14 mission.[3]

This period of time from September 18 to October 14 is not long for the crystallization of a hypothesis.[4] It is long only in relation to the speed of the missile installation. This sort of time difference is a perpetually agonizing aspect of intelligence interpretation. Collection, checking of sources and interpreting all take time. There is always delay between the intelligence source and the evaluation center, and between the center and the final report to the decision-maker. Even then, the decision-maker may merely request more information before taking action. In the meantime, the opponent moves forward.

In the Cuban missile crisis, for example, there were delays in the identification of surface-to-air missiles. From July 29 to August 5, Cuban refugees reported that "an unusual number of ships" unloaded cargo and passengers at the ports of Havana and Mariel. All Cubans were excluded from the dock. By August 14 these reports reached U.S. intelligence agencies, which the next day requested U-2 photo coverage of the suspect areas. On August 29 the flight was made. From the first visual observation on July 29 to the overflight on August 29 a full month passed.

This August 29 flight turned up the first hard evidence of surface-to-air missiles in Cuba. During September, surveillance flights seem to have been stepped up: the U-2 flew on September 5, 17, 26, 29, and on October 5, 7 and 14. On the September 5 flight, which took in the San Cristobal area a hundred miles east of Havana, the photographs showed no evidence of medium-range missiles. A flight scheduled for September 10 was canceled, perhaps because a U-2 had been shot down over Red China the previous day. According to the American press, all U-2 flights stopped while the United States waited for the world reaction.

Secretary McNamara testified that available evidence indicated the first landing of mobile M.R.B.M.s occurred on September 8, and that construction of the sites did not begin before September 15 to 20. It is possible that September 10 photography might have shown some activity at the San Cristobal site. The September 17 flight was of little use because cloud cover obscured the areas photographed. However, between September 18 and 21 further Cuban reports came to U.S. intelligence, and these were evaluated on September 27. They eventually led to the flight on October 14, again over San Cristobal. This flight produced the first reliable evidence of medium-range missiles on the island.

In spite of the frequency of the U-2 flights, there is a lag of 33 days from the first visual observation made by a Cuban exile on September 8, and reported on September 9, to October 14, the day that hard evidence was obtained. There is a lag of 39 days between September 5 and October 14, during which no flights covered the San Cristobal area. This gap in coverage was not apparent until some inquiring Congressmen pressed their cross-examination. When William Minshall of Ohio asserted that the U-2 flights had been covering the wrong end of the island, General Carroll pointed out that it was necessary to cover the eastern and central portions also. Secretary McNamara supported him by pointing out that the September 5 flight over San Cristobal "showed absolutely no activity whatsoever." He also recalled that this was the hurricane season, "and the weather in that part of the Caribbean is very bad. We had a number of flights canceled during that period." Mr. Minshall then produced the official weather report showing clear days in the vicinity of Havana, and said that "the weather from September 25 to October 2, at least at 7:00 in the morning, was generally clear." No one pointed out at that time that weather forecasts, not actual weather, determined the schedule of U-2 flights.

Photographic coverage, then, was apparently being scheduled on the assumption that any Soviet construction would proceed at a pace which might be considered rapid according to our own experience in installing similar equipment. Secretary McNamara repeated several times that there was no missile construction activity in the Havana area on September 5, as if this, coupled with the pressing need to get clear pictures of other parts of the island, were sufficient reason for not covering the area again until October 14. This judgment, with hindsight, may have been correct, but in the absence of the full intelligence picture the layman can only wonder why it was not possible to cover more than one section of the island on a single U-2 sortie, or why it was not possible to make several simultaneous sorties when good weather prevailed. Perhaps Secretary McNamara's statement, made under pressure of Mr. Minshall's criticism, to the effect that "we were facing surface-to-air missile systems that might be coming into operation," indicates that the flight schedule was sensitive to the political atmosphere. The fact is that there *were* increasing dangers to our pilots as the SAM sites became operational. With the Republicans now in opposition, it was easy for some of them to forget the extreme embarrassment of the Eisenhower régime at the shooting down of the U-2 over the Soviet Union in 1960 and the collapse of the Paris summit that followed. Certainly after the publicity given to the U-2 shot down over Red China on September 9, the United States would not want to lose such a plane over Cuba. U-2 planes are never armed; and the August 29 flight had showed surface-to-air missile installations in western Cuba.

Naval photography shows a somewhat similar gap. Photographs of the crates containing IL-28 bombers were taken on September 28 but not evaluated until October 9, and not disseminated until October 10. This identification of bombers capable of carrying a nuclear or non-nuclear payload of 6,000 pounds and with a combat radius of about 700 nautical miles [5] came together with a report of October 15 evaluating the U-2 photographs of M.R.B.M.s.

This sort of delay can easily be paralleled in the Pearl Harbor intelligence picture. In the handling of the coded messages, there was inevitably a delay —from interception of the message at the intercept station through transmission to the decoding center in Washington, determination of priority in handling, assignment for full decoding, assignment for translation and the actual translation, to final delivery to the approved list of recipients. The longest delay recorded in the Congressional hearings is 54 days between interception and translation. Part of the delay is a function of the time necessary for transmission. Part of the delay comes from checking the accuracy of the reports, which is necessary for responsible decision. But these delays in response must all be seen against the forward march of events.

In Cuba, the rapidity of the Russians' installation was in effect a logistical surprise comparable to the technological surprise at the time of Pearl Harbor. Before September 1962 we were scheduling U-2 flights approximately two weeks apart, because we couldn't believe that capabilities could change significantly within a shorter period. But Secretary McNamara testified in his first background briefing (October 22) that the medium-range mobile missiles were planned to have a capability to be de-activated, moved, re-activated on a new site and ready for operation within a period of about six days. The Stennis Report, which reviewed the entire intelligence operation, refers to "a matter of hours." [6] In one instance, between two sets of photographs separated by less than 24 hours, there was an increase of 50 percent in the amount of equipment visible. On the date of withdrawal, October 28, the medium-range missiles were fully operational. Intelligence estimates set December 15 as the outside date for the non-mobile I.R.B.M.s to be operational.

This kind of technological or logistical surprise may be either a secret so carefully guarded that it doesn't reach our intelligence agencies until after the event; or it may happen too swiftly, too near the outbreak of the crises, to be transmitted and evaluated in time. In the case of Pearl Harbor, there were two technological changes that failed to reach either the intelligence agencies or the commanding officers who needed the information: (1) that the Japanese had fitted fins to their torpedoes which would permit bombing in the shallow waters of Pearl Harbor; and (2) that the combat radius of the Zero fighter plane had been stretched to 500 statute miles, making possible aerial attack on the Philippines from Formosa. Both of these developments came to fruition only a few weeks before Pearl Harbor.

IV

Besides technological surprise and the inevitable physical delays involved in transmission and checking, there are more subtle obstacles to accurate perception of signals. First, there is the "cry-wolf" phenomenon. Admiral Stark actually used this phrase in deciding not to send Admiral Kimmel any further warnings about the Japanese. An excess of warnings which turn out to be false alarms always induces a kind of fatigue, a lessening of sensitivity. Admiral Kimmel and his staff were tired of checking out Japanese submarine reports in the vicinity of Pearl Harbor. In the week preceding the attack they had checked out seven, all of which were false.

General Carroll had the same problem with missiles in Cuba. Refugee reports of missiles had been coming in for a year and a half and the first San Cristobal report of September 9 describing that suspect area, later confirmed as harboring medium-range missiles, was "comparable to many other reports . . . similarly received and checked out," and found to reveal not surface-to-surface missiles, but surface-to-air or nothing at all. This history of mistaken observations by the refugees tended to reinforce the feelings of fatigue and disbelief. There was also a justifiable reaction to the fact that refugee exaggerations of anti-Castro ferment in Cuba had not been properly discounted at the time of the Bay of Pigs, and that their self-interest in wanting to return to Cuba had not been properly weighed. This background increased the reluctance of the intelligence agencies to credit their reports without careful verification. Besides the refugees, members of the Congressional opposition were also using exaggeration and pressure, because they had an interest in overstating provocation in order to indicate laxness on the Administration's part. Senator Keating claimed to have hard evidence at a time when, it seems, such evidence did not exist. Opposition pressure tended to evoke a natural counter-pressure from the Administration, which responded by charging irresponsibility in its critics, and which insisted on caution and the necessity for special evidence before entering on such serious action. In this way the opposition served in some respects as rein rather than simply as spur.

Another obstacle to objective evaluation is the human tendency to see what we want to see or expect to see. The Administration did not want open conflict with the Soviet Union. It was working on a program of trying to relax tensions, of which a test-ban agreement was one important though distant goal. It most definitely did not want an offensive Soviet base in Cuba, in the same way that Zermatt, the famous Swiss ski resort, did not want typhoid fever and refused to acknowledge its existence until epidemic proportions had been reached. Just as President Roosevelt wanted no war in the Far East—no war on two fronts—and didn't want to believe that it could happen, so we didn't want to believe that the Soviets were doing what they were doing.

When this is the background of expectation, it is only natural to ignore small clues that might, in a review of the whole or on a simple count, add up to something significant. For example, the large ships that turned out to be the villains in the Cuban case had especially large covered hatches. They were unloaded at night by Soviet personnel, and all Cubans were excluded from the docks. The contents, whatever they were, were moved at night. The decks were loaded with 2½- and 5-ton trucks and cars. But these ships, in transit, had been noted to be riding high in the water. If intelligence analysts in the American community had been more ready to suspect the introduction of strategic missiles, would this information have led them to surmise, before as well as after October 14, that these ships carried "space-consuming [i.e. large volume, low density] cargo such as an M.R.B.M." [7] rather than a bulk cargo? Roger Hilsman points out that these vessels had been specially designed for carrying lumber, and "our shipping intelligence experts presumably deduced that lumbering ships could be more easily spared than others." "We knew," Hilsman writes, "that the Soviets had had some trouble finding the ships they needed to send their aid to Cuba." [8] This is a good illustration of the way we can adjust (without doing violence to the facts) a disturbing or unusual observation to "save" a theory—in this case that the Soviets would not send strategic missiles to Cuba.

Our estimate of Soviet behavior included, of course, some expectation of how the Russians would react to what we were telling them, to our warnings in words and acts. However, we overestimated the clarity of our signals. General Maxwell Taylor had visited Florida bases on August 25 with a great deal of publicity. Naval reconnaissance of ships approaching Cuba had been stepped up to the point where U.S. planes were shot at by nervous Cubans on September 2. Castro reacted with great restraint in commenting on this incident—a fact which might in itself have been thought suspicious. But above all, on September 4, President Kennedy announced the installation of surface-to-air missiles in Cuba which had been confirmed by the photographs of August 29. He said with the greatest care that we would not tolerate an offensive base or the installation of missiles capable of reaching U.S. territory. He made the distinction between offensive and defensive weapons, and he did this publicly in a way that put him on the spot. To anyone familiar with the workings of the American political system, this should have indicated that we were "contracting-in." The President was deliberately engaging his own prestige and that of the country. He was reacting to the Republicans as well as to Castro. He was justifying not acting up to a certain point, but making it more likely that he would act beyond that point. In other words, he was drawing a line, and he was making it extremely unlikely that we would back down if that line were crossed. Again on September 13, the President called attention to the firmness of his commitment.

To the official Administration statements, we must add the formal announcements by the opposition party. Senator Everett Dirksen of Illinois and Charles Halleck of Indiana, the Republican Congressional leaders, both issued statements on Cuba on September 7. Halleck warned that the increases in armaments and numbers of military technicians supplied by the Soviet Union to Cuba made the situation there "worse from the point of view of our own vital interests and the security of this country." Senator Dirksen invoked the Monroe Doctrine and defined current Soviet military aid to Cuba as a violation of that doctrine. He pointed out that, in view of our treaty commitments, either the Organization of American States should immediately agree on a course of action or, quoting President Kennedy's speech of April 20, 1961, the United States should act on its own, "if the nations of this hemisphere should fail to meet their commitments against outside Communist penetration."

American elections and their accompanying distractions have been the subject of world-wide speculation and concern. Yet they are not always easy for an outsider to understand. These protests from the opposition were taking place in a setting of pre-election debate, and Khrushchev may have hoped to exploit that fact. He may not have been aware that the alarm expressed by the Republicans was something President Kennedy could not ignore. In addition to explicit proposals and resolutions about the Monroe Doctrine, there was the President's request for Congressional authorization to call up 150,000 reserves. This action too should have been a warning signal; it did trigger a Soviet reassurance that Moscow had no need for an offensive base in Cuba. However, the Soviets did not find these warnings weighty enough to reverse their plans for installation.

V

Another major barrier to an objective U.S. evaluation of the data was our own estimate of Soviet behavior. The Stennis Report isolated as one "substantial" error in evaluation "the predisposition of the intelligence community to the philosophical conviction that it would be incompatible with Soviet policy to introduce strategic missiles into Cuba."[9] Khrushchev had never put medium- or long-range missiles in any satellite country and therefore, it was reasoned, he certainly would not put them on an island 9,000 miles away from the Soviet Union, and only 90 miles away from the United States, when this was bound to provoke a sharp American reaction.

In considering this estimate of Soviet behavior, let us remember that the intelligence community was not alone. It had plenty of support from Soviet experts, inside and outside the Government. At any rate, no articulate expert now claims the role of Cassandra. Once a predisposition about the opponent's behavior becomes settled, it is very hard to shake. In this case, it was reinforced not only by expert authority but also by the knowledge both conscious and unconscious that the White House had set down a policy for relaxation of tension with the East. This policy background was much more subtle in its influence than documents or diplomatic experience. For when an official policy or hypothesis is laid down, it tends to obscure alternative hypotheses, and to lead to overemphasis of the data that support it, particularly in a situation of increasing tension, when it is important not to "rock the boat."

In the case of Pearl Harbor, there was a concentration on Atlantic and European affairs, which led to a kind of neglect of, or tendency to ignore, Far Eastern signals, and to a policy of staving off the outbreak of a Pacific war as long as possible. In the last months especially, this tendency was combined with a desire to avoid incidents. The wording of the final warning messages to the Army and Navy reflected this concern:

If hostilities cannot repeat not be avoided the United States desires that Japan commit the first overt act. This policy should not repeat not be construed as restricting you to a course of action that might jeopardize your defense. Prior to hostile Japanese action you are directed to undertake such reconnaissance and other measures as you deem necessary but these measures should be carried out so as not repeat not to alarm civil population or disclose intent. . . . Undertake no offensive action until Japan has committed an overt act.[10]

These directives have been frequently characterized as "do-don't."

Another attempt to avoid incidents was the Navy order of October 17 to re-route all trans-Pacific shipping to and from the Far East through the Torres Straits (between New Guinea and Australia), thus clearing the sea lanes to the north and northwest of the Hawaiian Islands. This order followed a warning of possible hostile action by Japan against U.S. merchant shipping. We avoided any incidents in these sea lanes, and at the same time we cut off the possibility of visual observation of the Japanese task force bound for Pearl Harbor.

In the Autumn of 1962, pursuing a policy of reducing tension, the Kennedy Administration made very little allowance for deception in Soviet statements, for false reassurances that would quiet justifiable American fears. On September 2, TASS published a joint communiqué on Soviet military aid to Cuba, referring to the August 27 visit to Moscow of Che Guevara and Emilio Aragones. The Soviet Government announced assistance in metallurgical work and the sending of technical specialists in agriculture to Cuba. They added that

views were also exchanged in connection with threats of aggressive imperialist quarters with regard to Cuba. In view of these threats the government of the Cuban Republic addressed the Soviet government with a request for help by delivering armaments and sending technical specialists for training Cuban servicemen.

The Soviet government tentatively considered this request of the government of Cuba. An agreement was reached on this question. As long as the above-mentioned quarters continue threatening Cuba, the Cuban Republic has every justification for taking necessary measures to insure its security and safeguard its sovereignty and independence, while all Cuba's true friends have every right to respond to this legitimate request.[11]

This was reassuring in a negative understated way: it limited military aid to vague "armaments" and "technical specialists." On September 11, in response to the President's request to call up reserves, a higher-keyed, if not hysterical, pronouncement was issued by TASS. This started with an attack on "bellicose-minded reactionary elements" and "the provocations the United States Government is now staging, provocations which might plunge the world into disaster of a universal world war with the use of thermonuclear weapons." In the U.S. Congress and in the American press, the Soviet Government claimed, an unbridled propaganda campaign was calling for an attack on Cuba and on Soviet ships "carrying the necessary commodities and food to the Cuban people." "Little heroic Cuba" was pictured as at the mercy of American imperialists, who were alarmed by the failure of their economic blockade and calling for measures to strangle her. Particularly serious was the President's action in asking Congress' permission to call up 150,000 reservists. The statement then embarked on a series of jeers at the ridiculous fears of the American imperialists. The peace-loving Soviet Union was sending agronomists, machine-operators, tractor-drivers and livestock experts to Cuba to share their experience and knowledge and to help the Cubans master Soviet farm machinery.

What could have alarmed the American leaders? What is the reason for this Devil's Sabbath? . . . Gentlemen, you are evidently so frightened you're afraid of your own shadow. . . . It seems to you some hordes are moving to Cuba when potatoes or oil, tractors, harvesters, combines, and other farming industrial machinery are carried to Cuba to maintain the Cuban economy. We can say to these people that these are our ships and that what we carry in them is no business of theirs. . . . We can say, quoting a popular saying: "Don't butt your noses where you oughtn't." But we do not hide from the world public that we really are supplying Cuba with industrial equipment and goods which are helping to strengthen her economy.[12]

A bit farther on, having had its fun, TASS recalled that "a certain amount of armaments is also being shipped from the Soviet Union to Cuba" and that Soviet military specialists had also been requested by the Government of Cuba. However, the number of Soviet military specialists sent to Cuba "can in no way be compared to the number of workers in agriculture and industry sent there. The armaments and military equipment sent to Cuba are designed exclusively for defensive purposes and the President of the United States and the American military just [like] the military of any country know what means of defense are." The statement went on to imply that any threat to the United States was a figment of the American imagination. The major reassurance then followed:

The Government of the Soviet Union also authorized TASS to state that there is no need for the Soviet Union to shift its weapons for the repulsion of aggression, for a retaliatory blow, to any other country, for instance Cuba. Our nuclear weapons are so powerful in their explosive force and the Soviet Union has so powerful rockets to carry these nuclear warheads, that there is no need to search for sites for them beyond the boundaries of the Soviet Union. We have said and we do repeat that if war is unleashed, if the aggressor makes an attack on one·state or another and this state asks for assistance, the Soviet Union has the possibility from its own territory to render assistance to any peace-loving state and not only to Cuba. And let no one doubt that the Soviet Union will render such assistance just as it was ready in 1956 to render military assistance to Egypt at the time of the Anglo-French-Israeli aggression in the Suez Canal region.

This sort of reassurance had also been privately delivered to the President, and the misuse of the private channel apparently shocked President Kennedy as much as the creation of the strategic base in Cuba.

President Kennedy and his staff had believed the Soviet reassurances. Their reaction to what they regarded as deception was one of genuine outrage, for one of the President's basic tenets had been that a state of mutual trust between the great powers was an important part of the problem of relaxing tension. And there is a considerable body of literature which goes farther and isolates the attitude of mutual suspicion itself as the central danger today in international relations.

It is a permanent problem of diplomacy to know where to draw the line in extending trust to unfriendly states. A certain amount of healthy suspicion of the opponent's public statements is in order. The President deliberately tested the willingness of Gromyko to lie, after the President knew the truth, but before the Russians knew that he knew. The trap set by the President aroused the indignation of some of those very Americans who urge mutual trust. But the President of the United States would be simple indeed if he did not build his trust cautiously on the basis of many such probings. The Russian performance in the fall and winter of 1962 made it perfectly clear that we cannot take at face value Russian statements—even those made only to the top American leadership in privacy and without those constraints that might be imposed by having the Chinese or other Communist powers or the non-aligned or our own allies listening.

In periods of high tension it is commonly accepted that deception will be an enemy tactic. Before the Pearl Harbor attack Japanese deception was very refined and ingenious. It involved, among other things, giving shore leave to large numbers of Japanese sailors, reinforcing garrisons on the northern border of Manchuria to give an impression of a thrust to the north, issuing false war plans to Japanese commanders and substituting true ones only days before the attack, and on the diplomatic side continuing the appearance of negotiation. For deception is not confined to statements, but must also be translated into actions.

It is important for the enemy's security that he keep his signals quiet. On the Soviet side this meant that all movement on the island of Cuba must take place at night. The Cubans were excluded from the docks and from many of the missile construction areas. Troops were kept below decks, and unloaded equipment was camouflaged or hidden under the trees. On our own side, in the period before October 22, tight security was important to preserve the initiative. And this tight security was maintained through the next few weeks. The members of the group close to the President, known as the Executive Committee or EXCOM, were directly supervising decisions normally left to lower command levels and were doing paper work normally handled by their staffs. This sort of procedure is fine for a couple of weeks, but it means the neglect of other areas of government and, in particular, other areas of foreign policy.[13] Richard Neustadt, a keen observer, reminds us that the Sino-Indian conflict was in progress at the same time, and offers a "lay impression" that "at least one side effect of Cuba" was to tighten the time and narrow the frame of reference of the decision—then in the making—on Skybolt.[14] Under conditions of tight security, there is also a danger that we may keep signals not only from the enemy but also from ourselves. There are a good many who feel that careful study by a wider range of experts might have been useful at the time and would be useful now, particularly with regard to the Kennedy-Khrushchev communications. These, like MAGIC, were very closely held during the crisis and had to be read and interpreted swiftly at the time.

Another set of signs we may have misread or missed were those appearing in official Cuban statements. Castro is so verbose and temperamental that we tend not to listen carefully to his speeches. And his controlled press is so dull that we are equally careless about that. In addition, the policy of embargo and explicit isolation of the island tends to carry over in a curious way to ignoring the voice of Cuban officialdom.

It is interesting now to review the Cuban press of 1962 for clues we might have picked up. After Raoul Castro's July visit to Moscow, the warmth of the references to the Soviet Union increased noticeably. Thanks and praise became the order of the day. On September 11, the day of the falsely reassuring TASS statement, the Cuban newspaper *Revolución* underlined the threat of thermo-nuclear war invoked by TASS. The front page was printed with a single white headline on a black background, and it said: "Rockets Over the United States if Cuba is Invaded." Forcing the Soviet Union's hand in this way had been Cuban policy for some time, so that it was natural for our experts to take this as another instance of Cuban wishful thinking.

Finally, in intelligence work the role of chance, accident and bad luck is always with us. It was bad luck that September–October is the hurricane season in the Caribbean, so that some reconnaissance photography was unclear and certain flights were canceled. It was bad luck that the Red Chinese shot down a U-2 on September 9. In 1941 it was bad luck that we had cut all traffic on the Northwest Passage to Russia, and thereby made visual observation of the Pearl Harbor task force impossible. It was bad luck that there was a radio blackout in the Hawaiian Islands on the morning of December 7, and that Colonel

French of the Communications Room then decided to use commercial wire instead of recommending the scrambler telephone for the last alert message.

VI

To sum up then, in both the Pearl Harbor and Cuban crises there was lots of information. But in both cases, regardless of what the Monday morning quarterbacks have to say, the data were ambiguous and incomplete. There was never a single, definitive signal that said, "Get ready, get set, go!" but rather a number of signals which, when put together, tended to crystallize suspicion. The true signals were always embedded in the noise or irrelevance of false ones. Some of this noise was created deliberately by our adversaries, some by chance and some we made ourselves. In addition, our adversary was interested in suppressing the signs of his intent and did what he could to keep his movements quiet. In both cases the element of time also played against us. There were delays between the time information came in, was checked for accuracy, evaluated for its meaning, and made the basis for appropriate action. Many of these delays were only prudent, given the ambiguities and risks of response.

The interpretation of data depends on a lot of things, including our estimate of the adversary and of his willingness to take risks. To make our lives more complicated, this depends on what he thinks the risks are, which in turn depends on his interpretation of us. We underestimated the risks that the Japanese were willing to take in 1941, and the risks that Khrushchev was willing to take in the summer and fall of 1962. Both the Japanese and the Russians, in turn, underestimated our ultimate willingness to respond.

It is important to understand that the difficulties described are intrinsic. By focusing on misestimated capabilities, dispositions and intentions, we obscure the fact that, without a very large and complex body of assumptions and estimates, the data collected would not speak to us at all. If there were no technological constraints whatsoever—if, for example, a large missile installation could be put in place in an instant—no reconnaissance, no matter how frequent, could provide assurance that we would not at any moment face a massive new adversary. The complex inferences involved in the act of interpreting photographs are made possible only by a large body of assumptions of varying degrees of uncertainty, ranging from principles of optics and Euclidean geometry through technological, economic and political judgments. The inferences from the interpretations themselves in turn are based on an even wider range of uncertain beliefs. But just because a very large body of partially confirmed beliefs and guesses is involved in interpreting a reconnaissance photograph or the observations of a Cuban refugee or intelligence agent, it is possible to interpret the photograph or observations in many differing ways. Our beliefs, as Willard Van Orman Quine has put it, are "underdetermined" by our experience, and they do not face experience separately, statement by statement, but always in mass, as a collection. We have a good deal of freedom as to what statements to adjust in the light of any new and seemingly disturbing report.

An observation or its report does not seize us, then, and force any specific interpretation. This relatively free situation of hypotheses in intelligence is no different in kind from that of hypotheses in the more exact sciences such as physics. A more naïve empiricism once suggested that statements in physics could be refuted definitively by observation, by the result of a crucial experiment. But a great many physicists and students of the logic of science, at least since Pierre Duhem, have shown that even the interpretation of the simplest experiment depends implicitly on comprehensive theories about the measuring instruments and a great deal else. It is always possible therefore to "save" a theory or hypothesis by altering some other one of the large set of our beliefs that connects it with any given observation.

If this is true in the more exact sciences it is most obviously true for the role of observations and their interpretation in such spheres of practical activity as the operation of an intelligence agency, and the inferences and decisions of an executive. Here the assumptions that shape interpretation are likely to be more multifarious and also less explicit and therefore often less tentatively held. This puts it mildly. Some of the relevant assumptions may be held passionately. They are likely to include wishful or self-flattering beliefs, items of national pride or claims at issue in partisan debate. In the case of Japan, some of the critical assumptions concerned technology—the range, speed and manœuvrability of the Zero plane, the supposed inability of the Japanese to do any better than the Americans in launching torpedoes in shallow water. In the case of Cuba again some critical assumptions were technological; for example, the minimum time required to put into place and make operational a medium-range ballistic missile. Others concerned the politics and character of the Soviet, Cuban and American leadership and their estimates of each other's willingness to take a chance. Our expectations and prior hypotheses guide our observations and affect their interpretation. It is this prior frame of mind, now changed, that we forget most easily in retrospect. And it is this above all that makes every past surprise nearly unintelligible—and inexplicable except perhaps as criminal folly or conspiracy.

The genuine analogies between Pearl Harbor and Cuba should not obscure the important differences. A study of the Pearl Harbor case makes clear that the problem of getting warning of an impending nuclear raid today is much harder than the problem of detecting the Japanese attack some 20 years ago. It is against this increased difficulty that we must balance improvements in intelligence techniques and organization. But the missile crisis illustrates something else, namely that there are other acts very much short of nuclear war of which we want to be apprised, and here our improved techniques and organization can put us ahead of the game. Action *was* taken during the missile crisis and taken in time to forestall Soviet plans. For while we can never ensure the complete elimination of ambiguity in the signals that come our way, we can energetically take action to reduce their ambiguity, by acquiring information as we did with the U-2. And we can tailor our response to the uncertainties and dangers that remain.

In the Cuban missile crisis action could be taken on ambiguous warning because the action was sliced very thin. After reconnaissance reduced the ambiguity, the response chosen kept to a minimum the actual contact with Russian forces, but a minimum compatible with assuring Khrushchev that we meant business: quarantine, the threat of boarding, the actual boarding of one Lebanese vessel chartered to the Soviet Union. Further, it was a response planned in great detail as the first in a sequence of graded actions that ranged from a build-up of U.S. Army, Marine and Tactical Air Forces in Florida and our southeastern bases to a world-wide alert of the Strategic Air Command. We had been partially prepared for such sequences of action short of nuclear war by the Berlin contingency planning, and this put us in a position to use the warning we had accumulated. If we had had to choose only among much more drastic actions, our hesitation would have been greater.

The problem of warning, then, is inseparable from the problem of decision. We cannot guarantee foresight. But we can improve the chance of acting on signals in time to avert or moderate a disaster. We can do this by a more thorough and sophisticated analysis of observers' reports, by making more explicit and tentative the framework of assumptions into which we must fit any new observations, and by refining, subdividing and making more selective the range of responses we prepare, so that our response may fit the ambiguities of our information and minimize the risks both of error and of inaction. Since the future doubtless holds many more shocks and attempts at surprise, it is comforting to know that we do learn from one crisis to the next.

NOTES

1. Flights over the island took place on September 5, 17, 26, 29, October 5, 7 and 14. The irregularity is attributed to bad weather.

2. See testimony, September 17, 1962: United States Senate, Committee on Foreign Relations and Committee on Armed Services, *Situation in Cuba*, 87th Cong., 2d Sess., 1962, pp. 7, 12; *U.S. News and World Report*, November 19, 1962 (distributed week of November 12), p. 87; and speech to the Senate, October 12, 1962.

3. U.S. Congress, House of Representatives, Subcommittee on Department of Defense Appropriations, *Department of Defense Appropriations for 1964*, 88th Cong., 1st Sess., 1963, pp. 45–46. These hearings contain most of the intelligence data cited in this article.

4. According to Roger Hilsman, the request for a U-2 flight covering the western end of the island was made on October 4—ten days before the flight was actually made. "The Cuban Crisis: How Close We Were to War," *Look*, August 25, 1964, p. 18.

5. According to W. W. Kaufmann, *The McNamara Strategy*, Harper & Row, 1964, p. 270. According to John Hughes, Special Assistant to General Carroll, "about 600 nautical miles," *Hearings*, p. 15.

6. U.S. Congress, Committee on Armed Services, Preparedness Investigating Subcommittee, *Investigations of the Preparedness Program, Interim Report on Cuban Military Build-Up*, 88th Cong., 1st Sess., 1963, p. 3.

7. "Department of Defense, Special Cuba Briefing by the Honorable Robert S. McNamara, Secretary of Defense, State Department Auditorium, 5:00 P.M., February 6, 1963." A verbatim transcript of a presentation actually made by General Carroll's assistant, John Hughes.

8. *Op. cit.*, p. 18.

9. *Op. cit.*, p. 3.

10. U.S. Congress, Joint Committee on the Investigation of the Pearl Harbor Attack, Pearl Harbor Attack, 79th Cong., 2d Sess., 1946, Part 14, p. 1407.

11. *The New York Times*, September 3, 1962.

12. Text of Soviet statement, *The New York Times*, September 12, 1962.

13. According to Secretary Rusk, "Senior officers did their own typing; some of my own basic papers were done in my own handwriting, in order to limit the possibility of further spread. . . ." *C.B.S. Reports,* televised interview of Secretary Rusk by David Schoenbrun, November 28, 1962.

14. U.S. Congress, Senate Subcommittee on National Security Staffing and Operations of the Committee on Government Operations, *Administration of National Security,* 88th Congress, 1st Session, 1963, Part 1, p. 97, testimony of March 25, 1963.

19.

Alain C. Enthoven: Planning, Programming, and Budgeting in the Department of Defense

Centralization of decision-making and control, and more rigorous analysis, were among the goals of the "McNamara revolution" in the Defense Department which introduced the Programming-Planning-Budgeting System—unifying decisions on strategy, forces, programs, and budgets—and introduced the use of systems and cost-effectiveness analysis.

The author of the following selection, Alain Enthoven, was head of the Office of Systems Analysis (which was established by McNamara) and was instrumental in implementing the "revolution."

Statement of Dr. Alain C. Enthoven, Assistant Secretary of Defense (Systems Analysis) on Planning, Programming and Budgeting in the Department of Defense

Mr. Chairman and Members of the Committee:

I am very happy to testify before this committee. Over the years this committee and its predecessors have provided a most valuable public service as a forum for thoughtful, professional, non-partisan study and discussion of national security policy machinery, staffing, and operations. I have followed this work with interest and personal benefit. I consider it a distinct privilege to be asked to contribute.

I am especially pleased to have the opportunity to discuss with you the Planning-Programming-Budgeting System in the Department of Defense. For this committee, like others in the Congress, called for many of the reforms that are now summarized by the letters "PPBS." It is fitting that you should now review the record to derive conclusions that will serve as a foundation for future progress.

WHY PPBS?

One way to explain PPBS, and why it is needed, is to contrast it with the way Defense budgets were prepared prior to 1961. In doing this I do not in any

Alain C. Enthoven, "Planning, Programming, and Budgeting in the Department of Defense," in *Planning, Programming, Budgeting,* Subcommittee on National Security and International Operations of the Committee on Government Operations, U.S. Senate, 1970, pp. 221–32, 246–59.

way wish to criticize the previous administrations of the Defense Department or to belittle their very substantial contributions to better management. I simply want to discuss where we were so that you can see clearly what direction we have taken and what distance we have covered.

Before 1961, Defense budgeting and the planning of the strategy and forces were almost completely separate activities, done by different people, at different times, with different terms of reference, and without any method for integrating their activities. Forces and strategy were developed by the military planners; budgeting was done by the civilian secretaries and the comptroller organization.

The strategy and force recommendations of the Military Services and the Joint Chiefs of Staff were developed, for the most part, without any explicit reference to costs. Systematic information on the full financial costs of alternative strategies or forces was not available.

The Defense budget was based on a predetermined financial ceiling. This ceiling was in turn based on judgments about the nation's capacity to pay, but without explicit reference to military strategy or requirements. Systematic information on the implications for strategy or forces of different budget levels was not available.

If bought and fully supported, the forces recommended by the Services and the Joint Chiefs of Staff would have cost much more than the Administration was willing to pay. This is not surprising or unusual. The bargaining process by which the recommended forces and the budget ceiling were reconciled, however, led to serious problems. As the budget examiners bore down to meet their predetermined targets, the Services held on to their force structures and their most glamorous weapon systems. What normally gave way were the less glamorous support items: ammunition and equipment inventories, support personnel, spare parts, etc. The result was unbalanced forces that could not have been readily deployed into combat. The glamorous weapon systems had been retained, but at the cost of reducing important items of supply to a few days or weeks. . . .

Military planning was done in terms of missions, weapon systems, and forces—the "outputs" of the Defense Department. Budgeting was done by object classes or appropriation titles—Procurement, Operations and Maintenance, Military Personnel Research and Development, and Construction—the "inputs" to the Department. There was no machinery for translating appropriations into the forces or missions they were to support. Thus, it was not possible for the Secretary of Defense, the President, or the Congress to know in meaningful terms where the Defense dollars were going. . . .

Thus, the Defense budget was not the vital policy instrument it should have been. . . . The fact that Defense financial planning was done on a year-by-year basis was particularly detrimental to good planning. . . . Finally, the Defense Department lacked measurable criteria by which to evaluate the effectiveness of alternative programs. . . .

WHAT PPBS IS AND IS NOT

First and fundamental is the fact that since 1961, the Secretary of Defense has not operated with any predetermined budget ceiling. Rather, he judges each proposal on its merits, considering the need, the contribution of the proposal to increased military effectiveness, and its cost in national resources. The total Defense budget recommended by the Secretary of Defense to the President, and by the President to the Congress, is the sum of many such judgments about military need and effectiveness and their relation to cost.

While it is inevitable that many will disagree with the Secretary of Defense on specific decisions, it seems clear to me that this is the most rational and balanced way to approach the Defense budget. Moreover, I believe the Secretary of Defense sits in the best place to make such judgments, subject, of course, to review by the President and the Congress.

I recall the reaction by a friend of mine, then in Programming in the Joint Staff, to the first presentation by Mr. Hitch of the principles of PPBS: "Good. From now on, whenever the Secretary of Defense wants to cut the Army's budget, he will have to name the units." That is true, and as it should be. Of course, this approach makes great demands on the Secretary of Defense because it forces him, with the help of his staff, to become acquainted in detail with the merits of many proposals. It gives the Secretary of Defense a lot of homework to do. It is clearly much tougher than simply decreeing across-the-board cuts based on some arbitrary financial limit.

To consider these proposals, the Secretary must have a systematic flow of information on the needs, effectiveness, and cost of alternative programs, including differing opinions on them when they exist. We are organized to provide this information.

Second, decision making on strategy, forces, programs, and budgets is now unified. A decision to increase our forces or to start a new weapon system is a decision to add the required amounts to the financial plan. The machinery by which this is done is the Planning-Programming-Budgeting System.

The key to this system is decision making by missions, i.e., by the "outputs" of the Department of Defense rather than solely by the "inputs."

We call the basic, mission-oriented building block of the programming structure a "program element." A program element is an integrated activity, a combination of men, equipment, and installations whose military capability or effectiveness can be related to our national security policy objectives. For example, B-52 wings, infantry-battalions, and attack submarines, each taken together with all the equipment, men, installations, and direct support required to make them effective military forces, are program elements. The program elements are then assembled into "major programs" defined by mission. A major program contains closely related elements which must be considered together in arriving at high-level management decisions. For example, Strategic

Retaliatory Forces, General Purpose Forces, and Airlift-Sealift Forces are major programs.

A program element has both costs and benefits associated with it. The benefits are the ways in which it helps us to achieve broad national security objectives. The costs include the total system cost, regardless of appropriation category, projected systematically five to ten years into the future.

PPBS enables the Secretary of Defense, the President, and the Congress to focus their attention on the major missions of the Department of Defense, rather than on lists of unrelated items of expenditure. For example, in making decisions about Strategic Retaliatory Forces, the Secretary looks at the threat, at our national objectives, and at alternative plans to meet our objectives, their effectiveness, and their costs. He reviews the data on these matters with the Joint Chiefs of Staff and the Services, obtains their advice, and makes decisions on the forces. From there on, the breakdown of the budget by Service and appropriation title is largely derivative, a process left mostly to the staff.

The advice of the Joint Chiefs of Staff is systematically sought and included in this process. In particular, they now have cost data that enable them to estimate the financial implications of their force recommendations. Thus, force requirements and strategy are effectively related to costs early in the decision making process.

Each spring, the Joint Chiefs and the Services send the Secretary of Defense their recommendations on forces, together with supporting data. The Secretary reviews these recommendations, and, during the summer, sends the Joint Chiefs of Staff and the Services the results of his review in the form of memorandums —called Draft Presidential Memorandums. These drafts summarize the relevant information on the threat, our objectives, the effectiveness, and cost of the alternatives he has considered and his tentative conclusions. With rare exceptions the Joint Chiefs and the Services have a month to review and comment on each of these drafts. They comment in detail. The Secretary reviews the comments thoroughly. He revises his tentative decisions, has more discussions with the Chiefs and the Services, and gradually develops a program and a budget. This dialogue continues for months. It is in sharp contrast to the situation the Senate Preparedness Subcommittee found in 1959:

> Furthermore, the Joint Chiefs as a group were given only 2 days to consider the total program and never considered such important aspects as the size of the Army, whether to include an aircraft carrier or—most fundamental of all—what deterrent forces are needed.

The results of the process are summarized in the Five Year Defense Program. It includes an eight-year projection of all approved forces, and a five-year projection of costs, manpower, procurement, construction, etc. This document enables all top Defense officials to be readily informed about the total Defense program and its components.

The decisions in the Five Year Defense Program do not represent a five-year commitment by the President or even by the Secretary of Defense. Nor do these decisions "tie the President's hands." The President and the Secretary of Defense retain their flexibility to change these decisions as they should. Rather, the Five Year Defense Program represents the sum total of programs that have been tentatively approved for planning purposes by the Secretary of Defense. You might say it is an official set of assumptions about what forces we currently plan to request authorization for in the future, assumptions from which the financial planners can derive the budget requests required to support these forces.

Moreover, the Five Year Defense Program is not a complete master plan calculated in minute detail at the top and handed down to the troops for execution. It is a set of broad planning guidelines that help us all to pull together in the same direction instead of at cross-purposes. It is not a substitute for individual initiative or for the many benefits that we get from competition among and within the Services. The Planning-Programming-Budgeting System is not what makes the Department of Defense run. The initiative, the drive, the imagination, the dedication, the judgment, and the hard work of a great many people, makes the Department of Defense run ánd progress. PPBS is a flexible tool to channel this creative energy, as much as possible, along rational and useful lines.

WHAT SYSTEMS ANALYSIS IS AND IS NOT

Hardly a week goes by that I don't read some fantastic description of systems analysis in the Pentagon. The more I read about it in the public press, the more I get the feeling I must not be doing it. According to some accounts, the essence of systems analysis is the application of computers and fancy mathematics to reduce all issues to numbers, with lots of attention to cost and none to effectiveness, and with a complete lack of interest in military judgment or anyone else's judgment. If I believed that even a small fraction of such descriptions were accurate, I would recommend to Secretary McNamara and Deputy Secretary Nitze that they fire me; I am sure that if they believed I was trying to replace their judgment with a computer, they would not wait for my recommendation.

In fact, systems analysis is just one name for an approach to problems of decision making that good management has always practiced. The essence of systems analysis is not mysterious, nor particularly complicated, nor entirely new, nor of special value only to Defense planning. Rather, it is a reasoned approach to highly complicated problems of choice characterized by much uncertainty; it provides room for very differing values and judgments; and it seeks alternative ways of doing the job. It is neither a panacea nor a Pandora's box.

Decisions must be made by responsible officials on the basis of fact and judgment. Systems analysis is an effort to define the issues and alternatives clearly, and to provide responsible officials with a full, accurate, and meaningful summary of as many as possible of the relevant facts so that they can exercise well-informed judgment; it is not a substitute for judgment.

You might object, "But you're merely describing disciplined, orderly thought;

why call it 'systems analysis'?" Most labels are imperfect; this one is no exception. We use the phrase "systems analysis" to emphasize two aspects of this kind of thinking.

First, every decision should be viewed in some meaningful context. In most cases, decisions deal with elements that are parts of a larger system. Good decisions must recognize that each element is one of a number of components that work together to serve a larger purpose. The strategic bomber, the airfield, the pilot, the fuel, and the spare parts are all parts of a weapon *system*. One cannot make sense out of airfield requirements without looking at the objectives the bomber is intended to achieve. For some purposes, it is necessary to look at the airfield construction program as such; there would be no sense in building a new bomber base if a perfectly good transport base were being vacated a few miles away. Systems analysis emphasizes the airfield as a part of the weapon system. Similarly, to make sense of strategic bomber requirements, you need to look at other strategic offensive weapons, such as missiles.

There is nothing mysterious about this kind of thinking. Informed men in the Congress, the Executive Branch, and elsewhere have been pointing out the need for such an approach for years. We are doing it, and we have given it a name.

The word *analysis* is used to emphasize the need to analyze complex problems, that is, to reduce them to their component parts. Then each of the component parts can be studied by methods appropriate to it. Logical propositions can be tested logically; questions of fact can be tested against the factual evidence; matters of value and uncertainty can be exposed and clarified so that the decision makers can know exactly where to apply their judgment.

Systems analysis is not a substitute for judgment; it is an aid to judgment. It helps by isolating those areas where judgment must be applied and by indicating to the decision maker the potential significance of each of the alternatives he might choose. Systems analysis is not a "wholly rational basis for decision making? . . . [a] technocratic utopia where judgment is a machine-product?"

Far from it. It is based on the fact that most decisions in Defense are at least partly susceptible to rational treatment, and it tries to deal with these in a disciplined way, leaving the responsible decision makers more time to ponder the imponderables and weigh the intangibles.

One of the foundations of systems analysis in the Department of Defense is the concept of "open and explicit analysis." Unfortunately this is not something that is discussed in the formal literature on analytical methods, but it is very relevant to the concerns of this committee. In fact, this concept is the single most important idea I have to communicate today.

An analysis is "open and explicit" if it is presented in such a way that the objectives and alternatives are clearly defined, and all of the assumptions, factors, calculations, and judgments are laid bare so that all interested parties can see exactly how the conclusions were derived, how information they provided was used, and how the various assumptions influenced the results. We do not achieve this in every case, but this is the objective, and important issues are almost always approached this way.

In other words, systems analysis is a method of interrogation and debate suited to complex, quantitative issues. Systems analysis is a set of ground rules for constructive debate; it gives the participants useful guidelines for proceeding to clarify and resolve disagreements. It requires the participants to make their methods of calculation and their assumptions explicit so that they can be double-checked; it helps to identify uncertainties, makes these uncertainties explicit, and aids in evaluating their importance; and it identifies and isolates issues.

In cases of substantial disagreement, it is much better to join your adversary in a joint analysis than to restate without change last year's arguments for last year's frozen position. Joint analyses often narrow the differences, and sometimes lead to agreement, by helping the adversaries to persuade each other of the merits of their arguments and by identifying new alternatives that are mutually more satisfactory.

This is an especially important aspect of systems analysis as it operates in the Department of Defense. Frequently, when there are differing points of view on the value of a proposed program, the Secretary of Defense asks us to prepare a memorandum listing points of agreement and disagreement. For each of the points of disagreement, an agreed calculation is performed which shows the implications of each person's assumption. The Secretary of Defense is then able to see exactly what the issues are, how important they are, and what judgments he must make in order to resolve them.

For example, last year the Secretary of Defense got conflicting estimates from my office and from the Army of the probable damage to the United States and the USSR resulting from various possible thermonuclear wars, with alternative anti-ballistic missile defense systems. He asked the Secretary of the Army and me to prepare a joint memorandum describing points of agreement and disagreement in such a way that the total difference would be explained explicitly, and our arguments would meet "head on." The Secretary of the Army and I explored the calculations in considerable detail and identified the assumptions that accounted for the difference. We then discussed each of these assumptions, reached agreement on some, and agreed to disagree on others. We then prepared a set of calculations and a table of results which we both agreed was a fair representation of what would happen under each set of stated assumptions.

The value of such a table to the Secretary of Defense, the President, members of Congress, and other officials in government is that it isolates the important assumptions and calls to their attention the key judgments that must be made. Systems analysis thus aids and focuses judgment; it does not replace it. Incidentally, this table was used in summary form in Secretary McNamara's presentation of the anti-ballistic missile defense issue to the Congress last winter.

I might add that, partly as a result of that dialogue and similar work with the Joint Staff and the Services, we now have an agreed set of methods for calculating the results of thermonuclear war under alternative assumptions. We can all make the same assumptions and get the same answers. We don't always agree on the assumptions, but the agreement on methods of calculation now permits the Secretary of Defense, the Joint Chiefs of Staff, the Services, and others to concentrate their attention on determining which assumptions they consider most realistic. This is one valuable contribution that systems analysis makes to decision making.

The open and explicit approach is fundamental to systems analysis as it operates in the decision making process of the Department of Defense. Open and explicit analysis is our best protection against persistent error. Also, the open and explicit approach makes it very difficult, if not virtually impossible, for any group to rig or manipulate the results. When the Air Force sends the Secretary of Defense an analysis of the requirements for a new bomber, a copy is also sent to my office. We take it apart and see what makes the analysis come out as it does. When my office or the Office of the Director of Defense Research and Engineering does an analysis on bombers, a copy goes to the Air Force. If you think Harold Brown and his staff are going to let my analysts get away with rigging an assumption to prove a point, then you don't know Harold Brown and his staff. And, of course, we try to provide them with the same assistance. I can assure you that the Secretary of Defense hears all sides, and when he gets a joint analysis, he gets a much more precise statement of the issues than would otherwise be the case.

We don't succeed in doing this in every case, sometimes because of the pressure of time, sometimes because one of the interested parties is unable or unwilling to pursue a joint analysis. Nevertheless, this is our objective, and we are achieving it in a growing number of cases.

Systems analysis usually includes some calculations. Where appropriate, it includes the application of modern methods of quantitative analysis, including Economic Theory, Mathematical Statistics, Mathematical Operations Research, and various techniques known as Decision Theory. However, systems analysis is not synonymous with the application of these mathematical techniques, and much of the most important systems analysis work in the Department of Defense does not use them.

Systems analysis is not an attempt to measure the unmeasurable. But one of the opportunities that systems analysis offers for creative work is seeking ways of giving valid measurement to things previously thought to be unmeasurable. A good systems analyst does not leave considerations that cannot be quantified out of the analysis. Inevitably such considerations will be left out of the *calculations,* but a good analyst will and does list and describe such factors.

Systems analysis is definitely not synonymous with the application of computers. We sometimes use computers, we also use pencils, paper, slide rules, telephones, etc. The computer aspect has been grossly overplayed in many discussions of systems analysis. The use or misuse of computers is too minor an aspect of this subject to be relevant to the serious concerns of this committee.

"COST-EFFECTIVENESS" ANALYSIS AND THE RELEVANCE OF COST

Some of the main tools of systems analysis come from Economics. Where appropriate, we approach problems of choice by defining the objectives, identifying alternative ways of achieving the objectives, and identifying the alternative that yields the greatest effectiveness for any given cost, or what amounts to the same thing, that yields a specific degree of effectiveness for the least cost. In other words, the main idea is to find the alternative that yields the greatest military effectiveness from the resources available.

Systems analysis includes a critical evaluation of the objectives. It recognizes that most ends are, in fact, means to still broader objectives. For example, an ability to destroy a particular target is not likely to be an end in itself; it is a means to some more basic end such as deterrence. Therefore, a good systems analyst will seek to determine whether or not the pursuit of certain intermediate objectives is the best way of pursuing the broader ends.

Thus, systems analysis is often associated with "cost-effectiveness" or "cost-benefit" analysis. The term "cost-effectiveness" analysis is often misunderstood. It seems to suggest to some people a notion of "cost-effectiveness" that is somehow to be contrasted to "military-effectiveness" or just plain "effectiveness." It might be better if we used the expression "military effectiveness in relation to cost," or simply "the best mix of military forces."

The point is that every weapon system we buy has both benefits and costs associated with it. You cannot get "effectiveness" without paying a "cost." Each program uses up resources that could otherwise be put to some other useful purpose. Sensible decisions on the use of these resources must depend on the costs incurred in relation to the military effectiveness obtained. "Cost-effectiveness" analysis is nothing more than an attempt to identify the alternatives that yield the most effectiveness in relation to the money spent and other costs incurred.

The main line of attack on "cost-effectiveness" analysis is an attack on the relevance of cost. One frequently hears statements to the effect that considerations of cost have no place in matters of national security.

I certainly agree that we cannot afford to buy less than the military forces we really need, and that we must not let defense spending be constrained by arbitrary financial limits that are unrelated to military needs. But it is simply naive to assert, as some people do, that the cost we pay for our military power is irrelevant. Our experience with the war in Southeast Asia each day demonstrates the opposite conclusion. We are in the midst of a great national debate over whether the objectives we are fighting for are worth the cost. Whatever the merits of the particular arguments, it is clear that the cost is relevant if for no other reason than that it affects popular support for the war effort.

I think the key point on the relevance of cost was made by the distinguished chairman of this subcommittee 6 years ago when he said:

Rich as we are, we cannot do all the things we would like to do to assure the national safety and provide for the general welfare.

The job of the President is to rank the competing claims on our resources in terms of their national importance—to distinguish between what cannot wait and what can wait.

One hears other criticisms of "cost-effectiveness" analysis. Does PPBS *necessarily* lead to an overemphasis on cost? It does not. I would like to know how anyone who claims that it does can reconcile that conclusion with the sharp increase in Defense budget requests in the two years after 1961.

Cost in any program merely represents "effectiveness foregone elsewhere." The reason that the Secretary of Defense cares about the cost as well as the effectiveness of proposed weapon systems is because he recognizes that the dollars used to support a particular program represent resources that could possibly be used to greater benefit elsewhere. Cost and effectiveness must be related to achieve national policy goals, just as the front and rear sights of a rifle must both be used to hit the target. The position of the rear sight matters only in relation to the front sight. Likewise, the cost of a program matters only in relation to the military effectiveness provided, and *vice versa*.

Does "cost-effectiveness" analysis stifle innovation? On the contrary, such analysis has given the proponents of good ideas a better way of making their case and of getting prompt and favorable decisions. I would cite, as examples, such new systems as the Minuteman II, Minuteman III, and Poseidon strategic missile systems; Multiple Independently-targetable Re-entry Vehicles (MIRVs) that enable one ballistic missile to destroy many separate targets; the Short Range Attack Missile known as SRAM; the Sprint and Spartan anti-missile missiles and the new phased array radar that will guide them; the A-7 fighter bomber; the C-5A transport aircraft; the Fast Deployment Logistic Ships; and the Airmobile Division. In each case, some very good ideas were identified early and sold on the basis of "cost-effectiveness" analysis. Also, by helping to cut back programs that are based on poor ideas, "cost-effectiveness analysis" helps to leave more resources available for the most effective programs.

Does "cost-effectiveness" analysis always lead to a preference for the cheapest system on a unit cost basis? The record shows it does not. I just mentioned a number of systems that were justified on the basis of "cost-effectiveness" analysis, each of which costs more per unit than its predecessor. However, in each case the margin of extra effectiveness per unit is worth the extra cost.

A popular remark among the critics of PPBS is that we would never have developed and procured the Polaris weapon system if it had had to pass the "cost-effectiveness" test because it costs more per missile than Minuteman. This charge is particularly ironic in view of the facts. One of the first things that Secretary McNamara did as Secretary of Defense was to more than triple the rate of Polaris submarine construction in order more rapidly to achieve an invulnerable retaliatory force. The Navy's recent proposal to develop Poseidon also got very prompt and favorable treatment from the Secretary. Poseidon missiles will cost much more than the Polaris missiles they will replace, but analysis makes it clear that their extra margin of performance is worth the extra cost.

Does "cost-effectiveness" analysis or systems analysis lead to an over-emphasis on factors that can be reduced to numbers? Not necessarily. A good analysis of the numerical factors leaves the decision makers more time and energy to weigh the intangibles.

In this connection, let me comment on an example that is used in support of the opposite view. Your *Initial Memorandum* says:

Skybolt presumably did not meet the Defense tests of cost-effectiveness, but one wonders whether, in estimating the costs of its cancellation, allowance was made for the impact on the British Government and perhaps on French policies in Atlantic and West European affairs.

Yes, allowance was made for the impact on the British. There is no question that the Secretary of Defense and his main advisors were keenly aware of the political implications of Skybolt for the British. In fact, Skybolt was kept alive for many months and millions of dollars longer than it otherwise would have been precisely because of the British interest. But, it finally got to the point that the expected effectiveness of Skybolt fell so low, and the projected costs rose so high in relation to competing systems, such as Minuteman, that the President and the Secretary of Defense, reached the conclusion that Skybolt would not be satisfactory for the British, and was clearly unsatisfactory for us. Continuation of Skybolt would have only postponed the political problem, not avoided it.

CENTRALIZATION OF DECISION MAKING

The Planning-Programming-Budgeting System has provided the Secretary of Defense with some of the tools he needs to make major strategic decisions and to see that they are carried out. After careful consideration of the advice of the Joint Chiefs of Staff, the Services, and his civilian advisors, the Secretary of Defense decides what the Department's recommendations to the President and the Congress will be.

I am convinced that there is no sensible alternative to centralization of the major strategic decisions. They were decentralized before 1961 and the result was clearly unsatisfactory. The Army was trying to prepare for one kind of war while the Air Force was trying to prepare for another. The result was that we could not effectively fight either kind of war.

Centralization of these decisions has not led to a Defense program based on a single view of strategy or a single vision of the future. On the contrary, PPBS has helped to improve the ability of the Joint Chiefs of Staff and the Services to comment on, and to debate thoroughly, the totality of our military posture in order to make their contributions to insuring that it can deal effectively with a wide range of contingencies.

Moreover, it is not entirely coincidental that the introduction of PPBS was accompanied by a major change in military strategy. Since 1961, we have moved from a rigid, inflexible reliance on the threatened massive use of nuclear weapons to the strategy that has been characterized as "flexible response." This latter strategy includes balanced, ready forces that are able to deal appropriately with aggression at each point across the broad spectrum of warfare from anti-guerrilla war to thermonuclear war. The themes, "options," "flexibility," and "choice," have become as fundamental to our military strategy as they have been to our approach to analysis and planning of the defense program. The charge that centralized decision making leads to an inflexible strategy based on a single set of assumptions is refuted by the historical facts.

Has the greater centralization of decision making and control made it easier for the Office of the Secretary of Defense to suppress dissent or to ignore opposing arguments? I don't think anyone who reads the newspapers will believe that dissent is suppressed in the Department of Defense. There is plenty of debate now; but I like to think that it is now enlightened by more information and analysis and more sharply focused on the important policy issues than it was a decade ago.

Does PPBS help the Secretary or his staff ignore opposing views? It does not. In fact, just the opposite is true.

I remember well the experience of an Admiral who worked for Secretaries of the Navy in the program decision process before and after 1961. When one of Secretary McNamara's first "Draft Presidential Memorandums" on Naval Forces was sent to the Navy for review and discussion, some of the Admiral's colleagues reacted negatively to the idea. They did not accept some of the Secretary's assumptions and they did not agree with some of his conclusions. They questioned why the Secretary should be sending such a document. My friend's reaction was: "No, no, don't try to make him stop sending these drafts. All we got from previous Secretaries of Defense was the decision, without explanation or analysis. McNamara sends us his analysis, assumptions and all. If we don't agree, we've got something to attack and if we can prove him wrong, he'll change his mind."

The fact is that the Secretary of Defense sends drafts of all important program decision documents to the Joint Chiefs of Staff and to the Service Secretaries for review and comment before he makes up his mind. Rather than suppressing dissenting points of view, his procedure "smokes them out" and gets them out in the open where they can be analyzed and discussed. The PPBS procedures we use encourage the expression of opposing views, and the result is better analyses.

ACHIEVEMENTS OF PPBS IN THE DEPARTMENT OF DEFENSE

PPBS has led to a major and general improvement in the quality of the decision and planning process in the Department of Defense. It has also led to a major improvement in the quality and relevance of debate over requirements issues. The Secretary of Defense, the Joint Chiefs of Staff, and the Services have more and better data on the effectiveness and costs of alternative programs.

Many studies have been done, and others are underway throughout the Department on each major force requirement issue. Procedures have been established so that these studies can be followed and reviewed in an open and professional way by the Office of the Secretary of Defense, the Joint Staff, and the Services.

PPBS provides an official force plan which gives the planners and analysts in the whole Department a firm foundation for their planning and a solid point of departure for their analyses. Now the procurement, facilities, and personnel branches can be confident they are providing equipment, facilities, and manpower for the same forces, thus greatly reducing the confusion and waste that occurred when there was no unified, approved plan as the basis for these activities. Today we have a firm force structure base from which to analyze the additional effectiveness and cost of new programs. The left hand has a better idea of what the right hand is doing in force and financial planning.

By unifying programming and budgeting, PPBS has closed the "gap" between force and financial planning. This has led to the acquisition of ready, more balanced, and better supported combat forces. There have been the inevitable difficulties in detailed execution, and I do not doubt that one could find minor examples to the contrary. But, for the most part, since instituting PPBS, the forces that have been authorized and approved by the Secretary of Defense have been procured together with the manpower, equipment, facilities, etc., necessary to make them balanced and combat ready. The systematic viewing of all requirements on an overall basis, rather than on the basis of a single Service, has led to the elimination of much unnecessary duplication.

One of the results of PPBS has been the development of unified analyses of requirements for Strategic Offensive and Defensive Forces and the Airlift and Sealift Forces. I believe that these developments are quite important and representative of what the system can achieve.

We have come a long way since 1961. . . .

In 1961, Secretary McNamara asked a group of military planners to study strategic offensive force requirements for the next ten years. I worked with them as an observer and friendly critic. The group displayed a very high degree of professional competence, and the study was by far the best that had been done on that subject to date. The study group developed a list of all strategic targets and, using the best available intelligence and their own judgments, projected the growth of these target lists over the next ten years. They then estimated the performance and operational characteristics of the various available weapon systems and calculated how many would be needed for destruction of 75 percent and 90 percent of the targets in each of the next ten years. These calculations were summarized and forwarded to the Secretary of Defense.

The study was excellent, but it raised many more questions than it answered. Why 90 percent or 75 percent? What were we really trying to do? What was the purpose of having the power to destroy these targets, not in terms of the narrow technical criteria of the force planner, but in terms of broader criteria of interest to the Secretary of Defense, the President, and the Congress? The study had other limitations. For one thing, it treated only strategic offensive forces and gave no indication of the relationship of strategic offensive to strategic defensive forces. Moreover, it assumed the Soviets would not react to major changes in our own forces.

I point to these limitations not to criticize those who did the study; I was one of them. My purpose is to indicate the state of the analytical art at that time. Since then a great deal of questioning, debate, exploration, study, calculation, and research have illuminated many of these questions. First, as to criteria, we asked: What national purpose is served by being able to destroy those targets? There were two purposes. The first was deterrence. By having the power to destroy Soviet society in a retaliatory strike, we hope to deter the Soviets from attacking or threatening to attack us. The second was that the power to destroy bomber bases and missile sites might reduce the amount of damage that Soviet forces could do to us in case of a nuclear war. The first criterion we now call Assured Destruction; the second, Damage Limiting.

Then it became clear that strategic offensive forces bought for Damage Limiting needed to be compared systematically with strategic defensive forces bought for the same purpose. It would make no sense, for example, to spend an additional $10 billion on strategic offensive forces, primarily for Damage Limiting, if we could save the same or a greater number of lives by spending a billion dollars on fallout shelters. Thus, we developed methods for integrating the treatment of strategic offensive forces and strategic defensive forces.

Next, we observed that the U.S. anticipates and reacts to Soviet moves such as their deployment of an anti-ballistic missile defense system. So we began exploring the implications of various assumptions about how they might react to our moves.

Of course, the effectiveness of different combinations of systems will vary a great deal depending on the assumptions about how the war starts, how it is fought, how each side responds to what the other side does, and many other uncertain factors. So, the analytical procedure must be developed in such a way that the assumptions can be varied and the implications of different assumptions explored.

Now, after six years of steady work on this problem, we have an agreed set of numerical representations of the outcome of nuclear war under alternative assumptions. Basic contributions to the development of these models have been made by all components of the Department of Defense: by military planners in the Service staffs, by study groups in the Joint Staff, by the Joint Strategic Planning Staff, and by the Office of the Secretary of Defense. Today, the experts are all pretty much in agreement on how you go from any single set of assumptions to the results those assumptions produce. This makes it possible for the top level officials, who are not themselves technical experts in nuclear planning, to understand which assumptions are important and to concentrate their attention on the crucial judgments. . . .

Let me now summarize briefly.

First, before 1961, several committees of the Congress, including the one before which I have the honor of appearing today, justly criticized the budgetary process in the Department of Defense because:

(1) it was based on arbitrary and predetermined financial limits unrelated to military strategy or needs;

(2) it was done entirely by objects of expenditure which were unrelated to the missions of the Department of Defense;

(3) it was a piecemeal, one-year-at-a-time-effort, without adequate attention to long-run consequences; and

(4) it paid insufficient attention to measures of performance or effectiveness.

Since 1961, we have developed a Planning-Programming-Budgeting System in the Department of Defense that:

(1) starts with a review of strategy and military needs, develops a program to meet them, and derives an annual budget without regard to predetermined financial limits;

(2) is based on a financial plan that identifies Defense spending by the major military missions subdivided into meaningful "output-oriented" program elements;

(3) projects forces eight years into the future, costs at least five years (and to completion for major systems); and

(4) focuses attention on explicit measures of effectiveness.

For the very reasons that the Congress called for these reforms, I believe that they enable us to manage the Department of Defense better.

Second, open and explicit analysis, reviewed and commented on by all interested parties is fundamental to the working of PPBS in the Pentagon. No major force issues are decided by the Secretary of Defense on the basis of analysis by any one office or department alone. The analyses underlying the Secretary's decisions are circulated for comment and review by all interested parties, and their comments go directly to him. The procedures are designed so that the Secretary will hear all sides, so that no one has a monopoly on the information going to the Secretary. This open and explicit approach is our best protection against persistent error; it makes it virtually impossible for any group to rig the analysis without that point being made clear to the Secretary. It ensures that all assumptions are made explicit and that all opinions are considered.

Third, systems analysis is an integral part of PPBS. Systems analysis is not synonymous with the application of mathmatical techniques or computers. Systems analysis is not a substitute for judgment; it is an aid to judgment.

"Cost-effectiveness" analysis does not lead to an over-emphasis on cost. It does not stifle innovation; on the contrary, it helps it. It does not always lead to buying the cheapest system; there are numerous examples to the contrary. "Cost-effectiveness" analysis does not lead to an over-emphasis on factors that can be reduced to numbers; on the contrary, good systems analysis frees the decision maker to concentrate on the intangibles and uncertainties.

Fourth, PPBS has not led to a single set of assumptions dominating military strategy; it has not led to a single, rigid military strategy; it has not eliminated flexibility; and it has not over-centralized the Defense decision making process. On the contrary, PPBS in the Department of Defense has been associated with a change from the inflexible strategy of "massive retaliation" to a strategy of "flexible response." Moreover, it has been associated with large increases in our military strength to give us the balanced, ready forces we need to support this strategy.

Fifth, the potential of PPBS is great in clarifying debate over program issues, in stimulating and recognizing new solutions to problems, and in helping the Government to spend money wisely. Within the limits of what any improvement in management can do, I believe that PPBS has the potential to be a most important innovation in government management.

20.
James R. Schlesinger: *Uses and Abuses of Analysis*

A strong case for systems analysis was made in the previous selection by Alain Enthoven. In this selection a sympathetic critic and practitioner responds with his assessment of the role of systems analysis, dealing in particular with "its relation to decisions and decisionmakers, its functioning in a political environment where conflicting objectives exist, and its utility for improving the resource allocation process."

James R. Schlesinger is the chairman of the Atomic Energy Commission and was formerly an assistant director of the Office of Management and Budget. He is the author of *The Political Economy of National Security.*

The Subcommittee's invitation to assess the role that analysis may play in governmental decisionmaking is gratifying for a number of reasons. In its current stocktaking, the Subcommittee is accomplishing something of a turnabout: the analysis of systems analysis. This evaluation takes place at a critical time. Like other offspring in American life, analysis has been absorbed into an environment which has been at once both too permissive and too resentful. There is ample evidence that such a pattern is beneficial to neither the offspring nor the environment. Currently there is a risk that reaction against what may be termed the exuberance of certain claims and activities of analysis could result in the discarding of the substantial benefits that analysis does offer. I shall be attempting to bring out the instances of undue gullibility as well as undue skepticism, but in so doing I should perhaps make my own position clear. My attitude has long been one of two-and-a-half cheers for systems analysis. I recognize—and have emphasized—its limitations. I will make no excuses for offenses committed in its name. But despite the limitations and distortions, I remain an unabashed, if qualified, defender of the value of analysis in policy formation.

In the pages that follow I shall deal with some salient issues regarding the

James R. Schlesinger, "Uses and Abuses of Analysis," in *Planning, Programming, Budgeting,* Subcommittee on National Security and International Operations of the Committee on Government Operations, U.S. Senate, 1970, pp. 125–36.

role of analysis: its relation to decisions and decisionmakers, its functioning in a political environment where conflicting objectives exist, and its utility for improving the resource allocation process.

The Authority of Analysis

Systems analysis has been variously defined. In the most ambitious formulation it has been described as "the application of scientific method, using that term in its broadest sense." Certain attributes of science—objectivity, openness, self-correctability, verifiability, etc.—are alleged to apply to systems analysis. Would that it were so, but realistically speaking such assertions must be rejected. Even for science—as those who are familiar with the history of scientific investigations will recognize—this represents a rather romanticized view. In science, however, competition takes the form of establishing hypotheses regarding the workings of the natural order. Evidence and experiments are reproducible, and institutions and personalities consequently play a smaller long-run role. In scientific investigations the search for truth is by and large unfettered. By contrast, in the search for preferred policies such encumbrances as social values and goals, constraints, institutional requirements (both broad and narrow) pertain. Truth becomes only one of a number of conflicting objectives and, sad to relate, oftentimes a secondary one.

An alternative definition described systems analysis as "quantified common sense." By some expositors this definition has been treated as the equivalent of the earlier one, but is really quite distinct. However high the regard in which common sense, quantitative or otherwise, is held in the American community, it never has been regarded as synonymous with scientific method. Nonetheless, the definition is far more apt. Common sense, for example, will accept that within a complicated bureaucratic structure distortions inevitably creep into the process of acquiring and organizing evidence. What one sees depends upon where one sits—an earthy way of describing what is more elegantly referred to as cognitive limits. It may be inferred that a systems analysis shop attached to the Office of the Secretary of Defense will be quite responsive to the perceptions and prejudices of the Secretary and the institutional requirements of his Office. This should be no more surprising than that the Operations Analysis shop at Omaha will be influenced by the doctrine, present activities, and aspirations of the Strategic Air Command.

In the early years of the introduction of the PPB into the Department of Defense, faith in the ease with which scientific objectivity could be attained tended to be high in OSD. For Service staffs, this was a rather painful period for rather invidious distinctions were drawn regarding *their* objectivity. In recent years an enormous change has taken place regarding the nature of the analytical dialogue. Undoubtedly this new attitude reflects experience and the growing awareness that past decisions and past commitments limit the openness and the freshness with which the OSD staff can address issues in controversy.

This new realism has been reflected in a number of ways. Especially in private appraisals analysis has been justified with increasing frequency and frankness as part of an adversary proceeding. But such an interpretation is symptomatic of a substantial change. Whatever the merits of an adversary procedure —and these are substantial where there exist clashes of interests and goals and where evidence is difficult to unearth—no one has ever suggested that adversaries seek to be wholly objective. One may hope that the result will be the elucidation of the best possible case for and the best possible case against. But, unfortunately, the emphasis tends to shift to a search for the winning argument as opposed to the correct conclusion. In view of the uneven distribution of debating skills, one cannot fail to have qualms about the probable outcomes. One senior official has observed, only half facetiously, that experience in debate is the most valuable training for analytical work.

Acceptance of the tug-of-war concept, as opposed to the objective-scholar concept, of analysis has coincided with recognition of an even greater limitation on analysis as a guide to policymaking. In recent years it has been recognized in public statements (as well as the textbooks) that analysis is not a scientific procedure for reaching decisions which avoid intuitive elements, but rather a mechanism for sharpening the intuitions of the decisionmaker. Once again this is right. No matter how large a contribution that analysis makes, the role of the subjective preferences of the decisionmaker remains imposing. Analysis is, in the end, a method of investigating rather than solving problems. The highest strategic objectives, the statement of preferences or utility, must in large part be imposed from outside. Poor or haphazard analysis may contribute to poor decisions, but good analysis by itself cannot insure correct decisions. This implies two things. First, whatever the complex of decisions, legitimate differences of opinion will persist. Second, disagreement with the decisions should not automatically cast doubt on either the role of analysis in general or on the quality of specific analyses. These must be examined in and of themselves.

To be sure, the judgment of the decisionmakers regarding major objectives and what is or is not important is likely to feed back and influence the analysis. This is not always true, but there are strong pressures to make it come true. Studies are driven by the underlying assumptions, and these may be imposed directly or indirectly from above. Specific terms of reference may indicate which scenarios are acceptable, which unacceptable, and which contingencies should or should not be considered. It is perfectly appropriate, if not obligatory, for the analyst to point out deficiencies in study assumptions or terms of reference. Yet, many will lack the perception or the inclination, while others would regard such action as personally imprudent. In these cases the analysis will only play back to the decisionmaker a more sharply defined version of what was already implicit in his assumptions. The role of analysis then becomes not so much to *sharpen* the intuitions of the decisionmaker as to *confirm* them.

Under these circumstances analysis is not being used in its most fruitful form, that of raising questions. But analysis is a tool that can be used in a variety of ways. Much depends upon how the decisionmaker decides to employ it. Considerable fear has been expressed that analysis will usurp the decisionmaking role, that the decisionmaker will become passive, and let analysis (implicitly) make the decisions. This is possible; it is also improper. But whether the decisionmaker will control the tool rather than letting it run away with him strikes me as a less important question than whether he will employ it properly in another sense. Will the decisionmaker tolerate analysis—even when it is his own hobby horses which are under scrutiny?

How many hobby horses are there?

Are they off limits to the analysts?

Dr. Enthoven has quite properly objected to the canard that analysis is somehow responsible for what are regarded as the mishaps of the TFX decisions, pointing out that the new procedures were only tangentially involved. A more penetrating question, it seems to me, is: why did the analysts steer away from the issue?

A slightly different issue arises in the case of Vietnam. Numerous blunders are alleged to be chargeable to analytic errors. But analysis has been employed in the Vietnamese context in only the most cursory fashion. In this context neither the high-level civilian nor the military authorities have been eager to exploit the full potentials of analysis. Once again, rather than blaming analytic efforts for the failures, the appropriate question should be: why has analysis been so little employed?

An acquaintance, who has been deeply involved in analytic activities in one of the Departments, recently commented to me on his experiences. Analysis he felt had been relevant in only a small proportion of the decisions. Half the time a decision had been foreclosed by high-level political involvement: a call from the White House, interest expressed by key Congressmen or Committees. In an additional 30 percent of the cases, the careers of immediate supervisors were involved. Analysis could not influence the recommendations; it could serve only as an irritant. But, he argued, in something like 20 percent of the issues, analysis was unfettered and contributed to much improved overall results. This was only the experience of one individual. In other cases the proportions might be quite different. The point is that analysis should be judged on the basis of only the minority of cases in which its influence is in some sense instrumental. Analysis is a useful tool, but it is only a tool. It would be a mistake to turn over a new proverbial leaf—and generally find fault with tools rather than craftsmen.

Practitioners versus Instruments

Accepting that analysis only sharpens the intuitions of decisionmakers, that its powers may be curtailed by unquestioned (or question-begging) assumptions or by imposed terms of reference, and that it is increasingly viewed as a contest between adversaries permits us to be more realistic about analysis in a number of ways. The inflated claims, periodically made in its behalf, may be rejected—along with the misplaced criticisms made in response. Questioning of decisions is turned into questioning of decisionmakers' judgments rather than the role of analysis. And analysis itself can be employed more effectively in clarifying the underpinnings of policies, thereby creating the potential for designing more effective ones. We should understand that analysis provides no formula for solving problems, no prescription for sensible policies. It cannot and should not be employed to "demonstrate" that one's own policies are so right and those of others, so wrong.

What analysis provides is an exercise in logical coherence, hopefully with knowledge of and respect for the underlying technical, economic, and organizational data. Coherence does not insure the "correctness" of policy. In fact, an incoherent policy will sometimes be closer to correct than a coherent one. But the incoherence itself scarcely makes a contribution. It is almost invariably a source of waste, and typically of policy muddles.

Analysis may make a contribution, but we should be very clear what it cannot do. It does not provide an instant cure for pigheadedness. In fact, it does not provide an instant cure for anything—not because of its theoretical deficiencies, but because it has to be employed by people and by organizations with divergent goals and views and with stringently limited information about actual conditions.

It is a mistake to identify analysis with the particular judgments, prejudices or arguable decisions of some of its major proponents. Especially is this so when analysis has been employed as a weapon of political conflict. The political process being what it is, it is hardly advisable to admit error in public; that would prove too costly. Human emotions being what they are, it is also unlikely that error will be admitted in private. This does not gainsay the value of analysis before policy commitments are made—or when they are being seriously reconsidered. What it does say is that we should avoid tying analysis to the personal proclivities of the particular individuals who were instrumental in introducing it into government. To do so may be flattering to the individuals. Some may even be inclined to treat their own attitudes and commitments as synonymous with analysis. It would be a serious error for others to accept this view.

Disciplined, orderly thought is the characterization given to analysis, but disciplined, orderly thought suggests certain traits: reflectiveness, self-criticism, and the willingness to reconsider past commitments without self-justification. However rarely or frequently encountered in the general human population, these are not traits characteristic of the action-oriented, incisive individuals who reach policymaking positions. Questioning and self-doubt lead to Hamlet-like decisionmakers.

Analysts themselves may be self-doubting, bemused by uncertainties, frighteningly candid, but different tactics have been required of the missionaries who have proselytized in behalf of analysis. I do not need to develop this point at any length. It should be plain, for example, that the actual decision to introduce analysis on a government-wide basis (as previously within the DOD) required an act of judgment and courage passing beyond the confines of analysis. Some analysts found the manner in which analytical procedures were instituted disquieting. This no doubt reflects a certain naivete on their part regarding political processes. But analysis was introduced rather suddenly. There was little advance preparation, little attempt to assess resource availability or calculate short-run costs. There was no "program definition phase." What occurred was that the political conditions were ripe,[1] and the opportunity was seized—for analysis.

I have perhaps belabored the distinction between analysis and judgment and the fact that the act of deciding occurs in the nonanalytical phase. These matters need to be emphasized right now. It is important that analytical procedures in the DOD or elsewhere *not* be identified with particular sets of policies, decisions, or individuals. If analysis comes to be confused with the idiosyncrasies of a few dominant personalities, there is some risk that it will disappear along with its original proponents. Its potential benefits for U.S. policy would then be lost for some time to come.

Admittedly there have been overstated claims, planted stories, and an impression generated among the *cognoscenti* of a new, scientific means for grinding out decisions. Admittedly the limitations appeared in the footnotes and not in the fanfare. But these are just the accoutrements of attention-getting. Analysis itself should scarcely be discarded on these grounds. Even if some decisionmakers or analysts have failed to display the mental elasticity that analysis in principle demands, this is only a reflection of the human condition. Why throw the baby out with the bathwater?

Payoffs

What is the baby? I seem to have devoted most of my attention to the reasons for refraining from that last half cheer for analysis, and virtually no attention to the reasons for the two and one-half cheers. In part this is due to the excellent set of papers and comments that the Subcommittee has published. Therein the potential benefits of program budgeting and analysis are fully presented. Lengthy reiterations of either the potential advantages or the accomplishments seem unnecessary. However, there are some points on which I should like to add a few words.

First, analysis has great value in turning debates over resource allocation toward the realities and away from simple statements of noble purpose. Analysis is not scientific method. Neither will it necessarily be objective in an organizational context. Yet, within the adversary relationship, analysis at least focuses the debate on what particular systems can accomplish and what numbers are required. The emphasis is on the real rather than the symbolic function of weapon systems. Disappointed as many in the Services have been with major policy decisions of the OSD, I believe most knowledgeable officers would agree that the new methods have been beneficial in this respect.

Second and closely related, analysis is oriented toward outputs rather than toward inputs. In this way expenditures can be tied to specific goals, and those expenditures which satisfy primarily the traditions or well-being of individual agencies are brought into question. There are difficulties with goal or output orientation, particularly since we so frequently lack complete understanding of the mechanism that ties inputs to outputs. But the orientation is correct. The government structure is subdivided into agencies that typically concentrate on inputs. Dams, warships, trees, post offices, bombers, nuclear power, supersonic transportation, and, I may add, research expenditures are often treated as ends in themselves—with little examination as to how these instruments serve public purposes. Conscious output orientation, with as much quantitative backup as possible, points in the right direction. It forces agencies to shift attention from their beloved instruments and to explain the goals they serve rather than the functions they perform—and this at a level more practical than the usual rhetoric of noble purpose.

Third, the attempt is made to design systems or policies with practical budgetary limits in mind. The time-honored gap between the planners and the budgeteers has been widely discussed, along with the difficulties it causes. There is little point in plans too costly to be implemented or systems too expensive to be bought in the requisite quantity—if some reduction in quality will provide a feasible and serviceable, if less ideal, posture. (Here we are discussing capabilities and postures which would be effective, if bought—keeping in mind that so many expensive proposals serve little purpose at all.)

Fourth, an attempt is made to take spillovers into account and to achieve better integration between the several Services and Commands. Once again, this is more easily said than done. For example, we are belatedly becoming aware of the spillovers and the integration problems between the strategic offensive force under Air Force management and the new Sentinel system under Army control. This indicates that the attempt to take spillovers into account has not been overwhelmingly successful, but the goal is a correct one. The nation would not wish to duplicate SAC's capabilities for SACEUR or the Polaris force for CINCSAC.

Fifth, the attempt is made to take into account the long-run cost implications of decisions. Perhaps, it is more appropriate to say . . . the attempt *should* be made. There has been a certain inconsistency on this account. The costs of some systems have been carefully investigated, before a choice is made. For other (preferred) systems this has not been the case. The Program Definition Phase was originally introduced to insure that technology was in hand and the long-run costs considered before force structure decisions were made. Yet, curiously, in the programmed forces for the '70s our strategic forces are scheduled to become increasingly dependent on MIRVed vehicles, even though the technology is not yet in hand and we have only an inkling of the ultimate costs. The appropriate review of alternatives and hedges did not take place. But this represents, not a criticism of the objective, but a plea for more consistency in its pursuit. It hardly negates the desirability of the careful weighing of alternatives with the long-run cost implications taken into account.

These attributes and precepts of analysis seem unexceptionable.

They are.

An appropriate inference is that many of the complaints couched in terms of "too much analysis" or "the errors of analysis" should be altered into "better and more consistent analysis." In this connection, an editor and friend recently suggested a paper on the impact of systems analysis: "not the general appraisals, we've had enough of that; tell us whether systems analysis has ever really been employed in the Department of Defense." An exaggeration perhaps, but as the MIRVing case suggests, analytic techniques have not been consistently applied.

Bernard Shaw observed somewhere that the only trouble with Christianity was that it had never really been tried. An epigram is at best a half truth, designed as someone has commented to irritate anyone who believes the other half. In DOD systems analysis has at least been tried. But there is an element in Shaw's remark that needs to be taken into account. In assessing the success of analysis, both the incomplete implementation and the resistance should be kept in mind.

Budgets

Military posture is determined in large measure by the total volume of resources the society is willing to divert from non-defense to defense uses. Yet, understanding the determinants of this resource flow presents a most perplexing problem. No good mechanism or rationale exists for deciding what diversion is proper. Some analysts have shied away from the problem arguing that the main objective should be the efficient employment of whatever resources are provided. A limited feel for appropriate diversion may be obtained by asking such questions as how much more is needed for defense than is needed for other purposes. In principle, senior policymakers may find it no harder to decide on allocation between damage limiting and urban renewal than between damage limiting and assured destruction. They will certainly find it no easier. For a number of practical reasons, they may find it far harder actually to bring about such a resource shift.

The amorphousness of this decision area combined with the repudiation of what were regarded as the rigidities of the Eisenhower years led to some bold words in 1961: there would be no *arbitrary* budget limits; in addition, every proposal would be examined on its own merits. These guidelines have since been regularly reasserted—with perhaps somewhat falling conviction. Originally they might be attributed to sheer enthusiasm; now they can only be taken as either propaganda or self-deception.

However, no matter the source, they will not stand up to *analysis*.

At any time there exists a rough political limit on defense expenditures. For members of this Subcommittee—in fact for any practicing politician—such an assertion will seem like a truism. Something like a consensus develops regarding proper levels of defense expenditures—and in the absence of external shocks this sum will not be substantially augmented. Of course, the *arbitrary* limit is always the *other fellow's*. One's own limit is only proximate and is wholly reasonable. Yet, defense expenditures do tend to become stabilized for years within rather narrow limits. Inevitably, new pressure for funds leads to the sacrifice of programs previously desirable on their own merits. That is as simple as arithmetic.

The only time that budget limits are not pressing (and more or less arbitrary) is when, as during the early Kennedy years, a political decision has been made that much more can be spent on defense. After a brief period of exuberance, the old constraints reappear. The decision does not have to be announced by the President or the Budget Bureau. The Secretary of Defense may get a feel for what is feasible, or he may be trusted to bring in a reasonable figure. But within a rather narrow range he will face a limit, which he may not transcend without either creating a minor fiscal crisis or straining his own credit with the President of the United States.

Save in the rare periods of budgetary relaxation, this, rightly or wrongly, is the way the system works. There is no point in kidding oneself. One may erect a facade intended to demonstrate that there are no arbitrary budget limits and each proposal is examined on its own merits. The pretense can be partially successful, but only because the criteria for choice are so imprecise. Standards can be made increasingly stringent, yet no one can prove how large was the role of budgetary pressures.

Nonetheless, no one should be deceived. What happens is that various alternatives and hedges are discarded; programs become less pressing and are stretched out. The practices are well-known from the bad, old meat-axe days. Under budgetary pressure (arbitrary or not) it is truly remarkable how many options one discovers one can do without. Multiple options just become less multiple. Before uncertainties are resolved, commitments are made and hedge programs are terminated. In the well-advertised adversary relationship, the negotiator-analysts become much harder to persuade. If they are not directly instructed, *they know*.

These are not hypothetical possibilities. With the intensification of budgetary pressures stemming from the Vietnamese war, there has, for example, been a wholesale slaughter of programs in the strategic area. It is important not to be misled regarding the critical role of budgetary pressures—and thus come to believe that so many programs, previously regarded as meritworthy, have suddenly lost their merit. Otherwise, we might gradually come to believe that we are doing far better than is actually the case. One should remain aware that the decimation of a program has long-run postural implications. That is, after all, the message that PPB attempts to convey.

These are elementary propositions. I do not dwell on certain theoretical problems and inconsistencies bearing on the relationship of overall defense spending to the optimality of programs. Suffice it to say that the *quality* of what one buys depends upon how much one wants to spend. This connection between level of demand and cost/effectiveness creates a dilemma in that *neither* the character of the programs nor the size of the budget can be determined initially. But that is a theoretical nicety, the direct consequences of which may not be of major importance.

The vital point is the way in which budgetary limits may control force posture and therefore strategy. Shifting sands seems the best way to characterize the strategic rationales of recent years. In 1961 the suicidal implications of massive retaliation were underscored: the United States would be faced with a choice between humiliation or holocaust. Interest then developed in damage-limiting and coercion. But there has been little willingness to invest money in either. Since 1965 the merits of Assured Destruction have been emphasized —with little attention paid to the suicidal implications found so distressing in prior years. The principal rationale for the current emphasis on Assured Destruction reflects certain recently-developed notions of arms control. It clearly falls within the province of the decisionmakers to adopt a strategy of measured response to any Soviet buildup with the long-term objective of preserving U.S. Assured Destruction capabilities. One should note, however, that to accept this particular guide to action implies that the buildup of the Minuteman force in 1961–62 was a mistake. These newer arms control criteria may be the preferred ones, but they rest on the judgments and intuitions of the decisionmakers. They certainly do not emerge by themselves from analysis.

May one infer that the oscillations in strategy have something to do with budget limits, or in this case something more specific: a preconception regarding how much this nation should spend on the strategic forces? I find the conclusion irresistible. The evidence antedates the current phase-down in the face of the Soviet buildup. Once again, these lie within the decisionmaker's prerogatives, but particular beliefs regarding budget limits or the "adequacy" of specific strategies should not be attributed to, much less blamed on, analysis.

A Useful if Oversold Tool

Whatever resources are made available to defense (or any other mission), choices will have to be made.

Allocative decisions inevitably are painful; many claimants will be sorely disappointed.

Few will find fault with their own proposals, almost all with the machinery for selection.

Any procedures for allocation will be criticized—even in a hypothetical case in which the conceptual basis is unarguable and no errors are made. Analysis provides the backup for a selective process. What does it contribute? How does it compare with real-world alternatives—not with mythical alternatives in which all claimants get their requests and no one is disappointed?

It has been emphasized that analysis cannot determine the appropriate strategy. It can shed light on costs and tradeoffs. But the choice to press arms control or arms competition or to rely on tactical nuclears or nuclear firebreaks must be determined by the decisionmaker sustained primarily by hope, conviction, and prayer. Even if a decision could be demonstrated as correct at a given moment in time, there is the certainty that objectives will change over time. For these higher level problems analysis is an aid, but a limited aid. The toughest problems, dominated as they are by uncertainties and by differences in goals, do not yield to analysis.

Happily many problems are more mundane and more tractable. Where analysis has proved its highest value is in uncovering cases of gross waste: points at which substantial expenditures may contribute little to any stated objective. It might be thought that a problem of diminishing returns exists for analysis in that the cases of gross misuse of resources are likely to be uncovered at an early stage. Thus, as the opportunity for major savings through elimination of irrational forms of waste theoretically recedes, analysis would be forced into the more ambiguous areas in which strategic choices become intimately involved. In some cases, where information is readily available and objectives and conditions relatively unchanging, this could prove to be true. The very success of analysis would then undermine near-term expectations of additional returns. However, in defense this turns out to be irrelevant, since the problems are so volatile and information so difficult to unearth.

To say that analysis works best in cases of gross waste should not be taken to imply that analysis accomplishes little. The simple cases involving so-called dominant solutions may involve billions of dollars. The volume of government resources that may be lavished on the care and feeding of white elephants is simply staggering.

Here we have "quantified common sense" in its most direct form. In bureaucracies, units at all levels are concerned with organizational health. Rather than making the hard choices, the tendency is strong to maintain morale by paying off all parties. Analysis provides a means for coping with this problem. The big issues may not be directly involved, though they are likely to be dragged in by the proponents of particular programs.

Should the assessment of analysis be much influenced by the annoyance felt by those whose proposals have failed the tests? Certainly not in the general case. No more than should the decisionmakers be permitted to hide their judgments behind the camouflage of analysis, should the patrons of doubtful proposals be encouraged to argue that acceptance would and should have come—if *only* analysis had not been employed. Budgets are limited and hard choices must be made. If nobody were annoyed analysis would not be doing its job—of questioning both routinized practices and blue-sky propositions. Disappointment is unavoidable. The question is not the existence of annoyance, but to strive to annoy in the right way and for the right reasons.

In this light it may be desirable to examine the issue of the generalist versus the specialist which has been touched upon in the Hearings. In the nature of things specialists become committed to particulars: a piece of hardware, a technological criterion, a disciplinary blind spot. It is a case of suboptimization run wild. Proponents of specific capabilities or gadgets tend to become monomaniacs. In a sense that is the way they should be: totally dedicated to their tasks. But one does not turn to them for detached judgments. There is no substitute for the *informed* generalist. There is a recognizable risk that the superficiality of the generalist may match the monomania of the specialist.

However, that need not be the case. Although the generalist's knowledge cannot match that of the specialist in detail, analysis can once again play a useful role, by permitting the organization for the generalist of more specialized information than he alone could master.

How does this relate to the limits of the analyst's role? Two distinctions should be kept in mind: that between the technical specialist and the analytical generalist and that between the analyst and the decisionmaker. The analyst's tools are not circumscribed by discipline or even by subject matter. But general tools are not immediately convertible into broad policies. Many analysts are, in some sense, specialists in the use of general tools. Being a good analytical generalist does not necessarily imply possession of such additional qualities as breadth, judgment, and political attunement. These latter qualities are what many have in mind when they speak of the generalist as policymaker.

Conclusion

In closing I should like to underscore three points.

First, the position of the decisionmaker employing analysis is somewhat ambiguous. For tactical purposes this ambiguity may be deliberately augmented. Intermittently he may choose to stress *analysis* or *judgment,* and to shift hats according to the tactical requirements of the moment. His policy judgments may be obscured or defended by cryptic references to detailed analyses which allegedly force the policy conclusions. On the other hand, if any limitations or inadequacies in the analyses should come to light, these can be waved away with the reminder that all issues are ultimately matters for the decisionmaker's judgment.

Moreover, the pattern is in reality far more complicated than the standard exposition in which the analyst produces an *objective* study, and the decisionmaker's judgment enters at a later stage erected on the foundation of these objective results. That makes the analytical and judgmental stages seem clean-cut. Few studies are that pure. The decisionmaker's judgments quite typically are dumped in at an early stage in the form of guidance, assumptions, and terms of reference. The more political a study, the less likely is it to be pure. In fact, the process can be (and has been) far more corrupted, when questionable (phony) numbers are introduced. Since judgment and analysis are thoroughly intertwined in all but a few studies, the attempt of decisionmakers to shift roles by referring to fundamental analyses should be treated with some skepticism. The decisionmaker should not be permitted to escape the full burden of responsibility by the invocation of analysis.

The temptation for those who have introduced analytical techniques into the government to treat their own positions or careers as identical with analysis is understandable. No outsider should yield to the same temptation. The roles and even the temperaments of decisionmaker and analyst are quite distinct. The confusion tends to disguise the heavy personal burden borne by the decisionmaker. More important, if analysis is treated as synonymous with particular decisions or personalities, there is a risk that it will be throttled or abandoned after their departure. From the standpoint of public policy this would be a major loss.

Second, we should avoid the erroneous belief that the performance or potential power of analysis will be uniform in all contexts. If a town is considering building a bridge, a number of difficult analytical problems must be addressed: does demand warrant construction, where should the bridge be built, what should be its capacity, and so on. But once these questions are resolved the engineer falls back on a solid technical base. By contrast, for such goals as deterrence, assured destruction, controlled nuclear warfare, damage limiting, to say nothing of welfare benefits, we fall back, not on a firm technical base, but on what may be scientific mush. The distinction is not always appreciated. The difficulty is sometimes dealt with by referring euphemistically to *the model problem*. But our ability to formulate models depends upon our knowledge of the mechanics of the real world. For many problems our knowledge is meager, and the proffered models are misleading or downright erroneous. The lack of good models in many problem areas simultaneously limits the power of analysis, while increasing the burden placed on judgment. In treating analysis as a uniformly efficient problem-solving technique, the variability of analysis, which reflects the variability of the knowledge base, is ignored.

Though analysis is a powerful tool, specific analyses vary greatly in quality. Some are little more than trash. But we need to discriminate, rather than to reject analysis *in toto*. At the present time there is some risk that we will do the latter. In an address some years ago Secretary Enthoven observed: "My general impression is that the art of systems analysis is in about the same stage now as medicine during the latter half of the 19th century; that is, it has just reached the point at which it can do more good than harm." That was a frank and realistic, if somewhat pessimistic, assessment of the state of the *art*. Scientifically speaking, there are numerous blind spots in medicine. Yet, most of us ultimately are inclined to accept the doctor's diagnosis, if not his advice. Quite plainly at the present time Congress and the public are having second thoughts regarding how much trust to put in systems analysis. No doubt it is necessary to develop a greater ability to discriminate. Nonetheless, I suggest that policy will benefit substantially from the analysts' diagnoses.

Third, there is little doubt that analysis has been oversold. That strikes me as a rather standard result in matters political. But the reaction against the overselling could be more costly than the overselling itself. Analysis is a powerful instrument: with it our batting average has been far higher than without it. Analysis is also an adaptable instrument. The McNamara regime has in many respects been a highly personalized one. Its performance should not be taken as defining the limits of this flexible tool. Admittedly, analyses vary substantially in quality. Each should be taken with a large grain of salt. On the other hand, if one does not demand too much of it, analysis will prove to be a most serviceable instrument.

NOTES

1. This episode suggests why the politician in his role may find analysis both incomplete and frustrating. Analysis deals in a rather abstract way with resource usage and efficient allocations. It does not deal with the attitudinal issues of support-generation, coalition-gathering or with timing which are so important in the political context.

WEAPONS RESEARCH AND DEVELOPMENT

21.

Charles L. Schultze: The Fiscal Dividend after Vietnam: Military versus Civilian Spending

Allocations for the military budget have an impact on resources available for domestic national priorities for many years to come. One hope—for a fiscal dividend from the reduced Vietnam expenditures—has been dashed due largely to many continuing military and nonmilitary programs. In the following selection Charles Schultze examines the basic factors that contribute to rising military budgets, including the impact of technology, planning that is based on a "greater than expected threat," "modernization inflation," and the fact that some of the fundamental decisions affecting the military budget are seldom subject to public debate or outside review. He calls upon Congress to focus its debate on the basic priorities and choices facing the nation by examining the assumptions underlying the military budget.

Formerly Director of the Bureau of the Budget, Charles Schultze is now Senior Fellow at the Brookings Institution.

M r. Chairman, members of the subcommittee: The subcommittee's decision to hold hearings on the military budget and national economic priorities is not only welcome but timely. Over the next several years, the Executive and the Congress will be faced with a series of basic decisions on military programs and weapons systems, whose outcome will largely determine not only the nation's security and its military posture, but also the resources available to meet urgent domestic needs. It would be most unfortunate if these decisions were made piecemeal, without reference to their effect on non-military goals and priorities. Moreover, any one year's decisions on military programs—and, in fact, on many elements of the civilian budget—cast long, and usually wedge-shaped shadows into the future. Their cost in the initial budget year is often only a small fraction of the costs incurred in succeeding years.

For these reasons there are two major prerequisites to informal discussion and decision about military budgets:

Charles L. Schultze, "The Fiscal Dividend after Vietnam: Military versus Civilian Spending," in *The Military Budget and National Economic Priorities,* Hearings, Subcommittee on Economy in Government of the Joint Economic Committee, 91st Congress, 1st session (1969), pp. 57–70.

First, the benefits and costs of proposed military programs cannot be viewed in isolation. They must be related to and measured against those other national priorities, which, in the context of limited resources, their adoption must necessarily sacrifice.

Second, the analysis of priorities must be placed in a longer-term context than the annual budget, since annual decisions—particularly with respect to large military forces or weapons systems—usually involve the use of scarce national resources, and therefore affect other national priorities, well into the future.

I might also add, parenthetically, that a review of military budgets in the context of a long-run evaluation of national priorities can directly serve the interests of national security itself. In the past year there has sprung up a widespread skepticism about the need, effectiveness, and efficiency of many components of the defense budget. This is a healthy development. But it must be harnessed and focused. In particular it must not be allowed to become a "knee-jerk" reaction, such that any proposed new military program is automatically attacked as unneeded or ineffective. We still live in a dangerous world. Effective and efficient provisions for the national security should rightfully be given a high priority. I believe that a proper balancing of military and civilian programs can best be achieved by a careful and *explicit* public discussion and evaluation of relative priorities in a long-term budgetary context. Neither the extreme which automatically stamps approval on anything carrying the national security label, nor its opposite which views any and all military spending as an unwarranted waste of national resources, has much to recommend it as a responsible attitude.

In this context I should like to discuss with the Committee three major aspects of the problem of national priorities:

A five-year summary projection of federal budgetary resources and the major claims on those resources.

A more detailed examination of the basic factors which are likely to determine the military component of those budget claims.

Finally, some tentative suggestions for improving the process by which defense budget decisions are made, designed particularly to bring into play an explicit consideration and balancing of national priorities, both military and civilian.

I. The Budgetary Framework

By definition, the concept of "priorities" involves the problem of choice. If, as a nation, we could have everything we wanted, if there were no constraints on achieving our goals, the problems of priorities would not arise. But once we recognize that we face limits or constraints, that we cannot simultaneously satisfy all the legitimate objectives which we might set for ourselves, then the necessity for *choice* arises.

There are various kinds of constraints. There is probably some limit to the public "energy" of a nation. Psychologically, the nation and its leaders cannot enthusiastically pursue a very large number of energy-consuming goals at the same time. The psychic cost is too high. Sometimes we face limits imposed by the scarcity of very specific resources. What we can do quickly, for example, to improve the availability of high quality medical care is limited in the short run by the scarcity of trained medical personnel. But the most pervasive limit to the achievement of our goals, even in a wealthy country like the United States, is the general availability of productive resources. If the economy is producing at full employment, additions to public spending require subtractions from private spending—and vice-versa.

From the point of view of public spending, the practical constraints we face are even tighter than this. I think it is a safe political prediction that during the next five years or so, and particularly once a settlement in Vietnam is reached, federal tax rates are unlikely to be raised. Reforms may and should occur. But the overall yield of the system is unlikely to be increased. If this judgment is correct, then the limits of budgetary resources available are given by the revenue yield of the existing tax system—a yield which will, of course, grow as the economy grows. And even those who believe that the needs of the public sector are so urgent as to warrant an increase in federal tax rates are likely to agree that an examination of long-term budgetary prospects should at least start with a projection of revenue yields under current tax laws.

Assuming for purposes of projection an initial constraint imposed by existing tax laws, it is then possible to determine roughly how large the budgetary resources available to the nation will be over the next five years, for expanding existing high-priority public programs, for creating new ones, for sharing revenues with the states or for reducing federal taxes. The magnitude of the budgetary resources available for these purposes—the "fiscal dividend"—will depend on *four basic factors:*

1. The growth in Federal revenues yielded by a *growing economy;*

2. The budgetary savings which could be realized from a *ceasefire and troop withdrawal in Vietnam;*

(These two factors, of course, *add* to fiscal dividend available for the purposes listed above. The next two *reduce* the fiscal dividend.)

3. The "built-in" or "automatic" increase in *civilian expenditures* which accompanies growing population and income. (This expenditure growth must be deducted before arriving at the net budgetary resources available for discretionary use.)

4. The probable increase in non-Vietnam military expenditures implicit in currently approved military programs and postures. (This increase must also be deducted in reaching the net fiscal dividend which can be devoted to domestic needs. Needless to say, of course, changes in military programs, policies, and force levels can affect this total.)

The net result of these four factors—the revenue yield from economic growth, the savings from a Vietnam ceasefire, the built-in growth of civilian expenditures, and the probable growth of the non-Vietnam military budget—measures the fiscal dividend available for meeting domestic needs.

Let me summarize the likely magnitude of each of these four budgetary elements five years from now. More precisely, I will attempt to project them from fiscal 1969 to fiscal 1974.

If we assume that economic growth continues at a healthy but not excessive pace, and that—optimistically perhaps—the annual rate of inflation is gradually scaled down from the current 4½ percent to a more tolerable 2 percent, *Federal revenues should grow each year by $15 to $18 billion*. This is, of course, a cumulative growth, so that by the end of five years federal revenues should be about $85 billion higher than they are now. It is highly likely, however, that once the war in Vietnam is over, or substantially scaled down, the present 10 percent surcharge will be allowed to expire. The yield of the surcharge five years from now would be some $15 billion. This must therefore be subtracted from the $85 billion revenue increase, leaving a net $70 billion growth in federal revenue between now and fiscal 1974.

A second potential addition to budgetary resources is the expenditure saving which could be realized upon a *Vietnam ceasefire and troop withdrawal* and a return to the pre-Vietnam level of armed forces. The current budget estimates the cost of U.S. military operations in Vietnam at about $26 billion. As I have pointed out elsewhere, however, this figure overstates somewhat the *additional* costs we are incurring in Vietnam. Even if our naval task forces were not deployed in the Gulf of Tonkin, they would be steaming on practice missions somewhere else. Hence some of the costs of those forces would be incurred even in the absence of fighting in Vietnam. Similarly our B-52 squadrons, if not engaged in bombing missions, would be operating on training exercises. And the same is true for other activites. As best I can judge, the truly incremental, or additional, costs of Vietnam—which would disappear if a ceasefire and a return to pre-Vietnam force levels occurred—amount to about $20 billion. These savings would not, of course, be available the day after a ceasefire occurred, but would gradually be realized as withdrawal and demobilization occurred.

With perhaps 18 months to two years after a ceasefire, this $20 billion in budgetary savings would be available to add to the $70 billion net growth in budget revenues—a total gross addition of $90 billion to resources available for other public purposes.

From this $90 billion, we must, however, make several deductions before arriving at a net fiscal dividend freely available for domestic use.

We can expect a fairly significant built-in growth in federal civilian expenditures over the next five years. As the GI's come home from Vietnam, educational expenditures under the GI bill of rights will naturally increase. Even if interest rates rise no further, the roll-over of older debt into new issues will increase interest payments. Expenditures under the Medicaid program will rise, although at a slower pace than in the last few years. A larger population and income almost automatically lead to higher public expenditures in many areas: more people visit national parks and the Park Service's outlays grow; more tax returns are filed and the Internal Revenue Service must expand to handle them; as airplane travel increases, federal expenditures on air traffic safety and control rise; and so on down the list. Social security benefits will almost certainly rise sharply if past practice is followed under which the Congress tends to raise benefit levels more or less in line with payroll revenues. For all of these reasons, I believe one must allow for a "built-in" growth of federal expenditures by some $35 billion over the next five years. Subtracting this $35 billion from the $90 billion additional resources calculated above leaves $55 billion for the fiscal dividend.

But yet another deduction must be made. Barring major change in defense policies, military spending for *non-Vietnam* purposes will surely rise significantly over the next five years. There are *five* major factors working towards an increase in military expenditures.

1. *Military and civilian pay increases.* There are now $3\frac{1}{2}$ million men in the Armed Forces. In addition some 1.3 million civilian employees, about 45 percent of the federal total, work for the Department of Defense. As wages and salaries in the private sector of the economy rise, the pay scales of these military and civilian employees of the Defense Department must also be raised. The military and civilian pay raise scheduled for this coming July 1 will add some $2.3 billion to the Defense budget. If we assume, conservatively, that in succeeding years private wage and salary increases average 4 to $4\frac{1}{2}$ percent per year, the payroll costs of the Pentagon will rise by about $1\frac{1}{2}$ billion each year.

2. *The future expenditure consequences of already approved weapons systems.* A large number of new and complex weapons systems have been approved as part of our defense posture; the bulk of the spending on which has not yet occurred.[1] Some major examples are:

The Minuteman III missile, with MIRV's; cost, $4\frac{1}{2}$ billion.

The Poseidon missile, with MIRV's; cost, including conversion of 31 Polaris subs, $5\frac{1}{2}$–$6\frac{1}{2}$ billion.

The Safeguard ABM system, with a currently estimated cost, including nuclear warheads, of some $8 billion, plus hundreds of millions per year in operating costs.

The F-14 Navy fighter plane in three versions; the 1970 posture statement indicates that the entire F-4 force of the Navy and Marine Corps may be replaced by the F-14. If so, the total investment and operational cost of this system over a 10-year period should be well in excess of $20 billion.

A new F-15 air-to-air combat fighter for the Air Force.

Three nuclear attack carriers at a currently estimated cost of $525–$540 million each.

62 new naval escort vessels, at an investment cost of nearly $5 billion.

A number of new amphibious assault ships.

A new Navy anti-submarine plane, the VSX, at a cost of $2–$2\frac{1}{2}$ billion.

A new continental air-defense system, including a complex "lookdown" radar and an extensive modification program for the current F-106 interceptor.

These do not exhaust the list of new weapon systems already a part of the approved defense posture. But they do give some idea of the magnitude of the expenditures involved.

3. *Cost escalation.* The weapons systems costs given for each of the systems listed above represent current estimates. But, as this Committee is well aware, past experience indicates that final costs of complex military hardware systems almost always exceed original estimates.

A study of missile systems in the 1950's and early 1960's revealed that the average unit cost of missiles was 3.2 times the original estimates.

The nuclear carrier Nimitz, now under construction, was estimated in 1967 to cost $440 million. One year later the estimate was raised to $536 million. No new estimates have been released but given the rapidly rising cost of shipbuilding, it is almost certain that this latter figure will be exceeded.

In January 1968 the Defense Department proposed a plan for building 68 naval escort vessels at a total cost of $3 billion. In January 1969 the estimated costs of that program had risen to $5 billion.

The cost of modernizing the carrier Midway was originally given as $88 million, and the work was scheduled to be completed in 24 months. In January 1969 the cost estimate was double, to $178 million, and the time estimate also doubled, to 48 months.

The Air Force's manned orbiting laboratory (the MOL) was originally announced by President Johnson at a cost of $1.5 billion. The latest estimate was $3 billion.

In many cases the rising unit costs of these systems forces reevaluation of the program and a reduction in the number purchased. The F-111 program is a classic case in point. Consequently the *aggregate* costs of the procurement budget do not rise by the same percentage as the inflation in *unit* costs. Nevertheless, cost escalation does tend to drive the total military budget upward.

4. *Weapons systems under development, advocated by the Joint Chiefs of Staff, but not yet approved for deployment.* In addition to weapons systems already approved, there are a large number of systems, currently under development, which are being advocated for deployment by the Joint Chiefs. Among these items are:

The AMSA—advanced manual strategic aircraft—a supersonic intercontinental bomber designed as a follow-on to the B-52. President Johnson's proposed 1970 budget requested $77 million for advanced developments. Secretary Laird proposed an additional $23 million to shorten design time and start full-scale engineering development. This $10 million will be supplemented by $35 million of carryover funds. The investment costs of the AMSA, if procurement decision is made, are difficult to estimate, but it is hard to see how they could be less than $10 billion.

The new main battle tank is now in production engineering. Depending on the number purchased, a procurement decision will involve investment costs of $1 to $1½ billion.

A new advanced strategic missile in super-hard silos is being advocated by the Air Force.

A new attack aircraft, the AX, is under development for the Air Force.

The Navy is proposing a major shipbuilding and reconversion program to replace or modernize large numbers of its older vessels.

A new continental air defense interceptor, the F-12, is being advocated by the Air Force.

A new underwater strategic missile system (the ULMS) is under development for the Navy.

In the normal course of events, not all of these new systems will be adopted in the next five years. But, in the normal course of events, some will be.

5. *Mutual escalation of the strategic arms race.* The United States is currently planning to equip its Minuteman III and Poseidon missiles with multiple independently targeted reentry vehicles (MIRV's). MIRV testing has been underway for some time. The original purpose of MIRV's was as a hedge against the development of a large-scale Soviet ABM system, in order to preserve our second-strike retaliatory capability in the face of such Soviet development. Recently, however, Pentagon officials have indicated that we are designing into our MIRV's the accuracy needed to destroy enemy missile sites—an accuracy much greater than needed to preserve the city-destroying capability of a retaliatory force. Secretary of Defense Laird, in recent testimony before the Armed Services Committee for example, asked for additional funds to "improve significantly the accuracy of the Poseidon missile, thus enhancing its effectiveness against hard targets."

Putting MIRV's with hard-target killing capabilities on Poseidon alone will equip the U.S. strategic forces with 4,000–5,000 missile-destroying warheads. Viewed from Soviet eyes the United States appears to be acquiring the capability of knocking out Soviet land-based missile force in a first strike. It might be argued that the difficulties of attaining a hard-target killing capability on our MIRV's are so great that the objective will not be realized for many years, if ever. But without attempting to evaluate this observation, let me point out that what counts in the arms race is the Soviet reactions to our announcements. And, like our own conservative planners, the Soviets must assume that we will attain our objectives.

The United States has announced that in answer to the 200-Soviet SS-9's—which may be expanded and MIRV'd into 800 to 1,000 hard-target warheads—it will build an ABM system. What must the Soviet reaction be when faced with the potential of 4,000–5,000 hard-target killers on Poseidon alone? As they respond—perhaps with an even larger submarine missile force than now planned, or by developing mobile land-based missiles—we may be forced into still another round of strategic arms building. This may not occur. But its likelihood should not be completely discounted.

I have seen several arguments as to why a new round in the strategic arms race will not be touched off by current U.S. policy. I think they are dubious at best. One argument notes that the U.S. development of MIRV's and ABM is being made against a "greater-than-expected" threat—i.e., a Soviet threat larger than current intelligence estimates project. Hence, runs the argument, should the Soviets respond to our new developments, this response has already been taken into account in the "greater-than-expected" threat against which we are currently building. Consequently, we would not have to respond ourselves with a still further strategic arms buildup. But this misses the very nature of "greater-than-expected" threat planning. Once the Soviets proceed to deploy a force which approaches the *current* "greater-than-expected" threat, then by definition a *new* "greater-than-expected" threat is generated, and additional strategic arms expenditures are undertaken to meet it. This is the heart of the dynamics of a strategic arms race.

Another argument is often used to discount the mutual escalation threat posed by MIRV's. Multiple warheads, it is argued, make an effective large area ABM practically impossible to attain. Hence, deployment of MIRV's destroys the rationale for a large-scale, city defense, ABM. So long as MIRV's do not have the accuracy to destroy enemy missiles on the ground, this argument might indeed have some validity. But once they acquire hard-target killing capability —or the Soviets think they have such capability—they are no longer simply a means of penetrating ABM's and preserving the second-strike retaliatory force; they provide, in the eyes of the enemy, a first-strike capability, against which he must respond.

Given these various factors tending to drive up the cost of the non-Vietnam components of the military budget, by how much are annual defense expenditures, outside of Vietnam, likely to rise over the next five years? Obviously, there is no pat answer to this question. Any projection must be highly tentative. But assuming the increase in civilian and military pay mentioned earlier, calculating the annual costs of the approved weapons systems listed above, and allowing for only modest cost escalation in individual systems, it seems likely that on these three grounds alone non-Vietnam military expenditures by 1974 will be almost $20 billion higher than they are in fiscal 1969. They will, in other words, almost fully absorb the savings realizable from a cessation of hostilities in Vietnam. And this calculation leaves *out* of account the possibility of more than modest cost escalation, the adoption of large new systems like the AMSA, and a further round of strategic arms escalation.

I might note that the 1970 defense budget—even after the reductions announced by Secretary Laird—already incorporates the first round of this increase. From fiscal 1969 to fiscal 1970, the *non-Vietnam* part of the defense budget will rise by $5½ to $6 billion, after allocating to it the Pentagon's share of the forthcoming military and civilian pay raise. In one year, almost 30 percent of this $20 billion rise will apparently take place.

Starting out with an additional $70 billion in federal revenues over the next five years, plus a $20 billion saving from a ceasefire in Vietnam, we earlier calculated a $90 billion gross increase in federal budgetary resources. From this we subtracted the $35 billion growth of "built-in" civilian expenditures and now we must further subtract a $20 billion rise in non-Vietnam military outlays, leaving a net fiscal dividend in fiscal 1974 of something in the order of $35 billion, available for discretionary use in meeting high priority public needs or additional tax cuts. That $35 billion, in turn, is itself subject to further reduction should major new weapons systems be approved, or should another round in the strategic arms race take place.

Let me make it clear, of course, that there is nothing inevitable about this projection of military expenditures. Some of the weapons systems I listed are in early stages of procurement. Other areas in the military budget can be analyzed, reviewed, and if warranted, reduced as a budgetary offset to the new systems. Hopefully, disarmament negotiations if held quickly, may prevent mutual strategic escalation. My projection assumes that no changes in basic policies, postures, and force levels occur. It is obviously the whole purpose of these hearings to examine that assumption, in the context of other national priorities.

II. The Basic Factors Behind Rising Military Budgets

While the budget projection summarized above discusses some of the specific weapons systems which are likely to cause the defense budget to expand sharply in the next five years, it does not address itself to the underlying forces which threaten to produce this outcome. In the first half of the 1960's the military budget ran at about $50 billion per year. With those funds not only were U.S. strategic and conventional forces maintained, they were sharply improved in both quantity and quality. Both land- and sea-based missile forces were rapidly increased. Similarly dramatic increases in the general purpose forces were undertaken. Fourteen Army divisions, undermanned, trained primarily for tactical nuclear war, and short of combat consumables were expanded to over $16\frac{1}{3}$ divisions, most of them fully manned. Equipment and logistic supply lines were sharply increased. The 16 tactical air wings were expanded to 21. Sea-lift and air-lift capability were radically improved.

In short, on $50 billion per year in the early 1960's, it appeared to be possible to buy not only the maintenance of a given military capability, but a sharp increase in that capability. By the early 1970's, taking into account general price inflation in the economy plus military and civilian pay increases, it would take $63–$65 billion to maintain the same purchasing power as $50 billion in 1965. Yet, as I have indicated earlier, even on conservative assumptions the non-Vietnam military budget is likely to approach $80 billion by fiscal 1974—$15 to $17 billion more than the amount needed to duplicate the general purchasing power the pre-Vietnam budget had—a budget which already was providing significant increases in military strength. Why this escalation? What forces are at work?

While there are a number of reasons for this increase, I would suggest that four are particularly important.

First, the impact of modern technology on the strategic nuclear forces. During most of the 1960's the primary goal of our strategic nuclear forces was the preservation of an "assured destruction capacity"—the ability to absorb an enemy's first strike and retaliate devastatingly on his homeland. In turn this capability provided nuclear deterrence against a potential aggressor. In general this could be described as a stable situation, in part because of the technology involved. To mount a first strike, an aggressor would have to be assured that he could knock out all—or substantially all—of his opponent's missiles. Since missiles did not have 100 percent reliability and accuracy for this task, more than one attacking missile would have to be targeted on the enemy missile force. For every missile added by the "defender," the attacker would have to add more than one. Hence, it was easy to show that first-strike capability could not be attained, since the opposing side could counter and maintain his second-strike capability at a less-than-equal cost. And, of course, the existence of mobile submarine launched missiles made the stability of the system even greater.

But the development of MIRV's, and more critically the development of guidance systems which are designed to make them accurate enough to "kill" enemy missiles on the ground, changes this balance. Now a single attacking missile, with multiple warheads, can theoretically take out several enemy missiles. The advantage to the first attacker rises sharply. Strategic planners on both sides, projecting these developments into the future, react sharply in terms of the danger they perceive their own forces to be facing. Add to this the development of ABM, which—however initially deployed—raises fears in the minds of enemy planners that it can be extended to protect cities against his submarine launched missiles, and escalation of the strategic arms race becomes increasingly likely.

The impact of changing technology on strategic arms budgets, therefore, is one of the driving forces which changes the prospects of post-Vietnam military expenditures from what they might have seemed several years ago.

The second major factor in driving arms budgets up is the propensity of military planners to prepare against almost every conceivable contingency or risk. And this applies both to force level planning and to the design of individual weapons systems. Forces are built to cover possible, but very remote, contingencies. Individual weapons systems are crowded with electronic equipment and built with capabilities for dealing with a very wide range of possible situations, including some highly unlikely ones.

If military technology were standing still, this propensity to cover remote contingencies might lead to a large military budget, but not to a rapidly expanding one. As technology continually advances, however, two developments occur: (1) As we learn about new technology, we project it forward into the Soviet arsenal, thereby creating new potential contingencies to be covered by our own forces; (2) The new technology raises the possibility of designing weapons systems to guard against contingencies which it had not been possible to protect against previously.

Continually advancing technology and the risk aversion of military planners, therefore, combine to produce ever more complex and expensive weapons systems and ever more contingencies to guard against.

Let me give some examples.

According to Dr. John S. Foster, Jr., Deputy Director of Defense Research and Engineering in testimony before the Senate Armed Services Committee last year, the Poseidon missile system was originally designed to penetrate the Soviet TALLINN system—a system originally thought to be a widespread ABM defense. When this system turned out to be an anti-aircraft system, the deployment decision on the Poseidon was not revised. Rather it was continued as a hedge against a number of other possible Soviet developments, including in Dr. Foster's words the possibility that "the Minuteman force could be threatened by either rapid deployment of the current Soviet SS-9 or by MIRV'ing their existing missiles and improving accuracy."

Once the Soviets began to deploy the SS-9 in apparently larger numbers than earlier estimated, however, this gave rise to the decision to deploy a "Safeguard" ABM defense of Minutemen sites.

In short the sequence went like this: (1) The Poseidon deployment decision was made against a threat which never materialized; (2) despite the disappearance of the threat against which it was designed, the Poseidon was continued, presumably as a hedge against other potential threats, including faster-than expected Soviet deployment of the SS-9; (3) but now a decision has been made to hedge against the SS-9 by building a "hard-point" ABM—so we are presumably building the Poseidon as hedge against a number of possible Soviet threats, including the SS-9, and then building a hedge on top of that; (4) finally, new technology has made it possible to design a hard target killing accuracy into the Poseidon—an accuracy not needed to preserve our second strike capability against either the SS-9 or a Soviet ABM. The technology is available—why not use it! Yet the existence of that capability may well force a major Soviet response.

Another example of hedging against remote threats is the currently planned program of improvements in our continental air defense system. The existing SAGE system cost $18 billion to install but is apparently not very effective against low-altitude bomber attack. Although the Soviets have no sizable intercontinental bomber threat, the decision has been made to go ahead with major investments in a new air defense system. The major reasons given for this decision are these: to deter the Soviets from deciding to reverse their long-standing policy and develop a new bomber; to guard against one-way Kamikaze-type attacks by Soviet medium-range bombers; and to protect those of our missiles which would be withheld in a retaliatory strike. There is admittedly no direct threat to be covered. But a number of more remote threats are covered. And since we cannot defend our cities against Soviet missiles, it gives small comfort to have them protected against as yet non-existing bombers or Kamikaze attacks.

Another case in point is the new F-14 Navy aircraft. Both the F-111B and its successor, the initial version of the F-14, were designed to stand off from the carrier fleet and, with the complex Phoenix air-to-air missile, defend the fleet from a Soviet supersonic bomber plus missile threat, in the context of a major Soviet attack against our carrier forces. But as the Senate Defense Preparedness Subcommittee noted last year, this threat is "either limited or does not exist." Or as Chairman Mahon of the House Appropriations Committee noted, "The bomber threat against the fleet, as you know, has been predicted by Navy officials for some time. It has not, of course, developed to date."

The problem of what contingencies and risks are to be guarded against goes to the very heart of priority analysis. Primarily what we buy in the military budget is an attempt to protect the nation and its vital interests abroad from the danger and risks posed by hostile forces. We seek either to deter the hostile force from ever undertaking the particular action or if worst comes to worst, to ward off the action when it does occur. Similarly, in designing particular weapons systems, the degree of complexity and the performance requirements built into the systems depend in part on an evaluation of the various kinds of contingencies which the weapon is expected to face. Now there are almost an unlimited number of "threats" which can be conceived. The likelihood of their occurrence, however, ranges from a significant possibility to a very remote contingency. Moreover, the size of the forces and complexity of the weapons systems needed to guard against a particular set of threats depends upon whether the threats materialize simultaneously or not. If they do not occur simultaneously, then very often forces developed to meet one contingency can be deployed against another. But the probability of two or more remote contingencies occurring simultaneously is obviously even lower than either taken separately.

Clearly we cannot prepare against every conceivable contingency. Even with a defense budget twice the present $80 billion, we could not do that. The real question of priorities involves the balance to be struck between attempting to buy protection against the more remote contingencies and using those funds for domestic purposes. In any given case, this is not a judgment which can be assisted by drawing up dogmatic rules in advance. And, since it is a question of balancing priorities, it is not a question which can be answered solely on military grounds or with military expertise alone—although such expertise must form an essential component of the decision process.

For what it is worth, it is my own judgment that we generally have tended in the postwar period to tip the balance too strongly in favor of spending large sums in attempting to cover a wide range of remote contingencies. And, as I have pointed out, this tendency—combined with the relentless ability of modern technology to create new contingencies and new systems to combat them—threatens to produce sizable increases in the defense budget.

A third important factor which is responsible for driving up the size of defense budgets is "modernization inflation."[2] The weapons systems we now buy are vastly more costly than those we bought 10 or 20 years ago. The F-111A and the F-14A, for example, will cost 10 to 20 times what a tactical aircraft cost at the time of Korea. A small part of this increase is due to general inflation. But by far the largest part is due to the growing complexity and advanced performance of the weapons. In the case of tactical aircraft, speed, range, bomb load, accuracy of fire, loiter time, ability to locate targets, and other characteristics are many times greater than models one or two decades older. The same kinds of performance comparison can be drawn between modern missile destroyers and their older counterparts, and between modern carriers and their predecessors. We pay sharply increased costs to obtain sharply increased performance. Yet seldom if ever is this advance in "quality" used to justify a reduction in the *number* of planes or carriers or destroyers or tanks. If bomb carrying capacity and lethal effectiveness is doubled or tripled, then presumably a smaller number of new planes can do the same job as a larger number of old planes. But the numbers generally stay the same or increase. As a consequence, modernization inflation primarily causes a net increase in military budgets rather than providing—at least partially—a reasoned basis for maintaining military effectiveness while reducing the level of forces.

In some cases, of course—for example, Soviet fighter aircraft—rising enemy capabilities may reduce the possibility of substituting quality for quantity. But the same kind of argument is hard to adduce for such weapons as carriers or attack bombers.

The fourth, and perhaps most important, reason for increasing military budgets is the fact that some of the most fundamental decisions which determine the size of these budgets are seldom subjected to outside review and only occasionally discussed and debated in the public arena. This problem is most acute in the case of the budget for the nation's general purpose forces. The fundamental assumptions and objectives of the strategic nuclear forces are more generally known and debated. But the assumptions, objectives and concepts underlying the general purpose forces—which even in peacetime take up 60 percent of the defense budget—are scarcely known and discussed by the Congress and the public. Congress does examine and debate the wisdom and effectiveness of particular weapons systems—the TFX, the C-5A, etc. But choices of weapons systems form only a part of the complex of decisions which determine the budget for our general purpose forces.

Those decisions can conveniently be classified into four types:

1. What are the nation's *commitments* around the world? While our strategic nuclear forces are primarily designed to deter a direct attack on the United States, our general purpose forces have their primary justification in terms of protecting U.S. interests in other parts of the world. At the present time, we have commitments of one kind or another, to help defend some 40-odd nations around the world—19 of them on the periphery of the Soviet-Eastern European bloc and Communist China. Almost all of these commitments were made quite some time ago, but they are still in force. Unless we wish to rely solely on "massive retaliation" as a means of fulfilling our commitments, they do pose a fundamental "raison d'etre" for general purpose forces of some size.

2. Granted the existence of these commitments, against what sort of *contingencies* or *threats* do we build our peacetime forces? A number of examples will help illustrate this aspect of decision making:

Pre-Vietnam (and, barring changes in policy, presumably *post*-Vietnam), our general purpose forces were built to fight *simultaneously* a NATO war, a Red Chinese attack in S.E. Asia, and to handle a minor problem in the

Western Hemisphere, à la the Dominican Republic. Obviously the forces-in-being would not be sufficient, without further mobilization, to complete each of these tasks. But they were planned to handle simultaneously all of the three threats long enough to enable mobilization to take place if that should prove necessary.

The Navy is designed, among other tasks, to be capable of handling an all-out, non-nuclear, protracted war at sea with the Soviet Union.

The incremental costs of maintaining in-being a force to meet the Chinese attack contingency, probably amounts to about $5 billion per year. When in 1965 the nation decided to begin Federal aid to elementary and secondary education—which has subsequently been budgeted at less than $2 billion a year—a major national debate took place. To the best of my knowledge, there was no public comment or debate about the "Chinese contingency" decision. Yet the decision was not classified—it was publicly stated in the unclassified version of the Secretary of Defense's annual posture statement several years running. This is not to say that the decision was necessarily wrong. Rather, I want to stress that it has a very major impact on the defense budget, yet was not, so far as I know, debated or discussed by the Congress. This lack of debate cannot be laid at the door of the Pentagon, since the information was made available in the defense posture statement.

3. Granted the commitments and contingencies, what *force levels* are needed to meet those contingencies, and how are they to be based and deployed?

The Navy, for example, has 15 attack carrier task forces. The carrier forces are designed not merely to provide quick response, surge capability for air power, but to remain continually on station during a conflict. As a consequence, because of rotation, overhaul, crew-leave, and other considerations, one carrier on station generally requires two off-station as back-up. Thus for *five* carriers on station, we have *ten* back-up carriers. (The "on-station" to "back-up" ratio depends on the distance of the station from the carriers' base. The 2/1 is an average ratio.)

The pre-Vietnam Army comprised 16⅓ active divisions with eight ready reserve divisions. The 16⅓ division force is supported by a planned 23 tactical air wing (only 21 were in-being pre-Vietnam).

The Navy has eight anti-submarine carrier task forces.

Defense plans call for a fast amphibious assault capability, sufficient to land one division/air wing in the Pacific and ⅔ division/air wing in the Atlantic.

The force levels needed to meet our contingencies are, of course, significantly affected by the military decisions and capabilities of our allies. The U.S. situation in NATO, for example, is strongly affected by whether or not the divisions of our NATO allies are equipped with the combat consumables and rapid fire-power weapons enabling them to conduct a prolonged conventional war.

4. With what *weapons systems* should the forces be equipped? Such questions as nuclear versus conventional power for carrier and carrier escorts, the

F-111B versus the F-14, the extent to which the F-14 replaces all the Navy's F-4's, must, of course, be decided.

Let me hasten to point out that there is no *inexorable logic* tying one set of decisions in this litany to another. Do not think that once a decision has been made on commitments that the appropriate contingencies we must prepare against are obvious and need no outside review; or that once we have stipu‧ lated the contingencies that the necessary force levels are automatically determined and can be left solely to the military for decision; or that once force levels are given, decisions about appropriate weapons systems can be dismissed as self-evident. There is a great deal of slippage and room for judgment and priority debate in the connection between any two steps in the process.

Some examples might help:

There is no magic relationship between the decision to build for a "2½ war" contingency (NATO war, Red Chinese attack, and Western Hemisphere trouble) and the fact that the Navy has 15 attack carrier task forces. In the Washington Naval Disarmament Treaty of 1921, the U.S. Navy was allotted 15 capital ships. All during the nineteen twenties and thirties, the Navy had 15 battleships. Since 1951 (with temporary exception of a few years during the Korean war) it has had 15 attack carriers, the "modern" capital ship.[3] Missions and "contingencies" have changed sharply over the last 45 years. But this particular force level has not.

If one assumed, for example, that the Navy's carrier force should provide "surge" support to achieve quick air cover and tactical bombardment during an engagement, and then turned the job over to the tactical Air Force, the two-to-one ratio of back-up carriers to on-station carriers would not have to be maintained and the total force level could be reduced, even with the same contingencies. The wisdom or lack of wisdom in such a change would depend both upon a host of technical factors and upon a priority decision—does the additional "continuation" capability as opposed to "surge" capability buy advantages worth the resources devoted to it, on the order of $300–$400 million per year in operating and replacement costs per carrier task force.

Similar questions arise in other areas. Does the 16⅓ division Army peacetime force need 23 tactical air wings for support, or could it operate with the Marines' one-to-one ratio between air wings and divisions? Granted the 15 carrier task forces, must all of their F-4's be replaced by F-14's as the Navy is apparently planning.

In short there is a logical order of decisions—commitments to contingencies to force levels to weapons systems—but the links between them are by no means inflexible, and require continuing review and oversight.

As I mentioned earlier, I am impressed by the fact that the Congress tends to concentrate primarily upon debate about weapons systems to the exclusion of the other important elements of the general purpose component of the defense budget. Many of the elements involved in military budget decision making cannot, of course, be made subject to specific legislation—I find it hard to see how the Congress could, or should, legislate the particular contingencies against which the peacetime forces should be built. But the Congress is the nation's principal forum in which public debate can be focused on the basic priorities and choices facing the country. It can, if the proper information is available and the proper institutional framework created, critically but responsibly examine and debate *all* of the basic assumptions and concepts which underlie the military budget. And it can do so in the content of comparing priorities. The Congress can explicitly discuss whether the particular risks which a billion dollar force level or weapons systems proposal is designed to cover are serious enough in comparison with a billion dollars' worth of resources devoted to domestic needs to warrant going ahead. By so doing, the Congress as a whole can create the kind of understanding and political climate in which its own Armed Services and Appropriations Committee, the President, his Budget Bureau, and his Secretary of Defense can effectively review and control the military budget.

This brings me to my next point. The size and rapid increase in the defense budget is often blamed on the military-industrial complex. Sometimes it is also blamed on the fact that the Budget Bureau uses different procedures in reviewing the military budget than it does in the case of other agencies.

The uniformed Armed Services and large defense contractors clearly exist. Of necessity, and in fact quite rightly, they have views about and interests in military budget decisions. Yet I do not believe that the "problem" of military budgets is primarily attributable to the so-called military-industrial "complex." If defense contractors were all as disinterested in enlarging sales as local transit magnates, if retired military officers all went into selling soap and TV sets instead of missiles, if the Washington offices of defense contractors all were moved to the West Coast, if all this happened and nothing else, then I do not believe the military budget would be sharply lower than it now is. Primarily we have large military budgets because the American people, in the cold war environment of the nineteen fifties and sixties, have pretty much been willing to buy anything carrying the label "Needed for National Security." The political climate has, until recently, been such that, on fundamental matters, it was exceedingly difficult to challenge military judgments, and still avoid the stigma of playing fast and loose with the national security.

This is not a reflection on military officers as such. As a group they are well above average in competence and dedication. But in the interests of a balanced view of national priorities we need to get ourselves into a position where political leaders can view the expert recommendations of the military with the same independent judgment, decent respect, and healthy skepticism that they view the budgetary recommendations of such other experts as the Commissioner of Education, Surgeon General, and the Federal Manpower Administration.

I think the same approach can be taken with respect to the procedures used by the Budget Bureau to review the Budget of the Defense Department. In all other cases, agency budget requests are submitted to the Bureau, which reviews the budgets and then makes its own recommendations to the President subject to appeal by the agency head to the President. In the case of the Defense budget, the staff of the Budget Bureau and the staff of the Secretary of Defense jointly review the budget requests of the individual armed services. The staff make recommendations to their respective superiors. The Secretary of Defense and the Budget Director then meet to iron out differences of view. The Secretary of Defense then submits his budget request to the President, and the Budget Director has the right of carrying to the President any remaining areas of disagreement he thinks warrant Presidential review.

Given the complexity of the Defense budget and a Secretary of Defense with a genuine interest in economy, efficiency, and effectiveness, this procedure has many advantages. It probably tends to provide the Budget Director with better information on the program issues than he gets from other Departments. I think the procedure might perhaps be strengthened if the practice were instituted of having the Budget Director and the Secretary of Defense *jointly* submit the budget recommendation to the President, noting any differences of view.

But essentially, this procedural matter is of relatively modest importance. The Budget Bureau can effectively dig into and review what the President wants it to review under this procedure or many others. It can raise questions of budgetary priorities—questioning, for example, the work of building forces against a particular set of contingencies on grounds of higher priority domestic needs—when and only when the President feels that *he* can effectively question military judgments on those grounds.

In my view therefore, the issues of the military-industrial complex, and of budget review procedures are important. But they are far less important than the basic issue of public attitudes, public understanding, and the need to generate an informed discussion about the fundamentals of the military budget in the context of national priorities.

NOTES

1. For most of the systems listed below, the decision to procure the item has already been made. In a few cases, such as the Navy's VSX antisubmarine plane, procurement has not yet been approved, but development is well along, and official statements of Defense Department officials have already indicated that the system is most likely to be approved.
2. This is the term used by Malcolm Hoag.
3. This observation is reported by Desmond P. Wilson, *Evolution of the Attack Aircraft Carrier: A Case Study in Technology and Strategy*, Ph.D. Dissertation, M.I.T., February 1966.

22.

George Berkley: The Myth of War Profiteering

In the preceding selection, Charles Schultze maintained that public attitudes and the need for informed discussion were more important issues concerning the military budget than the military-industrial complex. The two selections that

George E. Berkley, "The Myth of War Profiteering," *The New Republic*, December 20, 1969, pp. 15–18. © 1969 by Harrison-Blaine of New Jersey, Inc. Reprinted by permission of *The New Republic*.

follow, however, address themselves directly to one controversial aspect of the military-industrial complex issue. The claim that munitions makers have a vested interest in war has a long history, going back in the United States to the Senate investigations between the two world wars. The authors of the two selections debate the particular question of Vietnam war profiteering by defense industries. George E. Berkley offers various arguments to support his view that "the industrial end of the military industrial complex is seeking to extricate itself from the dubious and often dismal fortunes of war." In seeking to refute this view, Victor Perlo (selection begins on p. 323) points to the profits that are hidden, for example, in subcontracting and in government supplied capital, concluding that Berkley exaggerates the shift of defense industries to civilian production.

George E. Berkley teaches political science at Northeastern University; Victor Perlo, an economist, is author of *Militarism and Industry*.

Although America's munition makers are thought to be reaping a financial bonanza from the Vietnam War, the facts indicate otherwise. In 1965, the top five defense contractors were General Dynamics, Lockheed, Douglas, General Electric and United Aircraft. By the beginning of 1969, one of the big five, Douglas, had been squeezed out of existence; a second one, Lockheed, was in trouble. Of the three remaining, two were under severe financial pressure. For many war contractors, Vietnam has been a headache; for others it has been disaster.

Look at the balance sheets. General Dynamics earned $4.48 a share in 1965, the year the Vietnam build-up got underway. By 1968, its per share earnings had dropped to $2.83. Lockheed netted $4.89 a share in 1965. By 1968, its per share earnings, computed on the same basis as those of 1965, came to only $1.64. General Electric's profits were running at $3.93 a share in 1965. In 1968, they amounted to $3.95, a miniscule gain of 2 cents. United Aircraft scored the only earnings improvement during these war years. Its profits rose from $4.57 to $5.05, an increase of about ten percent.

Even these figures overstate the munition makers' war "prosperity" for they fail to allow for inflation. If we assess their earnings records in terms of constant, 1965 dollars, we find that United Aircraft marked time during these years, General Electric's earnings went down by nearly ten percent, General Dynamics' decreased by almost one-half and Lockheed's plummeted by more than two-thirds.

On January 1, 1969, *Forbes* published a summary of how the top 500 American corporations had fared in earnings growth during the previous five years. How did the prime war contractors place in this comparative ranking? General Dynamics, the biggest defense supplier, ended up almost at the bottom of the list, placing 481. The other three held the following rankings on the earnings growth list: Lockheed 390, General Electric 371, United Aircraft 243. In other words, during the war buildup, those companies furnishing the sinews of that war were faring a good deal less well financially than most of those firms denied such opportunities. Statistics such as these lead us to ask a further question: Were the blotched earnings record of the big war contractors representative of those war contractors generally? Did small defense suppliers make out as poorly as their larger colleagues?

Generally speaking, they did. Grumman Aircraft for example, is number 11 on the list of defense suppliers, but since it is smaller than some of the others its government contracts make up over 80 percent of its gross revenues. The company earned $3.03 a share in 1965, and $2.68 a share in 1968. AVCO, another corporation that does nearly four-fifths of its business with the Defense Department, listed its earnings as $2.88 a share for the 12-month period ending November 1965. For the same period ending November, 1968, the figure was $2.54. Both these companies experienced better than ten percent declines as measured in inflationary dollars. Measured in constant dollars, the declines were closer to 20 percent.

Some companies turning out war products fared much better. Raytheon's earnings more than doubled, leaping from $1.03 in 1965, to $2.07 in 1968. McDonnell Aircraft, which took over the financially tottering Douglas in 1967, managed to log an earnings record of $3.38 in 1968 compared to $2.62 per share three years earlier. Boeing succeeded about as well as General Electric, its per share earnings inching up from $3.82 to $3.84 during the three-year period.

However, these brighter spots are largely explained by special factors. Wall Street analysts attribute Raytheon's increase to an earnings turnaround brought about by new management, reorganization and a multi-pronged drive into such nondefense activity as textbook publishing and home appliance manufacturing. McDonnell-Douglas' sudden upsurge in profits in 1968—it had run deficits for 1966 and 1967—was attributed by a Standard and Poor investment letter to stepped-up deliveries of DC-8 and DC-9 commercial jets. The same investment letter claimed that Boeing's ability to at least mark time during the war years was based on its success with its commercial planes, primarily the 707 and 727.

As one combs through investment letters, designed solely to help stock market speculators make decisions on their investments, one finds recurring evidence of the discrepancy between the amount of revenue that companies derive from war contracts and the amount of *profit* they obtain from such orders. Thus, in reporting on Boeing on March 13, 1969, Standard and Poor notes that "over *half* of billings and the *bulk* of profits now come from commercial jetliners." (Emphasis added.) In appraising AVCO on September 15, 1969, Standard and Poor says, at one place, that "in 1967–8 about 77 percent of earnings came from commercial operations with the balance from government billings." Some paragraphs later, we find the sentence, "The Government Products Group accounts for the major portion of revenues." Similarly, Value Line investment service, in appraising North American Rockwell on July 25, 1969, notes that the company's commercial business was expected to reach 40 percent of its gross revenues in 1969, while accounting for over 50 percent of profits. In the same investment letter, Value Line noted that Ling-Temco-Vought had reduced its aerospace business to less than 20 percent of its gross revenue. In commenting on this, the service pointed out that the company's aerospace division had generated after tax profits of less than 0.3 percent last year.

Common sense tells us that such figures are wrong. After all, who should benefit from a war if not those who furnish its weapons? And haven't the defense contractors always been hungry for government business. Common sense told the Italians of the sixteenth century that if two unequal weights were dropped to the ground, the heavier would hit the ground first. But Galileo dropped two unequal weights from the top of the Tower of Pisa to prove that common sense was wrong.

Early this year, the Logistics Management Institute released a study showing that the average profit margin for all US industry was 8.7 percent of sales, but that the average profit margin on defense work was only 4.2 percent of sales. Since the all-industry average included the low-profit defense work, the actual profitability gap between defense and nondefense orders may be even greater than the better-than-two-to-one ratio that the figures suggest. The study was attacked in some quarters because it was based on data supplied by the defense contractors themselves. However, for reasons having to do with the stock market, which we will examine shortly, there is more of a tendency for defense manufacturers to overstate rather than understate their profits on war contracts. Furthermore, there are additional data to show that, if anything, defense work is even less remunerative than the LMI study indicates.

Once again let us turn to *Forbes*. Every year it publishes separate listings, ranking the top 500 corporations in terms of revenues, assets, profits, etc. If we extract the rankings of the top ten war contractors in 1968 from the list of revenues, and similarly take their rankings from the list of profits, we obtain a graphic picture of the return on defense work:

Top 10 War Suppliers	Rank Based on Total Revenue	Rank Based on Total Profit
General Dynamics	34	220
Lockheed	43	190
General Electric	5	13
United Aircraft	41	118
McDonnell-Douglas	17	60
AT & T	2	1
Boeing	22	74
Ling-Temco-Vought	31	232
North American Rockwell	6	94
General Motors	1	2

Now, in examining this list, let's first exclude American Telephone and Telegraph and General Motors. These corporations are so large that even though they are among the top ten, their defense business comes to only one or two percent of their gross revenues. In every single instance, the ranking of the remaining eight companies in terms of total profits earned is far, far below their rank in terms of total gross revenues. Moreover, all these companies have at least some nondefense business and, as already seen, such commercial business earns them much more, proportionally, than do their defense orders. Without their commercial business, the gap between their revenue position and their profit position would widen further.

Why are profit margins so poor and why, anomaly of anomalies, do they seem to be even poorer in war time than in peace time?

To answer this we should first note that defense orders were not always the mixed blessing for armaments makers that they are today. During the 1950's, many firms flourished on such business. It was the advent of Robert McNamara as Secretary of Defense that made the difference. McNamara changed the Defense Department's purchasing policy from a cost-plus to a fixed fee basis. The old cost-plus arrangement had allowed the military suppliers to charge the Pentagon whatever the project cost with a guaranteed profit added on. Furthermore, crafty contractors often found ways of including in costs, work that would benefit them in other areas. The fixed fee arrangement did away with blank checks. Contractors now have to stay within the bounds of the predetermined price if they expect to make a profit. Modern munitions-making is a complex business, however, and frequently unforeseen problems lie in wait for even the shrewdest. Lockheed's heavily publicized troubles with its C-4 Air Force Transport is one of many such instances.

Another problem besetting the defense industry is that its outlets for civilian business have grown markedly during the past decade. The economic lethargy of the Eisenhower years is behind us; the New Economics is established policy. The American economy picked up a startling momentum in the 1960s. In addition, various technological breakthroughs have given many aerospace companies considerable nonwar-related business. When the war buildup began in 1965, many of them suddenly found themselves with too much business. The influx of war orders piled on top of civilian billings, forced them into uneconomic practices. These included giving employees extensive overtime work, which means paying them 50 or 100 percent more for work which, because of increasing fatigue, becomes increasingly less satisfactory. Too many orders may also mean hiring less skilled employees, overutilizing plant and machinery and doing other things that can narrow profits and even turn them into losses.

It was precisely such factors which drove Douglas to the wall, transforming its $14.6 million of profits in 1965 into a $27.6 million loss in 1966. A *New York Times* financial writer noted in late 1968 that Boeing was beginning to experience a similar situation: "There were signs . . . that Boeing's tremendous commercial backlog [added to "low return government work"] was producing some of the strains that ruined the Douglas Aircraft Corporation— too rapid a buildup of business, a squeeze on plant and manpower capacity and, in the case of Douglas . . . production problems and deficits." Boeing in the first six months of this year earned $1.03 per share compared to $1.85 in the first half of 1965. In constant dollars, this would constitute an earnings drop of over 50 percent. The firm was expected to do less well in the second half of '69.

As noted earlier, AVCO's earnings declined from 1965 to 1968. In February

1969, a New York stock brokerage house, Goodbody and Company, issued an investment appraisal of the firm, assessing its prospects if peace should come. Although nearly 80 percent of AVCO's business comes from the Defense Department, the brokerage house found that peace would actually enhance AVCO's investment appeal. Its letter noted, for example, that ". . . profit margins on helicopter engine business . . . have been adversely affected by uneconomic production schedules created by the heavy demands of the Vietnam War. With a slowdown in hostilities, which would probably bring a more even flow of production, profit margins should improve."

A final factor must be considered in explaining the wilting profit margins of so many munitions makers during recent years: inflation. The Keynesian-oriented, welfare-state capitalism that has characterized European economies since World War II, and which began to take hold in the United States during the 1960s, has reversed the normal capitalist imbalance. Where at one time capitalism tended to suffer from too much supply in relation to demand, it now tends to enjoy the opposite. I say enjoy because this situation keeps up employment and wages and encourages growth. However it makes inflation a persistent threat. Thus, war which was once an elixir to capitalism has become anathema instead. Lack of military spending has brought many blessings to Japanese capitalism in recent decades. Too much military spending in the United States is reducing 1969 business profits, adjusted for inflation, to a level below that of 1965. And 1970 will probably be worse.

The military suppliers are, if anything, more susceptible than other branches of American industry to these ravages of inflation. Not only do they find their costs rising, but often they have a harder time passing such costs on to the consumer—in this case, the government. Inflation for a full-throttle economy is not a boon but a bane, and for a defense contractor, working under a deluge of orders on a fixed fee basis, and requiring a high proportion of scarce skilled labor to meet them, it can prove a disaster.

There is yet another problem that plagues munitions makers—the impact of Wall Street.

Stocks do not sell on profits alone. The auction market, which is the American securities industry, takes into account a variety of factors in determining what price a company's share will command. In 1969, the stocks of military suppliers were selling, on an average, at about 8 or 9 times their earnings. The average stock on the New York Stock Exchange, meanwhile, was selling at about 16 times earnings. (The average price-earnings ratio on the American Stock Exchange was higher still.) Thus, firms with a high defense component in their production operations have not only tended to make less money but have also been less able to capitalize on such earnings as they do make. This discrepancy between marketability of defense company stock compared to those of other companies is not simply a result of the prospective end of the Vietnam war. The gap between what their earnings can command in the financial markets vis-à-vis what other companies can obtain has existed for years.

A good price for its stock offers many desirable advantages for a business firm and its managers. First, it increases the managers' personal wealth. Much has been said in recent years about the separation of ownership from management in American industry but this should not obscure the fact that managers usually own some stock in the firms they run. If Wall Street chose to give armament industries the same price-earnings multiple that it gives other technological companies, the men who run America's armaments would realize a windfall of personal profit.

The managers of munitions industries have other reasons for wanting to see their stock priced at the levels of nondefense firms. The higher price increases management prestige and stockholder satisfaction. The latter factor can be quite important. There are many individuals and companies on the prowl in Wall Street these days, seeking firms with disgruntled stockholders who might be receptive to an acquisition offer. At the same time, a host of stock brokerage firms and investment counselors are constantly checking out reports, comparing company performances and suggesting ways in which the private investor can best put his money to work. Such elements put increasing pressure on those who run defense industries to appease their stockholders with better prices for their shares.

Meanwhile, war contractors are on the lookout themselves for tempting acquisition possibilities. They too have been showing an increasing predilection for taking over other firms and this makes an attractive price for their stock almost mandatory. Most mergers are based on an exchange of securities between the merger and the merged, and the higher the evaluation that Wall Street places on the shares of the former, the better the terms he can offer to the latter. Thus, the heavy discount which defense contractors' stock sells for these days is putting a severe crimp in their expansion plans, and making them vulnerable to raids by Wall Street predators. This helps explain why they are more apt to overstate rather than understate the profitability of their war contracts. Lockheed, for example, sought to minimize its losses on the C-4 air cargo plane for the Air Force.

One may wonder why business firms want defense contracts at all. Some industries *are* avoiding them. In January, 1967, *Iron Age,* the steel industry magazine, reported that steel makers were refusing to bid on defense work. Despite the fact that the Vietnam War was choking off steel orders in such areas as construction and auto production, the companies were showing little desire to compensate by going after defense contracts.

Those industries specifically geared for defense contracting do remain in the armaments-making race and often bid zealously on such work. Despite the flood of defense orders which the Vietnam War has brought them, however, most munitions makers have succeeded in gradually increasing their commercial business. The industrial end of the military-industrial complex is seeking to extricate itself from the dubious and often dismal fortunes of war.

Many such firms are finding expanded opportunities in the commercial aircraft sector. In 1968, such private business accounted for 47 percent of McDonnell-Douglas total sales. By the start of 1969, its commercial orders had increased to 68 percent of the company's backlog. Today, it is engaged in heavy competition with Lockheed for the coming wave of air bus production. It claims to have signed up 184 customers for its DC-10 which will carry about 300 passengers and will gross the company about $14.5 million each. Lockheed claims to have 181 orders for its L-1011 Tristar air bus, which will sell at the same price, and is counting on a total market of 1400 planes during the 1970s. (Its backlog of orders for these planes by the end of last year had a dollar value of 2.5 billion, 15 percent more than its entire billing for all work in 1968.) Boeing, meanwhile, says it has orders for 183 of its still larger air buses, the 747, which will be priced at $20 million each. Boeing's commercial orders had already reached 86 percent of its backlog by the end of last year, as compared to only 50 percent of its sales during the year, and the proportion of such backlog orders will undoubtedly cross the 90 percent mark at the end of 1969.

The aerospace industry has assembled the greatest pool of technological manpower in the world, and our ever increasingly technological society is beckoning them into newer civilian fields. United Aircraft's Sikorsky Division, long associated with helicopters, has built the experimental turbo trains that now run between Boston and New York. The apparent success of these trains offers the division numerous opportunities to transfer its energies to peacetime uses. Lockheed, in addition to its commercial aircraft business, is moving heavily into underseas technology, computers and medical information retrieval systems. LTV Aerospace is developing and marketing new systems for controlling automobile traffic. The aerospace industry is tooling up for a peacetime world of the 1970s that will in all probability earn it much more money than the war years of the late sixties.

Some munitions makers are even stepping outside their accustomed areas of competence to strengthen their tie-in with more profitable civilian activity. AVCO has taken over finance and insurance companies and is planning to build an entire community in California. Such endeavors will receive a great boost once the Vietnam War ends and the expected housing boom, long stifled by war-caused high interest rates, gets underway. Raytheon is counting on a post-war housing boom to provide opportunities to sell its new home heating system, as well as to increase orders for its home appliances division. The company's newly acquired textbook division also stands to benefit considerably from a shift of the country's resources to nonmilitary purposes.

These promising developments will not take most of the munitions makers out of munitions-making completely. Despite the low profitability of such work and the existence of more profitable opportunities in the civilian sector, any new contracts that arise for defense work will probably find at least some suppliers ready to bid. As they diversify into the civilian sector, however, they should become a less troublesome element in American society. Improbable though it may seem, many defense suppliers, motivated by sheer greed, may eventually join other industry leaders, Wall Street speculators and such business-oriented magazines as *Fortune* and *Forbes* in calling for a curtailment in defense spending and a shift to the more lucrative pursuits of peace.

23.
Victor Perlo: Arms Profiteering: It's Not a Myth

Part of the domestic pacification program is the attempt to convince us that nobody makes a financial killing out of our soaring wartime tax load. For example, not too long ago a Defense Department-financed outfit, the Logistics Management Institute, got considerable publicity with a study purporting to show low defense profits. But sophisticated people could easily identify this in-house propaganda. And it was followed by sensational reports of billions in "cost overruns" on weapons systems, climaxed by the recent firing of an Air Force official, Arthur Ernest Fitzgerald, who persisted in exposing the waste and profiteering.

Now, however, we have a seeming refutation of the war profiteering charge from a presumably disinterested source, George E. Berkley, a political scientist at Northeastern University, who in *The New Republic* of December 20, 1969, drew us a picture of sharply declining military profits during Vietnam War years. Mr. Berkley's try is no better than the others. Here's why:

1. He leaves out the Big-Five contractor with the best profit record. The Big Five Pentagon contractors in fiscal 1969 were Lockheed, General Electric, General Dynamics, McDonnell Douglas, and United Aircraft. Berkley uses four of these, and mentions Douglas, not the merged successor, McDonnell Douglas, though we have comparative figures for the entire period.

2. He picks the wrong year to show the effects of the Vietnam War on profits. The first year of a war buildup always shows the most dramatic profit rise, at least on paper—cf. 1941 in World War II, 1950 in the Korean War. By comparing 1965, the first year of the Vietnam War, with 1968, Berkley omits the main profit increase of this war.

3. He uses "per share earnings" instead of dollar net income, which results in downward distortions as a result of continued issuance of additional stock for options, stock dividends, acquisitions, etc.

4. His most "dramatic" earnings decline (Lockheed's) is simply a gross misstatement of the 1968 per-share figure. Berkley cites a net earnings for Lockheed of $1.64 per share in 1968, compared with $4.89 in 1965. But the actual figure as reported in Moody's Industrial Manual, was $3.95 in 1968 compared with $4.65 in 1965.

Berkley attributes much of the alleged decline in war profits to McNamara's tight management. For proper comparison I have tabulated profits of the Big Five in 1960, the last year before McNamara; 1964, the last year before the Viet-

Victor Perlo, "Arms Profiteering: It's Not a Myth," *The New Republic,* February 7, 1970, pp. 23–25. © 1970 by Harrison-Blaine of New Jersey, Inc. Reprinted by permission of *The New Republic.*

nam War, but after considerable buildup; and 1968, the latest full year for which statistics are complete. I used company reports as presented in Moody's.

The combined net income of the five companies increased from $137 million in 1960 to $395 million in 1964 and $587 million in 1968. The combined stockholders' equity increased from $2376 million in 1960 to $3036 million in 1964 and $4107 million in 1968. If we omit General Electric, the largest of the five, and the one with the largest proportion of civilian business, the trend for the remaining four is even more favorable. The statistics are shown in the table on page [325].

The increases in profits and property values exceed the increases over the same period in gross national product, national wealth, the military budget, corporate profits as a whole, or prices.

The record of the new armament-based conglomerates is still more dramatic. LTV (seventh among Pentagon contractors in 1968) increased net income from $4 million in 1964 to $36 million in 1968; net worth from $25 million to $104 million. Textron (16th on the list) increased profits from $22 million in 1964 to $74 million in 1968, and net worth from $116 million to $462 million. Comparable 1960 figures aren't available for these two companies: Litton Industries (21st among Pentagon contractors) increased net from $7 million in 1960 to $30 million in 1964 and $58 million in 1968. Its net worth went up from $51 million in 1960 to $155 million in 1964 and $597 million in 1968.

Berkley attributes Douglas' troubles in 1966–67, which led to the McDonnell merger, to the effects of military business. But it is common knowledge that Douglas' losses then, like Lockheed's and General Dynamics' huge losses a few years earlier, were in civilian plants. If one may generalize, they all tried to get away with the same grossly wasteful practices that paid off in military business.

Similarly, Mr. Ling's operation is in the deep red because the methods which worked in the Texan's defense production lost hundreds of millions when tried on his steel industry acquisition, Jones & Laughlin.

Berkley cites the customary arms-makers' "evidence" of a lower-than-average profit rate by taking profits as a percentage of sales. But it is well known that a large part, and often a major part of the fixed capital, as well as many billions of working capital, are supplied by the government.

Economist Robert J. Gordon, in the June 1969 *American Economic Review* lead article, found "a $45 billion treasure chest of plant and equipment which the US government has purchased for the use of private firms since 1940, but which has never been counted as part of the private US capital stock. . . . Even today, 123,000 employees of private firms work in plants and laboratories owned by the Atomic Energy Commission, having a gross book value of over $8 billion. *Much of the aircraft and ordnance production for the Vietnam war has been carried on by private firms with government-owned plant and equipment.* And, similarly, almost all of the construction, testing and firing of rockets in the US space program has been performed by private contractors in government-owned facilities. *In addition, the production of commercial aircraft is*

carried on partially through the use of government-financed equipment."
[Italics added.]

Similarly, much of the working capital of armament contractors is supplied by the government in the form of progress payments, and this practice has increased immensely during the Vietnam War. In 1960 Lockheed carried $237 million of inventories, against which it had received $61 million, or about one-fourth, in progress payments and advances. But by 1968 it carried $1382 million of inventories, against which it had received $1096 million, or four-fifths in progress payments and advances.

Also, the armament business is many-layered; a number of slices of profit are taken out of each dollar of Pentagon purchases.

One of the most striking examples is brought to mind by the recent award of more than $200 million in an initial contract to Western Electric as prime contractor on the Safeguard anti-missile system, for which President Nixon fought so hard. The American Telephone and Telegraph manufacturing subsidiary inherited this business from the Old Nike program. Western Electric did only one-fifth of the work on the Nike missiles in its own shops. The rest was subcontracted, mainly to the "second-tier" firm, Douglas, which passed on four-fifths of its work to "third-tier" subcontractors.

The main operation of Douglas and Western Electric was in their billing departments, where liberal profit markups were added onto the bills submitted by lower-tier manufacturers. Western Electric finally submitted the total bills, with all the layers of profit padding, to the Pentagon.

Western Electric did actual work of $276.9 million in its shops. To this, and to the four-times larger volume of work done by subcontractors, it added $82.4 million for general and administrative expenses and $112.5 million for profits.

FIVE LARGEST PENTAGON CONTRACTORS
NET INCOME AND STOCKHOLDERS' EQUITY
1960, 1964, AND 1968

(millions of dollars)

Company	Net Income			Stockholders' Equity		
	1960	1964	1968	1960	1964	1968
Lockheed	−43	45	44	103	239	371
General Electric	200	237	357	1,513	1,888	2,433
General Dynamics	−27	43	30	289	300	336
McDonnell Douglas	−7 *	41	95	182 *	294	464
United Aircraft	14	29	61	289	315	503
Totals	137	395	587·	2,376	3,036	4,107
Total excluding General Electric	−63	158	230	863	1,148	1,674

* Sum of figures for Douglas and McDonnell.
Source: Moody's Industrial Manual, 1969 and 1966.

The combined addition of $194.9 million equalled 70.4 percent of the work done by Western Electric.

Obviously, there have been huge rates of profit on invested capital, the only standard that counts in the long run. The munitions industry economist, Murray Weidenbaum, who is very much of the Establishment—he is now Assistant Secretary of the Treasury—compared profit margins on sales and net worth for defense and nondefense industrial firms. He found the defense firms had 2.6 percent on sales, the nondefense 4.6 percent in 1962–65. But the former had a profit rate on net worth of 17.5 percent as compared with 10.6 percent for the latter. [*Hearings, Subcommittee on Economy in Government, Joint Economic Committee, November 1968, Part 2, Page 11.*]

Then there is the whole business of hidden profits, never reported on the books, which go into the pockets of the controlling stockholders in the big munitions firms, to the banks, lawyers and propagandists associated with them, to the hundreds of ex-generals and admirals employed to get them business, and to the swollen top bureaucracy and military-science executives of the armament firms.

Hidden profits run deep throughout American industry, for well-known tax reasons. They are especially large in the munitions industry, because of the lack of competition and the amiable relations with the Pentagon which permit soaking away large profits as "costs." The men of the Renegotiation Board try hard, and have recovered tens of millions. But budgetary and legal limitations restrict their recovery possibilities to a minor fraction of overcharges.

Admiral Rickover, the veteran battler for economy in procurement, testified last year before the House Appropriations Committee:

"Contractors are able to hide profits in their costs. . . . One large defense contractor reported a lump sum figure as subcontracted costs. Actually, the work was subcontracted to another division of the same company, and a 25-percent profit was hidden in the cost of the subcontracted work. Another contractor certified to a 20 percent general and administrative expense rate and a three percent profit rate. . . . The government auditor determined that the true general and administrative expense rate was only 12 percent, so that the actual profit on the order was really 10 percent, instead of the three percent . . . certified."

A contractor, he reported, "may double a legitimate cost estimate without concern for the Truth-in-Negotiations Act if he attributes the doubling to 'judgment.'" The Admiral quotes Dr. Howard Wright's "Accounting for Defense Contracts"—a guide for contractors: "No cost is unallowable under fixed-price contracts." [*House Appropriations Committee Hearings, Fiscal Year 1970 Defense Appropriations, page 825.*]

In short—write your own ticket. Between 1960 and 1968 the percentage of the value of contracts of this type increased from 57.4 percent to 77.6 percent of the total, according to the office of the Secretary of Defense, and various government studies have shown that they yield higher profits than the other "cost-plus" type. Incidentally, part of McNamara's unearned kudos for economy was based on his stress on the "fixed-price-incentive" type contract.

As indicated above, much of the hidden profits is stashed away under the "general and administrative" category. Between 1960 and 1967 Lockheed's cost of sales increased 71 percent, while its general, administrative, engineering and development expense increased 175 percent. Rickover gave five examples, in a 1968 hearing, of the difference between reported profit and actual profit, as uncovered by the incomplete and relatively rare government audits:

Contractor	Profit Reported	Actual Profit by Government Audit
A	4.5	10.0
B	12.5	19.5
C	11.1	16.9
D	2.0	15.0
E	21.6	32.7

What about the trend of profit rates during the Vietnam war? A General Accounting Office study showed that in 1966 the rate of profit on Pentagon business averaged 26 percent higher than in 1959–63. A Defense Department "refutation" of this study showed an increase in the profit rate of "only" 22 percent.

Mr. Berkley makes much of the recent decline in stock market prices of armament firms. Of course. Their stocks zoom at the beginning of a war, and drop drastically as the belief spreads that the war is coming to an end. If the military-industrial complex has its way, and armament contracts are stabilized at present levels, and then start up again, there will undoubtedly be a fresh upturn in prices of these stocks—and the upturn will take place well before the general public is aware of the next big surge in munitions profits.

Berkley exaggerates the extent to which the munitions firms have switched to civilian work, by giving the percentage of their backlogs in civilian business. Commercial plane orders are placed years ahead for popular models. But military contracts are placed only for a relatively short period, even when the program is effectively scheduled out for many years. Thus a company may have 80 percent of its backlog in commercial planes, but do more than 50 percent of its business for the military.

The latest example of how the armament contractors are "running away" from military business was the bitter struggle between McDonnell-Douglas and North American for the F-15—the largest aircraft program initiated in years. McDonnell gambled $10 million of its own funds and $20 million of Air Force funds in research for it; while North American, the loser, sank $20 million into it. "McDonnell Flies High" . . . "McDonnell Will Move Quickly to Slice F-15 Pie With Subs"—headlined *Metalworking News*. "NAR to Keep Punching" was the lead on another article. A company spokesman admitted "disappointment. . . . Our military aircraft expertise is now being concentrated on another competition for a new aircraft, the B-1 bomber."

Not, note well, a substitute civilian program. The trade paper commented that North American's "steadily declining sales in this field [i.e. the military] have become a serious drain on its over-all profit picture," and quoted a West Coast financial analyst as saying: "If North American loses out on the B-1, they'll slide right down the Kazoo."

I do not consider the armament manufacturers the decisive force getting us into wars, but they play their part. Now we have the Lockheed Aircraft Corporation acting as wedgemaker for an Air Force attempt to set up a base in Singapore by establishing a major repair and maintenance base there, which "among other things" will "service United States military aircraft from all over Asia." The need for the private business entry is because, "in the present mood of congressional and public disaffection with United States military involvements overseas, it is thought quite likely that the Defense Department is not eager to show too keen an interest in Singapore. However, a number of senior American military officers . . . have been paying discreet visits to Singaport over the past few months" (*New York Times,* December 2, 1969).

In contrast, Berkley ends his article with a pollyanna picture of "the aerospace industry . . . tooling up for a peacetime world of the 1970s," the defense contractors becoming "a less troublesome element in American society," and "through sheer greed" joining the demand for a curtailment in defense spending.

Unfortunately, life is never so simple. Supporters of a nonmilitary priority still have powerful opponents in the profiteers from armaments. It will take continued efforts, against the resistance of military contractors, to assure the end of the war in Asia and a major reduction in the $80 billion Pentagon budget.

THE POLITICS OF DEFENSE DECISIONS

24.

David W. Tarr: *Military Technology and the Policy Process*

A pluralistic response to the power-elite or military-industrial complex interpretation of the policy process is offered in the following selection, which emphasizes the political basis for making national security policy. Despite the fact that the

David W. Tarr, "Military Technology and the Policy Process," *The Western Political Quarterly,* Vol. 18 (March 1965), pp. 135–36, 138–42, 146–48. Reprinted by permission of the University of Utah, copyright holder.

military policy process—essentially a series of incremental, tactical decisions—is gravely affected by the ramifications of military technology, it is, according to David Tarr, "not irresponsible, only somewhat removed from direct public accountability."

Professor David Tarr, a political scientist at the University of Wisconsin, is the author of *American Strategy in the Nuclear Age.*

Military policies are formulated in an environment that is increasingly affected by developments in military technology and by the civilian and military elites associated with that technology. Rapid advances in science and technology cause strains on the policy process in two major respects: (1) with regard to American foreign and military policies the problem of developing military instruments that are relevant to our national policy objectives is exacerbated by rampant extensions in the range, complexity, and destructive power of modern weapons systems; (2) with respect to our domestic political system the secrecy and technical complexities inherent in the new weapons technology impose limitations on the responsiveness of military policy to traditional democratic control arrangements.

Military power is the most potent instrument of policy available, yet it is also the most difficult element of national power to render manageable for political purposes.[1] The nation's political objectives are always plural and often conflicting. Which policy goals should military policies serve? It has been the tendency of American military policies both to contribute to and to reflect the conflicting and ambiguous state of our foreign policy objectives. As Professor Huntington has pointed out, "military policy is not the result of deductions from a clear statement of national objective. It is the product of the competition of purposes within individuals and groups and among individuals and groups. It is the result of politics not logic. . . ."[2] Disharmonies in military policy are a consequence both of the character of the policy process and of the difficulties involved in attempting to relate military means to the great variety of political ends at stake. Defense policies are formulated within a framework of competing groups, interests, and values and the decisions precipitated are usually the product of the vigorous bargaining efforts of the participants. It should not be surprising, therefore, that the product of the process is often not clearly related to the foreign policy objectives it is supposed to serve.

While policy relevance is obfuscated by the process through which policies are developed, democratic controls over military policies are difficult to maintain because new developments in military technology must, for security reasons, be shielded from public view and participation confined to a limited technological and political elite. Information about policies related to military technology more often comes to light *after* policy is established rather than before. Faced with a *fait accompli,* opponents and critics can engage in attacks on Administration policy that may modify implementation, but they are seldom able to contribute to the *formulation* of policies themselves. Such contributions can only be expected if the policy critics are included within the policy-making structure and this structure is strictly circumscribed according to political role and government office.[3] Information that does become available is sometimes rooted in highly technical details beyond general public understanding. The environment in which competing policy proposals are considered, therefore, is severely limited both in terms of the participants involved and in what is allowed to become public knowledge.

The problem of controlling military power, of rendering it useful within a democratic framework to the political purposes of the government, is thus complicated by the demands of democratic politics, by the pace and complexity of military technology, the threats to our survival posed by our enemies, and the need for secrecy inherent in the development of military programs in the context of a technologically oriented arms race. These are interacting complications. Secrecy impedes democracy. Technology confounds laymen. Informed opinion is scarce. The political leadership grows increasingly dependent on scientific and technical experts for advice and counsel, but secrecy and technical data impose barriers to the kinds of communications which are necessary for the proper functioning of democratic controls.

This essay examines the military policy process from the standpoint of problems which arise from the pressures of the revolution in military technology and the Soviet-American arms race as they impinge upon the strategy-making functions of the national government. In focusing on the processes by which military policies are formulated, it suggests that the crucial question is one of control and guidance of the decision system in ways which minimize the determination of policies by purely technological factors and maximize the capacity of our political leaders to determine basic defense policies themselves, to explain their needs to the scientific and military elites, and to convey the fundamental issues in a meaningful way to the larger political community to which they are responsible and from whom they require support. . . .

The formulation and execution of national security policies is an enormously complex task requiring great organizational skills and careful orchestration of the human and material resources of military power. Overseeing the defense policy process are clusters of top-level political leaders and their staffs—the President and his principal advisers, the National Security Council, the Bureau of the Budget, the Atomic Energy Commission, the Central Intelligence Agency, various groupings of cabinet and sub-cabinet officers, and key members and committees of Congress. The bureaucratic core of the defense policy process is naturally located in the Pentagon, the control center of the military establishment, where more than 25,000 civilian and military personnel[4] labor to devise, establish, and maintain effective military postures and capabilities. The Department of Defense is a huge and complicated organism employing in excess of 3.7 million people (armed forces included);[5] there are, of course, many other agencies, public and private, involved in the national defense effort, most of them having an impact on national security policies. The over-all defense community is, in short, a large and disparate system, difficult to manage under any circumstances, and particularly lacking in authoritative control devices because of the democratic and pluralistic environment in which it must operate.

The term "policy process" is perhaps too neat a phrase to describe the network of activities which generate policy alternatives and the arenas in which such proposals are fought to conclusions, stalemates, or oblivion. It is clear, however, that activities related to policy-oriented research, analysis, advocacy, and opposition go on at almost all levels of government at once. Moreover, while the bureaucratic hierarchies of the government tend to impose structure and a degree of rationality on the effort, they do not confine activities to formal organizational contexts and lines of communication. The "conflict-consensus" model suggested by Roger Hilsman several years ago [6] aptly epitomizes the policy process as essentially a *"political"* activity, one in which the issues at stake require conciliation of diverse values and the groups that have become identified with them; reconciliation is accomplished through series of pressures and counterpressures, bargaining and compromise, alliance and counteralliance; there are few who see themselves as decision-makers, "but only as inputers, recommenders, vetoers, and approvers"; and in the ensuing conflict and consensus, the relative power of the groups identified with particular goals and policies appears to be as relevant to the final outcome as is the cogency of the arguments used in supporting the policies in contention.[7]

Furthermore, the decision process less often approximates a rational and comprehensive effort wherein all possible alternatives and their consequences are considered, than it does what Lindblom has colorfully described as a system of "muddling through," an activity which he sees as consisting of a series of "incremental adjustments" related to certain desired objectives but made within a framework of action in which "what is desired itself continues to change under reconsideration."[8] The "process" of making decisions as seen in such a context is not so much chaotic in character as it is supremely *political*—where ideas and interests are in conflict and where the beginnings of policy consensus are built. The level at which particular policy issues are considered depends, in part, on the functions of interested agencies, the interests of specific participants, and on the importance of the values at stake. No one has a monopoly on good ideas, but quite obviously the more influential the source of the idea, the greater the potential for success.

Fundamental decisions on weapons and strategy are made within the bureaucratic structure of the executive branch, usually within the Pentagon itself. Proposals are developed, support is aroused, opposition develops, and negotiating and bargaining ensue among various agencies and individuals. Outside influences may be felt, from Congress or elsewhere, but normally the process is internal and secret, and neither Congress as a whole nor the public at large becomes aware of the issues involved until the decision is announced (if, indeed, it is ever announced). In short, the locale of the military policy process is largely executive rather than legislative and policies are formulated outside the public purview.[9]

These may strike the reader as truisms about the decision-making processes in military affairs, but they are offered in order to make a particular point: the policy process is not easily subject to guidance, direction, and control by the political leadership. It is difficult for Congress and the public to understand and influence the policy process. Policy innovations tend to involve incremental rather than radical departures from current policies. Because most policy alterations are subtle in content, they sometimes are not identified as "decisions," *per se,* and they often lack the dramatic impact that might otherwise bring wider recognition and understanding. When masked by the complications of secrecy and technology, as decisions involving military affairs so often are, this is even more the case.

Because the policy process is "political" in essence, effective leadership over it is probably best exercised through traditional political action—by defining the basic objectives and building support for them through coercion, bargaining, and compromise—in much the same way that political leadership is exercised in the mainstream of American politics. But in military affairs there is a critical difference. It is very difficult to generate wide understanding and consensus under the cloak of secrecy. Moreover, the political ramifications of many technological developments often are understood neither by the scientists involved nor by the political authorities under whose directions the military programs are advanced. More often than not weapons grow out of the impetus of what is technically possible—especially major or "strategic" weapons systems— and their military and political values tend to be defined after the fact. Weapons tend to search for strategies rather than strategies for weapons. Arms programs developed in an environment of technological innovation and international competition have a momentum of their own and the direction the programs take is determined as often by the vagaries of technology as they are by the needs articulated by the political and military leadership. Those who provide policy guidance find themselves "riding herd" over forces that are hard to understand and difficult to control.[10]

Yet having made this observation, one must nevertheless conclude that there is no alternative to technologically determined military capabilities, for technology obviously delimits the capabilities within reach. This is not to say, however, that the over-all strategies and operational policies adopted are inevitably determined by technological considerations. They are limited by whatever military capabilities are available. But what is to be done with the military instruments—from the point where choices are made as to which instruments should be produced, to the point where decisions are made respecting the deployment and use of the military forces available—is a political problem involving the ends and means of national policy that no amount of scientific advice or military hardware can resolve.

When one views this process from the perspective of interservice competition it can be seen that although one or another military service may appear dominant at a particular moment in time, each of the services is able to hold its own in the contest. Consistency in strategic doctrine need not be the hobgoblin of military minds. For example, during the "Admiral's Revolt" in 1949, when

Secretary of Defense Louis Johnson eliminated a Navy "supercarrier" from the defense budget, the Navy charged the government with relying upon an Air Force strategy of strategic bombing that was morally and militarily unsound and also claimed that the United States was buying an aircraft that was obsolete.[11] The Air Force won the day and the B-36 intercontinental bomber was produced in large numbers (and, incidentally, quickly considered obsolete even by the Air Force). During the Korean War funds were finally provided for the Navy supercarrier program. In the late 1950's the tables were partly reversed. The Navy developed the Polaris missile system premised on the finite deterrence strategy of "city-busting" which the Air Force charged was morally abhorrent and militarily useless. The issue in both cases was Air Force insistence upon its monopoly over strategic retaliatory forces. Ultimately, the Air Force strategic view prevailed, for it is at least the announced intention of the present Administration to develop military options that could exclude or at least defer strikes against enemy cities, placing primary emphasis on the destruction of military forces and capabilities. Yet in the strategic compromises that are now emerging, manned aircraft have been de-emphasized (a setback for the Air Force) and the Navy's Polaris missile system has been awarded a major role in the strategic bombardment mission of the armed forces. But the Air Force will retain a large strategic bomber force into the late 1960's and will continue to control America's intercontinental ballistic missile forces. In the meantime, re-emphasis on the role of ground forces, tactical warfare, and counter-insurgency techniques, has enhanced the bargaining position of the Army, which has won its struggle to increase its manpower, to build its own air arm, and even has hopes of producing an operational anti-missile missile (a sophisticated version of the Nike-Zeus, designated the "Nike-X").[12]

In short, while strategies and weapons systems compete in the policy-making arena, the clash tends to be resolved through military bargains that produce "mixes" of military forces and hardware which are compatible with the basic views of the three military services but may represent contradictory elements in the over-all strategic picture. This probably has more economic costs than it does political, because even though it is more expensive to produce multiple military systems it also produces a wider range of military and political options. However, it may undermine the development of coherent strategies. Over the past fifteen years there have been times when the United States has appeared to have, militarily speaking, a little bit of everything, but not enough of anything.[13]

Since the military policy process has a momentum and continuity that is characterized by incremental adjustment on the basis of internecine bargaining and consensus, decisions at any particular point in time are not likely to be recognized as critical. They may be controversial, in the sense that budgetary limitations require the selection of one system over another. Technical and cost factors may produce agreement to cancel a program altogether. But controversial issues are not always critical ones. Controversy is usually the product of severe reductions or cancellations of major weapons projects but the debates that are a consequence of these decisions rarely clarify the strategic issues which underlie such programs as the Navy supercarrier, the Army Nike-Zeus, the Air Force RS-70, or the "TFX" all-service aircraft. In retrospect one may be able to identify crucial decisions, decisions which represent turning points in American strategy, but they are seldom recognized *at the time* as being so fundamentally important.[14]

Most of our military policies are legacies of the immediate past, the most recent configuration of forces based on the changes caused by technology, the shifting requirements of international politics, and the consensus of the moment within the defense community. Policy alterations by incremental adjustments are aptly summarized by Warner Schilling's phrase "how to decide without actually choosing."[15] Schilling provides a most illuminating example of the policy process. He examines the events leading to the decision to produce the hydrogen bomb and concludes that "through a sequence of minor 'tactical' or minimal decisions" the American government found itself adopting a "new 'strategic' position without ever having made the major choice to get there."[16]

The procession of defense policies by a series of "tactical" rather than "strategic" decisions is the usual way of the policy process. The momentum of policy is hard to overcome. Each previous decision sets in motion actions that will affect the next decision. Each step, only an adjustment in existing policy, often represents too small a departure to gain the stature of a recognizably critical point in the decision process. Yet as step follows upon step, defense programs move in directions which are easier left to meander as dependencies of the vagaries of military technology and the policy process than to the more difficult task of conscious direction and control. . . .

To sum up, it has been argued here that the translation of resources of military power (through what has been called the "policy process") into instruments of policy appropriate to our national objectives through methods compatible with the democratic processes of the United States is gravely affected by the techniques, complexities, and elites associated with military technology on the one hand, and by the compromising nature of the policy process and the multiplicity of policy objectives on the other. Military technology limits the circle of effective participants in the policy process and the policies produced are more likely to represent bargains struck between contending forces than basic resolutions of underlying strategic issues. Furthermore, the momentum of military programs, the special influence of military scientists, and the incremental character of the decision process itself, serve to undermine the real authority of top-level policy-makers. Those who are responsible for military policy are, therefore, to a certain extent victims of the process which they seek to control.

Unfortunately there are no practicable grand alternatives to the current system of policy-making. The military policy process may be less democratic than we would like it to be, but even though it takes place in an arena partly hidden from public view it must also be acknowledged that the pluralistic setting, although circumscribed, does often provide higher political authorities with sufficient leverage to impose their own views because contending forces advocate contradictory policies and technical advice.

The policy process is also inherently deficient when measured against the principle of the political utility of military force. A system of "muddling through," highly suited to solutions based on bargaining and compromise, is not guaranteed to precipitate policy arrangements best suited to the international environment. There is hardly ever a consensus of conceptions of the national interest and what unity does exist is apt to be fragmented by specific interests.

This all leaves top-level policy-makers in a precarious position in the policy process. Their conceptions of their own political roles are perhaps more significant than the particular organizational arrangements in which they find themselves. Secretary of Defense McNamara, for example, believes that it is his responsibility to retain basic control over decisions in *all* important areas of military planning and programming.[17] This conception has led to centralized policy control. But central control of policy, especially when accomplished in association with greater use of automated techniques in decision-making (as Secretary McNamara and his staff have done), may interfere with normal consensus-building processes, resulting in policy statements that may be tightly argued and logically sound, but lacking the support and understanding necessary for successful implementation because traditional bargaining processes have been short-circuited by centralized control procedures.

Intelligent and authoritative participation in the policy process is not an unreasonable requirement of our political leadership and the special complications of secrecy and technology should not be accepted as excuses for a failure to grasp the policy reins in military affairs. Hans Morgenthau is undoubtedly correct in arguing that "participants in our democratic processes can come to know the politically relevant secrets of the nuclear age if they gain confidence in their ability to judge for themselves on the basis of common sense and if the scientific elites let them in on the secrets of their trade."[18] Most basic decisions on weapons and strategies involve political rather than technical choices. Within the limits of what can be done, the fundamental question is now, as it always has been, "What *should* be done?" Should we, for example, conduct more nuclear tests, build more Polaris submarines, add more conventional forces? What purposes will these systems serve, and how much of each kind of defense should we buy? Political leaders responsible for such decisions need the advice and counsel of their military and scientific confreres, but the decisions are rooted in political issues which only responsible political leaders are suited to resolve.

In the final analysis the political relevance and democratic responsiveness of the policy process depends greatly upon the understanding, outlook, and courage of those political leaders charged with responsibility for military policies. These leaders are, in the main, members of the executive branch of government, which is the locus for military policy formulation, innovation and implementation. The leaders of the executive branch most concerned with the development of military policies, in particular, the President and the Secretaries of State and Defense, have an obligation to present to Congress and the public coherent statements of American military strategy, relating major weapons programs to the over-all policy goals of the United States. There is, unfortunately, no traditional or functional occasion for such a presentation. Testimony before the House and Senate Committees on Armed Services, Appropriations, Foreign Affairs and Relations are fragmented by the particular legislative proposals at hand. What is needed at the very least is an American equivalent of the annual British White Paper on Defense. But ours is not a parliamentary system and it would be difficult indeed to establish a tradition of annual debate over American military policy. Moreover, even if it were possible, such a debate could not be expected to have a very great impact upon the daily policy formulating processes through which specific policy alterations emerge.

In short, the present system of formulating national security policies is likely to continue without radical alterations. It is not an insidious process, but it does suffer from operating too frequently and unnecessarily within the confines of military secrecy. Moreover, weapons programs appear to develop rather far before they are related to specific strategies and policy objectives. The military policy process, affected as it is by the impact of technology and the elites associated with it, is perhaps less democratic and less often addressed to basic questions of national purposes than one might demand, but it does operate within a system that is responsive to wider public interests. It is not irresponsible, only somewhat removed from direct political accountability. It is, in brief, also more democratic and relevant to the conduct of American foreign relations than one might expect.

NOTES

1. An excellent discussion of the political utility of military power in international relations is provided by Robert E. Osgood in *Limited War* (Chicago: U. of Chicago Press, 1957), pp. 13–27. Osgood argues that military power should be understood primarily as an *instrument* of policy. He also notes what here is argued at length: ". . . that military power does not automatically translate itself into national security." *Ibid.*, pp. 14–15.

2. Samuel P. Huntington, *The Common Defense* (New York: Columbia U. Press, 1961), p. 2.

3. *Ibid.*, pp. 175–90.

4. U.S. Department of Defense, Office of the Secretary of Defense, Directorate for Statistical Services, *Selected Manpower Statistics*, 2 February 1962, p. 13.

5. *Ibid.*, pp. 19, 61.

6. Roger Hilsman, "The Foreign-policy Consensus: An Interim Research Report," *Journal of Conflict Resolution*, 3 (December 1959), 361–82.

7. *Ibid.*

8. Charles E. Lindblom, "The Science of 'Muddling Through,'" *Public Administration Review*, 19 (Spring 1959), 79–88.

9. Not all defense issues are decided in secret, of course, but those bearing on basic questions of weapons and strategy usually are. A full and brilliant account of this process is contained in Huntington, *op. cit.*, chap. III. Huntington refers to the "legislative" character of strategy-making in the executive branch, an insightful contribution to an understanding of the nature of the policy process.

10. Henry S. Rowen, Deputy Assistant Secretary of Defense for Policy Planning, International Security Affairs, Department of Defense, likened policy-makers in the Defense Department to ants riding on a log that is floating downstream. Each ant, he observed, believes it has some control over the direction the log takes. (Remarks at Annual Conference of the District of Columbia Political Science Association, December 9, 1961, Washington, D.C.)

11. See U.S. Congress, House, Committee on Armed Services, *Hearings on the National Defense Program—Unification and Strategy,* 81st Cong., 1st sess., 1949.

12. See testimony of Secretary of Defense Robert McNamara, U.S. Congress, House, Committee on Armed Services, 88th Cong., 1st sess., January 30, 1963.

13. Some compromises appear in retrospect to be absurd. For example, a failure to decide in favor of one of two competing intermediate range missiles, the Air Force Thor and the Army Jupiter, led to the production of *both* missiles with operational jurisdiction assigned to the Air Force. Yet neither IRBM had much military value. They were highly vulnerable weapons suitable only to a first-strike strategy, a strategy which the United States has never embraced. Only a few years after their emplacement the Thors and Jupiters were removed for just the reasons cited.

14. In this respect I would take issue with Huntington's *Common Defense* which identifies a number of critical strategic decisions over the past fifteen years without stressing adequately the point that at the time the decisions were made the participants were not fully aware that the decisions involved critical departures from previous strategic positions. These departures "grew" out of the policy process rather than springing forth full-blown.

15. Warner R. Schilling, "The H-Bomb Decision: How to Decide Without Actually Choosing," *Political Science Quarterly,* 76 (March 1961), 24–46.

16. *Ibid.,* p. 44.

17. See excerpts from remarks of Deputy Secretary of Defense Roswell L. Gilpatric to the National Defense Committee of the National Association of Manufacturers, *Aviation Week and Space Technology,* February 11, 1963, p. 32.

18. Hans J. Morgenthau, "Decisionmaking in the Nuclear Age," *Bulletin of the Atomic Scientists,* 18 (December 1962), 7–8.

25.

Samuel P. Huntington: Strategic Planning and the Political Process

Drawing a parallel to the legislative process in Congress, Samuel P. Huntington describes the strategy-making process as inevitably a political one of conflict, bargaining, and compromise that involves the groups represented in the National Security Council and the Joint Chiefs of Staff. Although the decade that followed publication of the article saw the strengthening that he expected of the Secretary of Defense and the Assistant for National Security Affairs, Huntington's conclusion still holds: "Decisions on strategic programs are simply too important to be fitted into a symmetrical and immaculate model of executive decision-making. Clarifications of the chain of command and legal assertions of formal authority may reduce bargaining, but they can never eliminate it."

Professor of Government at Harvard University, Samuel P. Huntington has contributed widely to the analysis of national security policy with books like *The Soldier and the State* and *The Common Defense.*

For a decade or more statesmen and scholars have been unhappy about American methods of making decisions on strategic programs—that is, decisions on the over-all size of the military effort, the scope and character of military programs (continental defense, anti-submarine warfare), the com-

Samuel P. Huntington, "Strategic Planning and the Political Process," *Foreign Affairs,* January 1960, pp. 285–99. Copyright by the Council on Foreign Relations, Inc., New York. Reprinted by permission of *Foreign Affairs.*

position of the military forces (force levels), and the number and nature of their weapons. The most common criticisms have been:

1. National security policy lacks unity and coherence. Decisions are made on an ad hoc basis, unguided by an over-all purpose.

2. National security policies are stated largely in terms of compromises and generalities. The real issues are not brought to the highest level for decision.

3. Delay and slowness characterize the policy-making process.

4. The principal organs of policy-making, particularly the National Security Council, are ineffective vehicles for the development of new ideas and approaches. They tend to routinize the old rather than stimulate the new.

5. Policy-making procedures tend to magnify the obstacles and difficulties facing any proposed course of action.

6. These deficiencies are primarily the product of government by committee, especially when the committee members must represent the interests of particular departments and services.

Few persons familiar with the processes by which strategic programs are determined would challenge the general accuracy of these allegations. The persistence of the criticism since World War II, moreover, suggests that the defects are not incidental phenomena easily remedied by exhortations to high-mindedness, assertions of executive authority, or changes in personnel or Administration. Instead, it suggests the necessity of viewing the defects in the context of the political system of which they are a part, and of analyzing the functions which they serve in that system and the underlying causes which have brought them into existence.

II

In domestic legislation, it is often said, the Executive proposes and Congress disposes. Except when a presidential veto seems likely to be involved, the political processes of arousing support or opposition for bills are directed toward the Congress. In determining strategic programs, on the other hand, the effective power of decision rests not with Congress and its committees but with the President and his advisors.

Congressional incapacity to determine force levels and strategic programs is often attributed to the lack of proper information and technical competence. This is indeed a factor, but it is only a contributory one. Congressmen often tend to consider broad questions of general military policy as technical while at the same time they do not hesitate to probe thoroughly and to render judgments about highly specialized and detailed questions of military administration. The inability of Congress to act effectively on strategic programs derives primarily not from its technical failings but from its political ones.

The initiation and elimination of programs and the apportionment of resources among them are highly political decisions involving conflicting interests and groups. They can be made only by bodies in which all the conflicting interests can be brought in focus. The principal groups concerned with the determination of strategic programs are the armed services, the Office of the Secretary of Defense, the State Department, the Treasury, the Budget Bureau, plus a few other governmental departments. The military programs have to be weighed against each other, against conflicting interpretations of the security threats and military requirements, against domestic needs and non-military foreign policy programs, and against probable tax revenues and the demands of fiscal policy. No congressional committee is competent to do this, not because it lacks the technical knowledge, but because it lacks the legal authority and political capability to bring together all these conflicting interests, balance off one against another, and arrive at some sort of compromise or decision. Congress cannot effectively determine strategic programs because the interests which are primarily concerned with those programs are not adequately represented in any single congressional body. The armed services, appropriations, finance, foreign relations, space and atomic energy committees are all, in one way or another, involved in the process. No one of them can have more than a partial view of the interests involved in the determination of any single major strategic program. Every congressional action in military affairs is to some extent *ex parte*.

Congressional bodies may become advocates of particular programs, but they lack sufficient political competence to determine an over-all program. After World War II, except when confronted by similar competing programs, Congress *never* vetoed directly a major strategic program, a force-level recommendation or a major weapons system proposed by the Administration in power. Nor did Congress ever achieve this result, with one partial exception (the Navy's second nuclear carrier), through the failure to appropriate funds recommended by the Executive. The relative inviolability of the military requests was striking when compared with those for domestic or foreign-aid appropriations. Almost regularly, of course, Congress reduced the *total* military request, but it virtually never did this in a manner which seriously affected a major strategic program. Quite properly, Congressmen generally feel that they are ill-equipped to be responsible for the security of the country, and they have, by and large, recognized and accepted the decisive role of the Executive in formulating strategic programs. "God help the American people," Senator Russell once remarked, "if Congress starts legislating military strategy."

The inability and unwillingness of Congress to choose and decide does not mean that congressional groups play no role in the formulation of strategic programs. On the contrary, with respect to strategy, Congress has, like Bagehot's queen, "the right to be consulted, the right to encourage, the right to warn." The most prominent congressional role is that of prodder or goad of the Executive on behalf of specific programs or activities. With the Executive as the decision-maker, Congress has become the lobbyist. Congressional groups engage in sustained campaigns of pressure and persuasion to produce the desired strategic decisions on the part of the Executive, just as in other areas the Administration uses pressure and persuasion to move its legislation through Congress.

In lobbying with the Executive, Congress employs three major techniques. First, congressional groups may attempt, through letters, speeches, investigations and threats of retaliation in other fields, to bring continuing pressure upon the Administration to construct certain types of weapons. The Joint Committee on Atomic Energy, for instance, has been an active lobby on behalf of nuclear weapons: its members played important roles in prompting executive decisions on the hydrogen bomb, the nuclear powered submarine, the intermediate-range ballistic missiles. On the other hand, no lobby ever scores 100 percent, and the Committee was somewhat less successful with the Polaris speed-up and the nuclear-powered airplane.

Second, congressional groups may establish force-level minimums for their favored services or appropriate more money for the services than the Administration requested. In these cases, Congress attempts to use its ancient powers of authorization and appropriation for the positive purpose of establishing *floors,* whereas these powers were designed originally for the negative purpose of establishing *ceilings* to prevent a tyrannical executive from maintaining military forces without the consent of the people. Such actions undoubtedly influence the Administration in planning future force levels, and in two cases involving the National Guard and the Marine Corps, the Administration formally complied with congressional wishes. In the final analysis, however, no way has yet been evolved of compelling an Administration to maintain forces it does not wish to maintain or to spend money it does not wish to spend.

Third, Congress can bring pressure upon the Executive through investigation and debate. Although it is generally held that Congress' power to investigate rests upon its power to legislate, in actual fact Congress investigates, in the grand manner, matters which it cannot legislate. The activities of Senators McCarthy and Kefauver are obvious examples, but more reputable and worthwhile ones are furnished by the great investigations of strategy: the 1949 inquiry into "Unification and Strategy," the 1951 MacArthur investigation, the 1956 Symington airpower hearings, and the Johnson missile investigation of 1957–1958. None of these directly produced legislation but they did compel the Administration to make a public defense of its policies, enabled Congress to bring pressure to bear on the Executive and helped to educate the attentive public on strategic issues.

III

Strategic programs are thus decided upon in the Executive rather than in Congress. The process of decision within the Executive, however, bears many striking resemblances to the process of decision in Congress. It retains a peculiarly legislative flavor. Legislative and executive *processes* of policy-making do not necessarily correspond to the legislative and executive *branches* of government. A policy-making process is legislative in character to the extent that (1) the units participating in the process are relatively equal in power (and consequently must bargain with each other), (2) important disagreements exist concerning the goals of policy, and (3) there are many possible alternatives. A process is executive in character to the extent that (1) the participating units differ in power (*i.e.* are hierarchically arranged), (2) fundamental goals and values are not at issue, and (3) the range of possible choice is limited.

Strategic programs, like other major policies, are not the product of expert planners rationally determining the actions necessary to achieve desired goals. Rather, they are the product of controversy, negotiation and bargaining among different groups with different interests and perspectives. The conflicts between budgeteers and security spokesmen, between the defenders of military and non-military programs, among the four services, and among the partisans of massive retaliation, continental defense and limited war, are as real and as sharp as most conflicts of group interests in Congress. The location of the groups within the executive branch makes their differences no less difficult to resolve. The variety and importance of the interests, the intensity of the conflicting claims, the significance of the values at stake, all compel recourse to the complex processes of legislation. The inability of Congress to legislate strategic programs does not eliminate the necessity to proceed through a legislative process. It simply concentrates it in the executive branch.

To be sure, the specific techniques for innovating proposals, mobilizing support, distracting and dissuading opponents, and timing decisions may differ in the executive "legislative" process from those in the congressional "legislative" process. None the less, in its broad outlines the development of a major strategic program, such as continental air defense, lacks none of the phases involved in the passage of a major piece of domestic legislation through Congress. The need for the program is recognized by an executive agency or some skill group (nuclear physicists) or consulting group close to the executive branch. The agency or group develops policy proposals to deal with the problem and arouses support for them among other executive agencies, congressional committees and, possibly, some non-governmental groups. Opposition develops. Alternative solutions to the problem are proposed. Coalitions pro and con are organized. The proposals are referred from committee to committee. Consultants and advisory groups lend their prestige to one side or another. The policies are bargained over and compromised. Eventually a decision or, more accurately, an agreement is hammered out among the interested agencies, probably through the mechanisms of the Joint Chiefs of Staff and the National Security Council, and is approved by the President. The locus of decision is executive; the process of decision is primarily legislative.

The building of a consensus for a particular strategic program is as complex and subtle as it is for either domestic policy or foreign policy. At a minimum, within the Executive, it involves complicated interlocking patterns of vertical bargaining along the executive hierarchy and horizontal bargaining through a conciliar structure. In almost no executive hierarchy is the exercise of power all in one direction: the actual authority—even the influence—of administrative superiors over their subordinates is hedged around by a variety of inhibiting considerations. Underlying the hierarchy is a set of bargaining relationships, explicit or implicit. The dispersion of power in American society and the separation of powers in government tend to reinforce this tendency. Agencies and officials in subordinate positions often are substantially independent of their administrative superiors. At best the superior may be able to persuade; at worst he may be openly defied.

Vertical bargaining is exemplified in the efforts of the Administration to secure the concurrence of the Joint Chiefs of Staff, individually and collectively, in its budgetary and force-level decisions. On the one hand, each Chief presses for what he believes is essential for his service; on the other, the Administration attempts to cut back and fit service demands into its strategic plan and budgetary goals. Each side has to balance the risks involved in alienating the other against the benefits gained in shaping the final decision. The interlarding of hierarchical and bargaining roles inevitably enhances the possibilities for ambiguity and confusion. As subordinates the Chiefs would be expected to accept but not necessarily to approve decisions made by their administrative superiors. "I'd be worried," Secretary Wilson once declared, "if Ridgway didn't believe in the good old Army."[1] On the other hand, the semi-autonomous position of the Chiefs enhances the value of their approval to their superiors. An administrative decision derives legitimacy (as well as effectiveness) in part from its acceptance and support by the subordinate officials and agencies affected by it. Consequently, great efforts are made to secure the Chiefs' concurrence. "The pressure brought on me to make my military judgment conform to the views of higher authority," General Ridgway declared, "was sometimes subtly, sometimes crudely, applied."[2] The intensity of the pressure applied was tribute to the value of the approval sought.

While vertical bargaining plays a crucial role in strategic decision-making, horizontal bargaining is probably even more widespread and important. Theoretically, of course, authority to determine strategic programs rests with the President and the Secretary of Defense. Actually, the compromising and balancing of interests tends to focus about the two most important committees in the executive branch of the national government: the J.C.S. and the N.S.C. On the surface, it seems strange that two committees should play such important roles in the formulation of military policy and national security. These are areas where one might expect clear-cut lines of authority and executive decision-making. Within the executive branch, few committees of comparable stature exist in domestic areas of policy-making. The J.C.S. and the N.S.C. are significant, however, precisely because they do perform essentially legislative rather than executive functions. They have what Congress lacks: the political capability to legislate strategy. Just as agricultural policy is the product of conflict, bargaining and compromise among the interested groups represented in Congress, military strategy is the product of conflict, bargaining and compromise among the interested groups represented in the J.C.S. and the N.S.C. Hence, the same criticisms are now leveled at these committees which have long been leveled at Congress: logrolling prevails; over-all objectives get lost in the mechanism; a premium is put upon agreement rather than decision. Just as Congress often wrote tariff legislation by giving each industry the protection it wanted, the N.S.C. and the Joint Chiefs make decisions on weapons by giving each service what it desires. The individual members of these bodies suffer the classic conflict known to members of all legislatures: on the one hand, they must represent the interests of their departments or constituencies; on the other, their decisions are expected to be in the national interest.

IV

In strategy, as elsewhere, effective policy requires some measure of both content and consensus. Strategic programs, like statutes or treaties, are both prescriptions for future action and ratifications of existing power relationships. A strategy which is so vague or contradictory that it provides no prescription for action is no strategy. So too, a strategy whose prescriptions are so unacceptable that they are ignored is no strategy. Consensus is a cost to each participant but a prerequisite of effective policy.

In strategy-making, as in congressional legislating, one means of avoiding disagreement is to postpone decision. The proliferation of committees serves the useful political end of facilitating and, in some cases, legitimizing the avoidance of decision. Issues can be referred from committee to committee, up and down the hierarchy. Normally the same service and departmental interests are represented on all the committees; agreement in one is just as unlikely as agreement in any other. Controversial decisions may also be removed entirely from the jurisdiction of the N.S.C. or the Joint Chiefs and devolved back upon the interested agencies; the "decision" is that each will pursue its own policy. Disagreement on major issues also may be avoided simply by devoting more time to minor ones. The J.C.S. "dips into matters it should avoid," Vannevar Bush complained in 1952, "it fails to bring well considered resolution to our most important military problems, and it fritters away its energy on minutiae." [3] The Joint Chiefs, however, were treading a classic legislative path. In almost identical terms, political scientists for years have accused Congress of refusing to grapple with major issues of public policy and of wasting time and energy on minor matters of administrative detail.

Where stringent limits are imposed from the outside, the decision-makers are especially prone to compromise. As the $14 and $13 billion ceilings firmly succeeded each other in the late 1940s, the tendency to divide the funds equally among the three services became more and more pronounced. On the other hand, if the limits permitted by superior executive authority are relatively undefined or broad, logrolling enables each agency to obtain what it considers most important. The result is "Operation Paperclip," in which Army, Navy and Air Force proposals are added together and called a joint plan. Duplication in weapons systems—Thor and Jupiter, Nike and Bomarc—is simply the price of harmony. It is hardly surprising that the J.C.S. should be referred to as "a trading post." This, after all, is the traditional legislative means of achieving agreement among conflicting interests. As one Congressman remarked to his colleagues:

If you are concerned, you politicians, with getting unanimity of action, I refer you to the Joint Chiefs of Staff. There is a classic example of unanimity of action on anything: You scratch my back and I will scratch yours. "Give me atomic carriers," says the Navy, "and you can have your B-52s in the Air Force." I do not know why General Taylor is going along, because I have never been able to find anything that the Army is getting out of the deal.[4]

The political and legislative character of the strategy-making process also casts a different light on the argument that the N.S.C. and J.C.S. have failed to initiate new policy proposals. As many observers of the domestic legislative process have pointed out, relatively few statutes actually originate within a legislative assembly. They are first developed by interest groups or executive agencies. It is therefore not surprising that relatively few strategic programs originally come to life in the committees or staffs of the N.S.C. or J.C.S. The latter necessarily serve as negotiating bodies; the responsibility for innovation lies with the participating agencies.

Just as much of the early criticism of Congress stemmed from a failure to appreciate the political roles of that body, so much of the criticism of the N.S.C. and J.C.S. stems from the application to these bodies of nonpolitical standards. At times in the past, it has been assumed that through investigation and debate all members of a legislative body should arrive at similar conclusions as to where the public interest lay. More recently, conflict within a legislature has been viewed as normal, and policy thought of as the result, not of a collective process of rational inquiry, but of a mutual process of political give and take. Congress is seldom criticized today because of conflicts and disagreements among its members. To a considerable extent, however, the J.C.S. and the N.S.C. are judged by the former theory: in them disagreement is still considered inherently evil. As one naval officer wryly commented: "How curious it is that the Congress *debates,* the Supreme Court *deliberates,* but for some reason or other the Joint Chiefs of Staff just *bicker!*"[5]

Significantly, the Joint Chiefs have also been criticized for employing precisely those mechanisms designed for reaching agreement: delay, devolution, referral, platitudinous policies, compromise, logrolling. On the one hand, the Chiefs are criticized because they cannot resolve major issues; on the other hand, they are criticized because they do resolve them through the classic means of politics.

Much criticism of strategic decision-making has failed to appreciate the tenuous and limited character of hierarchical authority in American government. Reacting against the prevalence of horizontal bargaining, the critics have advocated the abolition of committees and the strengthening of executive controls. In brief periods of emergency, presidential coördination may partially replace the normal bargaining processes. But no presidential laying on of hands can accomplish this on a permanent basis. Decisions on strategic programs are simply too important to be fitted into a symmetrical and immaculate model of executive decision-making. Clarifications of the chain of command and legal assertions of formal authority may reduce bargaining, but they can never eliminate it. Each of the three reorganizations of the military establishment since 1947 has purported to give the Secretary of Defense full legal authority to control his department and yet each succeeding Secretary found his control circumscribed if not frustrated. The existence of counterparts to the N.S.C. and J.C.S. in virtually every other modern state suggests that the causes which have brought them into existence may be pervasive and inherent in the problems with which they deal.

The problem of legislating strategic programs is thus the dual one of producing both content and consensus. On the one hand, little is gained by assuming that effective policy can be achieved without compromise, or that the political problems of strategy-making can be eliminated by strengthening the executive chain of command. On the other hand, it is also impossible to accept what emerges from the bargaining processes as ipso facto in the national interest. Too often, this has blatantly not been the case, and national purposes have been lost in bureaucratic feuding and compromise. The road to reform begins with recognition of the inherently complex political and legislative character of strategic decision-making. The need is for methods which will, at best, contribute both to the substance and the acceptance of policy, or, failing that, at least contribute more to the improvement of one than to the impairment of the other.

V

When the strategy-making process is viewed as essentially legislative in nature, the critical points appear to be not the prevalence of bargaining but rather the weakness of legislative leadership and the limited scope of the strategic consensus.

In the traditional legislative process, interest groups and executive agencies originate proposals, the President integrates them into a coherent legislative program, Congress debates, amends and decides. In the strategy-making process, executive agencies and related groups originate proposals, the N.S.C., the J.C.S., the President and Secretary of Defense debate, amend and decide upon them. But who plays the role of the legislative leader? Who winnows out the various ideas in the light of an over-all set of priorities or grand strategy and integrates these proposals into general programs which can then be discussed, amended and ratified? In the decade after World War II no clear concept developed as to which official or agency had the responsibility for leading the J.C.S. and the N.S.C. in their deliberations. In actual practice, leadership tended to rest with the Chairman in the J.C.S. and with the Department of State in the N.S.C. However, the case was frequently made for expanding the N.S.C. staff in the Executive Office of the President and for strengthening the Special Assistant for National Security Affairs. Similarly, it was often urged that the Secretary of Defense be provided with a mixed civilian-military policy staff which would, at the least, give him an independent source of advice, and, at most, enable him to play a stronger role in making strategic decisions. Other suggestions[6] include the creation outside the executive hierarchy of a council of elder statesmen, a "supreme court" for foreign and military policy, or an "academy of political affairs" (modeled on the National Academy of Sciences) which could study national security problems, issue reports and advise the President directly.

It seems likely that either the leadership functions of the Secretary of State and the Chairman of the Joint Chiefs will become more fully recognized and clarified, or the Special Assistant and Secretary of Defense will develop the staff facilities necessary to perform these functions, or new organs of policy recommendation will come into existence. Such developments would not only facilitate consensus but also would probably improve the content of strategic decisions. The form in which issues are presented for decision often drastically affects the nature of the decision. The problem in the Executive today resides not in the presence of bargaining but rather at the point at which bargaining begins. The development of more effective leadership organs in the N.S.C. and J.C.S. would permit bargaining to be more limited and focused. The starting point would become not three separate proposals advanced by three separate departments but rather one set of proposals advanced by the legislative leader. The requirements of consensus might still cause those proposals to be torn apart tooth and limb, but, at the very least, the clear visibility of the mutilation would have certain restraining effects. It has had them in Congress.

A related and perhaps more important problem concerns the relatively limited scope of the strategic consensus. The strategy-making process goes on largely within the Executive, and the consensus arrived at, if any, is primarily an executive one. As a result, it tends to be both tenuous and tentative. Although the effective power of decision rests with the executive branch, the possibility always exists that it may be upset by forces from the outside. Consequently the activity of the Administration is largely devoted to defending a policy which has been decided upon rather than advocating a policy which has yet to be adopted.

In the traditional legislative process, an issue is debated first within the Executive and then publicly within and about Congress. All the debate, however, contributes directly or indirectly to shaping the final product: to pushing the legislation through without change, amending it in one direction or another, or defeating it entirely. When the President signs the bill, the policy-making process is over, and the debate stops—or at least lessens—for a while. In strategy-making, debate among the various executive agencies and related groups also contributes directly to shaping the measure. Once the decision is made, this debate subsides, but as soon as the decision becomes known to non-executive agencies and groups, the public debate begins. The likelihood of such debate may have had its effects upon the executive policy-makers before the decision was reached, but their anticipation of public reaction to policy often is, at best, an informed hunch and, at worst, a rationalization that the public will not accept policies which they do not accept themselves. Public debate of a strategic decision may also affect its implementation and may influence subsequent decisions. Coming after the initial decision, however, the debate necessarily loses much of its force and value.

It is striking that both the Truman and Eisenhower Administrations, different as they are otherwise, have been regularly criticized for not exercising "leadership" in national security policy. In each case, it is alleged, the President has failed to take the initiative in bringing strategic issues to the people, in arousing support for foreign and military policy proposals, and in educating the public to its responsibilities in the nuclear age. Such criticism assumes that the President should play the same leadership role in strategic matters that he does in domestic legislation. In the latter, the President must be the source of energy for his program, and it is normally in his interest to dramatize the issue and to broaden the public concerned with it. The concept of presidential leadership is that of Theodore Roosevelt, Wilson, F.D.R. rallying support for a legislative program which he is urging upon a recalcitrant Congress.

In the strategy process, however, the President's role is very different, and the domestic model is inapplicable. Here, the President and his Administration have little reason to desire public debate and many reasons to fear it. The decision has been made; the policy is being implemented. The extension of the public concerned with the policy can only lead to pressure to change it in one respect or another and to the exploitation of the issues by the opposition. The primary role of the Administration has to be defensive: to protect the balance of interests, the policy equilibrium which has been laboriously reached within the Executive, against the impact of profane forces and interests outside the Executive. Mr. Cutler put the matter bluntly when he declared:

There is another seamlessness in our complex world: the fabric of our national defense. Perhaps the most potent argument against public disclosure of secret projects or of short-falls (which inevitably always exist) in any one aspect of our national defense is that such disclosure builds up a Potomac propaganda war to rectify that defect or over-finance that project. But if you devote larger resources to one area of national defense, you are apt to imbalance the rest.[7]

Given the nature of the decision-making process, this concern is a natural one. The cold-war Presidents have evolved a variety of means to limit public interest in strategy, to minimize the concern of external groups with force levels and weapons, and, most particularly, to insulate and protect the executive balance from the disruption of outside interests. Hence the tendency of both Presidents and their Administrations to reassure the public, to pour on the "soothing syrup" which has so exasperated the Alsops and others, to limit the information available on American deficiencies and Soviet achievements, to discount these achievements and to minimize their significance, to preserve discipline and to suppress leaks, to discourage dissenting and disquieting testimony before congressional committees, and in general to maintain an air of calm assurance, an imperturbable façade. All these actions stem from a fear of the fragility of the executive consensus and of the irrationality and uncontrollability of the external political forces. These are the new "defensive" weapons of presidential leadership, as important to an Administration in the formulation of strategy as the old "offensive" techniques are in the promotion of domestic legislation in Congress.

A striking feature of the past dozen years has been the extent to which expressions of alarm at the decline of presidential leadership have occurred simultaneously with expressions of alarm at the growth of executive power. This apparent paradox simply reflects the fact that the increasing responsibility of the executive branch in making crucial decisions on strategic programs has undermined the ability of the President to lead. The more the President becomes, at least in theory, the judge, the less he can be the advocate. Yet, in practice, even his power to decide strategic issues is difficult to exercise. To be sure, the N.S.C. and the J.S.C. are theoretically only his advisors: no policy exists until he has approved it. But in part this is a myth to preserve the appearance of presidential decision-making. Surely the President does not override united opinion among his top advisors much more often than he vetoes acts of Congress. The theory that the President makes the decisions, in short, serves as a cloak to shield the elaborate processes of executive legislation and bargaining through which the policies are actually hammered out. Consequently, the President may be less influential as a decision-maker than he is as a legislative leader. The latter function is personal to him. The former is one which he shares with a variety of other groups in the executive branch.

Whatever defects may exist in this situation cannot be removed by shifting the point of decision away from the executive branch. The tenuous character of the decisions and the defensive role of the Administration could be modified only by broadening the scope of discussion and concern in the early stages of the policy process—*before* key decisions are made. Once adequate legislative leadership emerges in the executive branch, the debate could focus on the proposals of this leadership, provided they were made public to the fullest extent possible. Greater publicity for and public participation in strategy-making at an earlier stage would tend to restrain some of the more gross forms of "horse trading" in the Executive, and should enhance the President's actual power of decision. At present, one way in which issues are brought to the top and forced upon the President for decision is through the lobbying activities of congressional committees. Broader and earlier public discussion of strategic programs would in all probability have a similar effect, and instead of interested guesses we would be provided with concrete evidence of what "the public will support." Certainly, discussion is more useful before decisions are made than afterwards. Broadening the scope of the policy consensus could well go hand in hand with improving the quality of the policy content.

NOTES

1. Duncan Norton-Taylor, "The Wilson Pentagon," *Fortune,* December 1954, p. 94.

2. General Matthew B. Ridgway, "My Battles in War and Peace," *The Saturday Evening Post,* January 21, 1956, p. 46.

3. "Planning," speech at Mayo Clinic Auditorium, Rochester, Minnesota, September 26, 1952, p. 8.

4. Rep. Daniel J. Flood, *Congressional Record* (85th Congress, 1st Session), May 27, 1957, p. 7733.

5. Vice Admiral H. E. Orem, "Shall We Junk the Joint Chiefs of Staff?" *U.S. Naval Institute Proceedings,* February 1958, p. 57.

6. See Walter Millis, "The Constitution and the Common Defense," New York: The Fund for the Republic, 1959, p. 36–46.

7. "The Seamless Web," *Harvard Alumni Bulletin,* June 4, 1955, p. 665.

26.
Warner R. Schilling: Scientists, Foreign Policy, and Politics

The scientist as expert has become a familiar figure in the post-World War II debate over national security policy, first with the debate over atomic and hydrogen bombs, and more recently with the one over the ABM. The selection by Warner Schilling offers an illuminating analysis of the scientist's policy predispositions (based on expert skill, knowledge, and experience) and suggests a number of procedures to be followed by the nonscientist in the face of conflicting scientific advice.

Warner Schilling, Professor of Political Science at Columbia University, is author of numerous works on national security affairs and international relations, including "The Politics of National Defense: Fiscal 1950," in Schilling, Paul Y. Hammond, and Glenn Snyder, *Strategy, Politics, and Defense Budgets.*

. . . As an integral part of the efforts of governments to become both more responsive to and responsible for the development of science and technology, scientists have been invited into the highest councils of government, and it is with some of the problems occasioned by the presence of these "new" participants in the making of national policy that the remainder of this article will be concerned. Although some illustrative material will be drawn from the experience of other governments, the paper focuses on problems associated with the participation of scientists in the American policy process.

Needless to say, the problems in policy-making that may arise will vary greatly with the kind of scientist participating (oceanographer, theoretical physicist, specialist in space medicine, industrial chemist), with the nature of the policy issue at stake (weapons development, science education, public health, the exploration of space, the allocation of funds for basic research), and with the manner in which the scientist is involved in the policy process (member of the attentive public, adviser to the President, worker in a government

Warner R. Schilling, "Scientists, Foreign Policy, and Politics," *American Political Science Review,* Vol. 66 (June 1962), pp. 288–300. Footnotes omitted. Reprinted by permission of the *American Political Science Review* and the author. An earlier version of this paper was prepared for discussion at the Fifth Congress of the International Political Science Association in Paris, September, 1961. The points made in it owe much to the comment and counsel of William T. R. Fox.

laboratory, official in an executive department or agency). This article will make no attempt to deal systematically with the combinations possible among these three variables (profession, issue, and involvement). The discussion will be confined to a few of the central problems that the layman and the scientist are likely to encounter in working together on national security issues; and the treatment, as will become evident, will be of a very general and suggestive order.

In their general character, the problems occasioned by the participation of scientists in the determination of high policy are not nearly so novel as is generally supposed. The scientist has been brought into the councils of government because he possesses specialized skills and information believed relevant to the identification and resolution of particular policy probems. His relationship to the policy process is therefore a familiar one, that of an expert. Just as Sputnik I precipitated the establishment of a Special Assistant to the President for Science and Technology, so the earlier problems of fighting World War II and insuring postwar employment had brought the Joint Chiefs of Staff and the Council of Economic Advisers into the Offices of the President.

The central problems in policy-making posed by the entry of scientists into the policy process are thus formally no different from those associated with any other expert involved in the determination of national security policy. In particular, four such problems can be noted. (1) Like all experts, scientists will at times disagree, and the non-scientist (be he politician, administrator, or an expert in some other field) will confront the problem of choosing a course of action in the face of conflicting scientific advice. (2) Like all experts, scientists will at times evince certain predispositions toward the resolution of the policy problems on which their advice is sought, and the non-scientist will confront the problem of identifying the policy predilections peculiar to scientists and being on his guard against them. (3) The non-scientist and scientist will confront one problem in common, and that is how to organize themselves to maximize the contribution that science can make to the government's programs, opportunities, and choices. Finally, (4) the scientist will confront a problem common to all experts who participate in the American policy process, and that is how to engage in politics without debasing the coinage of his own expertise.

II

The difficulties the non-scientist confronts in choosing a course of action in the face of conflicting scientific advice seem inherently no more formidable than those a non-expert would face in deciding what to do in the event of conflicting advice from economists, soldiers, or specialists on Soviet foreign policy. There are at least seven procedures that the non-expert can follow in such circumstances, singly or in combination, and they appear to have about the same promise, for better or for worse, regardless of the kind of experts involved.

The first step the non-scientist can take is to make certain that it is really conflicting *scientific* advice he is receiving. In the fall of 1949 President Truman asked Secretary Acheson to look into the disputes then current within the

Atomic Energy Commission and elsewhere about the consequences of undertaking an intensive effort to make an H-bomb. Upon investigation the Secretary of State concluded that the scientists involved were not really very far apart except on the foreign policy issues that were his and Truman's responsibility to decide.

Procedures two and three are simple: the non-scientist may be guided by quantitative or qualitative features of the division (he can side with the majority, or with that side whose past record is the more confidence-inspiring). Failing these, there is, four, the "principle of least harm" and, five, the "principle of minimal choice." In the former, one chooses that course of action which appears to involve the least cost if the technical premise on which it is based proves to be wrong. Thus in World War II, given the American belief that the Germans were hard at work on an A-bomb, it seemed more sensible to spend $2 billion on the assumption that the bomb could be made than to do little or nothing on the assumption that it could not. In the case of the "principle of minimal choice," one chooses that course of action which seems to close off the least number of future alternatives. This was the character of President Truman's first decision on the H-bomb. He decided to go ahead in the effort to explore the feasibility of an H-bomb, but nothing was decided about technical steps of a greater political or military consequence (for example, testing a device if one were fabricated, or preparing to produce the materials that would be required for weapons production in the event of a successful test).

In the case of procedure six the non-scientist can make his choice among conflicting scientists on the basis of whichever technical estimate is most in accord with policy on which he was already intent. (In contrast to the first procedure, where the non-scientist endeavors to factor out of the conflict the policy preferences of the scientists, here he is factoring into the conflict his own policy preferences.) In the spring of 1942, the British scientists Henry Tizard and F. A. Lindemann (Lord Cherwell) diverged greatly in their estimates of the destruction that could be accomplished by an intensive bombing of the homes of the German working class. There was general agreement among the soldiers and politicians involved that if the lower estimate were correct there were better military uses for the resources the bombing campaign would require, but in the end the campaign was made in the expectation that the higher estimate would prove to be the more accurate (which it did not). This choice was clearly influenced by Churchill's interest in presenting the Russians with a dramatically visible contribution to the war against Germany and by the fact that British air doctrine had long presumed the efficacy of strategic bombing.

In procedure seven the non-scientist is guided by his own sense for the scientific and technical problems involved. In the 1949 H-bomb debate, some of the politicians involved were little deterred by the fact that the scientists were by no means confident that they could make such a weapon and by the possibility that an all-out but failing effort might entail very high costs for the A-bomb program. These politicians were willing to press ahead in part because of their belief that the scientists were not really aware of their own potential. Similarly, when the German soldiers, scientists, and engineers engaged in the development of the V-2 divided on the question of whether it should be launched from mobile or fixed batteries, Hitler's own technical enthusiasm for large, hardened bunkers led him, unwisely as it turned out, to decide on behalf of the latter.

In concluding this survey of the problem of conflicting advice, it should be noted that one of the more likely outcomes is that the actions of the contending scientists may prove much more influential than the procedures followed by the non-scientist. Divided experts will not always be equal in their physical or personal access to the decision-maker, in the persistence with which they state their case, or in the force and clarity of their arguments. Thus, in the H-bomb debate, there were instances where equally qualified scientists differed greatly in the time and energy they spent circulating their views of the technical (and political) prospects, and such differences were by no means without consequence for the judgments of others.

III

The discussion of the policy predispositions displayed by scientists must be entered with considerable caution. The major theoretical premise involved is that all experts will evidence certain predilections with regard to policy and policy-making which are the result of the character of their expertise: their skills, knowledge, and experience. Since experts differ in the skills, knowledge, and experience they command (or in the responsibilities with which they are charged), they will differ in the biases they characteristically exhibit. Thus scientists, soldiers, and diplomats jointly concerned with a policy problem are likely to approach the question of how and in what manner it should be resolved with rather dissimilar predispositions.

These points, however, are easier stated than demonstrated. To begin with, it should be clear that, insofar as policy is concerned, "the scientific mind" is as much a chimera as "the military mind." Scientists, like soldiers and the rest of us, differ greatly in the ideas they have about the political world and the things that will (or ought to) happen in it, and their views on foreign policy matters are far more likely to be reflective of these differences than conditioned by their common professional skills and interests. Moreover, even if differences in expertise or responsibility were the only factors determining the views of policy-makers (and they certainly are not), one would still have to take account of the fact that scientists are as varied in their professional skills and pursuits as soldiers. The perspectives of a theoretical physicist engaged in basic research are no more to be equated with those of an organic chemist engaged in applying extant knowledge to the improvement of an industrial product than is the outlook of a staff officer in Washington drafting a war plan to be considered identical with that of a general in charge of a theatre of operations.

In addition to these difficulties, analysis must also contend with the fact that it is directed toward a moving target. The policy perspectives that a physicist may have developed as a result of two decades in a university laboratory are unlikely to endure without change after a few years on a Washington advisory committee. Many American scientists are well along the same route that transformed the policy perspectives of large numbers of the American military profession during the war and immediate postwar years. As a result of new problems and new responsibilities, these soldiers acquired new skills, knowledge, and experience. In consequence, with regard to their approach to foreign policy, some are, for all practical purposes, interchangeable between the Pentagon and the State Department, and one could wish that there were more diplomats equally well equipped to work on both sides of the Potomac.

With these reservations in mind, six policy perspectives will be presented here which seem moderately characteristic of many scientists, most of them physicists, who have participated in national security policy in recent times. Most of these predispositions were first evidenced during their work with the military during World War II, and the extent and manner in which they have been later operative in reference to larger foreign policy issues is not always easy to document, since most of the sources are still classified. Needless to say, in outlining these predispositions, one is presenting a cross between a caricature and a Weberian ideal type, not describing real people. In discussing these predispositions, the present writer does not mean to convey the impression that they are either "good" or "bad" from the point of view of policy or policy-making, or that one or another of these predispositions may not also be evidenced by groups other than scientists. The point to this discussion is that if certain orders of scientists are indeed prone to these or other policy predispositions, the non-scientist will be wise to be alert to them, even if in the event he should conclude that they are all for the good.

Naive utopianism or naive belligerency. C. P. Snow has described the scientist as an impatient optimist in his approach to social wrongs; he is quick to search for something to do and inclined to expect favorable results. Certainly, the scientist's profession inclines him to look at problems in terms of searching for a solution to them. When this perspective is turned to problems of international politics, however, the scientist's approach often appears open to the characterization of "naive utopianism or naive belligerency." His approach to international relations appears simplistic and mechanistic. It is almost as if he conceives of policy being made primarily by forward-looking, solution-oriented, rational-thinking types like himself.

In these perspectives the scientist is likely to find little in common with the diplomat (who is inclined to believe that most of his problems have no solution, and who is in any event too busy with the crises of the day to plan for tomorrow), or with the politician (whose approach to problems is so spasmodic as to seem neither analytical nor rational, and whose policy positions are anyway soon blurred by his efforts to accommodate to the positions of others), or with the professional student of international politics (who, when the opportunity permits, lectures the scientist on the elegant complexity of the political process, but who never seems, to the scientist at least, to have any really good ideas about what to do). It is perhaps these differences in perspective that lead the scientist on occasion to seem "intellectually arrogant"; it is as if he concludes that those who have no promising solutions or are not seeking them cannot be very bright. In his predisposition toward action and solutions, the scientist comes closest to sharing the predilection of the soldier for decision, which may be one reason why their partnership has been so spectacularly successful.

The whole problem approach. The first grant made by the United States Government for experimental research was in 1832 to the Franklin Institute. The scientists were asked to investigate the reasons for explosions in steamboat boilers. They reported back not only with a technical explanation but with a draft bill to provide for Federal regulation of steamboats. In this they evidenced the scientist's predilection for the "whole problem approach." The reluctance of scientists to apply their expertise to mere fragments of the total problem, especially under conditions where those who prescribe the fragments do not reveal the whole of which they are a part, was evident in the work of both British and American scientists during World War II. Military officials initially approached the scientists with requests for the development of particular weapons and devices without revealing the military problems or reasoning responsible for their requests. The scientists objected to this procedure, and they were eventually able to persuade the soldiers to inform them of the general military problems involved in order that the scientists might reach their own conclusions about the kinds of weapons and devices the military would need to meet those problems.

In 1952, in connection with an Air Force project on air defense, a group of American scientists were asked to review the prospects for improving the nation's continental air defense. The scientists concluded that some new and promising systems were possible, and they submitted an estimate of what the developments might cost. They also recommended that the money be spent. The Air Force did not approve the recommendation, and as is customary in Washington the disputants on both sides began to search for allies and to leak their cases to the press. Certain Air Force officials, who feared that additional funds for air defense would come at the expense of dollars otherwise available for the Strategic Air Command and who were convinced that this would be militarily undesirable, charged that the scientists by entering into matters of military strategy and budget policy had exceeded both their assignment and their expertise. Commenting on this charge, one of the scientists involved later explained that he would have little interest in working on a study project that did not have the potential for leading into the question of whether the conclusions should be acted upon.

The predisposition to want to be told and to deal with the whole problem no doubt has its base in the professional experience of scientists (and one of the central credos of science) that good ideas on a problem may come from the most unexpected quarters and that the widest possible dissemination of information about a problem will significantly enhance its chances for an early solution. Still, there are problems and problems; some are open to determinate solutions, and others can be resolved only through the exercise of political power. The point about the "whole problem approach," as the air defense example illustrates, is that it not only helps propel the scientists from an advisory to a political role but it serves to make the scientist somewhat blind to the fact that he is so moving. In its most extreme form, the "whole problem approach" coupled with the "intellectual arrogance" perspective can lead to such instances as when, on one high-level advisory committee concerned with several areas of national security policy, a scientist whose formal claim to participation was a knowledge of infra-red ray phenomena was reportedly quite free with his proposals for what political policies should be adopted with regard to the United Nations.

Quantum jumps versus improvements. A number of scientists have advanced the proposition that the military tend to be more interested in improving existing weapons than in developing radically new ones, and they have urged that a separate civilian agency be established to undertake such development. Both scientists and soldiers have explained this difference in their approach to military research and development, "quantum jumps versus improvements," with the hypothesis that the soldier's interest in developing entirely new weapons must always be inhibited by his concern for the possibility that war may come in the near future, since in this event his interests are best served by improving existing weapons. It has also been suggested that military leaders, who must be prepared at any time to ask others to take up the weapons at hand and fight with them, cannot afford to let themselves or others become too impressed with the deficiencies of those weapons as compared with others that might have been had.

An explanation less flattering to the military for this difference is the occasional assertion by scientists that theirs is a profession which stimulates original and creative thought, while that of the military tends to develop minds which accept the existing situation without too much question. As indicated in the discussion of the first predilection, this is a judgment which the scientist may extend to the diplomat and the politician as well. The structure of both the domestic and the international political process is normally such as to make "quantum jumps" in policy infeasible. Diplomats and politicians are accustomed to seeing the same old policy problems come around year after year, and they are generally intent on policies which promise only slow and modest change. Scientists, on the other hand, have been demanding and searching for quantum jumps in foreign policy ever since the end of World War II. It is symptomatic that the first proposal developed by the Advisory Committee on Science and Technology to the Democratic National Advisory Council, established in 1959, was for the creation of a new scientific agency, independent of the State and Defense Departments, whose function would be "to face all the problems of disarmament."

Technology for its own sweet sake. In the summer of 1945, after the A-bomb had been tested but before the first drop on Japan, the Director of the Los Alamos Laboratory, J. Robert Oppenheimer, suggested to his superior, General Leslie Groves, that if some improvements were made in the design of the bomb it would be more effective. Groves decided against the improvements because he did not want to incur any delay in the use of the bomb, which he expected would end the war with Japan. In the summer of 1943, after the Director of the German V-2 project, General Dornberger, had finally secured a first-class priority for the use of the weapon, those responsible for producing it in quantity were increasingly handicapped by the scientists and engineers who kept improving but changing its design. Dornberger was finally obliged to issue a flat order against any further improvements.

There was nothing irresponsible in these scientists' actions. Charged with the technical development of weapons, they would have been remiss in their responsibilities if they had failed to call attention to the prospects for improvement. The point to the examples is that scientists and engineers, in the pursuit of their own responsibilities and interests, may easily lose sight of those of the policy maker.

The scientists on the General Advisory Committee to the Atomic Energy Commission who recommended against the development of an H-bomb in 1949 did so in part because of their concern for the foreign-policy consequences of introducing a weapon of such destructive power into the world. Oppenheimer, the Chairman of the Committee, later stated that the thermonuclear design developed by Edward Teller in 1951 was "technically so sweet" that, if it had been available in 1949, the Committee would probably not have made the recommendation that it did. Since, with a technically more promising design at hand, one might suppose that the Committee's foreign-policy concerns would have been all the greater, some observers have concluded that in the pursuit of his technical interests the scientist can also easily lose sight of his own policy concerns.

Such a judgment ignores the complexity of the Committee's position. For example, one of the reasons why the Committee thought the United States should take the initiative in renouncing the H-bomb was precisely because the device then in view seemed likely to be both difficult to make and of dubious military value. It was thought that for this reason the Russians might be willing to follow the American example and that, if they did not, the United States would not have risked much by the delay. These were considerations which obviously would have been changed if a technically more promising design had been available in 1949. Still, the comments of several scientists close to these events are not without relevance. It is their feeling that there are times when the technician does take over, that when the scientist is faced with an interesting and challenging problem his inclination is to get to work on it, and that under these circumstances he should not be the first person to be expected to keep larger policy considerations in balance.

This predisposition, "technology for its own sweet sake," appears to have its roots in two more of science's central credos: the belief in the value of pursuing knowledge for its own sake, and the belief that the best motivation for the direction of research is the strength and character of individual curiosities. But the direction and strength of scientific interests and curiosities is not necessarily coincident with the requirements of military or foreign policy. One of the most recent examples of the scientist's capacity to get caught up in a challenging problem (assigned, to be sure, by policy-makers) is afforded by the ingenious techniques scientists conceived for evading nuclear-test detection systems and for the design of new systems to meet those evasions. In the light of the later course of negotiations, an American statesman who believed there was considerable foreign-policy gain in a test-ban treaty and who believed that the Russians were at one time seriously interested in such a treaty might well conclude that the formula developed by Watson-Watt, the scientist who fathered radar, with reference to the problem of meeting wartime military requirements was not without its implications for meeting peacetime foreign policy requirements: "Give them the third best to go with; the second comes too late, the best never comes." This observation is not intended as an argument that the interests of the United States would have been better served by a test-ban treaty with a "third best" detection system than by no treaty at all. The point is that the policy maker must be sensitive to the prospect that, because of the constant advance of technology, his only real choices may be of this order.

The sense for paradise lost. This predisposition is likely to be more characteristic of the scientists who had their graduate training and early professional experience in the years before World War II than of those who have known only war or Cold War conditions. The prewar scientists took it as an article of faith that certain conditions were essential for the progress of science, in particular that scientists be free to select their research problems and that both scientists and scientific information be free to move among as well as within nations. All of these conditions were violated during World War II, and as a result of the Cold War they were never fully re-established. The nuclear physicists had had perhaps the most highly developed sense of international community. They were relatively few in number, had intimate personal relationships at home and abroad, and had been experiencing an exciting exchange of discoveries since Rutherford identified the nucleus in 1911. They also lost the most, for theirs was militarily the most sensitive knowledge, and the pages of the *Bulletin of the Atomic Scientists* offer eloquent testimony to their ideological disturbance.

The result is that the senior scientists tend to be especially sensitive to possibilities which hold some promise for restoring the former order. They may usually be found on the side (or in front) of those urging freer exchange of scientific and military information with allied governments, less secrecy in the circulation of scientific (and sometimes military) information, and more extensive cultural, and especially scientific, exchanges with the Soviet Union. Similarly, the major activities of the Foreign Policy Panel of the President's Science Advisory Committee and of the Office of the Science Adviser to the Secretary of State have been in connection with the Science Attaché program, the facilitation of international scientific programs and conferences, and the exchange of scientists with the Soviet Union.

Science serves mankind. For at least 300 years the western scientific tradition has assumed that the unrestricted generation of new knowledge about the world was a social good. Over these years science in its purest form (the discovery of the facts of nature for knowledge's sake alone) became increasingly an autonomous social institution; research scientists were largely disassociated from the practical applications of their discoveries, but they took it for granted that these discoveries would ultimately benefit mankind. The advent of nuclear and bacteriological weapons systems which have the potential of destroying so much of mankind and his works has called this faith sharply into question. It does not take much imagination to wonder if man, in view of his apparent inability to escape from the order of conflicts which have historically resulted in war, would not be better off in a world where the knowledge that has made the new weapons possible did not exist. For some of the senior nuclear physicists this is more than a philosophical question. They are unable to avoid a sense of real personal responsibility; they reason from the premise that they were few, and if they had acted differently weapons development might not have taken the turn it did.

In the immediate postwar years, the apparent contradiction between the good of science and the evil of war was resolved by the expectation that the very destructiveness of the new weapons would lead man to renounce at last the folly of war. The course of foreign policy in later years has weakened these expectations but not destroyed them, as the recent flurry of arms-control proposals premised on the rational self-interest of both sides in avoiding mutual destruction testifies.

The need to preserve their sense of service to mankind led some American scientists to refuse to work on weapons. Similarly, there are reports that several Russian scientists were imprisoned, exiled, or placed under surveillance for refusing to participate in weapons work between 1945 and 1953, and in 1957 a number of Germany's elite physicists announced that they would have no part in nuclear weapons work. Such cases are dramatic, but nowhere have they prevented the development of weapons on which governments were determined. The more consequential resolutions have been those in which scientists have simply identified the good of mankind with the strength of their nation or have endeavored to develop new weapons systems which would be as effective as the old in promoting national policy but which would result in less slaughter if used. This was part of the rationale behind the recommendation made by a group of American scientists in 1951 that the government undertake the development and production of a large number of A-bombs for tactical use in the ground defense of Western Europe. Their hope was that such an innovation would relieve the United States of the burden of having to rely solely on the threat of strategic bombing to contain the Red Army.

The failure of the United States to orbit a satellite before the Soviet Union did was the result of the State Department's insensitivity to the political implications of the event and the decision of the President and the Secretary of Defense not to let a satellite program interfere with military missile programs. A small part of the story, however, is to be found in the reluctance of some of the American scientists involved in the programming of the International Geophysical

Year to see an American IGY satellite propelled by an operational military weapon. Their preference for the less developed but non-military Vanguard over the Army's Redstone appears to have reflected a combination of the "sense for paradise lost" and the "science serves mankind" predispositions, in this case an interest in showing the world the peaceful side of science and in demonstrating that the scientists of the world could cooperate in the interests of knowledge as well as compete in the interests of nations.

IV

With regard to the two remaining problems to be discussed—how to organize relations between science and government, and how the scientist can participate in policy-making and still keep his expert standing—four points seem deserving of special emphasis: (A) the problem of organization, especially in the area of foreign policy, is still very much in the research and development stage, and so it may long remain, considering the precedent set by the problem of how to relate military experts and foreign policy; (B) in many areas of policy it will never be possible to specify what constitutes "the best" organization; the way in which policy-makers are organized is not without influence on the kind of policies they will produce, and so long as there are differences over policy there will be no agreement about organization; (C) in the American political system, at least, the science expert at the high-policy level has no real hope of keeping out of politics; his only choice is in the character of his political style; and finally, (D) it should not be forgotten that organization and policy-making are not the same as policy; successful instances of foreign policy capitalizing on or guiding developments in science and technology will not automatically follow just because scientists have been liberally injected into the policy-making process.

Organization. Current American organization in the area of science and foreign policy still reflects the emergency responses to the Russian ICBM and Sputnik I. One effect of these events was that scientists were rushed to the most important single center of power, the Office of the President, by means of the creation of the Special Assistant to the President for Science and Technology and the President's Science Advisory Committee.

The President certainly needs men around him sensitive to the areas of interaction between science and foreign policy. But a case can be made for the proposition that the center of gravity for the input of scientific advice into the policy-making process should be at a lower level than the White House. The President's political interests lie in keeping the staff about him small and generalized. Well-developed plans and programs will have a better chance of maturing in the larger and more diversified facilities that departments and agencies can provide. Secondly, as C. P. Snow concludes in his account of the differences between Tizard and Lindemann, there are risks in having a single science adviser sitting next to the center of political power. Although it should be noted that Churchill fared better with a single science adviser than Hitler did with none ("The Führer has dreamed," Dornberger was told, "that no [V-2] will ever reach England"), Snow's point has merit and it holds for institutions as well as for individuals. The President will generally find his choices facilitated by the existence of multiple and independent sources of scientific advice.

This is a condition that already prevails in the case of many of the departments and agencies whose actions have significant foreign policy consequences, especially in the use of scientists by the Department of Defense, the Atomic Energy Commission, and the National Aeronautics and Space Administration. It is, however, a condition notably absent in the case of the Department of State. As it now stands, the President has more scientists to advise him on the scientific and technical aspects of various foreign policy issues, particularly in the national security field, than has the Secretary of State.

Excluding the science attachés overseas, the Department of State's Office of the Science Adviser numbers six people of whom three, including the director, are professional scientists. There are no scientists, full or part-time, in the Department's offices for policy planning, space and atomic energy, or political-military affairs. As might be inferred from these arrangements, many of the policy-makers concerned believe that their needs for scientific advice are adequately met through formal and informal communication with scientists employed in the operating agencies and departments and with the President's own Science Advisory Committee. (It should also be noted that in at least one office the need for additional political personnel is clearly more urgent than the need for scientists). The Department's Science Adviser, who participates in the work of both the President's Committee and the Federal Council on Science and Technology, serves to facilitate such communication; otherwise both the demands placed on the Office and its own interests have limited its activity, as previously noted, to a relatively narrow range of foreign policy problems.

Whether the interests of the Department of State would be better served by a larger "in-house" scientific competence is a question that an outside observer cannot easily answer. Much depends on the validity of the expectations that the Department can rely on the scientists of the operating agencies to alert it to developments and information relevant to foreign policy. Even more depends on how determined the Department is to play an active and influential part in shaping the scientific and technical programs of the government to conform to its own conception of national needs and priorities. Should this determination be high, it is difficult to avoid the hypothesis that if the President has found it useful to have a relatively large science advisory body to help him monitor and direct the course of science and technology as they affect foreign and domestic policy, so too might the Secretary of State in the area of his own more limited but still extensive responsibilities.

Organization and purpose. Since administrative organizations exist for the purpose of serving policy goals and implementing policy programs, it is to be expected that those who differ on the goals and programs of policy will differ about the proper design of administrative organizations. The desire of many scientists in 1945 to see atomic energy used for peaceful rather than military purposes was one of the reasons for their political campaign to place the postwar atomic energy program in the hands of a civilian commission instead of the War Department. Similarly, more recent differences about how to organize the government's space effort reflect, in part, policy differences about whether space will or should be an area for major military operations.

The same point can be seen in the proposal to create a Department of Science and Technology which would include the variety of "little" science programs now scattered throughout the Executive structure (for example, those of the Weather Bureau, National Bureau of Standards, the Antarctic Office) but would exclude those of the Department of Defense, the Atomic Energy Commission, and the Space Administration. The hope behind this proposal is that, combined together, the "little" programs would be able to compete more effectively in the struggle for government dollars with the "big" science programs of the military, atomic energy, and space organizations.

The question of the "best" science organization is thus inescapably tied to the question of what is the "best" science policy. But who can demonstrate whether science and foreign policy would be better served by allocating dollars to a program to control weather or to a program to explore Mars? There are no determinate solutions to problems of this order. Neither, for that matter, is there any "one right amount" of the nation's scientific resources that should be allocated to basic as compared to applied research. Differences on policy questions such as these are unavoidable among scientists and non-scientists alike, and they can be resolved in but one manner: through the interplay of power and interest in a political arena.

This condition, plus the increasing dependence of scientific programs and research on government funds, plus the increasing consequences of the choices the government makes in allocating those funds, all promise to put the politicians and the scientists under increasing pressure. As the opportunities for further development in each of a thousand different scientific fields mushroom with the acceleration of scientific knowledge, whatever the government decides to support, it will be deciding *not* to support more. Indeed, it is not too difficult to see the scientists becoming practiced advocates and lobbyists for the government's support of their cherished fields and projects, or to imagine the day when the politicians start to complain about "interscience rivalry" and begin to fancy that, if only there were a single Chief of Science, competition and duplication could be ended and the nation could have an integrated science policy.

Scientists in politics. The American political system is not one that insulates its experts from the politics of choice. The scientist involved in high-policy matters is likely to find himself propelled into the political arena, either by a push from behind or by his own interest in seeing that the "right" choices are made. Some of the incentives the scientist may have, to follow up his advice with an effort to see that it is accepted (and to take a hand in a few other matters while he is at it), were outlined and illustrated in the preceding section. It is equally important to recognize that the scientist may find himself on the political firing line, placed there by a politician interested in using the scientist's prestige as an "expert" to disarm the critics of his (the politician's) choices.

Thus, prior to the moratorium on nuclear tests, the Eisenhower administration appeared to be using scientists and their scientific facts on fall-out as a means of justifying and defending a policy that was obviously compounded of a variety of considerations besides that of the radiological hazard. The comparison with Truman's use of the prestige of the Joint Chiefs of Staff to defend his choices in the Korean War comes easily to mind. So, too, do the statements of various Republican leaders that they had lost confidence in the Joint Chiefs and their determination, when they came to power, to get rid of the "Democratic" Chiefs and to appoint Chiefs in sympathy with Republican policies.

The scientist, in short, is not likely to orbit the centers of political power emitting upon request "beeps" of purely technical information. He will inevitably be pulled into the political arena. If his participation there is to be either productive or personally satisfying, both the scientist and the non-scientist need to be highly conscious of the character of their activity and the problems involved. The scientist (and many a non-scientist) must learn that the making of foreign policy is not a quest for the "right" answers to the problems of our time. There are only hard choices, the consequences of which will be uncertain and the making of which will often seem interminable in time and irrational in procedure.

The debate and disagreement over these choices will be heated and confused under the best of circumstances, but emotion and misunderstanding can be eased if scientists and non-scientists are both alert to the limits as well as the potential of the scientist's contribution. On the scientist's part, there is the obvious need to exercise the utmost care in making clear to himself and to others the areas where he speaks as a concerned citizen and those where he speaks as a professional expert. More difficult will be the task of learning how and to whom to address himself in each of these capacities when he is dissatisfied with the outcome of a policy decision in which he has participated. There is, as Don Price has pointed out, no clear code in Washington to govern the conduct of dissenting experts, only a "flexible" set of possible relationships with one's immediate superiors and those whose authority competes with or exceeds that of one's superiors. In contrast to the soldier, who can find some although not complete guidance in the doctrine of "civilian control," the very nature of the scientist's intellectual habits and many of his policy predispositions may make especially difficult his task in determining the limits to which he can stretch his dissent.

On their part, the non-scientists need to recognize that scientists can hardly be expected to remain politically indifferent or inactive about the policy issues with which they are involved (especially when no one else in Washington practices such restraint). It was the naivete of this expectation that was so appalling in the conclusion of the Gray Board that Oppenheimer was a security risk because (among other reasons) "he may have departed his role as scientific adviser to exercise highly persuasive influence in matters in which his convictions were not necessarily a reflection of technical judgment, and also not necessarily related to the protection of the strongest offensive military interests of the country." It is unlikely that "civil-scientist" relations will ever get any worse than this. With time and experience one can expect many of these problems to be eased, but it would be unrealistic to expect them to disappear. Military experts have participated in the making of foreign policy far longer than scientists, and the question of how they can best do so is still the subject of more than a little disagreement.

Policy processes and policy. In closing this discussion of scientists and the problems of their organizational and political relationships to others engaged in the determination of foreign policy, it is important to remember that the policy process can bring minds together but it cannot make them think. It is worth noting that, in the political and administrative structure of the Soviet Union, no scientist is as institutionally close to the Premier as is the Special Assistant for Science and Technology to the President of the United States and that there is no equivalent of the Science Advisory Office in the Russian Ministry of Foreign Affairs. Yet one would not say that the foreign policy of the Soviet Union has appeared either ineffectual or insensitive in its response to developments in science and technology.

The circumstances attendant on the development of radar by the British from 1935 to 1940 provide a useful insight into both the potential and the limits of effective organization. Essential, obviously, were the scientific and technical ideas that Watson-Watt and his colleagues had in mind in 1935, ideas which in turn were the result of the earlier years of research they had been free to conduct in the facilities of a government laboratory. Certainly, it was important that there were administrative scientists in the Air Ministry who were so alert to the military problems of the Air Force that they could see on their own initiative the need to establish a special scientific committee for the study of air defense (the Tizard Committee) and who were so alert to the work of the scientific community that they made their first request for information to Watson-Watt. Of consequence, too, was the fact that the personal and political relations of the members of the Tizard Committee with the members of the military, administrative, and political hierarchies whose interest and cooperation were vital for the subsequent progress of the research and development program were relations characterized by mutual ease, respect, and understanding.

But these conditions would not have led from the formation of the Tizard Committee in 1935 to a chain of operational radar stations by 1940 and a Fighter Command practiced in their use if it had not been for the military ideas of members of the Royal Air Force. It was they who first thought of the formation of a committee to look specifically into the problem of detection, they who recommended more funds than those first proposed by the Tizard Committee for the development of an electromagnetic detection system, and they who were responsible for the decision to start constructing the stations and training the personnel while the equipment was still under development. The explanation for this interest and support is to be found in their theories about the next

World War. They believed the Germans were planning to engage in the strategic bombing of Great Britain, and they wished to be prepared for it.

The point is obvious but important. British scientists and science organization were in the final measure but ready tools. They were good tools, but the use to which they were put was the result of the kind of ideas the military men had about war. The same will hold in the other areas in which science may affect foreign policy. The contributions that science and technology will bring to international politics will largely turn, not so much on the particular arrangements of scientists in the policy-making process, but on the purposes of statesmen and the theories they have about the political world in which they live.

27.

Eugene J. Rosi: Public Opinion and National Security Policy: The Nuclear Testing Debate

The impact of public opinion in the policy-making process is difficult to assess as governmental and nongovernmental elites—such as the press, interest groups, prominent individuals—interact in debating security issues. The following selection analyzes a number of such interacting components in the ten-year public controversy (1954–63) over the testing of nuclear weapons.

> Whereas . . . the vast majority of these lines of strategy [presented by the Foreign Policy Association in its Great Decisions Program] reflect positions inimical to the best interests of the United States . . . [and] equal weight is sometimes given to issues contrary to our national interest . . . now, therefore, be it Resolved . . . that vital decisions affecting survival arrived at by the President and the Congress of the United States demand concerted support of all citizens. In this hour when free nations are facing their most critical trials, all our efforts and resources must be united behind decisions that are clearly directed to survival. PATRIOTISM IS NOT DEBATABLE.
>
> Resolution of The American Legion, September 1961

> Not the violent conflict between parts of the truth, but the quiet suppression of half of it, is the formidable evil; there is always hope when people are forced to listen to both sides. . . .
>
> John Stuart Mill, On Liberty

This article was written especially for this volume, incorporating some of the author's material that appeared previously in the following articles: "How 50 Periodicals and the Times Interpreted the Test Ban Controversy," Journalism Quarterly (Autumn 1964), pp. 545–56; "Mass and Attentive Opinion on Nuclear Weapons Tests and Fallout, 1954–63," Public Opinion Quarterly (Summer 1965), pp. 280–97; and "Elite Political Communications: Five Washington Columnists on Nuclear Weapons Testing, 1954–58," Social Research (Winter 1967), pp. 703–27. The data analyzed for the 1954–63 period include 18 national opinion surveys, more than 700 articles from 50 periodicals, 194 New York Times editorials, 200 articles by Washington columnists, and numerous publications of 33 interest groups and three scientists.

American national security policy on nuclear weapons tests during the period from March 1954, when the fission-fusion-fission bomb blanketed a large area of the Pacific with fallout, to August 1963, when the partial Test Ban Treaty was signed, was made within a context conditioned by domestic public opinion. Public opinion was hailed by some advocates of test cessation for bringing about the suspension of tests in 1958 and 1963; it was condemned for the same reasons by some opponents of test cessation, who criticized policy-makers for bowing to its demands. Rejecting both these judgments, other observers have maintained that as an accelerating technology confronts the American people with "assured destruction" and "multiple independently targeted reentry vehicles," the public opinion that has often been glorified as omnicompetent in the past is becoming increasingly incompetent in the nuclear age.

The aim of this study of the ten-year test-ban issue is threefold: to describe mass and attentive public opinion on the issue; to draw inferences about the interaction of general opinion, elite opinion, and the decision-makers; and to evaluate the contribution of nongovernmental elites to the public debate of the issue.

One assumption of the study is that the opinion-policy process is neither town-meeting democracy nor power-elite tyranny. Instead, mediating between the government and the mass public is a nongovernmental elite structure that was initially described in Gabriel Almond's pioneering work, *The American People and Foreign Policy*.[1] These nongovernmental elites include interest groups, the press, and prominent individuals. Within broad value boundaries delineated by the general public, a division of labor or influence exists in which the nongovernmental elites compete before an audience made up of the attentive public—that small portion of the population which follows policy deliberations—interacting with each other, with the governmental elites, and with the attentive public. In this way, and not merely by mandate or manipulation, are government and public opinion linked.

A second assumption is that public debate of issues by nongovernmental elites and the attentive public in advance of governmental decision is fundamental to the national security policy process in a democracy. The contributions of debate can include: (1) clarification of the value positions of the participants in the debate; (2) establishment of the facts and of the need for more information; (3) distinguishing the value positions from the facts; (4) improvement of proposed administration policy through searching criticism from counter-experts; (5) generation of new alternative courses of action; (6) making more explicit the possible risks and consequences in administration-proposed policy and alternatives, thereby reducing potential disillusionment, psychological let-downs, and volatile swings of opinion; (7) widening the base of support for the selected course of action; (8) education of the participating publics for future debates.[2]

The mass public is often criticized for its well-documented ignorance of many public issues, yet it can hardly be expected to be well informed on the complexities of national security policy. The nongovernmental elites, however, can be held responsible for the public debate of these issues. This study therefore assesses these elites according to criteria that are frequently applied to the mass public with disappointing results. The public communications of the nongovernmental elites have been examined not only for information but for the frames of reference communicated (including values, goals, and means or policy advocacy to achieve these goals), as well as for the style of presentation. For example, the testing debate was replete with references to prohibition both of the use and testing of nuclear weapons (atomic and hydrogen; clean and dirty), to genetic and somatic damage from radioactive fallout, to unilateral and multilateral cessation, to inspection and detection of tests, and so on. Left unexplained, unclarified, and unstructured, these terms become blurred and interchangeable, promoting only confusion. Analyzed and placed in a framework for observing the political world, they could become part of the working vocabulary of the nongovernmental elites and of the attentive public that intelligently participates in the debate. Such analysis should not be presented in the abstruse discourse of a technical expert; on the contrary, it should be lucid enough to make sense to the intelligent layman—although complex enough not to distort reality.

The communications of the elites were analyzed using the following framework (a thematic, qualitative content analysis was used for the media):

(1) *Direction of opinion:* Was it for, against, or noncommittal on unilateral/multilateral test cessation?

(2) *Values:* Were judgments based primarily on humanitarian or on security values? (The connotation of "security" as used herein lies between the strict military meaning and the broad meaning of preserving the basic values of a society.) *Goals:* Were they primarily in political, military, or humanitarian areas? Were they short, middle, long, or utopian in time perspective? *Means to these ends:* Were they mainly political, military, or other—such as public opinion, education, moral regeneration?

(3) *Style:* Were issues oversimplified, presentations biased, issues considered in a political context? Was an attempt made to inform, clarify, guide, suggest alternatives? Was the tone in regard to radioactive fallout one of emotionality (near despair) at one extreme, reassurance (near insensitivity) at the other, or concern between the two? *Authority:* Were particular groups or individuals referred to with approval or disapproval? Were their competence or patriotism called into question? Was administration policy accepted without questioning?

(4) *Perspectives on the political process:* Was there an understanding of politics as a continuing group competition for scarce values by means of persuasion, negotiation, and coercion; an appreciation of the need for flexibility and of the omnipresence of risk and uncertainty; some understanding of the nature of deterrence, the potential of arms control, and the continuity and change in Soviet policy?

The "mediating" elite components analyzed in this study comprise interest groups, the mass media, Washington columnists, and three scientists.[3] Interest groups included national organizations that had a general interest in foreign and national security policy or a specific interest in the issue in question. Magazines were selected for analysis instead of newspapers since it was judged that such a technical issue was more a subject for intra-elite rather than intra-mass public discussion; *New York Times* editorials were included because of its status as an influential "prestige paper." Five Washington columnists, who may serve as "reference individuals" for faithful readers, offered a liberal to conservative spectrum: Walter Lippmann, James Reston, Joseph and Stewart Alsop, Arthur Krock, and David Lawrence. The three scientists—Linus Pauling, Ralph Lapp, Edward Teller—represented both the most vocal and, broadly, the principal points of view in the scientific community.

The discussion will proceed as follows: first, considering general and attentive opinion in the context of events; next, presenting the analysis of nongovernmental elite communications; finally, offering inferences about possible relationships among mass and attentive opinion, nongovernmental elites, and decision-makers. The ten-year period will usually be divided at approximately the halfway mark—1958—when the United States and the Soviet Union stopped testing without a formal agreement.

General and Attentive Public Opinion in the Context of Events, 1954–63

Two generalizations about national opinion are suggested by an examination of Figure 1 and Table 1:

(1) From 1954 to 1958 the American public seemed to differentiate between multilateral and unilateral test cessation (i.e., cessation by agreement of all the nuclear powers or by the United States alone without such an agreement), strongly opposing unilateral American suspension while generally approving a multilateral agreement by fairly large majorities.

(2) Numerous and wide fluctuations of opinion occurred: (a) shortly after the 1956 election, approval of a multilateral agreement dropped twenty points to a minority, only to climb back to a majority the following April 1957; (b) in November 1959, 77 percent of the people approved a continuation of the testing moratorium that had begun the year before; (c) in mid-1961, attitudes plummeted to disapproval of continued cessation; (d) in November 1961 and January 1962, the nation was evenly divided on the issue of America's resuming atmospheric tests; (e) two months later, 67 percent of the public favored resumption of such tests; (f) and seventeen months after that (August 1963), a majority swung to approval of the partial Test Ban Treaty.

These swings in opinion must now be placed in the context of events. Between 1954 and early 1956, before the election campaign, the general public could scarcely have understood the implications of test cessation. Most likely, unilateral suspension was equated with unilateral disarmament or surrender of the nuclear weapons which were considered the primary defense of the

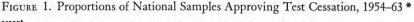

Figure 1. Proportions of National Samples Approving Test Cessation, 1954–63 *

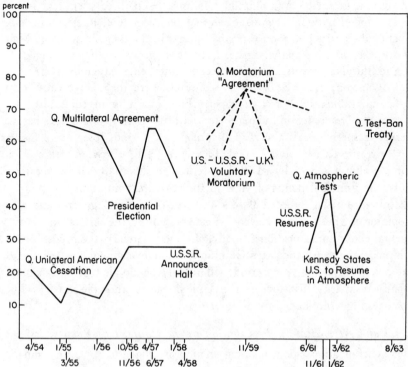

*Based on AIPO and NORC surveys. For the complete data, see Table 1. Responses to "resumption" questions in 1961–62 have been reversed.

West; the main appeal of a test-ban agreement may have been the felt need for cooperation in view of the special nature of the atomic bomb or the overtones of the word "agreement" in the survey question. Cues supporting both positions could have been derived from the Eisenhower Administration's emphasis on the importance of nuclear weapons, continued testing, the insignificance of fallout, and its goal of a comprehensive disarmament agreement to control nuclear weapons.

The opinion shifts around election time in 1956 seemed due largely to party affiliation. During the campaign, Democratic candidate Adlai Stevenson proposed a test cessation that, in its original form, could have been interpreted as unilateral American suspension; the Republicans tended to oppose cessation in any form other than with "foolproof" inspection and comprehensive disarmament. In addition to partisanship, the reversal of opinion concerning an agreement shortly after the election was most likely due to the convincing "expert judgment" of the administration on an esoteric subject; the Suez crisis; the Russian repression of the Hungarian revolution; and, because of the latter crises, the enhanced role of President Eisenhower as leader of all the people and foremost military expert.

Partisanship subsided in the months that followed. The swing in attitudes back toward approval of an agreement in April and June 1957 was possibly attributable to the dissociation of the issue from Stevenson and from the extremism exhibited by both sides during the campaign. Moreover, the administration appeared more favorable: the President on several occasions in the

TABLE 1. NATIONAL OPINION ON TEST CESSATION, 1954–63
(in percent)

Date	Unilateral American [a]				Multilateral [b]			
	For	Against	DK	(N)	For	Against	DK	(N)
4/6/54 [c]	21	72	7	(1,435)				
1/21/55 [d]	11	84	5	(1,209)				
3/11/55 [d, e]	15	80	5	(1,225)	65	28	7	(1,225)
1/26/56 [d, e]	12	83	5	(1,238)	62	29	9	(1,238)
10/16/56 [c]	28	53	19	(1,049)				
11/15/56 [d]					42	52	6	(1,286)
4/23/57 [c]					64	28	8	(1,602)
6/25/57 [c]					64	22	14	(1,515)
7/16/57 [e, f]								
1/22/58 [c]					49	36	15	(1,543)
4/14/58 [c]	28	61	11	(1,433)				

Date	For	Against	DK	(N)
11/10/59 [c, g]	77	10	13	(1,636)
6/21/61 [c, h]	27	53	27	(1,625)
11/15/61 [c, i]	44	42	14	(1,523)
1/9/62 [c, i]	45	45	10	(1,618)
3/6/62 [c, i]	25	67	8	(1,600)
8/13/63 [c, j]	61	18	21	(1,246)

[a] Most questions asked something like "Should the United States stop nuclear (atomic, hydrogen bomb) tests?" or "continue tests?"

[b] Most questions asked something like the phrase in footnote a, but added, "if all other nations, including Russia, stop."

[c] Date sent out by the American Institute of Public Opinion (AIPO).

[d] Date sent out by the National Opinion Research Center (NORC).

[e] This question first asked if the United States should continue tests, then asked those who wished tests to continue if they favored an agreement by all countries, including the United States and Russia, to stop tests. The total in favor of the multilateral ban here includes those who stated their approval first of unilateral American cessation, the assumption being that they would also approve of an agreement.

[f] This ambiguous question did not specify multilateral or unilateral cessation; the results: 40 percent for (5 percent qualified); 43 percent against (3 percent qualified); 17 percent DK.

[g] The testing moratorium was misleadingly called an "agreement" in this question.

[h] ". . . should the U.S. resume tests at this time?"; responses reversed.

[i] ". . . U.S. should or should not start tests in the atmosphere"; responses reversed.

[j] Those who heard or read about "the agreement with Russia to have a partial ban on the testing of nuclear weapons" (78 percent of the sample) were asked, "Do you think the Senate should vote approval of this ban or not?"

spring of 1957 included approval of a test ban as part of a general disarmament agreement.

In the spring of 1958, despite (or partially because of) the Soviet test suspension and despite the concern over fallout by more than one-third of the population, the public opposed American test cessation, 61 to 28 percent. President Eisenhower had called the Soviet cessation announcement a "gimmick" and the USSR had refused the President's suggestion for a study of inspection measures. Yet in November 1959, a year after the test moratorium had begun, the American public strongly approved the suspension of tests, in contrast to the disapproval expressed in April 1958.

Several reasons for the shift from disapproval to approval suggest themselves. The administration was continuing to endorse the moratorium, albeit cautiously, conditional upon the success of the Geneva disarmament talks; this may have given the cessation a kind of official sanction. Additional support might have stemmed from the question wording, which mistakenly called the moratorium a Soviet-American "agreement" (presumably the general public would not be sophisticated enough to consider the implications of "tacit" agreements).

By June 1961, however, the majority had reversed, now favoring resumption of American testing by 53 to 27 percent. Tension was then mounting over the Berlin crisis and public doubts were expressed by the Kennedy Administration over adhering to a test halt without progress toward a treaty or assurance that Russia was not testing clandestinely. The President ordered a scientific inquiry to determine whether evidence indicated a Soviet violation of the moratorium.

Four months later the issue became the resumption of atmospheric tests by the United States, since underground operations had begun after the USSR resumed experiments in the atmosphere in September 1961. The American public was now split evenly. Significant events included Soviet explosions up to 56 megatons; the Berlin crisis; and President Kennedy's order for preparations to test in the atmosphere if it became necessary. Radioactive fallout did not appear decisive at this time since a majority of the people (61 percent) did not consider it a danger. Opinion remained deadlocked in January 1962, as the Geneva talks seemed headed for a dead end.

But in March 1962 a large majority (67 to 25 percent) emerged in favor of American testing in the atmosphere. The survey revealing this was made shortly after President Kennedy's national television address announcing the US decision to resume atmospheric explosions.

The final reversal of opinion occurred seventeen months later, when in August 1963 a majority (61 to 18 percent) approved Senate ratification of the partial Test Ban Treaty signed in Moscow. The President had called the treaty a "victory for mankind" and the administration strongly supported it in Senate hearings being conducted during the interviewing period.

The Attentive Public

In an attempt to separate empirically—however crudely—a more interested, informed, and involved public from the general public discussed above, nine criteria derived from the survey data were used as filters: (1) whether or not the respondent voted; (2) respondent's educational level—grammar, high, some college, or college graduate (numerous studies have indicated that voters and the better educated tend to be more interested, informed, and involved in public affairs); (3) a combination of educational level and vote; (4) interest in world affairs and hydrogen bomb tests; (5) a sample of respondents selected from *Who's Who;* (6) awareness or knowledge of fallout; (7) whether or not the respondent correctly explained in his own words the Kennedy Administration's plan to increase trade with other countries; (8) a combination of education, vote, and fallout awareness; (9) a combination of education, vote, and correct understanding of the trade plan. The last criterion is illustrated in the following table, which shows how voters on each educational level who had a correct understanding of the trade plan responded to the question of test resumption in March 1962.

TABLE 2

Correct on Trade Plan and Voted	*% for Resumption*	*% Against Resumption*	*% Don't Know*	*(N)*
Grammar school	67	19	14	(15)
High school	82	11	7	(82)
Some college	85	7	8	(87)
College graduate	88	5	7	(56)

Source: AIPO poll, March 1962.

A rough idea of the size of the attentive public that was located within the general public can also be illustrated by the above data: voters who answered the trade plan question correctly made up about 17% of the total national sample; voters answering the trade question correctly who had attended college or were college graduates made up, respectively, 6% and 4% of the national sample. The smaller figures seem to offer a more realistic approximation of the size of the public that is regularly attentive to the often abstruse national security debates.[4]

The nine criteria contribute support to the following generalizations about the trend of attentive public opinion compared to general opinion. Before the moratorium (1954-58), the attentive public was more opposed to unilateral American suspension than the inattentive public. In April and July 1958 it was roughly 75 to 25 percent against such action. With regard to a multilateral agreement, a shift of the attentive public had occurred in 1957. Up to that time the college-educated voters gave the smallest majority of the educational groups in favor of such an agreement. In April and June the college group became the largest majority in favor of the ban. January 1958, however, saw a reduction in the overall majority for the ban, with the college group once again the least in favor. A *Who's Who* sample in July 1958 (55 percent approved the agreement) also indicated a decline from the favorable percentage of the previous June (67 percent).

After the moratorium began, the attentive public generally manifested greater approval of test resumption than the inattentive public from November 1959 (a smaller majority in favor of the moratorium) to March 1962 (an overwhelming majority in favor of resuming tests). Before reaching such protesting proportions, however, the attentive segment divided more closely than the inattentive in June 1961. Finally, in August 1963, the attentive sector presented the largest majority in support of a partial test-suspension agreement.

From the data presented in the preceding pages a number of inferences can be drawn concerning mass and attentive opinion on fallout and the nuclear test ban:

1. Large numbers of persons (ranging from 31 to 35 percent of the sample, roughly representing 31 to 35 million people) were concerned with the health effects of fallout. Yet fear of such effects appeared to play less of a role in attitudes toward test cessation than one might have expected; and this role diminished as time passed, at least until March 1962. Education was the most significant variable; the amount of anxiety was directly inverse to the level of education.

In April 1957 those more concerned over fallout were more in favor of an agreement, but 59 percent of those not thinking fallout was a hazard also favored an agreement. Anxiety over fallout would not have affected the nearly three-quarters of the grade-school educated who had not heard of it (58 percent of whom approved the test-ban agreement), nor the 38 percent of the college group that did not think it was harmful. The college-educated were least concerned with fallout and most in favor of the test-ban agreement.

In the spring of 1958, about half the respondents who had heard of fallout were concerned with its effects on health (35 percent of the sample). Once again the degree of anxiety diminished with increase in education. But in April 1958 those concerned with the effects of fallout divided evenly on unilateral suspension (in contrast to the three-to-one approval of an agreement in April 1957); those not concerned were overwhelmingly opposed to a unilateral suspension (90 percent compared with 7 percent—yet 59 percent of this group had favored an agreement in 1957). Security considerations appeared to have driven one-fourth of the fallout conscious and twice as many of the unconcerned from approval to opposition in one year. A large majority of the populace therefore seemed willing to take the risks involved in continuing American tests rather than cease them without an agreement. The public seemed far from hysterical over fallout at this time, and appeared even less so in November 1961, when majorities in nearly every breakdown of the sample saw no danger in fallout, and also in March 1962, when the resumption of atmospheric testing was widely approved. Increased knowledge about fallout apparently produced a decrease of anxiety about its effects.[5]

2. The climate of general opinion seemed relatively moderate and stable. No panic over fallout was registered. Security considerations apparently outweighed humanitarian concerns, and large portions (31 percent and 47 percent) of even those who were fearful about the effects of fallout accepted the risks of continued testing.[6] Rather than being attributable to volatility, most of the swings in opinion appeared to be in the same direction as changes in official policy (further comment on this appears below). Public attitudes were polarized on testing in only two surveys—in November 1961 and January 1962, over the resumption of atmospheric tests.

Cessation of testing by agreement of the nuclear powers generally received favorable majorities over the ten-year span; however, the public seemed to disapprove of American cessation while Soviet explosions continued (Figure 1 could be interpreted as reflecting these tendencies). Doing business with the USSR was accepted, unaccompanied by expectations of utopia or catastrophe. A public preference for limited goals was demonstrated in the differing responses to queries on the Test Ban Treaty and on agreement with Russia to reduce armaments and armed forces; only 46 percent approved the latter (40 percent disapproved),[7] compared to the 61 percent which favored (18 percent disapproved) the Test Ban Treaty at about the same time. Recognizing the limited nature of the treaty, the public seemed unlikely to suffer a psychological letdown when the millennium did not follow—a possibility which had troubled some opponents of the test ban in 1958. The attentive segment in particular would very likely have been aware of the limitations, being more sensitive to the administration's campaign at the time emphasizing the restricted scope of the treaty. This may partially explain the greater approval by the attentive compared with the inattentive, a reversal of the 1959 relationship. Russia's breaking of the moratorium and the possibilities of Soviet cheating might have been salient in the minds of the inattentive; information on the treaty limits might not have percolated down sufficiently. The attentive public, however, would have been more cognizant of the limitations and the difficulties in cheating without detection.

3. Differences observed between the attentive and inattentive were often considerable but they were not drastic cleavages. For example, in January 1962 —while the national sample divided evenly 45 percent for, 45 percent against, and while nonvoters as a whole opposed the resumption of American tests 53 to 34 percent—college-graduate voters favored the resumption of tests by 54 to 38 percent.

In several instances the data suggest that the process of opinion formation and change in the attentive and inattentive publics was dissimilar. More of the attentive public appeared to respond positively and rapidly to the firm setting of policy by the administration; when no such direction was offered less pronounced stands were taken. The inattentive reacted to the contrary: they gave clear-cut policy decisions less support and took longer to do so; when policy was in flux, compared to the attentive, the inattentive public at times took stronger —or even opposing—positions.

There is some evidence for this generalization in the pre-moratorium period: for example, the high percentages of the inattentive public favoring an agreement from 1954 to early 1956, before the test-ban debate had begun; and the decline of these high percentages as the attentive public increased their approval of an agreement in 1957, when encouraging reports were emanating from the "businesslike" London disarmament negotiations and the administration was publicly favoring a disarmament agreement.

Stronger support for the generalization appears after the moratorium. In June 1961 the attentive public favored test resumption by a smaller ratio than the inattentive; in November the attentive ratio was diminished but still slightly favorable to test resumption (the inattentive reversed itself to opposition); in January 1962 attentive opinion favored test resumption by an expanded proportion (inattentive opposition increased); in March 1962 a consensus (81 percent of the college-graduate voters) was approached by the attentive majority approving test resumption (the inattentive reversed itself once again to approval of test resumption by a majority smaller than that of the attentive public). In August 1963 both publics switched to approval of the test-ban treaty, with attentive support being much greater.

Attentive opinion in 1961–62 appeared to have crystallized sooner; several months before inattentive opinion reacted, it seemed to begin shifting gradually in the direction policy was headed. This is not to maintain that the attentive public was ahead of the government but that it was more sensitive to the accumulation of cues pointing toward test resumption. The volatile inattentive sector changed directions twice and was unresponsive to these cues; instead it may have reacted to fears generated over fallout (more of the less educated were fearful and an ample part of the inattentive shift in favor of a test halt in January 1962 seemed to come from the larger number of "no opinion" responses in November 1961). Although the inattentive public did not perceive the more subtle cues, it was apparently reached by President Kennedy's nationwide television speech in March 1962.

In view of the many studies in which college-educated people are found to manifest greater foreign policy optimism and internationalism,[8] and more favorable attitudes toward disarmament and dealing with the Russians, one might have expected more approval of test cessation by the attentive sector. Yet in all but three of the surveys over the ten years the attentive public tended to be less in favor of test cessation than the inattentive. One can perhaps interpret this finding as an increased but not doctrinaire security orientation in the attentive public, which was illustrated by the strong approval it gave both the resumption of American testing and the Test Ban Treaty.

Nongovernmental Elites

To generalize on the articulate publics in the 1954–58 pre-moratorium period, let us consider them in three broad categories according to their approaches to the issue and its context—as Idealists, Pragmatists, and Pessimists—setting out for each group a brief description of values, goals, means (policy advocacy), and style in their contributions to the public debate.[9] Subsequently for the 1959–63 years, we will single out some of the participants for brief discussion along the same lines.

Idealists (a group which overwhelmingly favored test cessation, as well as many a unilateral US halt). Subsumed here are a large proportion of the interest groups studied (the peace groups—e.g., Fellowship of Reconciliation—and many of the religious organizations); a few of the mass media (*Saturday Review, Christian Century,* and the editorials of the *Bulletin of the Atomic Scientists*); and one elite individual, scientist Linus Pauling.

The core values of this group included pacifism, moral absolutism, legalism, and humanitarianism; their goals embraced the abolition of war and nuclear weapons, total disarmament, the establishment of world government under world law, and the regeneration of mankind. For the more extreme members of this group the cessation of nuclear tests tended at first to be too limited for attention; and later seemed not the first of many steps, but perhaps the penultimate step to their objectives. A major obstruction in the path according to this group seemed to be a conspiracy of obsolete sovereign states against "the people," who were naturally good, with a nearly limitless ability to control their futures if they put their minds to it. Idealist values fostered a faith in the existence of common interests between the USSR and the West and an optimism about the prospects for change within the Soviet Union and its behavior in response to western initiatives.

A substantial portion of the means for achieving these Idealist objectives was the power of a compelling public opinion—domestic and world—which had decided that "human destiny was too important to be left to governments." Somewhat less general were the functionalist methods advocated by the Idealists: education, people-to-people contacts, scientific cooperation, and the application of the scientific method to international political problems. Dissemination of the facts, such as those concerning the destructiveness of nuclear bombs and tests, would bring enlightenment and moral regeneration. Most of the Idealists inclined toward nonviolence; to consider one's own advantage seemed somewhat unethical; negotiation was not mutual activity to work toward adjustment but unilateral action—goodness and will on one side would suffice.

The values of the Idealists were manifested in the style of their communications, which were largely characterized by oversimplification—and often ignorance—of political, technical, and strategic implications of the test-ban issue. In a manner that was generally one-sided and categorical (at times tending to claim moral and intellectual superiority), some of the Idealists delineated only one alternative to their prescriptions—nuclear holocaust; concomitantly, some risks lay in their choice but certainty in any other. Although the temporary necessity of deterrence was reluctantly admitted by some, the complicated nature of that system was not explained. No compromise was permissible: if war could be limited by agreement, it could be abolished.

Pessimists (a group which adamantly opposed both multilateral and unilateral test cessation). Included were three of the mass media (*U.S. News and*

World Report, National Review, and the *Saturday Evening Post*), three elite individuals (scientist Edward Teller, columnist David Lawrence, and to a lesser extent columnist Arthur Krock), and one interest group (the American Legion).

Preoccupied with the rampant communist conspiracy at home and abroad to conquer the United States, the Pessimists emphasized security—using that word almost entirely in the military sense—and dismissed humanitarian concerns. Disarmament was a myth for most of them and the test ban a first step to disaster. Since enmity only and not common interest could exist between the United States and the USSR for as long as they could envision, their goals were predominantly oriented toward military security—until the remote day when the Soviet Union became an open society.

From the sheaf of political instrumentalities these guardians of security selected only the threat and use of coercion, placing their faith in the power of nuclear weapons. Much of the blame for the American test cessation was ascribed to the pressure of domestic and world opinion which had been stirred up by communists and their "dupes." (Many Pessimists deplored debate of the issue in the name of patriotism.) Negotiation with the Soviet Union was a "snare" and/or a "delusion," most of the Pessimists dismissing negotiation by repeating what seemed to be almost a motto: "Agreements with the Soviets are not worth the paper they are written on."

Like those of the Idealists, the communications of the Pessimists were dogmatic and tended toward oversimplification politically, strategically, and technically. The alternative to continued testing was simply nuclear surrender. While emphasizing massive retaliation to offset the communist "hordes," some Pessimists saw no inconsistency in advocating a ban on the use of nuclear weapons and not on tests. Some were satisfied with a comprehensive, foolproof, riskless agreement that opened up Russia. As long as the administration supported such a position, its views were treated reverentially. Proponents of different opinions were suspect as to their sincerity or loyalty.

Although the Idealists and the Pessimists were on opposite sides of the test-ban issue, their approaches to the problem were similar in several respects: (1) A propensity for absolutes—absolute morality or absolute security—and a gravitation toward single-value and single-alternative solutions (humanitarian values or military security). Compromises in either case were dubious; the preference was for all or nothing (world government, an open Soviet society) rather than limited change. The significance of a test ban as a "first step" depended on the basic goals and values, as both groups associated *testing* with the *use* of nuclear weapons: the Pessimists feared the prohibition of testing because it meant to them a ban on the use of the bomb—and therefore disaster for the West; the Idealists wanted a test ban because it meant to them a ban on the bomb—without which mankind was doomed. (2) Espousal of essentially unilateral methods of action in international politics. Whether one's antagonists were converted by good example or conquered by military might, in neither instance did multilateral techniques—e.g., negotiation—play an important role. (3) An attribution of considerable power to public opinion, although they disagreed as to whether "the people" or their leaders were wiser. (4) A dogmatic tone, with intolerance for opposition, each implying its own superiority: one a supposed superiority in knowledge, morality, and mental health; the other a supposed superiority in knowledge, political "realism," and patriotism. One side wanted its opponents' heads examined; the other its opponents' loyalty. (5) A tendency to attribute policy they opposed to conspiracy (on the part of communists, governments in general, or the Defense Deartment and industry). (6) A generally nonanalytical, one-sided, and vague style of presentation.

Some of the media at the opposite ends of this Idealist-Pessimist spectrum, such as the *Saturday Review* and the *National Review*, at times seemed to be having a dialogue between themselves, reacting to each other's hopes and fears. For example, the persistent terror about nuclear holocaust in the *Saturday Review* could be compared to the frequent undertones in the *National Review* of wanting to "roll back" the Soviet empire; the hopes for world government and internationalism in the former could be compared to the nationalism and trauma about world government in the latter; and the appeals to world public opinion in the former could be compared to the denunciations of the pressures of such opinion in the latter.

Pragmatists (a group in which a large majority approved a multilateral ban with various conditions and most disapproved unilateral American cessation). In this category were most of the media which committed themselves on the issue; a handful of groups (National Planning Association, Federation of American Scientists, National Council of the Churches of Christ, Commission of the Churches on International Affairs, American Veterans Committee); and four elite individuals (columnists Walter Lippmann, Stewart and Joseph Alsop, and James Reston; and scientist Ralph Lapp). It should be noted that some of the Pragmatists tended to lean to varying degrees in the direction of the Idealists or Pessimists: for example, the mass-circulation media—*Time, Life,* and the *New York Times* (for the first four years studied)—leaned toward the Pessimists; some of the quality magazines, several of the groups, and Ralph Lapp leaned toward the Idealists.

Multiple values underpinned the orientations of most of the Pragmatists. Security measures, humanitarian concerns, and a step-by-step approach to more practicable disarmament goals could be entertained at the same time. (The Pragmatists approved gradual or limited change in the direction of disarmament, while the Idealists sought radical change and the Pessimists no change at all.) For the Pragmatists, the test-cessation question did not simply evoke a moral imperative, nor was it devoid of moral overtones. Although some assumed a common interest with Russia and others denied it, for most the issue was to discover possible common interests rather than to presume their existence or nonexistence.

Negotiation was the primary instrument for this endeavor (without ignoring the roles of coercion and persuasion, relying on omniscient world opinion, or requiring Soviet conversion). Lippmann perhaps placed undue faith in this tool; other Pragmatists—such as *Time, Life,* and the *New York Times*—occasionally displayed an apprehension about negotiating with the USSR similar to that of the Pessimists.

As the foregoing suggests, the basic characteristic of Pragmatist style was moderation. They tended to be undogmatic—to be aware of uncertainties, possibilities, and risks on all sides of the issue. Pragmatist conditions placed on a multilateral ban did not in effect preclude any type of agreement (as some Pessimist conditions did), nor were they equivalent to unilateral suspension (as some Idealist conditions were). More analytical and less categorical, the Pragmatists were critical of governmental and nongovernmental participants in the debate without hysteria or conjuring devil theories. On the other hand, some of the weaknesses of the Idealists and Pessimists were evident among the Pragmatists: systematic analyses, balanced and disinterested presentations, and strategic sophistication were sparse.

In sum, few of the Idealists and Pessimists—but many of the Pragmatists—could view the test ban as a possible partial and stabilizing measure and not necessarily a ban on the bomb, a defeat for the West, or a catastrophe for mankind. Both of the doctrinaire extremes were essentially outside the frame of reference of politics in the conduct of international affairs. The values of both extremes fell far short of Max Weber's ethic of responsibility, and their means and style were not conducive to what W. T. R. Fox called the "reconciliation of the desirable and the possible." Unlike the Idealists and Pessimists, the Pragmatists operated more often within a political-oriented framework. Their communications, however, generally seemed to be drowned out in the public debate by the noise of the latter groups, whose contributions were not likely to improve the quality of policy choices or expand the capacity of other elites and the attentive public to understand and participate in the political process.

In what other ways were the communications of these nongovernmental elites during the 1954–58 pre-moratorium period functional or dysfunctional for the conduct of public policy debate? In general, the task of separating fact from value was inadequately performed by the articulate publics. One would not expect the Idealists and the Pessimists to accomplish such a task; but even among the Pragmatists, *New York Times* editorials and the columns of Walter Lippmann were lax in clarifying the relationships of the value judgments of the scientists involved in the debate over testing to the facts. The best elite performance was perhaps in the dissemination of information about radioactive fallout. Although over the period considerable information on fallout was revealed, biased selection and exaggeration were frequent. Both extremes overlooked the unknowns: the Pessimists, the unknowns of fallout; the Idealists, the unknowns of test inspection and detection. Yet in the pursuit of information on fallout, considerable pressure was placed on a seemingly reluctant administration, which then released information it otherwise might have kept secret. Counterexperts were prominent in this activity, with the debate allowing those scientists to be heard who felt their ideas were not getting sufficient attention from the scientific representatives within government. However, few of the articulate publics offered disinterested interpretation and guidance toward improving administration policy; the most vocal were the least practical.

Nonetheless, the Idealists were functional to the extent that they challenged established patterns of thought; called attention to an issue whose existence the administration and others at times seemed reluctant to admit; forced the latter and the apathetic moderates to think about and address themselves publicly to the issue sooner and more precisely than they otherwise might have; and emphasized some of the values to be "reconciled with the possible." As Max Weber wrote in *Politics as a Vocation,* politics "takes both passion and perspective . . . man would not have attained the possible unless time and again he had reached out for the impossible." If the Pragmatists supplied perspective for the debate, the Idealists supplied the necessary passion.

On the other hand, the Idealists were dysfunctional to the degree they promoted emotionalism and obscurantism, a faith in easy solutions, and an intolerance for methods other than their own. The Pessimists were dysfunctional in similar ways—and to the extent they undermined the role of debate in the policy process. They were functional chiefly by substantively complicating the facile policy prescriptions of the Idealists. As Albert Wohlstetter has pointed out, for example, Edward Teller was ingenious in considering enemy countermeasures to thwart control systems (both sides in the debate ignored the countermeasures which did not suit their arguments).[10]

From 1959 to 1963 few changes were discernible in the basic approaches (values, goals, means, style) of most of the nongovernmental elite participants in the debate. Some of the extremes, however, inched toward the middle, resulting in somewhat less emotionality/insensitivity and in a broader area of agreement that fallout was unhealthy. In several instances an increased balance and sophistication in the use of strategic and technical information was evident.

Interest Groups. Most of the active interest groups (falling in the Idealist category) tended to disapprove of the resumption of American tests in 1961–62, supporting the cessation of testing throughout the period; a score of them testified in favor of the treaty before the Senate Foreign Relations Committee in August 1963. One of the few organizations in opposition was the Veterans of Foreign Wars, which declared that Russia "could not be trusted." A skeptical American Legion endorsed the treaty only with the assurance that it was not a step toward disarmament and the surrender of national sovereignty.

Anxiety over nuclear weapons and their proliferation seemed to stimulate a proliferation of peace groups, such as Women Strike for Peace and Turn Toward Peace, the latter a group coordinating the efforts of peace organizations.[11] These new peace groups, according to a member of one, "know their [Herman] Kahn and their [Edward] Teller." Yet an examination of the contributions to the test-ban debate of these and other peace organizations from 1959 to 1963 did not offer convincing proof that sophistication had expanded sufficiently to match the complexities of the issues confronted.

More than a third of the nationwide advertisements by the National Committee for a Sane Nuclear Policy (SANE), for example, seemed intended to evoke only moral and visceral rather than anlytical responses. Asserting that the question was not "will" but *when* will" nuclear war occur if changes are not made, Steve Allen wondered in one SANE advertisement, "how many people who believe in Hell have ever asked themselves how many souls would be plunged into Hell by a nuclear war resulting in, say, 200 million deaths." When the United Nations Report on Radiation (released in 1962) indicated areas of uncertainty, it was criticized by a SANE spokesman for opening the doors for opponents of the test ban: "The scientifically conservative have had their way over the scientifically objective and over those concerned with the social implications of their findings." Less publicized policy statements contained more analysis of disarmament—yet here also appeared suggestions of "almost instantaneous disarmament" which would obviate the necessity for endless negotiation on the balance of forces.

Quality Magazines. The Idealist *Saturday Review* was more moderate in its approach in 1959–63 than before the moratorium was declared. The editorials of Norman Cousins tended much less toward emotionality in discussing fallout; the resumption of American explosions in the atmosphere in 1961 did not receive the type of condemnation one would have expected in 1957–58: "traditional, national thinking" had to be transcended with a sense of ultimate responsibility to the condition of man and not nations. The Test Ban Treaty was regarded as the "first dent in the theory that superior force can provide safety."

As in 1954–58, the largest proportion of material devoted to the issue was published in the *Bulletin of the Atomic Scientists*. Balanced, analytical articles (on inspection, evasion, the nth-country problem, etc.) were generally offered, frequently by recognized scholars. As in the earlier period, articles usually diverged from the writings of the editor, Dr. Eugene Rabinowich, whose main theme became the inadequacy of disarmament ("survival can't be bought so cheaply") and the necessity of an even more radical transformation—extensive international cooperation especially in science and technology.

The Pragmatist *Reporter* grew more concerned over the security aspects of the issue compared with its previous positions and with the other quality magazines. It tended to approve the resumption of American tests in the atmosphere in 1962 due to the stubbornness of the Soviet Union in negotiations, while the *New Republic* and *Nation* opposed resumption. The *New Republic* was not sufficiently convinced by the President's explanation to the American people of the need for the tests. Although the treaty was favored by all three magazines, the *Nation* and *Reporter* were at variance in their evaluations: while the *Nation* called for following up the treaty with more decisive steps, the *Reporter* was concerned with maintaining military and technological preparedness in all fields, being critical of the "meaningless formula" of general and complete disarmament, and fearful of American delusion and Soviet reneging.

The potential danger of fallout was belatedly recognized by the Pessimist *National Review,* which was somewhat less flippant than before the moratorium; indeed this was one of its reasons in 1959 for supporting a ban on atmospheric tests while allowing underground explosions, although it remained reassuring about the "myth of fallout." In 1963 the *National Review* changed its position and refused to support any ban "even if it had the tightest of controls," since there was much to lose and nothing to gain. The spread of nuclear weapons?—"on the whole it would aid rather than injure our security, decrease the chances for total war." An arms race?—"our interest is to compel the Soviet Union to compete in an intense and unrelenting arms race, above all in the nuclear sector. . . . Our economy can take it. Theirs can't."

News and Mass-Interest Magazines. As in 1954–58, the most balanced accounts appeared in Pragmatist *Newsweek,* with *Time* displaying bias in favor of continued testing. During the Senate debate over the treaty in 1963, for example, a series of items in *Time* over six weeks emphasized skepticism and arguments attacking the treaty. Compared to 1954–58, Pessimist *U.S. News and World Report* contained considerably less distortion and reassurances about fallout, although the "inside dopester" headlines were frequent. Despite a number of balanced items, more articles tended to approve testing.

The mass-interest magazines—*Life, Reader's Digest,* and *Saturday Evening Post*—were generally opposed to test suspension throughout the period. An article in the *Post* saw the "real meaning" of the ban as the prevention of China's becoming a nuclear power, implying a Soviet-American agreement to destroy the Chinese capability ("accidents happen").

New York Times editorials. After four years of opposition to both unilateral and multilateral test cessation, the *Times* shifted to approval in 1958. Thereafter, while maintaining its previous concern with the Soviet "drive for world domination" and its disgust over the "mockery" the USSR made of the test-ban negotiations, it nevertheless regretted the premature resumption of American explosions underground in 1961 and was in a dilemma over the possibility of further atmospheric tests. It seemed torn between US responsibility to "defend the free world" and responsibility for the health of the world's peoples and future generations. From October 1961 forward, the *Times* repeatedly asked for an explanation to the American people if atmospheric experiments should be decided upon by the President, calling for a revaluation of secrecy and "Papa knows best" policies. President Kennedy's address in March 1962 which announced the resumption of tests was described as having "fully explained to the American people" in clear and understandable language the necessity for such experiments.

Although numerous editorials presented arguments on both sides of the issue (unlike the 1954–58 editorials revealing anti-ban bias), the *Times* repeatedly referred to the risks of continued explosions as being greater than an acceptable test ban. The signing of the treaty was therefore a "cause for rejoicing," notwithstanding the recognized limitations and the criticism during the Senate hearings, which was smothering the treaty in a "blanket of fear and distrust."

Washington Columnists. As the United States and the Soviet Union exploded weapons in 1961–62, Walter Lippmann seemed resigned to the fact that a treaty would not be forthcoming until both sides were satisfied that they had learned all they could. Perhaps because he believed the issue was fundamentally a scientific one, he observed that the testing decision must be left to the experts. The treaty of 1963 was therefore a consequence of hardheaded calculation and mutual recognition that the absolute weapon (an anti-ballistic missile) could not be achieved ("if there were a real chance of achieving it, the risks of not testing would be absolutely enormous"). Taking issue with the treaty's adversaries, Lippmann pointed out the limitations ("a complete ban would be a very different proposition") and foresaw the cold war smoldering for generations; yet he welcomed this important first step toward limiting the arms race because there was "no alternative to nuclear peace."

Within the strategic context that he had stressed in 1954–58, Joseph Alsop approved of American experiments in the atmosphere in 1962, having little concern for "so-called world opinion." In his eyes, "naked power counted far more than virtuous intention"; because of the technological revolution the wise course was to "hope for the best and prepare for the worst." Nevertheless, Alsop favored the partial Test Ban Treaty, which "may be a great turning point" in international relations.

The generally balanced and politically conscious columns of James Reston continued in 1959–63. Implying that the United States should resume tests in 1961–62 following Soviet explosions, but continue negotiating, Reston noted that Russia had "always been generous regarding principles but stingy when it came down to cases." In mid-1961 (presciently, a year before the Cuban missile crisis), he recorded the growing confidence of Russia and the possible dangers of a Soviet miscalculation of the United States. As he had from the early years of the testing debate, Reston pointed out that despite the scientific and military testimony from equally sincere and well-informed men on both sides, the issue was in the end philosophical and political rather than technical.

The military-security orientation of Arthur Krock led him to regret the President's preference for considerations of foreign policy ("could bring disaster"); to attribute to world opinion an "unfortunate" power over American decisions; to ventilate mainly the arguments opposing test cessation; and to express frequently a fear of possible secret experiments by the USSR which would lead to radically new weapons. While viewing the treaty from the humanitarian aspect as a step "toward one of the greatest accomplishments of civilized statecraft," Krock was worried about possible loopholes (e.g., a commitment not to use nuclear weapons) or a secret agreement to consolidate the Russian empire, and skeptical, implying that national security was being risked on the good faith of the USSR.

David Lawrence's Pessimist views appeared to have mellowed somewhat in several respects since the 1950's: for example, the "communist plans" for prohibiting tests were now abetted by scientists, politicians, and citizens who were "naive and sincere" rather than the "dupes" they were usually called in previous years. But although he was somewhat less certain than previously about fallout's harmlessness—"scientists disagree"—Lawrence nevertheless termed fallout a "red herring" that (quoting Edward Teller) can "allegedly harm"; he asked why the administration had not debunked fallout for the millions of Americans who had been persuaded by the Soviet Union, pacifist groups, and misguided scientists that it was a terrible danger.

Extensive comments were offered by Lawrence on the loopholes in the 1963 treaty and on America's "peace at any price" behavior. In his search for explanations of Soviet motives, Lawrence's fear of trickery seemed to be balanced by the trend he perceived toward equilibrium and mutual forebearance due to the prospect of mutual suicide from war.

Scientists. On October 10, 1963, the day that the Test Ban Treaty came into force, Idealist Linus Pauling was awarded the 1962 Nobel Peace Prize in recognition of his impassioned opposition to nuclear weapons' testing. Although his approach to the issue from 1959 to 1963 was generally similar to that of 1954–58, in an article assessing the effects of testing through December 1962, however, Dr. Pauling offered the kind of scientific qualification that was sometimes missing from his assertions in 1958. He noted, for example, that the number of persons affected genetically could be greater or less by 15 times (radioactive fallout) or 50 times (carbon-14).[12]

The position of the principal scientific opponent of test suspension, Pessimist Edward Teller, also remained largely unchanged. Although briefly in 1960 Teller supported an agreement to halt explosions in the atmosphere but not underground or in space, in 1963 he vehemently opposed the partial treaty. He saw "grave consequences for US security" because atmospheric tests were absolutely necessary to develop an anti-missile missile.[13]

Mass and Attentive Opinion, Nongovernmental Elites, and Policy-Makers—Possible Relationships

This discussion of possible relationships between general and elite opinion and the decision-makers begins with the pre-moratorium period (1954–58) and then broadens to include the entire decade of the test-ban issue (1954–63), with references to earlier and later commentary on American public opinion in the atomic age.

From 1954 to 1958 most of the general public's contact with material on testing was probably with anti-ban opinion picked up from administration cues in newspaper headlines or on radio/television (as late as spring 1958, the administration was deflating the test ban), or from the mass-interest magazines, many of which tended to oppose a test-ban agreement as well as unilateral suspension. That a majority of the general public favored an agreement (especially in 1957) seems to indicate that they attended more to the administration rather than the mass-interest magazines, since the administration's goal of a comprehensive disarmament agreement could be interpreted by the uninformed as approval for a separate test-ban treaty. But for many of the nonreaders of magazines (one-third of a national sample in 1957), who were among the least educated, it is likely that even the vague cues from the administration were remote. To the extent that the mass public paid attention to nongovernmental elite communications, they probably would have more often encountered material which was against unilateral cessation and moderately concerned-to-reassuring on fallout. (Newspapers may have been sensational about fallout in their news columns, but editorially it seems likely that a majority would have backed the administration's views on the subject.) The less educated and less informed sector of the general public, who were most aroused about fallout, were least likely to have encountered the messages of the Idealists (studies have shown, for example, that most voluntary organizations reach few persons in the lower income/education sectors of society).

The attentive public could be expected to be more attuned to the elite communications studied here than the general public. Recall that while majorities of the attentive public favored a ban agreement most of the time and strongly opposed a unilateral cessation, the most vocal elite publics deviated from this pattern: many of the Idealists tended to favor a unilateral American suspension as well as an agreement; the Pessimists opposed suspension in any form. Closest to resembling the ratio of the attentive public were the Pragmatic elites: a majority favored an agreement but few approved a unilateral cessation.

The attentive public was among that 11 percent of the public that read the quality and news magazines.[14] Most of the latter periodicals were in the Pragmatist category and were concerned about fallout (generally avoiding emotionality and reassurance) and split on the ban (most of the limited-circulation quality magazines being pro-ban and the mass-circulation, news magazines tending in opposition—with U.S. News strongly opposed). The views of the attentive public—less aroused about fallout, favoring a multilateral agreement, but against unilateral suspension—tended to parallel roughly the stands of a majority of the quality and news magazines and to contradict the positions of both extremes. Broadly speaking, then, the movements of attentive and mass opinion tended in the direction of the moderate segment of elites and in the direction of the administration's variations in position. Whether because of lack of interest, apathy, moderation, or the administration's reassurance (and President Eisenhower's silence), the public seemed not overwrought by the more extreme declarations on fallout which were disseminated by various elite groups and individuals in 1957–58; rather it seemed aware of security considerations.

What was the possible relationship of public opinion to the Eisenhower Administration's decision to cease testing in the fall of 1958 without an agreement? Aside from other explanations for the decision (such as the President's strong desire to break the disarmament impasse or the changing of the scientific guard—James Killian and Hans Bethe for Lewis Strauss and Edward Teller), it seems doubtful that the administration would have stopped testing at that precise time and under those conditions if there had been no domestic and worldwide public agitation.[15] For example, Harold Jacobson and Eric Stein wrote in their book Diplomats, Scientists and Politicians: The U.S. and the Nuclear Test Ban Negotiations[16] that American policy-makers felt constrained by the pressure of opinion: one of the motives behind the American proposal for a Conference of Experts in the summer of 1958 was to "neutralize the public pressures against testing so that the United States could conduct its planned series of nuclear weapons tests" that summer (p. 487); declaring a moratorium in October 1958 before achieving a treaty was considered necessary "because of the pressure of public opinion and to create the most propitious atmosphere for the diplomatic negotiations" (p. 91).

Our data suggest the contrary about public attitudes, however. The general and attentive publics and the substantial Pragmatic elites were not in favor of a test cessation without an agreement *before* the Conference of Experts and the 1958 moratorium: indeed, both mass and attentive publics strongly opposed unilateral suspension; the Pragmatic elites were not demanding unilateral suspension; and the Pessimist anti-ban elites grew more vociferous in 1958. Yet the administration decided to cease tests without many of the preconditions it has required for years.

Although public opinion was not in fact constraining, it is possible that the policy-maker's perceptions of opinion had changed, with their decisions of course depending on how they perceived reality. In the previous year, for example, Secretary of State Dulles reportedly believed that the public was not behind the administration's "bold" disarmament ideas. Yet that period marked the high point of mass and attentive public approval of a test-ban agreement and perhaps the high point of elite pro-ban relative to anti-ban activity. At that time the Secretary's image of public opinion may have been colored by his own apprehensions about taking such a disarmament step.[17]

What may have contributed to the change in 1958? How the decision-makers perceived public attitudes may have been disproportionately affected by the more vocal pro-cessation groups. The vocal Idealist organizations whose arguments permeated the debate may have received more attention because none of the other groups usually interested in foreign policy made themselves heard in support of more moderate approaches. (The latter groups—e.g., labor, business—might have been silent for several reasons: they may have preferred not to voice opposition to a cause which seemed to have great popular support; they may have hesitated to oppose the administration when it began to favor a ban; they may have been uninterested since their special concerns were unaffected; they may have feared a split in their own ranks.)

The moral aspects of the issue and the possibility that the public might have been more excitable than in the past because of the awareness of the health danger may also account for any greater influence (directly or indirectly) the vocal Idealist groups might have exerted on the administration in comparison to what usually has been a minimal influence in foreign policy matters.[18] The result may have been that the Idealists had more success in affecting the administration's perception of public opinion than in modifying that public opinion itself. Vociferous but small proportions of the articulate elites do not, however, seem sufficient reasons in themselves for the impact of what was perceived as public opinion. Part of the explanation may lie in the interaction of domestic and world opinion. The uproar in world opinion may have acted as an amplifier: the concern over fallout and testing of various groups, eminent individuals, and governments in allied and nonaligned nations may have magnified the resonance of the minority at home. For the policy makers the domestic voices may have been noisy representatives and reminders of that world opinion.

The constraint felt by decision-makers in 1958 due to public opinion therefore seems attributable in part to their own perceptions of opinion and to a vociferous minority opinion stimulated in some measure by the administration's own declarations and actions over a number of years—including the extremely reassuring views about fallout which tended to provoke opposite-extreme reactions. The 1958 moratorium decision was not compelled by mass public opinion, in other words; the responsibility lay with the governmental and nongovernmental elites.

In the years following the moratorium there are additional examples of the pressure of public opinion on the policy-makers to test or not to test, according to Jacobson and Stein:[19] (1) In December 1959, "that no one [in the administration] urged resuming atmospheric tests reflected both the extent to which public opinion, or fear of an adverse public reaction, could inhibit United States policy, and the conscience of American policymakers" (p. 232); (2) among the pressures to resume testing in mid-1961 were those of public opinion (p. 277); (3) within the administration those who argued in the winter of 1961–62 against resumption of atmospheric tests were "concerned about the widespread public opposition to nuclear testing both within the United States and abroad and the effects of the expression of this opposition in such forums as the United Nations" (p. 346). Thus, the reexamination of the American position that began in April 1962 was largely triggered by "the reaction in the Eighteen Nation Committee, among world-leaders, and within the United States to the resumption of atmospheric testing. The widespread opposition to atmospheric testing made American leaders hesitant to order its resumption and also compelled them to search for ways of avoiding such action in the future" (p. 381).

Our data support point (1) from Jacobson and Stein. With reference to (2)—the pressure to resume tests in mid-1961—Jacobson and Stein cite a Gallup poll made after a somber television speech by President Kennedy following the Vienna summit meeting, in which the President stated that the chances for a test cessation were slim. Our data show that although several columnists favored resumption at this time, the *New York Times* was one of several articulate voices not approving. Public pressure in general to resume testing was probably stimulated largely by the intragovernmental debate itself that had been reported by the mass media in the spring and by the President's speech in June. As to (3), which pointed out administration concern about the widespread opposition to testing in early 1962 and in April when the United States was reexamining its position: a survey which was made following the President's speech explaining why it was necessary to resume tests showed a large proportion of the public, especially the attentive portions, favoring such a resumption. Numerous Pragmatic elites also tended toward a resumption (many before the President's speech)—including the *New York Times,* all five columnists analyzed in this study, and the mass-circulation magazines and news magazines. We would conclude that the policy-makers in 1961 and 1962 were not faced with a compelling or constraining public opinion, but with a permissive one. The changes in public attitudes were not simply due to volatility but were very likely in response largely to cues from the political elites as they debated and modified policy (coupled with events and elite interpretation of events in the debate).

A volatile mass opinion did not "enfeeble . . . the executive [at] . . . critical junctures" examined in this study,[20] thereby forcing the United States to start or stop tests contrary to national security interests. The Eisenhower Administration stopped tests in October 1958 due in part to its perception of a constraining public opinion that did not altogether match reality. The Kennedy Administration, however, seemed capable of mobilizing opinion in support of policy —whether the policy was to resume or to halt tests—as shown by: (1) the strong approval of test resumption in March 1962 after several months of closely divided general opinion, with the administration evidently reaching and reversing the opinions of even the most inattentive groups; (2) approval of the test-ban treaty in August 1963 and the communication of its limited scope. The attentive public seemed responsive to discriminating leadership, demonstrating flexibility and tending to be neither volatile nor prone to absolute means and goals. While the greatest support for policy stemmed from the informed sector that attended the elite debate, majorities of the inattentive mass were also generally forthcoming and radical cleavages did not occur.

In this interaction of opinion, elites, and decision-makers, what briefly were the roles of the two administrations and the nongovernmental elites? Neither administration appeared to be simply "manipulating" opinion: the policy-makers were in part reacting to what they believed were the demands of the public, apparently without being aware of the permissiveness of opinion; not merely uninformed masses but attentive and elite publics were responding to political leadership in 1961–63; and the Idealist minority appeared to have had some influence on the decision to stop testing in 1958.

The Eisenhower Administration seemed reluctant to debate publicly the testing issue, and seemed vacillating in its policy. When policy was changed and the moratorium declared, the administration failed to explain clearly why many of the preconditions were dropped. The President's press conference statements contributed to the confusion and misinterpretations.[21] The Kennedy Administration delayed a full explanation of the need to resume atmospheric tests until the decision had been made, for which it was criticized. When that time came, however, the President appeared on television to explain elaborately the reasoning behind the resumption, and later his administration campaigned extensively to educate the public and Congress on the test-ban treaty. Furthermore, in contrast to President Eisenhower, President Kennedy "made himself an expert"[22] on the issue. Overall, the Kennedy administration seemed to make a more determined and concerted effort for a test ban. "No other single accomplishment in the White House," wrote Theodore Sorenson, "ever gave [President Kennedy] greater satisfaction.[23]

Among the nongovernmental elites, who are responsible for offering relevant criticism of administration policies, impartial observers were generally lacking. Although most of the mass media were one-sided on testing, surprisingly few were hysterical about fallout. Nor were they "pro-war," as newspapers have sometimes been described by some peace spokesmen; a large majority of the magazines were moderate in their views. The quality media generally offered multiple-value, politically-aware orientations to the issue but few presented systematic analysis of both sides. A number of the mass-circulation magazines leaned toward single-value, politically-simplified frameworks. Greater balance appeared during the later years of the period in the editorials of a less conservative *New York Times,* which seemed to appreciate more in the 1960's the possible modifications in the international environment due to nuclear weapons and changes in Soviet policy.

The major failings of the interest groups were (1) the relative inactivity of a number of world affairs and educational organizations, especially before the moratorium (the issue was not considered at any time by the League of Women Voters; the Foreign Policy Association published some valuable material but did not include the issue in its Great Decisions discussion series); (2) the comparative silence of the large economic interest groups; and, hence, (3) the predominance in the group debate of the peace groups.

Of the three scientists studied, the best combination of information, clarification, and balance in the fallout controversy came from Ralph Lapp, who tended to keep the ranges of probability and uncertainty in the forefront rather than select that extremity which favored one policy predisposition. To the contrary, Linus Pauling and Edward Teller not only seemed to lack appreciation of political phenomena, but their exposition of the "scientific facts" was less than scientific (e.g., each tended to ignore the qualifying conditions and probabilities that did not suit his political predilections). With hindsight, some may conclude that the scientists were in basic agreement on the "facts"; yet at the time many of the elites, including senators and columnists, were confused —let alone the mass and attentive publics. And it seems unfair and incorrect to blame the confusion primarily on the inadequate questions and understanding of nonscientists, as one observer did,[24] particularly when some of the most vocal scientists were not employing scientific methods in their public appeals.

The Washington columnists, considered individually, with one exception did not generally offer other elites and the attentive public the kind of information and interpretation required for comprehending the ramifications of the testing issue. The exception was James Reston: his mainly balanced and dispassionate articles provided information and clarification on central questions in the debate (e.g., fallout, detecting underground tests) and related them to more general aspects of democratic foreign policy-making (e.g., the scientific revolution, Congress, public opinion), all within a politically-oriented framework.[25]

As a group, however, the columnists made a number of contributions to the debate. For example, all of them were security-oriented; most encouraged neither moods of apathy nor panic; [26] three appreciated the role of elite debate in the democratic system, and revealed a greater awareness of the political implications of test cessation than many other elites and the general public at that time.

Some of the foregoing conclusions are interesting in light of a study of the reactions of fourteen Washington columnists to the atomic bomb from 1946–49.[27] This examination showed that the columnists then were neither more nor less irresponsible or original than other opinion leaders; not clearly much ahead or behind general opinion; not extremely aggressive or hysterical but at times not very realistic (Lippmann, for example, entertained the view that world opinion would enforce world law). The present study indicates that the competence and confidence of the columnists (as represented in this sample) in dealing with aspects of the same subject had progressed from the sense of confusion and groping that was found to be general in the early years of the atomic age.

Despite the many deficiencies in elite participation, an improvement in the quality of some elite communications was evident over the decade. A number of elites displayed more balance, less emotionality, and greater understanding of arms control and strategy in the years following the commencement of the moratorium. What seems essential in an era of rapid technological innovation, however, is more elites knowledgeably coming to grips with an issue sooner than they did on the test ban—in order to prevent a widening of the gap between the complex reality of national security policy and the perspectives of nongovernmental (and many Congressional) elite participants, not to mention the attentive and mass publics. Too wide a breach may reduce most elite publics to largely ineffectual post-decision deliberation, leaving predominant over a permissive general public the experts of the administration and a vocal opposition or supportive group, none of whom might have exhausted the implications of a policy proposal.

There were some manifestations of such a pattern in our study. Before the important moratorium decision in 1958, as we have seen, a sophisticated debate was not conducted by the elites. After this decision, the various shifts in administration policy seemed to be reflected in the views of some of the media, a number of the columnists, and several major economic interest groups (as well as the mass and attentive publics). On the question of resuming tests in the atmosphere in 1961–62, Walter Lippmann seemed to be looking toward the technical experts for the answer. The *New York Times* tended to accept the administration's views before the moratorium decision in 1958 and in 1961–62 appeared to be waiting on the administration's response concerning the resumption of atmospheric tests. ("It is impossible for the layman to say whether the newest tests are absolutely required by military necessity.")

Participating knowledgeably in the debate of vital issues does not imply presuming to make detailed military-strategic decisions. But these "technical" decisions rest on fundamental value choices for the nation, and the unwillingness or inability of responsible, pragmatic elites to offer independent analysis and judgment leaves public evaluation to the administration and to irresponsible extremes—in the testing debate, the elite sector that made the most noise and showed the least evidence of having increased in sophistication. The tendency of some elites to remain silent or to follow the lead of the administration rather uncritically was doubtless due in part to the technical complexity of this issue. But it is precisely such technical complexity which requires greater effort by the nongovernmental participants in the debate to narrow the gap between the reality and their perception (and therefore representation) of it.

The permissiveness of opinion that we found in this case places a heavy burden not only on the nongovernmental elites but even more on the administration, because effective public policy debate depends on the role the policy-makers play. The administration is responsible for not crossing from the "mobilization" to the "manipulation" of opinion; for striking a balance between secrecy in the interests of national security and the publication of accurate information in advance of decisions in the interest of public debate; for enhancing public understanding and confidence in governmental competence and promoting appreciation of the role of elite debate in democratic policy formulation. Little or no public debate preceded the decisions in the Bay of Pigs invasion in 1961 and the Vietnam commitment in 1964. The outcomes suggest that a danger opposite to nongovernmental elite "irresponsibility"—of which the *New York Times* was accused for releasing the Pentagon Papers—may be "over-responsibility": after the Bay of Pigs disaster, according to the managing editor of the *Times,* President Kennedy stated that if the *Times* had printed more of what it knew before the operation was launched, it "would have saved us from a colossal mistake." [28]

Let us conclude by relating some of the findings from this case study to other writings on American public opinion in the atomic age, beginning with Almond's classic work, *The American People and Foreign Policy.* Although in 1950 he stressed the instability of the mass public's mood (mood being the "lack of intellectual structure and factual content" of their foreign policy attitudes), Almond suggested as well that "the era of great fluctuations in America may have passed"; in the new introduction to the 1960 edition he concluded that the public was indeed more stable, security conscious, responsible, and aware of the hazards of the nuclear age without being panicked.[29] The present study generally supports Almond's assessment: recall the lack of hysteria over fallout, and in the spring of 1962 the approval of the resumption of American atmospheric testing at a time when the fallout levels were highest due to Soviet multimegaton tests. Although two shifts by the inattentive sector indicated some volatility, most of the major fluctuations we found could be attributed largely to changes in policy and the elite debate over issues and events. Nor was it likely that these fluctuations indicated a public opinion ahead of its leaders, as one author put it, since the public would probably have looked to governmental and nongovernmental experts for guidance on a subject with such technical ramifications.[30]

"Through a disciplined democratic elite and a broad attentive public," wrote Almond, "foreign policy moods may be contained and gross fluctuations in attitude checked." We criticized on several counts the elite performance in the test-ban debate, but noted an improvement in their participation over the decade. Since the early 1960's, additional sophisticated participants from the universities and research institutes like RAND and the Institute for Policy Studies have joined the policy debate. Although these "defense intellectuals" have advanced the "most impressive arguments" on both sides of the ABM issue (e.g., see the Rathjens-Wohlstetter exchange in Part II of this volume), Aaron Wildavsky believes the bad arguments have driven out the good ones when "eminent spokesmen for peace would seriously contemplate a launch-on-warning policy, or would pledge themselves to rush into huge provocations in the 1970s if a Soviet threat materializes, or would glory in the vulnerability of the populace as a guarantor of restraint." [31]

Among the foreign policy elites, our large Pragmatist group roughly approximated Almond's "foreign policy consensus" in their general agreement on political procedures and their multiple-value orientation. The segments outside the consensus—in this case, the Idealists and Pessimists—revealed only slight improvement in their approaches to political problems since the period of Almond's analysis (shortly after World War II). At that time Almond viewed the academic elites as a source of "moral wishful thinking." Although this case study did not single out the academic elites, the introduction to Part I of this volume speculates that for some academics and other intellectuals, the pendulum may have swung too far toward "realism" in the 1960's.

The foreign policy elites, Almond observed in the 1960 introduction to *The American People and Foreign Policy,* "can rely . . . on a large critical audience." We have identified the "attentive public" on the testing issue and traced it empirically by means of crude criteria of information, involvement, and interest—suggesting differences in opinion formation between the mass and attentive publics. Although we have not compared the size of the attentive to the general public, one scholar concluded that the attentive public is increasing relative to the general public, concerning both public affairs in general and international affairs specifically.[32]

One of the main conclusions of this case study—that concerning the permissiveness of public opinion—supports Almond's suggestions in both 1950 and 1960 that the political leadership has had discretion in making national security policy. This permissiveness has been found also in other security/foreign policy issue areas of narrow and broad interest, such as trade, defense, the Japanese peace treaty, and the Korean War.[33] Some evidence of permissiveness (and stability) of the public can be found in the Vietnam issue as well, although that can also serve to illustrate the pressure of public opinion on the policy-makers. A study in the spring of 1967 found a "relatively permissive majority behind the President" on Vietnam (and contrary to our findings, that the informed and uninformed displayed little difference in policy preferences)—this despite the tragic consequences that were much more vivid and immediate than the consequences of radioactive fallout.[34] Another analysis concludes that "the administration, particularly in the short run, has more flexibility in war policy than might at first appear." Poll data supporting this analysis indicated the gradual decline in support for the Vietnam war until a majority appears against it in August 1968. Support for withdrawal increased considerably in 1969 and 1970, when a kind of withdrawal had become official policy, suggesting "shifts in public opinion . . . after policy changes." [35]

Public "followership" of elite leadership seems to be illustrated by the China issue as well. A compilation of survey data on attitudes toward admission of the People's Republic of China to the United Nations concluded that official American opposition to China's admission had been "uniformly" in accordance with American public opinion. From a low of 7 percent in the 1950's that favored mainland China's presence in the UN, the total reached only 35 percent in October 1970 (49 percent were opposed).[36] Yet in May 1971, following the various efforts of the Nixon Administration to increase contacts with the People's Republic, for the first time more people favored admission of the People's Republic (45 percent to 38 percent).[37] Republican respondents shifted the most, going beyond the Democrats (from 30 percent in 1970 to 45 percent, compared to a 34-40 percent Democratic shift), suggesting their greater susceptibility to Republican presidential cues on a controversial issue.[38]

We have suggested several cases of public response to elite leadership, yet we have also maintained that the leadership is at times constrain by opinion. How policy-makers respond to public opinion depends on how they perceive it. A recent study illustrated how national survey data can conceal differences among publics in intensity, activity, information, etc.; although the Vietnam "hawks" were only 18 percent of a 1967 national sample, for example, they formed 30 percent of the group that had written letters on Vietnam. As the authors of the study put it, the complex reality of public opinion includes both sets of data.[39] This underscores the significance of the images in the minds of the policy-makers—which publics do they perceive as reflecting the "reality" of opinion? (This perception in turn depends in part on the policy-maker's own conceptual framework for interpreting the political world.) Recall that our study found that the intense and vocal but small Idealist segment, interacting with world public opinion, may have influenced the perceptions of the policy-makers concerning the cessation of tests in 1958.

Public opinion has developed in the post-World War II period as publics, elites, and policy-makers interacted in response to events. In the late 1940's, facing a perceived Soviet threat and with images of prewar isolationist opinion in their minds, the policy-makers believed it imperative to mobilize the American public to support worldwide responsibilities in the atomic era. Establishing the necessary security orientation was helped by events, policies, and elite cues. (Recall that the New York Times opposed a test ban until 1958 and was fairly "hard" towards the Soviet Union.) In later years, policy-makers favoring tension-reducing actions felt constrained by a hard-line public opinion—albeit one which they had helped create (e.g., Secretary Dulles's view on disarmament initiatives in 1957; China policy). Even the Kennedy Administration decision-makers who mobilized opinion favoring the test ban, encouraging pro-ban pressure, were reportedly relieved and somewhat surprised at "how little public indignation had been aroused by the test ban." [40] Yet evidence from various studies suggests that the development of a security orientation among the public did not preclude a degree of permissiveness on national security issues greater than the policy-makers realized. This permissiveness, which has gone hand in hand with Congressional acquiescence, evidently reached its limits in the late 1960's on the Vietnam war and defense expenditures. Even so, the short-run prospects for substantial defense cuts are slim and the Vietnam war is slackening gradually. [41]

Opinion before World War II was characterized by isolationism; in the 1950's and 1960's, by support for worldwide cold war involvement; in the 1970's, perhaps by support for reduced, discriminating involvement in an era of partial detente. Beyond the 1970's?—A recent study of young American elites indicates that the conceptual frameworks and the perceptions of the past quarter-century of these future leaders fundamentally challenge those of the present leadership. [42] In terms of what "reality" will they seek to mobilize the publics? While their decisions will be based on their perceptions of the world and domestic environments, as Harold and Margaret Sprout have written, the consequences of the decisions will be affected by what is actually out there.

At a time when the international and national patterns of the cold war years are changing—producing subtle international challenges and pressing domestic demands, when technology continues to accelerate exponentially, when millions of new young voters are joining the electorate, responsible public debate of national security issues is vital. The role of public opinion has not been made obsolete because of the MIRV or the FOBS. The American people are not helplessly dependent on a single "assured destruction" decision to be made by the President on a millisecond's notice. Ever having to face such a decision will depend on many choices to be made beforehand, the most fundamental being not technical but value preferences. National security, the democratic process, and the people would seem best served, therefore, if the public is mobilized in support of policy that has benefited from intelligent public debate by governmental and nongovernmental elites, rather than policy that has been decreed by philosopher-kings, scientist-kings, or the "Queen of the World" [public opinion]. [43]

NOTES

1. Gabriel Almond, *The American People and Foreign Policy* (New York: Harcourt, Brace and World, 1950; New York: Praeger, 1960).
2. See Almond's discussion of the role of foreign policy elites, *ibid.,* Chap. 10.
3. Various participants in the policy process were examined in the case study on the Japanese peace settlement by Bernard Cohen, *The Political Process and Foreign Policy* (Princeton, N.J.: Princeton University Press, 1957). The communications of the nongov-

ernmental elites examined here are considered the upper limits of quality and quantity that were available for the public on this issue—all of which would be differentially diluted because of the selective exposures, selective perceptions, and selective memories of the various audiences.

4. With reference to the size and composition of the attentive public: Angus Campbell *et al.*, concluded in *The American Voter* (New York: Wiley, 1960) that only 10 percent of even the college-educated had a relatively high level of political conceptualization and that 5 percent of the grade-school educated had close to a fairly high level (as did 8 percent of the high school and 22 percent of college respondents). We found that 8 percent of the grade-school educated correctly defined "fallout" as early as 1955, when 58 percent of the college-educated had no opinion. The latter findings support the requirement in V. O. Key's *Public Opinion and American Democracy* (New York: Knopf, 1961), for political activists sprinkled throughout the system.

5. However, anxiety apparently diminished only where their educational background enabled respondents to assimilate and evaluate the information presented. From 1955 to 1958 many of the less educated were unaware of fallout; when they were aware, more of them were vague about it and afraid of the health danger than those in other educational levels. Before 1958, if more of them had heard of fallout, national anxiety might have been greater and the pressure for unconditional test cessation heightened.

6. Contrast Japanese opinion on security and fallout during roughly the same period: in 1954 only 11 percent of a national sample agreed with a statement by the Premier that Japan should cooperate with the United States regarding nuclear testing for the sake of security; in 1957, 76 percent of the public—91 percent of the well-educated, the reverse of the American pattern—feared the effects of fallout; 90 percent favored the prohibition of tests. Douglas Mendel, *The Japanese People and Foreign Policy* (Berkeley: University of California Press, 1961).

7. AIPO poll released September 20, 1963.

8. For the citation of a number of such studies, see Alfred O. Hero, *Americans in World Affairs* (Boston: World Peace Foundation, 1959).

9. This division is intended to suggest general tendencies and not that all individuals, interest groups, or mass media within a category fit all the characteristics described. Classification is necessarily judgmental, but no disparaging connotations are intended in the use of the three terms. For a more differentiated classification scheme with new terminology, see Robert A. Levine's *The Arms Debate* (Cambridge, Mass.: Harvard University Press, 1963), in which the Idealists are called the "systemic anti-war school"; the Pessimists, the "systemic anti-communist school"; and the Pragmatists, variously, the "marginal anti-war school," the "marginal middle school," and the "marginal anti-communist school."

10. Albert Wohlstetter, "Strategy and the Natural Scientists," in *Scientists and National Policy Making,* Robert Gilpin and Christopher Wright, eds. (New York: Columbia University Press, 1964).

11. For a discussion of the "peace establishment" in the early 1960's, see Arthur Herzog, *The War-Peace Establishment* (New York: Harper & Row, 1963).

12. Linus Pauling, "Genetic Effects of Weapons Tests," *Bulletin of the Atomic Scientists* (December 1962), p. 18. In a letter to the editor (June 1963), this article was viewed by geneticist Bentley Glass as having corrected Pauling's earlier statements. Dr. Pauling's rejoinder (September 1963, p. 30) maintained that no correction had taken place; rather, that Glass's views were due to his own misinterpretation or misunderstanding of the original statements.

13. Dr. Teller changed his position in April 1967, saying he was starting to believe that a satisfactory defense system "may be based on underground testing and the ingenious combination of experiment and theory." As to the problems in using nuclear explosives, "with the restrictions, we have done more than I had expected we could do" (*New York Times,* April 28, 1967).

14. *The Public Impact of Science in the Mass Media* (Ann Arbor: University of Michigan Survey Research Center, 1958).

15. The proposal was made before the results of the ongoing test series had been evaluated (in April the President had stated that a cessation hinged upon satisfactory information from the test series); the cessation proposal was also unaccompanied by a cutoff in the production of fissionable material, a condition that had been required for years, and as late as June 9, 1958.

16. Harold Jacobson and Eric Stein, *Diplomats, Scientists and Politicians: The U.S. and the Nuclear Test Ban Negotiations* (Ann Arbor: University of Michigan Press, 1966).

17. Executive notions of public opinion on disarmament were related to fears of loss of support for defense expenditure because of public disaffection. Samuel Huntington points out in *The Common Defense* (New York: Columbia University Press, 1961) that the administration's belief in public disaffection on arms spending did not jibe with attitude surveys. Rather, administration values modified their images of opinion, which were then used to legitimize the reduced defense budget. For discussions of "images," see Herbert C. Kelman, ed., *International Behavior* (New York: Holt, Rinehart and Winston, 1965).

18. See Bernard C. Cohen, *The Influence of Nongovernmental Groups on Foreign Policy Making* (Boston: World Peace Foundation, 1959) and Lester W. Milbrath, "Interest Groups and Foreign Policy," in *Domestic Sources of Foreign Policy,* James Rosenau, ed. (New York: Free Press, 1967).

19. Above, n. 16.

20. The U.S. executive was often "enfeebled" by mass opinion in this century, according to Walter Lippmann's *The Public Philosophy* (New York: New American Library, 1956), pp. 19, 23. In our study mass opinion did not compel the government to be, in Lippmann's words, "too pacifist in peace" (nor in the Vietnam conflict "too bellicose in war"). Lippmann also described the democratic Executive as being "enfeebled . . . by the representative assembly." In national security affairs from the end of World War II until the late 1960's, however, the U.S. Congress was generally acquiescent, and for a number of years the decline of the western European parliaments has been noted. For a critique of Lippmann's approach see David B. Truman, "The American System in Crisis," *Political Science Quarterly* (December 1959), pp. 481–97.

21. Commenting on criticism of his news conferences, President Eisenhower stated in his memoirs that "By consistently focusing on ideas rather than on phrasing, I was able to avoid causing the nation a serious setback through anything I said in many hours, over eight years, of intensive questioning." Dwight D. Eisenhower, *Mandate for Change* (Garden City, N.Y.: Doubleday, 1963), pp. 232–33.

22. Jerome B. Wiesner, *Where Science and Politics Meet* (New York: McGraw-Hill, 1965), p. 11.

23. Theodore C. Sorenson, *Kennedy* (New York: Harper and Row, 1965), p. 740.

24. "Yet if the questions put to the scientists were adequately formulated and the answers received properly understood, the public and the political leadership would have easily found out that the two groups of experts had nearly the same answers." Eugene Rabinowitch, "Decision-Making in the Scientific Age," in *The Scientific Revolution,* G. W. Elbers and Paul Duncan, eds. (Washington, D.C.: Public Affairs Press, 1959), p. 23.

25. Criticism of the columnists must take into account, however, the three-to-five-columns-a-week deadlines they faced.

26. For a discussion of the need for interpretation to avoid the creation of apathy or excessive anxiety, see Harold Mendelssohn, "Socio-Psychological Perspectives on the Mass Media and Public Anxiety," *Journalism Quarterly,* Vol. 40 (Autumn 1963), pp. 511–16.

27. Janet Besse and Harold Lasswell, "Our Columnists on the A-Bomb," *World Politics* (October 1950), pp. 72–87.

28. *New York Times,* June 2, 1966.

29. See William R. Caspary, "The 'Mood Theory': A Study of Public Opinion and Foreign Policy," *American Political Science Review* (June 1970), pp. 536–47, for a criticism of the "mood theory," which seems to give insufficient credit to Almond's judgment in both 1950 and 1960 concerning the increase in stability and the permissiveness of the public.

30. Reviewing the foreign policy attitudes of the American people in *American Credos* (New York: Harper, 1962), Stuart Chase wrote that "the United States government followed the wish of the city-dwellers and resumed testing." (59 percent of the respondents in New York City, Chicago, and Los Angeles favored American testing in August 1961.)

31. Aaron Wildavsky, "The Politics of ABM," *Commentary* (November 1969), p. 62. A report by the Operations Research Society of America criticized experts on both sides of the ABM debate for analyses which were often "inappropriate, misleading, or factually in error," with experts too frequently failing to distinguish between the role of analyst and advocate; misleading argumentation which was not apparent to laymen could have been "quite effective in public debate" (*New York Times,* October 1, 1971).

32. James Rosenau, *The Attentive Public on Foreign Policy* (Princeton, N.J.: Center of International Studies, Princeton University, March 1968).

33. Raymond A. Bauer, *et al., American Business and Public Policy* (New York: Atherton, 1963); Samuel P. Huntington, *The Common Defense* (New York: Columbia University Press, 1960); Bernard C. Cohen, *The Political Process and Foreign Policy* (Princeton, N.J.: Princeton University Press, 1957); Kenneth Waltz, *Foreign Policy and Democratic Politics* (Boston: Little, Brown, 1967).

34. Sidney Verba, *et al.,* "Public Opinion and the War in Vietnam," *American Political Science Review* (June 1967), p. 321.

35. John E. Mueller, "Popular Support for the Wars in Korea and Vietnam," *American Political Science Review* (June 1971), pp. 358–75.

36. Hazel Erskine, "The Polls: Red China and the UN," *Public Opinion Quarterly* (Spring 1971), 123–35.

37. Gallup Poll, *New York Times,* May 30, 1971.

38. The possible constraints of public opinion are also suggested by the China issue. Since administration trial balloons in the early 1960's were not followed up with substantial changes in policy, one can only speculate about what effects an earlier policy change toward China and its consequences might have had on the perceptions of policy-makers concerning a war in Vietnam.

39. Sidney Verba and Richard Brody, "Participation, Policy Preferences, and the War in Vietnam," *Public Opinion Quarterly* (Fall 1970), pp. 325–32.

40. Milton J. Rosenberg, "Attitude Change and Foreign Policy in the Cold War Era," in *Domestic Sources of Foreign Policy,* James Rosenau, ed. (New York: Free Press, 1967), p. 129.

41. Testifying before Congress shortly after the Moscow SALT agreement was signed, Defense Secretary Laird urged continued funding for new submarine and bomber systems to maintain bargaining strength in future SALT talks (*International Herald Tribune,* June 6, 1972). In Vietnam, although American troops were at nearly one-tenth the 1968 level, the North Vietnamese offensive in spring 1972 was met with massive US bombing of North Vietnam and mining of its ports.

42. Graham T. Allison, "Cool It: The Foreign Policy of Young America," *Foreign Policy* (Winter 1970–71), pp. 144–60.

43. Pascal's phrase, as quoted in V. O. Key, *Public Opinion and American Democracy* (New York: Knopf, 1961), p. 7.

Interaction of the Domestic and International Environments

We have been following a simple framework for explaining the operation of the national security policy process—a framework which includes an examination of values and goals, the nature of the world environment, and the domestic response to the challenge of the world environment. Reality is not so simple: except for analytical purposes (and sometimes not then), the component parts of the process are not easily separated or placed in order of priority, but overlap and interconnect. The policy outcomes are subject to similar qualifications; one or more of a variety of methods of projecting American power into the international arena may be chosen to protect perceived security interests. But the projection of power is not one-way. Because the domestic and international arenas overlap, policy is conditioned in the domestic arena also by the feedback from external sources—arriving not only in the diplomatic cables to the White House, State Department, or Pentagon, but also from the news services and television networks which transmit the information to elites and attentive and general publics. "NATO's reverse impact on American policy processes," for example, was studied by William T. R. Fox and Annette Baker Fox, who found that "United States membership in NATO has altered the position of various parts of the executive branch in relation to each other and to Congress. It has provided new ways for them to influence and be influenced by the NATO allies, and it has made the NATO institutions themselves participants in the 'legislative politics' of the executive branch."[1] Such interaction of the internal and external arenas, which has been called "linkage politics," may involve "linkage groups" that connect both the domestic and international systems.[2]

The dynamics of the national and international systems in the post-World War II period have influenced the techniques of national security policy. On the international level we have mentioned the impact of technology, the decline of cold war hostility, the rise of new powers such as China and Japan, polycentrism in the communist world, the growing economic strength of Europe, and the ferment in the Third World. On the national level, within the United States numerous problems are demanding attention—among them, urban blight, the racial problem, pollution, inflation and unemployment, and health.[3] In the following pages we will discuss four of the techniques of implementing national security policy: alliances, foreign aid, arms control and disarmament, and limited war. (Another technique which will not be specifically considered—negotiation—is an integral part of all four of the other techniques, including war, since negotiation does not generally stop when the guns begin to fire and start again only when the guns are silent.) [4]

Less than a quarter-century ago the United States entered its first peacetime foreign entanglement since George Washington's farewell counsel. Our foremost alliance bond—the North Atlantic Treaty Organization—has involved us in what Washington referred to as "the toils of European ambition, rivalship, interest, humor or caprice." What began as essentially a paper structure was transformed in the early 1950's to a flesh and blood organization, due largely to the impetus of the Korean War.

How American officials thought the NATO alliance would serve American interests has been described as follows by William T. R. Fox and Annette Baker Fox: (1) to "promote both 'self help' and 'mutual aid' "; (2) "raise the morale of the Europeans"; (3) "provide an instrument for coordinated action"; (4) "deter aggression by being prepared to meet it"; (5) "build an Atlantic community"; (6) "serve economic purposes"; (7) "provide a channel for communication and diplomatic pressure"; (8) "extend the area and resource base" of the United States; and (9) "help manage the problem of Germany." Policy-makers, according to Fox and Fox, also perceived seven distinctive roles for the United States in the alliance which were without precedent for America in peacetime: (1) to "make good the deficiencies of the alliance as a whole"; (2) "act as pilot in the strategic planning of the alliance"; (3) "guide the general policies of NATO"; (4) "induce, energize, and stimulate actions which its allies can only undertake by themselves"; (5) "fill the principal military commands in the alliance"; (6) "manage the nuclear deterrent for the alliance"; (7) in conventional defense to "demonstrate by example what other allies might also profitably do." [5]

Reflected in the foregoing lists are some of the traditional functions of alliances—described by Robert Osgood as being principally "accretion of external power, internal security, restraint of allies, and international order" [6]—as well as some of the modifications brought on by the nuclear era. For the first time coalition planning and an infrastructure (e.g., airfields and hundreds of miles of pipelines) were provided in peacetime because a large-scale war would be fought with forces-in-being and not after a long mobilization period. At the same time, alliances in the nuclear age are intended more to deter than to fight a war; indeed some of the debates within NATO have revolved around the relative emphasis given deterrence capacity as compared to the ability to fight if deterrence failed. (It was felt by some that the latter would undermine deterrence.) Nuclear weapons have also diminished the credibility of the guarantor nations, symbolized by the question "Would the United States sacrifice New York for Berlin?" Doubts have indeed existed in Europe—due in part to memories of America's rapid departure after World War I and to awareness of competing interests in the coming decades—but Europeans have not generally espoused the position of General Gallois of France that alliances are obsolete in the nuclear age since no one can trust anyone else to accept nuclear destruction on his behalf.

Under the nuclear umbrella, meanwhile, smaller powers have found greater freedom of action both within and without alliances, as the nuclear giants fear the use of force which may lead to nuclear escalation. At the same time, however, the holders of the nuclear umbrella—the superpowers—have occasionally acted above the heads of their allies in the interests of world stability as they perceived it. Witness the reluctance to distribute nuclear weapons to their allies and the Suez incident, in which the United States and the Soviet Union sided against Britain and France. (See Richard Neustadt's analysis of Anglo-American negotiations during this crisis, selection 28.)

American predominance during the first decade of NATO's existence was due mainly to Europe's weakness, America's strength, and the threat of the the Soviet bloc. By the mid-1960's President DeGaulle could cite changes in the communist world, the loss of US credibility, American involvement around the world, and the growth of French power and stability. His conclusion that France need no longer be a "protectorate" of the United States, as she was in 1949 applied to much of Europe as well.

What Europeans viewed as American paternalism in the alliance was exacerbated in the early 1960's by what other observers considered an American insensitivity to political and psychological factors and an overemphasis on the logic of technology.[7] Although the United States had encouraged Europe to move toward independence politically and economically, it continued to dominate strategy. The city-sparing doctrine of the early 1960's, for example, demanded centralized command and control; since the United States possessed the technological and strategic expertise, a division of labor seemed logical to many American policy-makers, with the Europeans handling the conventional forces. As the debate raged back and forth over the Atlantic, one critic of the American position, Stanley Hoffman, said that "cursing DeGaulle is not a policy." Some Europeans were indignant that the United States seemed to trust its enemy more than its allies, assuming that the Europeans would be more "trigger happy" than the Russians.

Preventing the spread of nuclear weapons provided part of the strong American impetus to develop the Multilateral Force (MLF), which would have created a ship-launched missile force (at first submarines were suggested) with mixed manning but not mixed control of nuclear weapons by the NATO nations. After considerable pressure was brought to bear on the Europeans for several years to accept the MLF, the plan was dropped by President Johnson in 1964. Forging ahead to create an independent French nuclear force, DeGaulle reportedly called the MLF an ANFL—American Naval Foreign Legion.

Due to the debate in the alliance and the withdrawal of France from the NATO structure (but not from the treaty), it was common in the mid-1960's to read of NATO's "disarray." W. T. R. Fox and Annette Baker Fox commented, however, that "It may be clever to say the king has no clothes on when he is in fact naked. But when he is arrayed, even if somewhat unspectacularly, it is dangerous to deny it."[8] The growth of the detente atmosphere in the late 1960's—including in 1970 West Germany's Non-Aggression Pact with the USSR and her frontiers' agreement with Poland, both ratified by the West German parliament in 1972—has encouraged domestic pressure in the United States for a reduction of American commitments in Europe and encouraged interest internally and abroad in a European Security Conference. Immediate disengagement is the logical action for cold war revisionists, who maintain that NATO was never necessary in the first place; the demand that the prosperous Europeans do more for their own defense has come from Congressional critics. NATO supporters point to the Soviet invasion of Czechoslovakia; the Brezhnev Doctrine of intervention in socialist states; Germany's vital position; and the growing Soviet Mediterranean fleet, whose political influence has caused concern especially among the Mediterranean members of the Alliance. As for the disproportionate costs to the United States of the alliance, Bruce Russett suggests that this is the "price of primacy" and in a sense a measure of the alliance's success: efforts to shift the burdens to our allies are "very unlikely to succeed. To extract a very much larger contribution from others we would have to cut our own by so much as really to diminish our allies' sense of security."[9]

By 1971 a new troops-in-Europe debate seemed to be generating, two decades after the debate that initiated our NATO commitment. Proposed amendments by several Senators to cut American troops by one-half over periods ranging from six months to three years reflected the changing domestic and international setting, and the conflicting institutional and personal perspectives we have been describing. Congressional critics in this debate who cited domestic priorities and the Europeans' reluctance to bear their share were opposed by an administration stressing the use of troop cuts as a "bargaining chip" in negotiating mutual and balanced force reductions with the East. In 1972, following the Nixon-Brezhnev summit meeting, the ratification of West Germany's Eastern Treaties, and the Big Four Berlin accord, the way seemed clear to conferences on European security and cooperation, and on mutual and balanced force reductions in 1973.[10]

What are the future prospects for alliances as instruments of national security policy? Rather than the dismantling of NATO that some critics have called for, more likely in Robert Osgood's phrase, is "the mitigation of the burdens of American predominance." In what will be a more pluralistic international system with new centers of diplomatic influence and power, writes Osgood, "Instead of trying to organize the 'free world' against 'international communism,' [the United States] will have to expend its energy in promoting, through selective support, inducements, threats, and sanctions, a more complex balance of power in which the distinctions between foe and friend break down into numerous gradations along a broad spectrum of conflict and alignment." [11] More probable for Adam Yarmolinsky is a "new version of non-entanglement, involving abrogation or modification of existing treaties with the end of insuring that, except for the defense of Western Europe or Japan, the United States will not be in danger of having to employ ground forces or to deploy any forces at all except as part of a broad-based multilateral military effort." [12]

A supplement to formal alliances as instruments of national security policy has been the use of foreign aid in various economic and military forms. Originating with Marshall Plan aid for European economic recovery, over the past two decades more than $120 billion has gone to countries around the globe. The geographic shift from Europe to Asia and Latin America is one of several discernible trends in American aid patterns; others include increased use of loans instead of grants and limited expansion of multilateral over bilateral transactions. Annual Congressional debates have pitted liberal supporters of the aid program against conservatives who saw American dollars going down foreign "ratholes" or who asked if the United States was indeed "financing public baths for Egyptian camel drivers." Arguments that sought to assuage the conservative critics—such as the fact that perhaps four-fifths of military assistance dollars are spent in the United States—have bolstered the attacks of the radical critics, who labeled the aid program part of American "neo-imperialism." In the past half-decade, opposition has emanated as well from liberals, who had been staunch supporters of foreign aid in the past—in the mid-1960's, for example, Senator Fulbright began calling for greater multilateralization of foreign aid in order to avoid future American intervention of the Vietnam type; in October 1971 liberal and conservative votes defeated the Senate foreign aid authorization bill.

Unlike economic aid, the military-assistance program—originating with the Greek-Turkish (Truman Doctrine) aid in the late 1940's and providing training, equipment, and advice [13]—has frequently been under liberal attack. In 1971, with indications that military assistance would be increased in accordance with the Nixon Doctrine aim of promoting self-help,[14] pressure from Senator William Proxmire forced the administration to disclose for the first time in advance the list of military-assistance recipients and the dollar amounts for fiscal year 1972: a worldwide total of 49 countries receiving $2.35 billion.[15] (The $3.19 billion foreign-aid appropriations bill was signed in March 1972, eight months after the start of the fiscal year.)

The economic and military-assistance labels conceal considerable confusion over the objectives of and the expectations for foreign aid. Much of the practice of foreign economic aid, writes Professor Hans J. Morgenthau, has rested on a number of unfounded assumptions represented by the following series of "causal" relationships: between the infusion of capital and technology and economic development, between economic development and social stability, between social stability and democratic institutions, and between democratic institutions and a peaceful foreign policy. One can readily agree that economic development depends upon "intellectual, moral, and political preconditions" without, however, accepting other implications in Professor Morgenthau's statement that "as there are bums and beggars, so there are bum and beggar nations." [16] Nevertheless, it must be recognized that political leadership, administrative skills, and motivation are of primary importance; for as economist Wilfred Malenbaum has written, "non-economic forces, not economic forces, are the prime movers in the growth process." [17]

In recent years organizations such as the United Nations Conference on Trade and Development and the Committee for Economic Development have advocated that developed nations allocate one percent of their GNP to foreign aid.[18] Setting such a goal is part of what Samuel P. Huntington calls the "purist rationale" for foreign aid, which makes economic development an end in itself and divorces it from foreign policy. One can no more justify the foreign aid budget this way than the military budget, Huntington observes. As both he and Morgenthau emphasize, foreign aid is part of the domestic and foreign policy process; its goals, especially in a period of mounting domestic demands, must be evaluated in competition with other claims for limited resources. Rather than an arbitrary percentage of the GNP, Huntington offers the following American national interests to be served by a foreign aid program: (1) "to enhance the military security of selected countries"; (2) "to encourage the economic development of the Third World in general" ("a limited but real interest"); (3) "to promote the economic development of selected countries as one element of overall U.S. foreign policy toward these countries"; and (4) "to encourage the emergence of pluralistic societies" (a goal "quite separate" from the foregoing and best promoted "indirectly rather than on a government to government basis"). While the major purposes of American foreign aid since World War II may be characterized as European recovery in the 1940's, mutual security in the 1950's, and economic development in the 1960's, new purposes for the 1970's include American leadership of international cooperation for maintaining the quality of life on earth.[19]

The specter of possible atomic war directs attention to the third technique of national security policy—arms control and disarmament. Yet despite the concerns special to the nuclear age, one finds fewer examples of "disarmament" —reduction of weapons—than in pre-atomic decades. Caught in the security dilemma and having participated for more than a decade in intense cold war hostility, the fearful and mistrusting superpowers have hesitated to take any steps that might jeopardize their perceived security. Disarmament negotiations at times have been characterized by advocacy of sweeping plans for general and complete disarmament (GCD) that seemed to serve mainly propaganda purposes. Indeed, one pessimistic account described the negotiations as "gamesmanship" in which each side sought to "weaken the political and military posture of the other side," using "jokers" such as "ban the bomb" (USSR) or "inspection and control" (US) in each proposal to protect its interests, while ensuring the proposal's rejection by its opponent.[20]

The disappointing results of the disarmament talks are obvious without accepting the gamesmanship thesis. What about "arms control"? As defined by

Thomas Schelling and Morton Halperin, arms control includes "all forms of military cooperation between potential enemies in the interest of reducing the likelihood of war, its scope and violence if it occurs, and the political and economic costs of being prepared for it," with the "essential feature [being] the recognition of . . . common interest, of the possibility of reciprocation and cooperation. . . ."[21] Unlike the failures of disarmament, gains have been made in arms control, which began coming into prominence in the late 1950's as negotiations shifted away from GCD (the last proposal was in 1962) to partial measures such as a nuclear test ban. The most recent success was the 1972 Moscow Summit agreement. This and other arms control measures, such as the mutual development of invulnerable retaliatory forces, the Hotline Agreement, and the Non-Proliferation Treaty, have contributed to stability in the international system. A mutual learning process has produced increased sophistication about technological and strategic problems, which is reflected in the summit negotiations and in *Pravda's* description of an action-reaction type arms spiral in discussing the Strategic Arms Limitation Talks (SALT).[22]

It has become clearer in the past decade also that arms control negotiation does not simply involve discussions by representatives of foreign offices or defense ministries in the style of eighteenth-century cabinet diplomacy. The transformations in the international system—which include the blurring of lines between domestic and foreign policy—are reflected in the interaction of domestic and international factors concerning arms control. While it remains basically true that armaments reflect underlying clashes of political interests, still the existence of armaments may contribute to further increases through an action-reaction effect. Vested interests in the domestic bureaucratic structures may work to maintain their respective weapons systems. Hardliners and softliners in the United States and the Soviet Union may be supportive of each other. Whether the USSR will accept strategic parity with the United States or press for a margin of "superiority" will presumably depend in part on which groups in the Soviet military and political bureaucracy prevail. The interaction of domestic and international factors is illustrated as well in the Nixon Administration's two-way use of the ABM as a "bargaining chip" in the SALT talks in 1970: the administration received double value for its "chip" by using the argument to encourage the Senate to pass the ABM appropriation and then presumably using the latter in the SALT negotiations.

The latest arms control negotiations—the SALT talks—got underway in late 1969. Two and one-half years of negotiations marked by a minimum of propaganda were capped with the agreement signed by Nixon and Brezhnev in mid-1972. The United States and the USSR were restricted to two anti-ballistic missile systems each (one defending the national capital; the other, an ICBM base); and their ICBM's and SLBM's were frozen until 1977 at the numbers in existence or under construction at the time of the agreement. The leaders of the two superpowers also agreed to continue the SALT talks beyond this first step to seek further arms limitations.

The signing of a formal treaty is not the only value of the SALT talks. As

Jerome H. Kahan has suggested, the US-USSR "strategic dialogue" can help clarify intentions and misunderstandings and can mutually increase knowledge of frames of reference. Moreover, arms control measures may result without formal agreement, by means of "reciprocal-action" procedures—informal arms control arrangements such as the test-ban moratorium of 1958–61.[23] A useful outcome of the talks would also be, Hedley Bull observes, a reexamination of the basic assumptions of the balance of terror, and an expansion of Soviet-American cooperation to include other major powers—such as China—that are significant for arms control and international security.[24]

Although nuclear war is "unthinkable" as a rational instrument of policy, the use of force remains as a technique of defending national interests, despite a decline in its utility.[25] Countless armed conflicts have occurred in the nuclear age involving nations on all points of the conceptual compass—East-West, North-South (e.g., USSR, the United States, China, India, Israel), but without a direct confrontation of superpower forces. Even conventional war appears to be unthinkable among the Western European democracies (a condition that was quite thinkable before World War II); but among the Third World nations, intra- and interstate conflicts have proliferated due to tribal, religious, and racial differences.

American use of force in the past quarter-century has ranged from the dispatching of troops for short periods to Lebanon in 1958 and the Dominican Republic in 1965, to the large-scale wars in Korea and Vietnam; and the spectrum of US limited-war capabilities has included counterinsurgency techniques and tactical nuclear weapons. Arguments against crossing the nuclear threshold that prevailed from the late 1950's through the 1960's have recently been under pressure, according to Earl C. Ravenal:

There has lately been a quickened advocacy of nuclear reliance in the public writings of middle grade military officers, journalist-strategists, and defense academics. There is now strengthened institutional support for nuclear alternatives within the Office of the Secretary of Defense—notably among the International Security Affairs staff—that reinforces the persistent nuclear orientation of the Joint Chiefs of Staff and such significant unified commands as CINCPAC.[26]

The powerful domestic impact of America's use of force in Vietnam is manifest in the demand for "No more Vietnams!" But as the Munich analogy has at times distorted foreign policy judgments in the past two decades, will the Vietnam analogy improve or impair judgment about American foreign policy in the coming decades? Addressing themselves to the possible use of American military forces in the future, three analysts suggest that a case for possible intervention be judged on the basis of these factors: the American sense of interest (mainly in terms of the world balance of power and substantial domestic concerns); and the estimated probability of success relative to costs and risks. In proposing the introduction of "new presumptions" in American policy, these analysts distinguish three categories of cases: first, "overt aggression" (significant numbers of organized units crossing frontiers) by a major communist power against an American ally, in which the presumption should be that the United States will intervene; second, overt aggression by any state against a nonally, in which there should be a presumption against American intervention if no other major power is involved; and third, internal violence jeopardizing a friendly state, in which the strong presumption should be against American intervention, even when there is outside encouragement and aid.[27]

An analytical framework such as this is of course fraught with difficulties, such as the definition of aggression or the perceptions of the decision-makers. But however complex or imprecise, the process of choosing to use or not use force cannot be avoided. In choosing, judgments about the utility of force rest ultimately on perception and values: "The utility . . . which a nation, or its leaders derives from military power—that is, from its maintenance and use—depends on the satisfaction of certain values . . . and the accrual of certain costs. . . ."[28]

Choices concerning the use of force are at the heart of the national security process; and the costs of maintaining a vast defense establishment and using the various instruments we have been discussing are sooner or later felt by the society at large. (The impact of the Vietnam war includes societal effects, costs in human life, and dollar costs recently estimated at nearly $200 billion.)[29] The defense establishment in America has been described as a "military-industrial complex" (MIC), theoretical support for which was offered by C. Wright Mills's *Power Elite.* Some recent observers have expanded this term to "Military-Industrial-Labor-Academic Complex"; others would include Congress; and still others maintain that American society is itself a military-industrial complex. (For various perspectives in this volume on the theory and practice of the MIC, see the articles by Pilisuk and Hayden and by Yarmolinsky in this part (selections 32 and 33), the selections by Mills and Rose in Part I (selections 5 and 6), and the Berkley-Perlo exchange in Part III (selections 22 and 23). The passing of the MIC was recently noted by Seymour Melman, who maintains that the "loose collaboration [of the MIC], mainly through market relations" has been replaced by Pentagon "state management."[30]

Among the critics of the MIC, interpretations of the military's role vary, with some emphasizing the expanding power of the military. Richard Barnet suggests this at one point of *The Economy of Death,* but subsequently he states that, more importantly, civilians have become militarized without "the soldier's professional caution."[31] For Gabriel Kolko, the role of the military has declined, contrary to Mills's "military ascendancy" thesis, and the business community is dominant: "not a mythical 'military-industrial complex' but civilian authority and civilian-defined goals are the sources of American foreign and military policy—and the American malaise." The military "conforms to the needs of economic interests."[32]

Although some of the writings on the MIC offer considerable statistical information, evidence supporting the claimed linkages is sparse and of course the data can be interpreted in diverse ways. For example, material on the MIC often cites the more than 2000 retired military officers working for defense-related industries in 1969. Discussing the same data, Adam Yarmolinsky's *The Military Establishment* indicates that only 11 percent of retired officers work in aerospace and electronics; 17 percent in manufacturing of any kind; and more than 40 percent in governmental, educational, medical insurance, or other non-profit institutions. Based on his reading of the statistics, Yarmolinsky finds it "hard to make a persuasive case suggesting that there is a remarkable concentration of retired military in war industries." [33] Lobbying by the MIC, which is of concern to some critics, is viewed by Bruce Russett as follows: "It is not surprising, nor is it censurable, that the armed services and their suppliers should undertake political activities. . . . In fact, without bureaucratic politics by the military services, military needs might well be neglected." [34] In examining the relationships of the Pentagon with industry, Yarmolinsky maintains that "adverse impacts . . . are becoming evident" and that the "Defense Department has slowly taken over (either directly or indirectly) many of the decision making functions which are normally the prerogatives of business management. . . ." [35] These relationships are interpreted more direly by Professor Melman, however, as manifestations of the "Pentagon capitalism" which, among other things, seeks to "prevent the conversion of its industrial empire to civilian use." [36]

One of the few attempts to marshal some empirical evidence for linkages between defense spending and Congressional voting, Bruce Russett's *What Price Vigilance?* turned up mixed results. Supporting the critics of the MIC is Russett's finding that the larger the share of Defense Department employment (e.g., military bases) in a Senator's state, the more "conservative" his votes are on arms issues. But, to the contrary, the awarding of contracts to industries in Congressional constituencies seemed unrelated to Congressional attitudes on arms issues. One of the conclusions Russett draws from the first finding points up another cost to society; the distortion of the political system by a large defense establishment that very likely "helps sustain the hawkish and most uncompromisingly anti-communist forces in American political life." [37]

The foregoing comparisons illustrate one of the themes of earlier discussions —that how one interprets data depends on the conceptual lenses one looks through. The command to "face the facts" may often mean "face the facts the way I see them." American society may be a military-industrial complex as Pilisuk and Hayden say, or the American people may by and large "get the kind of military establishment they deserve" as Yarmolinsky says. Has this situation with respect to the military establishment developed mainly because the people have been manipulated by elites, or because of a complex of reasons? —For example, initial perceptions of threat to their values may not have changed and the costs of the military establishment may not have been weighed against other competing values. If change is necessary, can it only come about by destroying the system, or can it work within the system through countervailing forces? (Richard Barnet suggests that such countervailing forces should include students, scientists and technologists, businessmen who are not clients of the Pentagon, and members of Congress.)

Some combination of continuity and change is always a part of national security policy. Because policy change usually occurs incrementally in response to perceived environmental demands, one hesitates to suggest environmental transformations of "watershed" or "end of era" dimensions. Yet the early 1970's are not the early 1950's, and we have alluded to various patterns in the international and domestic environments which have been more fluid in recent years.

America's future role in the world in response to these changes is not easily predictable. Here are examples of some recent thinking. Only a few years ago one writer described an "imperial" role for the United States, with the USSR as a regional power.[38] Another "globalist" viewpoint offered in the selection in this part by Zbigniew Brzezinski (selection 35) is that America should lead in the establishment of a community of developed nations. A "limitationist" critic of globalism, Senator Fulbright, believes America would best serve the world by setting an example in the way we run our own society.[39] Implied in his and other limitationist writing is a world divided into spheres of influence. An economic determinist such as Gabriel Kolko maintains that the American economic system's need for raw materials will not "permit the rest of the world to take its own political and revolutionary course in a manner that imperils the American freedom to use them."[40] On the other hand, in advocating an evenhanded benevolent policy toward all Third World nations, Max Singer and Aaron Wildavsky argue that "developing nations cannot affect America's national interests. . . . These countries are far more dependent on selling than America is on buying."[41] Positing the acceptance of change itself as the fundamental starting point, Marshall Shulman proposes two worthy principles for American policy: "noninterference by force in processes of internal change," and free political and economic access, which "permits nations to compete, not for the control of territory but for the establishment of mutually beneficial and nonexploitative relations, and thereby for political influence." American and Soviet acceptance of "tacit rules of engagement" which permit competition for political influence would not constitute a division of the globe into spheres of influence.[42]

Although the limitationist critique of globalist policy has not yet provided many operational alternatives for American policy,[43] some kind of American involvement in a world growing more interdependent is unavoidable. We can't stop the world so we can get off; neither can we simply run it, especially since our presence in the world is itself part of the problem. The nature of America's involvement is therefore what has to be decided.

Although the interdependence of the global system makes many aspects of the nation state increasingly obsolescent, the prospects are for a continuation of the nation state and nationalism as powerful forces. The security dilemma therefore remains. National security policy will depend on how the dilemma is interpreted; the means for response will depend on perceptions of the international and domestic systems, as costs and benefits of maintaining and using particular instruments of national security policy are weighed in comparison to the sacrifice of other values at home—for example, health, education, the natural environment, individual privacy, freedom of the press. Since the ultimate choices are value choices, the process of deciding is one which must in a democratic society rest ultimately on the public and its political representatives.

In thinking about the choices to be made, it may be useful to expand the concept of national security interests. "National interest" grew out of the "reason of state" doctrine, a doctrine followed by the new kingdoms of Europe and one which replaced Medieval western Christendom's pursuit of the "heavenly interest." Since global "system maintenance" now has far more than academic relevance, consideration should be given in calculating national security interests to the larger system of which we are a part—not the "heavenly interest" for other worldly salvation, but the "planetary interest" for earthly salvation.

NOTES

1. William T. R. Fox and Annette Baker Fox, *NATO and the Range of American Choice* (New York: Columbia University Press, 1967), p. 227.

2. James Rosenau, ed., *Linkage Politics* (New York: Free Press, 1969). The term "Linkage Groups" is used by Karl Deutsch in "External Influences on the Internal Behavior of States," in *Approaches to Comparative and International Politics,* R. Barry Farrell, ed. (Evanston: Northwestern University Press, 1966), p. 12.

3. For a discussion of the mounting "social services" pressures on security allocations in twentieth-century Britain and the implications for all political communities, see Harold and Margaret Sprout, "The Dilemma of Rising Demands and Insufficient Resources," *World Politics* (July 1968), pp. 660–93.

4. See Fred Iklé, *How Nations Negotiate* (New York: Harper & Row, 1964); *Every War Must End* (New York: Columbia University Press, 1971); and *How Wars End,* The Annals of the American Academy of Political and Social Science (November 1970).

5. Fox and Fox (above, n. 1), pp. 35–44, 59–72.

6. Robert E. Osgood, *Alliances and American Foreign Policy* (Baltimore: Johns Hopkins Press, 1968), p. 21.

7. For the views of one of these observers, see Henry A. Kissinger, *The Troubled Partnership: A Re-Appraisal of the Atlantic Alliance* (New York: McGraw-Hill, 1965).

8. Fox and Fox (above, n. 1), p. 313.

9. Bruce Russett, *What Price Vigilance?* (New Haven: Yale University Press, 1970), pp. 125–26.

10. On negotiating force reductions, see Timothy W. Stanley and Darnell M. Whitt, *Detente Diplomacy: United States and European Security in the 1970's* (New York: Dunellen, 1970).

11. Osgood (above, n. 6), p. 14.

12. Adam Yarmolinsky, *The Military Establishment* (New York: Harper and Row, 1971), p. 131. A chapter from this book appears in this part (selection 33).

13. See Paul C. Davis and William T. R. Fox, "American Military Representation Abroad," in *The Representation of the United States Abroad,* Vincent Barnet, ed. (New York: Praeger, 1965), pp. 129–83.

14. The Nixon Administration has also proposed a reform of the administration of foreign aid which would divide the Agency for International Development into separate development loan and technical assistance institutions.

15. *New York Times,* July 10, 1971.

16. Hans J. Morgenthau, *A New Foreign Policy for the American People* (New York: Praeger, 1969), p. 96; originally published as "A Political Theory of Foreign Aid," *American Political Science Review* (1962).

17. Wilfred Malenbaum, "Economic Factors and Political Development," in *New Nations: The Problem of Political Development,* The Annals of the American Academy of Political and Social Science (March 1965), p. 51.

18. See, for example, *Assisting Development in Low Income Countries,* and *Development Assistance to Southeast Asia,* Committee for Economic Development (September 1969; July 1970).

19. Samuel P. Huntington, "Foreign Aid for What and for Whom" and "Does Foreign Aid Have a Future?" *Foreign Policy* (Winter 1970–71; Spring 1971), pp. 161–89, 114–34.

20. John W. Spanier and Joseph L. Nogee, *The Politics of Disarmament: A Study in Soviet-American Gamesmanship* (New York: Praeger, 1962).

21. Thomas C. Shelling and Morton H. Halperin, *Strategy and Arms Control* (New York: 20th Century Fund, 1961), p. 2.

22. Quoted in *New York Times,* July 8, 1971.

23. Jerome H. Kahan, "Strategies for SALT," *World Politics* (January 1971), pp. 171–88.

24. See selection 30 in this part.

25. See Klaus Knorr, *On the Uses of Military Power in the Nuclear Age* (Princeton, N.J.: Princeton University Press, 1966). A chapter from this book appears in Part II (selection 8). For a dissenting view on the continuing utility of force, see Walter Millis, "The Uselessness of Military Power," in *America Armed,* Robert A. Goldwin, ed. (Chicago: Rand-McNally, 1963), pp. 22–42.

26. Earl C. Ravenal, "The Political-Military Gap," *Foreign Policy* (Summer 1971), p. 37.

27. Graham Allison, Ernest May, and Adam Yarmolinsky, "Limits to Intervention," *Foreign Affairs* (January 1970), pp. 245–61.

28. Knorr (above, n. 26), pp. 8, 9.

29. *Washington Post,* July 11, 1971.

30. Seymour Melman, *Pentagon Capitalism* (New York: McGraw-Hill, 1970). For a statement of Melman's views, see selection 32 by Pilisuk and Hayden. A critical review appears in Stephen J. Cimbala, "New Myths and Old Realities: Defense and Its Critics," *World Politics* (October 1971), pp. 126–57.

31. Richard J. Barnet, *The Economy of Death* (New York: Atheneum, 1970), pp. 80–83.

32. Gabriel Kolko, *The Roots of American Foreign Policy* (Boston: Beacon Press, 1969), pp. xiii, 31.

33. Yarmolinsky (above, n. 12), pp. 64–65.

34. Russett (above, n. 9), p. 22.

35. Yarmolinsky (above, n. 9), p. 67.

36. Melman (above, n. 31), p. 223.

37. Russett (above, n. 9), p. 180.

38. George Liska, *Imperial America: The International Politics of Primacy* (Baltimore: Johns Hopkins University Press, 1967).

39. J. W. Fulbright, *The Arrogance of Power* (New York: Vintage, 1966), p. 258.

40. Kolko (above, n. 32), p. 53.

41. Max Singer and Aaron Wildavsky, "A Third World Averaging Strategy," in *U.S. Foreign Policy,* Paul Seabury and Aaron Wildavsky, ed. (New York: McGraw Hill, 1969), pp. 18, 23.

42. Marshall Shulman, "What Does Security Mean Today?" *Foreign Affairs* (July 1971), pp. 614, 615. The Nixon-Brezhnev summit declaration of twelve "basic principles" can be viewed in part as a codification of some tacit rules of conduct that have developed.

43. Charles Gati, "Another Grand Debate? The Limitationist Critique of American Foreign Policy," *World Politics* (October 1968), pp. 133–51.

TECHNIQUES OF IMPLEMENTING NATIONAL SECURITY POLICY

28.

Richard E. Neustadt: Alliance Politics

One characteristic of America's pursuit of its aims in the international system since World War II has been its participation in peacetime alliances, dubbed "pactomania" by some of the critics of the 1950's. Two failures in the US-British

From Richard E. Neustadt, *Alliance Politics,* Columbia University Press, 1970, pp. 56–74. Reprinted by permission of Columbia University Press and the author.

"special relationship"—the crises over Suez in 1956 and over America's cancellation of the Skybolt missile in 1962—are analyzed by Richard Neustadt in his book *Alliance Politics,* a chapter of which is reprinted below. The production of an *"inter*allied outcome" through interaction of *"intra*governmental" bargaining is what the author terms "alliance politics," with the Washington and London decision-makers being "players in two intricate and subtly different bargaining arenas, interacting on each other by and through the side effects of their internal games. . . ."

Richard Neustadt is Professor of Government at Harvard University and a member of the staff of the John Fitzgerald Kennedy School of Government. He has had more than a decade of service in Washington, including service in the Bureau of the Budget. Professor Neustadt's best-known work is the widely praised *Presidential Power.*

As history may read them, Suez and Skybolt are unlike. Especially is this the case in British terms, where one was an event of enduring significance, the other a mere episode. Yet despite all differences of symbolism, timing, issues, outcomes, the same pattern of behavior runs through both. Let us pause over this pattern. It has much to tell about the task of maintaining friendly relations —at least between such friends as Washington and London.

My previous chapters make the pattern plain. It is woven from four strands: muddled perceptions, stifled communications, disappointed expectations, paranoid reactions. In turn, each "friend" misreads the other, each is reticent with the other, each is surprised by the other, each replies in kind. A spiral starts, and only when the one bows low before the other's *latest* grievance does the spiral stop. That spiral rose much higher over Suez than over Skybolt, which testifies mainly to Kennedy's detachment. Had his ego been as much engaged as Eisenhower's or his stakes as high, or had he felt committed to his Europeanists, Nassau would have set off a new turn.

I

What explains the crisis pattern? Why do governments so closely linked engage in such behavior? These are my questions for this chapter. Answers bring us a long way toward understanding what may be the hazards for our government when it endeavors to pursue its aims by means of a peacetime alliance.

Personalities afford a partial answer, often taken for the whole. As such it warms the hearts of journalists and diarists, and devil-theorists everywhere. In many English memories and memoirs, "Suez" is spelled "Dulles," the self-righteous-devious-schemer. Americans quite often spell it "Eden," the illusioned-nervous-fumbler. Far be it from me to downgrade the impact of human personality on governmental conduct. But obviously this is insufficient to explain repetitive behavior of successive human beings. Indeed it does not suffice even for the same men in successive contexts. No doubt the personalities of Dulles and Eden—in reality, not caricature—contributed to the severity of Suez. So did their lack of empathy for one another. But Macmillan and Kennedy are quite another matter, while Thorneycroft and McNamara started on the best of terms. Yet the Suez pattern is discernible in Skybolt. By contrast, before 1956

Eden had made do with Dulles (and *vice-versa*) on numerous occasions where that pattern does not show.

Divergences of policy afford another explanation, comforting for those diplomatists and theorists who reify the State into a single calculator, rationally pursuing its determinate self-interest. But this is no more a sufficient answer than the last. Policies there no doubt were in London and in Washington. One can, at least, find trend lines in their actions over time and label each a policy by hindsight. But trends of action emanating from these capitals run parallel, in most respects, both before 1956 and before 1962. Differences in emphasis exist, of course, also in effort applied. There are, however, no discernible divergences of trends so wide as to account for the collision we experienced in each of those two years. Nor are there signs that either side deliberately intended quarrelling with the other. Quite the contrary, they both espoused and actually pursued the policy of keeping company with one another. Their actions toward each other ran on trend lines of successive compromises and accommodations, not least regarding Egypt during 1954 and nuclear weaponry in 1960. The crises in these spheres thus broke the trend in their relations, belying this aspect of policy, not reinforcing it. And outcomes in both cases show how unprepared they were for that. These crises came upon them as bolts from the blue. Deliberate intention? Far from it.

Another partial explanation lies in orders of priority. Both governments took actions of all sorts in many spheres at once, pursuing many things besides accommodation with each other. Each crisis shows divergence of priorities. Nasser and his Canal, Moscow and its threats, Bomber Command and its deterrent, Paris and the EEC, even the "special relationship" itself were not viewed quite alike by Washington and London. Out of these shades of difference they derived a different weighting for one sphere as against others. But differences of these sorts occur all the time. A government's priorities derive from resources, geography, and public moods, and from the life experience of those who rule, together with the history they learned at school. From Washington to London different orders of priority are commonplace. Yet we do not have a crisis every day. The question remains, why the behavior in these crises? If personalities and policy are not sufficient answers, neither are established orders of priority.

This brings us to the rationality of individual decisions, to the good sense, or its absence, in a given act of choice. Had Dulles but backed SCUA * with the wherewithal for boycott, or had Eden but insisted on a better war plan, or had Macmillan on a simpler weapon, or had McNamara but deferred his cancellation, it is likely that these crises would have blown away or never come at all. Yet the reasonableness of each such choice is readily defended. Considering American conditions, the Secretary of the Treasury could not pledge dollars for a boycott while Egyptians safely piloted our ships through the Canal, whence shippers much preferred to go. Considering British unpreparedness, Musketeer ** was a triumph of improvisation—also of coordination—executed well and fail-

---

* Suez Canal Users Association.
** Code name for the British military operation at Suez.

ing technically in only one respect: blockage of the Canal. Considering intended British uses, Skybolt appeared to have no major flaw except the need for guidance to city-sized targets, a relatively modest technical requirement; besides, it was the cheapest thing in sight and kept the Navy quite as happy as the Air Force. Considering the American budgetary process, Skybolt's cancellation in December was a coup: exclusion from the January budget left its friends on stony ground where they must lobby for an increase, rather than against a cut, should they appeal from President to Congress.

The case for the defense goes deeper still. Beneath these reasonable surfaces lie virtual necessities: imperatives of bureaucratic politics. On each occasion— and not these alone—no better way was open to the man who made the choice, in light of his relations with his governmental colleagues. Dulles had to do his best for Eisenhower's peace, and also for the Eisenhower budget of which Humphrey was a guardian. Especially was Humphrey guardian of credits under Treasury control. Eden had to satisfy his activists within the terms set by his generals. These emphatically included sea-borne landings. Macmillan had to base his nuclear symbol on a durable consensus both in Cabinet and among his Services. What better than a weapon which caused no one harm? McNamara had to cancel Skybolt or risk cumulative loss of $2.5 billion in successive fiscal years. Immediate action held the key to Air Force and congressional acquiescence.

For these men, I have said, no better way was open. Theoretically, each had the option to give up. But this they were determined not to do. Dulles was determined to hang on to Eden's coattails. Eden was determined to have Nasser's head, or at least save his own. Macmillan was determined to remain a member of the Nuclear Club. Kennedy, with McNamara, wanted all that money. Eden and Macmillan had their lives at stake, politically, at least in their own estimations. Dulles had at stake his credit with his President. Kennedy was only after money, which goes far to show why Skybolt is the lesser of these crises. But the money mattered to him; otherwise there would have been no crisis.

Americans may boggle at my claims for Musketeer. Englishmen may find our budgeting incomprehensible. Never mind for now; I soon shall have occasion to elaborate.

Meanwhile, where does this leave us? It leaves us with a clue: what seemed "cockeyed" from abroad was rational when viewed in terms of home.

II

Foreign relations begin at home. What went wrong in those instances—and others of the sort—was their external impact, *not* their inner logic. The makers of these choices did not err in their own terms. Rather, their choices ran afoul of someone else's terms. The fatal flaw in SCUA was not lack of teeth to monitor Egyptian management, but rather London's passion to unseat that management (and Nasser too). The fatal flaw in Musketeer was not its time schedule as such, but rather the effect of a delay in Washington. The fatal flaw in Skybolt was not British uses but American requirements. The one thing wrong with McNamara's budgeting was Thorneycroft's desire—and Macmillan's—for a quiet life.

Did not the makers of those choices see what they were courting overseas? They saw the "big picture" but blurred fine details. Dulles saw that Eden wanted war, he spent months trying to stop him. Having got him well entangled in UN negotiations Dulles evidently thought he had him stopped. Eden saw of course—how could he help it—that Washington was eager for a peaceful outcome. But "Ike" would "lie doggo" until election; besides, he would be conscious of analogies to Panama. Macmillan knew, even in 1960, that topside at the Pentagon there was no little skepticism about Skybolt. But he had done his "deal," implicit though it was; the tactics that achieved it should suffice to keep it. McNamara knew very well that cancellation could make trouble for the British. But they were "clever chaps." When they had worked it out he would be helpful.

Not only did these men have blurry vision when they looked abroad, but also they took sightings by the kindly light of hope. Dulles evidently thought "public opinion" spurred by Labour opposition weakened Eden's hand. Eden evidently thought that lying doggo meant a passivity extending even to Ike's jaws. Macmillan evidently thought our Chiefs of Staff might be a match for McNamara, even as they had been for his predecessors. McNamara, in turn, apparently supposed that Thorneycroft's reaction would be like his own had trouble been reversed. Hopes like these abounded in both crises. By no means were they confined to these instances alone.

In this there are two ironies. For one, each hopeful estimate of friends abroad was grown at home, rooted in the inner politics of home; indeed it was the only estimate consistent with the chosen course of action. In effect, these men saw what they had to see if what they felt they had to do stood any chance to work. And second, what they chose to do turned out to be in fact the one thing that their friends found hardest to endure in their terms, their own politics, not as perceived across the water but as actually pursued by them.

I offer you these ironies as further clues. Again they point us toward concerns at home. In terms of home, what suited "A" the best hurt "B" the worst. So Eden, by October 1956, saw no way to his war save Musketeer under Israeli cover, which precluded sailings while the lid went on. He estimated—probably correctly—that his transatlantic friends would acquiesce in a *fait accompli*. But the one thing Eisenhower saw no way to do was acquiesce in something that remained undone. So Dulles earlier scaled SCUA's teeth to Humphrey's size, while Eden, who had bought it, then confronted colleagues all of whom felt "sold." So with McNamara and Thorneycroft in Schlesinger's "Pinero drama of misunderstanding." So later with Macmillan reading Kennedy's TV remarks on Skybolt: "The lady had been violated in public."

No wonder the behavior patterns we are probing show successive expectations crowned by disappointment, with surprise inducing paranoid reactions. The expectations suited felt necessities. The disappointment ran to treasured projects. The surprise was genuine. The pain was real. And the suspicion was commensurate. How could such harm be caused by inadvertence? Above all from a friend: "How could he do that to me?" This was the plaint, in turn, of Eden, Dulles, Eisenhower, Thorneycroft, McNamara, Macmillan, and even Kennedy. It is easy to see why.

What then of reticence, another thread through both our crises? What accounts for the successive spells of stifled communication? Clearly these contributed to faulty expectations, hence to unintended pain. Why should communications fail between allies so sorely needing to guess right about each other? To answer is to offer one more clue.

The summaries before you show an evident evasiveness on our side in the first two months of Suez: Dulles weaves and bobs. Then there is Eden's turn to the UN without informing Dulles, followed by the blackout in October 1956 on word of what the British meant to do with France and Israel. And in the Skybolt case there is the silence between Thorneycroft and McNamara—to say nothing of others—which lasted for five weeks.

Superficially, these instances are of two sorts, one turning on embarrassment, the other on retaliation. But beneath these motives we find others, less obvious. Those others seem to have a common source: between London and Washington the wall of sovereignty was full of holes.

How could McNamara unveil his plans to Thorneycroft with assurance that the RAF would not learn and so inform the USAF before he wanted his subordinates to know of his decision? Or *vice versa?* How could Eden whisper into Eisenhower's ear plans he was keeping secret from his permanent officials, to say nothing of his Parliament and press? Eden feared, reportedly, that Eisenhower surely would turn Dulles loose to badger him again. Behind that fear presumably lay an awareness that our State Department would arouse his Foreign Office regulars; these at the very least. Badgering from Dulles would be seconded at home, and thereby magnified.

If Dulles, for his part, was less than candid at an earlier stage, consider the embarrassments of candor. He walked a tightrope in London. Presumably he did so because he was walking a tightrope at home. For him to bare his breast in Eden's company might have been most imprudent, and not only for the reason that they did not like each other. Dulles worked for Eisenhower and was dependent on him. Eden had been Eisenhower's friend for many years. Besides, there was a telephone from Downing Street to 1600 Pennsylvania Avenue. Should Dulles have counseled in August that the President never would countenance force? But Nasser might yet run amok. Or should Dulles have "winked" in October, as Lloyd later asked? But "peace" was the word at the White House. On the merits it is hard to see what candor could have offered; certainly not signals of this sort. And signals of whatever sort could get back to the White House not as Dulles phrased them but as Eden recalled them; whether in complaint or thanks he might pick up that telephone.

In an alliance such as this the membrane between sovereign states is paper-thin and porous. Transatlantic reticence is of a piece with reticence at home. For any word to friends across the ocean may come back to other ears at home.

As well, a word to friends at home may skip across the water. The relationship is reciprocal. Either way the motive is the same; prudence counsels reticence.

The stifling of communication in these instances afforded self-protection to the men who did it, protection for their causes and accordingly for them. They were guarding exposed flanks—their own. And what they had to guard against was not only 3,000 miles away, far from it: their exposed positions offered targets to associates; the threat was at close quarters. These men of reticence were vulnerable at home. Their vulnerability becomes a final clue. It points us in the same direction as the other clues: toward the bureaucratic politics of home.

III

How then are we to characterize the hazards in relations between governments like Washington and London? Plainly we begin with an acknowledgment that these hazards arise out of necessitous relations *inside* governments.

What do our clues show? They show each side comprised of men intent upon their own concerns, and upon negotiation to advance them—Londoners with Londoners, Washingtonians with Washingtonians. Their self-absorption is a day-and-night affair; it never flags. They calculate accordingly and act to suit. So do their counterparts inside the other government. From one side to the other, awareness filters through their self-absorption. Comprehension of the other's actual behavior is a function of their own concerns. What occurs across the water tends to register in terms of its effects upon their calculations. So with perception of the other side's concerns. What they see across the water tends to be a virtual projection of those calculations. Habituated to regard the other side as friendly, they habitually expect accommodation for themselves. When both sides happen to produce compatible outcomes, or when one sees reason to adjust in its own terms, the alliance "works." When mutual expectations turn out to be mutually exclusive, crisis follows: thus it was in 1956 and 1962.

What made these allies crisis-prone was not the high priority they gave their own concerns. All governments do that at every time. The men inside each government have grown up there, gained power there, and exercise it there. They will retain or lose it there. Moreover, they are governing a nation, and their sense of obligation turns upon the task as so defined. These men did not propel themselves toward crisis when they registered the other side's behavior only as it bore on their concerns. In Washington and London men who govern draw their pay for this. At any given time these men deal first with what they must deal next. Priorities are set by their own business. What happens on the other side deserves attention when and as it bears upon their business. All else is tourism. No one is paid for that except researchists and diplomatists, who do not govern. So it always is, yet there is not always a crisis.

Crises were brought on by the next step in their performance: their perception of the other side's concerns. The villain of the piece is blurry vision by the light of hope, as each side looked abroad to gauge the other's bind and bite. These men made few mistakes when they took note of what the other side was *doing*. Perception of its actual behavior was not the problem. Comprehension of what lay behind behavior was the problem. There they made innumerable mistakes.

They did so because they repeatedly projected onto the other side two things stamped "made at home": an outcome which would suit their own convenience, and a series of alleged constraints sufficient to induce it. The other side's concerns were read accordingly.

The critical mistake in such a reading ran to their perception of the other side's constraints. For the alleged constraints seem powerfully to have reinforced considerations of convenience. Had Dulles known the British were unlikely to be hobbled by internal opposition, the sheer inconvenience of another outcome probably would not have been enough to keep him hopeful. Had Eden known that Eisenhower probably would want to dissociate Americans emphatically from allied intervention, he might not have been content to leave him in that posture for a week. Had Macmillan known how critical for Kennedy were budgetary tactics, he might not have waited on events. Had McNamara known that Thorneycroft was sitting still he almost certainly would have bestirred himself. In all such instances, a faulty reading of the other side lent these men confidence that its behavior would match their convenience. Otherwise, despite the inconvenience, they might well have taken thought about their chosen course: back to the drawing board.

Whence came these misperceptions of the other side's constraints? Sometimes they came from false analogies with past occasions on the other side as those had been enshrined, usually incorrectly, in one's own beliefs—thus, for example, Whitehall's view of Truman's Jewish vote analogized to Eisenhower's forthcoming election. Washington's view of Whitehall's clever chaps is probably in the same class, a false analogy from men who had been young in World War II and thrilled by Winston Churchill at a distance. Sometimes the misperceptions came from false analogies with past occasions of one's own, which would constrain if the positions were reversed. In the back of Eden's mind, reportedly, as he considered Ike-the-doggo, was a British General Election, where government stops stock-still. Evidently in the front of McNamara's mind lay the presumption that his counterpart-by-title was his counterpart in function.

Either way, these men dredged their perceptions of the other side's constraints out of their own heads. They reasoned by analogy and drew conclusions for the other side, and thereupon perceived what they projected. In this there is an interesting tautology: perceptions reinforced their own convenience which had led them in the first place toward selection of analogies on which to base perceptions. Thus they drew aid and comfort in proceeding on their own side to do what they felt they had to do within their own constraints. Thereby they set the stage for their own disappointment and its aftermath in paranoid reactions.

Projection of constraints, reasoning by analogy, compensates a busy man for unfamiliarity in an uncertain world. Someone else's government machine is something of a mystery. What may emerge from it by way of future action cannot help but be a speculative matter in advance. It thus saves time and trouble to analogize; it also short-cuts arguments which by their nature cannot be pre-tested. And to select analogies that reinforce one's own convenience is to do no more than keep one's eye on one's own business. The impulse is as natural as breathing to a man who has to manage by and through his own machine. . . .

Necessitous relations inside governments, productive of behavior in these terms, go far to help us characterize the hazards in relations between friends like Washington and London, but not far enough. We have seen this behavior lead to crisis, straining relations hard. But if behavior of this sort is rooted in such natural responses as I now suggest, why are there not hard strains upon relations of all sorts and everywhere at once? Blurry vision by the light of hope seems usual, not exceptional. What makes it so pernicious in encounters between Anglo-Saxon cousins?

Misperceiving others in this fashion is not confined to situations of such close alliance. Leaving aside London for the moment, there seem to be innumerable instances in Washington's appraisals of estranged or hostile governments. During the early 1960s Americans had wishful thoughts aplenty of de Gaulle constrained by costs in nuclear development as though he were a bourgeois Finance Minister. During the later 1960s some of us, in highest places, clung to thoughts of Ho Chi Minh constrained by "pain" as though he were a Senator hungry for public works. And inside our own government the tendency can be as marked when one department's bureaucrats size up another's. Between officials of Defense and State, or Education and Justice, wishful elements are often just as strong.

The same thing can be said of reticence, of stifled communication, which aggravated the misreadings in our crisis by sustaining them. This too is a phenomenon found in hostile relations as in friendly ones, and internally as well as internationally. The sievelike quality of sovereignty, at least for us, is not the product only of relationships among bureaucracies in an alliance. It also is the product of news media and their pervasive links with Washingtonians. In an age of instantaneous transmission, it takes few words from a foreign source of any stripe to let one part of Washington hear "prematurely" what another part has planned. We sometimes can rely upon an adversary—especially if dictatorial—not to let the "wrong" words slip at the "wrong" time to the "wrong" newsmen. But always this is risky, the more so with neutrals or friends, perhaps, than with acknowledged enemies. Although he may be spared collegial air forces or foreign offices, the prudent Washingtonian still finds reasons for reticence toward those with whom he deals, even as he ponders their constraints. Since reticence invites a like response, he thus adds to the prospect that if he has misperceived he will persist in doing so.

I speak just now of Washington and Washingtonians. With some adjustments of detail in cultural and institutional respects the same points seem to me to hold for London and for Londoners.

IV

The crisis pattern with which I began this chapter contains elements found frequently in situations of non-crisis. Two strands of the pattern are pervasive in Anglo-American behavior: muddled perceptions and stifled communications. It follows that their corollary, the third strand, is commonplace: disappointed expectations. Yet relatively speaking, the fourth strand is a rarity. Paranoid reactions do not always or inevitably stem from disappointment. When they do, the stage is set for crisis.

With one exception, men in our machine seem rarely to be shaken by the blighting of their hopes for outcomes in another machine. Witness our response when Soviet troops invade a satellite, or when Hanoi turns down another peace feeler (or witness the State Department's response when—as so often happens— our Treasury Department turns out to be conducting its own foreign policy). In instances of these sorts there is surely disappointment, but it does not seem to induce paranoia, or not for long; rather the result seems usually to be a relatively cool recalculation. As with Washington, so with London; the two appear substantially alike in this respect. Contrast the consequences in my crisis summaries. These speak to the exception: paranoid reactions are associated with relations bearing something like the burden of an unrequited love.

Misperceptions evidently make for crisis in proportion to the intimacy of relations. Hazards are proportionate to the degree of friendship. Indifference and hostility may not breed paranoia; friendship does.

In theory, friendship should provide a form of compensation: closeness spells acquaintance. If there is special risk in one friend's reading of another, there also is a special chance for accuracy. Both are fruits of friendship. Theoretically, these ought to cancel out. But evidently they do not.

In practice, as my crisis summaries suggest, acquaintance has wrapped up in it a faulty sense of competence, hence misplaced confidence. Instead of countering inaccuracy this contributes to it. Remember the cliche: "a little knowledge is a dangerous thing." So with acquaintance between friends, at least when they resemble Washington and London. For these, the two most intimate of peacetime allies known to modern history (excepting only Berlin and Vienna fifty years ago), acquaintance did not render misperception less. In the Suez case, still more in Skybolt, their knowledge rather aided and abetted their misreadings. It opened up to each side a rich storehouse of analogies and hid from sight uncertainties attendant on their use. All too seldom did the men on either side address the question: if we do harm to others in their terms what could they do to us in ours? That is the classic question asked of adversaries. It focuses attention on the other's terms and hedges confident analogizing. In the instances before us, "they," alas, were "friends."

Throughout these crises signs abound that close acquaintance was more burdensome than beneficial, more conducive to misreading than to accurate perception. Consider the degree to which chief officers of government on either side took their own word for what constrained the other side, played their own hunches, drew their own conclusions. Acquaintance ran so deep that each American conceived himself an expert on the British, and *vice versa*. Such are the consequences of a common language, a shared history, wartime collaboration, intermarriage, all abetted by air travel and the telephone. But confidence in one's own expertise diminishes one's sense of need to probe, reduces one's incentive to ask questions, removes from sight the specialists of whom these might be asked, and also pushes out of sight the usefulness of feedback. Recall what happened in the critical pre-public stages of these crises to that "private wire," the secure telephone, linking chiefs of government in Washington and London. It went unused. This serves us as a symbol for the burdensome effects of close acquaintance.

Still, I would guess that these Americans and Englishmen knew more of one another than the specialists in their regimes. could claim to know about most of their counterparts in other major governments. A little knowledge may be dangerous, but, relatively speaking, these self-constituted experts knew a lot. Yet we have seen how frequently they read each other wrong, how often their perceptions were inaccurate enough to risk the very things they sought from one another and to store in their own heads the stuff of paranoid reactions, hazarding a breach in their relations.

This· raises an insistent question: should these men have been able to do better than they did? Granting them their troubles but considering their resources, should they not have been capable of less misunderstanding?

The question goes to the heart of the alliance task these men confronted. Each worked from his own side of the alliance to shape outcomes stemming from the other side. When one side seeks to influence the conduct of another, everything depends upon the accuracy with which those who would wield influence perceive constraints impinging on the other side's behavior (and apply what they perceive in their own actions). As between London and Washington, you may think this an easy task, the easier for ties of language and the like. If so, my cast of characters will seem a foolish lot. Far from it; they were mostly men of high intelligence and wide experience. Each acted reasonably within his own constraints. Each failed to grasp some aspect of a foreigner's constraints. But this too becomes reasonable in the degree to which it actually was foreign. The difficulty of their task cannot be unrelated to the subtleties of difference they encountered in the inner workings of their governments. A judgment of their capability to do better depends in part upon a judgment of those subtleties as sources for misunderstanding.

29.

David A. Baldwin: *Foreign Aid, Intervention, and Influence*

Since the Marshall Plan was put into practice in the early postwar years, billions of dollars have left the United States in the form of private and public aid. Third World nations have attacked American "neocolonialism" while demanding preferential trade arrangements. Characterizing intervention as "influence" and aid-giving as a "political process," David Baldwin explores the relationship of foreign aid to intervention; points out that intervention can be two-way (e.g., with Vietnam exerting influence on the United States as well as vice versa); and suggests the importance of domestic groups with respect to the aid-giving process, in both the donor and recipient nations.

David Baldwin is an Associate Professor in the Department of Government at Dartmouth College and author of *Economic Development and American Foreign Policy*.

Foreign aid can be "related" to intervention in many ways. Some argue, with Senator J. W. Fulbright, that aid tends to precede intervention and to increase the probability of intervention.[1] Others would say that aid follows intervention, contending, for example, that American aid to Vietnam was evidence of a prior diplomatic commitment. Still others see aid as an alternative to intervention—if we give aid now we are less likely to have to intervene in the future. Another group would contend that the aid-giving process may *constitute* intervention.[2] It is with the views of this last group that most of this article deals. In examining them, we shall focus on three topics: (1) the links between foreign aid and influence; (2) the links between particular types of aid and what is often called intervention; and (3) the possibility of functional equivalents for aid that do not involve intervention. There are some conceptual problems, however, that we must address first.

I. The Concept of "Intervention"

Conceptual difficulties abound in thinking about the relationship of aid to intervention.[3] Although much has been written about intervention and "dollar diplomacy," most of these writings have employed a traditional concept of intervention that is too limited for use today. This traditional concept shares

David A. Baldwin, "Foreign Aid, Intervention, and Influence," *World Politics,* Vol. 21 (April 1969), pp. 425–447. Copyright © 1969 by Princeton University Press. Reprinted by permission of the publisher. This is a revised version of a paper delivered at the Conference on Intervention and the Developing States sponsored by the Princeton International Law Society, November 10–11, 1967. The author has benefited from comments on earlier drafts by Howard Bliss, Charles Frank, Christian Potholm, Laurence Radway, Richard Sterling, and W. Howard Wriggins.

legalistic and military connotations with many other terms in the standard vocabulary of the student of international politics. The old definitions of intervention in terms of illegal military infringement of national sovereignty are simply inadequate at a time when non-military techniques of statecraft are becoming increasingly important. Spokesmen for the developing states have found it frustrating to try to describe twentieth-century phenomena with a nineteenth-century vocabulary. They have resorted to such terms as "neo-colonialism," "economic imperialism," and the like, in an attempt to overcome some of these semantic obstacles.

How, then, should we proceed in a discussion of foreign aid and intervention? One way is to equate "intervention" with "influence."[4] This would have three advantages. First, almost everyone's definition of intervention would be included, since there is widespread agreement that intervention is a type of influence. Second, normative arguments that are unlikely to lead to agreement would be avoided. The breakdown in the consensus regarding what kinds of influence are legitimate and what kinds illegitimate often mires discussions of intervention in fruitless arguments over values. A third advantage of equating "intervention" with "influence" is that it helps us understand what the developing states are really complaining about. Reasonable and responsible leaders from developing nations have applied the label of "intervention" to almost every conceivable form of influence during the last twenty years. Only a very broad definition of intervention will allow us to discuss the matter in a way that is relevant to the concerns of these nations.

II. Foreign Aid and Influence

Although few would deny the connection between aid and influence, there is very little agreement on the precise nature of this connection or on analytical methods to be used in studying the problem. Some general questions about the aid-influence relationship need to be asked: What does it mean to say that aid is "political"? How can donors "control" their aid? Must aid be given in order to constitute intervention? Who wants this kind of intervention? Does the sword of intervention through aid cut two ways?

POLITICAL AID

Since the proposition that foreign aid is "political" is not self-explanatory, we would expect those who state it to explain it. Unfortunately, they rarely do. Lucian Pye, for example, alleges that Americans wrongly view their aid program as "inherently 'nonpolitical.'"[5] He neglects to tell us precisely what this means, however.[6] Perhaps the most common meaning given to the proposition is that aid donors are motivated by self-interest, which in turn is usually equated with a desire to acquire power. Defining political aid in terms of motivation, however, can lead us to overlook important dimensions of the problem of intervention through aid. Must intervention be motivated by a desire to intervene or by other ulterior motives? The elephant who dances among the chickens may be accused of intervention regardless of his intentions.

Likewise, many of the complaints of the developing states concern the effects of big powers' actions rather than the motivation for such actions. In the eyes of many developing states, the big powers intervene in their affairs simply by existing.[7]

Many of those who believe that foreign aid is political have in mind consequences rather than motivations of the donors' actions. Given the importance of wealth as a power base, it would be difficult to imagine a foreign aid transaction that did not change the distribution of influence both within and among nations with respect to several issues.

In addition to those who would focus on the motivation or consequences of foreign aid are those who define its political nature in terms of the process by which it is given. Political processes, according to Quincy Wright, involve groups of people seeking to advance their purposes against the opposition of other groups.[8] The foreign-aid transaction process clearly qualifies as "political" in this sense. Within any aid-giving nation there are groups who disagree as to the priority that should be given to foreign aid relative to alternative ways of using the resources, and who attempt to get their views accepted as government policy. Although we may not be able to name him, we may reasonably assume that Otto Passman has a Russian counterpart. More directly relevant to foreign intervention is the existence of conflicts between aid-donors and recipients. Such conflicts may concern amounts, repayment terms, fiscal policy, land reform, or myriad other issues.

Foreign aid may constitute intervention in terms of motivation, consequences, process, or all three simultaneously. Fruitful discussion of foreign aid and influence, however, requires us to differentiate among these three plausible meanings of the statement that "aid is political."

CONTROLLING AID

If we are to recognize effective intervention, it helps to have some idea of how donors can control the impact of their aid. As an example of a "penetrated political system" Rosenau has suggested "the operation of any foreign aid program in which the aiding society maintains some control over the purposes and distribution of the aid in the recipient society."[9] A clear understanding of what constitutes "control" of aid is required before we can identify such a situation in the real world.

Three methods are frequently suggested as "controls" for foreign aid— auditing the books, setting up formal coordinating machinery, and furnishing aid in the form of commodities. None suffices as evidence that control is actually being exercised by the donor. Measuring effective control requires an estimate of the extent [10] to which things are different in the recipient society from what they would have been in the absence of aid. The world's most efficient auditors can go over the books of the donor nation and learn nothing about the actual impact of the donor's aid. Earmarking aid shipments for bookkeeping purposes and controlling the impact of aid are two different operations.

Likewise, elaborate, fully-staffed aid missions in the recipient nation may not exercise control. If they participate in the making of decisions that would have been made even without their participation, they are not controlling much of anything. On the other hand, to the extent that they participate in decisions that would not have been made in their absence, they are exercising some control.[11]

Similarly, providing aid in the form of particular goods fails to ensure that the donor controls the impact of his aid. Food aid does not necessarily feed people; nor does aid in the form of tanks necessarily bolster military forces. If the recipient of tanks reduces its own military budget by an offsetting amount and spends the saved money on housing, the effect of the tanks has been to build houses.

The point is that some alleged "controls" on distribution of aid may not be intervention at all. Some strings constitute intervention; others do not. A string that asks the recipient to do what it would have done anyway can hardly be considered intervention. On the other hand, control may be taking place without many outward appearances. If the donor can accurately estimate how the potential recipient would allocate its resources [12] in the absence of aid, he is then in a position to exercise tight control over the use of his aid-funds without many of the formal trappings of control. In short, intervention may be real but not apparent, or apparent but not real.

"NON-AID" AS INFLUENCE

There is more to the aid-influence relationship than controlling the use of aid actually given. At least as important, in both theory and practice, is knowing how and when *not* to give aid. This is not just a matter of playing with words. Although much has been written about how to give aid, very little has been written about how not to give it. There are several possible ways to say "no"—as every woman and every political candidate knows—and there are several possible ways not to give aid. Some of the more common ways to say "no" to a request for foreign aid include: (1) "My government would like to help you, but we have no (time, money, etc.)." (2) Ignore the request or pigeonhole it. (3) Interpret the request to mean what the party saying "no" wants the request to mean. (4) "My government will study your request and let you know." (5) "Not at this time—come back next (month, year, decade, century, etc.)." (6) Say "no" in advance by establishing well-publicized policies. (7) "How dare you make such an outrageous request! Such behavior raises questions about your good sense and may affect my evaluation of your future requests." (8) No. (9) *No.* (10) NO! Although each method says "no," political influence is likely to vary from one method to another. How one says "no" does matter.

Suppose the United States wants to encourage developing states to be more hospitable to private foreign investors. Suppose, also, that American policy-makers believe that the attitudes of governments in developing states toward private foreign investors depend in part on their expectations regarding alternative sources of funds. In such a situation, the United States might adopt a tactic that game-theorists call the "commitment." "In bargaining, the commitment is a device to leave the last clear chance to decide the outcome with the other party, in a manner that he fully appreciates; it is to relinquish further initiative, having rigged the incentives so that the other party must choose in one's favor." [13] Thus, the United States government may try to commit itself not to provide an alternative source of funds for developing states, in a way that they fully appreciate, in order to leave the developing states with the last clear chance to avert disaster. The United States would thus be using "non-aid" to get developing states to do something they would not otherwise do—i.e., be nicer to private foreign investors.

It is one thing to cite a hypothetical example; it is another to show counterparts in the real world. Has non-aid ever been seriously proposed as a technique for influencing the developing states? Yes, responsible members of the governmental, business, and academic communities have all argued for non-aid as a technique for influencing these states. During the preliminary planning for the Bretton Woods institutions, Secretary of the Treasury Morgenthau expressed the hope that the International Bank would "*scrupulously* avoid undertaking loans that private investors are willing to make on reasonable terms." [14] Now, there is a great difference between not making loans for which private capital is available and "scrupulously avoiding" such loans. The difference, in terms of bargaining theory, is that between neglect and blackmail. Similarly, the "General Policy Statement of the Export-Import Bank of Washington" in 1945 included a special section devoted to outlining what the Bank would *not* do. [15] The Randall Commission Report in 1954 exhorted the government to make it "abundantly clear to prospective borrowers" [16] that American public lending would not be a substitute for private investment. Such abundant clarity was supposed to remove the uncertainty about American aid policies that the Commission believed affected "the willingness of foreign countries to accept private capital from abroad." [17] Using similar logic, the Clay Report in 1963 advocated "judicious withholding of funds" in order to encourage "internal reform" in developing nations. [18]

The American business community has also advocated non-aid. Perhaps the clearest statement of this position was made in 1951 by the National Foreign Trade Convention. In bargaining terminology the following excerpt is clearly a call for the American government to try to influence foreign governments by increasing the credibility of the promise not to provide aid to foreign governments:

> It cannot be expected that economic environments conducive to the investment of American private capital will be established in these foreign lands so long as the governments concerned have reason to believe—as they do have reason to believe— that they will continue to be the beneficiaries of the hand-outs our own Government has given them for so long. They have every right to assume, on the evidence afforded, that this profligate practice will continue to be the order of the day. It is clear why this is so: our own Government, conscious of the fact that economic devel-

opment abroad is highly desirable, has proceeded on the unfortunate assumption that private enterprise is unwilling or unable to undertake the task, and that, in consequence, the free provision of Government funds for the purposes in view is the only course open. This attitude has been seized upon by foreign governments as justification for their refusal to do the things they would otherwise find it necessary to do in order to attract the private capital they need. The dilemma is one which cannot be resolved until our Government brings itself to announce, as a fundamental element of our foreign economic policy, that we look upon industrial development abroad as the particular function of private enterprise, and that, until the receptive and cooperative attitudes called for are shown, no United States Government funds will be made available for *any* purpose except those of the most exigent military or humanitarian nature.[19]

Similar logic appears in a thorough and clearly reasoned study prepared by academics and presented to Congress in 1957, entitled "American Private Enterprise, Foreign Economic Development, and the Aid Program." [20]

Although strategic use of non-aid has been an important means of influencing developing states, its significance is rarely recognized. Even foreign-aid experts can look directly at this phenomenon and fail to understand it. Witness the following statement by a veteran aid administrator:

During the 1950's, U.S. aid policy was dominated by the curious notion that aid should be denied countries that are potentially attractive to U.S. investors. Latin America was considered capable of attracting all the foreign capital it needed from private sources; aid was considered to be a palliative that discouraged countries from creating appropriate conditions to attract foreign investors.[21]

Why should this be regarded as a "curious" situation? It is precisely the kind of behavior we should expect from a nation for which avoidance of competition with private capital is one of the basic guiding principles of its aid program. After we grow accustomed to thinking of non-aid as a technique of statecraft, there is nothing at all puzzling about the situation described. It was clearly United States policy to withhold aid from certain countries in order to force (encourage?) them to rely on foreign private investment. The same author notes that since the ten states that harbor two-thirds of all U.S. private investment in developing areas have received less than 7 percent of U.S. postwar economic aid, the United States cannot be accused of allocating its aid funds so as to further the interests of its private investors.[22] Precisely the opposite conclusion can and should be drawn. For twenty years American private investors have been exhorting the government to withhold aid funds from areas where they might compete with private capital. Official policy statements have repeatedly committed the government to comply with this exhortation. The empirical evidence is consistent with an American aid policy designed to help private investors, that is, designed to use non-aid to influence foreign investment climates. If we are to understand the relationship between foreign aid and intervention in developing states, we cannot afford to overlook the significance of non-aid.

Analysis of aid and intervention is further complicated by the difficulty of determining whether intervention is being resisted. Nations are not the monolithic corporate entities that we often imply they are. Within the government of an aid-recipient there are usually many groups with a variety of opposing views on policy matters. "To 'intervene,'" says Schelling, "is usually to encourage or support one part of the government rather than another, or one political force rather than another." [23]

Sometimes the intervention might be on behalf of the government vis-à-vis domestic political pressures. For example, the government might want to adopt measures to control inflation but might fear that it would thereby lose domestic popularity. Intervention by an aid donor on behalf of an anti-inflationary policy would strengthen the hand of the government by giving it a scapegoat on which to blame the unpopular measures. It is rumored that the International Monetary Fund has played the role of scapegoat on several occasions. The point here is that the desires of the donor and the recipient government may actually coincide even though they appear to conflict. Politics defined as group conflict may be more apparent than real.

TWO-WAY INTERVENTION

Karl Deutsch has pointed out that a nation can increase its autonomy in two ways. Either it can break its linkages with the outside world or it can reverse the flow of influence while maintaining the links.[24] This second possibility is rarely acknowledged in discussions of foreign aid. Although intervention of the donor in the recipient's affairs comes up often, we almost never find references to the converse situation. Even though they may not use the vocabulary of intervention, many American Negro leaders have made it quite clear that they think the plight of their people has been worsened by the activities of Marshal Ky and his countrymen.

This is not to say that Vietnam exercises more influence vis-à-vis the United States than the United States does vis-à-vis Vietnam. It is to say that Vietnam now has more influence on American affairs than it would have had if the United States were not injecting massive aid into Vietnam. We live, as one study put it, in "the era of reciprocal involvement." [25]

III. Types of Aid and Intervention

It is often suggested that particular types of foreign aid involve more intervention in the recipient's affairs than do other types. Let us examine four types that are frequently mentioned in this context: (1) loans as opposed to grant aid; (2) economic as opposed to military aid; (3) multilateral as opposed to bilateral aid; and (4) private as opposed to public capital.

GRANTS VS. LOANS

During the 1950's a frequently suggested means for eliminating intervention by aid donors in recipients' affairs was a shift from grants to loans. Loans were often described as a more "businesslike" way to provide aid. Loans allocated on the basis of "strictly economic" considerations were alleged to be politically sterile. Such a contention, however, cannot withstand even cursory analysis. In the first place, it is impossible to judge the credit-worthiness of a nation without reference to broad considerations of fiscal and monetary policy, the probability of internal civil disorders, and the overall role of the government in the economy. "In a world where governments can expropriate property, manipulate exchange rates, and control the currency supply, it is nonsense to speak of evaluating the economic soundness of a project without reference to governmental behavior." [26] Raymond Mikesell has described "political factors" as "the most fundamental consideration in the determination of credit worthiness." [27]

The implication of the necessity for taking political factors into account in evaluating loan applications is that potential borrowers may have to take politically significant steps in order to qualify as credit-worthy. Controlling inflation, for example, is not a purely economic matter. Basic changes in the institutional structure of the society are involved. Joseph Schumpeter has described inflation as "one of the most powerful factors that make for acceleration of social change." [28] In spite of this, neither the International Monetary Fund nor the World Bank has hesitated to advise developing states to control inflation in order to qualify for loans on the basis of purely "economic considerations."

In addition to the argument that loans can be allocated by strictly economic criteria is the contention that loans provide "no excuse" for donors to interfere in the affairs of the recipient states. "So long as the payments of interest and repayments of principal are made in full on the due dates, as stipulated in the terms of the loan, the details of how it is spent are no concern of the creditor. The independence of the borrowing country remains inviolate." [29] This does not apply to grants, argues Frederic Benham. "A country which makes grants is entitled to make sure that they fulfill their purpose and are not frittered away in corruption and waste." [30]

Do loans provide no excuse for intervention by the lenders? The bank that lent me money to buy a car seems to think that it has a right to tell me how much insurance I should carry on that car. Likewise, foreign-aid lenders have often cited an outstanding debt as reason enough for them to take an extraordinary interest in the domestic affairs of a debtor. The World Bank maintains a "close relationship with its borrowers throughout the life of each loan" and claims the right to give "continuing attention throughout the life of each loan to the general economic and financial conditions in the borrowing country" in order to "ensure that the maintenance of service on Bank loans is not jeopardized by the emergence of conditions which might be prevented." [31]

It would seem that we could make a fairly good case for the proposition that loans provide more opportunity for intervention than do grants. A grant transaction is unlikely to extend over a time-span as long as a typical foreign aid loan-agreement—ten to fifty years. Thus, the apparatus for administering the repayment of the loan may provide a conduit for influence over a considerable period of time. A loan-agreement is not just an excuse for interesting oneself in another's affairs; it is an eminently respectable excuse. Also, a one-time grantor is in a very weak position to intervene. Although he may be "entitled" to make sure that his grant is not wasted, the recipient has no incentive to allow such intervention. It is the expectation of the next grant that provides this incentive. Similarly, the hope of getting future loans acts as an incentive for a borrower to let his creditors examine his books.

During the early 1950's there was one aspect of American grant-aid that strengthened the argument for loans as a means of reducing intervention. It was customary for the United States to require a recipient of grant-aid to place an "equivalent" amount of its own currency in a "counterpart fund." This fund was owned by the recipient government but could be used only by joint agreement between the governments. "The exercise of American influence over the use of counterpart funds inevitably raised the question of interference with the internal affairs of countries in receipt of assistance."[32] Counterpart funds and grant aid were gradually replaced by soft loans repayable in inconvertible local currency during the later 1950's.[33] This resulted in a rapid build-up of enormous amounts of American-owned foreign currencies and even greater fears about intervention than had been generated by the counterpart funds.[34] Once again the advantages of loans over grants proved to be illusory.

The most obvious weakness in the argument that loans do not involve intervention is that loans are not just an "excuse" for intervention; they are a *means* of intervention and have been advocated as such. One writer speaks of the desire to place aid on a loan basis "for the benefit of superior discipline";[35] another refers to "our efforts to employ loan assistance as a means of influencing or compelling economic reforms in developing countries."[36] Perhaps the single most frequently heard argument in favor of placing the American aid program on a loan basis was that of the desirability of ensuring that the funds would be used economically.[37] Other control devices would be unnecessary because the necessity of repayment would provide the discipline needed to prevent waste.

One final aspect of the loan-grant debate deserves attention. If loans do not involve less intervention than do grants, how do we explain the expressed preference for loans by several developing states during the 1950's? There are at least two plausible explanations that do not depend on an expected reduction of intervention. The first is that governments in developing states might not want to appear in the eyes of their domestic public as dependent on foreign charity. It might be good domestic politics to refuse grants—regardless of the real merits of grants as opposed to loans. A second explanation is in terms of Friedrich's "rule of anticipated reactions."[38] The growing preference of the American Congress for loans as opposed to grants during the 1950's was no secret. Yet, writers on foreign aid rarely consider the possibility that potential recipients decided to ask for loans not because they preferred them but simply because they thought they were more likely to get them.[39]

In sum, loan aid appears to offer at least as much opportunity for the donor to intervene in the recipient's affairs as does grant aid.

ECONOMIC VS. MILITARY AID

Those who want to limit intervention through aid often point to military aid as an especially odious type. Economic aid, on the other hand, is supposed to involve less intervention. The weakness in this line of reasoning stems from a failure to distinguish between the commodities actually financed by the aid and those to which the aid is tied in a bookkeeping sense. As we noted earlier, aid in the form of tanks does not necessarily add to military strength; it may, in fact, buy milk for babies. If the recipient nation had intended to allocate one million dollars of its own funds for tanks in the absence of aid, and if it then received the equivalent of one million dollars worth of tanks as aid, it would be free to take the one million dollars that it had intended to spend on tanks and spend it some other way. If it used the money for a school lunch program, the "military aid" would actually have financed a school lunch program. We can tell little or nothing about the net impact of aid by looking at its commodity content as described by the bookkeepers. Instead, we must estimate how the recipient would have allocated its resources in the absence of aid and then compare this with the actual allocation after aid has been given. Only thus can we tell whether the military sector of the economy is really being strengthened by what is often called "military aid." [40]

Measuring allocation of economic resources, however, is not the only way to measure influence. It may be that there are side effects of a military aid program that could be considered intervention. The administration of the program by military men may increase their ability to influence people in the recipient nation. In addition, a donor who gives aid labeled "military" may be perceived as giving a stamp of approval to the military establishment in the recipient nation, thereby bolstering its prestige. It is easy to see how reasonable men could describe either of these side effects as intervention.

One particular type of economic aid is often alleged to be especially free from overtones of intervention—technical assistance. To suggest that technical assistance may involve as much intervention as do other types of aid is to tread on what many consider to be sacred nonpolitical ground. Without repeating the previous discussion of military aid, it should be obvious that technical assistance is merely another way of labeling the commodity-content of aid; and it is no more indicative of the actual impact of the aid than is the label of military aid.

The technical-assistance label is a very useful public-relations device. A primary source of political opposition to foreign aid had always been the business community, who had traditionally feared and resisted government intervention in the economy. Use of the technical-assistance label was supposed to reassure private foreign investors that the government did not intend to compete with them. In fact, technical assistance did compete with private investment in at least two ways. First, the services provided under technical-assistance programs could and would have been provided by private firms if the price had been high enough. Second, indirect competition was given to potential direct investors. For example, surveys of investment opportunities might provide the government with enough information to enable it to establish a public enterprise instead of relying on private enterprise. The point is that investigating investment opportunities has always been one of the services offered at a price by potential direct investors, even though we are unaccustomed to describing their activities this way. Describing this aid as "technical" was a way of making it sound as if it were something other than "capital" assistance. The United Nations Special Fund's "pre-investment surveys" are merely an extreme form of the attempt to make technical aid sound noncontroversial. Using technical language to divert attention from controversial issues is an old political tactic, one that has worked well in the case of technical assistance.[41] The technical-assistance label implied a qualitative difference between this type of aid and other types. It implied that technical assistance involved services that the private investment community would be unwilling to provide *at any price*. It also benefited from the vague widespread feeling that the technical and the political are two mutually exclusive realms. Those who would understand the relationship between aid and influence, however, should not overlook technical assistance.

MULTILATERAL VS. BILATERAL AID

Perhaps the most frequently heard proposal for political sterilization of aid giving is to multilateralize it.[42] In this context it has been argued that multilateral aid is (1) non-political, (2) stringless, (3) more acceptable to recipients, and (4) insulated from the foreign policies of donor nations. These arguments will be examined in turn.

Is multilateral aid political in any of the three ways referred to earlier? It is difficult to see how the process of distributing multilateral aid could be anything but political in the sense of involving group conflict. Even if various nations could be effectively coordinated from the lending side, it is inconceivable that recipients and donors would agree on the amount of aid needed by the recipient. Given the limited amounts of aid likely to be channeled through international agencies and given the almost limitless needs of the poor nations, conflict seems inevitable. Some sort of impact on the distribution of political influence within and among nations also seems to be a necessary concomitant of multilateral aid. Thus, international aid would be political in this sense also. Whether multilateral aid would be politically motivated is more difficult to determine. Although it is doubtful that a desire for power as an end in itself would be an important motivating factor, it is highly probable that some attempt would be made to get recipients to do things that they would not otherwise do. The experience of the World Bank provides many examples of just such behavior.[43]

It is sometimes argued that multilateral aid does not carry with it the strings associated with bilateral assistance. The lending pattern of the Inter-American

Development Bank gives some credence to this argument. Its funds are apparently earmarked in advance for allocation to specific countries, thus eliminating competition for funds and making it fruitless for the Bank to attach many strings. It does not follow, however, that multilateral aid necessarily involves fewer strings. It is interesting to note that some advocates of multilateral aid see it as a way of increasing the effectiveness of intervention in recipient nations. One proponent of multilateral aid, for example, sees the relevant question as "to what extent and in what ways the United Nations may provide a better channel for such intervention than bilateral programs of economic assistance." [44] International agencies, so the argument goes, are less likely to be accused of intervention and are thus freer to intervene. Multilateral aid, then, has been proposed as a means of both impeding and facilitating intervention. Channeling aid through international agencies does not guarantee fewer or weaker strings; in fact, aid through the World Bank complex is likely to involve a limited number of very strong strings—perhaps even ropes.[45] Those who want stringless aid should be wary of proposals for channeling more aid through the IBRD and its affiliates.

The argument for multilateral aid is often bolstered by the statement that such aid, with or without strings, is more acceptable to developing states.[46] There is some evidence, however, that this may not be true. John Lewis has described a pronounced shift from bilateral to multilateral operations as "one of the last things the government of India wants." [47] He notes that the existence of several bilateral aid channels permits India to fend off intervention by playing off one benefactor against another. The Indian government, according to Lewis, "is no readier to surrender to the World Bank or the United Nations than it is to the United States or the Soviet Union." [48] The acceptability argument usually carries an implicit assumption that multilateral aid involves no increase in the amount of intervention in the recipient's affairs. Thus, it is usually implied that, "other things being equal," multilateral aid is more acceptable. Other things, however, may not remain equal. The centralized coordination that would probably accompany a massive shift to multilateral aid would make intervention by the international donor much easier than it is now for an individual donor nation. If the World Bank, for example, were the only major source of development aid, its bargaining position vis-à-vis borrowers would be enormously strengthened.

A fourth argument for multilateral distribution of aid holds that it prevents individual donor nations from using such aid as a tool of national policy. Henry Cabot Lodge, for example, describes such programs as "obviously insulated against political manipulations" by donor states.[49] Does channeling aid through international agencies neutralize it as a tool of national policy? An influential RAND Corporation study is based on the assumption that those interested in foreign aid as an instrument of United States foreign policy need not concern themselves with the activities of the International Bank.[50] There are three reasons to doubt the wisdom of this assumption, however. First, a donor nation may choose to distribute its aid through international agencies purely on the basis of its calculations of its own national interest. The United States, for example, "may seek the comparative anonymity of multilateralism when the recipient regime or local opposition suspect 'strings' or other undue influence by the donor." [51] Such a move would not mean political neutralization, however. "To seek a measure of anonymity," Liska rightly observes, "is not to suspend the primarily political character of aid; it is merely to adopt a politically more proficient method in situations where direct involvement may be onerous for either the donor or the recipient." [52]

A second reason for skepticism about the degree to which multilateral aid is insulated from national policy is that some donors exercise extraordinary influence on the activities of international aid agencies. The United States, for example, wields over one-fourth of the voting power in the World Bank, an institution that has always had an American president. When the United States diverts some of its funds from bilateral channels to the World Bank complex, it is not giving up as much influence over aid-distribution policies as it seems to be. Likewise, when the United States gives aid to the Inter-American Development Bank, it does not lose as much control over distribution of funds as the formal arrangements would indicate. Although Latin American nations can outvote the United States in the Inter-American Development Bank, their hope for future funds gives them an incentive not to do so. In Friedrich's terms, they are anticipating the reactions of the United States and acting accordingly. Note that the Inter-American Deveolpment Bank has never made a loan to which the United States specifically objected. Anticipated reactions are far more important as a link between aid and influence than are formal voting arrangements.

There is a third reason for rejecting the hypothesis that multilateral aid cannot be a tool of national statecraft. To the extent that any nation can predict the aid-distribution pattern of an international agency, it can use that agency as a tool of its foreign policy. That is, it can frame its foreign policy so as to allow for the activities of the international agency. Thus, if there is reason to suspect that Ruritania will be successful in getting a loan from the International Development Association to finance a dam that the United States had intended to finance, the United States may decide to take the funds it had earmarked for financing the dam and use them to promote some other foreign policy goal. Successful use of this foreign policy technique depends on one's ability to predict accurately the aid-distribution patterns of international agencies. Doing this permits one to identify those projects that will probably be financed anyway and those that are on the margin. By confining its aid to marginal projects, a nation can strengthen its bargaining position vis-à-vis aid recipients.[53] A former AID administrator's description of the American negotiating process indicates that the United States does try to strengthen its bargaining position in this way: "Before even a tentative program is put together, the resources available from other countries, the United Nations specialized agencies and foreign private business must be estimated. . . . Only at this stage does it become relevant to look at the resources available from the United States." [54]

In conclusion, there are several reasons to doubt Henry Cabot Lodge's assertion that multilateral aid programs are "obviously insulated against political manipulations" by individual states. Channeling aid through international agencies will not necessarily reduce the intervention in developing states; it may even increase it.

PRIVATE VS. PUBLIC CHANNELS

One of the great American myths is that the private sector of the economy is "nonpolitical." It is not surprising, therefore, to encounter the argument that private "nonpolitical" investment would involve less intervention in developing states than does "political" public foreign aid. [55] The following discussion will focus on two questions: First, is private capital "political" in the three ways mentioned earlier? Second, in what ways is private investment linked to foreign policies?

The motivation of private businessmen is usually described in terms of a desire for profit. Without denying the importance of the profit motive, we may point out that profit can be pursued in various ways by different organizations. The rationale that typically underlies a description of business as nonpolitical implies the existence of numerous small firms obedient to impersonal market forces. Such a rationale ignores one of the most important economic institutions in the world today—the giant corporation. We are only beginning to perceive the far-reaching political and economic implications of this form of social organization. [56] It is clear, however, that these firms are not the slaves of the market envisioned in the model of pure competition. Many of them own more assets than the annual GNP in several developing states. It is these giant corporations that account for most of the American direct investment abroad. Roughly one-third of this investment is in the petroleum industry, which is so well organized that it has been described as a private world government. [57] Pursuing power and pursuing profit are not necessarily mutually exclusive undertakings.

Regardless of the motivations of private foreign investors, it is difficult to deny the political impact of their actions. The provision of forty million dollars in revolving credit to South Africa by a group of American banks has a profound effect on the distribution of influence within the recipient nation and among various nations. This same group of banks is unlikely to extend similar credit to Cuba in the near future. This is not to imply any sort of devious plan by bankers to promote racism or any other ideology. The point is that in making judgments about what constitutes a "safe" investment they tend to favor certain social systems. This link between private international capital flows and particular social institutions was identified by Eugene Staley in his classic study, *War and the Private Investor*: "Indeed, the export of capital to countries previously untouched by capitalistic industrialism necessitates the simultaneous 'export' of specialized governmental forms and institutions, such as commercial law, and specialized economic institutions, such as the wage system. Out of this fact . . . a deep and inevitable conflict emerges between capital-importing and capital-exporting countries when their social institutions are radically different." [58]

Is international private investment a political process in the sense that it involves conflict among groups? There are at least two reasons to think that it is. First, many of the developing states, rightly or wrongly, associate private foreign investors with their former colonial masters. As long as these attitudes persist, friction between developing states and private foreign investors is to be expected. Second, a substantial degree of group conflict in the process of transferring capital from the developed to the developing states should be expected even if there were no colonial heritage to stigmatize foreign investors. Staley sees such conflict as inevitable: "The process of international investment establishes between a capital-importing and a capital-exporting country a relatively permanent capital-labor conflict, a creditor-debtor conflict, a conflict of vested interests with groups interested in social reform or revolution, not to speak of cultural conflicts unleashed by the industrialization which accompanies capital investment." [59]

It is quite possible for private foreign investment to be political in all three ways mentioned above and still be insulated from the foreign policies of the government in the lending country. Although we often hear allegations that foreign policy is molded to suit private investors, we rarely hear private investment described as a "tool" of foreign policy. The United States government, however, has clearly tried to use private foreign investment to promote some of its foreign policy goals in developing states. It has used diplomacy, investment guarantees, propaganda, and non-aid to stimulate the flow of private capital to developing areas.[60] The Advisory Committee on Private Enterprise in Foreign Aid recently pointed out that "private institutions may be far more effective instruments of national policy in some situations than government institutions." [61] The committee report went on to describe private investment abroad as an effective way to exert "pressure" on the developing states to adopt the kind of pluralistic social system that the authors of the report believe exists in the United States.[62] The report made it clear that the authors viewed private capital as a means of intervening in the affairs of developing states.

After examining several types of aid, we conclude that none of them offers much hope to those who oppose any and all intervention in the recipient's affairs. Each of them can serve, and has served, as a mechanism for intervention. Although there may be types of foreign aid that cannot be used by the donor to intervene, they are not among those examined here.

IV. Trade, Not Aid: A Way Out?

A commonly suggested substitute for aid might be thought to provide a way out for those interested in preventing donors from influencing recipients. "Trade, not aid" has been a slogan heard intermittently for the last twenty years. Preferential treatment of developing countries in their trade relations with the developed ones could serve as a functional equivalent for aid, at least to some extent. The United Nations Conference on Trade and Development in 1964 proposed a variety of ways to cloak foreign aid in the guise of special trading arrangements.[63] If this could be done, would donors still be able to intervene? There would be no need for annual Congressional appropriations, no negotiating for each project, and no need for aid missions. It would appear that many opportunities for intervention by donors would thus be foreclosed.

Appearances can be deceiving, however. International trade can also be an instrument of national foreign policy. Implicit in all trade among nations is the potential threat of each trading partner to terminate the trade.[64] Three potential sources of intervention are obvious: (1) actual termination of trade by a rich country, (2) threatened termination, and (3) actions by developing states anticipating potential reactions by the developed states. One cannot make an *a priori* judgment as to which nations would be in the strongest bargaining positions with regard to terminating or threatening termination of trade. Other things being equal, however, nations gaining the most from the trade would have the most to lose and would thus be more vulnerable to threats to end the trade. It is interesting to note, in this respect, that several of the Unctad proposals involve measures to increase the developing nations' gains from trade with the rich nations. We are presented with the irony of a situation in which the developing states ask the rich nations to do many of the same things that Hirschman views as ways to maximize a nation's potential influence over its trading partners.[65] The Unctad proposals may be worthwhile, but developing states are deluding themselves if they think that implementation of the proposals will necessarily insulate them from intervention by rich nations.

V. Conclusion

The preceding discussion focused on three major topics: (1) the links between aid and influence, (2) the links between particular types of aid and intervention, and (3) the links between trade and intervention. The section on aid and influence was devoted to highlighting some of the less obvious aspects of the relationship and to noting a variety of analytical problems that confront the student of foreign aid. The examination of several types of aid revealed that all were likely to involve significant amounts of intervention in the developing states. The third section held out some hope, but not much, for minimizing intervention by the functional equivalent of special trading arrangements.

We did not discuss the question of whether certain types of intervention are desirable—by whatever standard. The preceding analysis will seem to have isolationist policy implications only for those who refuse to recognize that the doctrine of nonintervention was "fashioned for a world in which nations were set apart in space and did not interact significantly; a world in which there were no countries so much more powerful than others that they 'intervened' simply by being and acting . . . a world that has ceased to exist."[66] To increase economic well-being and to ensure world peace, some types of intervention are probably useful, even necessary. We live in a highly interdependent world and might as well make the best of it. As a Syracuse University study pointed out several years ago: "We cannot undertake any significant action without becoming involved in some nation's internal affairs, either in technical assistance, in economic planning, or in military training. . . . The appropriate attitude toward this new role of ours is acceptance of involvement, or joint participation, as a permanent part of our international life and on this basis to participate as intelligently and usefully as we can." [67]

NOTES

1. J. William Fulbright, *The Arrogance of Power* (New York 1967), 232–37.

2. James N. Rosenau, "Pre-Theories and Theories of Foreign Policy," R. Barry Farrell, ed., *Approaches to Comparative and International Politics* (Evanston 1966), 27–92. See also Andrew M. Scott, *The Functioning of the International Political System* (New York 1967).

3. A thoughtful series of essays on the concept of intervention is found in the *Journal of International Affairs*, xxii, No. 2 (1968).

4. "Influence" is defined by Robert Dahl as "the ability of A to get B to do something he would not otherwise do." For elaboration on the use of this definition, see Robert A. Dahl, *Modern Political Analysis* (Englewood Cliffs 1963), 39–54.

5. Lucian W. Pye, "Soviet and American Styles in Foreign Aid," *Orbis,* iv (Summer 1960), 168.

6. For similar examples, see David A. Baldwin, "Analytical Notes on Foreign Aid and Politics," *Background,* x (May 1966), 66–90.

7. On this point, see Scott, 23, and Herman Kahn and Anthony J. Wiener, *The Year 2000* (New York 1967), 365.

8. Quincy Wright, *The Study of International Relations* (New York 1955), 130–32.

9. Rosenau, 66. Rosenau defines a "penetrated political system" as one "in which non-members of a national society participate directly and authoritatively, through actions taken jointly with the society's members, in either the allocation of its values or the mobilization of support on behalf of its goals." 65.

10. The word "extent" is somewhat misleading. We might be interested in at least three important dimensions of control: (1) scope, (2) weight, and (3) domain. Cf. Harold Lasswell and Abraham Kaplan, *Power and Society* (New Haven 1950).

11. Cf. Dahl, 53.

12. These "resources" can be political as well as economic.

13. Thomas C. Schelling, *The Strategy of Conflict* (Cambridge, Mass. 1960), 37.

14. *New York Times,* November 24, 1943, 9. Italics added.

15. *Department of State Bulletin,* September 23, 1945, 443.

16. Commission on Foreign Economic Policy, *Report to the President and the Congress* (Washington 1954), 23.

17. *Ibid.,* 18.

18. Committee to Strengthen the Security of the Free World, *The Scope and Distribution of United States Military and Economic Assistance Programs* (Washington 1963), 13. (Hereafter cited as the "Clay Report.")

19. *Report of the Thirty-Eighth National Foreign Trade Convention* (New York 1952), xxxii.

20. American Enterprise Association, "American Private Enterprise, Foreign Economic Development, and the Aid Program," *Foreign Aid Program: Compilation of Studies and Surveys,* 85th Cong., 1st sess., S. Doc. 52 (Washington 1957), 539–618, esp. 548, 558–59.

21. Jacob J. Kaplan, *The Challenge of Foreign Aid* (New York 1967), 179.

22. *Ibid.,* 179–85.

23. Thomas C. Schelling, "American Foreign Assistance," *World Politics,* vii (July 1955), 623. On this point, see also George Liska, *The New Statecraft* (Chicago 1960), 126–83.

24. Karl W. Deutsch, "External Influences on the Internal Behavior of States," *Approaches to Comparative and International Politics,* 10–12.

25. Maxwell Graduate School of Citizenship and Public Affairs, *The Operational Aspects*

of United States Foreign Policy, Senate Committee on Foreign Relations Committee Print, 86th Cong., 1st sess. (Washington 1959), 17.

26. David A. Baldwin, "The International Bank in Political Perspective," *World Politics,* xviii (October 1965), 69.

27. Raymond F. Mikesell, "Problems and Policies in Public Lending for Economic Development," Raymond F. Mikesell, ed., *U.S. Private and Government Investment Abroad* (Eugene, Ore. 1962), 325.

28. Joseph A. Schumpeter, *Capitalism, Socialism, and Democracy* (3rd ed., New York 1950), 421.

29. Frederic Benham, *Economic Aid to Underdeveloped Countries* (London 1961), 104.

30. *Ibid.*

31. International Bank for Reconstruction and Development, *Policies and Operations of the World Bank, IFC, and IDA* (Washington 1962), 42.

32. William Adams Brown and Redvers Opie, *American Foreign Assistance* (Washington 1953), 188.

33. The evolution of this process is traced in David A. Baldwin, *Economic Development and American Foreign Policy: 1943–1962* (Chicago 1966).

34. On this point, see Consultants on International Finance and Economic Problems, *The Problem of Excess Accumulation of U.S.-Owned Local Currencies: Findings and Recommendations Submitted to the Under Secretary of State,* April 4, 1960.

35. Thomas C. Schelling, "American Aid and Economic Development: Some Critical Issues," *International Stability and Progress* (New York 1957), 157.

36. Raymond F. Mikesell, "Capacity to Service Foreign Investment," *U.S. Private and Government Investments Abroad,* 406.

37. It should be noted that the repayment requirement provides an incentive to allocate aid resources to *financially* remunerative projects, not necessarily to *socially* remunerative ones, such as feeding babies.

38. Carl J. Friedrich, *Constitutional Government and Democracy* (Boston 1941), 589–91.

39. For some evidence that this was indeed the case, see Baldwin, *Economic Development and American Foreign Policy.*

40. On this point, see Charles Wolf, Jr., *Foreign Aid: Theory and Practice in Southern Asia* (Princeton 1960), 159–62, 187–89, 258, 417–19.

41. Cf. Scott, 210, and James Patrick Sewell, *Functionalism and World Politics* (Princeton 1966), 43–44.

42. For a useful review of the arguments for multilateral aid, not all of which concern intervention, see Robert E. Asher, "Multilateral Versus Bilateral Aid: An Old Controversy Revisited," *International Organization,* xvi (Autumn 1962), 697–719. On international organizations and non-intervention see Scott, 208–11.

43. See Baldwin, "The International Bank," 68–81.

44. Benjamin Higgins, *United Nations and U.S. Foreign Economic Policy* (Homewood, Ill. 1962), 11. For similar statements advocating multilateral aid as a means of facilitating intervention, see the following: Kaplan, 350; Advisory Committee on Private Enterprise in Foreign Aid, *Foreign Aid Through Private Initiative* (Washington 1965), 12; Clay Report, 15–16; Henry Cabot Lodge, "Mutual Aid Through the United Nations," *Department of State Bulletin,* April 4, 1960, 525.

45. For a description of the strings used by the World Bank, see Baldwin, "The International Bank," 75–79.

46. For examples, see Benham, 105; and Lodge, "Mutual Aid," 525.

47. John P. Lewis, *Quiet Crisis in India* (Washington 1962), 263.

48. *Ibid.,* 264. Jacob Kaplan contends that the "only instance of the expulsion of a Western aid mission for pressing unwelcome advice is that of the World Bank advisor who was resident in Turkey in the early 1950's." 361.

49. "Mutual Aid Through the United Nations," 525.

50. Wolf, 80 n.

51. Liska, 217.

52. *Ibid.*

53. On the importance of this, see Thomas C. Schelling, *International Economics* (Boston 1958), 443–44.

54. Frank M. Coffin, *Witness for AID* (Boston 1964), 14–15. See also Agency for International Development, *Loan Terms, Debt Burden, and Development* (April 1965), 23.

55. For examples, see Cleona Lewis, *The United States and Foreign Investment Problems* (Washington 1948), 277; American Enterprise Association, "American Private Enterprise, Foreign Economic Development, and the Aid Programs," *Foreign Aid Program: Compilation of Studies and Surveys*, 592; Clair Wilcox, *A Charter for World Trade* (New York 1949), 145; and John Pincus, *Trade, Aid and Development* (New York 1967), 344.

56. On this point see John K. Galbraith, *The New Industrial State* (Boston 1967); Adolph A. Berle, Jr., *Power Without Property* (New York 1959); and Michael D. Reagan, *The Managed Economy* (New York 1963).

57. Robert Engler, *The Politics of Oil* (New York 1961).

58. Eugene Staley, *War and the Private Investor* (Garden City 1935), 142.

59. *Ibid.*, 367. See, also, Leo Model, "The Politics of Private Foreign Investment," *Foreign Affairs*, xlv (July 1967), 639–51.

60. For details on the United States use of these techniques for promoting private foreign investment, see Baldwin, *Economic Development and American Foreign Policy.*

61. *Foreign Aid Through Private Initiative*, 5.

62. *Ibid.*, 6–8.

63. For a description and analysis of the UNCTAD proposals, see Harry G. Johnson, *Economic Policies Toward Less Developed Countries* (Washington 1967).

64. On this point, see Albert O. Hirschman, *National Power and the Structure of Foreign Trade* (Berkeley and Los Angeles 1945).

65. *Ibid.*, 34–35. See also Pincus, 44.

66. Scott, 23.

67. Maxwell Graduate School, *The Operational Aspects of United States Foreign Policy*, 17.

30.
Hedley Bull: Arms Control: A Stocktaking and Prospectus

For more than a decade, "new thinking" on arms control has predominated over traditional conceptions of disarmament. The interaction of the superpowers, according to Hedley Bull, includes " 'unilateral action' [which] is more important than the pursuit of agreements, and 'tacit agreements' [which] are more important than formal ones." In the selection that follows, Professor Bull recapitulates the main ideas of the new thinking of 1960, evaluates the amount of progress since then, and draws some lessons from what has happened.

For biographical information, see the headnote to "Strategic Studies and Its Critics," p. 163.

The foundation of the Institute for Strategic Studies ten years ago coincided with the beginnings of a great debate within the Western world about the implications of nuclear weapons for arms control and disarmament. One of the high points of that debate was the conference of the Institute held here at

Hedley Bull, "Arms Control: A Stocktaking and Prospectus," in Alastair Buchan, ed., *Problems of Modern Strategy*. Chatto and Windus, Ltd., London, and Praeger Publishers, Inc., New York, 1971. Originally published as an Adelphi Paper by the Institute for Strategic Studies, London. Reprinted by permission of Praeger Publishers and Chatto and Windus.

Oxford in 1960, when the "new thinking" on this subject that had been developing in the late 1950s, chiefly in the United States, was first presented to a wide international audience.

The "new thinking" of 1960 was not as new as it seemed to some of us at the time: much of it was a restatement of old principles, concerning the balance of power or the political control of forces, in new terms, or an application of these principles to new circumstances. But it seemed to herald the birth, or at all events the renaissance, of a subject that was both intellectually exciting and of great practical importance. Some of the central ideas of the "new thinking" may be briefly recapitulated.

First, there was a feeling of concern about the dangers of nuclear war, and of dissatisfaction with the existing policies of the nuclear powers, that was shared with radical disarmers and was much more intense and immediate than the concern that is felt now. Our anxieties were focused upon the possibility of war between the United States and the Soviet Union, arising especially out of the dangers of a premeditated surprise attack, a pre-emptive attack dictated by the need to disarm the adversary if war was imminent, or the unintended expansion of a local conflict in Europe. The policies of the United States in the period of the "New Look," of the United Kingdom after the 1957 Defence White Paper, and of the Soviet Union after Mr. Khrushchev's speech of January 1960 seemed to envisage the unlimited use of strategic nuclear weapons as the chief, if not the only means of conducting a major conflict in the nuclear age.

Second, representatives of the "new thinking," in common with advocates of unilateral nuclear disarmament, who were then a force to be reckoned with on the British political scene, were suspicious and distrustful of the goal of a negotiated general and comprehensive disarmament agreement, which was still powerfully upheld by men such as Philip Noel-Baker and Jules Moch, whose thinking about disarmament had been shaped in the League of Nations period, and whose ideas still provided the chief content of "disarmament" as a concept in the public mind. The goal of a general and comprehensive disarmament agreement was adopted in principle by the nuclear powers, and had recently been forcefully restated in the Soviet proposal of 1959 for "total disarmament." Like members of the Campaign for Nuclear Disarmament in Britain, those who gave expression to the "new thinking" were apt to draw attention to the gap which separated the professions of the major powers to a belief in negotiated disarmament and their actual practice, the predominance of propaganda over genuine negotiation in disarmament conferences, the atmosphere of dilatoriness and humbug that accompanied these meetings, and the urgent need to do something to reduce the dangers of war, without waiting for the great powers to reach agreement on remote and improbable schemes for transforming the world.

Third, by contrast with both the traditional disarmament doctrine stemming from the prewar period and the school of unilateral nuclear disarmament, which were inclined to regard defence and disarmament as opposed objectives of policy, and the influence of the military on disarmament policy as a sinister one, the "new thinking" insisted upon the unity of strategy and arms control, the continuing need for defensive measures under conditions of disarmament, the need for defence planners to take disarmament into account, and the subordination of both defence and disarmament to the objective of security. While this doctrine of the unity of strategy and arms control meant that traditional defence thinking, unrefined by the element of collaboration with the antagonist in military policy, was inadequate, it also carried the implication that arms control was not the preserve of radicals and rebels, but was a respectable pursuit that could be contemplated without alarm in the corridors of power. Radicals and rebels were quick to interpret the "new thinking" as essentially a capitulation of disarmament thinking to defence thinking, or as the new apologetics developed by the defence establishment to protect itself against the criticism to which it had become subject.

Fourth, implicit in the treatment of arms control rather than disarmament as the essential focus of concern, was a broadening of the scope of the subject and a perception of links between varieties of military activity hitherto thought separate. "The essential feature of arms control," Schelling and Halperin wrote, "is the recognition of the common interest, of the possibility of reciprocation and co-operation even between potential enemies with respect to their military establishments." [1] Along with disarmament agreements it was necessary to recognize formal agreements which restricted military policy without involving disarmament, tacit agreements arrived at without being given formal or even verbal expression, and unilateral actions undertaken in the pursuit of common interests. The effect of this broadening of the scope of the subject was to weaken the claims that advocates of disarmament had always made that theirs was a new and untried course. For a great deal of what counted as arms control in this extended sense was already a part of the established practice of states.

The broadened definition also introduced a note of obscurity and even of metaphysics into the discussion of arms control. For while we may easily recognize a formal agreement when we see one there are inherent difficulties in establishing the existence of an agreement which has never been alluded to in the statements of governments. The fact that the United States and the Soviet Union have both refrained from doing certain things (e.g. directly confronting one another in war, using nuclear weapons in war or stepping up their defence expenditure to World War II levels) does not mean that they have agreed not to do them. Moreover, it is also often difficult to determine whether unilateral military policies can in fact be regarded as instances of arms control: for steps taken to strengthen command and control procedures, to render retaliatory forces invulnerable to destruction or to avoid provocative deployments of forces, have a simple defence rationale, and if they are to be regarded as measures of arms control it has to be shown that they are motivated by a perception of interests shared with the adversary, or at all events that they result in the advancement of such interests, which is sometimes difficult to demonstrate.

Fifth, the "new thinking" was critical of the assumption that disarmament, in the sense of the reduction or abolition of armaments and armed forces, should be the objective of arms-control policy. It was argued that "total disarmament" was not qualitatively different from any lesser degree of disarmament; that whatever meaning could be given to the term, it still implied a situation in which war was physically possible. It was argued also that drastic disarmament, while it might or might not prove desirable, should be regarded as the objective of arms-control policy only in cases where it could be demonstrated that a reduction of armaments, rather than an increase of them or a maintenance of them at existing levels, promoted the over-riding objective of security.

In particular, it was suggested that while the uncritical pursuit of disarmament implied the dismantling of the Soviet-American balance of terror, the proper object of arms-control policy was rather to preserve or perfect it. Arms-control policy should distinguish between those military developments which tended to stabilize the balance of terror, and those which tended to destabilize it; and while restricting the latter it should tolerate or even encourage the former. From this perspective measures directed towards making retaliatory forces invulnerable, or towards the maintenance of the ability to threaten unacceptable damage, were welcomed as stabilizing, while measures directed towards the acquisition of a disarming capacity or the provision of an effective defence of cities against missile attack, were branded as "destabilizing."

And sixth, although the "new thinking" was directed in part towards destroying the illusions and exposing the humbug that surrounded the discussion of disarmament it was also deeply infected with optimism, especially the optimism of the social sciences in America. There was a sense of being at the threshold of a new era in arms control, reflected in proposals to expand governmental machinery for dealing with arms control, in hopes placed in the goal of what was called "stable deterrence," and above all in the confidence that was displayed in study and research as a means of improving the prospects of peace and security. One of the most memorable interventions in the discussion at Oxford in 1960 was that of Mr. (now Sir) Con O'Neill, who warned that the hopes now being placed in logic or mathematics in the search for a solution to the problem of disarmament might prove as illusory as those which had been placed by a previous generation in the moral transformation of mankind.

II

What progress has been made since 1960 towards the goals that the "new thinking" mapped out? The answer to this question presents something of a paradox. On the one hand the world is a great deal safer than it was at the beginning of the decade, at all events against the danger of major nuclear war. But on the other hand the progress of arms control, while it has not been negligible, has been slight and the contributions it has made to the strengthening of international security are problematical.

It is obvious that the sense of impending catastrophe that gripped the Western world during the late 1950s has now given place to a more relaxed view of the dangers of nuclear war. Disarmament has lost much of its urgency as a public issue in Western countries; governments are not so much on the defensive against radical groups pressing for action in this field, and radical groups themselves have found other matters on which to focus their protest.

This more relaxed attitude does not necessarily reflect an objective improvement in the position. Moreover, there may be some risk that the new mood of relaxation will itself help to resuscitate the old dangers. While the departure of panic and hysteria from the discussion of nuclear problems can only be welcomed, we should beware of assuming that the twenty-three years' nuclear peace we have had reflects the operation of inherent tendencies of the nuclear age that are in no need of encouragement from us, of neglecting the part that has been played in our survival so far by conscious efforts to remove the dangers and by sheer chance.

In fact, however, there has been an objective improvement in the position. We remain, it is true, in a world of states that are sovereign, armed and divided, and subject to the insecurity which this entails. If progress is to be measured by the degree to which we have altered the political structure of mankind by depriving states of their sovereignty, or their armaments, or by removing the political conflicts among them, we have made none. But within this framework a situation of relatively greater security has grown up.

First, the United States and the Soviet Union have devoted much effort and attention to devising procedures and techniques for ensuring adequate command and control of their own nuclear forces and weapons. The novels and films which depicted the outbreak of a nuclear war as the result of failure in command and control, whether or not they drew attention to dangers which actually existed in the 1950s or early 1960s, cannot be taken very seriously as warnings now. These dramatized warnings, exaggerated as they no doubt were, served a useful purpose; they played a part in stimulating the measures which the United States and Britain have taken to improve command and control measures in relation to nuclear weapons.

I believe it is desirable that the United States and other nuclear powers should make more information available to the public about the steps they have taken in this field. Information about command and control is, of course, necessarily subject to the highest security classifications. But at the present time the public can only take it on trust that in this vital area their interests are being adequately safeguarded. Moreover, there is reason to believe that the dissemination by the United States of information in this field to other nuclear powers, including unfriendly ones, might help to guard against common dangers.

Second, the United States has carried out the steps to ensure the invulnerability of its strategic nuclear forces, for which the strategic writings of 1958–61 called as if with one voice. Moreover, the Soviet Union in due course followed the United States in the multiplication, dispersal and hardening of land-based missile sites and developing a nuclear-submarine-based missile force, and added the technique of the mobile land-based ICBMs.

As a consequence of these measures it is not reasonable now, as it was in 1960, on the basis of the information then publicly available about the state of nuclear forces, to doubt the stability of the situation of mutual deterrence, in the sense of the tendency to persist of the situation in which the United States and the Soviet Union could each survive a first blow by the other side and retain a capacity for assured destruction.

It is true that the situation of mutual deterrence remains "delicate" or unstable in principle, in the sense that its persistence is not assured by the mere existence of nuclear weapons on both sides but only by constant attention to the measures that are necessary to provide an assured-destruction capability. It is true also that there are actual "destabilizing" trends perceptible, both in the measures being taken by the United States and the Soviet Union to provide ballistic missile defence of their cities, and in such harbingers of the development of a disarming capability as the MIRV (Multiple Independently Targetable Reentry Vehicle) and the improvement of submarine detection. But experts do not now expect that trends such as these will undermine the situation of mutual deterrence within the foreseeable future.

A stable balance of nuclear terror does not ensure the preservation of peace. The form of order it provides, moreover, as Osgood and Tucker have pointed out, labours under the disadvantage that "a *single* breakdown of that order in nuclear violence would be catastrophic." [2] But it does ensure that deliberate resort to the unlimited use of force by either side cannot be a rational act of policy. And it does reduce—while not eliminating—the incentive to get in the first blow in a situation in which war is believed to be imminent. For these reasons the increased stability which the balance of terror between the super-powers has come to possess in the 1960s has made for a safer world, despite the absolute increase in the size and destructive potential of the Soviet and American strategic nuclear forces, and in the money spent on them, during this period.

Third, we have much less reason now than we had in 1960 to assume that if the United States and the Soviet Union did become involved in hostilities these would necessarily expand or "explode" into an unlimited conflict. Perhaps even then there was reason enough to doubt any automatic tendency of a Soviet-American conflict to become unlimited, and evidence enough from the experience of the Berlin blockade, the Korean war or the Quemoy crisis of the ability of the super-powers to contain conflicts in which they were involved. But in the 1960s the United States has come to espouse a sophisticated doctrine of the need for and the possibility of limitation of war, at a variety of different levels; and the Soviet Union, although it began later and has not gone nearly as far, has moved in the same direction.

The United States and the Soviet Union, I believe, need to go much further in elaborating a doctrine of limited war. Because espousal of the idea of limited war implies acknowledging the place of war in international relations, because it appears to weaken the force of deterrent threats, and because, as the United States discovered when it sought to enunciate this doctrine within NATO, it raises awkward questions about the different interests of allies in the nature and extent of the limitations proposed, there are great obstacles to carrying the doctrine of limited war further. Once the United States and the Soviet Union, moreover, are directly engaged in hostilities, the pressures for expansion of the conflict must be great. But at least if the major powers accustom themselves to the idea of limited war, and allow for it in their strategic planning and preparations, there will be some possibility of limiting a Soviet-American conflict that has broken out. United States and Soviet policy-makers, although they have studiously avoided direct military conflict and have controverted those who argued that once the strategic nuclear balance was stable, war between the super-powers would be likely to occur at a lower level of violence, nevertheless do not now assume that any hostilities would be bound to become unlimited.

Fourth, outside the field of strategic policy there have taken place the changes in United States and Soviet foreign policies which we refer to as the *détente*. Each of the super-powers has developed a degree of confidence in the other's willingness to coexist with it, to avoid provoking situations fraught with the danger of war, and even to co-operate for some purposes. The likelihood of war on both sides is felt to be less, the problem of deterring attack or preparing to meet it has come to seem less urgent, the need to view every move of the adversary in the light of military security has come to seem less pressing, and the possibilities of acting upon other than "worst case" assumptions about his intentions and capability have been enlarged.

These respects in which the dangers of war between the United States and the Soviet Union have receded have to be set against the emergence of other dangers to which in 1960 we paid less attention. Since that time France and China have become nuclear powers and the hopes that some entertained, that Britain would cease to be one, have subsided. India is within easy reach of membership of the nuclear club, while others are not far behind. New political conflicts have arisen to complicate the pattern of international alignment and antagonism. China has come to divert some of the attention that the United States and the Soviet Union bestow on each other, and to preoccupy India and the states of South-East Asia. Military conflicts between China and India and Pakistan, Indonesia and Malaysia, the civil war in Nigeria and the six-day war have made us more conscious than we were of the potential of poor countries, supplied with obsolete equipment by the great powers, for organized violence, and more apprehensive about the role these countries may come to play if and when they undergo the process of modernization. But none of these other conflicts is yet capable of giving rise to the destruction and devastation that could follow a war between the United States and the Soviet Union.

If the world has become perceptibly safer against the danger of major nuclear war the hopes of 1960 for progress in the field of arms control have been fulfilled only to a slight extent. When the Soviet Union in 1959 advanced its "total disarmament" proposal the Western powers had to decide whether to respond with a comparable plan of their own, or to ignore this objective and concentrate on limited measures. This issue was decided by President Kennedy when, swayed by Adlai Stevenson's insistence on the need for a plan that would, in Schlesinger's words, "strengthen allied unity and beat the Soviet Union in the UN" he over-ruled the Joint Chiefs of Staff and the "extreme arms controllers" and ruled in favour of general and complete disarmament.[3]

There followed the McCloy-Zorin talks of 1961 and the "Agreed Principles" concerning GCD (General and Complete Disarmament) which they drew up; and the following year the presentation of Soviet and United States draft GCD plans to the new Eighteen Nation Disarmament Committee (ENDC). Perhaps because of the new element of professionalism injected into the planning of disarmament policy by the US Arms Control and Disarmament Agency the United States GCD plan of April 1962 was a reasonably sophisticated document which attempted to spell out the meaning of drastic disarmament in terms of the stages necessary to accomplish it, and the institutions necessary to verify and enforce disarmament measures and to maintain international order in a disarmed world. Under the impact of this professional argumentation Soviet plans for drastic disarmament became less frivolous than they had previously been. The period 1961–64 was one of sustained intellectual attention to the subject of drastic disarmament on the part of the ENDC, bureaucracies, and outside scholars and writers, and it resulted in the appearance of a great deal of material of interest to students of the subject.

But it never showed any sign of resulting in any agreement in this field, apart from "agreements of principle" like the McCloy-Zorin one which merely serve to obscure the differences between the parties and to create an illusion of progress. Since 1965, the discussion of GCD in the ENDC has become a perfunctory affair, the time set aside for this subject being devoted to the canvassing of measures such as a freeze in the production of nuclear delivery vehicles, which may be formally linked to progress in the field of GCD but have in fact been discussed as separate proposals. Critics of the pursuit of GCD have often argued that it distracted attention from the discussion of partial measures and imposed an obstacle to agreement on them. In recent years, however, negotiators have experienced no difficulty in detaching particular proposed agreements from the GCD framework, and discussion of the latter has become a ritual affair. It is also striking that among non-official students of arms control and groups interested in promoting arms control, advocates of drastic or comprehensive disarmament have ceased to exert a significant influence.[4]

The most tangible evidence of progress in arms control is provided by the formal arms control agreements, not involving disarmament, that have been signed in the 1960s. Following upon the Antarctica Treaty of December 1959 we have had the Partial Test Ban Treaty signed in August 1963, the tripartite declaration on outer space of October 1963, followed up by the Treaty on the Exploration and Use of Outer Space of January 1967, and the Non-Proliferation Treaty of 1968 (NPT). The Hot Line agreement of June 1963, although it imposes no restriction on military policy and hence cannot strictly be considered an example of arms control, nevertheless may be mentioned as giving effect to the objective of perceived common interests in military security and embodying a technique advocated by students of arms control.

The intrinsic effects of these formal arms-control agreements on military competition among states are not negligible. "Realists" argue that the Partial Test Ban Treaty is ineffective because it does not prevent nuclear explosions, but merely registers the fact that the powers who launched it had exhausted the utility of tests in the atmosphere. Or they argue that it had merely the effect of intensifying underground explosions. These are misleading half-truths. It did not in fact prove possible to terminate United States and Soviet bouts of competitive nuclear testing without the instrumentality of the Partial Test Ban Treaty. And although underground testing has been intensified, the prohibition of testing in the atmosphere, under water and in outer space represents a real restriction, which elements within the United States and the Soviet Union, and among potential nuclear powers that are signatories of the Treaty, undoubtedly find irksome.

The Antarctica and Outer Space agreements similarly prohibit the deployment of weapons in areas where the pressure for deployment is in any case not yet powerful. But they do add an additional inhibition to others which already make against the extension of armaments competition into these areas; and they serve to advertise and to define the intentions of signatory states and thus to reassure them about one another's intentions. The Non-Proliferation Treaty similarly has to be viewed as an instrument which cannot by itself arrest the spread of nuclear weapons, but which adds a legal inhibition to other more powerful factors already making against proliferation, and which helps signatory states to arrive at a more precise appreciation of one another's intentions than they would be able to make in the absence of a formal agreement.

No one would argue, however, that any of these agreements has vitally affected the course of military competition. The chief importance of these agreements lies not in their intrinsic effects upon the military policies they are designed to restrict, but in their symbolic effect. The signing of the Partial Test Ban Treaty, which demonstrated that arms-control negotiations were not necessarily forever without concrete issue, and that the United States and the Soviet Union were able to agree upon a tangible restriction in the nuclear weapons field, marked an important stage in the emergence of the political *détente*. Similarly, the chief importance of the NPT may lie in its qualities as a symbol of positive co-operation between the United States and the Soviet Union in promoting a universal arms-control measure in opposition to the policies of other states, and as a dramatization to the world at large of the possibility of taking action to arrest the spread of nuclear weapons.

A number of important expectations or hopes that were entertained in 1960 in relation to formal arms-control agreements have failed to bear fruit. There have been no agreements bringing about any actual reduction of armaments. There has been no progress in the application of international inspection machinery to arms-control agreements, contrasting with an immense investment by the United States in the study and development of techniques for such inspection, although the NPT will result in the extension of International Agency for Atomic Energy (IAEA) safeguards to the peaceful nuclear activities of non-nuclear weapons state signatories. Advancing technology has greatly improved the means of verifying some agreements without international inspection machinery, as illustrated by the Partial Test Ban Treaty and the role which satellite intelligence might play in a limitation on deployment of nuclear delivery vehicles. But many possible agreements still clearly require formal inspection procedures for adequate verification, and many students of arms control in 1960 placed great emphasis upon international inspection as something valuable in itself, as undermining military secrecy and establishing a momentum towards further measures of arms control.

Above all, no progress has been made towards a formal arms-control agreement, or series of such agreements, that would stabilize the balance of terror at a minimum level of force. Perhaps the chief specific objective that was singled out by the "new thinking" was in this field. It was thought that whether or not radical disarmament was a feasible ultimate objective, the first step was to stabilize the balance of terror; that this was unlikely to come about as the result of Soviet-American arms competition itself; and that arms-control agreements could be designed specifically to this end. This immediate goal, which was viewed by "disarmers" as part of the first stage of a GCD plan and by "arms controllers" as a subject for negotiation in its own right, could be pursued directly by means of a comprehensive agreement on strategic nuclear weapons which would proclaim the desirability of distinguishing "stabilizing" from "destabilizing" weapons developments, rather as plans in the inter-war period had proceeded deductively from the principle that "specifically offensive" weapons were to be restricted and "specifically defensive" weapons to be retained. Or the goal could be sought indirectly by means of agreements such as a freeze of nuclear delivery vehicle (NDV) production, a deal on numbers of deployed NDVs arrived at by "straight bargaining," a prohibition of antiballistic missile (ABM) deployment or a "bomber bonfire."

In fact, as has been noted, the United States and the Soviet Union, unaided by formal arms-control agreements to this end, have created a stable balance of terror. It is, however, subject to destabilizing tendencies as illustrated by the MIRV and the ABM; and in terms of the numbers and size of missiles and destructive potential of warheads available to both sides, it exists at a vastly higher level than the strategic balance of 1960. Within and around the Western defence establishments some progress has been made in thinking through the great complexities of this subject. President Johnson's 1964 proposal for a freeze on numbers and characteristics of nuclear delivery vehicles proposed a way of opening the discussion of this subject, but at the time it was presented it would have frozen a great United States superiority; it involved a great deal of intrusive inspection; and it would have frustrated such "stabilizing" developments as the hardening of Soviet ICBM forces. The "Gromyko proposal" of 1962 for a nuclear umbrella, which also led to some valuable thought on this problem, was never spelt out in detail nor detached from the framework of GCD.

What contribution has arms control made to the improvement of security against major war during this decade? Measures of "unilateral arms control," like the strengthening of command and control and the securing of retaliatory forces, have undoubtedly played an important part, although it is difficult to estimate whether the dimension of arms-control thinking was essential to the taking of them. The category of "tacit arms-control agreements," if by that we mean studied attention by the great powers to one another's moves in military policy, plus the attempt to jockey each other towards minimal solutions, is central to the present Soviet-American expectation of secure coexistence. But this remains an obscure field in which there are some illuminating notions about what might happen or could happen, but little hard evidence about what actually goes on.

Tangible, formal arms-control negotiations have resulted in some agreements, but these agreements have affected the course of events by virtue more of their symbolic than their intrinsic importance, and the negotiations themselves have contributed to international security more because of their side-effects, in the communication of strategic ideas and the definition of arms-control policies, than as the result of their pursuit of the central purpose of arriving at agreements.

III

What lessons can be drawn from this experience for the study and practice of arms control in the future? If the fruits so far of the "new thinking" have been disappointing, should we return to the pursuit of radical disarmament, bending our efforts once again towards a GCD plan, or some comprehensive proposal of this sort, rather than expending our energies upon measures which, even if they are implemented, are of slight significance?

Such a course would be disastrous. If progress in the negotiation of limited measures has been disappointing in the field of comprehensive disarmament there has been none at all. The detachment from such comprehensive plans of items for separate negotiation, beginning with the Surprise Attack and Test Ban negotiations that opened in 1958, was the most constructive step of the disarmament negotiations in the post-war years. The developments that have flowed from this step have brought arms control out of the realms of cynical propaganda and scholastic irrelevance and into that of serious international politics.

I believe on the contrary that the Western powers should seek to deprive GCD plans of the foothold they still enjoy in disarmament conferences. When this course is suggested to them, officials are inclined to argue that the public will not stand for it. Very frequently, however, when this subject comes up for discussion it is the officials who are in favour of continuing to negotiate about GCD and the members of the public present who wish to drop it. The vocal public in this field is in fact a good deal more sophisticated about this matter than it was in the 1950s.

It is certainly not possible, nor would it be desirable, to abandon official espousal of a disarmed world as an ultimate goal. It is desirable that our leaders should uphold the idea that military force is in itself repugnant, and that we maintain it and pay for it only because it is an unfortunate necessity. The notion of a world without arms, moreover, is a necessary point of reference in maintaining the momentum and sense of direction of an enterprise devoted to the reduction and limitation of armaments.

What should be eliminated is the pretence that plans to bring about general disarmament are a matter that can be negotiated about in good faith by governments now. GCD plans need not be dramatically disavowed but can be quietly dropped. The accomplishment of this task would be facilitated if the Western powers were able to interest the Soviet Union in some reciprocated restraint to this end.

Apart from this negative one what positive lessons can be drawn? First, we would recognize that among the different sorts of measures that go to make up arms control "unilateral action" is more important than the pursuit of agreements, and "tacit agreements" are more important than formal ones. This may have been implicit in some of the "new thinking" but it was nowhere clearly spelt out. It now seems to me that one of the defects of the "new thinking" was that it was not radical enough, and over-rated the importance of formal arms-control agreements in imposing severe curbs upon armaments competition, and especially the importance of international inspection.

Formal agreements in areas of vital military concern, such as that of the reduction and limitation of strategic nuclear weapons, are immensely difficult to negotiate not only because of the sensitivity of governments towards them and the suspicion with which their military advisers regard them, but also because of the inherent difficulties of translating the uncertain and constantly changing balance of power into the precision and fixity of a treaty.

For as long as states remain the primary actors in international relations and possess arms, which is for as long as we can foresee, what will chiefly determine international security will be the decisions these states make about the use of their arms. International agreements, even when satisfactorily concluded and brought into operation, are at best a means of influencing these decisions.

As has been argued above, the improvement of international security in the 1960s owes more to unilateral actions than to the pursuit of formal agreements. Accordingly it is regrettable that the major organizational innovation of the period, President Kennedy's Arms Control and Disarmament Agency (ACDA), is one primarily oriented towards the pursuit of such treaties. The ACDA has done valuable work, and its creation was a step forward. Nevertheless, the heart of the problem of international security lies in the defence or strategic policies of the major powers, and the negotiation of international understanding is necessarily subordinate to it.

The prime need is perhaps to inject a greater element of self-consciousness about the arms-control dimension of strategic policy into the defence and foreign policy establishments of these states. No doubt a good deal of awareness of this dimension already exists. But this awareness might be strengthened if there were established within the defence and foreign policy machine groups charged not merely with the search for agreements, but with the definition of interests shared with adversaries, and the study of ways in which these interests might be advanced.

An example may be given from the field of antiproliferation policy. The NPT in my view has a part to play in the control of proliferation. But the spread of nuclear weapons will be more vitally affected by the overall policy of the nuclear powers on this matter: the restraints they themselves practise in their nuclear weapons policy, the assurances they can provide, the inducements and pressure they can bring to bear. These wider considerations are not unknown to policy-makers but one may doubt whether they have received the degree of attention that has been bestowed upon the NPT.

Another example is the field of Soviet-American competition in strategic nuclear armaments. It is this field which is the most sensitive of all areas of military activity at the present time, because on it the whole structure of power in the world depends. Formal agreements may affect it, as up to a point the Partial Test Ban Treaty and the Outer Space agreement already have done. But in this area progress towards restraint and a scaling down of effort is more likely to come by means of reciprocated unilateral action than by treaty.

Second, we should recognize that the chief function of formal agreements may sometimes be the symbolic one of demonstrating "progress" and facilitating the conclusion of further agreements, rather than the intrinsic contribution they make to military security. The "new thinking," which was characterized by a certain intellectual purism in the pursuit of military security and by disdain for the merely political and theatrical, was inclined to overlook this. Thus we have had the Partial Test Ban Treaty dismissed as a "clean air bill," the Hot Line agreement disparaged as something that could as well have been arranged quietly between the United States and Soviet post offices, and the NPT derided as a merely declaratory instrument with inadequate provision for verification and none for enforcement. Such narrowly strategic appreciations of these agreements overlook the political dimension in disarmament negotiations, the force in the world of the desire for tangible evidence of action to curb the dangers of war, and the effect that can be produced upon relations among the negotiating countries by a dramatization of this evidence.

Clearly we must continue to insist on establishing the intrinsic utility of arms-control agreements before we set off in pursuit of them. In the accumulation of merely symbolic or hortatory treaties there is a risk that we shall repeat the errors of the 1920s and become the victims of our own illusion-making. But it should be recognized that the creation of a political effect can be a legitimate part of the utility of an agreement.

Third, given that disarmament talks frequently prove to be chiefly important in the function they have of providing opportunities for the exchange of ideas and for mutual education in strategic policy, there is a case for explicitly recognizing this function and assigning it an important place in the planning of arms-control policy. Jeremy Stone's recent study of the strategic dialogue brings out the extraordinary difficulty of conveying strategic ideas as between the United States and the Soviet Union.[5] The United States should give very careful attention to what it wants to say to the Soviet Union and how it can most effectively say it; and in making its voice heard through the interference, it would seem valuable to brief disarmament delegations explicitly to this end, and to include among them persons whose skills lie in their grasp of strategic ideas and their ability to expound them.

Fourth, the most important proximate goal of arms control remains the stability of the Soviet-American strategic balance. The ideas entertained in 1960 for surrounding the balance with a measure of control and for maintaining it at a lower level remain valid. A reduction, or cessation of expansion, of Soviet-American nuclear armaments remains important for its symbolic effect upon the *détente*, its possible economic benefits and its relation to the prospects of the NPT. The stability of the balance remains a chief foundation of peace and security.

It is unlikely, however, that this objective will be arrived at by means of a comprehensive arms-control agreement to this end. Such prospects of it as there may be depend upon reciprocated restraint, of the sort the United States was trying to practice until early this year in relation to the deployment of BMD. A stable balance at minimum levels might become the object of each side's negotiating policy, but it cannot be made the operative principle of an arms-control scheme, from which the numbers and sorts of the NDVs that each side is allowed to have will be deducted. Such a way of proceeding involves a rationalistic attempt to side-step the politics of arms-control discussion, and would founder on this rock. Formal agreements dealing with particular aspects of the strategic balance—a comprehensive test ban, a freeze on numbers of NDVs—could help indirectly to promote the objective of a stable balance at minimum levels.

Fifth, whereas the "new thinking" was focused principally on the dangers arising out of the Soviet-American relationship, it is necessary now to take more seriously into account other dangers to international security that have arisen in the world—not only from the spread of nuclear weapons but also from the acquisition of sophisticated armaments by new countries.

A great deal of attention has been devoted to the spread of nuclear weapons in the last few years, and the NPT is now under way. There may be some danger to arms control in the very success of the Treaty and in the developing consensus among the super-powers which it reflects. This is that the cause of arms control, like that of the League of Nations in the 1930s, will become identified with the interests of a particular power group and tarnished with the brush of ideology.

The United States and the Soviet Union do have a special position in world politics; and there is in fact a general interest in their co-operation for some purposes. It will be important, however, not to give priority to Soviet-American co-operation at the expense of failing to engage the interests of other major powers, including China, in the arms-control conversation. For the present there is clearly no possibility of engaging the interest of China, but it must surely be a high priority to bring China into the negotiations at the first opportunity, even at the expense of a lowering of consensus.

Sixth, it is time that the study of arms control was redirected towards an examination of fundamentals. Whereas the "new thinking" was remarkable for the questioning of old assumptions and the spelling out of new ones, the research that has been carried out since, now on a massive scale and under the aegis of large institutions, has tended to be encased within these latter assumptions, which are now ageing. The technical character, the professionalism and the absorption in detail of recent research in arms control, like research in the wider field of strategic studies, have tended to obscure the uncertainty of the starting points.

In particular, it is necessary to ask again how valid is the assumption that the balance of terror is the chief foundation of international security, and the preservation of it the first object of arms-control policy. If this assumption was valid at the time of the cold war, does it remain so in a period of declining concern about military security? If it does remain valid, do we have to accept Mr. McNamara's assumption that the objective of assured destruction requires an ability to destroy one-quarter to one-third of the Soviet population and two-thirds of Soviet industrial capacity, or can adequate deterrence be maintained at a lower level of assured destruction? What are the circumstances in which security would be enhanced rather than imperilled by the diminution of the capacity for assured destruction?

The importance of the debate about BMD is that it has tended to reopen these questions. The "classical" view of the arms controllers, that BMD of cities is unwelcome because it is "destabilizing," has come under attack from two directions: from "right wing" critics who accept that BMD is destabilizing but welcome it because they see in it the means of establishing preponderance; and from "left wing" critics who also accept that it is destabilizing but believe it will lead to the establishment of a "higher" form of stability based on defence rather than deterrence. In the new political and technological environment of the 1970s new basic assumptions may have to be thought out.

NOTES

1. Thomas C. Schelling and Morton H. Halperin: *Strategy and Arms Control* (New York: 20th Century Fund, 1961), p. 2.

2. Robert E. Osgood and Robert W. Tucker: *Force, Order, and Justice* (Baltimore, Md., and London: Johns Hopkins Press, 1967), p. 39.

3. Arthur M. Schlesinger, Jr.: *A Thousand Days: John F. Kennedy in the White House* (London: Deutsch, 1965), p. 418.

4. This is noted and deplored by R. R. Neild in *What Has Happened to Disarmament?* Annual Memorial Lecture, David Davies Memorial Institute of International Studies (London, April 1968).

5. Jeremy J. Stone: *Strategic Persuasion: Arms Limitation through Dialogue* (New York and London: Columbia University Press, 1967).

31.

Robert E. Osgood: *The Reappraisal of Limited War*

A body of limited-war doctrine was developed in the 1960's, spurred by the fears of nuclear war and by American containment policy. Reappraising limited war at what he considers to be the end of an era, Robert E. Osgood cites the relative neglect in this strategic doctrine of such political premises as the nature of the communist threat to American security and the willingness of the American government and people to support the costs of war. From the experience of the Vietnam conflict Professor Osgood attempts to draw lessons concerning a number of issues, including the impact of popular disaffection and the possible objectives and scale for a future use of limited force by the United States.

Robert E. Osgood's numerous works on national security issues include *Limited War* and *Alliances and American Foreign Policy*. He is Professor of American Foreign Policy at the Johns Hopkins University and Director of its Washington Center of Foreign Policy Research.

O ne of the most significant developments in international politics since World War II is the change of attitude towards armed force in the advanced Western countries. Between the two world wars total warfare was commonly viewed as virtually the only kind of warfare relevant to military preparedness and strategy. In such a war victory would depend on destroying in the most thorough way the enemy's capability and will to fight. But in the cold war quite a different view has become widespread—the view that the principal objective of military policies is the avoidance of general war and the limitation and control of lesser wars according to political ends short of traditional military victory. One aspect of this change of attitude is the great attention devoted to limited war strategy and preparedness in the United States, especially in the last ten or twelve years.[1]

To an extent that must amaze early proponents of limited war, who sought to overcome the formidable antipathy toward the concept during the Korean War and the Eisenhower-Dulles Administration, the rationale of limited war has gained widespread acceptance in the United States and, to a somewhat lesser degree, in allied countries. In the 1960s the United States went far in implementing the concept with strategies, weapons, and organization. Among research, academic and military analysts the concept of limited war inspired a great outpouring of strategic doctrine. In the Kennedy Administration lim-

Robert E. Osgood, "The Reappraisal of Limited War," in Alastair Buchan, ed., *Problems of Modern Strategy*. Chatto and Windus, Ltd., London, and Praeger Publishers, Inc., New York, 1971. Originally published as an Adelphi Paper by the Institute for Strategic Studies, London. Reprinted by permission of Chatto and Windus and Praeger Publishers.

ited war became official doctrine and achieved something approaching popularity.

But now the war in Vietnam, which has called so much into question, raises doubts about some limited-war concepts and the premises upon which they were based. It is not just Vietnam, however, that raises these doubts; it is the conjunction of Vietnam with basic changes in the international environment within which limited-war concepts arose and flourished. It is time, therefore, to reappraise limited-war thinking and experience during the past two decades, and such a reappraisal must take into account the international context in which limited war has come to command such unprecedented attention.

The reappraisal, however, should start with the antecedents of this attention, which lie in international developments before World War II. The concept and practice of limited war are as old as war itself; but the consciousness of limited war as a distinct kind of warfare, with its own theory and doctrine, has emerged most markedly in contrast and reaction to three major wars, waged between several major states, in behalf of popular national and ideological goals, by means of mass conscription and massive firepower: the Napoleonic Wars, World War I, and World War II. The contemporary interest in limited war springs partly from a determination to avoid World War III.

The relevance of limited war to contemporary international politics is manifest in the occurrence of more than fifty internationally significant local wars of various kinds since World War II, while there have been no general wars, and the armed forces of the most powerful states have come no closer to fighting each other than the American-Soviet confrontation in the Cuban missile crisis of 1962. The great majority of these wars, however, did not directly involve a nuclear or even a major power; most of them were insurgent or civil wars, none of them (except the Hungarian intervention in 1956) was fought between advanced industrial states or on the territory of an advanced state.[2] They were limited, as before World War II, by such factors as the restricted fighting capacity of the belligerents, the one-sided nature of the contest, or the inherent limits of internal war. With the diffusion of power and intensification of local conflicts, such wars in the Third World may become an increasingly disturbing element in international politics, if only because they could involve major powers. But the kinds of wars that have occasioned the systematic concern with strategies and weapons of limited war are wars that the United States fought, that might have expanded into much wider and more violent conflicts, but that remained limited because the United States and its adversaries deliberately refrained from conducting military operations with their full capacities. Equally important, the concern has arisen from the desire to deter or limit hypothetical wars that have not occurred—especially wars that might have resulted from limited aggressions impinging on America's vital interests abroad.

The detailed elaboration of a strategic doctrine of limited war, the formulation of specific plans for carrying out this doctrine, and the combined efforts of government, the military establishment, and private analysts and publicists to translate the doctrine into particular weapons and forces are developments peculiar to the nuclear age. They are products of the profound fear of nuclear war and the belief that the limitation of war must be carefully contrived, rather than left to inherent limitations upon military capabilities. But they are also products of American foreign policy in a particular period of history. Reappraising limited-war strategy as, in part, a function of American policy in the cold war will help us to distinguish between those aspects of limited-war thinking that are obsolescent or of only transitory relevance, because they reflect vanishing or short-run circumstances, and those that are likely to remain valid or become increasingly relevant, because they reflect fundamental conditions or significant international developments.

II

On the most general grounds the conception of limited war surely remains relevant—indeed, imperative. On grounds of morality and expediency alike, it is essential that states—especially nuclear states—systematically endeavour to control and limit the use of force where force is unavoidable. The fact that American public officials and spokesmen now generally take this for granted, while little over a decade ago high government officials commonly asserted that once war occurs it has no limits save those determined by the capacity to gain a military victory, must be regarded as a major and, hopefully, lasting triumph of reason over viscera.

But little about the feasibility and utility of particular limitations in specific conflicts, whether with respect to deterring or fighting a war, can be deduced from the general rationale of limited war. Nor can feasibility and utility be deduced simply by applying the logic derived from abstract models of conflict, although these may sometimes aid rational calculation. Judgments about the feasibility and utility of particular methods of limitation must, of course, take account of objective technical and physical facts, but these facts do not speak for themselves in strategic terms. Such judgments must depend largely on disciplined intuitions, informed and qualified by experience, about the way states actually behave when they are faced with war or the threat of war.

Yet experience is likely to be an inconclusive and misleading guide. If the test of a particular strategy lies in the results of actual warfare, how can one be sure whether the outcome is due to the characteristics of that strategy, to the way it was carried out, or to factors unrelated to strategy? If the test is deterrence, how can one know whether either the occurrence or non-occurrence of the act that one intended to deter was due to the strategy or to other circumstances? At best, experience is a partial representation of the full range of circumstances that might affect the feasibility and utility of strategies of limited war. Nevertheless, because strategy has no self-contained logic like mathematics, experience of one kind or another has been and must be the primary shaper of strategy in thought and action.

It is significant, in this respect, that limited war thinking has been conditioned by the perspectives common to a particular phase of the cold war, when the cold war expanded to Asia and the Soviet Union achieved the capacity to inflict terrible damage on the United States in any nuclear exchange. Limited-war strategy first blossomed in response to the Korean war (although the implications of nuclear weapons had led Bernard Brodie, Sir Basil Liddell Hart, and a few others to adumbrate concepts of limited war before). It flourished, especially among those out of office, during the Eisenhower-Dulles Administration. The appeal of limited-war strategy in this period was basically two-fold: on the one hand, the desire to mitigate the danger of nuclear war; on the other hand, the desire to support the policy of containment more effectively. The underlying disposition in both respects was to bring force under control as a rational instrument of policy, but the motive for control has been a combination of fear and determination in different admixtures at different times and in different minds.

In the course of applying the concept of limited war to changing international circumstances, it has become apparent that these two objectives may lead to different policy conclusions, depending on whether one emphasizes effective containment or the avoidance of nuclear war. They may lead to different conclusions not only about particular strategies, which have been copiously examined and discussed, but also about two issues that have scarcely been discussed at all by proponents of limited war: (1) when or whether to intervene in a local war; and (2) the proper intensity and scale of intervention within existing restrictions.

But even more important than the two objectives of limitation in shaping views on these questions are certain premises about the international and domestic political environment which have been relatively neglected in limited-war thinking. These premises concern (1) the nature of the Communist threat and its bearing upon American security; (2) the willingness of the American government and people to sustain the costs of fighting aggression; and (3) the identity and behaviour of potential adversaries.

It is not difficult to understand why the issues of intervention and the premises about the objectives and the political environment of limited warfare have received far less attention than strategies of limited war. The explanation lies partly in the familiar limits to man's ability to foresee basic changes in his environment or to imagine how new events and conditions might affect his outlook. Strategies, on the other hand, are adaptations to foreign policy in the light of realities and trends that are perceived at the moment. They are frequently rationalizations of existing military capabilities and domestic constraints. Man's political imagination is constrained by what is familiar, but his strategic imagination is relatively free to draw its inferences and design its plans until some unforeseen war tests its propositions—and most strategic propositions fortunately remain untested in the nuclear age.

But the explanation for the relative neglect of political premises in strategic thought also lies in the propensity of American civilian strategists to propound their ideas, often with brilliant ingenuity, as revelations of an esoteric body of learning (which to some extent they were) that would rescue military thinking from conventional wisdom and put it on a rational basis. In this respect, however, the deference of the uninitiated, overawed by the secrets and rituals of the strategic priesthood, has been more important than the pretensions of the priests.

III

Limited-war thinking has been conditioned by a period in which the overriding objective of American policy was to contain international Communism by preventing or punishing external and internal aggression. According to the prevailing consensus, a local Communist aggression even in an intrinsically unimportant place could jeopardize American security by encouraging further aggressions in more important places, leading to a chain of aggressions that might eventually cause World War III. This view, fortified by the lessons of fascist aggression, did not, as critics contended, depend on the assumption that international Communism was under the monolithic control of the Soviet Union—an assumption that the proponents of the consensus qualified as soon as its critics—but it did depend on an assumption that amounted to the same thing in practice: that a successful aggression by one Communist state would enhance the power of the Soviet Union, China, and other Communist states *vis-à-vis* the United States and the free world. By this reasoning American security interests were extended from Western Europe to Korea and, by implication, to virtually anywhere aggression threatened.

Proponents of limited-war strategy sought to strengthen containment. They hoped to make deterrence more credible and to bolster allied will and nerve in crises, like the one arising over access to Berlin. They argued their case as strategic revisionists seeking to save American military policies from the thralldom of misguided budgetary restrictions imposed at the expense of security needs. Conscious of America's superior economic strength and military potential, they rejected the thesis of the Eisenhower-Dulles Administration that the United States would spend itself into bankruptcy if it prepared to fight local aggression locally at places and with weapons of the enemy's choosing.

With the advent of the Kennedy Administration the revisionists came into office. Responding to a dominant theme in Kennedy's campaign, they were determined to fill the military gaps in containment. The United States, according to this theme, was in danger of losing the cold war because the governmentment had not responded to new conditions—particularly to the rise of Soviet economic power and nuclear strength but also to the shift of Communist efforts to the Third World. The most dramatic evidence of America's threatened decline of power and prestige was the Soviet Union's prospect of gaining the lead in long-range missile striking power, but the missile gap was thought to be part of a wider threat encouraged by misguided American political and military policies that had allegedly alienated potential nationalist resistance to Communist subversion in the Third World and forfeited America's capacity to deter or resist local aggression. To safeguard American security and restore American prestige it would be necessary, among other measures (reinvigorating the domestic base of American power, adopting policies better suited to the aspirations of the underdeveloped countries, and ensuring America's strategic nuclear superiority) to build up the United States' capacity to fight limited wars without resorting to nuclear weapons. If the Communists could be contained at the level of strategic war and overt local aggression, the new administration reasoned, the Third World would be the most active arena of the cold war and guerrilla war would be the greatest military threat.

In office, the Kennedy Administration not only increased the United States' lead in long-range missile power; it also built up her capacity to intervene quickly with mobile forces against local aggression at great distances, and it emphasized a strategy of "controlled and flexible response." Identifying the most dangerous form of Communist expansionism as "wars of national liberation," it created special forces to help combat aggression by guerrillas and concerned itself intensively with methods of counter-insurgency.

By 1964, after the Cuban missile crisis and before large numbers of American forces got bogged down in Vietnam, the United States looked so powerful that not only some Americans but others too (particularly Frenchmen) began to think of the world as virtually monopolar and of America's position in the world as comparable to that of a global imperial power. The only remaining gap in military containment might be closed if the United States could demonstrate in Vietnam that wars of national liberation must fail. To achieve that demonstration was America's responsibility to world order as well as to its immediate interests. In this atmosphere of confidence and determination there was no inducement to question the premises about the wisdom and efficacy of intervention that underlay the prevailing American approach to limited war. The tendency was, rather, to complete the confirmation of a decade of limited-war thinking by proving the latest and most sophisticated conceptions in action.[3]

We shall return to the impact of the adversities of Vietnam on American conceptions of limited war, but first let us review the development of limited-war thinking that had taken place in the meantime.

IV

Apart from the fascination with counter-insurgency in the early 1960s, the great outpouring of strategic imagination in the United States was inspired by efforts to deter or fight hypothetical conflicts in Western Europe. But these conflicts, in contrast to wars in the Third World seemed less and less likely as *détente* set in. So in this area it was not the discipline of war that impinged upon strategic thought but rather the discipline of restrictions on defence expenditures and changes in the international political atmosphere. Moreover, in the absence of war, merely the passage of time caused a certain attrition of ambitious strategic ideas, as the inherent implausibility of limited war in Europe and the difficulty of gaining agreement on how to meet such unlikely contingencies dampened successive sparks of strategic innovation.

In Europe, as in the Third World, the dominant objective of limited-war strategy was, first, to enhance the credibility of deterrence; second, to strengthen conventional resistance to local non-nuclear aggression; and, no less important, to bolster the West's bargaining position in crises on the brink of war. These three objectives were integrally related. But the objective of effective resistance was far more difficult to achieve in Europe because of the greater physical and political obstacles to limitation and the greater strength of potential adversaries.

The effort to formulate a strategy that would combine effective resistance with reliable limitations reached its logical extreme in 1957 with the theories of limited tactical nuclear war propounded by Henry Kissinger, Admiral Sir Anthony Buzzard, and others. But these strategies soon died from indifference and incredulity. The difficulty of settling upon a convincing strategy for integrating tactical nuclear weapons into limited warfare in Europe evidently remains overwhelming, and the interest in doing so has declined as the credibility of the West using any kind of nuclear weapons first, except in circumstances warranting the risks of general war, has declined.

While the cold war was still relatively warm the search for a strategy of limited war in Europe enriched the post-war history of military strategy with ingenious ideas, some of which now seem strangely irrelevant. Strategies for fighting large-scale limited wars (endorsed by Alain Enthoven and, apparently, by McNamara in the early 1960s) were condemned to irrelevance by the unwillingness of an ally to support them with the necessary expenditures and manpower, by the unlikelihood that a war involving such powerful adversaries in such a vital area would remain limited, and by the fear of allied governments that emphasizing large-scale conventional resistance would undermine the efficacy of nuclear deterrence. That left strategies (1) to enforce short conventional pauses and raise the threshold between conventional and nuclear war (first publicized by General Norstad); (2) to combine static with mobile, and conventional with tactical nuclear resistance in limited wars resulting from accident and miscalculation (most notably formulated by F. O. Miksche and Malcolm Hoag); and (3) to control escalation as a bargaining process using non-nuclear and nuclear reprisals and demonstrations (chiefly identified with Herman Kahn and Thomas Schelling).

All of these latter three strategies were attempts to accommodate the logic of limited war to the realities of limited conventional means. They were also responses to perceived security needs in an international political environment in which it was assumed that the threat of Soviet-supported limited aggression was undiminished—and even rising, according to many who foresaw the Soviet achievement of virtual parity with the United States in the capacity to inflict unacceptable second-strike damage. But this assumption became much less compelling or was abandoned altogether with the onset of *détente,* although the conception of raising the threshold of conventional resistance continued to gain adherents and in 1967 was finally embodied in NATO's official strategic position. Consequently, although the logic of flexible and controlled response prevailed on paper and in strategic pronouncements, the means to withstand anything more than the most limited attack for longer than a week were not forthcoming. France's withdrawal from most arrangements for collective defence only made this predicament more conspicuous.

Only the French government rejected the objective of avoiding an automatic nuclear response to a local non-nuclear incursion; but for all governments the objective of deterrence increasingly overshadowed the objective of defence. Yet despite the declining concern with strategies of limited resistance, the allies were less worried than ever about their security. This was not because nuclear deterrence was more credible. Indeed, one might suppose that Secretary of Defense McNamara's open admission that the United States could not prevent the Soviet Union from devastating the United States even if the United States struck first, would have undermined confidence in America's will to use the ultimate deterrent to defend its European allies. The allies felt secure because even a low degree of credibility was regarded as sufficient for deterrence under the new political conditions of *détente*.

In this atmosphere there was a tendency of strategic thought to revert to the conceptions of the Eisenhower-Dulles period. Proponents of limited-war strategy now took comfort in pointing to the deterrent effect of the danger that any small conflict in Europe might escalate out of control. Considering the nature of Soviet intentions, the value of the stakes, and the integration of tactical nuclear weapons into American and Soviet forces, they were prepared to rely more on this danger and less on a credible capacity to fight a limited war effectively. It is symptomatic that this view found support from Bernard Brodie, an outstanding former champion of local conventional resistance in Europe, who now saw the official emphasis on stressing the conventional-nuclear "firebreak" and increasing conventional capabilities as unfeasible, unnecessary, and politically disadvantageous in America's relations with its allies.[4]

In one respect, the limited-war strategy of the Kennedy-McNamara Administration underwent a modification that was tantamount to official abandonment. The most far-reaching application of the idea of contrived reciprocal limitation of warfare was the counter-force or no-cities strategy, which was intended to make possible the option of a controlled and limited Soviet-American nuclear exchange by holding the American assured-destruction forces (that is, the forces capable of delivering unacceptable damage on a retaliatory strike) in reserve and inducing the Soviets reciprocally to confine nuclear strikes to military targets.[5] When McNamara first publicly announced this strategy at Ann Arbor in June 1962, critics charged that it was intended to enhance the credibility of extended deterrence. This inference was not unwarranted, since McNamara's statement did reflect his view at the time that a strategic deterrent, to be useful, had to be rational to use. In a few years, however, McNamara came to view the strategy as no more than an option for keeping as limited as possible a nuclear war that might result from accident or miscalculation, not as a means of deterring or fighting such a war more effectively. In subsequent statements McNamara explained the objective of a counter-force strategy as exclusively damage limitation. He also explained the difficulties of inducing the Soviets to fight a limited strategic war in such a way as to cast doubt upon its feasibility.[6] Finally, in successive annual reports on the nation's defence posture he indicated that cost-effectiveness considerations dictated a relatively increased allocation of money and resources to maintaining a capability for assured destruction, as compared to the objective of damage limitation.

Summing up the fortunes of limited-war strategy with respect to Europe and central war, we can say that the basic rationale of limited war seems firmly established in the United States and in allied countries, with the possible exception of France, and that this rationale is to some extent implemented in operational plans, military policies, and weapons. But the high-point of limited-war theory—in terms of the inventiveness, thoroughness, and energy with which it was carried out in strategic thought and actual policies—was roughly in the period from 1957 to 1963. Since then economic restrictions and diminished fear of Soviet military action, together with the inroads of time upon novel plans for hypothetical contingencies that never occur, have nullified some of the most ingenious strategies and eroded others, so that limited-war thinking is left somewhere between the initial Kennedy-McNamara views and the approach of the Eisenhower-Dulles administration.

In military affairs, as in international politics, one senses that an era has ended but finds little intimation of the era that will replace it. Meanwhile, strategic imagination seems to have reached a rather flat plateau surrounded by a bland atmosphere in which all military concerns tend to dissolve into the background.

V

This was the state of limited-war thinking in 1965 when American forces became the dominant element in fighting Communist forces in Vietnam. At that time the only really lively ideas were counter-insurgent warfare and controlled escalation.

Some regarded the war as a testing ground for strategies of counter-insurgency. When the United States began bombing selected targets in North Vietnam, ostensibly in retaliation for attacks on American units at Pleiku and elsewhere in the South, some regarded this as a test of theories of controlled escalation. When American forces in South Vietnam engaged regular units of the North Vietnamese army in large numbers, a host of new strategic-tactical issues arose, such as the issue, which was surely oversimplified by polemics, between search-and-destroy and seize-and-hold methods and the equally overdrawn issue between a mobile and an enclave strategy.

The war in Vietnam should have been a great boon to strategic innovation, since it fitted none of the existing models of limited war, although it contained elements of several. But the lessons derived from the strategies that were tried have been either negative or inconclusive, yet it is not apparent that alternative strategies would have worked any better. Some critics of the conduct (as opposed to the justification) of the war assert that different political or military strategies and tactics, executed more skillfully, might have enabled the United States to gain its political objectives—primarily, the security of an independent non-Communist government in South Vietnam—more readily. Others assert that those objectives were either unattainable because of the lack of a suitable political environment in South Vietnam or attainable only at an unacceptable cost, no matter what methods had been adopted.

If it is difficult to make confident judgments about the efficacy of various strategies and tactics in Vietnam, it is even more difficult to draw lessons applicable to other local wars in which the United States may become involved, since the war in Vietnam is almost surely unique in its salient characteristics: the large size and effectiveness of North Vietnam's combat forces, the organizing genius of Ho Chi Minh, the North's appeal to the South on nationalist grounds stemming from the post-war independence movement, and the weak and fragmented nature of South Vietnam. Yet lessons will, and probably must, be drawn. Many have already been offered before the war has ended.

The most general lessons concern the political and other conditions under which the United States should intervene in revolutionary or quasi-revolutionary wars, and the proper scale of intervention. It is asserted, for example, that the lesson of Vietnam is that no regime too weak to defend itself against revolution or subversion without American military intervention will be able to defend itself with American intervention.[7] This may turn out to be true in Vietnam, although it is too early to tell. But even so, can one conclude from this single, sad experience that no kind of American intervention under any circumstances, regardless of the nature of external support for revolutionary forces and the characteristics of the defending government and nation, could provide the necessary margin of assistance to enable a besieged regime to survive? No such categorical rule is warranted. And if it were, what would be its utility? The rule does not tell one how to determine whether a regime can defend itself, and it may be impossible to tell in time for American assistance to be useful.

Rejecting any such sweeping rules of abstention, Hanson Baldwin draws a no less sweeping lesson of intervention. Future interventions against insurgency, he says, must be undertaken "under carefully chosen conditions and at times and places of our own choosing," and they must avoid the sin of "gradualism" by applying overwhelming force (including tactical nuclear weapons, if necessary) at an early stage.[8] Walter Lippmann, on the other hand, sees the lesson of Vietnam in such negative terms as virtually to preclude successful intervention in wars of insurrection under any circumstances. Impressed by the unsuitability of such wars for American genius and power, he asserts that Vietnam simply demonstrates that elephants cannot kill swarms of mosquitoes.[9]

Given the general disaffection with the war, Lippmann's conclusion is likely to be more persuasive than Baldwin's. Indeed, although overstated, it contains an important kernel of truth. Once the United States becomes involved in any local war with its own troops, it will tend to use its modern military logistics, organization, and technology (short of nuclear weapons) to whatever extent is needed to achieve the desired political and military objectives, as long as its military operations are consistent with the localization of the war. For every military establishment fights with the capabilities best suited to its national resources, experience, and ethos. In practice, this means that American armed forces (and the large non-fighting contingents that accompany them), when engaged in a protracted revolutionary war on the scale of the Vietnamese war, tend to saturate and overwhelm the country they are defending. If the war were principally an American operation, as the long counter-insurgency war in Malaya was a British operation, the elephant might nevertheless prevail over the mosquitoes in time, even if it had to stamp out in the crudest way every infested spot and occupy the country. But the war in Vietnam, like every other local war in which the United States has or will become engaged, has been fought for the independence of the country under siege—in this case the country nominally represented by various South Vietnamese governments. Therefore, despite South Vietnam's great dependence on the United States, the United States is also dependent on South Vietnam. The chief trouble with this situation is that in some of the most crucial aspects of counter-insurgency South Vietnamese forces and officials have been ineffective and the United States could do nothing about it. Moreover, where American pressure on South Vietnam might have been useful the very scale of the United States' involvement has deprived it of leverage, since its direct involvement gave it a stake in the war that militated against the sanctions of reducing or withdrawing assistance.

In one respect Lippmann's metaphorical proposition may understate the difficulty the United States must encounter in trying to apply containment to a situation like the Vietnam conflict. If South Vietnam lacks the minimum requisites of a viable polity, then no amount of leverage or control could succeed in establishing the independence of a country, even if the organized insurrection and its external support were defeated. In this case, the incapacity of the elephant would be more profound than its inability to kill mosquitoes. In this case, when the adversary were defeated, the task of establishing an independent country would have just begun.

The lesson—although it is not universally applicable—seems to be that if a country cannot defend itself from insurrection with assistance short of American regular forces, the United States can probably defend it only at a level of involvement that will contravene its objective of securing the sovereignty of that country; so that even if the United States should defeat the insurgents, it will be burdened with an unviable protectorate. To oversimplify the proposition: either the United States, under these internal circumstances, must virtually take over the country and run the war itself at the risk of acquiring a troublesome dependent, or it must keep its role limited at least to guerrilla operations and probably to technical and staff assistance at the risk of letting the besieged country fall.

Hanson Baldwin is probably right in thinking that an early massive intervention can, in some circumstances, achieve a limited objective more effectively than a sustained war of gradually increasing scale, but following this generality as a rule of action would entail great risks of over-involvement in quasi-revolutionary wars. Consequently, to condition American support of a besieged country on its ability to survive at a low threshold of direct American involvement seems like the more prudent strategy. This proposition, however, like others concerning the conduct of local wars, implicitly contains a consideration more basic than strategy and tactics: how important are the interests for which the United States may intervene? For if they are truly vital, a high-risk strategy is justified, and even under the most unpromising conditions intervention may be imperative.

America's intervention in Vietnam has suffered from ambiguity on this question of interests. South Vietnam was evidently not considered important enough to justify the costs and risks of a scale of intervention that, if undertaken early enough, might (or might not) have led to a more successful outcome. Indeed, probably no American leader would have considered the eventual scale of war worth the costs if he had known the costs in advance. The reason the United States got so heavily involved in Vietnam lies, not in its estimate of South Vietnam's importance to American vital interests, but in the United States' inability to limit an expanding involvement after it had drifted beyond a certain scale of intervention. Hence, the United States found itself fighting a small version of World War II without undertaking a commensurate mobilization of its resources and manpower—or of its moral energy. In this sense, the scale and costs of the war were greater than the nation was prepared to sustain.

If the larger lessons of Vietnam concerning the efficacy and scale of intervention are ambiguous, the validity and utility of subordinate lessons concerning the strategy of limited warfare are no less inconclusive. Perhaps the strategy that has come closest to a clear-cut failure is controlled escalation, as applied by means of selective bombing in North Vietnam. But even in this case it would be misleading to generalize about the efficacy of the same methods under other conditions. Controlled escalation is a strategy developed principally to apply to direct or indirect confrontations between the United States and the Soviet Union.[10] It envisages influencing the adversary's will to fight and his willingness to settle a conflict by means of a process of "bargaining" during a "competition in risk-taking" on ascending—and, hopefully, on the lower—levels of violence, which would culminate in a mutually unacceptable nuclear war at the top of the escalation "ladder." In the spring of 1965 the American government, frustrated and provoked by Hanoi's incursions in the South and anxious to strike back with its preferred weapons, put into effect a version of controlled escalation, borrowing language and style from the latest thinking on the subject.[11] Through highly selective and gradually intensified bombing of targets on lists authorized by the President—incidentally, a notable application of one of the tenets of limited-war theory: strict political control of military operations—the United States hoped to convince Hanoi that it would have to pay an increasing price for aggression in the South. By the graduated application of violence, the government hoped through tacit "signalling" and "bargaining" to bring Hanoi to reasonable terms. But Hanoi, alas, did not play the game.

Perhaps the experiment was not a true test of escalation, since the punitive purpose of the bombing was ambiguous. Indeed, in deference to public protests throughout the world, the United States explicitly stressed the purely military nature of the targets as though to deny their bargaining function. Perhaps the escalation was not undertaken soon enough or in large enough increments, thereby sparing the North Vietnamese a decisive dose of punishment and enabling them to make material and tactical adjustments. But it seems more likely that the failure of controlled escalation lay in inherent deficiencies of bombing as a punitive device. In any case, there are special difficulties in applying to an underdeveloped country a strategy that presupposes a set of values and calculations found only in the most advanced countries. Yet even in an underdeveloped country there must be some level of bombing damage that would bend the government's will to fight. Perhaps controlled escalation exerts the desired political effect only when there is a convincing prospect of nuclear war at the top of the ladder. Or perhaps it works only against a country fighting for limited objectives. Hanoi had unlimited ends in the South, but the United States had quite limited ends in the North. Whatever the explanation, controlled escalation failed to achieve its intended political effect; and that should be sobering to its enthusiasts, if any remain. Nonetheless, the experience does not prove much about the efficacy of a different strategy of escalation against a different adversary in different circumstances.

Nor does the war carry any clear lesson about the wisdom of granting or denying impunity from attack to a country supporting insurrection in an adjacent country. Critics contend that carrying the war to the north violated one of the few clear-cut rules of the game on which limitation might be reliably based, alienated world and domestic opinion, fortified North Vietnam's determination to fight for an unconditional victory, and distracted attention from the real war—the civil war—in the south, without substantially affecting that war. But advocates of carrying the war to the North argue that the attrition against North Vietnamese units and logistics was significant and might have been decisive but for self-imposed restrictions that were unnecessarily confining, that these operations were necessary to South Vietnamese morale and provided a valuable bargaining counter for mutual de-escalation, and that the denial of sanctuary is a valuable precedent for avoiding disadvantageous rules of the game in the future and may be a useful deterrent against other states who may contemplate waging wars against their neighbours. Moreover, it can be argued that when a local war cannot be won at a tolerable cost within the country under attack, the only reasonable alternative to a dishonourable withdrawal is to engage the source of external support directly, and charge it with a greater share of the costs, in order to secure a satisfactory diplomatic termination of hostilities.

Both the Korean and the Vietnamese wars indicate that the particular restrictions on military operations will be determined by such a variety of conditions and considerations that it is almost fruitless to try to anticipate them in advance. In some conceivable future circumstances, one can even imagine a sensible case being made for crossing the threshold that bars the United States from using tactical nuclear weapons. It is unlikely, however, that the prevailing reaction to Vietnam will be in the direction that Hanson Baldwin advocates when he condemns the constraints of gradualism and the "cult" of self-imposed limitations. For Vietnam does at least indicate that the United States will go a long and frustrating way to observe significant self-imposed restrictions on a war, rather than insist on obtaining a military victory by all means available.[12] It indicates that even when the nation is "locked in" to an unpromising local war with its own troops, it will prefer to follow the rule of proportionate response to enemy initiatives rather than incur the immediate risks of massive escalation.

It is significant how weak and ineffectual American all-or-nothing sentiment has been in the Vietnamese as compared to the Korean war. The idea of the United States confining itself to a limited war, which was novel and antithetical in Korea, has been widely taken for granted in Vietnam. Indeed, the most influential American critics have urged more, not less, stringent restrictions on combat despite the fact that the danger of nuclear war or of Chinese or Russian intervention never seemed nearly as great as in Korea.[13] Those (including some prominent conservative Senators and Congressmen) who took the position that the United States ought either to escalate the war drastically in order to win it or else disengage, clearly preferred the latter course. But their frustration did not manifest a general rejection of the conception of limited war but only opposition to the particular way of applying that conception in Vietnam.

Thus the popular disaffection with the Vietnamese war does not indicate a reversion to pre-Korean attitudes toward limited war. Rather, it indicates serious questioning of the premises about the utility of limited war as an instrument of American policy, the premises that originally moved the proponents of limited-war strategy and that underlay the original confidence of the Kennedy Administration in America's power to cope with local Communist incursions of all kinds. In Vietnam the deliberate limitation of war has been accepted by Americans simply from the standpoint of keeping the war from expanding, or from the standpoint of de-escalating it, whereas in Korea the desire to keep the war limited had to contend with a strong sentiment to win it for the sake of containment. In Korea the principal motive for limitation was the fear that an expanding war might lead to general war with China or nuclear war with the Soviet Union, but in Vietnam the limits were motivated as much by the sense that the political objective was not sufficiently promising to warrant the costs of expansion. This change of emphasis reflects more than the unpopularity of the war in Vietnam. It also reflects the domestication, as it were, of limited war—that is, of the deliberate, calculated restriction of the ends and means of fighting—as an operational concept in American foreign policy.

Some of the reasons for the strength of sentiment for keeping the war limited, however, bear upon the political question of whether to intervene in local wars at all. They suggest that the specific lessons about the strategy and constraints of limited war that one might derive from Vietnam are likely to be less important than the war's impact on the political premises that underlay American intervention.

VI

The political premises that Vietnam has called into question are more profound, yet more limited, and at the same time less explicit than the sentiment embodied in the popular refrain "no more Vietnams." If Vietnam exerts a fundamental impact on American policy with respect to limited-war interventions, it will not be merely because of the national determination to avoid future Vietnams and to restrict American commitments to a scope more compatible with American power and the will to use it. The whole history of the expansion of American commitments and involvements is pervaded with the longing to avoid new commitments and involvements. Yet a succession of unanticipated crises and wars has led the nation to contravene that longing. Sometimes the desire to avoid the repetition of unpleasant involvements had only led to a further extension of commitments, which in turn has led to further involvements. That is what happened when the Eisenhower-Dulles Administration formed deterrent alliances (including SEATO) to avoid another Korean War.

The reason for this contradiction is not really a sublimated national longing for power—at least not power for its own sake—but rather the nation's persistent pursuit of a policy of containment, which under the prevailing international conditions has repeatedly confronted it with predicaments in which the least objectionable course has seemed to be the exercise and extension, rather than the abstention or retraction, of American power. If a fundamental change in America's use of limited-war strategy as an instrument of policy takes place, it will be because the premises of containment are no longer convincing to the nation and Vietnam has acted as the catalyst to enforce this realization.

In effect, the United States has equated Communist aggression with a threat to American security. Although the relationship of Communist aggression in Asia or Africa to American security is quite indirect and increasingly far-fetched, this equation was plausible enough if one assumed—as Americans generally did assume until after the Korean War and the Sino-Soviet split in the late 1950s—that the cold war was essentially a zero-sum contest between the two super-powers and that a successful aggression by any small Communist state would shift the world balance of power towards the Communist bloc. Moreover, there was no need to question this view of American security as long as American efforts to counter aggression were successful at a tolerable cost.

But *détente* with the Soviet Union and the increasing divergencies of interest among Communist states and parties are changing the American view of international reality, and of the nature and intensity of the Communist threat in particular. Thus, a gain for China or even North Vietnam is not automatically seen as a gain for the Soviet Union or a loss for the United States, and opportunities for limited co-operation with the Soviet Union occasionally appear attractive. Moreover, the accentuation of national and subnational particularism outside the Communist world may have diminished what capacity the Soviet Union or China ever had to extend their control and influence through diplomacy, subversion, or revolution. In Africa, most notably, Americans are becoming accustomed to a great deal of disorder and Communist meddling without jumping to the conclusion that the balance of power or American security is jeopardized. To some extent China emerges as a new object of containment; but despite the long strand of American obsession with China, the Chinese do not yet—and may never—have the strength to pose the kind of threat to Asia that the Soviet Union could have posed to Western Europe, and Asia is simply not valued as highly on the United States' scale of interests as Western Europe.

American involvement in the Vietnamese war began on a limited scale at a time of national self-confidence and self-assertion in the Third World. The United States applied forceful containment there according to familiar premises about America's general interest in stopping Communist aggression without questioning the precise relevance of the war to the balance of power and American security.[14] The scope of American involvement grew in an effort to defeat North Vietnam's "war of national liberation" and to establish a secure non-Communist government in the South. But during this period the familiar American image of the Communist world and its threat to American security was changing. Furthermore, in contrast to the Korean war, the Vietnamese war never seemed to pose a threat to the security of Western Europe or Japan.

Nonetheless, if American objectives could have been achieved with no greater pain and effort than the Korean war, which was also unpopular but not beyond being resolved on satisfactory terms, the nation might have accepted the Vietnamese war as another vindication of containment—troublesome and frustrating but not so costly or unsuccessful as to call into question the premises of American intervention. In reality, however, the war became so costly and unpromising that, given its remote relationship to American security, Americans began to doubt the validity of the premises on which the government intervened. So, whereas the "never-again" reaction against the Korean war fostered the effort of the Eisenhower-Dulles Administration to apply containment more effectively to Asia at less cost by strengthening deterrence, the "no-more-Vietnams" spirit seems to challenge the necessity, if not the basic rationale, of strengthening military containment in any way that would increase American commitments.

At the least, these doubts seem likely to lead to a marked differentiation of interests in the application of containment—a downgrading of interests in the Third World and a greater distinction between these interests, and those pertaining to the security of the advanced democratic countries. Possibly, they will lead to abandonment of containment in Asia altogether, in so far as containment requires armed intervention against local aggression on the mainland. More likely, they will simply lead to a sharper distinction in practice between supporting present security commitments and not forming new ones, and between supporting present commitments with American armed forces when aggression is overt, and abstaining from armed intervention in largely internal conflicts. What they seem to preclude, at least for a while, is any renewed effort to strengthen military deterrence and resistance in the Third World by actively developing and projecting United States' capacity to fight local wars.

VII

On the other hand, it is misleading to reach conclusions about future American limited-war policies and actions on the basis of the nation's desire to avoid quasi-revolutionary wars like the one in South Vietnam, since the threat of local wars impinging on American interests could arise in many different forms. Thus, while the war in Vietnam seems to be waning and the prospect of similar national liberation wars in Asia is uncertain, the capacity and perhaps the incentive of the Soviet Union to support local wars that might spring from quite different circumstances is increasing. The Soviet will to exploit this capacity will depend, in part, on the American position. If Soviet leaders were to gain the impression that the United States is firmly set upon a course of neo-isolationism and the absolute avoidance of intervention in local wars, they might become dangerously adventurous in the Middle East and elsewhere. The United States would almost surely regard Soviet exploitation of local conflicts more seriously, than it would regard another war like Vietnam. So one of the military-political issues facing the United States in the late 1960s is how to respond to the growing capacity of Soviet mobile overseas forces.

Current trends seem destined to provide the Soviet Union with a significantly enlarged capacity to intervene in local conflicts overseas, a capacity of which the United States has heretofore enjoyed a virtual monopoly.[15] The buildup of Soviet naval, amphibious, air, and land forces in this direction has been accompanied by a substantial expansion of Soviet arms deliveries and technical assistance to Middle Eastern countries, as well as to North Vietnam, and the acquisition of technical facilities (although not permanent bases) in several Mediterranean ports. The experience of observing America's large-scale support of South Vietnam and providing North Vietnam with weapons and logistics support has given Soviet leaders a new appreciation of overseas local-war forces. At the same time, Soviet strategic doctrine has assigned a greater role to supporting Soviet interests overseas, both on the sea and in local wars on land.

These developments do not portend a mobile overseas capacity that can compete with America's capacity in an armed conflict, but they do provide Soviet leaders with new options for intervening in local wars. They provide new levers

of influence in the Middle East and elsewhere. And they impose new constraints on American intervention. The greatest danger they pose is that the
super-powers will unintentionally become involved in competitive interventions in local conflicts, where they lack control, and where the *modus operandi*
of avoiding a direct clash has not been established.[16]

VIII

The history of limited-war thought and practice in the last decade or so provides little basis for confidently generalizing about the feasibility, and utility
of particular strategies. Many strategies have never really been put to the test;
and where they have been tested, either in deterrence or war, the results
have been inconclusive. Moreover, strategies are very much the product
of particular circumstances—not only of technological developments, but also
of domestic and international political developments. This political environment is always changing. Developments that have made some strategies
seem obsolete—for example, the impact of *détente,* domestic constraints, and
the balance of payments on strategies of conventional resistance in Europe—
might change in such a way as to revive abandoned strategies or evoke new
ones. The limited-war strategies appropriate to the international environment
of the 1970s—especially if there should be a significant increase in the number
and severity of local wars, a more active Soviet policy of intervention in local
wars, a more aggressive Chinese military posture, or new nuclear powers—
might contain some interesting variations on strategic notions that were born
in past periods of intense concern with military security. Changes in military
technology, such as forthcoming increases in long-range air- and sea-lift capabilities, will also affect the strategies and political uses of limited-war capabilities.[17]

Yet one has the feeling, which may not spring entirely from a lack of imagination, that in the nature of international conflict and technology in the latter
half of the twentieth century there are only a limited number of basic strategic
ideas pertaining to limited war, and that we have seen most of these emerge
in the remarkable strategic renaissance of the past decade or so. These ideas
can be combined in countless permutations and combinations and implemented
by a great variety of means, but we shall still recognize trip wires, pauses, reprisals, denials, thresholds, sanctuaries, bargaining, demonstrations, escalation,
Mao's three stages, enclaves, seize-and-hold, search-and-destroy, and all the rest.

What we are almost certain not to witness is the perfection of limited-war
conceptions and practice in accordance with some predictable, rational calculus
and reliable, universal rules of the game. The conditions and modalities of international conflict are too varied, dynamic, and subjective for limited war to
be that determinate. Any search for the strategic equivalent of economic man
on the basis of which a grand theory of military behaviour might be erected is
bound to be ephemeral and unproductive. On the other hand, I think it is
equally clear that military conceptions and practices among the advanced states
are not going to revert to romantic styles of the past that glorified the offensive

spirit, war *à l'outrance,* the national will to victory, and overwhelming the enemy. If counterparts of the stylized limited warfare of the eighteenth century are unrealistic, counterparts of the total wars of the following centuries would be catastrophic.

The nuclear age has not made armed conflict obsolete, nor has it excluded the possibility of catastrophic war. It has, however, inculcated a novel respect for the deliberate control and limitation of warfare. That respect is a more significant and enduring achievement of limited-war strategists than any of their strategies.

NOTES

1. One symptom of the increased acceptance of the concept of limited war is the increased ambiguity of the term, since the concept of controlling war within rational limits relevant to specific political objectives has come to be applied to *any* kind of war, even one involving a nuclear exchange. A limited war is generally conceived to be a war fought for ends far short of the complete subordination of one state's will to another's and by means involving far less than the total military resources of the belligerents, leaving the civilian life and the armed forces of the belligerents largely intact and leading to a bargained termination. Although a war between nuclear states might conform to this definition, the term limited war is generally applied to relatively more likely local non-nuclear wars in which the interests and deliberately restricted means of the super-powers are involved on opposite sides, if only indirectly. The term local war is now often reserved for the great number of local conventional wars in which neither of the super-powers is directly or indirectly involved. The difficulty of defining limited war arises partly because the relevant limits are matters of degree and partly because they are a matter of perspective, since a war that is limited for one side might be virtually total from the standpoint of the other, on whose territory the war is fought. Furthermore, a limited war may be carefully restricted in some respects (e.g., geographically) and much less in others (e.g., in weapons, targets, or political objectives).

2. For a useful list and classification of armed "conflicts," see David Wood, *Conflict in the Twentieth Century,* Adelphi Paper No. 48 (Institute for Strategic Studies).

3. Beyond proving the efficacy of any particular strategy, a successful war in Vietnam would demonstrate America's psychological and political capacity to cope with limited war. As Secretary McNamara put it, "If you read Toynbee, you realize the importance of a democracy learning to cope with a limited war. The greatest contribution Vietnam is making—right or wrong is beside the point—is that it is developing in the United States an ability to fight a limited war, to go to war without the necessity of arousing the public ire. In that sense, Vietnam is almost a necessity in our history, because this is the kind of war we'll most likely be facing for the next fifty years." Quoted by Douglas Kiker, "The Education of Robert McNamara," *Atlantic Monthly,* March 1967, p. 53.

4. See Bernard Brodie, *Escalation and the Nuclear Option* (Princeton: Princeton University Press, 1966). Brodie's differences with the official position (which, incidentally, he exaggerated in attributing to it the objective of resisting conventionally a large-scale Soviet aggression) were no less significant for being differences of degree. For they were intended as an antidote to a strategic tendency, just as his earlier advocacy of preparedness for limited conventional defence was intended as an antidote to the Eisenhower-Dulles emphasis on nuclear deterrence in Europe. See, for example, *Strategy in the Missile Age* (Princeton: Princeton University Press, 1959), pp. 335ff.

5. An even more radical, but not necessarily less plausible, strategy for limited strategic nuclear war, based on striking cities selectively rather than sparing them had already attracted some academic attention. Klaus Knorr and Thornton Read, eds., *Limited Strategic War* (New York: Praeger, 1962).

6. On the one hand, he explained, the Soviet Union would be unlikely to withhold its counter-city capability as long as its missiles were relatively scarce and vulnerable; but on the other hand, he acknowledged that as Soviet missiles became more numerous and less vulnerable, the prospects of confining retaliatory damage from them would vanish com-

pletely. In any event, in each annual "posture statement" he stated in progressively more categorical terms that there was no way the United States could win a strategic nuclear war at a tolerable cost.

7. Former Ambassador Edwin O. Reischauer reaches the following "simple rule of thumb" on the basis of the Vietnam experience: "Any regime that is not strong enough to defend itself against its internal enemies probably could not be defended by us either and may not be worth defending anyway." See *Beyond Vietnam: The United States and Asia* (New York: Alfred A. Knopf, 1967), p. 188.

8. "After Vietnam—What Military Strategy in the Far East?", *New York Times Magazine,* 9 June 1968.

9. "Elephants Can't Beat Mosquitoes in Vietnam," *Washington Post,* 3 December 1967.

10. The concept and strategy of controlled escalation are set forth most fully in Herman Kahn, *On Escalation* (New York: Praeger, 1967), and Thomas C. Schelling, *Arms and Influence* (New Haven: Yale University Press, 1966), although both authors developed the idea in earlier writings. Needless to say, neither author believes that controlled escalation was properly applied in Vietnam.

11. Punitive bargaining, however, was only one of the objectives of the bombing. Two other principal objectives were to raise the morale of South Vietnamese and to impede the infiltration of men and supplies to the South. See General Maxwell D. Taylor, *Responsibility and Response* (New York: Harper and Row, 1967), pp. 26–28; Thomas C. Schelling, *Arms and Influence* (New Haven: Yale University Press, 1966), pp. 170ff.; and Tom Wicker, "The Wrong Rubicon," *Atlantic Monthly,* May 1968, pp. 81ff.

12. One indication of the magnitude of self-imposed restrictions is the number and kinds of military actions that the United States refrained from taking that it might have taken to defeat Communist forces. In Vietnam as in Korea a major restriction was on the number of armed forces mobilized and deployed. In both wars the United States reached an upper limit on these forces—higher in Vietnam than in Korea—beyond which it would not go even if it meant ending the war on less advantageous terms. Perhaps the most obvious restrictions—such as not bombing civilian targets and not invading the enemy's homeland—were in North Vietnam. Correspondingly, the most obvious limitations of political objectives have applied to North, not to South, Vietnam. Of North Vietnam the American government has asked, essentially, only that it stop supporting the war in the South materially and with its regular units. But in the South, too, the American government has become willing to settle for something considerably less than a total victory without arousing popular protest in the nation.

13. It should be noted, however, that one of the reasons that the danger of nuclear war did not seem so great was that the United States refrained from taking actions, like bombing Haiphong, which seemed to carry too great a risk of Chinese or Soviet intervention compared to their military or political value.

14. One indication of the generalized and unquestioned anti-Communist purpose of America's intervention is that, according to Bill Moyers, President Johnson's special assistant and White House Press Secretary, the containment of China was rarely discussed even as late as the deliberations about the escalation decisions of 1965. Rather, these decisions were taken simply to prevent a communist (that is, Viet Cong) victory. See, "Bill Moyers Talks About LBJ, Power, Poverty, War and the Young," *Atlantic Monthly,* July, 1968, pp. 30–31.

15. Thomas W. Wolfe, "The Projection of Soviet Power," *Survival,* May 1968, pp. 159–65 (reprinted from *Interplay,* March 1968); Curt Gasteyger, "Moscow and the Mediterranean," *Foreign Affairs,* July 1968, pp. 676–87; Claire Sterling, "The Soviet Fleet in the Mediterranean," *Reporter,* 14 December 1967, pp. 14–18. Since the Cuban missile crisis the Russians have made new investments in large long-range air transports and have built up the naval, infantry and amphibious forces, enlarged the merchant marine (including ships configured for military cargo) to put the Soviet Union among the two or three leading maritime powers, and established a greatly augmented naval presence in the Mediterranean, including two helicopter carriers for support of landing operations or antisubmarine warfare. There are no signs, however, that the Soviet government intends to create what the United States regards as a balanced naval force capable of coping with American naval forces.

16. Gasteyger, *op. cit.,* p. 687.

17. In particular, the C-5A air transports, now coming into operation, and fast-deployment logistics ships, not yet appropriated, will greatly increase the amount of troops, equipment, and supplies that can be lifted from the United States overseas in a short time. Such improvements in air- and sea-lift will provide increased capabilities and flexibility in supporting many different kinds of military tasks in remote places at all levels of conflict, and in varied physical and political conditions. By reducing or eliminating the need for a standing American presence overseas they will enable the United States to be more selective in establishing and maintaining bases and commitments. See Robert E. Osgood, *Alliances and American Foreign Policy* (Baltimore: Johns Hopkins Press, 1968), pp. 137–43.

THE MILITARY-INDUSTRIAL COMPLEX

32.

Marc Pilisuk and Tom Hayden: Is There a Military-Industrial Complex That Prevents Peace?

The huge military establishment that has developed in the past two decades has links with industrial, academic, Congressional, and other sectors of American society. In discussing the concept of a military-industrial complex and theories of political power in the United States, Marc Pilisuk and Tom Hayden dissent in part from both the power-elite and the pluralist viewpoints. In contrast to the argument of C. Wright Mills concerning a narrow elite and the argument of Arnold Rose, whose "position is not simply that power is pluralistic in American society, but that the society itself is pluralistic," Pilisuk and Hayden do not maintain "that American society contains a ruling military-industrial complex. Our concept is more nearly that American society *is* a military-industrial complex."

Marc Pilisuk is Professor in Residence in the School of Social Welfare, University of California, Berkeley, and Tom Hayden is on the staff of Liberation Magazine.

The notion of a military-industrial complex as a potent force or even indeed a ruling elite is not new in American history. From FDR who attacked the "merchants of destruction" and campaigned in 1932 to "take the profits out of war" to a more restrained warning by Eisenhower against the "unwarranted" power of the military-industrial complex, American politics and scholarship have often entertained such a concept. Many scholars, however, have rejected the "power elite" concept implicit in the charge of a military-industrial complex capable of dominating the entire American scene. Implicit in the writings of

Marc Pilisuk and Tom Hayden, "Is There a Military-Industrial Complex That Prevents Peace?" in Robert Perrucci and Marc Pilisuk, eds., *Triple Revolution Emerging: Social Problems in Depth,* Little, Brown, 1971, pp. 73–86, 89. Footnotes and bibliography omitted. (The article also appears in Marc Pilisuk, *International Conflict and Social Policy,* Prentice-Hall, 1972.) Reprinted by permission of Marc Pilisuk.

such pluralist writers as Daniel Bell, Robert Dahl, and Talcott Parsons is the basis for a denial that it is a military-industrial complex that prevents peace. The argument is:

1. It is held that the *scope* of decisions made by any interest group is quite narrow and cannot be said to govern anything so broad as foreign policy.
2. It is held that the "complex" is *not monolithic, not self-conscious,* and *not co-ordinated,* the presumed attributes of a ruling elite.
3. It is held that the military-industrial complex does not wield power if the term "power" is defined as the ability to realize its will even against the resistance of others and regardless of external conditions.

Since the arguments of the pluralists have been directed largely to the work of C. Wright Mills, it is with Mills that we will begin to analyze the theories which claim there *is* a military-industrial complex blocking peace.

The Thesis of Elite Control

Mills is by far the most formidable exponent of the theory of a power elite. In his view, the period in America since World War II has been dominated by the ascendance of corporation and military elites to positions of institutional power. These "commanding heights" allow them to exercise control over the trends of the business cycle and international relations. The cold war set the conditions that legitimize this ascendance, and the decline and incorporation of significant left-liberal movements, such as the CIO, symbolizes the end of opposition forces. The power elite monopolizes sovereignty, in that political initiative and control stem mainly from the top hierarchical levels of position and influence. Through the communications system the elite facilitates the growth of a politically indifferent mass society below the powerful institutions. This, according to the Mills argument, would explain why an observer finds widespread apathy. Only a small minority believes in actual participation in the larger decisions that affect their existence and only the ritual forms of "popular democracy" are practiced by the vast majority. Mills' argument addresses itself to the terms of the three basic issues we have designated, i.e., scope of decision power, awareness of common interest, and the definition of power exerted.

By *scope,* we are referring to the sphere of society over which an elite is presumed to exercise power. Mills argues that the scope of this elite is general, embracing all the decisions which in any way could be called vital (slump and boom, peace and war, etc.). He does not argue that *each* decision is directly determined, but rather that the political alternatives from which the "deciders" choose are shaped and limited by the elite through its possession of all the large-scale institutions. By this kind of argument, Mills avoids the need to demonstrate how his elite is at work during each decision. He speaks instead in terms of institutions and resources. But the problem is that his basic evidence is of a rather negative kind. No major decisions have been made for twenty years contrary to the policies of anti-communism and corporate or military aggrandizement; *therefore* a power elite must be prevailing. Mills might have improved his claims about the scope of elite decisions by analyzing a series of actual decisions in terms of the premises that were *not* debated. This could point to the mechanisms (implicit or explicit) that led to the exclusion of these premises from debate. By this and other means he might have found more satisfying evidence of the common, though perhaps tacit, presuppositions of seemingly disparate institutions. He then might have developed a framework analyzing "scope" on different levels. The scope of the Joint Chiefs of Staff, for instance, could be seen as limited, while at the same time the Joint Chiefs could be placed in a larger elite context having larger scope. Whether this could be shown awaits research of this kind. Until it is done, however, Mills' theory of scope remains open to attack, but, conversely, is not subject to refutation.

Mills' theory also eludes the traditional requirements for inferring monolithic structure, i.e., consciousness of elite status, and coordination. The modern tradition of viewing elites in this way began with Mosca's *The Ruling Class* in a period when family units and inheritance systems were the basic means of conferring power. Mills departs from this influential tradition precisely because of his emphasis on institutions as the basic elements. If the military, political, and economic institutional orders involve a high coincidence of interest, then the groups composing the institutional orders need not be monolithic, conscious, and coordinated, yet still they can exercise elite power. This means specifically that a military-industrial complex could exist as an expression of a certain fixed ideology (reflecting common institutional needs), yet be "composed" of an endless shuffle of specific groups. For instance, our tables show 82 companies have dropped out of the list of 100 top defense contractors and only 36 "durables" remained on the list from 1940 to 1960. In terms of industry, the percentage of contracts going to the automotive industry dropped from 25 percent in World War II to 4 percent in the missile age. At the same time, the aircraft companies went from 34 to 54 percent of all contracts, and the electronics industry from 9 to 28 percent. Mills' most central argument is that this ebb and flow is not necessarily evidence for the pluralists. His stress is on the unities which underlie the procession of competition and change. The decision to change the technology of warfare was one that enabled one group to "overcome" another in an overall system to which both are fundamentally committed. Moreover, the decision issued from the laboratories and planning boards of the defense establishment and only superficially involved any role for public opinion. The case studies of weapons development by Peck and Scherer, in which politics is described as a marginal ritual, would certainly buttress Mills' point of view.

Making this institution analysis enables Mills to make interesting comments on his human actors. The integration of institutions means that hundreds of individuals become familiar with several roles: general, politician, lobbyist, defense contractor. These men are the power elite, but they need not know it. They conspire, but conspiracy is not absolutely essential to their maintenance. They mix together easily, but can remain in power even if they are mostly anonymous to each other. They make decisions, big and small, sometimes with the knowledge of others and sometimes not, which ultimately control all the significant action and resources of society.

Where this approach tends to fall short is in its unclarity about how discontinuities arise. Is the military-industrial complex a feature of American society which can disappear and still leave the general social structure intact? Horst Brand has suggested a tension between financial companies and the defense industries because of the relatively few investment markets created by defense. Others have challenged the traditional view that defense spending stimulates high demand and employment. Their claim is that the concentration of contracts in a few states, the monopolization of defense and space industry by the largest 75 or 100 corporations, the low multiplier effect of the new weapons, the declining numbers of blue-collar workers required, and other factors, make the defense economy more of a drag than a stimulant. Certainly the rising unemployment of 1970 in the midst of expansion of the ABM system and extension of the Vietnam war to Laos and Cambodia show the flaws of relying upon defense spending for an economic stimulant. Mills died before these trends became the subject of debate, but he might have pioneered in discussion of them if his analytic categories had differentiated more finely between various industries and interest groups in his power elite. His emphasis was almost entirely on the "need" for a "permanent war economy" just when that need was being questioned even among his elite.

This failure, however, does not necessarily undermine the rest of Mills' analysis. His institutional analysis is still the best means of identifying a complex without calling it monolithic, conscious, and coordinated. Had he differentiated more exactly, he might have been able to describe various degrees of commitments to an arms race, a rightist ideology constricting the arena of meaningful debate, and other characteristics of a complex. This task remains to be done, and will be discussed at a later point.

Where Mills' theory is most awkward is in his assertions that the elite can, and does, make its decisions against the will of others and regardless of external conditions. This way of looking at power is inherited by Mills, and much of modern sociology, directly from Max Weber. What is attributed to the elite is a rather fantastic quality: literal omnipotence. Conversely, any group that is *not* able to realize its will even against the resistance of others is only "influential" but not an elite. Mills attempts to defend this viewpoint but, in essence, modifies it. He says he is describing a tendency, not a finalized state of affairs. This is a helpful device in explaining cracks in the monolith—for instance, the inability of the elite to establish a full corporate state against the will of small businessmen. However, it does not change the ultimate argument —that the power elite cannot become more than a tendency, cannot realize its actual self, unless it takes on the quality of omnipotence.

When power is defined as this kind of dominance, it is easily open to critical dispute. The conception of power depicts a vital and complex social system as essentially static, as having within it a set of stable governing components, with precharted interests which infiltrate and control every outpost of decision-authority. Thereby, internal accommodation is made necessary and significant change, aside from growth, becomes impossible. This conception goes beyond the idea of social or economic determinism. In fact, it defines a "closed social system." A "closed system" may be a dramatic image, but it is a forced one as well. Its defender sees events such as the rise of the labor movement essentially as a means of rationalizing modern capitalism. But true or false as this may be, did not the labor movement also constitute a "collective will" which the elite could not resist? An accommodation was reached, probably more on the side of capital than labor, but the very term "accommodation" implies the existence of more than one independent will. On a world scale, this becomes even more obvious. Certainly the rise of communism has not been through the will of capitalists, and Mills would be the first to agree. Nor does the elite fully control technological development; surely the process of invention has some independent, even if minor, place in the process of social change.

Mills' definition of power as dominance ironically serves the pluralist argument, rather than countering it. When power is defined so extremely, it becomes rather easy to claim that such power is curbed in the contemporary United States. The pluralists can say that Mills has conjured up a bogeyman to explain his own failure to realize his will. This is indeed what has been done in review after review of Mills' writings. A leading pluralist thinker, Edward Shils, says that Mills was too much influenced by Trotsky and Kafka:

Power, although concentrated, is not so concentrated, so powerful, or so permeative as Professor Mills seems to believe. . . . There have been years in Western history, e.g., in Germany during the last years of the Weimar Republic and under the Nazis when reality approximated this picture more closely. . . . But as a picture of Western societies, and not just as an ideal type of extreme possibilities which might be realized if so much else that is vital were lacking, it will not do.

But is Mills' definition the only suitable one here? If it is, then the pluralists have won the debate. But if there is a way to designate an irresponsible elite without giving it omnipotence, then the debate may be recast at least.

This fundamental question is not answered in the other major books that affirm the existence of a military-industrial complex. Cook's *The Warfare State* and Perlo's *Militarism and Industry* and several more recent works are good examples of this literature which is theoretically inferior to Mills' perplexing account.

Cook's volume has been pilloried severely by deniers of the military-industrial complex. At least it has the merit of creating discussion by being one of the few dissenting books distributed widely on a commercial basis. It suffers, however, from many of the same unclarities typical of the deniers. Its title assumes a "warfare state" while its evidence, although rich, is only a compilation of incidents, pronouncements, and trends, lacking any framework for weighing and measuring. From his writing several hypotheses can be extracted about the "face of the Warfare State," all of them suggestive but none of them conclusive:

1. The Department of Defense owns more property than any other organization in the world.

2. Between 60 and 70 percent of the national budget is consistently allocated to defense or defense-related expenditures.

3. The military and big business join in an inevitable meeting of minds over billions of dollars in contracts the one has to order and the other to fulfill.

4. The 100 top corporations monopolize three-fourths of the contracts, 85 percent of them being awarded without competition.

5. As much as one-third of all production and service indirectly depends on defense.

6. Business and other conservative groups, even though outside of the Defense establishment, benefit from the warfare emphasis because it keeps subordinate the welfare state that is anathema to them.

There is no doubt about Cook's data holding up for the years since his book was written. The federal budget of $154.9 billion for the fiscal year 1971 assigns 64.8 cents of every tax dollar to the cost of past and present wars and war preparation. The Vietnam war costs are concealed in the 48.4 cents per dollar for current military expenditures. Veterans benefits and national debt interest are also sizable items. The Nixon administration claims 41 percent of its budget to be on human resources. The figure, however, includes trust funds like Social Security (for which the government is merely a caretaker), veterans benefits, and even the Selective Service System in this category. The actual human resources figure is 17 percent, indicating that welfare is still being crushed by warfare.

Cook's work, much more than Mills', is open to the counterargument that no monolithic semiconspiratorial elite exists. Even his definitions of vested interests are crude and presumed. Moreover, he suffers far more than Mills from a failure to differentiate between groups. For instance, there is nothing in his book (written in 1962) that would explain the economic drag of defense spending, which Cook perceptively observed in a *Nation* article, "The Coming Politics of Disarmament," in 1963. One year he wrote that big business was being fattened off war contracts, but the next year the "prolonged arms race has started, at last, to commit a form of economic hara-kiri." "Hara-kiri" does not happen spontaneously; it is a culmination of long-developing abnormalities. That Cook could not diagnose them before they became common in congressional testimony illustrates the lack of refinement in his 1962 analysis. Cook's failure lies in visualizing a monolith, which obscures the strains that promote new trends and configurations.

It is in this attention to strains that Perlo's book is useful. He draws interesting connections between the largest industrial corporations and the defense economy, finding that defense accounts for 12 percent of the profits of the 25 largest firms. He adds the factor of foreign investment as one which creates a further propensity in favor of a large defense system, and he calculates that military, business, and foreign investments combined total 40 percent of the aggregate profits among the top 25. He draws deeper connections between companies and the major financial groups controlling their assets.

This kind of analysis begins to reveal important disunities within the business community. For instance, it can be seen that the Rockefellers are increasing their direct military investments while maintaining their largest foreign holdings in extremely volatile Middle Eastern and Latin American companies. The Morgans are involved in domestic industries of a rather easy-to-convert type, and their main foreign holdings are in the "safer" European countries, although they too have "unsafe" mining interests in Latin America and Africa. The First National City Bank, while having large holdings in Latin American sugar and fruit, has a more technical relation to its associated firms than the stock-owner relation. The Mellons have sizable oil holdings on Kuwait, but on the whole are less involved in defense than the other groups. The DuPonts, traditionally the major munitions makers are "diversified" into the booming aerospace and plutonium industries, but their overseas holdings are heavily in Europe. Certain other groups with financial holdings, such as Young and Eaton interests in Cleveland, have almost no profit stake in defense or foreign investments. On the other hand, some of the new wealth in Los Angeles is deeply committed to the aerospace industry.

Perlo makes several differentiations of this sort, including the use of foreign-policy statements by leading industrial groups. But he does not have a way to predict under what conditions a given company would actively support economic shifts away from the arms race. These and other gaps, however, are not nearly as grave as his lack of analysis of other components of the military-industrial complex. There is no attempt to include politicians, military groups, and other forces in a "map" of the military-industrial complex which Perlo believes exists. This may be partly because of the book's intent, which is to document profiteering by arms contractors, but, for whatever reason, the book is not theoretically edifying about the question we are posing. Nor does it refute the pluralist case. In fact, it contains just the kind of evidence that pluralist arguments currently employ to demonstrate the absence of a monolith.

The newer literature, since 1965, shows a somewhat more penetrating glimpse into the extent of the merger of the military and the defense industry. Lapp, *The Weapons Culture;* Weidenbaum, "Arms and the American Economy"; Galbraith, *The New Industrial State;* and Knoll and McFadden, *American Militarism 1970,* all show the heavy involvement of the Department of Defense with the corporate giants. The two recent and most striking works which provide the most concrete detail on the operation of this military-industrial network are Seymour Melman's *Pentagon Capitalism* (1970) and Richard Barnet's *The Economy of Death* (1969). Both are well written and a must for any serious student of contemporary policy. *Pentagon Capitalism* describes the result of the defense-industrial merger as a giant enterprise controlled by the civilian defense establishment, or "state-management." Through the elaboration of government controls over the firms that carry out defense contracts, the Defense Department's role has changed from that of customer to that of administrator over a far-flung empire of defense production. The Pentagon is able to divert capital and scientific and technical manpower to its own purposes, drawing resources away from productive activity to, what Melman calls, economically "parasitic" activity. He holds that the prime goal of the "state-management" *is to enlarge its decision power*. Thus wars, once begun, tend to expand; "security gaps" are invented, causing weapons systems to grow in size and sophistication; and international arms sales increase.

Barnet (*The Economy of Death*) sees the military-industrial complex as more decentralized, like a machine with several separate parts that run together smoothly. Each institution within the complex acts for its own purposes, and all contribute to justifying and maintaining the irrational and dangerous growth of military capability. Barnet documents the interchangeability of personnel between industry and the military. A major strength of Barnet's work lies in his willingness to be specific, to name the key names from among those in his study of 400 top decision makers who come from a handful of law firms and executive suites "in shouting distance of one another in fifteen city blocks in New York, Washington, Detroit, Chicago, and Boston." Many of the names are commonly known (although the extent of their financial-world connections is not)—Charles Wilson, Neil McElroy, Robert Anderson, George Humphrey, Douglas Dillon, John McCone, Adolph Berle, Averell Harriman, William C. Foster, John McCloy, Robert McNamara, Roswell Gilpatric, James Douglas, William Rogers, and Nelson Rockefeller. Men such as these are systematically recruited into the top Cabinet posts and become "national security managers." Their common backgrounds, even membership in the same elite social clubs, assures a measure of homogeneity around their task of defining who or what threatens this nation and what should be done about it. Their views on the national interest reflect their own success in judicious management of risk in the business world. Barnet's assumption about the homogeneity of their club is supported by Dumhoff's "Who Made American Foreign Policy, 1945–1963?" It is clear that a man like William Rogers with the right business background but no particular knowledge or background in foreign affairs can be made Secretary of State while a civil-rights leader, Martin Luther King, was admonished by official spokesmen for expressing a position against the Vietnam war.

Barnet believes it is the ongoing mechanisms of the system that keep it rutted in old paths. The evils are not incidental, he says, but built into the system. Military solutions to international problems seem more reliable, "tougher," than diplomatic solutions, and they are backed up by millions of dollars' worth of "scientific research"; so military solutions are preferred even by civilian defense officials. The military, the civilian defense establishment, and defense contractors constantly work together to develop new weapons systems to meet defense "needs"; so they feed one another's ideologies, and costlier, more elaborate weapons result. It is difficult and expensive for military contractors to convert to peacetime production, so they have done virtually no planning for conversion and many have abandoned all interest in such planning. Perhaps most important for Barnet, those in power see America's chief purpose as consolidating and extending American power around the world; hence military technology is an indispensable tool. Whether this collection of civilian managers is really in control or whether they are merely serving more powerful military bureaucracy is the point at issue, and Barnet leans toward the view of the ascendance of relatively smooth-working military hierarchy. Dumhoff, using very similar evidence, places the aristocratic economic elite at the top of the pinnacle.

Melman, in particular, presents a strong case to suggest that militarism in the United States is no longer an example of civilian corporate interests dictating a military role to produce hardware for profit from the governmental consumer and to defend the outposts of capitalism. Instead, he sees the system as one led by the military managers for their own interests in power, a state socialism whose defense officials dictate the terms of policy, and of profits, to their subsidiary corporations. Melman supports his case by the observation that not only the personnel but the actual procedural ways of operation demonstrate that the Defense Department and the corporations which serve it have interpenetrated one another's operations—to such an extent that there is for all practical purposes really only one organization. The horrible example that comes to mind is the rise of Hitler, first backed and promoted by industrialists who later lost their measure of control over an uncontrollable military machine. Melman's thesis differs from both the pluralist doctrine which sees various groups competing for power and the Marxist doctrine which sees the greed of the capitalists as the prime mover. In Melman's convincing analysis the military is fast becoming the King.

Melman's analysis may yet prove true. For the present, however, corporate capitalism has fared too well to alleviate all suspicions of the hidden hand. The nature of the new interlocking industrial conglomerates like Lytton, Textron, or General Dynamics is that they and the main financial houses of the United States provide an inner core whose interests are permanently protected even as individual corporations prosper or falter. For such centers of elite power, which Barnet shows to be the main source of top Defense Department and other foreign-policy-appointed officials, the terms of the military merger have been highly beneficial. The benefits must be seen not only in profits but in the retention of the entire profit-making system against the demands of a hungry and impatient world. Melman speaks of the drive of the new technocratic military bureaucracy to increase its power and control but deemphasizes what interests this power is protecting. Barnet specifies the community of interest and outlooks among the corporate decision managers who are recruited into the inner circles of foreign policy but does not state explicitly what beliefs lie at the core of the practices that are promoted.

Both Barnet and Melman believe that American militarism is a function of institutions directly involved with defense. It can be argued, on the other hand, that a description of something called a military-industrial complex should include all of the power centers of American society. Directorates of the major defense contractors are not separable from those of industries geared primarily to the production of consumer goods. Neither are the consumer industries independent of military and diplomatic actions which protect international marketing advantages. Barnet himself notes that it is not merely the faction of the labor movement directly employed in defense industries, but organized labor in general which is a political supporter of military-industrial power. The universities are heavily involved in defense interests as is the complex of oils, highways, and automotives. Even in education the armed services Project 100,000 has inducted a large number of former draft rejects for resocialization and basic educational development (followed by two years of applied study abroad in Vietnam for the successful graduates).

Barnet and Melman deal incompletely with the relationship of the sector they regard as the military-industrial complex to the rest of society. Both realize the tremendous power of the military, the civilian defense officials, and the defense industry combined. They are aware that the defense establishment has a powerful hold on public opinion through fear of enemy attack and through control over a large sector of the work force. Yet they seem to hope this power can be curbed by a loud enough public outcry. In the last analysis they too believe that the defense establishment has merely been allowed to get out of hand, and that now the exercise of some countervailing power may bring sanity back into American policy and make peace possible.

Revising the Criteria for Inferring Power

After finding fault with so many books and divergent viewpoints, the most obvious conclusion is that current social theory is deficient in its explanation of power. We concur with one of Mills' severest critics, Daniel Bell, who at least agrees with Mills that most current analysis concentrates on the "intermediate sectors," e.g., parties, interest groups, formal structures, without attempting to view the underlying system of "renewable power independent of any momentary group of actors." However, we have indicated that the only formidable analysis of the underlying system of renewable power, that of Mills, has profound shortcomings because of its definition of power. Therefore, before we can offer an answer of our own to the question, "Is there a military-industrial complex that blocks peace?," it is imperative to return to the question of power itself in American society.

We have agreed essentially with the pluralist claim that ruling-group models do not "fit" the American structure. We have classified Mills' model as that of a ruling group because of his Weberian definition of power, but we have noted also that Mills successfully went beyond two traps common to elite theories, viz., that the elite is total in the scope of its decisions, and that the elite is a coordinated monolith.

But we perhaps have not stressed sufficiently that the alternative case for pluralism is inadequate in its claim to describe the historical dynamics of American society. The point of our dissent from pluralism is over the doctrine of "countervailing power." This is the modern version of Adam Smith's economics and of the Madisonian or Federalism theory of checks and balances, adapted to the new circumstances of large-scale organizations. Its evidence is composed of self-serving incidents and a faith in semimystical resources. For instance, in the sphere of political economy, it is argued that oligopoly contains automatic checking mechanisms against undue corporate growth, and that additionally, the factors of "public opinion" and "corporate conscience" are built-in limiting forces. We believe that evidence in the field, however, suggests that oligopoly is a means of stabilizing an industrial sphere either through tacit agreements to follow price leadership or rigged agreements in the case of custom-made goods; that "public opinion" tends much more to be manipulated and apathetic than independently critical; that "corporate conscience" is less suitable as a description than Reagan's terms, "corporate arrogance."

To take the more immediate example of the military sphere, the pluralist claim is that the military is subordinate to broader, civilian interests. The first problem with the statement is the ambiguity of "civilian." Is it clear that military men are more "militaristic" than civilian men? To say so would be to deny the increasing trend of "white-collar militarism." The top strategists in the Department of Defense, the Central Intelligence Agency, and the key advisory positions often are Ph.D.'s. In fact, "civilians" including McGeorge Bundy, Robert Kennedy, James Rostow, and Robert McNamara are mainly responsible for the development of the only remaining "heroic" form of combat: counterinsurgency operations in the jungles of the underdeveloped countries. If "militarism" [1] has permeated this deeply into the "civilian" sphere, then the distinction between the terms becomes largely nominal.

The intrusion of civilian professors into the military arena has been most apparent in more than 300 universities and nonprofit research institutions which supply personnel to and rely upon contracts from the Department of Defense. About half of these centers were created to do specialized strategic research. One of these, the RAND Corporation, was set up by Douglas Aviation and the Air Force to give "prestige-type support for favored Air Force proposals." When RAND strategy experts Wohlstetter and Dinerstein discovered a mythical "missile gap" and an equally unreal preemptive war strategy in Soviet post-Sputnik policy, they paved the way for the greatest military escalation of the cold-war era, the missile race.

The civilian strategists have frequently retained an exasperating measure of autonomy from the services that support them. Such conflicts reached a peak when both the Skybolt and the RS 70 projects met their demise under the "cost effectiveness" program designed by Harvard economist Charles Hitch (then with RAND, later Defense Department comptroller, now President of the University of California). That the civilian and military planners of military policy sometimes differ does not detract from the argument. What must be stressed is that the apparent flourishing of such civilian agencies as RAND (it earned over 20 million dollars in 1962 with all the earnings going into expansion and spawned the nonprofit System Development Corporation with annual earnings exceeding 50 million dollars) is no reflection of countervailing power. The doctrine of controlled response under which the RS 70 fell was one which served the general aspirations of each of the separate services; of the Polaris and Minuteman stable deterrent factions, of the brush-fire or limited-war proponents, guerrilla war and paramilitary operations advocates, and of the counterforce adherents. It is a doctrine of versatility intended to leave the widest range of military options for retaliation and escalation in U.S. hands. It can hardly be claimed as victory against military thought. The fighting may have been intense but the area of consensus between military and civilian factions was great.

Consensus

All that countervailing power refers to is the relationship between groups who fundamentally accept "the American system" but who compete for advantages within it. The corporate executive wants higher profits, the laborer a higher wage. The President wants the final word on military strategies, the Chairman of the Joint Chiefs does not trust him with it, Boeing wants the contract, but General Dynamics is closer at the time to the Navy Secretary and the President, and so on. What is prevented by countervailing forces is the dominance of society by a group or clique or a party. But this process suggests a profoundly important point; that *the constant pattern in American society is the rise and fall of temporarily irresponsible groups.* By *temporary* we mean that, outside of the largest industrial conglomerates, the groups which wield significant power to influence policy decisions are not guaranteed stability. By *irresponsible* we mean that there are many activities within their scope which are essentially unaccountable in the democratic process. These groups are too uneven to be described with the shorthand term "class." Their personnel have many different characteristics (compare IBM executives and the Southern Dixiecrats) and their needs as groups are different enough to cause endless fights as, for example, small versus big business. No one group or coalition of several groups can tyrannize the rest as is demonstrated, for example, in the changing status of the major financial groups, such as the Bank of America which grew rapidly, built on the financial needs of the previously neglected small consumer.

It is clear, however, that these groups exist within consensus relationships of a more general and durable kind than their conflict relationships. This is true, first of all, of their social characteristics. In an earlier version of this essay we compiled tables using data from an exhaustive study of American elites contained in Warner et al., *The American Federal Executive* (1963) and from Suzanne Keller's compilation of military, economic, political, and diplomatic elite survey materials in *Beyond the Ruling Class* (1963). The relevant continuities represented in this data suggest an educated elite with an emphasis upon Protestant and business-oriented origins. Moreover, the data suggest inbreeding with business orientation in backgrounds likely to have been at least maintained, if not augmented, through marriage. Domhoff, in *Who Rules America?*, has shown that elites generally attend the same exclusive prep schools and universities, and belong to the same exclusive gentlemen's clubs. The consistencies suggest orientations not unlike those found in examination of editorial content of major business newspapers and weeklies and in more directly sampled assessments of elite opinions.

The second evidence of consensus relationships, besides attitude and background data indicating a pro-business sympathy, would come from an examination of the *practice* of decision making. By analysis of such actual behavior we can understand which consensus attitudes are reflected in decision making. Here, in retrospect, it is possible to discover the values and assumptions which are defended recurrently. This is at least a rough means of finding the boundaries of consensus relations. Often these boundaries are invisible because of the very infrequency with which they are tested. What are visible most of the time are the parameters of conflict relationships among different groups. These conflict relationships constitute the ingredients of experience which give individuals or groups their uniqueness and varieties, while the consensus relations constitute the common underpinnings of behavior. The tendency in social science has been to study decision making in order to study group differences; we need to study decision making also to understand group commonalities.

Were such studies done, our hypothesis would be that certain "core beliefs" are continuously unquestioned. One of these, undoubtedly, would be that efficacy is preferable to principle in foreign affairs. In practice, this means that violence is preferable to nonviolence as a means of defense. A second is that private property is preferable to collective property. A third assumption is that the particular form of constitutional government which is practiced within the United States is preferable to any other system of government. We refer to the preferred mode as limited parliamentary democracy, a system in which institutionalized forms of direct representation are carefully retained but with fundamental limitations placed upon the prerogatives of governing. Specifically included among the areas of limitation are many matters encroaching upon corporation property and state hegemony. While adherence to this form of government is conceivably the strongest of the domestic "core values," at least among business elites, it is probably the least strongly held of the three on the international scene. American relations with, and assistance for, authoritarian and semifeudal regimes occurs exactly in those areas where the recipient regime is evaluated primarily upon the two former assumptions and given rather extensive leeway on the latter one.

The implications of these "core beliefs" for the social system are immense, for they justify the maintenance of our largest institutional structures: the military, the corporate economy, and a system of partisan politics which protects the concept of limited democracy. These institutions, in turn, may be seen as current agencies of the more basic social structure. The "renewable basis of power" in America at the present time underlies those institutional orders linked in consensus relationships: military defense of private property and parliamentary democracy. These institutional orders are not permanently secure, by definition. Their maintenance involves a continuous coping with new conditions, such as technological innovation, and with the inherent instabilities of a social structure that arbitrarily classifies persons by role, status, access to resources, and power. The myriad groups composing these orders are even less secure because of their weak ability to command "coping resources," e.g., the service branches are less stable than the institution of the military, particular companies are less stable than the institutions of corporate property, political parties are less stable than the institution of parliamentary government.

In the United States there is no ruling group. Nor is there any easily discernible ruling institutional order, so meshed have the separate sources of elite power become. But there is a social structure which is organized to create and protect power centers with only partial accountability. In this definition of power we are avoiding the Weber-Mills meaning of *omnipotence* and the contrary pluralist definition of power as consistently *diffuse*. We are describing the current system as one of overall "minimal accountability" and "minimal consent." We mean that the role of democratic review, based on genuine popular consent, is made marginal and reactive. Elite groups are minimally accountable to publics and have a substantial, though by no means maximum, freedom to shape popular attitudes. The reverse of our system would be one in which democratic participation would be the orienting demand around which the social structure is organized.

Some will counter this case by saying that we are measuring "reality" against an "ideal," a technique which permits the conclusion that the social structure is undemocratic according to its distance from our utopian values. This is a convenient apology for the present system, of course. We think it possible, at least in theory, to develop measures of the undemocratic in democratic conditions, and place given social structures along a continuum. These measures, in rough form, might include such variables as economic security, education, legal guarantees, access to information, and participatory control over systems of economy, government, and jurisprudence.

The reasons for concern with democratic process in an article questioning the power of a purported military-industrial complex are twofold. First, just as scientific method both legitimizes and promotes change in the world of knowledge, democratic method legitimizes and promotes change in the world of social institutions. Every society, regardless of how democratic, protects its core institutions in a web of widely shared values. But if the core institutions should be dictated by the requisites of military preparedness, then restrictions on the democratic process, i.e., restrictions in either mass-opinion exchange (as by voluntary or imposed news management) or in decision-making bodies (as by selection of participants in a manner guaranteeing exclusion of certain positions), then such restrictions would be critical obstacles to peace.

Second, certain elements of democratic process are inimical to features of military-oriented society, and the absence of these elements offers one type of evidence for a military-industrial complex even in the absence of a ruling elite. Secretary of Defense Robert McNamara made the point amply clear in his testimony in 1961 before the Senate Armed Services Committee:

Why should we tell Russia that the Zeus development may not be satisfactory? What we ought to be saying is that we have the most perfect anti-ICBM system that the human mind will ever devise. Instead the public domain is already full of statements that the Zeus may not be satisfactory, that it has deficiencies. I think it is absurd to release that level of information.

Under subsequent questioning McNamara attempted to clarify his statement that he only wished to delude Russian, not American, citizens about U.S. might. Just how this might be done was not explained.

A long-established tradiiton exists for "executive privilege" which permits the President to refuse to release information when, in his opinion, it would be damaging to the national interest. Under modern conditions responsibility for handling information of a strategic nature is shared among military, industrial, and executive agencies. The discretion regarding when to withhold what information must also be shared. Moreover, the existence of a perpetual danger makes the justification, "in this time of national crisis," suitable to every occasion in which secrecy must be justified. McNamara's statement cited above referred not to a crisis in Cuba or Vietnam but rather to the perpetual state of cold-war crisis. And since the decision about what is to be released and when is subject to just such management, the media become dependent upon the agencies for timely leaks and major stories. This not only adds an aura of omniscience to the agencies, but gives these same agencies the power to reward "good" journalists and punish the critical ones.

The issues in the question of news management involve more than the elements of control available to the President, the State Department, the Department of Defense, the Central Intelligence Agency, the Atomic Energy Commission, or any of the major prime contractors of defense contracts. Outright control of news flow is probably less pervasive than voluntary acquiescence to the objectives of these prominent institutions of our society. Nobody has to tell the wire services when to release a story on the bearded dictator of our hemisphere or the purported brutality of Ho Chi Minh. A frequent model, the personified devil image of an enemy, has become a press tradition. In addition to a sizable quantity of radio and television programming and spot time purchased directly by the Pentagon, an amount of service, valued to $6 million by *Variety*, is donated annually by the networks and by public-relations agencies for various military shows. Again, the pluralistic shell of an independent press or broadcasting media is left hollow by the absence of a countervailing social force of any significant power.

Several shared premises, unquestioned by any potent locus of institutionalized power, were described as:

1. Efficacy is preferable to principle in foreign affairs (thus military means are chosen over nonviolent means).

2. Private property is preferable to public property.

3. Limited parliamentary democracy is preferable to any other system of government.

At issue is the question of whether an America protecting such assumptions can exist in a world of enduring peace. . . .

We agree fully with an analysis by Lowi [2] distinguishing types of decisions for which elite-like forces seem to appear and hold control (redistributive) and other types in which pluralist powers battle for their respective interests (distributive). In the latter type the pie is large and the fights are over who gets how much. Factional strife within and among military-industrial and political forces in our country are largely of this nature. In redistributive decisions, the factions coalesce, for the pie itself is threatened. We have been arguing that the transition to peace is a process of redistributive decision.

Is there, then, a military-industrial complex that prevents peace? The answer is inextricably embedded into the mainstream of American institutions and mores. Our concept is not that American society contains a ruling military-industrial complex. Our concept is more nearly that American society *is* a military-industrial complex. It can accommodate a wide range of factional interests from those concerned with the production or utilization of a particular weapon to those enraptured with the mystique of optimal global strategies. It can accommodate those with rabid desires to advance toward the brink and into limitless intensification of the arms race. It can even accommodate those who wish either to prevent war or to limit the destructiveness of war through the gradual achievement of arms control and disarmament agreements. What it cannot accommodate is the type of radical departures needed to produce enduring peace.

NOTES

1. We are defining the term as "primary reliance on coercive means, particularly violence or the threat of violence, to deal with social problems."

2. Theodore J. Lowi, "American Business, Public Policy, Case Studies, and Political Theory," *World Politics* (July 1964), pp. 676–715.

33.

Adam Yarmolinsky: Military Involvement in Foreign Policy

The rise and incipient decline of military influence in American national security policy is analyzed in the following selection by Adam Yarmolinsky, who attributes the "militarization" of American policy over the past three decades to

From Adam Yarmolinsky, *The Military Establishment: Its Impacts on American Society,* pp. 110–33. © 1971 by The Twentieth Century Fund, New York. Published by Harper & Row. Reprinted by permission of The Twentieth Century Fund.

civilian adoption of "military ways of thinking about political problems." As a result of recent changes in the domestic and international environments, however, "the force of military logic and the authoritative status of military professionals as spokesmen on foreign policy—or even on military matters—have diminished."

Adam Yarmolinsky served for five years in the Defense Department as Special Assistant to Secretary McNamara and Deputy Assistant Secretary for International Security Affairs and is presently Professor of Law at the Harvard Law school. The book from which this selection has been taken, *The Military Establishment: Its Impacts on American Society,* contains a wide-ranging analysis of its subject.

During the last thirty years, the military establishment has exerted much more influence on the making of American foreign policy than in any previous period. As indicated earlier, the Chiefs of Staff have acted as presidential advisers, often with a voice on foreign policy issues equal to or greater than that of key Assistant Secretaries of State. Since civilian Secretaries of Defense have continued to give advice on foreign policy and have at the same time acquired increased independent authoritativeness, the military establishment has sometimes dominated presidential councils. Such occasions have become all the more frequent partly because so much discussion of foreign policy concerned actual or imminent warfare or the complicated and compelling issue of nuclear balance, partly because foreign policy questions were posed by overseas commands or military aid or advisory missions.

Yet, even more important, policy-makers, civilian and military, became obsessed with the problem of the nation's security and gave to it the highest priority. In Europe, Asia, and the Middle East, successive American administrations opposed the expansion of Communist states and Communist political strength, taking the position that any such expansion would adversely affect the balance of military power, encourage the Soviet Union (or the Sino-Soviet bloc) to initiate war, and put the United States at a disadvantage if war came. Policy-makers adopted military staff habits of reckoning contingencies in terms of the capabilities rather than the intentions of potential enemies and, as has been pointed out, emphasizing readiness for the worst contingencies that might arise. These characteristics were slightly less in evidence in periods when the professional military had least access to the White House—the later Eisenhower years and the interval between the Cuban missile crisis and the Johnson decision to bomb North Vietnam—periods that saw the opening of dialogue between Washington and Moscow, the limited test-ban treaty, and American pressure for more broadly based and politically responsive regimes in Seoul and Saigon. But, in substance and in character, United States foreign policy has become substantially militarized.

It was not, however, the military establishment alone that gave the policy this cast. Basically, it was done by civilians. Civilians in the White House, the State Department, and in other policy-making and opinion-making centers shared the military establishment's view of the Soviet Union as an aggressive and threatening force. They also shared awareness that long-range aircraft, missiles, and nuclear weapons had brought to an end America's long era of what C. Vann Woodward called "free security." [1] They were strongly influenced by lessons alleged to be taught by recent history. Above all, they believed, with some justification, that Congress and public opinion would apply those lessons only if convinced that the continental United States faced danger. And to be convinced, Congress and the public had to hear testimony from those whose judgment they regarded as most detached, trustworthy, and authoritative—the spokesmen of the military establishment. The prominence of the military in the policy-making process has been a function of the priority of military security in American policy. It is essential to look for factors that explain *both* phenomena.

The impact of the military establishment on political decision-making is very much a function of the tasks assigned to the military establishment by the political decision-makers. Early in 1961, it became clear that the balance of payments problems would be an acute and continuing one for the United States, and that a major contributing factor to the big deficits registered by the United States was its overseas troop deployments, particularly the troops stationed in Europe under NATO commitments. While some reduction in the numbers of troops stationed overseas might have been achieved in the long run, through improvement of airlift and ingenious rotation policies, the immediate need was to reduce the outflow of dollars to Europe without reducing the number of troops.

After some investigation and experimentation, the Department of Defense concluded that the most effective way to reduce the military impact on the balance of payments was by agreements with the countries on whose territory the troops were stationed, principally Germany and Britain, to purchase military equipment in the United States in amounts approximately equal to the dollar expenditures arising out of the costs of American troops. The department pursued this policy so vigorously that it had some unanticipated consequences on American relations with Great Britain and Germany, even to the extent of indirectly encouraging sales of second- or third-hand military equipment by Germany to Third World countries. The Department of Defense arms sales policies and programs were monitored by the Department of State and by the National Security Council staff in the White House; but the creation of a vigorous and aggressive sales force within the Department of Defense, assisted and encouraged by the private sector of the defense establishment, developed a momentum that the political decision-makers had not anticipated and could not fully control, until finally it produced the congressional investigations of 1967, which resulted in congressional curbs on the credit mechanisms that were the principal instruments of foreign military sales promotion.

When Japanese troops seized Shanghai in 1937, it was the commander of the Pacific fleet who submitted a recommendation that the United States government reaffirm its intention to protect American nationals and reinforce its garrison in the international settlement as proof of its determination. The recommendation became for several days the focus of State Department and White

House debate.[2] As a rule, however, before World War II, military and naval officers figured as quite minor characters in major diplomatic decisions.

With World War II and the elevation of the Chiefs of Staff to virtual super-cabinet status, the reverse became true. General Eisenhower managed relations with the French regime in North Africa, and later he handled negotiations for Italy's surrender. Other American military commanders functioned with even greater political independence. Communication with De Gaulle was as much the responsibility of Admiral Harold R. Stark, the commander of American naval forces in Europe, as of any American ambassador. And in the Far East, General MacArthur, General Joseph Stilwell, and General Albert Wedemeyer dealt with the British Dominions, the Republic of China, and the Chinese Communists as the ranking representatives of the United States. Field commanders and their staffs had much to do with determining which foreign policy issues would be raised in Washington. The service staffs and committees of the Joint Chiefs recommended solutions. After the President made a decision, his instructions went back to the field commanders. From beginning to end, military men were involved in wartime foreign policy.

After 1944, relations with the U.S.S.R. became the most important foreign business of the United States government. These relations had not at any point been managed by the military. The small military mission in Moscow had remained subordinate to the embassy, and President Roosevelt had communicated with Premier Joseph Stalin either directly or through the American ambassador or special civilian emissaries. President Truman used similar channels. In dealing with liberated countries in Western Europe, Truman relied on the embassies, and he used Marshall in a civilian capacity in 1945–46 as a special envoy to China. Management of foreign affairs lay with the military only in occupied areas, although enough major problems arose so that General Clay in Germany, General MacArthur in Japan, and Lieutenant General John R. Hodge in Korea remained among the principal American agents abroad.

In civilianizing the foreign policy machinery after 1948, Truman attempted to change arrangements in Washington and overseas. In 1949 he replaced Clay with a civilian high commissioner, and in 1950 he opened negotiations for a Japanese peace treaty which, when completed, would mean the end of MacArthur's proconsulship. However, he concluded that the North Atlantic Treaty would not in and of itself deter a Russian attack on Europe, and the result was the organization of NATO forces under an American supreme commander. And, of course, the eruption of war in Korea meant that the American commander in the Far East—first MacArthur and then Ridgway—also had a great deal to do with fixing the terms in which Washington would debate foreign policy problems.

Through most of the 1950's and 1960's, the NATO command played a central role both in posing foreign policy issues and in championing particular policies. Successive supreme commanders and their staffs had much to do with establishing a case for German rearmament, promoting formation of a European Defense Community, defining the challenge involved in Khrushchev's proposal to sign a separate peace treaty with East Germany, and advocating creation of a multilateral nuclear force. Although President Johnson's final rejection of the multilateral force (MLF), followed by France's virtual withdrawal from NATO, reduced the stature and influence of the command, it retained a voice equal to that of any civilian agency on such matters as, for example, a means of reducing American expenditures in Europe in order to compensate for balance of payments deficits.

When President Eisenhower reorganized the defense establishment in 1953, he provided for a number of unified commands. After the Korean War, a commander in chief, Pacific, assumed control of Army and Marine units in Korea, Japan, Okinawa, Taiwan, the Philippines, and island areas, the Seventh Fleet, and United States Air Force groups stationed in the region. He, his headquarters staff, and subordinate commanders played a prominent role in defining the policy issues involved in French reversals in Indochina, Chinese Communist threats to Chinese Nationalist-held offshore islands, civil warfare in Laos and South Vietnam, and Communist movements in the Philippines and Indonesia.

As the level of American engagement in Vietnam increased, the Military Assistance Command, Vietnam (MACV), developed more and more of a separate identity while its influence in foreign policy debate was amplified by transmission through the Honolulu headquarters of the Pacific Command. Other military organizations, of course, figured in the foreign policy process. The Strategic Air Command, for example, participated in debate over the policy issues involved in test-ban negotiations. The issues on which policy-makers had to act were posed as often in cables from SHAEF, SCAP, SHAPE, SACEUR, COMPAC,[3] or MACV as in cables from American embassies or notes presented by foreign governments.

Aid funds earmarked for military purposes in the mutual security program made up almost half of United States foreign aid between 1950 and 1968. (See Table 1.) The figures tell only part of the story, since economic aid itself had to be justified to Congress primarily in terms of its contribution to effective military aid. The establishment of military advisory missions was a natural consequence. By 1968, missions were stationed in at least fifty countries. Military advisers, serving at least as quasi-diplomatic agents of the United States, outnumbered State Department personnel stationed abroad by almost two to one.

Like overseas commands, military aid missions contributed regularly to the policy process. Their cables framed questions that policy-makers had to answer. And to some extent this has been the case regardless of the degree to which the officers involved were technically subordinate to ambassadors or other civilians. For in countries where the military dominated political life, members of United States military missions almost inevitably had special entree. In the Dominican Republic between 1961 and 1965, for example, military aid constituted less than 4 percent of American assistance; the military mission never numbered more than forty-five, and presidential instructions plainly made the ambassador captain of the country team. Nevertheless, when civil warfare broke out in 1965, members of the Military Assistance Advisory Group were regarded in Wash-

TABLE 1. PERCENT OF FOREIGN ASSISTANCE PROGRAM 1950–69
REPRESENTED BY MILITARY ASSISTANCE
($ millions)

Fiscal Year	Total Foreign Assistance Program	Economic Assistance	Military Assistance	% of Program for Military Assistance
1950	$ 5,042.4	$ 3,728.4	$ 1,314.0	26.1
1951	7,485.0	2,262.5	5,222.5	69.8
1952	7,284.4	1,540.4	5,744.0	78.9
1953	6,001.9	1,782.1	4,219.8	70.3
1954	4,531.5	1,301.5	3,230.0	71.3
1955	2,781.5	1,588.8	1,192.7	42.9
1956	2,703.3	1,681.1	1,022.2	37.8
1957	3,766.6	1,749.1	2,017.5	53.6
1958	2,768.9	1,428.9	1,340.0	48.4
1959	3,448.1	1,933.1	1,515.0	43.9
1960	3,225.8	1,925.8	1,300.0	40.3
1961	4,431.4	2,631.4	1,800.0	40.6
1962	3,914.6	2,314.6	1,600.0	40.9
1963	3,928.9	2,603.9	1,325.0	33.7
1964	3,000.0	2,000.0	1,000.0	33.3
1965	3,325.0	2,195.0	1,055.0	31.8
1966	3,933.0	2,463.0	1,545.0	39.5
1967	2,935.5	2,143.5	792.0	26.8
1968	2,295.6	1,895.6	400.0	17.4
1969	1,974.1	1,599.1	375.0	19.1
Total	$78,777.5	$40,767.8	$38,009.7	Avg. 48.6

Sources: 1950–1968 in *Military Assistance Facts,* October 1968, Department of Defense, Office of the Assistant Secretary for International Security Affairs, 1968, p. 25. 1969 in *U.S. Code Congressional and Administrative News,* 90th Congress, 2nd Sess., 1968, Vol. III, p. 3973

ington as having better information about both warring factions than the embassy. Where the major stakes in a country's relations with the United States government are military aid funds, as was the case in Vietnam under Ngo Dinh Diem, American military personnel can become the chief focus of attention on the part of local politicians, with civilians in the embassy routinely playing second fiddle.

Major overseas commands and military missions have exerted an influence simply by their existence. The Seventh Army and Sixth Fleet in Europe constitute an important element in the balance of payments problem. Their estimates of increased force or supply requirements call forth high-level policy debate in Washington. American bases and garrisons in Spain, Turkey, North Africa, the Caribbean, Southeast Asia, Taiwan, Okinawa, and Japan have been the causes of comparable debates, either because they provided a focus for political agitation in the host country or because base or other rights had to be negotiated or renegotiated.

The military establishment has thus participated not only in counseling the President but also in putting foreign policy issues before him and, at least on occasion, in creating these issues. For example, there was evidence that an Air Force general, who was in charge of negotiations with his Spanish opposite numbers in Madrid, had acted in a high-handed fashion toward the American Embassy, while making all kinds of commitments in the name of the United States government to defend Spain in return for the base rights. The Congress (particularly the Senate) was alarmed, but not necessarily for the right reason. For it soon became apparent that the Air Force had been delegated the responsibility to pursue bogged-down negotiations in large part as a tactical move initiated by the State Department and warmly encouraged by Secretary Rusk, who handed over responsibility to the Defense Department, in particular to Deputy Secretary of Defense Paul Nitze, who delegated it to the Joint Chiefs, and its chairman, General Earl G. Wheeler, who wound up calling the shots, with Air Force General David Burchinal doing the actual negotiating.

The international posture of the United States has changed since 1940, and the change has coincided with an expansion of the policy-making role of the military. Until then, Presidents and Secretaries of State said ritually that the United States had three foreign policy objectives: the preservation of the Monroe Doctrine, the maintenance of the Open Door and the territorial and administrative integrity of China, and the avoidance of entangling alliances.

The first of the objectives embodied some concern for military security. The Monroe Doctrine rested on an assumption that the United States would be endangered if any foreign power increased its holdings in Latin America. The development of Pan-Americanism, culminating in Franklin Roosevelt's "Good Neighbor" pronouncements, however, subordinated this specific American interest to the collective interest of the inter-American community.

The Open Door doctrine contained no security component. Except for devotees of Homer Lea,[4] feverish about a yellow peril, few Americans imagined that barriers to trade in China or even the takeover of China by Japan or the Soviet Union would put the continental United States in danger. In fact, military planners and others who thought in security terms tended to side with a minority that voiced doubts about the traditional policy. Protests against Japanese encroachment on China, they held, needlessly irritated the Japanese and thus increased the risk of Japan's attacking the Philippines or Hawaii.

The third principle, nonentanglement, expressed a traditional belief that no change in the balance of power elsewhere would affect America's safety. But the United States emerged from World War II with a somewhat altered set of principles. The American government promised to cooperate with the other victors as it had not cooperated with its allies after World War I. Through the United Nations, it accepted responsibilities it had refused earlier. Collective security replaced nonentanglement as a watchword.

The Monroe Doctrine and Open Door policy were by no means discarded, as the Chapultepec and Rio conferences of 1945 and 1947 and the Marshall mission in Asia demonstrated. But a new element entered American policy when Truman called for aid to Greece and Turkey in 1947 in the name not only of collective security but of American security; he argued that ". . . totalitarian regimes imposed upon free people, by direct or indirect aggression, undermine the foundations of international peace and hence the security of the United States." [5]

Although the Marshall Plan, as originally proposed, did not preclude aid to the Soviet Union and other Communist states (Marshall said the program would not be "directed against any country or doctrine but against hunger, poverty, desperation, and chaos"),[6] once the Communist nations refused to take part, Marshall and other administration figures argued before congressional committees that United States economic aid could reduce the danger of Communist revolutions or electoral victories in the countries of Western Europe and hence make it less likely that these potential powers would line up against the United States in a new war. Significantly, the Secretary of Defense joined the Secretary of State in asking for the European recovery program. "Peace and security are not to be viewed merely in terms of great military power or wealth in the hands of the United States," said James V. Forrestal, adding that

France had its Maginot line . . . and ancient Rome had her legionnaires, but none of these gave real security. . . . In our own case the security of our nation has to be viewed not merely in the light of our military strength but in the light of the restoration of balance throughout the world.[7]

By 1949, spokesmen for the administration were stating this point more emphatically. Immediately after ratification of the North Atlantic Treaty, they sought funds for building up the military forces of the new allies. Dean Acheson, now Secretary of State, described Western Europe as America's first line of defense. So long as it remained militarily weak, he declared, "the United States is open to attack on its own territory to a greater extent than ever before." [8] American policy-makers began to take a similar attitude toward areas other than Europe after the outbreak of the Korean War. Almost immediately after authorizing American air and naval forces to defend South Korea, Truman announced that the Seventh Fleet would protect the Chinese Nationalist regime on Formosa. He also proposed to aid the French in their struggle against Communist-led guerrillas in Indochina.

Since the Indochinese rebels had support from the Chinese Communists, observed Dean Rusk, then Assistant Secretary of State for Far Eastern Affairs, in testimony before Congress, their war against the French was tantamount to Chinese aggression. "If that aggression succeeds in that area," Rusk declared, "it would bring added strength and impetus to Communist aggression in other parts of the world and it would seriously affect the basic power situation upon which our own security depends." If the Chinese prevailed, they would acquire new resources—"the bread basket of Southeast Asia." The "free world" would suffer "a sapping of sources of strength . . . ; strength in terms of raw-materials resources; strength in terms of strategic position; and strength in terms of potential manpower." Rusk went on to claim that "the loss of the province of Tonkin, where active operations are now going on . . . would make it extremely difficult to retain the remainder of Indochina. The loss of Indochina would make it extremely difficult to retain Burma and Siam in the free-world system." [9]

From 1950 onward, America's stand in Asia resembled its stand in Europe. The truce line finally established in Korea, the Formosa straits, and the line drawn in 1954 between Communist North Vietnam and the rest of Southeast Asia were treated as military frontiers. The United States engaged itself by treaty to defend South Korea against another attack, and some 50,000 American troops remained in the country. Similarly, the United States signed a mutual defense treaty with Nationalist China. In 1955 and 1958, when the Communists shelled Quemoy and the Matsus, President Eisenhower and Secretary of State Dulles warned that seizure even of those tiny islands situated just off the mainland harbor of Amoy might constitute a threat to the United States. By the Southeast Asia Treaty of 1954, the American government meanwhile committed itself to the proposition that any Communist aggression against South Vietnam, Laos, Cambodia, or Thailand would "endanger its own peace and safety."

In the Middle East, the United States gravitated to a position of defining as its vital interests the territorial and political integrity of non-Communist states. The Eisenhower Doctrine of 1957 pledged United States aid to any government in the region menaced by Communist attack or subversion. A memorandum prepared by various hands in the State Department and submitted by Secretary Dulles to the Foreign Relations Committee explained the logic behind this doctrine.

The Soviet Union aspires to control the Middle East, not because it needs or is dependent upon the resources or the transportation and communications channels of the area, but because it sees control of the area as a major step toward eventually undermining the strength of the whole free world. Africa might well be the first major objective. Control of the oil of the Middle East would almost insure control of Europe. . . . The Middle East offers an avenue for aggression against India, West Pakistan, and the Asian countries which lie to the east of them. Successful Soviet aggression in the Middle East could flow to the eastward as gains were consolidated.[10]

Concern for American security had clearly replaced concern for collective security. As Dulles saw it, the world situation has to be viewed in simple balance-of-power terms, because ". . . our national security cannot rest on the strength of the United States alone. We must have allies to join their strength with ours and we must also prevent their strength from falling into Soviet hands. . . . If the Soviets take over the great land masses of Europe, Asia, and Africa, the scales of world power would be heavily weighted against us." He told Congress that subversion posed an even greater danger than overt aggression, for successful subversion of a free government could give the Soviet Union control of a country with "its population unharmed and its industries and resources intact." [11]

All continents were viewed as arenas of competition. In the Western Hemisphere, the Eisenhower, Kennedy, and Johnson administrations were prepared to forgo inter-American cooperation in order to minimize the risk of a Communist gain. The United States acted in Guatemala in 1954, at the Bay of Pigs in 1961, and in the Dominican Republic in 1965 without prior consultation with other American republics. In Africa, the United States government supported United Nations intervention in the Congo on premises expounded later to the House Foreign Affairs Committee by one of Kennedy's Assistant Secretaries of State: ". . . when it comes down to a question of whether the Russians will put in the steel structure of government in the Congo or whether we will, I think we have to work for our doing it because of the danger to a world order of having country after country operated as responsive puppets to a central world Communist movement run out of Moscow." [12]

From the late 1940's until the late 1960's American thinking about foreign policy was substantially military in character. The globe was conceived as a potential battleground between Soviet Communist forces on one side and American and "free world" forces on the other. Any addition to the land or resources of any Communist nation (except possibly Yugoslavia) or any political successes by Communists or Communist sympathizers would, it was assumed, add to the relative strength of the Soviet Union and diminish correspondingly that of the United States. American statesmen were not only preoccupied with elements of military potential; they also adopted military habits of thought. One such habit is to avoid estimating a potential enemy's intentions but instead to appraise his capabilities and to assume that he will do whatever mischief he can. Dulles's adherence to this way of thinking was evident in his response to a Senator who asked whether he possessed actual evidence of Soviet designs on the Middle East. "No one can reliably predict whether, and if so, when, there would be Communist armed aggression," he replied, "but three things are known: (1) the Communist capability, (2) the temptation, (3) the lack of any moral restraints." [13]

A second, closely related habit is to emphasize readiness for the worst contingency that might arise, a rule best illustrated by American policy in Europe, in which priority consistently went to preparedness for a massive assault mounted in secrecy and launched suddenly and surprisingly by the Soviets. It was much more difficult, as a result, to test whether the U.S.S.R. might be willing to settle some European issues. Between 1950 and 1953, the Truman administration rejected all Soviet suggestions for negotiations on an all-German peace treaty. In 1957–58 the Eisenhower administration rejected Polish Foreign Minister Adam Rapacki's scheme for making Central Europe a denuclearized zone. On both occasions, as cautious and hard-eyed Western analysts now read the evidence, the Soviets may have had a genuine desire for some kind of agreement. [14] The United States did not follow up Soviet overtures in large part because if agreements were reached, it believed NATO would be less able to lay preparations for the worst contingency.

In other rimlands American diplomacy has concentrated on building up ready military force to the exclusion of almost all other considerations. Between 1953 and 1963, more than half of all United States aid in Asia went to Korea, Nationalist China, and South Vietnam. Each of these three states was ruled during all or most of this decade by dictatorial governments. Though President Eisenhower and President Kennedy both affirmed belief in principle that popularly based governments possessed much greater strength in the long run, neither mentioned this principle in connection with these Asian states until Kennedy in 1963 uttered some cautious criticism of the tottering Diem regime. American thinking was concentrated here, too, on a "worst contingency"—a full-scale North Korean, Chinese, or North Vietnamese invasion—and such thinking precluded the diplomacy of looking toward a longer run.

It is now a fashion among writers identified with the New Left to suppose that the postwar Soviet menace was invented in Washington.[15] Bent from the beginning on extirpating Communism, these revisionist writers contend, American officials provoked the cold war by attempting to install anti-Soviet regimes in Eastern Europe. This reconstruction ignores almost completely the cooperative spirit which Truman and his agents displayed time and again at Potsdam, in meetings of the Council of Foreign Ministers, and at sessions of the United Nations and its committees. It ignores the steady accumulation of evidence that Soviet-backed Communists not only brutally suppressed all potential political opponents in Eastern Europe but also did their utmost to provoke disorder and seize power in Italy and France. It ignores, too, the evidence of Yugoslav and Bulgarian aid to Communist rebels in Greece, the demands of the U.S.S.R. for a strategic trusteeship in Tripolitania and for territorial and other concessions from neutral Turkey, and Soviet support for separatism in Azerbaijan, coupled with failure of the Red Army to withdraw from that Iranian province. Anyone looking open-mindedly at the cables and memoranda crossing the desks of Truman and his key advisers between 1945 and 1947 can hardly fail to understand why they reached the conclusion that the Soviet Union aimed at control of Western Europe, the Mediterranean, and the Middle East.[16]

The subsequent refusal of Russia and her satellites to participate in the Marshall Plan, efforts by Western Europe Communists to defeat that plan, the Czech coup, and the Berlin blockade necessarily seemed confirmation of the original judgment. The solidarity with the Soviet Union shown by the triumphant Chinese Communists, together with guerrilla or subversive activity by other Communists in Korea, Southeast Asia, and India, appeared to be evidence that Soviet imperial ambitions ranged even more widely. The sudden North Korean attack on South Korean added final proof, for there existed no doubt that Soviet authorities dictated policy in Pyongyang and directed, through advisers at every major command level, the operations of North Korean military units.[17] A riot in Bogotá in 1948, allegedly inspired by Communists, suggested that Soviet ambitions extended to the Western Hemisphere. Meanwhile, unwelcome evidence that at least a few clandestine Communists had infiltrated the British, Canadian, and American governments made it seem that even during the period of the wartime alliance, the Soviet Union had regarded the English-speaking nations as enemies.

To apparent evidence of Soviet expansionism and hostility, American leaders need not, of course, have reacted by deciding to interpose American power. Aid to Turkey and Greece, the North Atlantic Treaty, the arming of NATO, the Southeast Asia Treaty, the Eisenhower Doctrine, and the use of American forces in Lebanon and Vietnam reflected judgment not only that the Soviet Union had imperialistic aims but also that it was so important to prevent those aims from fulfillment that it justified the risk of a large-scale war. To explain why Americans drew this conclusion, it is important to take into account not only the prevailing view of Soviet behavior but also another factor —awareness of advancing technology.

On the eve of World War II, Roosevelt and his civilian advisers believed that German bombers based in Brazil or the Azores could reach targets in the United States, and this belief heightened their concern about Nazi activity in Latin America and the Iberian Peninsula. By the end of World War II, intercontinental bombers were almost in production, and long-range guided or ballistic missiles were a possibility. The sense of peril grew as one generation of nuclear weapons gave way to a second, as tests proved the workability of a hydrogen bomb. Intelligence showed the Soviet Union rapidly catching up in nuclear technology. The threat of possible direct attack by the U.S.S.R. disturbed Truman and his civilian advisers. In the Eisenhower administration, when the Soviets demonstrated an intercontinental bomber fleet and a long-range missile capability, the anxiety of the White House grew.

Awareness of advancing technology could have led instead to less concern about geographic positions, manpower, and natural resources—elements of power which had determined the outcome of World War I and World War II. But a future war could be imagined only in vague outline while past wars could be recollected in detail. American participation in the two world wars had followed inevitably, it seemed, from crises in faraway places—the Balkans, Manchuria, Czechoslovakia, Poland. It seemed, therefore, that Americans could not—and should not—in the future ignore episodes abroad that reminded them of Sarajevo or the Manchurian affair or Hitler's descent on Czechoslovakia.

In the two world wars, moreover, Americans had had time to muster their resources while others held the enemy at bay. The new technology made such a grace period unlikely. Acheson, Dulles, Rusk, and others repeatedly argued that rather than take the expensive course of turning America into an armed camp of immediate preparedness, it would be wiser to seek allies who might give the United States at least a little leeway for mobilization. This kind of reasoning, mixing supposition about the future with inference from the past, justified many of the changes in American diplomacy. But neither this reason-

ing nor perceptions of Soviet intransigence and expansionism led inevitably
to the policies actually adopted. American statesmanship became preoccupied
with military security, with the capabilities of the potential foe, and readiness
for worst contingencies. In part, this preoccupation was a result of domestic
politics. American political leaders recollected the strength of isolationism
prior to World War II, and most officials in the executive branch, many Congressmen, and most members of the foreign policy establishment feared a
revival of isolationism. They read signs of its return into the Henry Wallace
campaign of 1948, congressional opposition in 1950–51 to stationing troops
with NATO, the public support for General MacArthur in 1951, the popularity
of Senator Joseph McCarthy in the early fifties, the campaign for the Bricker
Amendment, persistent criticism of foreign aid, the activities of such groups
as the Committee for a Sane Nuclear Policy, the Goldwater candidacy of 1964,
and the upsurge of protest in the sixties against the war in Vietnam.

The most effective exhortation involved warnings that the people of the
United States faced immediate danger. If stated convincingly, this argument
could subdue any doubts and was, therefore, used in every conceivable context.
Witness, for example, administrator Robert L. Johnson's testimony in support
of the International Information Administration budget for fiscal 1954:

> I think there are bonds that can be developed that are strong, and may prevent a
> third world war, and I think unless we win the cold war in the next two years we
> are apt to have a third world war. So I am anxious to use all the tools that honorable
> people can use to win the hearts and minds of the people of this world.[18]

Reliance on such arguments compelled the executive branch to send representatives of the military establishment to Capitol Hill to support foreign policy
recommendations. Though Truman took pains to separate the issue of subsequent military aid to Europe from the ratification of the Atlantic treaty, he
arranged for both the Secretary of Defense and the Chairman of the Joint
Chiefs to appear before the Foreign Relations Committee. For the first post-
Korean mutual security program, thirteen out of thirty administration witnesses represented the military establishment. Annually, thereafter, about one-
third of the executive branch witnesses for any aid program would come from
the Pentagon.

The tack taken by the executive branch responded also to the need of other
Representatives and Senators to justify themselves in the eyes of their constituents. Even if they themselves regarded the Executive's policies as wise, they
had to explain to voters why they accepted the risks involved in alliances and
why they contributed money to foreigners. Few felt it adequate to say that
they followed the lead of the President or the Secretary of State or the advice
of diplomats or other political analysts. Most preferred to portray themselves
as defenders of America's security. The fundamental logic of American policy
was the belief that the American people would respond first to what could be
called the logic of fear.

Although the foreign policies of the United States might have been rationalized in military terms in any case, the actual involvement of the Pentagon and military commands in the policy-making process has had the effect of intertwining with the rationale for certain foreign policies a rationale for increased defense spending. It has also entailed an increase in the number and variety of military options available to Presidents in crises, probably at the expense of making other kinds of options either less available or less visible.

But while members of the military establishment have become much involved in foreign policy, few have regarded this as their primary function. Whether in uniform or not, they continue to regard the protection and strengthening of the military services as their primary function. Of course, military men have sometimes supported foreign policies that worked against their parochial interests. Some officers and Pentagon civilians, for example, advocated the Baruch plan, the test-ban treaty of 1953, and other moves toward arms limitation.[19] Secretary McNamara's Montreal speech of 1966 stands as one of the most eloquent appeals for reconsideration of the priority given military security over other national needs.[20] But such instances are exceptions. Most of the time officers and civilians from the military establishment addressing foreign policy issues have taken positions consistent with advocacy of larger investment in military force.

At the end of World War II, these officers and civilians feared a complete dismantling of all American defenses. To an extent, it took place. The Army dropped from over eight million men in 1945 to below 600,000 in 1950. Officers were conscious not only of the time that had been needed to build up forces for World War II but of the fact that advancing technology made lead-time requirements longer than before. B-36 bombers, ordered in 1940, were not to be operational before 1947. A *Midway*-class carrier would not leave the ways until two years after construction began. Fearful lest the country fail to prepare for an unforeseeable future, officers and civilian secretaries in the Pentagon advising Truman inevitably stressed the military dangers that might arise from the diplomatic intransigence and ideological imperialism of the Soviet Union. Equally inevitably, men from the military establishment interpreted the Soviet moves of 1948—the Czech coup and the Berlin blockade—as steps preparatory to aggression. The alternative interpretation—that the U.S.S.R. was reacting to the Truman Doctrine and the Marshall Plan by building a defensive wall—did not lend itself as well to the case for military preparedness.

At subsequent stages, whenever issues turned on predictions regarding future Soviet or Chinese behavior, the military establishment, as a rule, associated itself with the direst forecasts. Such is the military tradition. It was no coincidence that such forecasts in turn provided a rationale for spending money on maintaining or expanding military installations and developing and producing new weapons. Secretaries of Defense usually tried to hold down service demands for funds, and differences of opinion sometimes arose between civilians and professionals over the degree of danger involved in foreign developments. For example, Gates and McNamara evidently took a more hopeful view than the Joint Chiefs of prospects for Soviet agreement to limitations on strategic weapons; both vetoed JCS proposals to proceed with development of full-scale antiballistic missile systems. In the later stages of the Vietnamese war, McNamara and Clifford differed with the Chiefs about the extent of peril entailed in ending that war with something short of victory.

But the range of disagreement over foreign policy between the Secretaries of Defense and the Joint Chiefs has usually been relatively narrow. Though civilian secretaries have fought for economics within the Pentagon, they have still had to go to the Budget Bureau, the White House, and Capitol Hill to demand and argue for immense expenditures. These expenditures have had to be justified in terms of probable perils. Civilians in the military establishment no less than professional officers have felt a positive responsibility to take a pessimistic, foreboding view of actual and potential international issues.

Representatives of civilian agencies should have been able, of course, to discount the biases of the Pentagon just as they might discount those of the Commerce Department or Agriculture Department. To an extent, all Presidents and presidential aides have done so. But, as a rule, they have had to assume that Congress and the public would not do likewise but would instead accept military judgment on foreign affairs as sage, detached, and disinterested. And because Presidents have been aware of the military establishment's prestige with Congress and the public, they have had to pay unusual deference to military opinion, even within their private councils.

The military establishment has gotten from Congress some of what it estimated as the military strength necessary to cope with the foreign contingencies which it forecast. (Not all, to be sure, for Congress has consistently shown a preference for high-technology hardware, involving contracts, profits, and jobs for constituents, over providing the services with manpower or everyday items like machine guns, mortars, and landing craft, and the services have adjusted to this fact by stressing such items in their budgetary planning.) One result has been the military's increasing capacity for suggesting to the President that he employ military force to deal with foreign problems.

At the time of the Berlin blockade, Forrestal and the Joint Chiefs could recommend a limited range of alternatives—send tanks down the *Autobahn* and, if they were halted, use SAC bombers; test whether the Soviets would stop an airlift; or get out. Despite the Korean War buildup, the Joint Chiefs of 1954 could offer Eisenhower only three choices in Indochina—the use of land-based and carrier-based bombers to rescue the French, followed perhaps by contingents of United States ground forces, or the use of nuclear weapons, or taking no military action at all. In the 1960's, on the other hand, with 10 percent of GNP being spent on military capabilities, Kennedy and Johnson could be presented with a variety of alternative military moves suited to defending Berlin, reacting to the placement of Soviet missiles in Cuba, coping with a revolution in the Dominican Republic, or supporting Saigon against the Vietcong. Given their possession of F-105's, F-4's, carriers, destroyers, patrol craft, mine-layers, helicopters Green Beret detachments, etc., etc., the military could, in the latter case, offer a different prescription for each worsening phase.

Theoretically, the President ought to possess the widest possible range of options when dealing with any critical international problem. Such is the meaning of "flexible response." Having on hand a varied mixture of military forces does not make it inevitable or even necessarily more probable that he will use them. It simply provides him the opportunity to do so if he judges such action wisest. But this abstract reasoning ignores at least two realities. In the first place, situations serious enough to entail contemplation of the use of force are almost certainly situations with built-in deadlines. The President cannot spend much time considering all imaginable courses of action; he has to focus on those few which his subordinates are best equipped to carry out. In the second place, the investment required for a wide range of ready military options diverts some resources from preparation and multiplication of other kinds of options. Although one less well-outfitted carrier task force would not convert into one better-equipped State Department country desk, insofar as both demand talent and money (and talent and money are scarce) the one may be had only at the expense of the other.

In practice, therefore, heavy investment in military forces, and most recently, in flexible response, probably has increased the likelihood that a President in a crisis will consider military options above other possible options.

The Cuban missile crisis of 1962 provides an illustration. From the discovery of the missiles on October 14 until October 28, when Khrushchev promised to remove them, the executive committee of the National Security Council (Ex Com) spent at least 90 percent of its time studying alternative uses of troops, bombers, and warships. Although the possibility of seeking withdrawal of the missiles by straightforward diplomatic negotiation received some attention within the State Department, it seems scarcely to have been aired in the Ex Com. At the same time, scarcely any attention went to possible uses of economic leverage. To be sure, any time spent on options other than a "surgical" air strike or a naval quarantine might have been time wasted. But it seems noteworthy that nonmilitary agencies should have had so few expedients to put before the President, and it seems at least possible that this would not have been the case if State, the Treasury, and perhaps some lesser agencies had also been manned and funded for flexible response.

The existence of a variety of military options has probably had less effect in noncrisis situations, when representatives of civilian agencies have had more leisure to reflect on what they might do if the President assigned them a task. Even in routine handling of foreign policy problems, however, the massive presence of the military establishment has very likely had some skewing effects. Officers from the services and the Joint Staff and civilians from the Office of the Secretary of Defense necessarily concentrate on military aspects of issues that come before them. If involved in administering a foreign aid program, they focus on military components. While they can consider and even urge development aid, they must do so in terms of its contribution to military strength. If they take part in preparing a paper on, say, post-Franco Spain, they have to emphasize security aspects. Otherwise, when sitting at a table with representatives of State, CIA, the Treasury, and other agencies, they lead from a weak suit.

While representatives of the military establishment may, and perhaps do, conclude that an economic or diplomatic or other approach to the problem would be preferable, they are precluded from going very far in developing or recommending strategies that involve primarily the resources of other parts of the government since military force is presumed to be their area of competence. Papers from the Pentagon could speak again and again of the crucial importance of Saigon's winning "the hearts and minds" of the Vietnamese peasantry, but their operative paragraphs necessarily dealt with more efficient methods for killing, maiming, or starving a battlefield enemy.

Interdepartmental memoranda on relatively routine foreign policy problems usually represent a blend of views and recommendations. On formal committees, such as assistant secretary level, interdepartmental regional groups of the Johnson administration or interagency groups of the Nixon administration, the military establishment has had two representatives, one from the Joint Staff and one from International Security Affairs. Often, military capabilities have received heavy emphasis in papers relating to noncrisis situations. In sum, while the preoccupation with military security characteristics of post-World War II American foreign policy has to be laid to events, changes in technology, perceptions of the past, and predilections of Congress and the public, the extensive participation of the military establishment in the policy process accentuated this preoccupation, keyed policy to defense expenditures and, in both crisis and noncrisis situations, tended to focus undue concentration on military responses.

The military establishment's participation in the policy process produced some distortive effects. It led to an overemphasis on NATO affairs, the nuclear balance, subversion in Southeast Asia, and other subjects with special implications for the Defense budget or for contests over roles and missions among the services or service branches. It also gave Presidents a richer variety of military options than of other kinds of options, when confronted either with crises or with longer-term problems. In these respects, the military establishment has had a direct and potent impact on foreign policy.

But the character and conduct of United States policy would probably have been the same had the military establishment taken no part at all. For the real or apparent preoccupation with military security reflected the attitudes and values of civilian policy-makers, and ultimately of the American people. The conspicuous role of military men and civilian secretaries in framing and defending foreign policy was traceable in part to belief that visible military support was a political necessity. Under the circumstances that prevailed since World War II, had there been no elements in the military establishment concerned with foreign policy, it is likely Presidents and Secretaries of State would have had to invent them.

The recent past has, however, witnessed changes in the basic factors shaping American foreign policy. The Sino-Soviet split, acute divisions among other Communist states, and shifts in Soviet policy toward the United States and the nations of Western Europe have changed the image of the enemy. In addition, Americans have grown used to the shrinkage of the world and the absence of a sense of invulnerability. The "loss" of Cuba and the outcome of the 1962 missile crisis suggested, at least to some, that localized Communist successes need not jeopardize America's safety quite so much as had been assumed. And, most important of all, the force of military logic and the authoritative status of military professionals as spokesmen on foreign policy—or even on military matters— have diminished.

Mere passage of time accounts in part for this last change. Only men and women of middle age and older remember World Wor II. Many voters scarcely recall Korea. But the prolonged war in Vietnam, where predictions of victory from high military men were once so frequent, has had a decisive impact on most Americans. If they have any image of the contemporary military professional, it is at best that of a technician like General Westmoreland, at worst, a caricature drawn from a novel like *Fail-Safe* or a movie like *Dr. Strangelove*.

Meanwhile, national priorities have changed very critically. Civil rights, the plight of the cities, the needs of urban and rural poor, the restlessness of students, and other such problems have, since the early 1960's, commanded a much larger share of public interest. Although the military establishment's resources occasionally can be used in coping with them, its expertise is largely irrelevant to them. And the war in Vietnam, coinciding with this shift in priorities, and triggering some of them, stirred widespread concern about the expense of policies heretofore vouched for by the military establishment. The spread of this concern and a diminution in respect for military views on foreign policy were registered most visibly in public opinion polls relating to the war and in the surprisingly strong bipartisan movement in Congress against both Johnson's and Nixon's proposals for deploying antiballistic missile systems.

Nor was reaction confined to outspoken "doves." Senator Richard Russell of Georgia, long considered one of the military establishment's warmest supporters on Capitol Hill, indicated as early as 1965 skepticism about military testimony on the importance of Vietnam. "I don't think it has any value strategically," he said. During a hearing in 1968, Russell further declared, "I guess I must be an isolationist. I don't think you ought to pick up 100,000, or 200,000, or 500,000 American boys and ship them off somewhere to fight and get killed in a war as remotely connected with their interests as this one is." [21] Senator John C. Stennis of Mississippi, another longtime champion of the military establishment, asserted in 1967, "I believe that we are overcommitted. . . . I voted glibly for things around here in the fifties to guarantee this and guarantee that. I am certainly one that did not realize how hard it was going to be to carry them out." [22] Representative George H. Mahon of Texas, the shepherd of Defense appropriation bills, in the House declared that the military had "generated . . . lack of confidence" by their "many mistakes." [23] Issuing from such sources, these pronouncements were more than straws in the wind. They indicated that the authority previously attaching to military opinion had virtually disappeared.

These alterations in circumstances, in national priorities, and in public and congressional respect for military wisdom all suggest that major changes in basic American foreign policy are in prospect. Possibly, of course, the change will be temporary. The Korean War was followed by a "never again" mood, accompanied by a slight turn of public interest away from international affairs. Yet preoccupation with military security quickly reasserted itself. The same could occur after Vietnam. Some act of belligerence on the part of the Soviet Union or China could reawaken fears subdued or subsiding. So could a number of other events, including, for example, a sudden transfer of allegiance or collapse within a nation accounted a reliable American ally. Possibly, though, the change in United States policy will bring a long pendulum swing back toward isolationism such as that of the mid-1930's. But what seems more probable at this writing is the evolution of a trinity of operating principles superficially similar to those of earlier eras but different from them in scope and substance: first, a security-based but cooperative "Monroe Doctrine" embracing the great non-Communist industrial powers—the nations of Western Europe and Japan; second, an "Open Door" doctrine entailing support in various forms for economic and political development in less-developed countries, but with no actual or implied commitment to defend their governments against domestic or foreign foes; and, finally, a new version of nonentanglement, involving abrogation or modification of existing treaties with the end of insuring that, except for the defense of Western Europe or Japan, the United States will not be in danger of having to employ ground forces or to employ any forces at all except as part of a broad-based multilateral military effort. (Such a forecast must be accompanied by a caveat, that, if history teaches any lesson, it is that those developments which appear most probable at a given moment are rarely the developments that actually take place.)

It is possible to make slightly more confident predictions about the future of the military establishment in the foreign policy process. Even if the future sees simply a return to the policies of the fifties and early sixties, the Pentagon will probably have less to do with the framing and execution of those policies. For no event seems likely to restore the political charisma and air of infallibility which made support by military men seem almost indispensable for public acceptance of any major foreign policy decision. On the other hand, not even a violent swing toward isolationism could deprive the military establishment of all of its influence or function in the foreign policy process. The chances are that, while military professionals and Pentagon civilians will be less prominent and less influential than in the last three decades, they will continue to have a voice in formulating options and a hand in writing some of the cables and memoranda that form the stuff of foreign policy.

Such a prediction seems safe because the military establishment has developed such strong capabilities for dealing with foreign policy issues. The professional military men upon whom Roosevelt depended so heavily had to learn about international affairs while acting as presidential advisers. Of the wartime chiefs of staff, only Leahy, who spent eighteen months as ambassador to the Vichy regime, had had any experience outside his own service. Typically, by contrast, the service chiefs and other senior officers of the present day will have had prolonged involvement in the subtleties of international politics. General Wheeler (now retired), for example, became Chief of Staff of the Army after a career that included attendance at the National War College, three years of occupation service in Europe, four years with NATO, and three years on the Joint Staff. After moving up to the chairmanship of the JCS, he remarked to a congressional committee, "It is very hard to define where the military begins and the civilians leave off in our form of government." [24]

Senior officers not only possess background and qualifications for work on foreign policy problems; they possess a special organizational capability. The reliance placed on the military establishment by past Presidents has not been wholly a matter of choice. Truman stated an intention to centralize responsibility in the State Department. After acquiring some experience, he remarked regretfully on June 13, 1945, to Forrestal that "there wasn't much material in the State Department to work with." Kennedy started with a similar notion and came to the same conclusion. In the summer of 1961 he found the State Department a "bowl of jelly." [25]

While Truman and Kennedy did not necessarily judge fairly, it has been consistently the case that the State Department has not produced what the White House has wanted. Traditionally, Foreign Service officers have developed skill in reportage, representation, and negotiation. As a rule, they have not practiced reasoning out contingencies, analyzing alternatives, and planning detailed courses of action. Since professional military men do acquire these arts, the Pentagon can outperform the State Department in staff work on foreign policy problems. Though latent capacity for matching the Pentagon may exist in the Agency for International Development, the U.S. Information Agency, the Arms Control and Disarmament Agency, and certain reaches of State, it seems unlikely that the military establishment will be supplanted in this sphere so long as Foreign Service officers dominate the civilian foreign affairs community.

Furthermore, military men are apt to retain roles in the foreign policy process simply because they have them now. The President and his staff could sharply curtail consultation with the chairman and the Chiefs or with the Secretary of Defense. A simple executive order could decree that the military establishment be represented in interagency groups and other such bodies by a civilian or an officer from the Joint Staff, but not both. The State Department officials who ordinarily chair such committees could invite military representatives less regularly. Commanders overseas and chiefs of military aid groups could be directed to communicate with Washington on any subjects affecting foreign policy through State Department or other civilian channels.

But even if policy-makers would not be restrained from taking such steps by awareness of the unusual qualifications and capabilities of the military, they would probably not succeed in drastically civilianizing the process. At every level in State, CIA, and other foreign affairs agencies, consultation with the Pentagon has become an acquired habit, and the habits of bureaucracies are not easily altered. Similarly, overseas commands and military assistance groups have developed functions and procedures no arbitrary organizational change could quickly alter. It is almost inconceivable that the military establishment could be restored to the kind of marginal or fitful role in foreign policy that it occupied prior to 1940.

Finally, it is more than likely that the military establishment will continue to take part in the policy-making process because, regardless of how basic United States policies may change, many major issues are certain to be ones on which the military cannot be denied a voice. No foreseeable set of international agreements will do away with nuclear weapons or missile systems. No détente with the Soviet Union seems likely to end altogether the need for some American military presence in Europe and Asia. Even if there were no other reason, it would be called for in order to reassure Germany's western neighbors and to permit the Japanese to adhere to the arms limitation clauses of their constitution. In addition, it is a prerequisite for making workable any curb on the proliferation of nuclear power.

The military establishment can, of course, be ordered by the President to tailor strategic and general purpose forces to diplomatic ends. If opposition to military spending continues to grow in Congress, the services could find themselves in pre-1940 circumstances, with only a handful of friends on Capitol Hill. The size and composition of the forces could be determined almost wholly by the judgment of civilians outside the establishment, as was the case with the Navy between the signing of the Washington treaty in 1922 and the beginning of rearmament in the 1930's. Even so, generals, admirals, and civilian secretaries would—as in the twenties and thirties—have an undeniable right to be heard. Since the military establishment is now very different, since it possesses staff capabilities not equaled elsewhere in the government, and since it is inextricably meshed with the foreign affairs establishment, it seems most unlikely that military views will ever again, as in the past era, go unheard and unregarded.

Indeed, there seems little chance that the military establishment will be ignored in the framing of foreign policy. The history of the last three decades warns that the opposite danger is greater. The danger does not stem from the military establishment itself. Except possibly for MacArthur, no professional or civilian with any following in that establishment has sought to determine policy, as did Moltke, Schlieffen, Tirpitz, and Tojo. In the past, "militarization" of American foreign policy has developed because civilians adopted military ways of thinking about political problems. The influence of the military establishment on domestic politics or the domestic economy may be functions of its budget or size or power, but its influence on foreign policy depends on an altogether different variable—the extent to which civilians in the executive branch, in Congress, and among the public bear in mind or forget General Marshall's maxim that political problems, if thought about in military terms, become military problems.

NOTES

1. C. Vann Woodward, "The Age of Interpretation," *American Historical Review,* October 1960.

2. Dorothy Borg, *The United States and the Far Eastern Crisis of 1933–1938* (Cambridge: Harvard University Press, 1964), pp. 321–323.

3. SHAEF, Supreme Headquarters Allied Expeditionary Force; SCAP, Supreme Commander for the Allied Powers; SHAPE, Supreme Headquarters Allied Powers (Europe); SACEUR, Supreme Allied Commander, Europe; COMPAC, Commander, Pacific.

4. Homer Lea (1876–1912), American soldier and publicist; military adviser to Sun Yatsen; author of *The Valor of Ignorance,* Harper & Brothers (1909), a detailed prediction of a U.S.-Japanese war.

5. Statement of President Truman to a joint session of Congress, March 12, 1947.

6. *State Department Bulletin,* June 15, 1947, pp. 1159–1160.

7. *Hearings, European Recovery Program,* Congress, Senate, Committee on Foreign Relations, 80th Congress, 2nd Session, p. 480.

8. *Hearings, Military Assistance Program,* Congress, Senate, Armed Services and Foreign Relations Committees, 81st Congress, 1st Session, p. 7.

9. *Hearings, Mutual Society Act of 1951,* Congress, Senate, Armed Services and Foreign Relations Committees, 82nd Congress, 1st Session, pp. 533–537.

10. *Hearings, The President's Proposal on the Middle East,* Congress, Senate, Armed Services and Foreign Relations Committees, 85th Congress, 1st Session, pp. 30–31.

11. *Hearings, Mutual Security Appropriations for 1954,* Congress, Senate, Committee on Appropriations, 83rd Congress, 1st Session, p. 77.

12. *Hearings, United Nations Operation in the Congo,* Congress, House, Committee on Foreign Affairs, 87th Congress, 1st Session, p. 21.

13. *Hearings, The President's Proposal on the Middle East,* p. 5.

14. Adam B. Ulam, *Expansion and Coexistence: Soviet Foreign Policy, 1917–1967* (New York: Praeger, 1968), pp. 504–514, 610–613.

15. As examples, see Denna F. Fleming, *The Cold War and Its Origins, 1917–1960,* 2 vols. (New York: Doubleday, 1961): Gar Alperovitz, *Atomic Diplomacy: Hiroshima and Potsdam—The Use of the Atomic Bomb and American Confrontation with Soviet Power* (New York: Simon and Schuster, 1965); David Horowitz, *Free World Colossus* (New York: Hill and Wang, 1965); and, as the most responsible statement of such a position, Walter LaFeber, *America, Russia, and the Cold War, 1945–1966* (New York: John Wiley, 1967).

16. Some of this correspondence is now published in *Foreign Relations of the United States, 1945—*Vol. I: *General: The United Nations* (Washington, D.C.: Department of State, 1968), Vol. II: *General: Political and Economic Matters,* Vol. III: *European Advisory Commission, Austria, Germany,* Vol. IV: *Europe,* Vol. V: *Europe,* Vol. VIII: *The Near East and Africa,* and *Foreign Relations of the United States, 1946,* Vol. V: *The British Commonwealth; Western and Central Europe,* 1969.

17. Roy E. Appleman, *South to the Naktong, North to the Yalu, June–November, 1950* (Washington, D.C.: Office of the Chief of Military History, Department of the Army, 1961), p. 7.

18. *Hearings, Overseas Information Programs of the United States,* Congress, Senate, Committee on Foreign Relations, 83rd Congress, 1st Session, p. 869.

19. In the case of the nuclear test-ban treaty, however, the Joint Chiefs of Staff attached a set of conditions to their agreement to support the treaty: that withdrawal from the obligations of the treaty be as easy as possible; that the government pursue an aggressive program of underground testing, not barred by the treaty, and that other research and development facilities, for testing in those environments forbidden by the treaty, be kept intact and ready for action should the treaty be broken. *Nuclear Test Ban Treaty,* Hearings

before the Committee on Foreign Relations, U.S. Senate, 88th Congress, 1st session, 1963, pp. 274–275. All of the Chiefs testified that, unless their conditions were, in fact, met, they would have to oppose the treaty. During the Senate hearings, for example, General Wheeler, then Army Chief of Staff, reminded the committee that "in the purest sense of the term any agreement or treaty which limits the manner in which we develop our weapons systems represents a military disadvantage." *Ibid.*, p. 355. The treaty was ratified by a vote of 80 to 19.

20. Robert S. McNamara, *The Essence of Security* (New York: Harper & Row, 1968), pp. 141–158.

21. Interview on CBS television, August 1, 1965, quoted in Theodore Draper, *The Abuse of Power* (New York: Viking, 1967), p. 154; *Hearings, Department of Defense Appropriations for 1969*, Congress, Senate, Committee on Appropriations, Part V, p. 2545.

22. *Hearings, Worldwide Military Commitments*, Congress, Senate, Committee on Armed Services, 90th Congress, 1st Session, Part II, p. 133.

23. *Congressional Record*, 91st Congress, 1st Session, Vol. 115, Part 10, p. 13128.

24. *Hearings, Department of Defense Appropriations for 1964*, Congress, House, Committee on Appropriations, 88th Congress, 1st Session, Part II, p. 131.

25. Walter Millis and Eugene S. Duffield, eds., *The Forrestal Diaries* (New York: Viking, 1951), p. 62; Arthur M. Schlesinger, Jr., *A Thousand Days: John F. Kennedy in the White House* (Boston: Houghton Mifflin, 1965), p. 406.

IMPERIAL OR EXEMPLARY AMERICA?

34.

Wolfgang Friedmann: Interventionism, Liberalism, and Power Politics: The Unfinished Revolution in International Thinking

Some critics of American "globalism" have advocated disengagement or reduction of commitments abroad. Others, who are fearful of "neoisolationism," emphasize continuing American responsibilities in the world arena. In the selection that follows, Wolfgang Friedmann discusses aspects of the fundamental revolution in international thinking that has broken the Wilsonian alliance of liberal humanitarianism and international activism and has contributed to America's "imperialist strategy of interventionism."

The late Wolfgang Friedmann was Professor of International Law at the Columbia University Law School; his many publications include *Introduction to World Politics* and the *Changing Structure of International Law.*

The deepening debate over the role to be played by the United States in the world, and in particular the widening split over the rights and wrongs of the Vietnamese war, conceals a revolution in international thinking of fundamental proportions. It will be the purpose of the present article to survey the

Wolfgang Friedmann, "Interventionism, Liberalism, and Power Politics: The Unfinished Revolution in International Thinking," *Political Science Quarterly*, Vol. 83, No. 2 (June 1968), pp. 168–89. Reprinted by permission of the *Political Science Quarterly*.

major aspects of this revolution. It will be suggested that the Wilsonian alliance, even identity, between liberal humanitarianism and international activism—which began after World War I and lasted for nearly half a century—has broken up. The continuing weakness of the United Nations—in the areas of international security as well as of international protection of self-determination and human rights—accompanied by an explosive increase in the number of new, economically, militarily, and politically weak states—has accentuated the global strategic and political conflict between the superpowers. This has led to an imperialist strategy of interventionism supported in the United States by right-wing nationalists and opponents of international organization. The strategists of empire are, however, divided between those who recognize a "spheres of interest" accommodation between the United States and its two major opponents and those who claim a universal police role for the United States.

The Alliance of Humanitarians and Internationalists

For nearly half a century—since the end of World War I and the establishment of the League of Nations—certain broad alignments and a high degree of continuity in the approach to international affairs prevailed. Humanitarians, liberals, and internationalists could combine in support of the ideals of the League of Nations, in the Wilsonian objectives of substituting international authority for national power, collective security for the national use of force and old-type alliances, the rule of law in international affairs for the supremacy of the sovereign national state. The transfer of the right to use force from individual states to a universal international organization meant protection of the weak states against the strong, the use of law as an equalizer. This was a fundamental revolution in international affairs, for up to 1919 international law had served essentially as a means of regulating diplomatic intercourse between states *in times of peace*. Once a state decided that its national interests or appetites required the use of force, there was no principle of international law to restrain it from doing so.

Together with this new concern of international law for the protection of the weak states against the strong, through an international organization founded on law, went humanitarian concern for the welfare of the individual on an international scale. Its first token was the International Labor Organization, founded together with the League of Nations, and articulating for the first time the concern for the social welfare of people all over the world as an international responsibility. The reorganization of the international community after World War II greatly widened the range of international preoccupations with the individual, not only through the creation of such international welfare agencies as the World Bank, the Food and Agriculture Organization, or the World Health Organization, but also through continuing efforts to formulate international standards of human rights. The 1948 Universal Declaration of Human Rights was followed in 1966 by the Covenants of Human Rights passed by the General Assembly of the United Nations. More important, perhaps, the European Convention on Human Rights sponsored by the seventeen-nation

Council of Europe set up for its member states an effective supranational administrative and judicial machinery to protect the rights of individuals even against their own government.

In all these respects, the objectives of humanitarian liberals and of what Arthur Schlesinger has called in a recent article in *Foreign Affairs* the "universalists," went hand in hand. Method and objectives were, on both counts, interventionist. If, in the initial stages of the League of Nations, there was a certain confusion between pacifists and advocates of collective security, the successive crises calling for armed intervention by the League against an aggressor —of which the most blatant were Japan's annexation of Manchuria in 1931 and Italy's invasion of Abyssinia in 1935—soon showed that an effective League meant not the abolition of force but the transfer of legal and political authority to use it to the international community. Correspondingly, the concern with welfare, justice, and individual rights on an international scale could become effective only if these matters were made the object of international legislation and judicial institutions empowered to enforce international standards.

Two Kinds of Nationalism

Skeptical of, or openly opposed to, the coalition of humanitarian liberals and universalists were the believers in the nation-state as the ultimate source of power and the focus of individual allegiance and loyalty.

But anti-internationalist attitudes—the disbelief in either the possibility or the desirability of a supranational order that would derogate from the absoluteness of national sovereignty—has always taken two very different and, in many ways, antithetic forms: one is an inward-looking nationalism, the desire to develop national interests and policies with a minimum possible entanglement in foreign affairs and foreign nations; the other is an outward-looking and usually expansionist nationalism, an assertive and often militaristic stance which would inevitably clash with the competing national interests of other nation-states and thus provoke conflict. The second form of nationalism is more highly developed in the major states because it is dependent on military and economic power. Smaller powers can practice expansionist nationalism on a limited, usually regional, scale, as is notably shown by the turbulent history of the Middle East. But even the large powers show the conflict between inward-looking and expansionist nationalism. In nineteenth-century Britain the conflict of attitudes was symbolized by the rival philosophies of the "little Englander" Gladstone and the imperialist Disraeli. On the whole, however, the very fact of world-wide interests—political, military, or commercial—as a country like Great Britain had them since at least the beginning of the seventeenth century made an inward-looking attitude impossible. A maritime power in particular, which must develop and protect world-wide commerce on the seas, cannot but be drawn into the outward-looking and expansionist form of nationalism. Thus Britain—like other colonizing and seafaring powers (Holland, France, Spain, and Portugal)—had to develop a navy capable of protecting its possessions and commercial interests on all the oceans. It had to fight Spain and France in the

West Indies, intervene in the Russian-Turkish conflicts, and finally face the major challenge of Germany to its colonial and maritime predominance.

Where one major power achieves such pre-eminence that it cannot be effectively challenged by any other—as did the Roman empire at the height of its power—the progressive expansion of nationalist ambitions leads to the suppression or subjugation of other nationalities. Rome developed from a tribe to a nation, and from a nation to an empire controlling most of Europe, North Africa, and the Near East. There was no rival superpower to contest its law-making supremacy, and it was only gradually, from within the empire, that the conquered peoples developed toward a status of legal and civil equality.

In modern times the claim to empire has to proceed by the suppression of rival national claims. Driven to its ultimate logic, this leads, for example, to the short-lived attempts of the Nazi empire based on the suppression or extinction of other nationalities and races. The Nazi ideology was not the fulfillment but the antithesis of nationalism.

Contradictions in United States Policy

The history of the United States reveals a split personality. Throughout the nineteenth and early twentieth centuries, one dominant theme was the turning away from the conflicts of the nations of Europe. This coincided with a period of relative naval weakness and was progressively modified as the United States became a major maritime and international commercial power. The attempts of the United States in the first phase of World War I to maintain and enforce its neutrality came to an end with the sinking of the *Lusitania,* America's entry in the war, and the turn from an inward-looking aloofness to the universalist conception of Wilson and the League of Nations. The Neutrality Act of 1935 represented the last desperate attempt to enforce a semi-isolationist kind of neutrality by insisting on "cash and carry" in cargoes, that is, payment in advance and transfer of title taken by any belligerent from the United States. The effectiveness of this last fling at neutrality by a great power was eroded by Lend-Lease and political sympathies even before Pearl Harbor turned the United States into a major belligerent and shocked it into consciousness of its world-power position. This still left open the alternatives between the "spheres of interest" and the "universalist" views (Schlesinger's antithesis), but effectively ruled out the inward-turning isolationist form of nationalism.

In inter-American affairs the United States had, however, always asserted the privileges of a major power, claiming an imperial role in the regulation of continental affairs. Although the Monroe Doctrine of 1823 has never been recognized as part of international law, and although it has been repudiated by many Latin-American states, it has been a pillar of United States policy for a century and a half. Franklin Roosevelt's "Good Neighbor" policy was a partially successful attempt to alter the image of the United States by stressing voluntary coexistence with equals rather than the privileged status of the overmighty. The political significance of American intervention in the Dominican Republic in 1965 lay in the fact that it revived the memory of dozens of similar armed interventions by the United States in the affairs of her smaller neighbors. Unlike earlier interventions, however, this was undertaken in defiance of the emphatic affirmation, in Articles XV and XVII of the OAS Charter, of the absolute integrity and territorial sovereignty of all the member states. It is for this reason that the turn from the original limited objective of protecting the safety and property of a limited number of United States citizens to the claim, made in President Johnson's Baylor speech of May 5, 1965, that the United States could not and would not tolerate a Communist regime in the hemisphere, was seen widely as a return to the older philosophy of continental hegemony. Nor can the Dominican intervention or United States action in the Cuban Missile Crisis of October 1962 be taken as an acceptance of the "spheres of interests" philosophy. The deepening involvement of the United States in Vietnam and in other parts of Asia is an expression of a *global* "containment" policy which does not concede regional hegemony to China or any other regional paramount power in a manner corresponding to the hegemony claimed by the United States on the American continent. Present official policy of the United States is, therefore, a combination of a policy of regional hegemony—that is, a "spheres of interest" imperialism—and a "universalist" philosophy with regard to the rest of the world. But it is universalism with a difference. U.S. interventions, especially in Vietnam—whether based on international law or on national interest—are not predicated on collective action by the United Nations or even by a regional defense organization such as SEATO. The intervening power decides unilaterally that its intervention is required; it is both judge and prosecutor. And when the invocation of international law becomes tenuous, old-fashioned national interest takes its place, as in President Johnson's Texas speech of October 1967, justifying United States intervention in Vietnam. Where an intervening power becomes the self-appointed executant of a global policy, the universalism of the League Covenant or the UN Charter becomes a pale shadow. The only conceivable justification for such a dichotomy of attitudes is the assertion that the United States stands, globally and regionally, as a defender of self-determination and freedom, a guardian of the principles of the Charter which the United Nations itself is unable to enforce. In the absence of any international determination or authority, however, such a claim carries no conviction except with those who for reasons of their own are allied with the United States. The assertion of moral ideals or the invocation of law is seen by the opponents of the United States as a thin disguise for the exercise of its national power.

Nationalism and the Smaller Countries

It is essentially a limited number of small or medium-sized, developed, and satisfied states that can practice inward-looking nationalism, concentrating on the development of their material and spiritual resources, defending themselves as best they can against encroachments but not reaching outward aggressively. The states that spring to mind as being clearly in this category are the smaller countries of Western Europe, notably the Scandinavian states, the Netherlands, Switzerland, and, on this side of the Atlantic, Canada. It is significant that it is these very countries that have, since the end of World War I and even more strongly since the end of World War II, played a leading role in the strengthening of international organization and the struggle for the substitution of international authority for the use of national force. They have repeatedly supplied contingents for United Nations emergency forces, in the Gaza Strip, in Cyprus, in the Congo, or provided mediators for international disputes. They are part of the Western world, that is, they belong to the group of nations that was until very recently responsible for the development of international law. It is because they are, on the one hand, satisfied nations and, on the other hand, too small to be able to aspire to political and military expansion in the mid-twentieth century that they are the chief champions of a moderate "universalism." The attitudes of the newer countries are on the whole more complex and ambivalent. None of them—from giants such as India to dwarfs such as the Maldive Islands—can afford to rely on its own political, military, and economic power. Neither can they accept the *status quo,* in the way that the smaller nations of Western Europe can, because they are to a greater or lesser extent dissatisfied with the present distribution of political and economic power. They will support universal, international organizations, such as the United Nations and the specialized agencies, to the extent that they will reflect and foster the aspirations of the newer countries. The accession of more and more new and weak countries to the United Nations has altered the balance of voting power, though not of military and economic strength. The newer countries will use the General Assembly of the United Nations to the utmost, since it reflects the principle of the equality of nations, big or small, by giving one vote to each. They will support the World Bank and its sister institutions insofar as they are the chief recipients of the aid dispensed by these organizations, and they will strongly support such newer organizations as UNCTAD, in which the developing countries form a special group of their own, designed to improve the terms of trade and other economic relations of the developing vis-à-vis the economically developed world. On the other hand, their attitude has generally been one of aloofness and skepticism toward the International Court of Justice which they take to reflect by and large the international legal system as developed by the Western world. The recent judgment of the International Court in the Second Southwest Africa Case, which, blandly repudiating an earlier judgment to the contrary, rejected the claim of Liberia and Ethiopia to have standing to challenge the apartheid policy of the Union of South Africa in Southwest Africa, has greatly increased the distrust of the newer countries in the role of the Court.

Postwar Developments and the Change of Fronts

It is a remarkable fact that the alliance between the internationalists, the humanitarians, and the liberals generally held firm, from the early days of the League of Nations through the various crises of the League of Nations, the Spanish Civil War, World War II, and most of the postwar period. A number of factors combined to keep these various ideological groupings together. It was not so surprising that the League of Nations in its first phase received the enthusiastic support not only of the internationalists but also of humanitarian liberals. After the carnage and devastation of the war, the new belief in the substitution of international law for national force was still fresh and untried enough to put the various idealisms together, especially as the International Labor Organization and the establishment of the Permanent Court of International Justice were symbols of the concern for social welfare and international justice. In the supreme crisis of the League of Nations—the question of the application of sanctions against Italy after the invasion of Abyssinia—the front held, since the desire of the internationalists to stop and punish so naked an act of aggression went together with the liberal and humanitarian hostility to the Fascist regime of Mussolini's Italy and the corresponding desire to protect a small and unaggressive country. The emasculation of League sanctions—from which coal, steel, and oil, the most important items, were exempted—gravely weakened faith in the effectiveness of international security organization. The Spanish Civil War put a further strain on the old alliance of forces, since, on the one hand, devoted Catholics generally felt bound to follow the strong support of the Catholic Church for the Franco regime and, on the other, liberals and moderate Socialists found themselves in an alliance of necessity with Communists and the Soviet Union in support of the Republican government. By that time the League of Nations was already too much weakened by the disaster of the Abyssinia episode to play any role. But, generally, those who supported strong League action against Italy in the Abyssinia invasion also favored the Republican forces in the Spanish Civil War, especially in view of the blatant political and military support given to Franco from the very beginning by Hitler and Mussolini. And it was on a much larger and more decisive scale that the anti-Fascist forces joined the supporters of universalist ideology to form the great coalition of World War II. On the one side were the Fascist and aggressive powers, Hitler's Germany, Mussolini's Italy, and, later, the Japan of Pearl Harbor and the "Co-Prosperity Sphere"; on the other side were the remaining democracies of Western Europe and, later, the United States. The world-wide coalition against fascism was also a world-wide coalition against aggression. The association of the Soviet Union with the Western democracies was made possible because she was a victim of aggression and her support was needed to make victory over the Fascist powers possible. The problems which were later to take prominence in the cold war phase were not yet of primary importance. The Atlantic Charter could combine the proclamation of resistance to Nazi aggression with yearning for freedom and social progress, a yearning which found notable expression in the 1945 Labor victory in Britain and the series of welfare-state projects and nationalizations of basic industries in Britain and France. The United Nations Charter embodied the aspirations of a more sober, more realistic, but still hopeful, world in the combination of the concept of world-wide security under the auspices of the Security Council with the predominance of the Big Five (in effect, Four) acting as joint guardians of world peace and joint custodians of a defeated, but soon to be reunited and reconstructed, Germany.

Anti-Communism and the Growing Split

Even the growing impact of the cold war—manifested in the division of Germany, the failure of the attempt to set up an international military force as provided by the United Nations Charter, and the increasing use of the veto by the U.S.S.R in the Security Council—still left the combination of liberal humanitarians and international activists basically intact. Liberals and believers in the idea of collective security generally supported the attempt to substitute in part regionally collective defense organizations, notably the North Atlantic Alliance, for the shattered structure of universal collective security. Creators of the NATO Alliance were such good internationalists as Lester Pearson of Canada and Senator Vandenberg of the United States. At the same time the Marshall Plan of 1947 laid the basis for a continuing and world-wide involvement of the United States in reconstruction and development aid, supporting the objectives of the International Bank for Reconstruction and Development and appealing equally to universalists and humanitarians. But the beginnings of future discords and reversals of attitudes began to be apparent in the growing significance of anti-Communist ideology. Those primarily preoccupied with ideological and strategic opposition to Communist expansion could go along with NATO and other regional defense organizations. But this became increasingly difficult as regional defense organizations such as OAS and SEATO were used as instruments by the United States of its power conflicts with major opponents. The growing depth of the ideological split and the passions engendered, especially in the United States, by the fear of "international communism" brought the first of a number of major shifts in the alignment of forces. On the one hand, many, though by no means all, liberals and humanitarians do not feel the same way about communism as they do about fascism. While strongly opposed to totalitarianism, dictatorship, and the suppression of human freedoms, they see in communism at least the potential of a liberating force, a concern with human values and social and economic progress together with a rejection of racial antagonisms. In fascism, on the other hand, especially in the Nazi version, they see nothing but a nihilistic lust for power, a rejection of any international order, the glorification of race hatred and even genocide, and the perversion of nationalism into a full-fledged imperialism that suppresses the autonomy of nations and self-determination. While, during the height of the Stalinist terror, the differences between the two types of regimes tended to recede, they have again come to the fore since the relative liberalization of the Soviet regime after the death of Stalin and the stabilization of positions at least in Europe. This meant that liberals and humanitarians would be less inclined to regard communism, and the danger of its advance, as an absolute evil comparable to the aggressive expansion of fascism. On the other side, many nationalists and isolationists—who had viewed the suppression of liberal and democratic forces in Europe with indifference or who had even welcomed the German Nazi regime as a counter-weight to, and possible destroyer of, Communist Russia—tended to become the ardent champions of an interventionist foreign policy by the United States, provided it was designed to keep communism everywhere in check or even to push it back. In the cry of resistance to International Communism two different objectives and perspectives often become inextricably confused: the hostility to communism as a social philosophy repugnant to the "American way of life"[1] and resistance to a conglomeration of powers that are considered a threat to the national security of the United States. In the official defense of United States involvement in Vietnam there is a constant shift between the two, so that it is impossible to ascertain whether the United States would feel compelled to continue to fight in the interest of national security even if a war-weary South Vietnam decided to make peace with the Communists and to accept the possibility of a Communist-controlled unified Vietnam. Where, as in the Cuban Missile Crisis, the ideological element was overshadowed by the national security confrontation between the United States and the U.S.S.R., U.S. intervention received almost universal support, domestically and internationally. In their extreme form, the anti-Communist interventionists support preventive war, against the Soviet Union, or, at a time when the Soviet Union appears less menacing, against Communist China. The ultimate reason for this conversion of neutralists and isolationists to interventionists—globally although even more emphatically within the American hemisphere—is their fear that communism might ultimately threaten their own essentially conservative and capitalist way of life and conception of society. It is generally the same forces—intensely nationalistic, ardent advocates of a strong military establishment, and passionately anti-Communist—that are also skeptical of, or downright hostile to, any development aid other than assistance to anti-Communist countries. They tend to look upon the new countries as potentially more susceptible to Socialist—which to most of them means the same as Communist—ideologies and influences. They are instinctively skeptical about the humanitarian motivations of foreign development aid and cynical about the usefulness of such aid except as a *quid pro quo* for the promise of military support. They also continue to see communism as a monolithic phenomenon, an international force united and clear in its purposes, in Cuba or North Vietnam or in the election of a left-wing government in the Dominican Republic.

The reverse side of this picture is that liberal humanitarians—and to a large extent the supporters of the United Nations as a collective force for peace—have adopted certain aspects of what superficially appears like isolationism in their hostility to ubiquitous American political and military entanglement. The new attitude is, however, more than a reaction to the interventionism of the onetime isolationist nationalists. It is supported by the disintegration of international communism as a monolithic force, the undoubted emergence of nationalist dissensions and policies within the Communist camp corresponding to the growing diversities and dissensions in the Western camp. The humanitarian liberals believe that diversity in communism counters the monolithic and aggressive character of the ideology. They therefore welcome the emergence of nationalist communism, although ideologically they, like the supporters of universal organization and security, reject nationalism in principle as an outdated phenomenon, inappropriate to the realities of the mid-twentieth century. A painful but inevitable consequence of this attitude of non-interference is the sacrifice of the humanitarian-universalist crusading zeal directed against oppressive regimes. Non-intervention means tolerance of foreign revolutions even if they are brutal and undemocratic and suppress human rights. This is in accordance with the fundamental principles of international law, which is based on the coexistence of sovereign states differing widely in their political and social structure. It is quite contrary to the Wilsonian tradition: in his first term, Wilson sought to withhold recognition from the revolutionary Mexican regime because of its "unconstitutional" methods. And many liberal internationalists would have supported foreign intervention against the internal brutality of the Nazi regime. If it is for the Vietnamese to settle their affairs without foreign interference, by civil war or otherwise, the same principle must be applied to South African apartheid, however brutal, as long as it remains within the borders of the Union. (Its application to the trust-territory of Southwest Africa raises, of course, international issues which have been the subject of successive actions before the International Court.) The justification for the shift in attitude is threefold. First, the United States has long abandoned the attempt to enforce democracy abroad. The majority of present-day governments are undemocratic; any general policy of seeking to topple or modify them would be vastly beyond the resources of any power. It would also be self-defeating, since foreign interferences stimulate nationalist resistance. Even the modest and benevolent American attempts to use Alliance for Progress assistance for internal changes have aroused opposition in Latin America. Second, the United States has been noticeably more tolerant of right-wing than of left-wing dictatorships, for example, in Latin America. It has had friendly relations with right-wing dictators like Perón of Argentina, Jimenez of Venezuela, Batista of Cuba, Stroessner of Paraguay, and, for most of the time, Trujillo of the Dominican Republic. But it intervened against left-wing regimes in Guatemala, the Dominican Republic, and Cuba, and, outside the Americas, in Greece (1947) and Vietnam. Since in the new countries nationalism and Communist left-wing movements are often allied, because both are directed against social and economic oppression—much of it linked with foreign interests—United States intervention against left-wing nationalism of necessity must often ally itself with reactionary forces and the social *status quo*.

Third, humanitarians and internationalists both support collective action against external aggression. In the Korean conflict of the early fifties United States intervention had their general support because it arose from an open—though not perhaps entirely unprovoked—act of aggression by North Korea and was sanctioned by the United Nations. The deep split over United States intervention in Vietnam stems from disagreement between government and opposition about the real character of the conflict. Whereas the government maintains that it merely resists aggression by North Vietnam against an independent South Vietnam, the opposition stresses that the original United States intervention in setting up a separate anti-Communist state of South Vietnam, in violation of the Geneva Accords, was designed to prevent Vietnamese unification under Communist auspices and antedated the introduction of organized North Vietnamese military forces.

The New American Interventionism and the Revolt of the Liberal Internationalists

It is opposition to the *unilateral* use of military and economic power for intervention in various parts of the world, as distinct from the use of military and economic force as international sanctions of law on behalf of the international community, that is the main reason for the growing rebellion of the liberal-internationalist group against the new American interventionism. The mere use of collective and legal phraseology—such as the "right of individual or collective self-defense"—ceases to carry conviction when the actual decisions to intervene, by military and economic means, are made, not by an international security organization—the United Nations or even NATO, SEATO, or OAS —but in the Pentagon and the White House. To the great majority of nations, as to a large number of Americans, the assertion that the United States intervenes in Vietnam or in the Dominican Republic in order to safeguard freedom and self-determination against aggression or tyranny is unconvincing. This is not the place to reiterate the legal debate on these issues, nor to weigh the political or moral aspects of intervention in a particular case. What matters is that a unilateral national decision to use military power is in essence a return to the pre-1919 policies, disguised by a fragile collectivist phraseology. Liberal and univeralist opinion is all the more opposed to such a return as it occurs in a kind of international society which was virtually non-existent in 1919 and barely discernible in 1945, a society in which the multitude of new states which until recently were in a colonial or quasi-colonial status are accorded the right of self-determination. While the sovereign equality of states has always been a theoretical postulate of international law, most of the nation-states of our day— Asian, African, and in effect though not in name most of the Latin American States—were excluded. Such emphatic assertions of territorial integrity, independence, and self-determination as the relevant articles of the OAS Charter or the "Principles of International Law concerning Friendly Relations Among States," formulated by a Special United Nations Committee in 1966, are recent expressions of both factual and ideological developments that postdate the United Nations Charter. Although the proliferation of nation-states, which has more than doubled the number of "sovereign" states in a decade, is an anachronism, at a time when the discrepancy between nominal and actual sovereignty is greater than ever and effective power concentrated in the hands of fewer and fewer states, it is a political reality. It has aggravated the dilemma of the United States. The growing gulf between the assertion of hegemonial power and the strategic interests of a world power, on the one hand, and respect for international law and the self-determination of nations, on the other, becomes more and more difficult to bridge. On the one side, there are those who believe that in the reality of the power struggle between the United States and its two principal rivals, the U.S.S.R. and China, respect for international law, self-determination, and the like must come second. Such principles will, in Dean Acheson's phrase—used on the occasion of the Cuban Missile Crisis—serve as "ethical restraint" but will yield to higher necessities. Not all of those who oppose this view are inspired by an overriding respect for the rule of law in international affairs or the self-determination of small and weak countries. An influential segment of the opposition comes from those whom Arthur Schlesinger describes as the advocates of a "spheres of interest" approach. The proponents of this view accept the reality of the big power struggle and the claim of any of the superpowers to some regional hegemony in areas and matters of paramount proximity and importance. They maintain that such a right must be reciprocal and that what the United States claims in the American hemisphere must be conceded to the Soviet Union and to China—even a Communist China—in their respective paramount spheres of influence. As earlier advocates of such an approach, Schlesinger mentions Wallace, Harriman, and Kennan. Among contemporaries, Walter Lippmann, Hans Morgenthau, and others, including some military leaders, may be added. By contrast, the heirs of the humanitarian and internationalist tradition believe that, in the contemporary world, the overwhelming physical and military power of a few superstates—which tend to neutralize each other short of a nuclear catastrophe—is countered by the increasing collective influence of the growing number of medium and smaller states, inside and outside the United Nations. Respect for the principles of international law—which are largely designed to protect the weaker states against the superiority of the large powers—is a vitally important factor in the balance of world politics. The adherents of this view also point out that the United States has been least successful and incurred the heaviest burdens where it has intervened directly and by military force, as in Vietnam, whereas some of the internal revolutions most beneficial to the anti-Communist world and the interests of the United States have occurred from within, as in Indonesia or Ghana, and that several of the new African states have revolted against excessive Chinese interferences in areas where the United States has abstained from intervention.

A small band of liberals still dares to argue in terms of moral issues rather than of *Realpolitik*. Thus, Senator Fulbright asserted recently that even if North Vietnam were defeated the U.S. intervention in Vietnam would be a moral wrong. A by-product of this deepening conflict is the fate of foreign development aid. It is not without bitter irony that men like Senator Fulbright —whose name first became known through his sponsorship of the use of lend-lease counterpart funds for the advancement of international educational exchanges and who has been an advocate of development aid for many years— should now oppose the United States program for development aid. The explanation of this change must be seen in the intimate association of economic and military assistance and the use of economic aid, directly or indirectly, for the bolstering of states and governments in which the United States has a strategic interest. Hence, Senator Fulbright advocates—though with scant hope of success—a far-reaching transfer of development aid to multinational institutions such as the World Bank or its affiliated agency, the International Development Association. Since any far-reaching transfer of United States and other national development aid to international agencies is extremely unlikely, the practical result of this attitude is, unfortunately, a net reduction of the total amount of development aid.

The Split of the Intellectuals

The collapse of the alliance between the different groups and movements which have for so long marched in step is reflected in a deep split between the approaches of intellectuals to the major foreign policy problems of this time. Whereas one group of intellectuals regards the danger of interventionist power politics as so overwhelming that it is willing to sacrifice much of the humanitarian concern for universal freedom and democracy, another, on the contrary, regards it as the foremost task of American intellectuals to accept the world-wide struggle of power and ideology as the controlling facet of international politics, and to formulate the objectives of United States policy accordingly. The latter approach is clearly shown in a recent article on "American Intellectuals in Foreign Policy." [2] In this article the author launches a broad attack upon the contemporary American intellectual community because it fails to give the "intellectual and moral guidance" to the imperial policy which the United States has to pursue

in order to sustain a world order that (a) ensures its national security as against the other great powers, (b) encourages other nations, especially the smaller ones, to mold their own social, political and economic institutions along lines that are at least not repugnant to (if not actually congruent with) American values, and (c) minimizes the possibility of naked, armed conflict.

The foregoing analysis should have shown that this formulation of the objectives of United States policy slurs over the clashes between these various objectives. The author asserts that the intellectuals of this country (and apparently intellectuals everywhere) have overwhelmingly been dissenters from national policy.[3] He observes that "no modern nation has ever constructed a foreign policy that was acceptable to its intellectuals." This is an astonishing assertion to make for a citizen of a country whose structure and policies were forged by the most eminent group of intellectuals ever to guide a nation—men like Adams, Franklin, Jefferson, Madison, Paine. They were not perhaps the type of intellectuals acceptable to Mr. Kristol, since their predominant philosophy was humanitarian and influenced by the rationalist enlightenment outlook of the *encyclopédistes* of the eighteenth century.

But the role of the intellectuals in the nineteenth century should be much more to Mr. Kristol's liking. For as Julien Benda has shown in his classic study *La Trahison des Clercs*, intellectuals have played a decisive role throughout the nineteenth and early twentieth centuries in the shaping of nationalist ideologies and the support of nationalist policies. Nor is this merely a question of intellectuals usually being ready to support the nation at "moments of national peril or national exultation." The influence of men like Fichte, Hegel, Nietzsche, Mazzini, Gentili, Barrès, or Maurras on the strident nationalism of Germany, Italy, and France, their influence not only on ideology but on the actions of political leaders such as Hitler, Mussolini, or de Gaulle can hardly be exaggerated. Nobody illustrates the capacity of intellectuals to rationalize nationalism and imperialism more powerfully than Hegel, one of the principal mentors of both German and Italian aggressive nationalism. By manipulating his dialectical categories so as to make the nation-state, pursuing its destiny by war, the ultimate instrument and fulfiillment of the *Weltgeist,* and by simultaneously extolling absolute monarchy against any form of democracy or liberalism, as a matter not of political choice but of dialectical necessity, Hegel provided spurious intellectual underpinning for the policies that culminated—and finally collapsed—in Hitler's Germany and Mussolini's Italy. More than any other intellectual, Hegel symbolized the role of the intellectual as the rationalizer of national ambitions.

Fortunately, there are others. As was pointed out some years ago by Marcus Cunliffe,[4] there have been essentially two types of intellectuals: those acting as spokesmen of the society in which they live, and those who are alienated from the assumptions on which their society rests. Insofar as one of the essential attributes of an intellectual is his power of critical analysis, it is natural that many, but by no means all, intellectuals should be critical of their society. But the days when intellectuals as a class, in America or elsewhere, were a dissident minority, regarded with universal suspicion and excluded from seats of power, are over. Today, as Hofstadter points out, the great majority of intellectuals, be they lawyers, political scientists, economists, or scientists, are exposed to conflicting pulls—to assume a detached and independent critical posture, or to accept the challenge of responsibility and the sharing of power. Mainly under the Roosevelt and Kennedy administrations, but also under the Johnson administration, intellectuals have played prominent parts in the articulation of policies and in their intellectual vindication. As senior policy-making officials or ambassadors, men like Adlai Stevenson, McGeorge Bundy, Arthur Schlesinger Jr., George Kennan, John Kenneth Galbraith, and many others who, whether professional academics or not can be described as intellectuals, have played leading roles. At the present time Eugene and Walt Rostow and Nicholas Katzenbach, all academics by profession, hold key positions in government. Moreover, some intellectual critics such as Senators Fulbright or Eugene McCarthy are part of the machinery of government even though they hold no executive positions of command. Kristol's contention that intellectuals generally refuse to descend from the level of abstraction to the concrete demands and conflicting aims and practical necessities which determine foreign policy is, at the very least, a gross exaggeration. It also ignores the fact that many intellectuals are almost pathologically afraid of being branded as "starry-eyed idealists." Emphasis on the realities of power, rejection of blueprints, a deliberately "value-neutral," scientific "behaviorist" approach to the consequences of a thermonuclear holocaust characterize a great deal of modern political and social science. To state an issue in terms of moral right and wrong is widely regarded as naïve. Most of the debate about U.S. interventions, in Vietnam and elsewhere, proceeds in terms of national interest and *Realpolitik*. Moral issues are left to religious leaders and even they often talk in terms of political strategy. If intellectuals as a whole were to concentrate on the task of formulating an imperial United States policy, the critical function of intellectualism as a public voice would disappear. Some intellectuals would retreat into seclusion, while the majority would become the obedient spokesmen of government, using their intellectual skills like many of the jurists and political scientists who formulated the philosophies of fascism and communism and supported their political masters through all their perversions and excesses.

Some Conclusions

The division of approaches to the conduct of international affairs which has been briefly surveyed here reflects the agony and travail of a country torn between a moralizing tradition and the demands and aspirations of an imperial power.

There is no indication that this conflict will be resolved in the foreseeable future. One way to resolve it would be the complete subordination of legal and moral restraints to global-power strategy. This may happen if the tensions between the United States and its major rivals become more acute, through a further escalation of the Vietnam War, through an intensification of the armament race, or through direct confrontation elsewhere, for instance, in the Middle East. Such a development would bring to the fore a coalition of military men, scientists, technocrats, politicians, and "realist" intellectuals who would combine a virulent anti-Communist ideology with an unrestrained primacy of military and strategic needs. It would lead to the gradual suppression of dissent and move the United States closer toward the society of 1984.

The opposite extreme would be a return to an inward-looking defensive nationalism, marked by a policy of non-involvement in foreign affairs except those immediately affecting the physical security of the United States. This would be a radical reversal of the entire postwar trend of American policy, of its world-wide economic and military investments, and is hardly imaginable without a radical revision of United States policies and commitments on all the continents except perhaps Africa, where the American involvement is limited.

A third, "universalist," solution, that is, a strengthening of international authority and law enforcing machinery, is less likely than at any time since World War II in view of the deep fissures within the United Nations and its growing inability to provide even limited order forces, let alone the major military security establishment envisaged in the Charter and based on joint policies and operations of the major powers.

Perhaps the only realistic alternative to the steady escalation of naked imperial power struggle is the strengthening of several regional collective organizations which would, to a large extent, take over security functions from the United Nations, although the latter would retain its reserve function as the world's only universal forum and ultimate arbiter. This would, however, imply an acceptance of the "spheres of interest" approach. In other words, neither the United States nor either of the other superpowers could assume responsibility and prerogatives outside its own sphere of predominant interest. The United States would obviously be the major guardian of a strengthened Western hemisphere organization and retain a major interest in the Atlantic sphere, depending on the importance of its military and logistic role and on the extent of Western European integration. The adjustment between the "Eurasian" and "East Asian" spheres—marked by clashes between the aspirations of the Soviet Union and China—remains uncertain. This last prospect looks remarkably like George Orwell's vision of the three empires of 1984, a grim but far from unrealistic vision. The only modification might be a stronger voice for the smaller and medium states inside the collective regional organizations, as a partial substitute for the fading vision of a universal organization entrusted with the guardianship of peace and security throughout the world.

NOTES

1. It would require a separate study to analyze the meaning of "American way of life" in this context. Briefly, it combines glorification of an ideology of private initiative and hostility to all kinds of socialism (mostly identified with public enterprise and social welfare schemes)—an ideology that bears little resemblance to the realities of contemporary American life—with belief in political democracy of the American style.

2. Irving Kristol, "American Intellectuals in Foreign Policy," *Foreign Affairs,* XLV (1967), 594 *et seq.*

3. Mr. Kristol's definition of an intellectual "as a man who speaks with general authority about a subject on which he has no particular competence" may be added to the list of deprecatory definitions of intellectuals given by Richard Hofstadter in his book, *Anti-Intellectualism in American Life* (New York, 1963), 9ff. Mr. Hofstadter himself describes as characteristic qualities of an intellectual (as distinct from a professional) "disinterested intelligence, generalizing power, free speculation, fresh observation, creative novelty, radical criticism" (p. 27).

4. "The Intellectual School in the U.S.," *Encounter,* IV (1955), 23ff.

35.

Zbigniew Brzezinski: Between Two Ages: America's Role in the Technetronic Era

America is becoming what Zbigniew Brzezinski has called a "technetronic society"—one that is "shaped culturally, psychologically, socially, and economically by the impact of technology and electronics"—and is in turn contributing to the

From Zbigniew Brzezinski, *Between Two Ages: America's Role in the Technetronic Era,* pp. 293–97, 301–9. Some footnotes omitted. Copyright © 1970 by Zbigniew Brzezinski. All rights reserved. Reprinted by permission of The Viking Press, Inc.

transformation of the world environment as the "principal global disseminator of the technetronic revolution." In place of isolationism, Pax Americana, or traditional Wilsonian universalism, therefore, Professor Brzezinski advocates the goal of a community of developed nations: "unless the United States, the first global society, uses its proponderant influence to give positive direction and expression to the accelerating pace of change, that change not only might become chaos . . . but could eventually threaten the effort to improve the nature and the character of American domestic life."

Zbigniew Brzezinski is Director of the Research Institute on Communist Affairs and Professor of Government at Columbia University. Formerly a member of the State Department's policy planning staff, he is the author of numerous books and articles, including the *Soviet Bloc: Unity and Conflict*.

. . . A community of the developed nations must eventually be formed if the world is to respond effectively to the increasingly serious crisis that in different ways now threatens both the advanced world and the Third World. Persistent divisions among the developed states, particularly those based on outmoded ideological concepts, will negate the efforts of individual states to aid the Third World; in the more advanced world they could even contribute to a resurgence of nationalism.

Western Europe and Japan

From an American standpoint, the more important and promising changes in the years to come will have to involve Western Europe and Japan. The ability of these areas to continue to grow economically and to maintain relatively democratic political forms will more crucially affect the gradual evolution of a new international system than will likely changes in American-Soviet relations. Western Europe and Japan offer greater possibilities for initiatives designed to weave a new fabric of international relations, and because, like America, they are in the forefront of scientific and technological innovation, they represent the most vital regions of the globe. . . .

Accordingly, an effort must be made to forge a community of the developed nations that would embrace the Atlantic states, the more advanced European communist states, and Japan. These nations need not—and for a very long time could not—form a homogeneous community resembling EEC or the once hoped for Atlantic community. Nonetheless, progress in that direction would help to terminate the civil war that has dominated international politics among the developed nations for the last hundred and fifty years. Though the nationalist and ideological disputes among these nations have less and less relevance to mankind's real problems, their persistence has precluded a constructive response to dilemmas that both democratic and communist states increasingly recognize as being the key issues of our times. The absence of a unifying process of involvement has kept old disputes alive and has obscured the purposes of statesmanship.

To postulate the need for such a community and to define its creation as the coming decade's major task is not utopianism. Under the pressures of economics, science, and technology, mankind is moving steadily toward large-scale cooperation. Despite periodic reverses, all human history clearly indicates progress in that direction. The question is whether a spontaneous movement will suffice to counterbalance the dangers already noted. And since the answer is probably no, it follows that a realistic response calls for deliberate efforts to accelerate the process of international cooperation among the advanced nations.

Movement toward a larger community of the developed nations will necessarily have to be piecemeal, and it will not preclude more homogeneous relationships within the larger entity. Moreover, such a community cannot be achieved by fusing existing states into one larger entity. The desire to create one larger, formal state is itself an extension of reasoning derived from the age of nationalism. It makes much more sense to attempt to associate existing states through a variety of indirect ties and already developing limitations on national sovereignty.

In this process, the Soviet Union and Eastern Europe on the one hand and Western Europe on the other will continue for a long time to enjoy more intimate relationships within their own areas. That is unavoidable. The point, however, is to develop a broader structure that links the foregoing in various regional or functional forms of cooperation. Such a structure would not sweep aside United States–Soviet nuclear rivalry, which would remain the axis of world military might. But in the broader cooperative setting, the competition between the United States and the Soviet Union could eventually resemble in form late-nineteenth-century Anglo-French colonial competition: Fashoda did not vitiate the emerging European entente.

Movement toward such a community will in all probability require two broad and overlapping phases. The first of these would involve the forging of community links among the United States, Western Europe, and Japan, as well as with other more advanced countries (for example, Australia, Israel, Mexico). The second phase would include the extension of these links to more advanced communist countries. Some of them—for example, Yugoslavia or Rumania—may move toward closer international cooperation more rapidly than others, and hence the two phases need not necessarily be sharply demarcated. . . .

The Communist States

The Soviet Union may come to participate in such a larger framework of cooperation because of the inherent attraction of the West for the Eastern Europeans—whom the Soviet Union would have to follow lest it lose them altogether—and because of the Soviet Union's own felt need for increased collaboration in the technological and scientific revolution. That Eastern Europeans will move closer to Western Europe is certain. The events of 1968 in Czechoslovakia are merely an augury of what is to come, in spite of forcible Soviet efforts to the contrary. It is only a matter of time before individual communist states come knocking at the doors of EEC or OECD; hence, broader

East-West arrangements may even become a way for Moscow to maintain effective links with the Eastern European capitals.

The evolution of Yugoslav thinking and behavior attests to the fact that the communist states are not immune to the process of change and to intelligent Western initiatives. Slightly more than twenty years ago, Yugoslav pronouncements were not unlike those of the Chinese today. Yet Yugoslavia now leads all communist states in economic reform, in the openness of its society, and in ideological moderation. In the late 1960s it joined GATT, and Yugoslavia's association with EFTA—and perhaps eventually with the Common Market—is a probability. While still committed to the notion of "socialism," Yugoslavia's views on international politics are moderate, and they have had a significant impact on communism in Eastern Europe.

Similar trends are slowly developing elsewhere in the communist world. To be sure, they are opposed by entrenched bureaucrats, but in the long run the reactionaries are fighting a losing battle. Social forces are against them, and the conservative elites are on the defensive everywhere. It is doubtful whether they can reverse, though they certainly can delay, the trend toward a more open, humanistic, and less ideological society. The resistance of those regimes dominated by entrenched conservative bureaucracies will be further weakened if the West views the Cold War as primarily due to the fading self-serving doctrines of the Communist rulers, if it approaches the Cold War more as an aberration and less as a mission.

Over the long run—and our earlier analysis indicates that it would be a long run—Soviet responsiveness could be stimulated through the deliberate opening of European cooperative ventures to the East and through the creation of new East-West bodies designed initially only to promote a dialogue, the exchange of information, and the encouragement of a cooperative ethos. The deliberate definition of certain common objectives in economic development, technological assistance, and East-West security arrangements could help stimulate a sense of common purpose and the growth of a rudimentary institutional framework. (For example, through formal links in the economic sphere between OECD and the Council for Mutual Economic Assistance (CEMA); in the security sphere between NATO and the Warsaw Pact, and through United States–Soviet arms-control arrangements; or by the creation of an informal East-West political consultative body.)

A larger cooperative goal would also have other beneficial effects. For one thing, it is likely that the Soviet Union would initially demonstrate hesitancy or even hostility in the face of Western initiative. Therefore, an approach based on bilateral American-Soviet accommodation—as advocated by some Americans—might prove to be abortive and would consequently intensify tensions. But efforts to create a larger cooperative community need not be halted by initial Soviet reluctance, nor can they be easily exploited by Moscow to perpetuate the Cold War. On the contrary, Soviet resistance would only result in more costly Soviet isolation. By seeking to cut Eastern Europe off from the West, the Soviet Union would inevitably also deny itself the fruits of closer

East-West technological cooperation. In 1985 the combined GNP of the United States, Western Europe, and Japan will be roughly somewhere around three trillion dollars, or four times that of the likely Soviet GNP (assuming a favorable growth rate for the Soviets); with some Eastern European states gradually shifting toward greater cooperation with EEC and OECD, the Soviet Union could abstain only at great cost to its own development and world position.

Risks and Advantages

The shaping of such a community may well provoke charges that its emergence would accentuate the divisions in a world already threatened by fragmentation. The answer to such objections is twofold: First, division already exists, and our present problem is how best to deal with it. As long as the advanced world is itself divided and in conflict, it will be unable to formulate coherent goals. The less developed countries may even be benefiting from the internal rivalries in the developed world, which incite it to compete in extending aid; but since such aid tends to be focused on short-term political advantages to the donor, it is subject to political fluctuations and may decline as the rivalry declines in intensity.

Second, the emergence of a more cooperative structure among the more developed nations is likely to increase the possibility of a long-range strategy for international development based on the emerging global consciousness rather than on old rivalries. It could hence diminish the desire for immediate political payoffs and thus pave the way for more internationalized, multilateral foreign aid. While the vexing problems of tariffs and trade with the Third World are not likely to disappear, they might become more manageable in a setting that reduces both the impediments to truly international production and, consequently, a given country's stake in this or that protective arrangement. The underlying motivation for such a community is, however, extremely important. If this community does not spring from fear and hatred but from a wider recognition that world affairs will have to be conducted on a different basis, it would not intensify world divisions—as have alliances in the past— but would be a step toward greater unity.

Its appearance would therefore assist and perhaps even accelerate the further development of present world bodies—such as the World Bank—which are in any case *de facto* institutions of the developed world geared to assisting the Third World. A greater sense of community within the developed world would help to strengthen these institutions by backing them with the support of public opinion; it might also eventually lead to the possibility of something along the lines of a global taxation system.

More specifically, America would gain several advantages from its identification with a larger goal. Such a goal would tend to reduce the increasing danger of American isolation in the world; this isolation is unavoidably being intensified by the problems associated with America's domestic leap into the future. Moreover, the United States cannot shape the world singlehanded, even though it may be the only force capable of stimulating common efforts to do so. By encouraging and becoming associated with other major powers in a joint response to the problems confronting man's life on this planet, and by jointly attempting to make deliberate use of the potential offered by science and technology, the United States would more effectively achieve its often proclaimed goal.

The quest for that goal cannot, however, be geographically confined to the Atlantic world, nor should its motivation be even implicitly derived from security fears stimulated by a major outside power. One reason for the declining popular appeal of the Atlantic concept is the latter's association with the conditions of post-World War II Europe and with the fear of Soviet aggression. While such a concept was a bold idea at the time, it is now historically and geographically limited. A broader, more ambitious, and more relevant approach is called for by the recognition that the problems of the 1970s will be less overtly ideological, more diffuse—they will more widely reflect the malaise of a world that is still unstructured politically and highly inegalitarian economically.

Such an approach would also tend to end the debate over American globalism. The fact is that much of the initiative and impetus for an undertaking on so grand a scale will have to come from the United States. Given the old divisions in the advanced world—and the weaknesses and parochialism of the developing nations—the absence of constructive American initiative would at the very least perpetuate the present drift in world affairs. That drift cannot be halted if the United States follows the path which it is now fashionable to advocate—disengagement. Even if, despite the weight and momentum of its power, America could disengage itself, there is something quaintly old-fashioned in the eloquent denunciation of United States global involvement, especially when it comes from Europeans, who have shown a less than admirable ability to maintain world peace. Moreover, even the most brilliant indictment of United States policy cannot erase the fact that, despite its allegedly long record of errors and misconceptions, the United States has somehow become the only power that has begun to think in global terms and actively seek constructive world-wide arrangements. In this connection, it is revealing to note that initiatives such as the Test-Ban Treaty or the Non-Proliferation Treaty were opposed by governments habitually praised by some critics of United States global involvement. This country's commitment to international affairs on a global scale has been decided by history. It cannot be undone, and the only remaining relevant question is what its form and goals will be.

The debate on globalism did, however, perform one useful function. Though much of the criticism did not provide a meaningful policy program,[1] the debate prompted greater recognition of the need to redefine America's world role in the light of new historical circumstances. Thrust into the world by its own growth and by the cataclysms of two world wars, America first actively promoted and then guaranteed the West's economic recovery and military security. This posture—of necessity heavily marked by military preoccupations

—has increasingly shifted toward a greater involvement with the less political and more basic problems that mankind will face in the remaining third of the century.

John Kennedy caught the essence of America's novel position in the world when he saw himself as "the first American President for whom the whole world was, in a sense, domestic politics." Indeed, Kennedy was the first "globalist" president of the United States. Roosevelt, for all his internationalism, essentially believed in an 1815-like global arrangement in which the "Big Four" would have specific spheres of influence. Truman primarily responded to a specific communist challenge, and his policies indicated a clear regional priority. Eisenhower continued on the same course, occasionally applying European precedents to other regions. These shifts were symptomatic of the changing United States role. With Kennedy came a sense that every continent and every people had the right to expect leadership and inspiration from America, and that America owned an almost equal involvement to every continent and every people. Kennedy's evocative style which in some ways appealed more to emotion than to intellect, stressed the universal humanism of the American mission, while his romantic fascination with the conquest of space reflected his conviction that America's scientific leadership was necessary to its effective world role.

Global involvement is, however, qualitatively different from what has to date been known as foreign policy. It is inimical to clear-cut formulas and traditional preferences. But this intellectual complexity does not negate the fact that for better or for worse the United States is saddled with major responsibility for shaping the framework for change. This point of view is subject to easy misrepresentation and is highly unpopular in some circles. World conditions do not call for a Pax Americana, nor is this the age of American omnipotence. Nevertheless, it is a fact that unless the United States, the first global society, uses its preponderant influence to give positive direction and expression to the accelerating pace of change, that change not only might become chaos —when linked to old conflicts and antipathies—but could eventually threaten the effort to improve the nature and the character of American domestic life.

To sum up: Though the objective of shaping a community of the developed nations is less ambitious than the goal of world government, it is more attainable. It is more ambitious than the concept of an Atlantic community but historically more relevant to the new spatial revolution. Though cognizant of present divisions between communist and non-communist nations, it attempts to create a new framework for international affairs not by exploiting these divisions but rather by striving to preserve and create openings for eventual reconciliation. Finally, it recognizes that the world's developed nations have a certain affinity, and that only by nurturing a greater sense of communality among them can an effective response to the increasing threat of global fragmentation—which itself intensifies the growing world-wide impatience with human inequality—be mounted.

There is thus a close conjunction between the historic meaning of America's internal transition and America's role in the world. Earlier in this book, domestic priorities were reduced to three large areas: the need for an institutional realignment of American democracy to enhance social responsiveness and blur traditional distinctions between governmental and nongovernmental social processes; the need for anticipatory institutions to cope with the unintended consequences of technological-scientific change; the need for educational reforms to mitigate the effects of generational and racial conflicts and promote rational humanist values in the emerging new society.

The international equivalents of our domestic needs are similar: the gradual shaping of a community of the developed nations would be a realistic expression of our emerging global consciousness; concentration on disseminating scientific and technological knowledge would reflect a more functional approach to man's problems, emphasizing ecology rather than ideology; both the foregoing would help to encourage the spread of a more personalized rational humanist world outlook that would gradually replace the institutionalized religious, ideological, and intensely national perspectives that have dominated modern history.

But whatever the future may actually hold for America and for the world, the technetronic age—by making so much more technologically feasible and electronically accessible—make deliberate choice about more issues more imperative. Reason, belief, and values will interact intensely, putting a greater premium than ever before on the explicit definition of social purposes. To what ends should our power be directed, how should our social dialogue be promoted, in what way should the needed action be taken—these are both philosophical and political issues. In the technetronic era, philosophy and politics will be crucial.

NOTES

1. Even a critic who identifies himself as sympathetic to the "isolationist or neo-isolationist" school concludes that the alternatives offered by the more traditional students of international politics, such as Lippmann or Morgenthau, have relatively little of a constructive nature to offer (Charles Gati, "Another Grand Debate? The Limitationist Critique of American Foreign Policy," World Politics, October 1968, especially pp. 150–51). Moreover, the propensity of even some perceptive writers to concentrate almost entirely on the shortcomings of American foreign-policy performance makes it difficult for them to account for its relatively respectable performance during the last twenty years as compared with, for example, that of the European powers. Thus, Stanley Hoffmann's massive (556 pages) and in places stimulating book, Gulliver's Troubles (New York, 1968), focuses almost entirely on the impatience, wrongheadedness, misunderstanding, self-righteousness, gullibility, condecension, inflexibility, and paranoid style of American foreign policy. This leads him, on a more popular level, to say in a magazine article ("Policy for the Seventies," Life, March 21, 1969) that "Americans . . . have been prepared by history and instinct for a world in black and white, in which there is either harmony or an all-out contest." He does not explain why, in that case, the United States and the Soviet Union were successful in maintaining peace, whereas in the past the European powers had failed to do so.

At the same time, traditionalists who emphasize the continued vitality of nationalism are inherently inclined to postulate policies that are no longer in tune with the times. Thus, on the very eve of De Gaulle's repudiation by the French people, Hoffmann could speak of a "fundamental rapprochement" with De Gaulle ("America and France," The New Republic, April 12, 1969, p. 22).